Techniques for Meeting Client Needs

Financial Advisor Series *C. Bruce Worsham, Editor*

Sales Skills Techniques

*Techniques for Exploring Personal Markets**

Techniques for Meeting Client Needs

*Techniques for Building a Financial Services Career**

Product Essentials

Essentials of Annuities

Essentials of Business Insurance

*Essentials of Disability Income Insurance**

*Essentials of Life Insurance Law**

Essentials of Life Insurance Products

Essentials of Long-term Care Insurance

*Essentials of Employee Benefits**

Planning Foundations

Foundations of Senior Planning

*Foundations of Estate Planning**

*Foundations of Retirement Planning**

Foundations of Financial Planning: An Overview

*Foundations of Financial Planning: The Environment**

***forthcoming titles**

Techniques for Meeting Client Needs

Glenn E. Stevick, Jr., MA, CLU, ChFC, LUTCF

THE AMERICAN COLLEGE
THE LEADER IN FINANCIAL SERVICES EDUCATION

270 S. Bryn Mawr Avenue, Bryn Mawr, Pa 19010

Library of Congress Catalog Card Number 2004100850
ISBN 1-57996-097-9

Printed in the United States of America

Contents

Preface

The mission of this book is to develop your professionalism as a financial advisor counseling prospects and clients about the need for life insurance. We intend to do this by teaching you about the benefits of life insurance in shaping your performance as a successful advisor. By gaining a deeper understanding of the life insurance contract and the economic needs it satisfies, you will become a better financial advisor. The text will also analyze the technical aspects of life insurance policies and study ways of comparing them. It will review the processes of selecting and classifying risks and examine the life insurance policy provisions. It is our hope that this book has the right blend technical knowledge and practical information to accomplish this mission.

While much of the text material will be new to you, some will, no doubt, refresh knowledge you acquired in the past. In either case, all of the text material is both valuable and necessary if you aspire to be successful in the life insurance marketplace. The benefits you gain from studying the text material will be directly proportional to the effort you expend. Read each chapter carefully and answer both the essay and multiple choice review questions for the chapter (preferably before looking in the back of the book for the answers); to do less would be to deprive yourself of an unique opportunity to become familiar with life insurance and to learn more about selling it.

The book includes numerous educational features designed to help you focus your study of life insurance. Among the features found in each chapter of the book are

- an overview and learning objectives
- a chapter outline, examples, figures, and lists
- key terms and concepts
- review questions (essay format)
- self-test questions (multiple choice format)

The back of the book includes a glossary, answers to questions section, and an index.

Finally, all of the individuals noted on the acknowledgments page made this a better book, and we are grateful. However, in spite of the help of all of these fine folks, some errors have undoubtedly been successful in eluding our eyes. For these we are solely responsible. At the same time, however, we accept full credit for giving those of you who find these errors the exhilarating intellectual experience produced by such discovery.

Glenn E. Stevick, Jr.
C. Bruce Worsham

Acknowledgments

This book was edited by Glenn Stevick, Jr., LUTC author/editor and Assistant Professor of Insurance at The American College.

For their valuable contribution to the development of this book, appreciation is extended to senior editor Todd Denton for editing the manuscript, to permissions editor Patricia Cheers, and to production assistants Susan Doherty and Charlene McNulty.

Very special thanks to Burton T. Beam, Jr. Associate Professor of insurance at The American College, Edward E. Graves, Associate Professor of Insurance and Chairholder of the Charles J. Zimmerman Chair in Life Insurance Education at The American College, and John McFadden, Professor of Taxation and Pensions and holder of the Robert K. Clark Chair in Executive Compensation and Benefit Planning, for their generous help and expertise in creating this book.

Special thanks is also extended to Roy M. Lerner, LUTCF, of Walnut Creek, California, a dedicated and experienced LUTC moderator, who offered his editorial comments in many extended phone calls to the author. It is the hundreds of dedicated people like Roy that make the LUTC program a special and exciting educational experience.

Special thanks is also extended to Norman G. Levine, whose ideas and experiences in life insurance selling, expressed in his book "A Passion for Compassion," are provided in this textbook with his kind and generous permission.

To all of these individuals, without whom this book would not have been possible, the College expresses its sincere appreciation and gratitude.

C. Bruce Worsham
Associate Vice President and Director
Educational Development
The American College

About the Author

Glenn E. Stevick, Jr., MA, CLU, ChFC, LUTCF, is an author/editor and Assistant Professor of Insurance at The American College. His responsibilities at the College include writing and preparing text materials for the LUTC *Techniques for Meeting Client Needs, Essentials of Long-Term Care* and *Essentials of Business Insurance* courses. He has also co-edited the *Essentials of Life Insurance Products* with Burke Christensen for the Financial Advisor Series. He writes articles for *Advisor Today,* the national magazine distributed to members of NAIFA. He also currently teaches the Insurance and Financial Planning course at the American College.

Before joining the College, Mr. Stevick worked for New York Life as a training supervisor for 15 years in its South Jersey office. He also served as an agent with New York Life for more than 2 years. Prior to his insurance industry experience, Mr. Stevick taught psychology at the college level and worked in various educational and mental health programs. Mr. Stevick earned his BA degree from Villanova University and his MA degree from Duquesne University. He holds the CLU and ChFC designations from the American College and the LUTCF designation from the American College and NAIFA (National Association of Insurance and Financial Advisors).

Special Notes to Advisors

Text Materials Disclaimer
This publication is designed to provide accurate and authoritative information about the subject covered. While every precaution has been taken in the preparation of this material to insure that it is both accurate and up-to-date, it is still possible that some errors eluded detection. Moreover, some material may become inaccurate and/or outdated either because it is time sensitive or because new legislation will make it so. Still other material may be viewed as inaccurate because a specific company's products and procedures are different from those described in the book. Therefore, the authors and The American College assume no liability for damages resulting from the use of the information contained herein. The American College is not engaged in rendering legal, accounting, or other professional advice. If legal or other expert advice is required, the services of an appropriate professional should be sought.

Caution Regarding Use of Illustrations
The illustrations, sales ideas and approaches in this book are not to be used with the public unless you have obtained approval from your company. Your company's general support of The American College's programs for training and educational purposes does not constitute blanket approval of the sales ideas and approaches presented in this book, unless so communicated in writing by your company.

Use of the Term Financial Advisor or Advisor
Use of the term "Financial Advisor" as it appears in this book is intended as the generic reference to professional members of our reading audience. It is used interchangeably with the term "Advisor" to avoid unnecessary redundancy. Financial Advisor takes the place of the following terms:

Account Executive
Agent
Associate
Broker (stock or insurance)
Financial Consultant
Financial Planner
Financial Planning Professional
Financial Services Professional
Health Underwriter
Insurance Professional
Life Insurance Agent
Life Underwriter
Planner
Practitioner
Producer
Property & Casualty Agent
Registered Investment Advisor
Registered Representative
Senior Advisor

Answers to the Questions in the Book

The answers to all essay and multiple choice questions in this book are based on the text materials as written.

About the Financial Advisor Series

The mission of The American College is to raise the level of professionalism of its students and, by extension, the financial services industry as a whole. As an educational product of the College, the Financial Advisor Series shares in this mission. Since knowledge is the key to professionalism, a thorough and comprehensive reading of each book in the Series will help the practitioner advisor to better service his or her clients. A task made all the more difficult because the typical client is becoming ever more financially sophisticated with each passing day and demands that his or her financial advisor be knowledgeable about the latest products and planning methodologies. By providing practitioner advisors in the financial services industry with up-to-date, authoritative information about various marketing and sales techniques, product knowledge, and planning considerations, the books of the Financial Advisor Series will enable many practitioner advisors to continue their studies so as to develop and maintain a high level of professional competence.

When all books in the Financial Advisor Series are completed, the Series will encompass 15 titles spread across three separate subseries, each with a special focus. The first subseries, *Sales Skills Techniques,* will focus on enhancing the practitioner advisor's marketing and sales skills, but will also cover some product knowledge and planning considerations. The second subseries, *Product Essentials,* will focus on product knowledge, but will also delve into marketing and sales skills as well as planning considerations in many of its books. The third subseries, *Planning Foundations,* will focus on various planning considerations and processes that form the foundation for a successful career as a financial services professional. When appropriate, product knowledge and sales and marketing skills will also be touched upon in many of its books.

When all 15 titles in the Series are completed, they will be divided among the three subseries as follows:

Sales Skills Techniques

- *Techniques for Exploring Personal Markets*
- *Techniques for Meeting Client Needs*
- *Techniques for Building a Financial Services Career*

Product Essentials

- *Essentials of Annuities*
- *Essentials of Long-Term Care Insurance*
- *Essentials of Business Insurance*
- *Essentials of Disability Income Insurance*
- *Essentials of Life Insurance Products*
- *Essentials of Life Insurance Law*
- *Essentials of Employee Benefits*

Planning Foundations

- *Foundations of Senior Planning*
- *Foundations of Estate Planning*
- *Foundations of Retirement Planning*
- *Foundations of Financial Planning: An Overview*
- *Foundations of Financial Planning: The Environment*

This book, *Techniques for Meeting Client Needs,* is the seventh book in the Series. Other books in the Series will be forthcoming over the ensuing months and years.

Overview of the Book

Techniques for Meeting Client Needs is the latest revision of the LUTC course, Meeting Client Needs. This book examines the fundamentals of selling life insurance. It is organized around the selling/planning process and covers the basics of life insurance, including insurance principles, product design, and the economic value of a human life. The course explains the selling/planning process step-by-step, helping the advisor learn how to present ideas in each step of the process of defining and meeting client needs. The advisor is guided through the following steps of the selling/planning process: meeting the prospect, gathering information, analyzing the information, presenting the plan, implementing the plan, and servicing the plan. Additional topics include the personal and family uses of life insurance, comparing costs between policies, policy illustrations, the selection and classification of risks, policy provisions and surrender options, settlement options, and ethical issues facing the financial advisor.

Chapter 1 introduces the economic basics of life insurance, with emphasis on the human life value approach and the economic justifications for its use. The concepts covered include the needs for and benefits of life insurance, how the premium is determined, common life insurance policy provisions and riders, and the taxation of life insurance. Chapter 2 provides an in-depth look at the selling/planning process, the buying cycle, and the client-focused selling approach. Chapter 3 examines the initial interview and total needs selling. Chapter 4 expands on the fact-finding process and effective communication. Chapter 5 examines the analysis of the client situation uncovered in the fact-finding process and reviews employee benefits and Social Security benefits. Chapter 6 discusses the development and presentation of the plan to meet client needs, life insurance products, methods of comparing policy costs, and components of policy illustrations. Chapter 7 reviews the implementation of the plan, dealing with objections, closing techniques, and the underwriting process. Lastly, in Chapter 8 the topics of policy delivery and service and settlement agreements are covered.

Overview of the Book

Techniques for Meeting Client Needs

1

The Meaning of Life Insurance

Overview and Learning Objectives

Chapter 1 explores the meaning of life insurance based on the financial needs of individuals and families, and the benefits they may derive from it. It is important for financial advisors to understand these fundamental reasons for having life insurance and the arguments that favor or discourage the personal purchase and ownership of life insurance products. This chapter will discuss how life insurance works and analyze the basic ingredients of a life insurance policy: mortality, interest, and expense. It will conclude with a review of the basic life insurance contract provisions and policy riders, and the taxation of life insurance.

By reading this chapter and answering the questions, you should be able to:

1-1. Identify the needs of individuals and families for which life insurance can provide a solution.

1-2. Define the concept of human life value and explain how it relates to life insurance.

1-3. Identify and describe the benefits of life insurance.

1-4. Explain the use of mortality tables to predict mortality and life expectancy.

1-5. Explain the three elements that create and structure a life insurance policy.

1-6. Identify and explain the common policy provisions and riders of a life insurance policy.

1-7. Describe general tax rules that typically apply to individual life insurance policies.

Chapter Outline

The Meaning of Life Insurance

Themes of the Course

Life insurance, one of the largest and most important industries in America, is a business with far-reaching social and economic implications. Its first concern is economic security. It provides individuals with an important financial planning tool through which they can obtain financial security for their families and businesses. It also serves the economy as an important channel through which capital is made available to individuals and businesses for economic growth.

Life insurance was once commonly considered an isolated financial product designed to protect policyowners from the financial consequences of premature death. Little attempt was made to integrate life insurance planning with the complete array of products sold by all types of financial institutions. In recent years, it has become increasingly difficult to view insurance products in isolation from a total and comprehensive financial planning process. This is in part due to the growing popularity of the financial planning approach, and in part due to the integration and amalgamation of the financial services industry, where a broad array of financial services products are commonly being made available within one financial organization.

As our world and economy change, the way we do business changes too. These changes are clearly seen evolving and merging in the financial services and life insurance businesses. The themes of this course reflect the way that the life insurance industry is moving into the future.

Life insurance means many different things to people. It can serve a variety of purposes in one's overall planning for the uncertainties of the future. Life insurance is a financial planning tool that can be combined with other financial products to provide efficient, comprehensive plans for individuals and businesses, especially when designing ways to attain financial goals under a variety of uncertain future conditions.

Life insurance creates capital with guaranteed results. It is property bought with a contract and contractual guarantees that will provide large amounts of money upon the death of the insured. The amount of death benefit payable is typically considerably greater than the premiums paid into the policy.

If we knew when we were going to die, then life insurance would be far less necessary. The necessary amount of money needed at that date could be saved systematically, through what is often called a sinking fund. However, if the person died before the desired amount was accumulated, there would be no way to assure that the needed money could be generated. Life insurance is essentially a financial mechanism that guarantees the desired accumulation by the time of death regardless of when death occurs.

Life insurance is not morbid and it is not for those who die. It provides for those who live, which is why it is called life insurance, not death insurance. Life insurance is concerned with the economic value of a human life, which is derived from an individual's earning capacity or economic value, and the financial dependence of other lives on that earning capacity or value. It is the only way you can provide a definite sum of money for an indefinite time in the future. The life insurance contract is the insurer's promise to pay the policy's face amount upon the proof of the death of the insured, backed by one of the oldest, largest, most regulated, and on the whole financially sound industries in the world today.

This chapter introduces three themes that are central to today's selling/planning process in the financial services industry. Financial advisors (see explanation of this term in the preface) explore financial needs with their prospects and clients, seeking to implement solutions for those needs. The selling/planning process serves as the organizing framework of this textbook, since it is the foundation of an advisor's professional relationship with his or her clientele.

The needs for life insurance are discussed in this chapter. The total needs approach and the client-focused sales/planning approach are discussed in Chapter 2.

The Needs for Life Insurance

A discussion of the needs for life insurance products is a main topic in this chapter. Additionally, a thorough review of the life insurance contract, contract provisions, features of ownership, benefits, taxation, and related topics are discussed.

Total Needs Approach

The total needs approach is a professional and comprehensive approach to insurance and financial planning. This method uses fact-finding to determine the client's overall financial and personal situation, goals, and needs in order to intelligently assist the client in achieving his or her objectives. As a financial advisor, your role is twofold. First, you help your clients and prospects identify and understand the financial problems and needs their death will create. Second, you encourage and help them to solve those problems and to meet those needs for their survivors.

The total needs approach is a necessary ingredient in the client-focused sales/planning process discussed in Chapter 2. In order to solve a prospect's problems and help a prospect achieve his or her financial objectives, the advisor must conduct a total needs analysis. Just as a medical doctor who makes a diagnosis and prescribes a treatment without doing a medical history would be guilty of malpractice, so too would the financial adviser be guilty of unprofessional behavior by recommending a plan without conducting a fact finding and suitability analysis based on the client's total personal and financial situation.

Client-Focused Selling/Planning Approach

This book emphasizes the role of the advisor as a professional counselor. It explains the importance of building client relationships and offering value to the customer in the sales/planning process. A client-advisor relationship based on trust is at the heart of this approach. The objective for the advisor in a *client-focused sales/planning approach* is to develop long-term, mutually beneficial relationships with clients. The benefit of this approach is developing a clientele who view the agent as a trusted adviser and financial professional. In the long term, it is a better way to do business—one that should lead to new sales and referrals, increased persistency, and additional cross-selling opportunities. The benefit to the clientele is finding a reliable, trustworthy professional advisor who has their best interest in mind and on whom they can depend for help in achieving their financial goals.

The Need for Life Insurance

A human life possesses many values, most of them irreplaceable and priceless, and certainly not easy to measure. These values are based on religious, moral, and social relationships. Many religions believe that human life is immortal and gifted with a value beyond the understanding of the human mind. Moral teachings and beliefs, often deeply connected to religious values, maintain that the human life is sacred and must be preserved and held in the highest regard. A person's relationship with other human beings creates a set of emotional and sentimental attachments that cannot be measured in monetary terms or replaced by material things.

These values, however important as they may be, are not the foundation of life insurance. Life insurance does have strong moral and social significance, but life insurance is concerned with the economic values of a human life, derived from its earning capacity and the financial dependence of others on that earning capacity. But the earning capacity of a human life does not alone create an economic value and serve as the basis of life insurance. A human life has an economic value only if some person(s) or organization depends upon or expects to receive some monetary benefit through that life. If an individual is without dependents and no other person or organization stands to benefit through his or her living, either now or in the future, that life has no monetary value that needs to be carried on.

Life insurance products can satisfy many purposes and needs, and provide numerous economic and psychological benefits to individuals and families. Some of the common uses of life insurance include the following:

Family/Survivor Income

The death of a working family member usually terminates an income stream that the family or other survivors have relied on. The costs of daily living for the spouse and children need to be provided for during the dependency period and beyond. There will be continuing costs for food, transportation and utilities. The surviving family members will want to continue their established lifestyle and generate the same level of expense they encountered before the death. This means a continuation of bills for cable TV services, magazine subscriptions, cellular phone service, newspapers, club memberships, entertainment and other miscellaneous costs. Changes in a family's living standard are usually accomplished through a certain amount of trial-and-error adjustment over a period that often exceeds one year.

This death can leave a surviving family adrift with unfulfilled dreams and expectations, as well as outstanding unfulfilled financial obligations, if care has not been taken to meet the needs of those left behind. It is common to classify the survivor's income needs into three categories:

Readjustment Income—The readjustment period is the interval of time—usually one to 3 years in duration, immediately following the insured's death, during which income is usually provided at or near the level enjoyed by the family during the insured's lifetime. In the dependency period thereafter, the income drops to a more realistic and sustainable level.

Few individuals are able to leave an estate, including life insurance, substantial enough to provide their dependents with an income as large as they enjoyed while the income earner was alive. This means that an adjustment will generally have to be made in the family's standard of living. To cushion the economic and emotional shock, however, it is desirable to postpone that adjustment for a period following the income producer's death. The length of the period depends largely on the magnitude of the change that the family will have to make in living standards. If the surviving spouse must refresh or acquire skills to gain employment, a longer period may be needed. Whatever the duration, the income during this readjustment period should be approximately equivalent to the family's share of the producer's earnings at the time of his or her death.

The emotional turmoil following the death of a close family member usually lasts about one year. As survivors cope with the emotions of anger, denial, depression, bargaining, and finally acceptance of the death, the grieving process often distracts them from concentrating on financial issues. They may forget to pay important bills, such as premiums on homeowner's and auto insurance that could worsen their financial position. Creditors insisting to be paid immediately can be an additional source of emotional stress at this time. Survivors who are able to convince these creditors that adequate life insurance will be available are usually not pressed for collection until proceeds have been received.

Dependency Period Income—The dependency period extends from the date of the insured's death until the youngest child is self-sufficient. For planning purposes, the dependency period is the interval between the end of the readjustment period and the youngest child's self-sufficiency, usually assumed to occur at age 18, unless a child is mentally or physically disabled. Minor children and other dependents may need support for a lifetime or at least many years until they become self-supporting. A surviving spouse may need to be supported during this dependency period as well, rather than being forced to enter the labor market. Life insurance proceeds can supplement any other income sources that the survivors may receive. The other sources of support available to the children, like all other needs of the family, obviously affect the children's financial needs.

Most people assume major responsibility for the support and maintenance of their dependent children during their lifetime. In fact, they consider it one of the rewarding experiences of life. In any case, the law attaches a legal obligation to the support of a spouse and children. Thus if there is a divorce or a legal separation, the court will normally decree support payments for dependent children and possibly alimony for the dependent spouse. In some cases such payments, including alimony, are to continue beyond the provider's death, if the children are still dependent or if the alimony recipient has not remarried. In such event the parent and ex-spouse are required to provide life insurance or set funds aside in trust.

Another group of family dependents that may have a relatively short and predictable period of dependency are the husband and wife's parents. The financial demands of providing parental support can be minimal—providing room and board in the home for example. At the other end of the spectrum, support of a parent in an institution can be very expensive.

Payments to enhance someone's lifestyle, however, are not necessarily restricted to children or other family members. Payments are sometimes extended to lifelong domestic partners, helpers, and caregivers as an informal pension, perhaps for the recipient's remaining lifetime. Life insurance can fund these payments if the benefactor dies first.

Life Income for Surviving Spouse—In life insurance planning, discussed in Chapter 5, it is necessary to break the widow(er)'s basic need for life income into two periods. One period runs from the youngest child's 18th birthday to the widow(er)'s 62nd, and the other starts when the widow(er) is age 62. This breakdown is necessary because the surviving spouse's income from Social Security terminates when the youngest child reaches age 18 (unless the child is totally disabled) and does not resume until the surviving spouse is age 62. A permanently reduced benefit is available at age 60. The period in between is usually called the *blackout period.*

The Moral Obligation to Provide Protection

From the family standpoint, life insurance is a necessary business proposition that may be expected of every person with dependents as a matter of course, just like any other necessary business transaction which ordinary decency requires him to meet. The care of his family is man's first and most important business. The family should be established and run on a sound business basis. It should be protected against needless bankruptcy. The death or disability of the head of this business should not involve its impairment or dissolution any more than the death of the head of a bank, railroad, or store. Every corporation and firm represents capitalized earning capacity and goodwill. Why then, when men and women are about to organize the business called a family should there not be a capitalization in the form of a life insurance policy of the only real value and goodwill behind that business? Why is it not fully as reasonable to have a life insurance policy accompany a marriage certificate, as it is to have a marine insurance certificate invariably attached to a foreign bill of exchange? The voyage in the first instance is, on the average, much longer, subject to much greater risk, and in case of wreck, the loss is of infinitely greater consequence.

Life Insurance, Dr. Solomon S. Huebner

The surviving spouse may require income beyond his or her eligibility for Social Security benefits and private pension plans. Supplemental income may be needed to support the surviving spouse indefinitely.

The family's economic security lies in the earning capacity of each income earner, which is an accumulation of his or her character, health, education, training, experience, industriousness, personality, initiative and judgment. If the individual lives and stays in good health, the total income potential will be realized, to benefit the family and others who depend on that income. If the income earner dies, the unrealized potential for his or her income will be lost, and those dependents may find themselves reduced to a lower income than previously enjoyed. The potential estate (what a family will need to live in the future) may be substantially larger than the existing estate on which the family has been living.

This situation need not happen, since by means of life insurance, an individual can assure that the family will receive the monetary value of those income-producing qualities that lie within his or her physical being, regardless of when death occurs.

Specific Cash Needs

The above-outlined needs are income needs in which an amount of money is needed over a period of time to sustain survivors; those below are identified as cash needs. *Cash needs* are those needs for money that are typically a one-time or otherwise lump-sum need for money, which can be planned for and set aside in the case of death.

Final Expenses—Funeral expenses are not the only expenses associated with death. Some people will incur large medical bills in a last illness that are not covered by insurance. Their medical care costs not covered by insurance could accumulate a big debt. Home or convalescent care is rarely covered by private insurance and has limited coverage under Medicare for those over 65. Prolonged medical care and rehabilitative treatment will often leave the family's finances devastated even before death occurs.

Many of the expenses associated with death are incurred after the funeral. There are costs of settling financial and property matters in closing the deceased's estate. Included are court fees, administrative costs, attorney's fees, probate expenses, possible investment and real estate management fees, and potential estate and inheritance taxes.

Managing the estate prior to final property disposition may be extremely complex. This may require the services of specialized investment managers and/or real estate managers to safeguard the property until it can be sold or distributed. The provisions of the will and the nature of the property involved may necessitate a long period of estate management before the estate can be closed. Some assets may be hard to sell in the economic conditions following death. The terms of the will may require the establishment of trusts and other legal work that is also very time consuming. Even the task of locating heirs or other beneficiaries of the estate may require a lengthy search to cut through the bureaucratic red tape to obtain death certificates for all potential recipients who predeceased the insured. The longer this process takes and the more complex it is, the more it will cost.

Emergency Fund—There is a general rule in financial planning that a person or family should have about 3 to 6 months expenses set aside for emergency needs. This is of increased importance in the case of death of an income producer. Possible damage to or repairs needed for cars, home maintenance, health costs, and other expenses that may occur unexpectedly should be anticipated.

The family should have an adequate source of emergency funds in liquid holdings to meet any need for immediate cash prior to or following the death of an income producer, as well as at any other time. Liquid holdings might include money market funds, mutual funds, bank balances, cash management accounts, and life insurance cash values.

Mortgage Cancellation—For many families it is important to know that in the case of the death of a parent or wage earner, the family would have a place to live debt-free. In the case of renters, a rent fund can be established that would accomplish essentially the same goal. If the family can occupy the home free of a monthly mortgage or rent payment, it will greatly reduce the amount of income that they would otherwise require.

Debt Liquidation—Some personal debts become due and payable upon the death of the borrower. This may include loans for automobiles, education, a business, debts for credit cards and other retailers, and the like. In any case, many families desire to have a debt-free situation when the wage earner dies. Debt can create an economic hardship for the survivors who do not have the funds to repay it. Adequate amounts of life insurance will give the survivors the option to pay off the debt or continue to repay it in installments. Standard types of life insurance policies may be lower in costs than credit life policies. Adequate amounts of life insurance will give the survivor the option of paying off the debt or continuing to repay it according to schedule.

Education Funding—Although educational goals vary widely from one family to another, children commonly need financial support to reach their educational objectives. The costs of college and professional education continue to climb annually. Life insurance can guarantee that the necessary money will be there in case a parent dies.

Educational needs of the family are not restricted to the children. A surviving spouse may need further education to increase future income potential to help support the family. The spouse may need a modest refresher course or training to return to a prior occupation. On the other hand, the spouse's need may be extensive, such as preparing to enter the job market for the first time or trying to upgrade to a higher-paying career. There is even the possibility that a surviving spouse may need training for a less demanding career if he or she has become permanently disabled in some manner.

Supplemental Retirement Funding—Life insurance proceeds can be an important source of funds for a surviving spouse. These funds can supplement other sources of retirement income from corporate pensions, IRAs, other qualified plans, savings and investments, and Social Security.

Charitable Donations—Life insurance can increase the value of a gift to charity. A charity can be gifted a policy, named as beneficiary, or be the owner and premium payer on a donor's life.

Life insurance can also be used for charitable giving even if the charity is not a beneficiary of the insurance policy. The donor can use adequate amounts of life insurance to fund all of the needs of surviving family members and thereby free up personal property and other assets for lifetime gifts to the charities.

Gift tax and estate tax considerations are often strong motives for making charitable gifts. Because tax laws can—and probably will—change, tax planning should be carefully coordinated by a knowledgeable tax adviser.

Gifts to Individuals—The beneficiary of a life insurance policy can be a trust for the benefit of heirs or other recipients for whom the insured cares. One advantage of life insurance gifts is that they generally are free of probate and are therefore not a matter of public record or subject to probate expenses. The grantor or donor of the gift can increase the value of the gift using life insurance when transferring property to younger generations. Very sophisticated arrangements can be created to maximize gifts and transfer assets, often with tax advantages.

Accumulation of Supplemental Cash for Future Needs such as Education and Retirement

Life insurance can provide supplemental funds for many financial needs. This can be accomplished by using the cash value of life insurance, through policy loans or cash withdrawals, prior to an insured's death. Partial surrenders or withdrawals and policy loans can be made without terminating the policy itself. The interest rate for policy loans is known in advance and is usually lower than the rate available on loans from other sources. It must be emphasized that the primary role of life insurance is protection; cash accumulation should normally be viewed as a secondary purpose. Any loans or withdrawals made from a policy will reduce the death benefit protection.

Many would argue that it is because life insurance provides a safety net, and guarantee of a certain sum in the case of death, that saving is possible at all. Saving involves time to save, and life insurance provides a hedge against the possibility of a savings period being cut short. This refers to the characteristic of life insurance as self-completing; that it provides the money that an otherwise healthy and capable income-earner cannot because of premature death.

Tax-advantages Vehicle to Save for the Future

Under current tax law, cash value life insurance policies have several tax advantages for accumulating money for the future. This type of policy is often referred to as "double-duty" dollars, because money can be made available for the future whether or not the insured dies. The internal buildup of cash value is tax deferred, and money can be taken from the policy in the form of loans, which are normally not taxable, providing tax-free income if the policy stays in force until the death of the insured. If the policy pays dividends, they can be withdrawn tax-free until the cost basis (the amount paid in) is recovered from the policy.

The Many Uses of Life Insurance, The Swiss Army Knife of Financial Products

You can use life insurance to:

- Provide a death benefit
- Provide income to survivors
- Secure a line of credit
- Fund a buy/sell agreement
- Guarantee future insurability
- Equalize an inheritance
- Pay estate taxes
- Create an estate
- Give to charity
- Supplement college, retirement, and other expenses
- Pay funeral and last expenses
- Pay mortgages and debts
- Provide an employee benefit
- Protect a business from financial loss

The Economic Bases of Life Insurance

Human Life Value

The human life value concept was developed to measure the economic value of life. The most comprehensive approach to the economic value of a human life was provided by Solomon Huebner, the founder of the American College. In his book, *The Economics of Life Insurance,* Huebner defined *human life value* as the production potential of the individual over his life expectancy. More precisely, human life value is a measure of the actual future earnings or service of an individual, that is, the capitalized value of an individual's net future earnings after subtracting self-maintenance costs. From the standpoint of dependents, an individual's human life value is the measure of the value of benefits that the dependents can rightfully expect from their breadwinner or supporter (from *Life Insurance* by Huebner and Black).

The basic economic premise for life insurance planning is that nearly everyone has a human life value that should be assessed and protected in the same manner as any other valuable asset would be. Those individuals who are capable of earning or providing service in excess of self-maintenance costs have an actual calculable monetary value to those who are dependent on them. Human life value for insurance and financial planning purposes is the present value (today's value) of a life-long stream of net economic contributions a person will make to his or her family.

In many cases an income producer's family is completely dependent on his or her personal earnings for subsistence and the amenities of life. In other words, the "potential" estate is far more substantial than the existing estate (the savings that the family has been able to accumulate). The family's economic security lies in the earning capacity of each income earner, which is represented by his or her "character and health, training and experience, personality and power of industry, judgment and power of initiative, and driving force to put across in tangible form the economic images of his mind," said Huebner.

Over a period of time, these economic forces are gradually converted into income, a portion of which is devoted to self-maintenance, a portion to support of dependents, and if the income is large enough, a portion to savings to meet future needs and contingencies. If the individual lives and stays in good health, the total income potential will eventually be realized, all to the benefit of the family and others who derive financial gain from his or her efforts. If an income earner dies or becomes permanently and totally disabled, the unrealized portion of his or her total earnings potential will be lost, and in the absence of other measures, the family will soon find itself destitute or reduced to a lower income than it previously enjoyed.

This need not happen, however, since there are contracts that can create a fund at death at least to partially, and possibly to fully, offset the lost income of the insured. Those contracts, of course, are life insurance. By means of life insurance, an individual can assure that the family will receive the monetary value of those income-producing qualities that lie within his or her physical being, regardless of when death occurs. By *capitalizing* this life *value* (creating a fund large enough to generate ongoing investment income similar to the salary or wages of the individual), an income earner can leave the family in the same economic position that they would have enjoyed had he or she lived.

Human life value is measured daily in wrongful death lawsuits. The economic loss to the family and other survivors is the basis for determining monetary awards in these cases. When a wrongful death suit is filed, both sides routinely retain economists to evaluate the human life value of the victim. This was the method used in determining the awards to families of victims of the World Trade Center attack. A family can be awarded large sums of money for their economic loss of income, services that would have been provided by the deceased, and loss of employee fringe benefits and household services. These judgments are based on the human life value concept. When a car is destroyed, it can be replaced through auto insurance. With life insurance, when the insured dies, he or she cannot be replaced; only the financial contribution he or she makes to the family is replaceable.

When you think about this, you can see that calculating this value is not an exact science. This is because much of the accuracy of the calculation is dependent on what actually happens in the future, a distinct unknown. There are also many non-economic contributions of a family member, which are more difficult to measure. Regardless of precision, the purpose of life insurance is to replace someone's human life value in the event of death. From this point of view, life insurance might more accurately be called *human life value insurance*.

How much is the appropriate amount upon which to base a life insurance recommendation? The human life value approach will play a significant role in defining the economic need for life insurance. Calculating life insurance amounts and planning techniques for this purpose will be covered in Chapter 5.

The Money Machine Analogy

An example of the application of the human life value concept in selling life insurance is the money machine analogy, where a person's income-producing capability is compared to that of a machine. The money machine analogy asks the prospect to imagine that he or she had a machine in their basement that could print money as it was needed. If possible, would he or she insure the machine to guarantee that if something happened to the machine, the money could continue to support the family and maintain their lifestyle? Most people would probably say yes. You then point out to the prospect that the income he or she produces makes them very much like a money machine. What would happen to the family if the prospect died or became disabled and was no longer able to produce income? Wouldn't it make sense for the prospect to insure his or her life and earning capacity?

Time Value of Money

If a 35-year-old man earned $30,000 net of taxes and expenses, and worked for 30 more years to age 65, without ever getting a raise, the economic value to his family would be $900,000 (30 years x $30,000). Of course, it doesn't take $900,000 to produce $30,000 for 30 years, since part of the required money would be earning interest through the 30-year period. Money has a *time value*, and that time value is based on interest earnings. Interest is the difference between the present value and the future value of a sum of money. To the investor, interest is the money earned on invested capital; to the borrower, it is the money paid for the loaned capital.

The sum that will be needed over the next 30 years can be discounted to a present value. *Present value* is a concept that expresses the value of money today that is to be received in the future. A simple way to calculate this amount is to divide the desired income by the after-tax interest rate assumed. This will determine a lump sum that will produce the required income at the assumed rate indefinitely. For example, $30,000 divided by 5 percent will produce a required capital amount of $600,000. We will discuss this process in much greater detail in Chapter 5.

Another way to illustrate the value of insuring the money machine (human life value) is to compare the relative risk of each type of event we insure and compare it to the risk of death. How many homes burn down or cars have accidents? How much do we pay for these types of policies? What financial loss would we suffer? How many people escape death? What financial loss would our survivors endure?

The Benefits of Life Insurance

What does life insurance do? What are its benefits? When they hear the phrase "life insurance," many people think of the policy that will pay for a funeral. Life insurance is and can do much more than that. It has emotional as well as economic benefits. Some of these benefits are explained below.

Provision of Time and Money

Life insurance could also be called "time insurance." When someone dies and the proceeds are paid to the beneficiaries, that money helps buy time until the survivors can adjust, financially as well as emotionally. Life insurance guarantees large amounts of cash to pay final expenses, repair the car if it breaks down, keep the mortgage payments current, keep the utilities turned on, and generally provide sufficient cash so survivors can maintain the same lifestyle as before the insured's death. Most of the people who come to the survivors to talk about money come with their hands out, providing services that will have to be paid for. Only the insurance advisor can walk into a tragic situation and bring new money to pay old and new bills. The insurance proceeds offer survivors the time they need to adjust and begin living again. This is the advisor's real contribution.

Peace of Mind

Life insurance may be the only product someone cannot buy when it is needed and desired the most, a product that is delivered during a time of urgency. Let's look at what life insurance offers to the person who buys the policy. First, there is the peace of mind in knowing that a sound and prudent decision has been made. The life insurance contract guarantees payments in the future when cash is needed. This is why we sell life insurance and why people buy it.

What Your Work Means to Your Clients

When a person can answer either of the following questions with a "yes," who could not say that the work he or she does makes a difference in people's lives?

- Does the product you sell make a difference in people's lives?
- Does the service you perform make a difference in people's lives?

All of you who sell life insurance, especially after careful consideration, should be able to answer yes to both questions. You have a noble calling. Think about the good your work does for society and particularly for the people who are privileged to call you "my insurance agent."

Life insurance proceeds are not generally part of the *probate* estate, which involves the passing of the will through the local court system where the deceased lived. Life insurance proceeds pass by provision of contract directly to the beneficiary, bypassing probate. Because of this arrangement, the proceeds can normally be paid promptly to the beneficiary, without the delay caused by the administration of the estate. There is no public record of the death benefit amount or to whom it is payable. The proceeds would become a part of the probate estate if they were paid to or for the benefit of the estate of the insured.

Life insurance policies typically have some protection against creditors of both the policyowner and the beneficiary. This protection varies widely from state to state, but can typically be of great benefit to those who may depend on the values of the life insurance policy or its proceeds. The principle behind these statutes is that creditors should not be permitted to make someone destitute and a potential ward of the state. Check the statutes in your area to determine what provisions apply.

Living Benefits and Financial Flexibility

One type of life insurance, *cash value* or *permanent life insurance*, can provide guaranteed funds in the case of financial emergency. It can

Ben Feldman

One of the greatest life insurance salesmen of all time was Ben Feldman. Ben was a master at explaining the meaning and purpose of life insurance in simple language, and his stories have become known as "Feldmanisms." Here is what Ben said about the meaning of life insurance:

And what could life insurance do for him? He needed time to accumulate the money to pay back the loan. Life insurance guaranteed the money in case he ran out of time. What did life insurance do for him? It underwrote time. Time to complete his plans. Time to do what had to be done.

And isn't it the same with everyone? We all must die someday. Never at the right time. Always at the wrong time. We never have quite enough time to complete our plans, make our dreams come true—and that's why it's always the wrong time. Who'll give us more time? Only The Man Upstairs. But we can give our clients the equivalent of time in the sense that we can give them the money to complete their plans. You know, we sell contracts for time and money. We can't guarantee the time—but we can guarantee the money."

"Creative Selling for the 1990's," Ben Feldman, Longman Financial Services Publishing, 1989.

supplement retirement income or provide money for other purposes while the insured is alive. A policy can be used just once, when the insured dies and the death benefit is paid to the beneficiaries, or it can be used often during the life of the insured. People who own life insurance turn to the cash value of a policy when all else fails and they face a financial emergency. They know that the funds are there to borrow or withdraw, normally without delay or qualification.

The guarantees of the policy contract are what people look to for peace of mind when they buy life insurance. Life insurance offers financial security and also demonstrates concern for a family's future financial well being.

No other financial institution can do what life insurance companies can do. No other industry backs its products with reserves as sound as those of the life insurance industry. In fact, during the Great Depression of the 1930s, when the stock market hit bottom and many banks went out of business, insurance companies provided security for their policyowners that was unavailable anywhere else. While well-established companies in other industries went bankrupt, fortunes were lost overnight, and income from real estate and other property evaporated, the failure of life insurance companies was unknown. In no case was there any loss to a continuing policyowner.

A Safe and Sound Financial Foundation with Many Guarantees

The record of strength and safety of insurance companies even under the most adverse conditions is a badge of pride to the insurance industry. For generations life insurance has been the standard of security by which others are measured. Guarantee Associations have been established in various states to provide further safety for the individual policyowner. No investment or other type of business has had a safety record superior to that of life insurance.

Part of the reason for this safety is the way insurance companies manage and invest their assets. They look for real estate, mortgages, corporate and government bonds, and other opportunities that will bring consistent returns without compromising quality. Insurance companies invest for the long term because they know that people buy insurance for the long term. These investments are designed to provide a consistent and stable return that gives the insurance company a dependable income to pay its obligations, and provide the safety that will not compromise the guarantees that make up the life insurance contract.

Tax Advantages

Life insurance generally offers a number of tax advantages:

- There is normally no income tax payable on death proceeds. Depending on the policy ownership arrangements and overall estate of a decedent, there may be federal estate taxes and state inheritance taxes due on the proceeds upon death.
- Cash value policies generally allow for *tax-deferred* internal buildup of cash value as long as the policy remains in force. If the policy is surrendered for cash or lapses, the gain on the policy is subject to federal income taxation. The gain is the amount by which the cash value and any outstanding loan exceeds the policyowner's *cost basis* in the policy. The cost basis in the policy equals the premiums paid in cash less dividends and tax-free withdrawals, if any.
- An individual can retrieve his or her investment in the policy before recognizing gains. The taxation is based on a *first-in, first-out basis (FIFO)* tax treatment, also known in tax law as the *cost-recovery rule*. A withdrawal is considered to be a non-taxable recovery of cost basis (premiums) until the policyowner's entire cost basis is recovered. At this point the owner's cost basis is zero, and any subsequent distribution from the policy would be considered taxable as a gain and taxed as ordinary income.
- Dividends paid to the policyowner are generally not subject to federal income taxation until the aggregate of dividends paid exceeds the aggregate of premiums paid into the policy.
- Policy loans are not considered income unless the policy is identified as a Modified Endowment Contract, which is discussed below. If done correctly, a combination of withdrawals and policy loans can produce tax-free income from a permanent life insurance policy for financial purposes while the insured is living. The client must be informed that policy loans reduce the death benefit, and that interest is charged on the outstanding loan.
- Generally there are no tax advantages for premium payments. Premiums are not deductible except in a few circumstances, such as when the life insurance premium qualifies as a charitable contribution for a charitable gift deduction, or as a premium payment for group life insurance for employees, or where the

premium is part of a contribution to a *tax-qualified retirement plan.*

- A policy that is a *Modified Endowment Contract (MEC)* has some different tax treatment than those general rules discussed above. Distributions or withdrawals anytime before death are treated like premature annuity or Individual Retirement Account (IRA) distributions, on a *last-in, first-out (LIFO)* tax basis. Under the interest-first rules, any distributions from a MEC representing gains are taxable as ordinary income. In addition, if such distributions are received before age 59½, the taxable portion of the distribution may be subject to an a additional 10-percent penalty tax.

The preceding points are general rules, and are subject to limitations and exceptions. More discussion of the taxation of life insurance appears at the end of this chapter.

Basic Insurance Principles

How the Product is Created

All life insurance products are mathematically and scientifically created by calculating the relationships of mortality, interest, expense, and the financial values attached to each based on time. These factors ultimately determine the premium at which a policy is sold. The premium must be adequate to pay the expenses incurred in creating, offering and maintaining the product, to pay all promised benefits, and to increase the profit and surplus of the insurer.

From an economic viewpoint, insurance is a system for reducing financial risk through the transfer of those risks from policyowners, and combining or pooling those losses by the insurer. From the viewpoint of society, insurance is a device for accumulating funds to meet uncertain losses of economic value, carried out through the transfer of the risks of many individuals to one person or to a group of persons. The social aspect of insurance involves the collective bearing of losses through contributions by all members of a group to pay for losses suffered by some group members.

Insurance substitutes certainty for uncertainty through the pooling of hazards to which groups of people are exposed. Uncertain risks of individuals are combined, making the possible loss more certain, providing a financial solution to the problems created by the loss. Small, periodic contributions by the individuals provide a fund from which those who suffer loss may be reimbursed. Insurance thus manages the uncertainty of one party through the transfer of particular risks to another party who offers a restoration, at least in part, of economic losses suffered by the insured individual.

From a business viewpoint, insurance achieves the sharing of risk by transferring risks from individuals and businesses to financial institutions specializing in risk. Lastly, from a legal standpoint, an insurance contract or policy transfers a risk (for a premium) from one party, known as the insured or policyowner, to another party known as the insurer. By virtue of a legally binding contract, the possibility of an unknown large financial loss is exchanged for a comparatively small certain payment. This contract is not a guarantee against a loss occurring, but a method of ensuring that payment will be received for a loss that does occur.

Every insurance company will add cost and pricing variables to the actual historical results of that company in designing and pricing its products. This is the same procedure as any product on the market, not just insurance. It also accounts for the variations in premiums between products that might appear to be the same. Variations can be created by differences in company operational efficiencies, investment performance and assumptions, underwriting practices, profit and marketing objectives, sales results, service practices, policy persistency, expenses and other issues.

Statistical Predictability

Mortality is statistically predictable. Everyone will die, eventually. Time becomes a critical factor when we recognize that we never know when someone will die, only that everyone will. Combine the reality of death with the uncertainty of when it will occur, and you have the basis for life insurance. It is the scientifically calculated pooling, growth, and distribution of money to satisfy two objectives for paying benefits:

- paying benefits to survivors of someone who dies
- providing distribution of benefits with guaranteed lifetime payments to either the insured or the insured's survivors

Only life insurance and annuities can do these things. To accomplish this, companies keep extremely accurate records about births and deaths, especially when (by age) and how (by cause of death) people die. The size of the statistical base, now hundreds of years old, enables insurance actuaries to predict average mortality for groups of people in many different categories. This precision study of mortality and how it works helps to make life insurance a risk management tool rather than a game of chance. It is an actuarial science—mathematical calculations of probability based on huge amounts of experience—that establishes mortality and the statistical tables used to create and price life insurance products.

The Law of Large Numbers

The statistical group that is observed for purposes of measuring the probability must have mass— that is, the sample must be large enough to allow the true underlying probability to emerge. The *law of large numbers* states that as the size of the sample (insured population) increases, the actual loss experience will more and more closely approximate the true underlying probability. This means not only that the insurer's statistical group must be large enough to produce reliable results, but also that the group actually insured must be large enough to produce results that are consistent with the underlying probability.

Risk Pooling

Life insurance uses what is called risk pooling or group sharing of losses. People exposed to a risk agree to share losses on an equitable basis. They transfer the economic risk of loss to an organization, the insurance company. Insurance is based on pooling the premiums of thousands of people and spreading the risk of losses across the entire pool. By carefully calculating the probability of losses that will be sustained by the members of the pool, insurance companies can equitably (fairly) spread the cost of the losses to all the members. The risk of loss is transferred from one to many and shared by all insureds in the pool. Each person pays a premium that is measured to be fair to them and to all based on the risk they impose on the company and the pool (each class of policies should pay its own costs).

Risk Pooling Examples

Homeowner's Insurance

Of 1000 houses, each worth $200,000, assume only one house per year is destroyed by fire. Each homeowner could contribute $200 per year into a pooled fund that could pay out the full $200,000 value to the homeowner of a destroyed home. Such pooling transfers the risk of bearing the full impact of a potential $200,000 loss by an owner.

Life Insurance

10,000 males aged 35 contribute to a life insurance pool. Twenty-one of them are expected to die (based on 1980 CSO mortality tables). The mortality charge is $2.10 per $1,000 of benefit. If each of the 10,000 contributes $210 to fund death benefits (ignoring costs of operation, a death benefit of $100,000 could be paid for each of the 21 expected deaths.

The Building Blocks of the Life Insurance Policy

Mortality, Interest, and Expense

Every life insurance product, regardless of type, must take into account these three major factors in the construction and operation of a life insurance product. The assumptions made concerning these three factors will determine the policy premium and structure of the policy. The actual results over time, called experience, will determine the profitability and solvency of the life insurance company.

Understanding Mortality Tables

Every 20 years or so, new mortality tables are developed for individual life insurance products by the *National Association of Insurance Commissioners (NAIC)*. In December of 2002, the NAIC adopted the 2001 *Commissioners Standard Ordinary (CSO) Mortality Tables,* the first step in replacing current insurance reserve valuations based on the 1980 CSO Mortality Tables. As the various states adopt the 2001 CSO tables, the impact on the life insurance industry will be significant. Although full adoption of these changes will extend over the next several years, expect changes to begin as companies develop and market products that will take advantage of these changes. Reflecting improving mortality over the last 20 years, the resulting tables should lower rates and affect many of the products you sell.

2001 CSO Tables—With the significant improvements in mortality over the last 20 years since the introduction of the 1980 CSO Mortality Tables, the new 2001 tables create expected reductions in the reserve requirements. For some term products the reduction is approximately 30 percent, for traditional whole life from 10-20 percent, and a modest reduction for universal and variable universal life products. These reductions should be reflected in future product pricing, resulting in lower rates. Generally, the reduction for males is more significant than for females, and for nonsmokers than for smokers. However, with this lower cost of insurance, companies may need to restructure expense loads to make up for lost policy revenues.

One significant change is the extension of life mortality to attained age 120 (compared with age 100 with the 1980 CSO), which compounds these effects. These changes will lower the statutory reserves required by state insurance departments on all life products, but conversely, insurers will have more flexibility to design products that meet the needs of the older population.

Predictions vary, but the American Academy of Actuaries projects that 20-year term could become 33 percent lower under the new tables. Longer period and level premium term policies and riders, like 20- or 30-year term, will be expected to show the largest reduction in premium, whereas it is expected that annually renewable term premium may be adjusted only slightly. Traditional whole life premiums would also be expected to fall.

All of these changes will take effect over the next few years as state insurance departments approve the new rates for policy reserve valuation. These changes will affect newly issued policies only, since in-force policies will continue under their prior mortality and expense criteria. Once adopted by 26 states, the new tables will take full effect for federal tax reserve valuation, necessary for the product to meet the tax definition of life insurance. This will take some time since there is a 3-year transition rule under the tax code once 26 states adopt the new rates, with full implementation to be mandated by 2009 at the latest.

The 2001 CSO tables encompass multiple mortality tables that vary by gender, smoking status, ultimate and select rates, and age-last-birthday and age-nearest-birthday bases. Select rates are for those insureds that have recently provided evidence of good health and have been underwritten. Ultimate rates are higher and used for renewal purposes, to account for the longer period since evidence of insurability was provided and the deteriorating pool of those insured.

Take a few minutes to review the following mortality charts and refer to them when reading about mortality and its effects on you and your prospects. Keep in mind that larger insurance companies use their own morality statistics to calculate their pricing of products. These CSO tables are primary for statutory (regulation by state and federal government) purposes such as reserve requirements and tax issues. These tables will have an impact on policy and company reserves, lowering the amount the company needs to charge for mortality costs and the amount of premium a policyowner can place in the policy under tax regulations.

Using Mortality Tables—The National Safety Council will estimate how many hundreds of persons will be killed on highways between the Friday and Monday of a summer three-day holiday weekend. The actual number will be remarkably close to the estimate. Of course, when it makes its estimate, the Council has absolutely no idea who will be killed.

It merely applies the laws of large numbers and probability to make its estimate. Because the Council has a great volume of historical information available, and because large numbers of people are involved, these predictions are generally quite accurate. For life insurers the process is similar.

Life insurance companies pool their information to construct mortality tables that will accurately indicate the number of insured persons in any large group who will die at any particular age. The 2001 CSO tables do exactly this. They indicate that about one of every thousand male babies born in America can be expected to die before their first birthday. After age 1, the death rate declines until age 4, and then begins to increase at age 6 and every year thereafter. Mortality in males averages less than one death per thousand each year until age 20 (using composite rates). Generally, people are more likely to die each year that they live beyond early childhood.

Life Expectancy—*Life expectancy* information is not yet available at this writing for the new 2001 CSO tables. Although the mortality rates for the 2001 Tables are lower than the 1980 Tables, we will use the 1980 table rates for illustrative purposes. According to the 1980 mortality tables, newborn males have a life expectancy of 70.83 years, females 75.83 years. If the male child survives to age 10, his life expectancy has increased to age 71.66. If still living at 60, his life expectancy is age 77.51. At age 80 he has a life expectancy of 6.18 additional years, or age 86.18. At 90 his life expectancy is 3.18 years or age 93.18. In the past, very few individuals survived past age 100, so the 1980 CSO table assumed that everyone died by age 100. With longer life expectancies, the 2001 CSO table extends to age 120.

The Rate is One

"(Prospect), I must admit that when it comes to mortality tables and other actuarial statistics, I am far from expert. I don't know the mechanics of how they work.

"But I do know and understand perfectly what they mean: the death rate is no more and no less than one per person. I am going to die . . . and you are going to die. We just don't know when.

The odds may be one in a thousand, but it happens to you, they are one in one and the other 999 don't matter"

Age and Expectation Differences—Notice that a person's life expectancy (age at death) is increased by each year the person survives, even though the expectation of the number of years to live decreases. Life expectancy is the combination of age and expectation, and the expectation decreases slower than age increases. You can see in the table that there is no age at which expectation decreases by a full year in any one year. Thus, the older a person is, the older he or she can expect to be when death occurs, all else being equal.

IRS Life Expectancy Table (Partial)		
Age Male	Age Female	Life Expectancy (Years
55	60	21.6
56	61	21.0
57	62	20.3
58	63	19.6
59	64	18.9
60	65	18.2
61	66	17.5
62	67	16.9
63	68	16.2
64	69	15.6
65	70	15.0

Remember, however, that life expectancy has significance only for groups of people. To an individual, life expectancy is a meaningless figure. A 30-year old will probably live to age 70 or 75, but could die today. If we had a group of 211,000 30-year-old men, all in good health, we could expect one to die every day during the next year (365 days divided by 1.73 x 1,000). Averages, however, are not applicable to individuals for predicting death. They only indicate how many people in a particular age group will probably die. Clearly, life expectancy and mortality tables are important to a life insurance company as a basis for determining the values and guarantees that go into policies, but they are generally meaningless to individuals.

Chance of Death—Mortality tables can be important to individuals only as a means of recognizing that young, healthy people will die every day of the year. Consider the 31-year-old prospect that wants to buy life insurance but also wants to wait to make the purchase. Shouldn't this person be made aware that some 31-year-olds will not live long enough even to buy the insurance they want and need, if they wait?

Although the chance of dying at age 31 is remote, it does exist. With odds better than 763 to 1 (1000 ÷ 1.13=763), it does not appear that there is a very large chance of dying within the year. Then why should this life be insured when the odds are so heavily in favor of survival for the next

12 months? The answer is plain and simple. Even with such favorable odds, the prospect might still be the 1 in 763 to die. If death would create financial problems, as it usually does, then insure. If death will not create any financial problems whatsoever, then there is no reason to insure. The focus is on solving the problems *when* death occurs, not *if* death occurs. Since knowledge of when death will occur is unknown, the need to insure is critical. It is the sensible answer.

2001 CSO Table—Male Lives—per 1000 lives			
Age	Composite	Nonsmoker	Smoker
0	0.97		
1	0.56		
2	0.39		
3	0.27		
4	0.21		
5	0.21		
6	0.22		
7	0.22		
8	0.22		
9	0.23		
10	0.23		
11	0.27		
12	0.33		
13	0.39		
14	0.47		
15	0.61		
16	0.74	0.74	0.79
17	0.87	0.85	0.97
18	0.94	0.92	1.11
19	0.98	0.94	1.21
20	1.00	0.95	1.27
21	1.00	0.95	1.33
22	1.02	0.95	1.40
23	1.03	0.96	1.46
24	1.05	0.97	1.54
25	1.07	0.98	1.63
26	1.12	1.02	1.71
27	1.17	1.07	1.81
28	1.17	1.05	1.82
29	1.15	1.03	1.81
30	1.14	1.02	1.80
31	1.13	1.01	1.80
32	1.13	1.01	1.82
33	1.15	1.04	1.87
34	1.18	1.06	1.94
35	1.21	1.09	2.00
36	1.28	1.15	2.11
37	1.34	1.20	2.23
38	1.44	1.29	2.40

2001 CSO Table—Female Lives—per 1000 lives			
Age	Composite	Nonsmoker	Smoker
0	0.48		
1	0.35		
2	0.26		
3	0.20		
4	0.19		
5	0.18		
6	0.18		
7	0.21		
8	0.21		
9	0.21		
10	0.22		
11	0.23		
12	0.27		
13	0.30		
14	0.33		
15	0.35		
16	0.39	0.39	0.41
17	0.41	0.41	0.46
18	0.43	0.42	0.5
19	0.46	0.45	0.54
20	0.47	0.45	0.58
21	0.48	0.46	0.61
22	0.50	0.48	0.65
23	0.50	0.48	0.67
24	0.52	0.50	0.72
25	0.54	0.50	0.77
26	0.56	0.53	0.81
27	0.6	0.57	0.87
28	0.63	0.58	0.92
29	0.66	0.62	0.99
30	0.68	0.64	1.03
31	0.73	0.68	1.12
32	0.77	0.72	1.19
33	0.82	0.76	1.28
34	0.88	0.82	1.39
35	0.97	0.89	1.53
36	1.03	0.95	1.65
37	1.11	1.03	1.79
38	1.17	1.07	1.88

39	1.54	1.37	2.57	39	1.23	1.13	2.00
40	1.65	1.46	2.77	40	1.30	1.20	2.12
41	1.79	1.58	3.03	41	1.38	1.27	2.26
42	1.96	1.73	3.33	42	1.48	1.35	2.43
43	2.15	1.90	3.69	43	1.59	1.45	2.63
44	2.39	2.10	4.12	44	1.72	1.57	2.86
45	2.65	2.33	4.57	45	1.87	1.71	3.13
46	2.90	2.55	4.99	46	2.05	1.87	3.43
47	3.17	2.79	5.46	47	2.27	2.07	3.81
48	3.33	2.93	5.72	48	2.50	2.29	4.28
49	3.52	3.09	6.02	49	2.78	2.53	4.81
50	3.76	3.32	6.45	50	3.08	2.81	5.39
51	4.06	3.59	6.96	51	3.41	3.12	6.02
52	4.47	3.96	7.66	52	3.79	3.47	6.71
53	4.93	4.36	8.45	53	4.20	3.85	7.44
54	5.50	4.87	9.44	54	4.63	4.25	8.24
55	6.17	5.50	10.56	55	5.10	4.68	9.08
56	6.88	6.14	11.70	56	5.63	5.18	9.98
57	7.64	6.83	12.91	57	6.19	5.70	10.94
58	8.27	7.42	13.86	58	6.80	6.26	11.87
59	8.99	8.10	14.96	59	7.39	6.82	12.90
60	9.86	8.92	16.29	60	8.01	7.40	13.97
61	10.94	9.92	17.94	61	8.68	8.03	15.08
62	12.25	11.14	19.93	62	9.39	8.72	16.33
63	13.71	12.51	22.14	63	10.14	9.43	17.58
64	15.24	13.95	24.40	64	10.96	10.20	18.90
65	16.85	15.47	26.63	65	11.85	11.05	20.34
66	18.47	17.01	28.78	66	12.82	11.99	21.87
67	20.09	18.57	30.87	67	13.89	13.02	23.59
68	21.85	20.25	33.07	68	15.07	14.17	25.48
69	23.64	21.99	35.25	69	16.36	15.43	27.53
70	25.77	24.10	37.89	70	17.81	16.82	29.82
71	28.15	26.46	40.78	71	19.47	18.42	32.43
72	31.32	29.56	44.71	72	21.30	20.21	35.31
73	34.62	23.83	48.66	73	23.30	22.15	38.41
74	38.08	36.27	52.65	74	25.50	24.28	41.81
75	41.91	40.03	57.29	75	27.90	26.64	45.23
76	46.08	44.13	62.23	76	30.53	29.23	48.96
77	50.92	48.89	67.94	77	33.41	32.08	52.97
78	56.56	54.45	74.54	78	36.58	35.23	57.29
79	63.06	60.87	82.05	79	40.05	38.63	61.96
80	70.14	67.87	90.07	80	43.86	42.43	66.99
81	78.19	75.84	99.05	81	49.11	47.59	74.07
82	86.54	84.14	108.11	82	54.95	53.41	81.76
83	95.51	93.09	117.61	83	60.81	59.21	89.25

84	105.43	103.00	127.94
85	116.57	114.07	140.09
86	128.91	126.34	153.39
87	142.35	139.74	167.69
88	156.73	154.10	182.72
89	171.88	169.25	198.27
90	187.66	185.06	214.13
91	202.44	199.93	228.43
92	217.83	215.43	243.02
93	234.04	231.78	258.10
94	251.14	249.05	273.74
95	269.17	267.19	291.05
96	285.64	283.79	306.33
97	303.18	301.49	322.44
98	321.88	320.38	339.45
99	341.85	340.54	357.42
100	363.19	362.10	376.40
101	380.08	379.21	390.77
102	398.06	397.44	405.92
103	417.20	416.84	421.83
104	437.56	437.48	438.57
105	459.21	459.13	460.15
106	482.22	482.15	483.10
107	506.69	506.62	507.51
108	532.69	532.63	533.44
109	560.31	560.26	561.01
110	589.64	589.59	590.27
111	620.79	620.74	621.35
112	653.84	653.80	654.35
113	688.94	688.91	689.38
114	726.18	726.15	726.56
115	765.7	765.67	766.01
116	807.61	807.59	807.86
117	852.07	852.05	852.26
118	899.23	899.22	899.35
119	949.22	949.22	949.29
120	1000	1000	1000

84	67.27	65.62	97.30
85	74.45	72.84	105.41
86	80.99	79.39	112.17
87	90.79	89.25	122.89
88	101.07	99.55	133.59
89	112.02	110.53	144.35
90	121.92	120.65	153.05
91	126.85	125.77	154.94
92	136.88	135.84	162.66
93	151.64	150.78	175.10
94	170.31	169.64	190.97
95	193.66	192.92	214.97
96	215.66	215.03	236.91
97	238.48	237.79	258.95
98	242.16	241.63	260.01
99	255.23	254.74	270.77
100	275.73	275.46	289.27
101	297.84	297.55	309.03
102	322.21	322.19	330.78
103	349.06	349.04	354.11
104	378.61	378.60	379.41
105	410.57	410.56	411.32
106	443.33	443.32	444.02
107	476.89	476.88	477.53
108	510.65	510.64	511.24
109	545.81	545.8	546.35
110	581.77	581.76	582.26
111	616.33	616.32	616.78
112	649.85	649.84	650.25
113	680.37	680.36	680.72
114	723.39	723.38	723.69
115	763.41	763.4	763.66
116	804.93	804.92	805.12
117	850.44	850.44	850.59
118	892.44	892.44	892.54
119	935.11	935.11	935.16
120	1000	1000	1000

Investment

Insurers invest the premiums that are received by the company and accumulate them for future claims and other obligations. The cash generated by these investments represents a large sum of money, and a significant portion of the capital needed to operate the company, pay claims, and provide profits. Life insurance company portfolios are traditionally long-term and emphasize safety of principal and predictable rates of return, based on the long-term obligations of the insurer. Typically two-thirds or more of this capital is invested in bonds and mortgages, which meet the above criteria. A smaller percentage of common stocks are represented, under 10 percent, due to their volatility.

The company will credit interest to policies based on the *new money rate* or on its *portfolio rate.* The new money rate reflects recent investment experience, returns on money that are recently invested. The portfolio rate reflects the insurance company's overall investment return on money invested at various times over the years. During periods of rising interest rates, new money rates benefit, and the reverse is true where rates are declining.

Since insurance companies expect a block of recently issued policies to have low claims experience as a whole until years later, there is an adjustment to the premium calculation for the time value of money (compound interest). Investment returns are assumed to be at some minimum rate and are factored into the premium calculation.

If the investment results exceed the guaranteed minimum, policyowners benefit either from participating dividends or from excess interest crediting to the policy cash value. The insurance company's operating results may benefit from any investment earnings that are not transferred to policyowners.

Is Life Insurance an Investment?—We need to keep in mind that the word *investment* means many things to many people. Life insurance is not an investment in the usual sense of the word. In fact, the product was not originally intended to be an investment in any sense. Having said this, there is some disagreement and even controversy as to what extent life insurance can be viewed as an investment vehicle.

Almost everyone needs life insurance. Its primary purpose is to offset the economic loss that results from premature death during productive years. Life insurance provides the needed money no matter when death occurs. No investment vehicle does this with the same degree of security and guarantees provided by a properly designed life insurance plan.

Life insurance should be the first type of protection to buy because it pays for the necessities of life at the very time the decedent (deceased) cannot. This makes insurance the foundation of financial security. This is the first of many steps that are needed to provide for the future of the decedent's survivors.

The principal economic purpose of life insurance is to provide capital. Although it should not be viewed primarily as an investment, this is essentially what life insurance is. All conventional investment vehicles serve the same purpose, but the unique feature of life insurance is that it assures a desired accumulation at the specific but uncertain time of the insured's death. No other investment makes such a guarantee.

Expense

The Cost of Doing Business—Just as with any other business, life insurance companies incur costs in the course of doing business. These break down into two principle types: *acquisition expenses* and *administrative expenses*. Acquisition expenses include all the costs incurred in obtaining the business and placing it in force, and can include some or all of the following items:

Acquisition Expense

- advertising and promotion expenses
- commissions and fees paid to agents and brokers
- underwriting expenses, such as medical exams, attending physicians' statements, inspection reports, and credit histories
- home office processing costs, policy printing, and related fees
- an addition to the insurer's reserve, surplus, and profits
- state premium taxes

Additionally, ongoing administrative expenses incurred by the insurance company must be covered by the premium:

Administrative Expense

- cost of collecting premiums and distributing dividends
- cost on continuing producer remuneration
- investment expenses
- home office overhead

Any cost the insurer incurs must be recovered, either through premium charges or reduced investment credit.

Reviewing the Life Insurance Contract

Few people take the time to read their life insurance policies cover to cover. Even if they did, they might not understand everything they read. They depend on you to explain their policies to them in a way that makes sense. Not only do you need to understand policy provisions and language; you must also be able to explain them thoroughly, carefully and, above all, accurately to policyowners. This is immensely important, for the exact language of the policy determines how the provision will operate. This varies from state to state, company to company, and policy to policy.

The standard provisions of life insurance policies are regulated by the individual states, which control the provisions and policy language that may or may not be used. The policy forms must be submitted to and approved by the insurance department of the state or jurisdiction where it is sold. Current discussion in the legislative and administrative bodies throughout this country concerns the possible federal chartering and regulation of insurers and insurance activity.

Most life insurance contract provisions are similar to one another because of similar state laws and NAIC model regulation adoption. You would probably have little difficulty finding your way through any company's contracts with some limited experience. To policyowners, however, a several-page policy with dozens of largely unfamiliar terms, charts, and tables may seem incomprehensible. You can remove some of the mystery by walking the policyowner through the contract page by page. In most cases he or she will appreciate your personal interest and concern.

A Policy Is a Contract

A life insurance policy is a contract between the policyowner and the life insurance company (the insurer), governed principally by state law. Under such a contract, the policyowner buys (or is given the option to buy) the right to a certain sum of money to be paid to a named beneficiary in the event of death, or to the owner if living at the end of a certain number of years. Usually the policyowner is the insured person, but the policy can be owned by someone other than the insured.

The policyowner has the contract as proof of the agreement. It is not the actual policy that is purchased, however; it is the right to the sum of money and to the future delivery of it. The life insurance policy is simply a statement of terms under which an individual is buying a given sum of money for future delivery. It is called a *unilateral contract* because it is the insurance company's guarantee that the money will be paid. A unilateral contract is an agreement in which only one party makes an enforceable promise. The policyholder's only obligation is to keep paying the necessary premiums to keep the policy in force.

The life insurance policy is also an *aleatory contract*, or one in which the values exchanged (that is, a small premium for a potentially large loss payment, or many premiums with no loss payment) are not equal. Both parties realize that, depending on chance, one may receive a value out of all proportion to the value that he or she gives. The essence of an aleatory agreement is the element of chance or uncertainty. It means that the agreement conditions performance by one party on the happening of an uncertain event.

A life insurance policy is also a *contract of adhesion*. The contract drafted by one party must be accepted or rejected by the other party as it is written. There is no negotiation over the terms of the agreement. The policy is prepared by the company and the policyowner must "adhere" to it. This is important in the case of a legal dispute, because the basic legal rule is that the contract should be interpreted most strongly against the party that drafted it. Anything unclear in the policy is given the interpretation most favorable to the policyowner or the beneficiary.

Policy Face Page

Regardless of the trade name that the company uses to market the product, the formal name of the policy is usually printed on the outside cover of the policy form. The outside page also gives the name and address of the company and may have a window through which the following information on the next page appears.

The insured's full name is usually listed along with the date the insurance officially went into force. The *policy date* is the date that controls premiums and anniversaries, and the *issue date* is the date the company issued the policy, controlling the suicide and incontestability provisions. When a policyowner writes or calls the company or agency about the policy, having the insured's name and policy number on hand will avoid needless delays.

The company's identification number for that policy and the face amount of the policy are typically included, as well as a general description of the type of insurance provided by that policy contract. For example, a traditional participating whole life policy might read as follows: *Whole Life—Level Face Amount Plan. Insurance payable upon death. Premiums payable for Life. Policy may be eligible for dividends. Dividends, dividend credits and policy loans may be used to pay premiums.*

This information includes any additional benefits or riders attached to the contract, the premium amount and the premium frequency for all riders of coverage, with the periods of coverage listed in years or by specific dates.

Also usually included are the policy's free look provision, the insurer's promise to pay, called the insuring clause (the heart of the insurance contract), and the signatures of the officers of the company, usually the president and secretary, which binds the company to the terms of the contract.

The beneficiary's full name may be listed on this same page. Be sure it is spelled correctly. If it is not, check the application to see what name was given. If an error was made on the original application, be sure to submit a change of beneficiary request to the home office or service office with the correct name at once.

Policy Provisions

Entire Contract Clause

Point out that the *entire contract* consists of the policy, a copy of the application, and any reports of the insured's physical condition. The policy cannot be changed arbitrarily by the company after it is issued, except in accordance with terms stated in the contract. The company also accepts all statements made in the application as representations. This means that even if they were later proven untrue, the company could not cancel or amend the policy except where fraud was proved. Everything that controls the contract is included in the policy.

Free-look Clause

Many states require companies to give policyowners a period of time, usually 10 days, to examine their policies and return them if they are not satisfied. No reason needs to be given. If this is done within the required time period, a full refund of premium will be made—no questions asked.

Incontestability Clause

This clause limits the period of time the insurer can use the defense of fraud, concealment, or material misrepresentation to end a contract. Life insurance companies voluntarily introduced this provision to provide greater assurance to the public that relatively innocent misstatements by applicants would not be the cause of a claim being denied. After a policy has been in effect for a period of time prescribed by the *incontestable clause* (typically 2 years), the insurance company cannot have the policy declared invalid.

Three exceptions to the incontestability provision are generally recognized by the courts:

1. where no insurable interest existed at the time of application
2. if the policy was purchased with the intent to murder the insured
3. if there had been a fraudulent impersonation of the insured by another person (for example, someone else takes the medical exam)

Under these circumstances the contract was invalid and void from its inception. A typical incontestability provision would read as follows: *Except for accidental death and disability premium payment benefits, we cannot contest this policy after it has been in force for 2 years during the insured's lifetime.*

After the 2-year (in some states, 1-year) period has passed, the policy is "incontestable" and the full death benefit will be paid if the company has taken no action to rescind the contract.

Suicide Clause

To protect insurers from paying death claims on behalf of insureds that might buy life insurance with the intent to commit suicide, contracts contain a suicide clause. This clause reduces the company's liability to a return of the premium if suicide occurs within 2 years of the issue date of the policy. With some policies, the term may be limited to one year. The clause is intended to discourage suicide as a reason to buy the protection. A typical clause would read as follows: *For the first 2 full years from the original application date, we will not pay if the insured commits suicide (while sane or insane). We will terminate the policy and give back the premiums paid to us less any loan.*

Grace Period Clause

This clause allows the policyowner 31 days (sometimes 30 and sometimes 60 days in universal life contracts) to pay premiums after the due date and still keep the insurance in force. If the last day of the *grace period* ends on a non-business day, the period is normally extended to the next business day. If the premium is unpaid at the end of the grace period, the policy normally lapses.

If the insured dies during the grace period, the company is permitted to deduct overdue premium plus interest (the insurer normally does not charge interest) from the settlement with the beneficiary. The purpose of the provision is to protect the policyowner against unintentional lapse. If not for this clause, payments received even one day late could require new evidence of insurability to reinstate the policy.

If your client paid a premium on the 29th day of the grace period, then died, the insurance would be in force. As you can imagine, this important policy feature is accountable for saving more protection from being lost than any other single factor.

If there is cash value in a policy when it has passed the grace period limit, one of two things will happen: The automatic premium loan provision, if selected, will activate, or the policy will be moved to one of the nonforfeiture options (cash surrender, reduced paid-up, or extended term).

It is important to distinguish between the grace period and a late remittance offer. A late remittance offer is not a contract provision and is made at the insurer's option. It is not a right of the policyowner or an obligation of the insurer. It is an offer after the end of the grace period for the policyowner to remit (send in) the premium and reinstate the policy, without evidence of insurability. Conditions imposed on such an offer include that the insured must have been alive when the late premium was made.

Automatic Premium Loan (APL) Option

The *automatic premium loan (APL)* provides that if a premium has not been paid at the end of the grace period, the company will automatically take enough money out of the cash value (if there is sufficient value there) to pay the amount due. The policy continues just as if the scheduled premium payment has been made by the policyowner. At the same time, the APL creates a loan against the cash value that will reduce its total amount and add an interest charge. The owner's available cash value will change based on the loan.

If subsequent premiums are not paid, the company pays the premiums again out of the cash value. It will keep doing this until premiums are paid by the owner or the policy lapses due to insufficient cash value to pay the premium. Some companies limit the number of consecutive APLs, for example three, to prevent inadvertent depletion of cash value. Usually APL is an optional part of the contract and must be elected. Be sure you know whether this provision is included.

Reinstatement Clause

Reinstatement allows a policyowner to put into force coverage under a policy that has lapsed. Lapsed policies may be reinstated (within a certain time frame, typically 3 years) if: they have not been surrendered for cash; proper evidence of insurability has been submitted and accepted by the company; and back and current premiums are paid, with interest. The company may require that any outstanding policy loan be paid, with interest. Although the company usually reinstates the policy with a simple statement concerning the insured's health, a complete physical examination may be required at the company's option.

Policy Loan Provisions

The law requires that permanent life insurance has policy loan provisions enabling policyowners to borrow money from their policies, within certain limits, anytime they wish.

Interest rates may vary up to a maximum set by state law. Most new policies have variable loan rates, replacing the traditional flat rate found in older policies. The money is there if the insureds need it, but advise them to exercise the policy loan provision wisely and with caution. Borrowing should only be done in an emergency or to take advantage of a significant financial opportunity or important financial obligation. Indiscriminate borrowing can erode the protection provided by the policy.

The term *policy loan* is really incorrect, for a loan carries with it an obligation to repay the loan. A life insurance policy loan has no fixed or required repayment schedule, nor any obligation to repay the money taken from the policy. It is really an advancement of the death benefit, prior to the time of required payment—upon death, secured by the death benefit, or the cash value, if the policy is surrendered or lapses. The amount of the loan plus any unpaid interest will be deducted from any policy values payable upon surrender or death.

Many ask why loan interest is charged if the loan is not really a loan. After all, it is the policyowners money, is it not? The policyowner is expected to pay loan interest on the "loan" because he or she has withdrawn assets from the insurer that were intended to support the level premium concept. In the initial calculation of the level premium, it was assumed in the calculation that the money paid as premium would be invested and earn some stated rate of interest. If the policyowner withdraws those assets, it is fair to expect him or her to pay an interest rate approximate to what the insurer would earn if the insurer had the money as assumed. Otherwise, the insurer would have to charge a higher premium.

Change of Policy Provision

Most insurance contracts have a change of policy provision, which allows the policyowner to change the policy to some other plan of insurance. If the change requested is from a lower to a higher premium (as from a whole life to life paid up at 65), the change could be made without a medical examination because there would be a reduction in risk to the company. However, when the change requested is from a higher to a lower premium, the company would usually require proof of insurability because the insurance risk would be increased.

In order to make a change from a lower premium to a higher premium, the usual practice is for the company to charge the difference in reserves between the two policies. This amount would have to be submitted before the change could take place. If the change is from a higher to a lower premium, an adjustment is made in favor of the policyowner on the basis of the difference between the reserves of the respective policies. The new policy will bear the same date as the original policy.

Change in Insured Provision

In some companies, this policy provision permits a change of insureds on a contract. This is very useful for corporate owners of life insurance plans. With this, a key employee's life insurance plan for the benefit of the corporation no longer would need to be surrendered upon retirement or termination. The change of insured provision, subject to evidence of insurability on the part of the new insured, eliminates the need to purchase new life insurance. It also eliminates the front-end costs that would otherwise be incurred on a newly purchased contract. This procedure can become complicated, so this provision is rarely used.

Assignment Provision

Policyowners may assign the ownership of their policies to another person or institution by following company provisions for temporary or permanent transfer of ownership. Normally the policyowner must notify the company in writing of his or her intention to make an assignment. If the insured dies, the company will pay the death benefit to the new owner, the assignee, or the designated beneficiary if they differ. If the assignment is contested, the company will generally let the court decide who is to receive the proceeds. An irrevocable beneficiary of a policy must also agree to any assignment of the policy.

The three ways that policyowners may assign or change the ownership rights to their policies are:

Change of Ownership—Through a legal form provided by the company, the right to control the provisions of the policy is assigned to another individual or institution.

Collateral Assignment—Most conditional assignments of life insurance policies are made to facilitate the insured's credit to obtain bank loans. The assignment will give the lender rights to the portion of the policy assigned if the insured defaults on the loan repayment or dies before the legal obligations have been completed. The named beneficiary of the insured or the insured (if cash values were used) would receive any remaining value. When the legal obligation of the assignment is repaid, the insured regains all rights to the policy.

Absolute Assignment—Under this arrangement, the assignee gets the entire amount of the insurance policy. This arrangement is also frequently used to secure a debt.

Misstatement of Age Clause

Because of the importance of the insured's age in determining policy premium and values, any *misstatement of age* must be corrected once it is discovered. The company reserves the right to adjust the policy to the insured's correct age at any time. Different procedures are followed, depending on whether the mistake is discovered at the insured's death or while the insured is still living.

At death, if the insured is younger than originally shown in the policy, the amount of proceeds would be increased to an amount equal to what the premiums would have purchased at the correct age. If the insured is older than shown in the policy, the proceeds would correspondingly be decreased.

If the insured is alive and is discovered to be younger than originally shown in the policy, the company may either adjust the premium downward and refund any money due the policyowner, or correct the amount of insurance by adjusting it upward in line with the premium. If the insured is older than shown in the policy, the company may either have the policyowner make up the difference in a cash payment and then pay the higher correct premium, or reduce the amount of insurance to match the amount of premium being paid.

Nonforfeiture Provisions

The level premium concept makes life insurance more affordable to older policyowners. In the earlier years of the policy the level premium is higher than necessary to cover the mortality costs. The excess portion of the premium in the policy's early years, and the interest it earns, builds a cash reserve that is used to pay the mortality costs at older ages, which may exceed the level premium. Nonforfeiture laws state that the policyowner is entitled to have the reserve set aside for the future.

These laws require insurers to provide policyowners with an option to voluntarily or inadvertently terminate their contracts and receive fair return of the value within those policies. They also require that after a cash value policy has been in effect for a minimum number of years, usually three, the insurer must use part of the reserved excess premium to create a guaranteed minimum cash value.

If a policy is terminated for any reason other than the insured's death, the *nonforfeiture provisions* allow the policyowner to receive the policy's cash value in one of three ways:

Cash Surrender—The cash value may be received as a lump-sum payment, or the policyowner may elect to receive it as income under one of the settlement options offered by the company. This will be discussed later.

Reduced Paid-up Insurance—Under this option, the cash value is used as a single premium on a policy of the same kind as the one being surrendered, except that the face amount is reduced. This is because the single premium is calculated on an attained-age basis and will not be sufficient to purchase the original amount at issue. While no further premium payments are made, the policy cash values continue to grow.

Extended Term Insurance—The cash value may also be used to buy extended term insurance of an amount equal to the face amount of the original policy. The extended term option uses the cash value to purchase the same amount of coverage for as long a period as the premium can be paid by the cash value. When the term period expires, there is no more protection. The extended term option usually goes into effect automatically if the policyowner does not elect one of the other options and has not asked for the automatic premium loan provision to be included in the policy.

Separate tables showing each of these provisions at different ages are provided in the policy. Review these provisions with your client. Point out the cash value in any of the years specifically mentioned in your life insurance proposal, such as at retirement or when the insured's children are in college.

Exclusions in Life Insurance Policies

There are several exclusions to policy benefit payments that might be found in a life insurance policy. Where an accidental death benefit is offered as the policy or as a rider to it, payment is restricted to the way that death occurred. This same situation applies to the suicide clause and incontestability clauses mentioned earlier. Other exclusions that may be added to a policy include death from hazardous occupations, hobbies, aviation, physical impairments, death resulting under the act-of-war clause or while committing a felony.

Aviation Restrictions—Restrictions are virtually universal on accidental death claims for all aviation-related deaths except for the insured passenger. At one time even the basic coverage payment was excluded, but with public acceptance of flying, most companies instituted more liberal rules. All companies cover fare-paying passengers on regularly scheduled airlines. Passengers on unscheduled airlines, such as corporate planes, are increasingly being accepted without policy restrictions or increased premium rates. You should be thoroughly knowledgeable of your company's interpretation of aviation restrictions and use of an aviation questionnaire when you take an application. The latter will be used in underwriting some types of pilots and crewmembers. Depending on the type of pilot license, planes flown (especially ultra-light aircraft), and hours of flight, there could be an extra rate for the coverage you sell.

Avocations—Some hobbies and avocations are important underwriting considerations. In a few states where law permits, participation in a hazardous activity may exclude payment of death benefits if it is related to the claim. Hazardous activities include skin diving (to depths over 50 feet), mountain climbing, competitive racing, hang gliding, and skydiving. The underwriting process will reveal these activities; companies have avocation questionnaires for use when applicants indicate participation in these hobbies. Riders for extra premium could be required. Companies are interested in the insured's activities at the time of application, not in hobbies taken up after coverage is in force. This is a situation you may have to deal with occasionally. Prepare yourself on how to handle it before it comes up in an interview.

War Clause—Most contracts in the past have excluded full payment of proceeds to those in the military services during time of war. The purpose has been to control adverse selection due to the reality of increased mortality among those who buy insurance during these periods. The clause normally provides for a return of premium with interest or a sum based on the policy's reserve to the beneficiary. Be sure you know how your company handles the war clause if a policy you deliver contains one. Under the status type of clause, the policy will not pay full benefits while the insured is in the military regardless of how death occurs. The more liberal clause, the so-called results wording, states that death must result from actual combat.

Delay Clause—Life insurance policies must contain a provision granting the company the right to defer payment of any cash value or policy loan (except for paying premiums) up to 6 months after the request is made for it. This provision is intended to protect the company against adverse situations where investments might have to be liquidated. This stems from the banking crisis of the Great Depression of the 1930s. It is intended to be used only under dire circumstances and is designed to protect the remaining policyowners as well as the company.

Dividends

The Divisible Surplus Provision—Dividends are a valuable ownership provision of participating policies. Companies include an additional margin in determining factors such as premium rates, mortality, and investment return. If their experience is better than anticipated, the additional money may be returned to the policyowner in the form of dividends. Although dividend performance may be historically good, adverse mortality experience or periods of sustained inflation could have negative effects on dividend payments. You should discuss dividends in the most conservative terms and show the effect on the policy of a reduced dividend projection. Of course, always emphasize that dividends are not guaranteed.

Instead of dividends, many companies (typically stock companies) usually offer lower premiums. This type of company takes on the risk of higher mortality, decreased interest earnings, and increases in expenses.

Dividend Options—Dividends are paid on participating policies and are considered to be the policyowner's share of the company's divisible surplus. Technically, they are defined as a return of unearned premium. They are based on the company's profits and could provide additional proceeds for the beneficiary at death. They are never guaranteed, are not part of the contract, and will vary based on actual experience of mortality, interest, and expense compared to original actuarial assumptions made in creating the policy.

There are five main dividend options. Dividends may be

- paid in cash
- used to reduce or offset premium payments
- used to purchase paid-up additional insurance
- left with the company and accumulate interest
- used to purchase one-year term insurance

The policyowner chooses an option at issue, but has the right to change this option anytime during the life of the contract. The dividend option that is in effect on the policy anniversary determines how the dividend will be paid that year, if one is paid. If the one-year term insurance option is selected, proof of insurability may be required by the insurance company.

An alternate form of additional income for the beneficiary may be found in nonparticipating and the newer interest-sensitive policies. Excess interest and any other earnings are earmarked to provide an increase in the policy's cash value, to reduce the level of future premium payments, or both.

Postmortem and Terminal Dividends—A postmortem dividend is payable at death and covers the period between the preceding policy anniversary and the date of death. A terminal dividend is a special dividend that a company pays upon the termination of a policy through maturity, death, or surrender. The terminal dividend is usually a percentage of the policy's surrender value. The mortality and maturity dividends may be a percentage of the face amount of the policy or of the reserve, the percentage varying by plan and duration of contract. Not all policies will have these types of dividends.

> **The Truth About the Insurance Agent's Work**
>
> Life insurance offers an efficient method towards economic security. There are four great threats to personal security: unemployment, disability, death, and old age. Life insurance is an instrument that offers some elements of security against these four threats. If there is ample cash value, some supplementary income can be generated. There is also the availability of disability waiver of premium. It is your responsibility to help the public discover these benefits.

Policy Riders

Formal descriptions of any riders that have been included in the policy appear in the contract. Review each of these carefully; note any special purposes and definitions that may be confusing to your client. Three of the most common riders include:

Guaranteed Insurability Option (GIO)—The GIO rider guarantees that the policyowner can buy additional life insurance in the future even if he or she should become uninsurable. Typically, additional life insurance in amounts equal to the face amount of the base policy may be purchased at 3-year intervals beginning at the insured's age 25 and extending to the anniversary date nearest the insured's age 40. Many companies offer options for additional purchase at marriage and at the birth or adoption of a child. When the option is exercised, the additional insurance premium is based on the insured's attained age at the time of each purchase. Generally, the insured has 90 days in which to exercise the purchase option at each of the purchase dates, but this may vary from company to company. The GIO is an especially important option for insureds whose life insurance needs will increase in the future, but who cannot currently afford as much protection as they will eventually buy.

Accidental Death Benefit (ADB)—ADB usually provides an extra sum of insurance, equal to the face amount, if the insured's death is the result of an accident. Accidental death is strictly defined and usually excludes accidents resulting directly or indirectly from any ailment or physical disability of the insured. Generally, ADB can be added at issue or after the fact (which may require the insured to provide evidence of insurability). Most companies do not offer new ADB after ages 55 or 60, and the benefit typically terminates after the insured reaches age 65 or 70.

Waiver of Premium—Waiver of premium is a form of disability benefit that can prevent a policy from lapsing for nonpayment of premiums if the policyowner becomes disabled. In such cases, the company will waive the payment of premiums and keep the policy in force. Most policies specify that the insured must be totally disabled for the waiver to take effect. To qualify, the insured must be continuously disabled for a specific length of time, usually 90 days or 6 months. The insured must continue to pay premiums that come due during the waiting period, but those premiums will be refunded if the insured is disabled long enough for the benefit to begin. The company pays all premiums during the policyowner's disability. If the policyowner recovers and returns to work, regular premium payments are resumed. This benefit period will expire at about age 60 in most policies. Any clause providing benefits in force would continue, but no new claims would be honored. Premium for the rider is not charged when the benefit period expires. The waiver will normally not be granted if the insured's disability is self-inflicted or the result of war.

Settlement Options

Originally, life insurance proceeds were only paid out as cash in lump sums. It is still possible for policyowners to specify that their death proceeds be paid in cash, or beneficiaries may elect this payment form if the decision is left to them. Although they are the most flexible of any payout options, a danger inherent in lump-sum settlements is that the money may be mismanaged, poorly invested, or spent foolishly, resulting in a serious loss to the beneficiaries. For these reasons—and because many surviving families need guaranteed income rather than cash—several other settlement options are available and may be selected by the insured or beneficiary. These options are discussed in detail in Chapter 8.

Explain Provisions Carefully

It is very important that the advisor understands the product and can explain it to the applicant. Interest-sensitive products such as universal life, variable, and variable universal life require special attention when you are reviewing provisions and features. For example, although many of the standard policy provisions discussed here are found in universal life policies, many universal life features such as the coverage, death benefit option, premium, cash accumulation account, monthly deduction, interest crediting, partial withdrawals, and surrender all differ from company to company and product to product. These need to be carefully explained.

When you sell a product, it is your obligation to know the details of your product's features and provisions in order to clearly explain them to policyowners. Many permanent policies will require attention to the cash value performance in future years, and your policyowners need to understand their responsibilities and the future options they will encounter.

The Taxation of Life Insurance

Historically, life insurance has been considered beneficial to the public good because it contributes to the financial preservation of families. Because of this, certain tax benefits are provided for life insurance products.

There are many features of the life insurance contract that provide potential tax benefits to a policyowner or beneficiary. Many of these features are not found in other financial contracts, and certainly very few if any can claim all of them. In most all cases it is not proper to purchase life insurance contracts because of the tax advantages alone. But when considering these benefits in addition to others found, the life policy has a combination of benefits worth considering.

Many of your prospects will have questions about the taxation of personal life insurance policies. Frequently asked questions include:

- "Are life insurance premiums tax deductible?"
- "Will my children have to pay income tax on the proceeds from this policy?"
- "Do I have to pay income tax on the dividends you told me about?"

- "Is this life insurance going to be included in my estate and subject to estate tax?"

To help you with these questions, this discussion will summarize the main points of federal and estate taxes for both life insurance death proceeds and the living benefits of a life insurance contract.

Premiums

Premiums paid for individual life insurance policies in the United States are usually considered a personal expense and are not deductible for income tax purposes. There are some exceptions to this, such as premiums paid for life insurance in an alimony agreement, which may be deductible as alimony payments. Premiums paid for life insurance that is owned by and that is paid to a charity as beneficiary may be deductible as a charitable contribution. In business situations, employers are allowed to deduct premiums for life insurance protection if paid in the form of a bonus to the employee. The employer may then deduct the amount of the bonus as a business expense. Also, if life insurance is part of a pension plan, the premiums are deductible as part of a contribution by the employer to a tax-qualified plan.

Death Benefits

Generally, death proceeds from a life insurance policy are exempt from income taxation when paid in a lump sum. This is because Congress recognizes that life insurance ownership achieves a social purpose and should be encouraged. There are some exceptions to this general rule, and not all state income tax laws follow the lead of the federal tax laws. If the deceased had any incidents of ownership in the policy, it would be included in the estate for estate tax calculations.

Accelerated Death Benefits

Amounts received under a life insurance contract covering the life of an insured who is terminally or chronically ill are now excludible from income as amounts payable by reason of the death of the insured if certain conditions are met. Terminal illness must be certified by a physician, and the illness or condition must typically expected to result in death within 24 months of the certification.

Transfer for Value

One exception to the general rule of income tax-free death benefits is encountered when a policy has been transferred from one owner to another in exchange for valuable consideration. There is then the possibility that part of the proceeds would be subject to federal income tax. The taxable income from the death benefit is reduced by the amount paid to transfer the policy from one owner to another. The net premiums made by the new owner would further reduce taxation at the death of the insured. This would most often arise in connection with business insurance or estate planning cases. Details of this rule will not be covered here, but keep in mind that this type of transfer could negatively impact income taxation of policy proceeds.

Certain transactions are exempt from the transfer for value rule, including situations where the policy is sold to the insured. This situation is often found in business applications of life insurance used to insure employees, partners, officers, and others. Another exception is when the policy is a bona fide gift.

Matured Life Contracts

Another exception to the tax-free treatment of policy proceeds is the policy benefit that becomes payable during the lifetime of the insured because the insured has reached the maturity date specified in the policy. The proceeds would not then be considered a death benefit, and any gains in the policy would be considered ordinary income for the tax year in which they are distributed.

Dividends

During the premium-paying period of the insured's lifetime, personal life insurance premiums generally enjoy no tax advantage; they are not deductible. Participating policies normally receive an annual dividend, which can be paid in cash. The cash dividend is taxable only when and if it exceeds the amount of premiums paid into the policy. Dividends are generally taxed on a first-in first out (FIFO) basis; that is, withdrawals are treated as a nontaxable return of capital to the extent of premiums paid. Withdrawals in excess of premiums paid are taxable.

If dividends are withdrawn or the policy is surrendered, the same type of calculation would be made to determine if proceeds received are in excess of premiums paid, in which case a profit results and ordinary income tax is due on this amount. For this reason, as well as others, paid-up addition is the generally recommended dividend option.

The reason for the dividend not being taxed is that an insurance policy's dividend is considered a refund of excess premiums that have been paid by the policyowner. In most cases, participating insurance providers build a margin into their premium for contingencies. These margins are for mortality experience, persistency, and other variables. If it is not necessary to use the additional premium dollars, the insurance company refunds them to the policyowner in the form of dividends.

If a policyowner chooses not to receive the dividends in cash, but allows the dividends to accumulate at interest with the insurance company, the interest earned on the dividends is subject to taxation as interest income. Such interest payments on the dividends are treated the same as interest on any type of savings account.

Loans

Another living benefit is the loan provision contained in most permanent policies. This gives the policyowner the right to borrow a percentage of the cash value that has accumulated in the policy. If a policy is surrendered with a loan outstanding, and if that loan, with other cash value, is greater than the cumulative premium payments made, then there will be a taxable gain. If there is no loan outstanding and the surrender value is greater than the premiums paid, then the difference will be taxed.

Cash Surrenders and Modified Endowment Contracts

So far most of our discussion has been about the taxation of life insurance proceeds when the insured dies. The rules that apply to mature endowments and to life insurance policies surrendered for the cash value are considerably different.

Cash Surrenders—To determine if income tax is due on the surrender of a (non-MEC) policy for cash or the maturity of an endowment, it must be determined if the amount received from the policy over the life of the contract exceeds the net premiums paid. *Net premiums paid* means the gross premium less any dividends received, less any outstanding loans. This is the cost basis, meaning the amount the policyowner paid with after-tax money. The total net premium is then subtracted from the amount of cash the policyowner receives upon surrender or maturity. Any excess or profit is fully reportable as ordinary taxable income in the year received. Exceptions to this rule would be government policies or GI insurance. Any gains realized with these types of policies are exempt.

Premiums paid for supplementary benefits such as waiver of premium or accidental death riders are not included in the cost basis. Policy loans and cash value withdrawals may also be affected.

Modified Endowment Contract (MEC)—The modified endowment contract or MEC, as it is commonly called, came into being with the 1988 amendment to the tax code (TAMRA, IRC Section 72 and Section 7702A). Prior to this time, people were putting large sums of money into life insurance contracts so they could accumulate funds on a tax-deferred basis. This was contrary to the tax viewpoint that life insurance was to be used primarily to provide a death benefit. TAMRA provided that if a policy was over-funded (whether at issue or at a later date), it would be classified as a modified endowment contract, and as a MEC, any distribution representing a gain from the policy would be taxed.

Two tests were established to determine if a policy should be classified as a MEC. One is the seven-pay test. In short, this establishes limits to the amount of premiums that can be paid into a life insurance policy within a period of 7 years. If the policy was over-funded, it would become a MEC. "Material changes" that occur to a policy once it is in force can cause a policy to be retested. The rules apply as if the changes existed since the beginning of the policy. Your home office should be able to guide you on the classification of a policy as a MEC in these situations.

The Consequences of a MEC—If a policy is or becomes a MEC, it is treated the same as any other life insurance policy with one exception. The exception is that some distributions from a MEC will be taxed on a LIFO (last-in-first-out) basis to the extent there is gain in the policy. In addition, the taxable gain will be subject to a 10-percent penalty unless the distribution is made after age 59½ or death, disability, or annuitization occur.

Distribution from a MEC includes:

- policy loans (including automatic premium loans)
- cash dividends
- withdrawals
- surrenders

If a policy becomes a MEC, it is tainted for as long as it exists. The taint carries over to any policy that is issued in exchange for a MEC, even if the new contract normally would not be classified as a MEC. This means that care must be taken when making a 1035 exchange.

A Section 1035 exchange (tax-free exchange where one policy is exchanged for another meeting certain rules) is a material change for purposes of the MEC rules. According to the IRS, the policy received in exchange will be treated as a newly issued policy with a new 7-year period beginning on the date of exchange. The new policy must be tested under the special seven-pay test. Cash values transferred from the existing policy will not count as premium. If the policy fails the material change test, it will be classified as a MEC. Once again, look to your home office for guidance on these situations.

Remember, even if a policy is a MEC, it is treated the same as any other life insurance policy for tax purposes unless certain distributions are made from the MEC. Only dividends paid in cash are considered distributions for MEC purposes. When dividends or excess interest are used to pay premiums, to buy paid-up additions, or to buy term insurance they are not considered a MEC distribution. Also, when paid-up additions are surrendered to pay premiums, they are not distributions for MEC purposes.

Section 1035 Policy Exchanges

When a policyowner exchanges an existing policy for a new one and does so in accordance with the Internal Revenue Code guidelines of Section 1035, no gain is attributed on the exchange. The adjusted basis of the old policy is carried over to the new one. Only the newly added premium will be measured for MEC status. A section 1035 exchange is allowed only when transferring cash values from an annuity to an annuity, life insurance to life insurance, or life insurance to an annuity contract.

Anticipated Effects of 2001 Mortality Tables

Life insurance must meet certain premium and cash value tests to qualify for the tax benefits afforded by the tax code. The new morality tables will lower the tax reserves required by IRC Sec. 7702 (definition of life insurance) and IRC Section 7702A (Modified Endowment Contract) rules, which will consequently lower cash values, nonforfeiture values, maximum cost of insurance rates, and surrender charges for most issue ages and risk classes. This will lower the amount of premium (5-20 percent, depending on gender and class) allowable for a policy to meet the definition of life insurance and modified endowment tests (7-pay rules). By lowering the maximum amount of premium in all cash value products, their value as accumulation vehicles will be somewhat diminished. These changes may usher in new protection-oriented and accumulation products as companies work to create a market niche and provide competitive products under the new rules.

Summary

The purpose of this brief review of federal taxation of life insurance is simply to alert you to the questions your prospects and clients may ask. It is not definitive, so you should not give tax advice based on this information. When a client believes that a personal tax problem might result from the use of life insurance, the client should consult his or her own tax adviser. Your company will be able to help you in specific cases.

You may depend upon your life insurance company to provide the client with accurate information when any notice of taxation is sent. Ask your agency for further information about the taxation of the products you sell.

An Advisor Speaks:

What's a Tear Worth?

> *Paul R. Jeffers, CLU, ChFC wrote this article for LUTC several months before he died in February 1996. He was a well-known, national figure who spoke about the sale of life insurance to groups in every state and from the main platform at MDRT. He was a past president of California's ALU as well as his own Sacramento association and served as a national committee chairman.*

When I began selling life insurance about 40 years ago, I came across an advertisement in one of the magazines of the day. This ad was for tombstones and covered two pages back-to-back. The first page showed a picture of the front of the tombstone, facing the lettering. A small boy, about 8 or 9, stood with his back to the camera, facing the tombstone. He wore a Cub Scout shirt, a hat, and an old pair of scruffy jeans. Just over the little boy's shoulder, you could read the word "Daddy" carved on the tombstone. As you turned the page, the same scene was photographed on the reverse page, but from the opposite direction. It showed the back of the tombstone and the little boy's face. This picture showed the boy giving the tombstone his Cub Scout's salute as a big tear rolled down his cheek. The caption read, "What's A Tear Worth?"

As I looked back-and-forth between these pages, suddenly I realized that this was an ad about life insurance, not the sale of tombstones. That father's dreams for this little boy's life rested with the plans he had made in the past. Had he protected his family's future? Would dreams of home, education, and the pleasures of growing up in a loving, sheltered environment be there for this young boy? Was this the tear of sorrow or of desperation?

If that father could do it again, how much life insurance do you suppose that tear would mean to him? Don't you think that he would buy all the life insurance he could afford and then some? I think he would. As I have thought about this ad with the tombstone over the years, I have been inspired again and again to urge my clients to buy all the life insurance they could afford. There is but one life for each of us to insure. None of us knows how long it will last, and there is no second chance. As an advisor, I have felt the obligation never to miss the opportunity to push for the maximum protection a family could be provided by a policy the family's breadwinner(s) purchased.

I believe I know what our life insurance product is. It is, in fact, the greatest language of love ever known. Let me give you a couple illustrations to show you why I believe this to be so.

Not long ago, I delivered a death claim check of $800,000 on a 42-year-old doctor who went out one morning for his usual 5- to 6-mile run. He came back to the house after running and walked into the kitchen to say something to his wife. He fell to the floor with his head on her slipper. He was dead! He had an aortic aneurysm and had died instantly. He left his widow and two children with the $800,000. His practice that had been paying him $436,000 per year was sold for $-0-. The widow didn't get a nickel for it. Do you know why? The other doctors told her, "why should we buy it, those people have to come to us anyway?"

The widow had a house that was paid for and the $800,000 in a trust. This money in trust was given to her as monthly income. With every check that doctor told his widow, "I love you."

I delivered another check to a friend of mine who lost his 54-year-old wife to cancer. I laid the $200,000 check on his office desk. He started crying and so did I. After he regained control, he told me the following: "Paul, do you remember the trouble I gave you when you sold this policy to me? I told you it was the dumbest thing I could do."

He continued, "You persisted and I probably bought it just to get rid of you. Paul, let me tell you this, if I did not have this insurance money right now, I would lose everything I have. My business would be gone and I would have to start over. Your insurance policy is keeping me from going bankrupt and, thank God, you kept after me to do something that I should have done without any urging. *"You saved my business and my life."*

So, what is a tear worth? If you don't have life insurance, is it worth the suffering your family will go through because you just didn't have enough sense to buy adequate amounts when you had the chance?

I like to think that life insurance premiums are always paid, either during your lifetime by paying for a life insurance policy, or at death, by the family doing without those things that are so important to them. Which way is the best way? I spend my life helping people decide what the worth of that tear really is.

Case History
Lighting the Fire

C.W. Girard, LUTCF, CLU, ChFC has been an insurance agent for 25 years in a large Midwestern community along the banks of the Missouri River. He related this story about the experience he had as young agent that awoke him to the true value of life insurance to survivors. He always tells the new agents in his office that it was a policyowner's death that made him into a salesman.

My Frame of Mind—I awoke early on a crisp day in November and went for a long walk to get some exercise before my family woke. My early morning walks have always been one of my stress relievers—they give me a chance to get out and think through the things on my mind without the phone ringing or other distractions.

Shocking News—When I returned home that particular day, my wife met me at the door, almost in hysterics. My first thought was that something happened to one of the kids. A shake of the head told me no, and she said, "It's Kathy." In a halting voice, she told me Kathy—one of our closest friends—had died suddenly, unexpectedly, during the night. Kathy's father-in-law had called for me when I was out and asked that I come over as soon as possible.

After my wife assured me she was all right, I drove to Kathy and Dave's home. There were several cars parked outside, and I was met at the door by Dave's father, whom I know from many social and family events. He quickly told me Dave was at the hospital and would be home soon. He wasn't sure what had happened to Kathy—perhaps an aneurysm or stroke while she slept. I waited with him and a few neighbors while we shared memories and coffee to pass the time. Everyone was in a state of shock.

Remembering the Sale—The next few days passed in a blur. I thought often of Kathy and Dave, and their three children. They were among my first clients and I'm sure their first purchases were made with more concern for my welfare than theirs. I remembered Kathy laughing when we wrote up her first policy—$250,000 term—when I called it "a small one." We converted part of it 2 years later, but that was all the coverage she had in force. At her funeral, I cried for all the usual reasons and some special ones too, knowing Dave would have enough money to take care of the kids' college education.

Help From the Agency—I talked with my manager about how to file the claim before I worked up the courage to talk with Dave. My manager told me to wait a few days, and just be a friend for now. Three days later she called me into her office and had a settlement check for me—she had called the home office to explain the circumstances, obtained a copy of the death certificate from the funeral home, faxed a copy of the obituary from the paper, and took care of the paperwork for me. She suggested I meet with Dave, hand him the check in a sealed envelope, and simply offer to help when he was ready.

I went directly to Dave's home that afternoon and found him there with his dad. They were looking at old photo albums and talking of Kathy and Dave's mother, who had passed away several years before. They were in surprisingly good spirits as they remembered the good times of the past. I joined them on a nearby chair. Dave saw my briefcase and commented we could take care of business later. After looking at the photos, the kids came home from school. Following a hug and a snack, Dave's dad said he would take care of them for a while so we could talk.

Help From the Beneficiary—I didn't know what to say, but Dave made it easy for me by asking if I had paperwork for Kathy. I nodded my head and handed him the envelope. "I know we can't bring Kathy back, but she wanted you to have this. I suggest for now you put this into a money market account, and we can talk some more when you are ready." He agreed, signed a form, took my hands in his and simply said, "Thank you." It seemed like minutes, but after a few moments he offered me another cup of coffee and we returned to the dining room.

Three months later, I reflected on the events that had happened. Dave did invite me over after a few weeks passed, having spent the holidays in Florida with his dad and the kids. He asked about investments for college, and I suggested a mix of mutual funds. He wrote a check for most of the settlement proceeds immediately. I mentioned also that this might be a good time to review his life insurance coverage and look at converting his term policy. For premiums, he could use some of the interest and growth from the investments, and the growth in cash values would be available for college or retirement, too. Dave liked this idea and then mentioned his dad wanted to talk to me. Asking if there was anyone else that might be able to benefit from my services, he brought out his address book and gave me 21 more names and told me to use his name. Never had a client been so willing to help me.

What I Learned—I learned a great deal from the loss of my friend. It was the first time I had experienced the death of someone my own age, someone I knew so well. It made me appreciate life even more. My wife and I grew closer than we ever had been, and we made a real effort to spend more time together with out family. We saw first-hand how life insurance can help, and my commitment to the business became stronger than ever before.

The Outcome—I am also closer to my associates at the office, many of whom have heard me relate over and over how much we help people when they need it the most. Our ties with Dave and his family are closer than ever before, too. He was able to take time off to be with his family and not worry about money. Kathy's dream that the children attend college is still alive. I know, too, that the next time I get discouraged I will remember my friends Kathy and Dave, and I will persevere to help others help themselves.

Chapter One Review

Key Terms and Concepts are explained in the Glossary. Answers to the Review Questions and Self-Test Questions are found in the back of the book in the Answers to Questions section.

Key Terms and Concepts

life insurance needs
total needs selling
client-focused sales/planning approach
income needs
readjustment income
dependency period
blackout period
cash needs
final expenses
emergency fund
human life value
capitalized value
present value
tax-deferred
reinstatement
assignment
nonforfeiture provisions
settlement options
aleatory contract
unilateral contract
automatic premium loan
National Association of Insurance Commissioners (NAIC)
FIFI/LIFO cost recovery rules
Modified Endowment Contract (MEC)
tax qualified retirement plan
law of large numbers
2001 CSO mortality tables
new money rate
portfolio rate
policy date
incontestability
grace period
mortality, interest, expense
automatic premium loan
probate
cost basis
policy loan
misstatement of age
guaranteed insurability
Section 1035 exchange
contact of adhesion
incontestable clause
policy riders

Review Questions

1-1. How can life insurance provide a solution for the economic loss of a breadwinner?

1-2. What is the concept of human life value and how does it relate to life insurance?

1-3. What are the benefits of life insurance?

1-4. What are the general insurance principles that are the basis for life insurance?

1-5. What three elements create and structure a life insurance policy?

1-6. How can mortality tables be used to predict mortality and life expectancy?

1-7. What is the importance of the policy provisions to a life insurance contract?

1-8. Define the following policy provisions:

entire contract
incontestability
automatic premium loan
reinstatement
assignment
nonforfeiture options
policy loan

1-9. What are the general tax rules that usually apply to individual life insurance policies?

Self-Test Questions

Instructions: Read chapter 1 first, then answer the following questions to test your knowledge. Circle the correct answer. When finished with the test, check your answers with the answer key in the back of the book.

1-1. The national organization that offers model regulations to the individual States to provide uniformity to insurance regulations is

(A) LUTC
(B) NAIFA
(C) SFSP
(D) NAIC

1-2. When the premium for Irene's life insurance policy was still unpaid at the end of the grace period, what action would the insurance company have taken on her 10-year-old whole life plan with $8,000 cash value and the APL (automatic premium loan) option?

(A) cancelled the policy
(B) surrendered the policy for the $8,000 cash value
(C) advanced the premium payment automatically as a loan from the $8,000 cash value
(D) moved the policy to an extended term plan under the settlement options

1-3. If the insured is found to be younger at death than was stated in the application for an insurance policy, the company will

(A) do nothing
(B) refund all premiums
(C) increase the coverage amount to what the premiums would have purchased
(D) decrease the coverage amount to what the premiums would have purchased

1-4. An insured policyowner has access to the cash value of a policy by electing to use which of the following?

(A) nonforfeiture option
(B) policy loan
(C) automatic premium loan
(D) all of the above

1-5. The human life value approach assumes that a person's economic value is an amount equal to the

(A) capitalized value of a person's gross future earnings
(B) capitalized value of the person's net future earnings
(C) needs of the family if the person should die
(D) life income needs of the surviving dependent spouse

1-6. Which of the following investments accounts for the largest share of assets of U.S. life insurance companies?

(A) bonds
(B) policy loans
(C) stocks
(D) real estate

1-7. The new mortality tables currently being introduced by the NAIC are called the

(A) 2001 CSO Tables
(B) 2002 CSO Tables
(C) 2003 CSO Tables
(D) new morality tables

1-8. Which of the following statements regarding the misstatement of age provision is (are) correct?

I. The company reserves the right to adjust the policy to the insured's correct age at any time.
II. Inaccurate statements about the insured's age are material misrepresentations and void (make invalid) the policy.

(A) I only
(B) II only
(C) Both I and II
(D) Neither I nor II

1-9. Three factors that contribute to the determination of the premium and the structure of a life insurance policy include all of the following EXCEPT

(A) expense
(B) investment
(C) mortality
(D) lapse rates

1-10. If a policy becomes a Modified Endowment Contract (MEC), taxation of all of the following may be affected EXCEPT

(A) withdrawals
(B) loans
(C) surrenders
(D) death benefits

2

The Selling/Planning Process for Life Insurance

Overview and Learning Objectives

Chapter 2 takes a close look at the selling/planning process from the viewpoint of both the advisor and the prospect. The buying cycle and the selling/planning process are the initial focus. Then in examining the client-focused sales approach and the total-needs approach to interacting with the prospect, we begin to look at the advisor's opportunities to build a long-term relationship based on trust and confidence. In discussing professional practice techniques, the chapter also reviews the obligations of the professional advisor and key issues of compliant and ethical behavior.

By reading this chapter and answering the questions, you should be able to

2-1. List and explain the five steps in the buying cycle.

2-2. List and explain the eight steps in the selling/planning process.

2-3. List and describe the steps in the financial planning process.

2-4. Describe the key points of the client-focused sales approach.

2-5. Describe the total-needs approach to selling.

2-6. List advisor obligations regarding the client, the industry, the company, and the public.

2-7. Explain key areas and issues of compliant and ethical advisor conduct.

Chapter Outline

The Buying Cycle

There are two sides to every purchase: something is bought and something is sold. In the professional sales/planning process, it is essential that the advisor understand the buyer's side of the situation. Because of the intangible nature of life insurance and a general aversion to the concept of personal mortality in our society, the advisor typically takes the initiative in the sales process. But sales do not happen without the buyer's cooperation and participation. In the client-focused sales process, discussed in this chapter, the buyer's realization and acceptance of needs and goals is of utmost importance. By understanding the buying cycle, the advisor can appreciate the process from the buyer's perspective. This is where empathy and client-focused behavior by the advisor plays a key role.

In this chapter, we will review the sale from the buyer's side, the steps a buyer goes through in making a purchase, the length of time it takes to complete a sale, the client-focused and total needs approach to the sales/planning process, and the ethical, professional, and compliance issues that every financial advisor should know and follow in a responsible manner.

The buying cycle is universal to all buying decisions. You engage it whenever you select a product or service and make a purchase. You use these steps when you buy a home, a package of cheese at the grocery store, a new coffee pot, or a financial product such as life insurance.

The five steps in the buying cycle are:

1. **Recognize the problem or need**. The buyer must recognize that there is a problem, an unfulfilled need or want, and the nature and extent of it must be identified and understood.
2. **Desire a solution**. A buyer must have a strong desire to solve the recognized problem. There must be a compelling reason to act now rather than later if a sale is to be made.
3. **Decide on the best available choice**. A buyer must believe that the solution proposed is the most appropriate one for solving the problem now. This should not depend on price alone. An

intelligent purchase should be based on value (quality relative to cost). Many factors affect the choice including price, product performance, expected service, the company's ratings and, of course, the salesperson. In many cases the salesperson is the deciding factor in favor of the purchase. Personal interaction and the value the advisor brings to the client are very important.

4. **Make the purchase.** A buyer must be able and willing to exchange money in order to solve the problem. Remember—people like to buy; they don't like to be "sold."
5. **Take delivery.** The purchase is completed when it is received in hand. This is a psychologically sensitive moment in the purchase. A buyer may experience regret or "buyer's remorse" because he or she may feel that, for whatever reason, this is not the best solution to the problem. The product may be returned and the sale lost. At this point satisfaction with the purchase is critical. Customer satisfaction is the advisor's continuing challenge because retention of clients is important for long-term success.

Let's look at the buying process using the purchase of a home as an example. First, the homeowner must be dissatisfied with the present home. Perhaps it is too small or the street has become too busy for children to play in the neighborhood. Second, the homeowner must be unhappy enough with the present home to want a new home somewhere else. Third, the prospective home buyer must be satisfied that the selected new house is better than the present one and that it is worth the money. Next, the prospect must be able and willing to spend the money to buy it. Not until the prospect signs the contract to close, arranges to pay, and takes possession is the sale complete. It takes work and desire on everyone's part to make this happen. The buyer and the seller must cooperate. They interact to achieve their needs and goals.

In trying to understand the buyer's perspective, the advisor should ask the following questions:

- How do I properly assist another to make a buying decision?
- How do I find out what the prospect wants and/or needs?
- How do I develop trust and rapport with my client?
- What goes through the consumer's mind while deciding to buy a particular product?

- How much will the prospect be willing to commit to the solution?
- Once committed to buying, how can I keep the client satisfied with the purchase?
- Will the client buy again?
- Will the client refer me to other prospects?

But there is something very important missing from the buying cycle. There is no post-purchase step for satisfaction with what was bought. You most likely have suffered buyer's remorse at one time or another. You feel regret when you realize that your purchase was not the right one or that you shouldn't have made a purchase in the first place. There are times when there is no remedy for a bad purchasing decision. When there is, you might act on your dissatisfaction. You might take the hammer back to the hardware store because the handle grip didn't feel right.

This regret after a purchase may be even greater for the person who buys a life insurance policy. Life insurance is an intangible product that promises to pay dollars in the future, typically many years from now, at the death of the insured. The policyowner trusts the money will be there, but he or she can't hold or touch this money today. There is no immediate pride and satisfaction as there is when the buyer looks at his or her beautiful new house or shiny new sports car. The experienced advisor recognizes this potential problem and handles it by developing good relationships, keeping in touch, offering and delivering quality service, and reminding the client of the reasons for the purchase.

Selling: Art or Science?

Life insurance selling is both an art and a science. The science is knowledge of the product. Anyone can learn the science. People fail in the insurance industry because they cannot master the art: prospecting, interviewing, and building relationships.

Another aspect of client satisfaction is that the advisor experiences his or her greatest feelings of success and satisfaction at the very moment when buyer's remorse could set in for the new policyowner. After the policy is issued and delivered and the sales commission is on its way, many advisors believe this case is completed. Yet there is an important psychological difference between the experiences of the advisor and the new policyowner. The wise advisor will always remember that the focus must center on the policyowner's peace of mind and continued satisfaction. The selling and buying cycle never really ends with a life insurance product. The client must continue to pay the premium. This topic will be discussed in detail in Chapter 8.

What the Customer Says

"I can't stand salespeople who call me, immediately say they have this great product and start pitching, or want to come to my office and waste my time in person. Nearly always, their pitches are way off target."

"I want someone who knows their product inside and out and can apply that knowledge to what I want. Get my attention quickly by telling me what you might be able to do, and be prepared to ask questions to learn what I want. Then you are ready to make a presentation. Getting the best value over the long haul is more important than a low price."

"Sales reps should think more about my needs and less about their sales."

"Good salespeople always seek to build relationships with their customers, but their quest for a relationship is almost always transparent."

"The old, back-slapping 'How yah doin', buddy, can I take you out to lunch?' approach really turns me off."

"I knew she hadn't heard anything I said. Her inability to listen and her persistence in her static sales approach showed that she was unaware of my needs and only wanted to wear me down so she could make her sale. How could I trust her when she didn't listen to me or care about my needs?"

"Too often salespeople are only interested in telling me what they offer. I've never yet had anyone ask me, 'What are your goals for this year?' Seldom does anyone take time for a needs analysis. Do a needs analysis and compare my needs with what you can offer. Then, based on this analysis, prepare some possible matches of offerings and needs."

"Don't ever make me call about the status of an application or a service request. Tell me the truth, and anticipate problems and have a solution before calling me."

Selling in Today's Climate

The massive array of available choices has caused today's buyer to adjust. The Internet and modern technology in the 21st century have brought almost unlimited options to the buyer. There is simply too much happening to absorb it all. Everyone is bombarded with new ideas and too much information about these ideas. We are asked to do more and to think about more. The "good old days" are gone.

What has been done about the rapid change and the value of information? Very little, and the result is a profound impact on how people handle the decisions of their lives. Most of us scramble to keep up. No one wants to make a mistake. A better deal seems to wait around every corner. It seems like technology introduces product and service innovations daily. Each of us wants to consider all of the options. This takes time and has led to what is described as the "extended buying cycle."

A large group of life financial advisors who were asked about this phenomenon said the extended buying cycle described their marketplace well. They are finding it takes longer to get an application signed. It doesn't matter whether the case is for a modest sum of life insurance or for a mega-dollar amount involving several decision makers. Consequently, completing a sale takes longer today, apparently the result of increased client sophistication and greater consumer awareness of financial products.

Although the buyer may be considering many options, there is no urgency to commit to one course of action. Many alternatives compete for a person's attention and dollars. This bombardment of ideas and options never lets up. When the moment of peak interest passes another distraction replaces it, and there is a new challenge that prevents a sustained interest in the proposed plan.

The Right Attitude

New attitudes must be developed to accommodate our changing world. A new attitude toward success will come from newly learned patience, superior knowledge, and a willingness to be the prospect's adviser over a long period of time.

The new environment of the extended buying cycle can discourage anyone who sells. Sales management and the need to earn a living pressure you to complete sales. This is how you build success. You need ongoing sales with a continuing stream of commission income to succeed.

A consequence of this urgency is that the slow buyer is often discarded. This is the person who will never say no but may never say yes either. You become frustrated and discard the names from your files of good, qualified prospects. Some of these people may be victims of the extended buying cycle. They are not about to be pushed into a decision they're not ready to make. The financial advisor interprets this as disinterest and stops calling them.

You must learn to work effectively with slow bloomers. The following points suggest how to work with them and cope with the frustrations of the extended buying cycle.

Know Your Buyer—The first step in working with people today is to gain an understanding of the buyer and why they buy. Learning about the factors involved in the buyer's decision-making process will be a tremendous advantage. Spend the majority of your time with the prospect asking questions, learning, and building confidence and trust. It is easy enough to ask how they choose products to buy. For instance, what kind of research did they do before they bought that shiny new car in the driveway? How long did they lookbefore selecting the car? The answers to these questions reveal a picture of how the advisor and the prospect might work together on the purchase of life insurance.

What about a buyer who makes it clear that he or she knows exactly what is needed? This can be a deceptive situation. It may take more than blindly preparing the proposal the buyer is asking for. Quite often, such openers are merely a way of announcing who's in charge. The buyer may also be trying to impress you with his or her knowledge of the insurance business or financial planning issues. He or she may be looking for respect or may be afraid of making the wrong decision. He or she may not want to lose control of the situation, appear uninformed, or face sales pressure.

In these cases, prepare yourself for the long haul. Do not quit too soon. Knowing that there are many people to see, you might overlook many sales that will take time to nurture through an extended buying cycle. Consequently, you may not be available when the prospect is ready to buy.

Make a statement of commitment to your prospects when you begin working with them on their life insurance needs. Share a philosophy that says, "I want your business and I'm here to work with you." This indicates to your prospects that you are interested and will remain interested for a long time. You are committing to servicing their needs and you are establishing an advisor-client type relationship that turns one-shot customers into long-term clients.

You may spend more time gaining a client than you ever expected. The client-focused approach is committed to not pressuring for closure until the buyer is ready. Just as important is the commitment to work with the buyer so that the purchase will take place.

The *Advertising Research Foundation* issued the following statistics: 35 percent of buyers surveyed took up to 90 days to make their buying decision; 28 percent took from 3 to 6 months, and 19 percent waited 6 months to a year. Interestingly, in this same study, the participants said that when it came to future purchases only 13 percent would buy within 90 days; 44 percent said they would need 6 to 12 months. It appears that participants in this study thought it would take a long time to make a decision, longer than it actually did. People today do not want to feel pressured to make a buying decision.

Relationship Builders and Breakers

Builders:	**Breakers:**
Treat customers like lifelong partners.	Simply wait for a problem to develop.
Deliver more service than you promise.	Focus only on making the sale.
Schedule regular service calls.	Over-promise and under-deliver.
Develop open and honest communication.	Wait for your customers to call you.
Take responsibility for mistakes made.	Lie or make exaggerated claims.
Become a solutions provider.	Knock a competitor.
Establish a firm foundation for a productive relationship.	Focus on your own personal gain.

You are the Buyer's Resource—The advisor's critical task is to become a helpful resource to the buyer. You may have to prepare yourself mentally for meeting people who will require a long-term buying cycle. This makes it even more critical to continue to offer the best service possible in order to address the new needs of those clients you have. This is the group where you have already established your expertise, your interest, and your patience. You understand them. They trust you with their future decisions and the purchases that secure the financial safety of their families and business interests.

What will long-term selling become? Financial advisors will need to change their thinking about the way they sell to the people who are trapped in the mentality of an extended buying cycle. The seeds of prospecting will take longer to sprout. If you want to do business with these types of prospects, you must be willing to work at their pace and with their sporadic levels of interest.

You can accomplish this by extending your planning periods. You should already have weekly, monthly, and annual sales goals. Consider extending the same concern and number crunching to periods of 3 to 5 years into the future. When you are able to shift your prospect's name from this week to this year or even to 3 years down the road, you will not become impatient and give up too soon. Your new prospecting will fill the holes as you expand your own selling cycle. Over the long haul your business will also increase because there are more seeds out there to harvest.

Your close attention during the extended buying cycle will keep your clients from considering the competition because you are building a relationship that is not easily severed. The client turns to the advisor, not a stranger, for answers.

Many advisors feel this extended buying cycle is changing their selling process. It will upset some who are used to going in and out of the door, never stopping to look at the customer again. They have already missed more repeat business than they have written. More astute advisors may view the extended buying cycle as another opportunity to educate the buyer while demonstrating their own professional sales abilities.

If You Ain't Sold, You Can't Sell!

Remember: The seller usually determines the cost of a product or service, but only the buyer can determine its true value.

If you are healthy, you might consider an artificial heart a very poor bargain at $3.98, but if your heart were failing rapidly, you would probably trade everything you had for it. Just because you personally would not pay the asking price for a house is no sign that someone else would not be delighted to get it for that price - even if they knew everything you know about it.

So, if you have difficulty understanding the value of what you are selling, keep in mind that ultimately it is always the buyer who decides how much it is worth to him or her. Remember, "Beauty is in the eye of the beholder."

You can only convince others of the value of what you are selling when you are convinced of its value. As salespeople, our task is not to impart value to products that have none, or even to determine the value of a product to the end user. Your task is to convince your prospects that what you are selling has more value than the money they would pay for it or for anything else they could ever buy with that money.

You can only do that when you are thoroughly convinced of the value of what it is you are selling. You've got to believe in what you are selling to make your customers believe in what they are buying. It's as simple and straightforward as that.

Bill Brooks

Source: ***www.billbrooks.com.*** *Reprinted with permission.*

Overview of the Selling/Planning Process

This textbook is designed to help you develop and improve your sales skills, your knowledge of the reasons to own life insurance, and the features and benefits of life insurance products. A thorough understanding of the selling and buying process will help you achieve sales success and produce satisfied clients. Working with the prospect means guiding that person through each step of the selling/planning process. If any step is omitted or inadequately completed, the result will be that a sale is not made, or the sale will be on an unstable foundation and may end in disappointment. By following the selling/planning process systematically, better results will be obtained for both buyer and seller because a more complete process will be achieved. If the sale is not successful, it provides you with an opportunity to analyze what took place between you and the prospect, and identify the areas that need strengthening and improvement.

The selling/planning process involves eight steps and culminates with satisfying the needs and wants of the buyer with the appropriate product or service solution. This matching plus your own creativity may convince the buyer to act now, to buy now, and to solve the need.

The Eight Steps of the Selling/Planning Process

1. **Identify the prospect:** Identify whom you are going to approach and why. Effective selling begins when you find prospects likely to need and afford your products. They appreciate you and your services and may be a source for repeat business and referrals. You need a system to consistently find potential clients in target markets. The secret to successful selling is prospecting and marketing.

2. **Approach the prospect:** Contact the prospect by telephone, by mail, or face-to-face and ask for the appointment, stating the reason why you are interested in meeting. As telemarketing and direct mail become less effective today, referral prospecting becomes more critical than ever. With the implementation of the "Do-Not-Call"lists, the use of caller ID, telephone answering machines, and the general displeasure and negative public attitude toward telephone solicitation, new efforts and outcomes of contacting the public will be tested. Perhaps direct mail will regain popularity by both the public and the financial services industry as an approach method, or other methods will emerge, such as affinity marketing. *(These first two steps of the sales/planning process are covered in another title in the Financial Advisor Series,* Techniques for Exploring Personal Markets*).*

3. **Meet the prospect:** In the initial interview you establish rapport and explain your business purpose. Make positive statements about yourself, your company, and the services you offer. Ask thought-provoking and challenging questions and encourage agreement to proceed with the gathering of relevant information about the prospect. Impress upon the prospect what makes you different from other providers and what you offer that is of added value. Interest by the prospect in pursuing solutions to uncovered needs must be established for the sales/planning process to proceed. This is the topic of Chapter 3.

4. **Gather information and establish goals:** Using the fact-finder, ask questions that will uncover the prospect's situation. This will include considerable information about goals, attitudes, and priorities, in addition to facts about their personal and financial lives. Ask the prospect to define his or her expectations for your relationship. What results does he or she want? This will help you find out what to deliver and how to deliver it.

   Information is required to define the prospect's current situation, determine his or her desired future situation and when it is to be achieved, and establish what the prospect is willing and able to do to achieve those goals. This information must be accurate, complete, up-to-date, relevant to the prospect's goals, and well organized. Otherwise, financial plans based on erroneous information, or lack of it, will be deficient, inappropriate, inconsistent with the prospect's other goals, or even dangerous to his or her well being.

Goal setting is important to creating a successful financial plan. By guiding the prospect through the goal-setting exercise, the advisor not only helps to establish reasonable, achievable goals, but also sets the tone for the entire financial planning process and the total advisor-client relationship. We will explore this topic further in Chapter 4.

5. **Analyze the information:** Once the relevant information about the prospect has been gathered, organized, and checked for accuracy, consistency and completeness, you need to analyze the prospect's present financial situation. The objective is to identify where the prospect is now in relationship to the goals that were established in the previous step.

   Although the prospect's situation may reveal a number of strengths, more than likely your analysis of the prospect's present situation will also reveal a number of weaknesses or conditions that are preventing achievement of the prospect's goals. The prospect may have excellent fringe benefits at work, including good life, medical, and disability insurance benefits. He may have just recently updated his will and installed a living will and included provisions that legally carry out his wishes in the case of death or catastrophic illness. On the other hand, the prospect may be using debt unwisely, amassing credit card and other debt, paying unnecessarily high federal income taxes, or be inadequately insured. A prospect's investment portfolio may be inconsistent with her investment objectives or risk tolerance.

   It may be that the prospect cannot realistically attain the goals stated, and they need to be revised. For example, the prospect's income and resources may prevent reaching a specified retirement income goal or retirement starting age. In this case, the advisor should help the prospect revisit the goal and revise it, or discuss what needs to be done to achieve that goal. Postponing retirement, saving more money, seeking higher returns, or deciding to deplete principal during retirement may be four ways to help the prospect achieve the retirement goal. Presented as alternatives, the advisor can help the prospect restate the original goal in terms that will more likely make it achievable.

You must identify real problems and needs to which your products and services will provide real solutions. You must then design a plan that responds to these problems and needs. We will cover this topic in Chapter 5.

6. **Develop and present the plan:** After the information has been analyzed and the objectives to be achieved confirmed, and if necessary revised, the next step is to devise a realistic plan for bringing the prospect from his or her present financial position to the attainment of those objectives. A good plan must reflect the prospect's needs, attitudes and goals. Remember, the plan must be the prospect's plan, not the advisor's plan.

   It is not likely that any individual advisor can maintain familiarity with all the strategies that may be available and appropriate for a given prospect's situation. Based on his or her education, experience, training and specialization, the advisor is likely to rely on a given number of proven strategies and products that typically work when encountering similar prospect circumstances. When additional expertise is needed, the advisor should always consult with another advisor who is a specialist in the field in question to help the advisor design that aspect of the prospect's plan.

   There is usually more than one way to achieve a prospect's financial goals. When this is the case, the advisor should present alternative strategies for the prospect to consider and should explain the advantages and disadvantages of each strategy.

   Your presentation should provide an answer to the problems and needs discovered in your analysis of the prospect's situation. You support the decision to buy now because your product is the best available solution. Of course, your prospect must agree with this conclusion. You want to anticipate client concerns and provide answers for them.

   After the plan is presented and reviewed with the prospect, the "moment of truth" arrives. The advisor must ask the prospect to approve the plan, or some compromise alternative, and commit to purchasing any products that may be a part of the plan's implementation. Planning does involve selling. We will address this topic and the life insurance products that support the solution in Chapter 6.

7. **Implement the plan:** You must motivate the prospect to act and help the prospect acquire all of the financial products and services required to put the plan into action. You must answer client concerns that may prevent him or her from implementing the plan. You need to then support the decision to buy those products. Complete the application(s) and all required forms, explain the process to the prospect, and verify that everything that is being done is understood. Perform or order all field underwriting requirements as needed. If the plan is limited in scope or complexity, it may be within the advisor's ability to implement the plan entirely. Otherwise, it may be necessary to call upon additional specialized professional expertise where needed. For example, legal instruments, such as wills and trusts, may need to be drawn up and executed. It is typically part of the advisor's responsibility to motivate and assist the prospect in completing each of the steps necessary to fully implement the plan. This topic is covered in Chapter 7.

8. **Service the plan:** This may be the most important step in preserving your hard work and expanding on it. Deliver the policy and reaffirm the decision to buy and the problems that can be solved by having this product. Reinforce the benefits you are providing. Get referrals. Service will help you build your long-term career as a financial services professional. Through service you enhance and cement your relationship with each new client, make additional sales, and set the stage to obtain quality referrals to new prospects.

   The relationship between the advisor and client should be an ongoing one. Normally the advisor meets with the client once a year, or more or less frequently as agreed upon, to review the performance of the vehicles selected to implement the plan, and to review any changes in the client's personal or financial situation, or in the world around him or her (economic, tax or financial environment) that would warrant making any changes to the plan. Service is the subject of Chapter 8.

Steps of the Selling/Planning Process:

Summary

These 8 steps in the selling cycle all contribute to implementing a solution to the client's financial concerns. The process is designed to first satisfy the prospect's needs and then motivate him or her to buy now. In summary, the actions you take are: identify the need, create the desire to solve it, build acceptance of your solution as the best way to solve it, and encourage your prospect to make the purchase today. There is naturally a delicate balance between serving as a counselor and advocate in the buying process and acting as a professional salesperson who needs immediate action and positive sales results. Within the context of the client-focused sales process, the professional salesperson has an obligation to strongly encourage the prospect to take immediate action to place needed life insurance in effect. Considering the possible deterioration of health or death, the cost of waiting could be serious and detrimental to dependents.

Each of the eight steps is critically important to the sale. If a step is missed or not covered sufficiently, the sale will have a greater chance of failing.

The First Two Steps of the Selling/Planning Process

This text is organized around the selling/planning process outlined above. It will cover those aspects of the advisor-prospect interaction that begin at the point where the advisor and prospect typically sit down together to engage this planning process. Let's briefly review those selling steps that are not covered in this textbook.

1. Identify the Prospect—It is a rare life insurance buyer who both recognizes a need and initiates the purchase. A very old industry expression states that life insurance is sold, not bought. This reflects the need for the life insurance advisor to initiate the sales process. It is important to recognize the tendency to procrastinate when prospects approach life insurance, which is often due to a general lack of knowledge of and the denial of the need for it. The role of the advisor is to use the client-focused sales approach to help a person recognize and accept a need, and to seriously consider resolving that need.

Effective and successful selling begins with getting in front of quality prospects on a consistent basis. You want to look for prospects that have a high probability of being qualified prospects; that is, they have a need, they are able to pay, they can qualify medically, and they are willing to see you. You want to find people who will value you and what you can do for people, and who will be a source for repeat business and referrals. A systematic approach will help you find target markets of potential buyers and will enable you to market efficiently and effectively.

> **Any man who doesn't believe in life insurance deserves to die once without having any.**
>
> **—Will Rogers**

The advisor must have a constant flow of prospects. You are a "work creator," meaning that you, not your company or agency, must provide the work for your position. Prospecting is an ongoing activity and must be attended to daily to maintain the flow of potential customers. Everyone who is successful at marketing and selling life insurance has a means to gather and organize names. They collect them consistently and systematically, so that they have new people to call every day, people who may be interested in addressing financial issues that concern them.

Finding Prospects—Potential prospects are everywhere. Yet the biggest reason for advisors leaving this business is the lack of qualified prospects. A closer look at their experience reveals that they simply did not have an ongoing, organized prospecting system. One survey showed that 65 percent of the insured respondents reported they had never been asked for a referred lead. In this business, buyers do not come to you. You must seek out and approach the buyers.

Referrals—Referrals are the most effective source of new names because a third party, usually a client, recommends them. The advisor is being given a powerful introduction to the prospect. The referrer thought enough of that advisor's work and professionalism to suggest that another person would benefit from it.

Prospects and clients should expect you to ask for referrals. You can pave the way for this by clearly informing the prospect that your business depends upon meeting new people. You introduce this idea early in working with the client, creating the expectation of receiving qualified names.

Your Natural Markets—Think about the many people you do business with and the people you see casually everyday on the street or in a restaurant or club. Make a list of names as you review this category of prospects.

Social Mobility—Social mobility means being involved in your community and giving people the opportunity to see you working for common interests. If you stop to think about it, you will understand that the places where you have social mobility are also the places where you have prospects and centers of influence. Look around the community among your natural circle of acquaintances. Many opportunities are available. You should become involved in activities you have the time for and strong interests in; never join anything just for the potential prospects. But do take your time and use the prospecting avenues that you have now, expanding gradually as you become more involved.

Centers of Influence—Centers of influence are influential people you know. They know you well enough, and have enough confidence in you, to refer you to prospects. An important aspect of a center is that they have a personal interest in helping you succeed. They may or may not be clients. They may be a friend of the family or someone you have worked with in the past, either in business or in a community activity. Often they may be people who have a good understanding of the needs for life insurance.

Like any other relationship, this one must be cultivated. You must think of this person's interests, and what you can do for them. You will find your center of influence willing to promote your cause if you promote his or her interests in return. Remember though, that he or she should be pleased with their relationship with you, and that you have earned the right to his or her help. In other words, this type of relationship often takes time to develop.

Networking—Networking is the process of continuous communication and sharing of ideas and prospects with others whose work does not compete with yours. Their clients might also be eligible to become your clients.

Of course you should network in all of your relationships. You want to offer value to others in what you know and what you do. Develop business friendships and provide others with help. Teach, educate, and provide financial and other information that makes you a valuable person to know. This positive outreach will come back to help you.

It Costs Too Much

"You say this protection costs too much, that the premiums are too expensive. Let me ask you this: What is the value of the dollar you would spend today for that protection compared to the many dollars that will be needed if you die tomorrow? The premium is not your problem. The premium is the solution to your problem. Is the small price tag for this protection really too much?"

Public Programs and Seminars—Some have found that public speaking is a wonderful way to prospect. Clubs and organizations often seek speakers for their meetings. This is a great way to mass market with the personal touch. The object is to become well known in your market and to develop a method of gathering new qualified prospects.

2. Approach the Prospect—In the pre-approach step of identifying prospects, you must find the prospect and qualify him or her as a prospect, then stimulate interest in what you have to say so that they will be receptive to your request for an appointment. These activities overlap with those mentioned above, under the topic of prospecting, and often occur simultaneously.

Activities designed to foster this stage of the process include contacting prospects by telephone, canvassing, direct mail, and the Internet. The purpose and main objective of the approach is to obtain an appointment to meet to discuss your company, products, and services that can help the prospect in finding solutions to financial needs, problems, and objectives.

The remainder of the sales/planning process is covered in the following chapters. We will now turn our attention to a related and largely a parallel activity, the financial planning process.

Financial Planning

This section discusses financial planning as a process closely related to insurance planning. There are many interpretations and definitions of financial planning and the work of a financial planner. Financial planning services cover a broad spectrum of client concerns such as investments, insurance, banking, taxes, real estate, financial counseling, retirement planning, estate planning, and so on.

We wish to focus on the comprehensive financial planning concept. According to this view, financial planning must consider all aspects of the client's financial position, including the client's total financial needs and objectives, and develop strategies for fulfilling those needs and objectives. It is very similar to the total needs analysis view of life insurance planning. This approach sees the personal and financial situation as an integrated whole, with each part potentially impacting any other. It encompasses all the personal and financial situations of clients to the extent that they can be uncovered, clarified, and addressed. It also utilizes all the techniques and expertise found in the various specialty areas of financial management, services, and products. The comprehensive sales/planning approach is a process that requires a disciplined approach and an open attitude by the prospect and financial advisor toward the development of a well-thought-out plan that follows through each step of the selling/planning process. It requires fairly complete disclosure of relevant personal information by the prospect and an insightful and technically correct as well as creative solution from the advisor.

Because of the wide range of expertise required to engage in comprehensive financial planning, effective performance commonly requires a team of specialists. The specialists may not necessarily work together, but the financial planner needs to coordinate the efforts of the team and be sure the client is obtaining the services of the appropriate specialists.

In its purest form, comprehensive financial planning is a service provided by the advisor on a fee-only basis. No part of the advisor's compensation would come from the sale of financial products, thus helping to ensure complete objectivity in all aspects of the plan. In practice, there are very few fee-only planners; most receive some combination of fees and commissions from the sale of products.

Financial Advising

The trend in financial services today is a move toward financial advising. There are several reasons for this. Financial advising is an in-depth process in which the practitioner's time and energy are spent on developing a comprehensive program that meets all of the client's financial needs, not just one or two of them. The steps of this process are very closely related to the sales/planning process. This process also resembles the client-focused sales model, which emphasizes good communication focused on achieving client goals through listening and fact-finding skills.

On a practical level, although it serves as an ideal or pure model, comprehensive financial planning is not always done for several reasons. First, not many clients want to invest the time or the money necessary to do comprehensive planning. Secondly, only more affluent people have the resources and consequently the need to do comprehensive planning. Lastly, comprehensive planning can be a bit overwhelming. Working with the totality of their financial needs, goals and difficulties can be confusing and frustrating. Consequently, most prospects and advisors prefer to concentrate on only one or a few related issues at a time. A comprehensive plan can be developed and implemented in incremental stages over time.

The Six Steps in Financial Planning—General Model

1. **Establish financial goals**—Encourage client to express concerns, hopes, and goals. Help the client restate goals that are specific and quantifiable. Prioritize competing goals.
2. **Gather relevant data**—Gather all relevant client information, both objective and subjective, through questionnaires, counseling, and examination of documents.
3. **Analyze the data**—Identify the strengths and weaknesses in the client's present financial condition as they affect the ability to achieve the client's goals. Revise the goals if necessary.
4. **Develop a plan to achieve goals**—Design a set of recommended strategies tailored to the client's circumstances and goals, including alternative ways of achieving those goals. Draw on outside experts as needed. Obtain client approval.

5. **Implement the program**—Motivate and help the client in acquiring all the necessary financial products and services to put the plan into action. Draw on outside experts as needed.
6. **Monitor the program**—Evaluate the performance of all implemented vehicles. Review changes in the client's circumstances and the financial environment. Revisit the steps when necessary.

As you can see, each step of this process mirrors the sales/planning process. Financial planning is a more comprehensive process that includes life insurance planning as one part. Its processes, skills, and topics greatly overlap with the sales/planning process, the focus of this text.

Elements of a Comprehensive Financial Plan

A comprehensive financial plan should contain an analysis of all pertinent financial and personal information relating to the client's financial situation. This listing represents a set of standards for advisors to follow in developing a plan. The plan should include, but not necessarily be limited to, the following:

1. personal data
2. client goals and objectives
3. identification of issues and problems
4. assumptions
5. balance sheet/net worth
6. cash-flow management (budget)
7. income tax
8. risk management/insurance
9. investments
10. financial independence, retirement planning, education, and other special needs
11. estate planning
12. recommendations
13. implementation

These are the components of a comprehensive financial plan. As you can see, a financial planning approach covers many of the same issues that an insurance planning or general financial approach to a prospect does.

The advisor is responsible for all elements of the comprehensive plan. The advisor may not implement all elements, since these may require other professionals, but the advisor should coordinate all areas, and encourage the client to complete each aspect of the overall plan.

The Five Parts of the Sale

Much of the following discussion was developed by Norman G. Levine, an insurance industry giant, highly successful agent, manager, trainer, speaker and salesperson. More detail on this discussion can be obtained from his book, "A Passion for Compassion, The Formula For Successful Financial Advisors,"Le Gesse Stevens Publishing, 2000.

These parts or steps, and the content, ideas and skills associated with each part, represent the subject matter addressed in this book. This section will serve as an overview, with further details developed through the following chapters. In a sense these steps are the sale within the larger selling/planning process.

The sales process described below is a procedure all good salespeople should follow. The sales process builds on skills that must be learned and techniques that must be personalized to fit the style and personality of the advisor. It can accompany a standard company sales presentation (which you may be required to give) or an individually created sales talk that has proven effective and is repeated from prospect to prospect. By including each step in every sales presentation, you should improve your sales ratio. Your sales talk should include all five parts listed below. When you critique a sales effort with a positive or negative outcome, be objective. Do not just focus on your close, but review your effectiveness in each of the five areas:

1. Selling yourself (rapport)
2. Selling your expertise and service (competence)
3. Finding the want or need (problem)
4. Selling the benefit (solution)
5. Selling the product (close)

Let's briefly review each step as an introduction. We will explore each step in greater detail in the chapters that follow.

1. *Selling yourself (rapport)*: People buy from, and share their personal and/or business lives with people they trust, respect, and come to know as people. Yet so often we skip that part of the sales presentation and get right down to business, without first selling ourselves. One way to do this is to ask a leading question and listen. Say as little as possible and get the prospect to talk about themselves. Allow the prospect to share special interest. This will help the relationship develop, and will provide significant information that may be of value later in the sales process.

2. *Selling your expertise and service (competence):* Here the sale is based on the foundation of a comfortable personal relationship and involves telling the prospect how good an advisor you are. The sale of one's competence requires self-confidence, education, and enthusiasm. We must communicate success and expertise as well as earn the industry credentials that stand the test of time.

3. *Finding the want or need (problem):* For any consumer to buy, he or she must recognize that a problem exists, as we discussed earlier. We must not take for granted what the prospect wants; the prospect's real unfulfilled wants must be identified. Salespeople must resist transferring their own values, ethics, morals and wants to the prospect. You must be completely open-minded and pose questions designed to determine the prospect's real dreams and wants.

4. *Selling the benefit (solution):* The solution, the benefit, and the product are not the same thing. You must separate the concept of the product from the concept of the solution. Prospects do not care about or understand the product. Rather, they want to know if purchasing the product will solve their problems and satisfy their wants. They do not care that the product is a whole life with term rider, guaranteed insurability and waiver-of-premium riders. They want income for their spouse and children to live on should the prospect die. We must distinguish between product features (what it is) and product benefits (what it does). Clients identify with benefits, so we must sell the benefits. This is where the expression, "sell the sizzle, not the steak"came from. Unfortunately, the instinct of most sales professionals is to sell the steak (the product) and the instinct of most prospects is to buy the sizzle (the benefit).

5. *Selling the product (close):* You have covered all of the steps up to this final step. You have not discussed any products, cost, or product features, and have exclusively addressed the wants and needs of the prospect. Sometimes all that needs to be done is to complete the application forms. At other times there is procrastination, indecision, concern, objection. and questions from the prospect. You must present the products and features and use your closing skills.

The Four C's of Successful Selling

1. Competence—you must have the knowledge and ability to do the job.
2. Conviction—you must believe in yourself, your company and your product.
3. Credibility—others must believe in you and your genuine interest in helping them.
4. Courage— you must have strength to overcome obstacles and get the job done.

—Ed Berube

The Sales Process

The sales presentation used to present these five parts of the sale can be any that the advisor and/or his or her company choose. It must be an organized sales track. The following parts of the sales procedure should be added to the organized (memorized) sales presentation. Norman G. Levine, in his book "A Passion of Compassion," outlines the sales procedure as follows:

1. Uncover the prospect's wants, goals, dreams, and aspirations.
2. Find out what the prospect has already done to achieve those goals and wants.
3. If what has been done is inadequate to achieve the wants, take away the prospect's want or dream and disturb them with compassion, not fear.
4. Offer to give back the dream or want.
5. Close the sale.

These ideas will be drawn out more in the following chapters. They are presented here simply to set the stage for what is to come.

Sales/Planning Process Flow Chart

Selling yourself (rapport)—Warm up conversation—Allow the prospect to speak and express his or her interests. Sell yourself by listening.

Selling your expertise and service (competence)—Express what you can do, how you can help, and how you are different. Stress your experience, your philosophy, the quality of your agency and company, and your service.

Finding the wants or needs (problems)—Conduct a fact- and feeling-finding process. Uncover the prospect's wants, goals, dreams, and aspirations. Find out what the prospect has already done to achieve those goals and wants. Analyze and determine the needs of prospects. If what has been done is inadequate to achieve the wants, take away the prospect's want or dream and disturb them. Get a verbal dollar commitment of what the prospect is willing to spend for solutions(s). Develop a written discovery agreement and share with prospect. Gain the prospect's agreement on how to proceed. Determine options and solutions.

Sell the benefit (solution)—Present the solution. Sell the benefits. Show how the solution solves the prospect's problem.

Sell the product (close)—Discuss objections and concerns. Ask for the sale.

Sales Professionalism

There are a number of areas that comprise a professional attitude and ethical conduct by the financial advisor. They include client-focused selling, total needs selling, and ethical and responsible conduct, which are discussed in the following section.

Client-focused Selling Concepts and Principles

This text favors the client-focused sales approach as a business practice. This sales philosophy rejects high pressure, hard sell methods and supports the counselor model of an advisor. The client-focused model contrasts with what is often called *transactional selling*, which focuses on the results of the transaction—the sale—and moves on to the next transaction.

The business world changes dramatically and rapidly. The global economy is a reality. Technology sprints into the future at breakneck speed, constantly introducing new ideas, products, and ways of doing things. Competition becomes tighter as more companies from different industries and even different continents, such as banks, brokerage firms, and mutual fund companies, enter the same markets and customers become more sophisticated and knowledgeable.

These changes and others have created an environment in which salespeople must adopt new attitudes, learn new skills, and gain a new understanding of how to approach their markets and work with customers. Today's customers buy differently than they did in the past, so salespeople must sell differently. Customers today are less likely to accept sales pressure because they have more buying choices. They have more information and can get it faster via the Internet than in the past. Buyers are demanding more honesty and integrity as well as better service from sellers. Good salespeople and good companies are readily accessible. To succeed you have to differentiate yourself and communicate to your potential customers that you offer something special in terms of quality, value, and/or service.

Hard-Sell or Soft-Sell

There is no such thing as "soft" sell and "hard" sell. There is only "smart" sell and "stupid" sell.

—Charles Brower

The client-focused sales approach emphasizes helping clients by providing solutions to their insurance and financial needs and helping them achieve their objectives. The key difference between this method and transactional sales techniques is that a client-focused advisor approaches the client with a genuine agenda of helping in an open, honest, and forthright manner. The client's satisfaction with the process and the results are truly central. The process focuses on the advisor's role in helping people recognize and understand their financial needs, providing needed information, removing obstacles to financial success, and assisting in taking positive action to achieve their goals. The objective of the process is to develop a long-term, mutually beneficial relationship between the advisor and the client.

Client-focused selling requires that the advisor thoroughly understand what clients want to accomplish and the resources available to them. This approach involves asking prospects and clients many questions; questions about what they want to accomplish financially, what their attitudes are toward a vast array of financial products, and what opportunities are available to them. The salesperson must comprehend how clients view their current situation and future possibilities regarding personal assets and liabilities. Only after understanding the client's life circumstances, attitudes, values, and objectives can recommendations be made.

In the "traditional" or transactional sales approach, the immediate sale is the focus. Transactional selling focuses on the product and fits the prospect to the product. A good example of this is in the old joke about needs selling. The advisor states that he uses "needs selling:" "yeah, I need a sale." This is exactly the type of situation we all wish to avoid. When the advisor needs the sale many undesirable outcomes can occur from a compliance and ethics viewpoint that can eventually harm the personal relationship we wish to build.

Effective, professional salespeople have operated using client-focused methods for many years. In fact, Dale Carnegie started delivering this message 80 years ago. Positive relationship building in a people business is natural. Good fact-finding and understanding the client's needs make common sense. Unfortunately some people have forgotten these ideas, yet relationship selling brings them back to the forefront.

Client-focused Selling

The traditional sales approach was largely developed after World War II. The demand for consumer goods was high and consumers were not very sophisticated. Selling techniques developed around the following scenario, says Dr. Tony Alessandra:

Traditional salespeople paid little attention to targeting their markets or planning their sales calls. They approached the market as a "numbers game," delivered a canned pitch to as many prospects as possible in the shortest amount of time. Good salespeople began by breaking the ice with a little small talk (and equated small talk with relationship building). Then they delivered razzle-dazzle pitches to wide-eyed, hopefully receptive prospects. There was little if any information gathering. Instead the sales process focused on a persuasive pitch, manipulative closing techniques, and the salesperson's skills in handling customer objections. Super salespeople were those who mastered the art of arm-twisting.

The traditional sales pitch was, by necessity, generic. All of the product's features and benefits had to be covered because salespeople had no way of knowing which features and benefits were relevant. It was a true shotgun approach in which salespeople tried to sell their products to every prospect, regardless of need. There was no follow-up after the sale. Traditional salespeople moved from one transaction to the next without looking back. Sales were perceived as one-shot deals.

Traditional selling has another Achilles' heel. It creates tension and could be construed as adversarial. Traditional salespeople often perceive their prospects as people with whom they must go to battle to win business. It is a win/lose situation, where one person must lose when another wins. This power struggle mind-set is supported by sales trainers who teach manipulative sales techniques and by books that have combative titles about selling. The commando approach to selling is obsolete. It does not foster referrals, references, repeat business, word-of-mouth advertising, customer satisfaction, or goodwill.

Dr. Tony Alessandra, Ph.D., CSP, CPAE, "Collaborative Selling," P.O. Box 2767, La Jolla, CA, 92038, www.alessandra.com.

Caring and Knowing

People don't care what you know, until they know that you care.

—Anonymous

Client-focused selling has been gaining general acceptance over the last few decades. It has been given many names, such as client-centered selling, collaborative selling, counselor selling, and consultative selling. These sales systems or philosophies have several key principles.

- The main objective is helping the client achieve goals or solve problems. The primary methods to achieve this are developing trust and rapport. Credibility and positive intent are essential to the development of trust.
- Fact-finding to determine the customer's current situation, needs, and goals must precede any attempt to sell.
- Developing a relationship with the customer is vital. Positive sales results evolve from relationship building. Outcomes in terms of new sales, referrals, persistency, cross-selling, and repeat sales all depend on a trusting and open relationship with the client. The client in turn can be more open, trusting, and loyal because the seller avoids exploitation. A long-term relationship is the focus; short-term gains are secondary.
- Sales techniques are secondary to sales principles. Ethics, honesty, full disclosure, and professional values are principles that on the whole replace sales techniques. Customer satisfaction is the ultimate measure of success. Service and follow-through must be beyond the customer's expectations. For the best results for all involved, service and client management should be proactive, not reactive.
- Value must be delivered to the customer. Client-centered selling means just that: the focus is on satisfying the client's needs and objectives. The product must have value or the client will go elsewhere. If the client does not see value, the salesperson may not be necessary.
- The salesperson must differentiate himself or herself from other competing providers. This difference must be communicated to the client or, again, the client might find another provider.

The commando approach to selling is obsolete. Asking challenging questions to help the client face responsibilities or accept his or her analysis of the situation is certainly still a part of the sales process. But high-pressure, exaggerated pitches, razzle-dazzle presentations, arm-twisting, and manipulative sales and closing techniques are now unacceptable sales practices. Problem solving that is in the client's best interests must not be based on manipulative techniques or sales pressure. In many ways, the old phrase, "Let the buyer beware" is being replaced by "Let the Seller beware."

> **The Ultimate Sale—Transactional Viewpoint**
>
> The ultimate transactional sale is selling someone something they really do not need. It is the pure expression of the skill of the salesperson, like selling ice to an Eskimo. Think about that for a minute. No wonder ethics and compliance is at the forefront today.

In contrast to the client-focused relationship, the transactional sales relationship can be an adversarial one that pits the salesperson and the client against one another in mortal combat over the client's money. Transactional selling is an endless series of one-shot deals and poor service, if any at all. In transactional selling, "the sale begins when the customer says no" and "close early and often" are statements that reflect an oppositional view toward the customer. The advisor must always outthink, outmaneuver, and outtalk the customer. In contrast, client-focused selling is doing things for and with the client—not to the client.

The client-focused approach should permeate every aspect of the selling/planning process. From the beginning, marketing and prospecting strategies focus on client needs. Target marketing is preferable to the "numbers game" of transaction selling. If the goal is to understand and satisfy the client's needs, then the advisor has to listen, ask questions, and listen some more. In traditional selling, the salesperson does most of the talking and very little listening. With client-focused selling, the process is reversed. The advisor must spend significant time listening to the client.

Traditional Selling	Client-focused Selling
Salesperson oriented	Client oriented
Creates needs	Discovers needs
"Talks at" client	"Discuses with" client
Acquires sales	Acquires clients
Increases fear and distrust	Increases trust and understanding
Persuasion model	Discovering and helping model
Presentation	Fact-finding
Salesperson talks	Client talks
Telling	Listening
Discovery occurs through objections	Discovery occurs through fact-finding
Closing techniques	Relationship building

The client wants to feel he or she bought value, not that he or she was "sold." People like to buy; they hate to "be sold." A sale should not be a victory for the salesperson alone, but for both the client and the salesperson. Client-focused selling elevates the sales experience for the seller and the buyer as well as the social status and respect for the life insurance and financial services industries.

Is the movement toward financial planning and the client-focused model of doing business the inevitable direction the financial services industry will take? Will the continued merging of products, services, and functions of insurance companies, banks, trust companies, brokerage and investment companies, and mutual funds reinforce this sales approach? Is selling as the art of persuasion a concept whose time has come and gone? Only time will tell.

Client-focused Selling Strategies

The basic concept of client-focused selling is to view the selling process as helping the customer solve a problem or achieve a goal through the use of the seller's products and services. Most salespeople are familiar with this concept, but are not aware of how to implement it. This is because most salespeople have been trained to sell a product by educating the customer on the product.

Such product-oriented selling is ineffective and inefficient, leading the salesperson to swamp the potential buyer with exhaustive information on product types and features that may have little to do with the problems and goals of the customer. This approach tends to alienate the potential buyer. It tends to make the salesperson a product evangelist, trying to convince the buyer of the merits and wonders of the product. The result is that the customer objects to this product pushing and failure of the salesperson to listen to what the customer really wants.

Company sales training has tended to emphasize product pushing because those who are in charge of the products are also responsible for training the sales force. These product managers have self-interest in product sales, but also may lack sales experience and knowledge of the sales process.

Several strategies may help in correcting this situation.

- First, begin to think of the sales process as a process, rather than an event. The most important aspect of this process is listening to the potential buyer to find what he or she needs, then showing how a product may fulfill these needs.

- Second, think of the sales process as a process of helping the customer, rather than a process of making a sale. Most salespeople think of selling as a process of convincing, persuading, and overcoming, activities that put the salesperson in an adversarial relationship with the buyer. Instead, the sales process should focus on helping the buyer see how you can help them solve their problems.

- Third, part of the initial sales process should be a disqualification of the prospect if that person does not need your product. Rather than trying to force a product on someone who does not need it, which can be a frustrating, irritating, and tiring process for both parties, the salesperson could focus his or her time and energy on those who could truly benefit from the product. Rather than survive by dogged determination and persistence, the salesperson should make it clear to prospects that he or she is willing to leave if the products offered cannot actually help the prospect.

- Lastly, the primary communication flow with prospects should be through questions, and listening, rather that statements and telling. Do not confuse telling with selling. Rather than talking to customers about your products, ask questions and listen to the prospect that will lead the prospect to see that they need your product because it will help them solve a problem or achieve a goal. Most people would rather buy than be sold.

The questions you ask should be designed to help the prospect articulate goals and needs by identifying potential problems and opportunities based on solutions that the advisor can offer. Once this is established, the questions should address the prospect's understanding of how those problems, needs and goals can be addressed and achieved through the products offered.

Total-Needs Sales Approach

Total-needs selling means collecting and analyzing detailed information about a client's life situation. It includes "feeling finding" as well as fact-finding information. Facts include the objective personal details of a person's life, whereas the feeling finding involves the subjective attitudes, values and emotions that lay behind the facts and give them meaning. By exploring both facts and feelings, the advisor can discover what is important personally as well as financially in a person's life in order to understand the total situation. As a result, an integrated and coordinated financial plan can be created to assist a client in achieving his or her personal goals. This process is similar and analogous to the comprehensive financial planning model described earlier.

Total-needs analysis is not only completely compatible with the client-focused sales approach; it is actually necessary to carry it out. An attempt to determine life insurance and other financial needs that does not rely on a fair amount of client information is of questionable value. Complete and accurate information about current income, potential future income, accumulated assets, investments, pensions, and other qualified plan holdings must be determined. In addition, a profile of the client's priorities and goals must be developed. Much time and energy are spent in gathering information before any recommendation can be made. The ultimate product of this total-needs selling process should be a coordinated life insurance and/or financial plan, as opposed to a product sale, where each financial product stands alone. The goal is to create a meaningful plan where all financial products are integrated and coordinated.

An unfortunate trend called "illustration" selling began many years ago with the advent of computers. This selling method involves showing a prospect an illustration of a life insurance or other financial product and selling the features and benefits without the aid of a fact-finding process that determines what the prospect has and needs (we will address this again later in the book).

The advisor who will succeed in the long run is the one who is responsive to client needs and who understands his or her situation, feelings, problems, and goals. This will require the advisor to first develop a trustworthy relationship with the client and differentiate him or herself from the competition. A needs analysis will facilitate this process.

The intent of this text is to encourage client-focused selling using a total needs approach, based on thorough fact finding and relationship building. Following these techniques results in a professional salesperson and financial advisor who is responsible, compliant and ethical. The following is a review of the ethical responsibilities of a professional financial advisor.

Compliance and Ethics

A career in the life insurance and financial services business carries with it a tremendous responsibility. You talk to others about protecting and improving their financial security. You offer advice and recommendations, which can impact families, individuals, or business owners in every aspect of their lives. You are in a fiduciary position; you offer professional advice about financial matters and are expected to act in the best interest of the client, as if you were acting on your own behalf. In doing so you have an absolute obligation to maintain the highest ethical standards. It is this responsibility, combined with the specialized training and knowledge required to be in this career, that raises financial services sales to the professional level.

What must you do to live up to that responsibility? Certainly you must comply with all applicable laws and regulations. But professionalism and ethical conduct demand more than simple compliance.

Burke A. Christensen, JD, CLU, former general counsel and vice president of the Society of Financial Service Professionals, suggests that "a professional is a person engaged in a field that requires (1) specialized knowledge not generally understood by the public, (2) a threshold entrance exam requirement, (3) a sense of altruism, and (4) a code of ethics" (Burke A. Christensen, *Journal of the American Society of CLU and ChFC,* January 1990). In applying this definition, specialized knowledge in the insurance and financial services field is immediately evident in the complexity and depth of the information that must be mastered by the practitioner. Advisors and others working in this industry also must pass licensing exams, maintain continuing education requirements, and keep up with current state and federal regulations and tax and legislative changes. The third requirement, a sense of altruism, is the characteristic that promotes adherence to the fourth requirement, a code of ethics. *Altruism* is defined as an unselfish regard for the welfare of others. Altruism does not mean working for free, or giving away your services. It does mean acting unselfishly, taking others' needs and concerns into account before your own. Demonstration of altruism can be its own reward; it often wins trust, confidence, and reliance, all-important to success as an adviser to others. Client-focused selling is a sound approach to developing good relationships with clients because it is focused on meeting client's needs.

Compliance and ethical conduct have taken an increased role in the insurance and financial services industry over the last several years. *Compliance* means following the laws and regulations, including company rules, that apply to the sales of insurance and financial products. These are the minimum standards. State and federal laws regulate the insurance and securities industries to protect consumers from unfair sales practices. Company rules are designed to make certain that the company and its advisors are following and state and federal requirements. They are designed also to make sure that the company is receiving complete and accurate information on which to base underwriting and claims decisions. Following these regulations and rules is the first step in professional conduct.

The desire to help a prospect and the necessity to earn a commission and meet your company's production requirements place the advisor in a naturally conflicting situation. Fair business practices, legal requirements, and company rules sometimes seem to interfere with your best sales efforts. How that apparent conflict is resolved is a matter of ethics, and it goes beyond simple compliance with the law.

Ethical behavior is doing the right thing. Professional *ethics* can be defined as behaving according to the principles of right and wrong that are accepted by your profession. Behaving ethically requires putting the prospect's best interest before your own, maintaining the highest possible standard in all your business dealings. You continue to develop your skills to provide the best possible service to those with whom you work. Representing the industry, its companies, and its advisors in the best possible light is the ethical thing to do.

In the life insurance industry, these principles have been defined by the *National Association of Insurance and Financial Advisors (NAIFA)* in The Life Underwriter Code of Ethics. By adopting and practicing this code, you will achieve the high standard of professionalism that insurance and financial sales require.

Ethical Dilemmas for Financial Advisors

Listed below are some questionable situations from LIMRA's publication "Selling Ethically: How Do I Benefit?" These ethical questions will be discussed in more detail later. Read them now so that you can reflect upon them as you read the material in this chapter.

- A client dies when his automobile crashes into a tree. His life insurance death benefit doubles in the event of an accident, which is how the police described the event. You learn from his widow that the client had entered into a diary his plans to commit suicide.
- A client sends you a letter complaining about your service and requests that you send it to the company president.
- You are aware that one of your associates has started to date the member of the administrative staff who has control of leads. You've also found that the advisor's sales are now increasing dramatically.
- A prospect you are interviewing mentions a meeting she had with another advisor who described one insurance company as being "nearly bankrupt." The prospects asks for your opinion of the company.
- Your prospect hesitates when answering a key medical question, the answer to which will significantly affect the underwriting chapter and policy premium.

Responsible Advisor Conduct

The financial advisor has many responsibilities, but none are more important than the following four.

- First, the advisor has a *responsibility to his or her clients.* These are the policyowners.
- Second, the advisor has a *responsibility to himself or herself and to the insurance profession.* It is his or her job to maintain that professionalism at all times.
- Third, the financial advisor has a *responsibility to the insurance carrier*, the company that provides the advisor with the product line to be sold. These responsibilities are explained in a signed contract and advisor handbook.
- Fourth, the advisor has a *responsibility to the public.* This encompasses adherence to regulations and laws legislated for the public good. The advisor is obligated to act for the benefit of society at large. Frequently, this obligation overlaps all the others.

Responsibility to Clients

Your professional obligation to clients is to help them determine and carry out the best solutions available to meet their financial needs. In identifying the need for insurance, and by helping the client understand that need and seek protection, you have fulfilled your professional obligation. If the client has a situation such as a medical condition that leads to a higher premium or rated policy offer, then your responsibility is to help the client decide if the rated policy still meets his or her needs and is still the best solution to the problems it was meant to cover.

Client Needs and Suitability—Clients expect their professional financial advisors not only to be accurate in their analysis but also to recommend suitable products to satisfy their needs and goals. In order to accomplish this, insurance professionals must do thorough fact-finding. They must uncover client needs for insurance as well as determine the client's personal goals.

A thorough fact-finding will also help the insurance professional determine the client's risk tolerance. Some clients will accept far more risk in their insurance portfolio than others. Determining needs, goals, risk tolerance, and time horizon provides the advisor with information necessary to make a product recommendation. Risk tolerance has to do with a person's ability to withstand a financial loss. Time horizon deals with the period of time involved in a financial need or decision. It also provides the advisor with guidelines regarding the *suitability* of a particular product for a particular client.

Client Confidentiality—The client is entitled to a high level of confidentiality regarding the personal information that is given to the advisor. It is expected that every advisor will keep this information private and not share it with anyone other than with those involved in the company's underwriting process. It is also necessary that the client be treated fairly, with honesty and respect, for this is the only way to foster a professional relationship that will benefit all the parties involved.

Responsibility to Oneself and the Profession

Professional Education—Professionalism requires specialized knowledge not generally understood by the public and remaining current with the latest developments in the industry. This includes being knowledgeable about new products and their uses and aware of updates to tax laws and other relevant information.

As with any profession, the insurance industry has its own professional designations such as LUTCF, CLU, ChFC, RHU, CPCU, CFP, and so on. It should be the professional's desire to obtain one or more of these designations as evidence that he or she is qualified. These designations represent another high standard of professionalism. Continuing education is not only a professional obligation but is also required by law. Currently, all 50 states, Puerto Rico, and the District of Columbia require some form of continuing education to maintain an insurance license.

Professional Organizations—Most professionals are active in their own professional organizations. The insurance industry is no exception. By being active in professional organizations, the insurance professional is aided in keeping current with important changes and events in the profession. Active membership also helps in networking with others to develop business relationships, study groups, and other alliances. Such networking is the hallmark of professional organizations. Many advisors, in addition to providing service to their clients, also provide service to their communities by being involved in community activities and organizations. This provides the advisor with exposure to other members of the community to possibly generate additional business relationships.

Responsibilities to the Company

The advisor has a number of duties and obligations to the company with which he or she is placing business. As an insurance producer, you function as a representative of the company you represent if you are an agent of that company. The concept of agency gives an advisor a limited right to speak for the company he or she represents. What you say and do as an advisor may be binding on the company. Clearly, companies must take extraordinary care to protect themselves from the possible misadventures of those representing them. The advisor's contract and/or an advisor's handbook explain company policies regarding advisor representation, duties, and obligations. These policies spell out implied and actual powers to act on behalf of the company.

Underwriting—The process of underwriting determines if insurance is a possible solution to the prospect's need and, if so, at what premium rate. Your obligation to both the prospect and to the company you represent is to provide the most accurate and complete information possible. Only then can the company decide if it is willing to offer a policy, and at what premium. As an agent of the company, you are the primary source of information about the proposed insured. You are a field underwriter, meaning you collect information firsthand, directly, face-to-face. No one else in the company has that opportunity in the underwriting process. The company's decision is based, to a large extent, on the information you collect. You have a primary duty to provide factual information to the company—a duty that supersedes the responsibility to secure coverage for the prospect.

The need to provide complete and accurate information about a prospect goes beyond the simple need to protect the company from inadvertently accepting extra risk. Failure to provide complete, accurate information, failure to record information provided by the prospect, or intentional misrepresentation of facts by the advisor or the prospect could void the insurance contract, leaving the prospect unwittingly unprotected. In the case of a contested or denied claim, the advisor and the company both may be held accountable for the misinformation. If the client is responsible, his or her family may suffer if the claim is contested and subsequently not paid. If the advisor is responsible, he or she could be held personally liable. This is where *errors and omissions*, or *malpractice insurance* can protect the advisor against large lawsuits and financial ruin. The risk to all involved is simply too great not to provide complete and accurate information.

Company Policies and Procedures—Company rules also have a value to advisors. They are designed to help advisors make sure that they meet all applicable legal requirements. Keep in mind that an insurance policy is a legal contract between the policyowner and the insurance company. If it is not carefully and properly executed, it could lead to serious legal complications for the insured, the company, and the advisor. A company's rules are designed to make sure that all legal requirements have been met.

This is the major reason companies require that the company home office approve all sales materials used by an advisor in advance. It is a simple way for the company to make sure that its products and benefits are not being presented in a way that violates federal or state regulations. Companies design their sales literature to make sure that they are in compliance with the laws of each jurisdiction in which they offer products.

Loyalty and Honesty—You have an obligation of loyalty once you sign a contract with an insurance company. The company expects you to act with integrity and honesty in all matters connected with your business and with your clients.

The advisor has an obligation to avoid conflicts of interest. This means that the carrier expects the advisor to place his or her business with that company. Requirements in this regard may be more stringent for the captive advisor than it would be for the independent advisor. In any case, it is always wise to find out your company's policy regarding writing business with another carrier. Many carriers provide the advisor with specific instructions regarding solicitation of business and client communication. It is you responsibility to obey these instructions as they are given to protect you and the carrier.

An advisor has a duty to seek out business that will be profitable to the carrier. This involves selecting healthy people who can afford the premium and need the product. Policies that do not stay on the books are not profitable and may effect future product pricing.

The financial advisor has a direct obligation to the insurance company to carry out his or her duties with reasonable care. The advisor should not engage in business that he or she is not qualified to perform. In other words, if you are dealing in an area in which you are not familiar or in which you are not properly licensed, bring in a specialist. This is the only way you can adequately provide for your client.

The advisor is obligated to carry out transactions within a reasonable time frame. This means that you complete and forward all applications and monies to the appropriate offices in a timely manner. Holding on to money or applications for longer period of time than necessary does not help you or your client, especially if a claim should occur.

It is vitally important that the advisor does not mix his or her funds with that of his or her clients. All policyowner monies should be kept separate from personal funds and all record keeping should be done in an accurate and timely fashion, ideally when transactions occur.

Unauthorized Insurance Carrier—A financial advisor has an obligation to make sure the company he or she represents is licensed to do business in the state where he or she solicits the sale of policies. Each state has laws specifying that only admitted carriers may issue policies within its boundaries.

Failure to follow this rule can have serious consequences for both the policyowner and the advisor. Policyowners are jeopardized because state guaranty funds typically are set aside to cover losses only of admitted carriers. This means that the policyowner may lose all benefits of coverage should the unauthorized carrier run into financial difficulties.

The risk to the advisor may come directly from state insurance laws, which hold the advisor personally liable for any client losses arising out of business placed with an unauthorized carrier. The advisor may also face additional legal action by the client based on more generalized concepts of malpractice.

Good ethical and business practice dictates that you investigate the company(ies) with which you place business. If you are uncertain as to whether or not a company is authorized to do business in a state in which you solicit business, call your home office or your state insurance department.

Responsibility to the Public—Insurance Industry Regulation

Federal Regulation—While the states are the primary regulators of the insurance industry, the primary responsibility for regulation of securities clearly rests with the federal government. Security products include the variable life, variable annuity, and mutual fund products now being offered by many insurance companies. To sell these products, an advisor must be properly registered with the National Association of Security Dealers (NASD). Without proper registration, an advisor is not allowed to discuss equity-based security investment products with a prospective buyer. There are continuing education requirements that must be met for license renewal.

Even for a licensed, registered representative, the regulations for marketing security products are extensive. The company must approve all advertising, including letters mentioning the sale or availability of security products. Stationery and business cards used by registered representatives must meet certain strict standards. Failure to follow any of these rules can lead to the loss of licensing, significant fines and penalties, and even a suspension of a company's right to do business. Clearly, a failure to follow the proper procedures can be a very costly mistake.

Licensing—Each state is responsible for approving and regulating advisors who will be licensed to sell approved products. Generally, advisors must hold a resident license in the state in which they live and also hold a nonresident license in any other state in which they do business. It is illegal for anyone to solicit insurance business unless he or she is properly licensed.

Licensing procedures vary from state to state, although all states require the successful passing of an examination before issuing a resident license. Nonresident licenses are usually granted through reciprocal agreements between the states, without additional testing. Licenses are granted for a specific time period, and most states now require proof of continuing professional education before a license is renewed.

Typically, the basic life and health insurance license allows its holder to sell most life insurance, health insurance, and fixed annuity products. Variable life insurance, variable annuities, and other investment or equity-based products are not covered by the basic license. These products require special licenses, registration with the *National Association of Security Dealers (NASD)* and, depending on state regulations, may require separate state licenses.

The licensing process is a state's way of providing some control over financial advisors' activities. If an advisor fails to comply with the state's regulations, the state has the right to rescind the license and may take legal action against the advisor and/or his or her company. The state's insurance department, which oversees licensing in the state, therefore serves as a place for consumers to turn if they have a complaint or feel that an advisor has misrepresented the facts in making a sale.

While state laws regulating insurance vary, the state commissioners work together through the *National Association of Insurance Commissioners (NAIC)* in an attempt to identify the issues of greatest importance to consumers and to set legislative standards through model legislation. Through their work, there is general agreement when it comes to some insurance sales practices. For example, all but two states—California and Florida—forbid rebating or the practice of sharing or returning part of a premium to a client as an inducement to purchase a policy.

Misrepresentation—All states are concerned with *misrepresentation* of insurance products and their benefits. Presenting an insurance policy as a savings plan, cash accumulation fund, educational savings plan, individual retirement plan, or as any other similar savings device, without making it clear that the underlying product is life insurance, constitutes misrepresentation and is illegal. Many companies in recent times have been sued and have paid millions of dollars in fines because of this issue. When selling life insurance, you must identify it as life insurance. Suggesting that a policy has certain features, benefits, values, or guarantees that are not specifically guaranteed in the written contract, is, likewise, misrepresentation. A failure to reveal limitations or exclusions of the coverage is just as much misrepresentation as implying false benefits.

Illustrations—One concern over misrepresentation comes from the use of illustrations in the sales process. A life insurance illustration is meant to give the prospect a summary of the current and potential costs and values of an insurance policy. Its purpose is to show the prospect the premium, the guaranteed cash values, and the guaranteed death benefits. Illustrations may also show hypothetical future values based on certain performance assumptions such as interest rates or dividend scales. This can be especially problematic when the cash value accumulation depends on variable interest rates or the value of underlying investments. This becomes a problem of major proportions when alternative payment plans are illustrated.

Prospects do not always understand the difference between guaranteed values and the more attractive illustrated values that are often shown in addition. If the difference is not explained carefully, the prospect can easily be misled into believing that the policy promises significantly greater values than those guaranteed in the contract. Allowing this misconception to exist, or fostering it through the sales presentation, is a serious form of misrepresentation. A complete illustration should clearly explain which values are guaranteed and which are not. The advisor should also make sure that the prospect has read and understands the limitations of any projections that have been made. A full illustration, including all footnotes and explanation pages, should be given to and reviewed with the prospect.

This is especially important when the illustration shows dividends or other cash values paying the premium at some future date. It is critical to show that the premium will still be required from the prospect if the values illustrated are not achieved. Lower credited interest rates, increases in administrative expenses, and an increase in mortality rates can all negatively affect the illustrated values.

Life insurance is an excellent product with an excellent track record of performance. If applied to the needs it was meant to meet, and presented properly, it can be sold successfully. It will do what it is guaranteed to do. Only when it is misrepresented do problems arise.

Replacement—Another major concern is the unjustified replacement of existing policies in order to sell a new policy. Replacement should always be in the best interest of the client. Careful compliance with state regulations is one way of ensuring that the client has the information necessary to decide whether the replacement is in his or her best interest. The NAIC has drafted a Replacement of Life Insurance and Annuities Model Regulation. Most states have adopted this regulation or similar laws. You should be familiar with the laws regarding replacement in each state in which you are licensed. These regulations exist to provide the policyowner with enough information to make a comparison between the current and the proposed coverage in order to protect his or her interests. The NAIC defines replacement as follows: *Replacement* means any transaction in which new life insurance or a new annuity is to be purchased, and it is known or should be known to the proposing advisor or broker or to the proposing insurer if there is no advisor, that by reason of such transaction, existing life insurance or annuity has been or is to be:

a. lapsed, forfeited, surrendered, or otherwise terminated
b. converted to reduced paid-up insurance, continued as extended term insurance, or otherwise reduced in value by the use of nonforfeiture benefits or other policy values
c. amended so as to affect either a reduction in benefits or in the term for which coverage would otherwise remain in force, or for which benefits would be paid
d. pledged as collateral or subjected to borrowing, whether in a single loan or under a schedule of borrowing over a period of time for amounts in the aggregate exceeding 25 percent of the loan value set forth in the policy

If replacement is involved, in most states the advisor must provide the policyowner with a special form called a *Notice Regarding Replacement*. This form advises the policyowner to make a comparison. It also advises them that the new company is required to notify the existing company of the impending replacement. This encourages the policyowner to discuss his or her options with the existing carrier. If replacement does occur, its reasons and justification should be clearly documented.

Advisors should be aware that failure to comply with state insurance laws and regulations could result in fines, license suspension, or termination. Material misrepresentation or nondisclosure where an equity product is involved, such as a variable life policy, can constitute a violation of the securities law.

Many insurance practitioners believe that the replacement of existing permanent life insurance is often not in the client's best interest. A newly issued policy is almost always more expensive than an old one. The new policy also creates new suicide and contestability periods. This puts the client's family at risk of not being able to collect benefits should there be a claim during those periods.

The practice of replacement also makes the industry and its advisors look dishonest and unprincipled. The advisor must convince the client that the original policy is not worth keeping. Often, to do this the advisor must present the product or company in a negative light. If one company or policy looks bad, this characterization can reflect on the entire industry. It also calls into question the ethics of the advisor, and in whose best interest the recommendation is being made, the client's or the advisor's.

By replacing a policy, the advisor is also telling the owner, indirectly, that they have made a poor decision, that they made a mistake, or that the policy did not perform as projected. As a result, the policyowner may be afraid to do anything. Worse yet, the policyowner may become angry with the advisor and with insurance in general, causing him or her to drop coverage entirely.

It is possible that many people with whom a financial advisor works do not have enough life insurance to adequately protect their families. If the advisor is satisfied with the easy sale by replacing an inadequate amount of insurance with a new policy that is inadequate, then the advisor has failed to meet the prospect's needs. A preferred approach is to help prospects understand their overall insurance need. Show them where their existing policies fit toward meeting that need. Then help them purchase the additional coverage needed to adequately protect loved ones. This approach helps provide the family with the total protection it should have, adheres to the professional standard of meeting client needs, and supports the validity of the industry, its products, and its advisors. Conversely, not all prospects see the need for our products the way we do. It is important to understand and respect this, even if we disagree. If a prospect wants a certain type of coverage, you can either walk away or sell them what they want and hope to educate them as you develop a relationship.

Advice—States are also concerned with the kinds of advice advisors give to their clients and even with what they call themselves. Advisors who call themselves financial planners or financial consultants may be breaking the laws of the state where they work unless they have obtained special licenses. In many states, financial advisors, planners, and consultants are considered a separate professional group and specific licenses are required. Likewise, even in routine contacts, a financial advisor's discussions with a client may touch on legal or tax matters. But giving a client or prospect legal or tax advice could well be construed as practicing law without a proper license. While discussing legal or tax matters with clients in very general terms is allowed, an advisor cannot give advice in these areas. Instead, when advice is requested, the advisor should always advise the prospect to consult an appropriate attorney or tax adviser.

Insurance Marketplace Standards Association (IMSA)—*IMSA* is a voluntary organization of life insurance companies seeking to promote ethical marketplace conduct. Adoption and implementation of IMSA's Principles of Ethical Marketplace Conduct and the Code of Life Insurance Ethical Market Conduct is required for membership.

There are six components of the Principles of Ethical Marketplace Conduct. They affect the sale of individually sold life and annuity products. These principles are

- to conduct business according to high standards of honesty and fairness and to render service to its customers, which, in the same circumstances, it would apply to and/or demand for itself
- to provide competent and customer-focused sales and service
- to engage in active and fair competition
- to provide advertising and sales materials that are clear as to purpose and that are honest and fair as to content
- to provide for fair and expeditious handling of customer complaints and disputes
- to maintain a system of supervision and review that is reasonably designed to achieve compliance with the Principles of Ethical Market Conduct

The Principles are designed to set general standards to foster ethical market conduct practices in the life insurance industry. A company gains IMSA membership following an assessment process that gauges the systems and programs it has designed to encourage ethical market conduct behavior. An independent third party assessor reviews the company's procedures to assure company-wide compliance. IMSA membership runs for 3 years. A company must repeat the assessment process to retain membership.

IMSA offers the industry an opportunity to improve its image with the public by providing a mechanism to reinforce good market conduct. IMSA should improve public confidence in the industry, which in turn will make your prospects and clients more receptive to you and your products.

Ethical Advisor Conduct

Advisors must communicate honestly with prospects and clients. The most important consideration of what we say to the public and how we advertise our products and services is that we are truthful and accurate.

Today, companies require that advisors use sales material that has been approved by the insurance company's compliance department. These requirements extend to material found outside of your company, such as this text. We must all remember that public trust in the insurance industry is perhaps the single most important factor contributing to its long-term success. Clearly, we must communicate to the public the ethical standards it can expect from us if we are to maintain this trust.

Following are a few basic guidelines for advisors to keep in mind:

- Don't assume your prospects and clients understand a product or service. Instead, assume they do not know anything about a product. You should provide the details to help your prospects determine if what you recommend meets their insurance needs.
- Make sure your prospects understand the type of insurance policy they are purchasing. If you sell life insurance, make sure they know the policy is life insurance.
- Steer clear of unfamiliar or technical words and insurance industry jargon. Take care to explain what you are recommending with words that everyone can understand.
- Avoid reference to insurance as an investment or a savings vehicle. Do not use misleading words like *low cost*, *cheaper*, *all*, *full*, *complete*, *comprehensive*, *unlimited*, *up to*, *as –high as*, or any other words that may exaggerate the benefits available from an insurance product. You must use the word *premium* to describe payments. You may not say *deposits*, *investment*, or

such words that may mislead the client to think they are buying something other than life insurance.

- If you are selling a special premium arrangement, such as a premium offset, be sure the client understands the concept and how it will affect the policy. The *premium offset* concept means that policy values projected under current (nonguaranteed) assumptions will allow the policyowner to stop premium payments before the maturity date. You should never use the words *vanish* or *paid up* unless the policy is truly paid up, which means that no more premiums are due on a guaranteed basis. Be sure that the client understands the differences between guaranteed and nonguaranteed policy values, that this arrangement is not guaranteed and future premiums may be necessary. Do not use the term *vanishing premium*, which is judged to be misleading.
- Avoid disparaging the competition. It is against state insurance regulations and will hurt the industry and your prospect's confidence in you. Instead, emphasize the strength of your recommendations and what you, your agency, and your company can offer that is of value to the prospect personally.
- Keep a written record of fact-finding material in the client's file. This accomplishes several objectives: It shows anyone inspecting the file that the sale was based on a professional needs analysis and that you performed your obligation to determine need and suitability. Should any complaint or legal action be taken against you or your company, written proof of the actions taken are available as evidence. It is also practical for future client contacts. Keeping notes and records of past conversations, actions taken, and service performed may help in pursuing new sales, referrals, and networking opportunities.

The National Association of Life Insurance and Financial Advisors
The Life Underwriters Code of Ethics

PREAMBLE: Those engaged in life underwriting occupy the unique position of liaison between the purchasers and the suppliers of life and health insurance and closely related financial products. Inherent in this role is the combination of professional duty to the client and to the company, as well. Ethical balance is required to avoid any conflict between these two obligations. Therefore, I believe it to be my responsibility

- to hold my profession in high esteem and strive to enhance its prestige.
- to fulfill the needs of my clients to the best of my ability.
- to maintain my clients' confidences.
- to render exemplary service to my clients and their beneficiaries.
- to perfect my skills and increase my knowledge through continuing education.
- to conduct my business in such a way that my example might help raise the professional standards of life underwriting.
- to keep informed with respect to applicable laws and regulations and to observe them in the practice of my profession.
- to cooperate with others whose services are constructively related to meeting the needs of my clients.

Adopted April, 1986, NAIFA Board of Trustees

Case History

Relationship Selling

Rob T. Reider met this client after being in the life insurance business for 1½ years. His approach demonstrates the success that can be achieved by mastering the central techniques of this text, client-focused and total needs selling.

At the time I began working with Dr. Robinson I was 33 years old and had been in the life insurance business for about 1½ years. I had come to this business seeking a way to become my own boss and reap the benefits of working for myself. I did not have any real experience in the insurance and financial services industry, but I had always maintained a personal interest in these areas. I had worked for a large property and casualty insurance company for 8 years after graduating from college and, after being laid-off due to a downsize, moved for a few years from job to job. I did have sales, customer service, and marketing experience, so it was a rather easy transition into my new career as an advisor. I was already comfortable talking with people and making sales presentations. What I did lack, as most new people in the industry will probably admit to, was prospects. I was constantly seeking new people to talk to through direct mail and the buying of leads. I was not really good at getting referrals, although I did always ask. Nor did I have a large natural market.

As fate would have it, I hurt my ankle in March. After seeing my family doctor, I was referred to a specialist, an orthopedic surgeon, Dr. Robinson. On my first visit with him, my ankle was placed in a cast and I was told to keep off my feet for a month. When I explained to Dr. Robinson that my income was dependent upon my ability to go out and see people, he agreed to 2 weeks. On my second visit the cast came off and I was scheduled for some physical therapy and follow-up visits. At the time of my third visit I started thinking to myself, "I would really like to have Dr. Robinson as a client; what is the best way to approach him?" My plan was this: Make small talk and hopefully generate some interest. My sales manager always spoke of personal observations as a great means to generate prospects, but how do I break the ice?

On my way to appointment I happened to catch the stock market update and several indices were having a really bad day. In my conversation with Dr. Robinson about how my ankle was doing, I casually mentioned the market update to him and asked him if he watched the market. He said no, that he did not really have time to keep abreast of such things. I mentioned that I watched the market on a daily basis due to the type of work I did, and of course he asked me what that was. I told him I was an insurance and financial professional. He seemed disinterested, and talk turned to our families. No problem, as I was seeing him again in a few weeks.

To my next visit, I brought one of my cards and my personal brochure. I suggested to Dr. Robinson that we had a lot in common. We both helped people, either with people's physical well being or with their financial well-being. I also asked if it would be okay to give him my card and brochure just in case he ever had a need of his own. He took a quick look at the brochure and indicated he needed to do some college planning. I suggested that we get together, but he did not seem very interested.

Over the next two visits or so, our talks remained very casual and we did not discuss business. Finally, on my last visit he said, "I would like to make an appointment with you." Of course I had my appointment book with me, and I booked him for some time together. He then asked me if there was anything he should bring with him. I said I had a list of "Pertinent Information for the First Meeting" which I would fax to him.

Our first meeting was held at my office. After some preliminary warm-up talk, I quickly realized Dr. Robinson had not brought any of his personal records. I took this as a sign that he was not ready to get down to business, so I proceeded very slowly. As with any initial appointment with a potential client, I introduced myself as a professional in the insurance and financial business, told him about my background, provided some information about my company, and talked about the way I like to work with people. In addition, I overviewed some of the products and services I provided. At this point, I indicated that in order for us to move forward, I must find out more about his current situation, as well as his goals and objectives, to be in the best position to make appropriate suggestions and recommendations. I related it to his profession in that he wouldn't write a prescription without a full history. Dr. Robinson was very impressed, and I think surprised, that I did not want to proceed without doing fact-finding and developing a relationship. As with most people who are looking for the insight of a professional in their insurance and financial matters, I immediately began to see his tension and anxiety melt away. After my talk of about 1015 minutes, we set another appointment for fact-finding, at which time he would bring his records. Dr. Robinson seemed very relieved that I wasn't going to give him a high-pressure insurance talk and very pleased that I had a professional fact-finding and client-centered approach.

I want to stress that I did absolutely nothing different with Dr. Robinson than I do with each and every person I meet with for the first time. I have a rehearsed talk, which evolved over some time. I have used this talk over and over again with very good success. The bottom line of the talk is that, rather than just making a sale, it reduces anxiety, builds trust, and sets the stage for building a relationship with a prospective client through fact-finding. I have come to believe in this system and will not now do it any other way.

I was able to accomplish my fact-finding early in our relationship, and after several months, we formulated an entire estate plan, set up his retirement plan, helped him with college funding, and helped him with some defined benefit plan options through his employer. To highlight some of our work from a product standpoint, an Irrevocable Life Insurance Trust (ILIT) was formed and funded with a Variable Universal Life Policy. In addition, Dr. Robinson transferred some 403(b) plans from prior employers, as well as some scattered IRA's for him and his wife, into annuities. He also opened some brokerage accounts for his children using 2503(c) trusts. Not a bad few months work!

I continued to work with Dr. Robinson to periodically review his plan and make sure his goals and objectives are being met. I have also enjoyed referrals to his friends and colleagues. I continue to use the same initial appointment talk I used with Dr. Robinson, even with people who have some idea as to why they are meeting with me. I have tried to deviate from this system, and every time it backfires. Therefore, I believe very strongly in this system for setting the appropriate tone for building a relationship with the client.

My company promotes a relationship-selling philosophy. To me it's a mindset. I don't want someone to do business with me because of my product. I want someone to do business with me because of my belief that I can help him or her better than anyone else in the business. Once you believe in yourself and the system, a trickle-down effect occurs that drives everything we do as insurance and financial professionals. It boils down to the idea of helping people buy rather than selling to people. If a prospect understands that my recommendations are being made to help them achieve something they haven't been able to achieve on their own, the sale is a natural progression of my recommendation, and it really doesn't matter what product I'm using to achieve that goal.

Chapter Two Review

Key terms and concepts are explained in the Glossary. Answers to the Review Questions and Self-Test Questions are found in the back of the book, following the Glossary.

Key Concepts and Terms

buying cycle (5 steps)
selling/planning process
prospect
client
financial planning process
suitability
replacement
altruism
ethics
malpractice insurance
client-focused sales/planning approach
transactional selling
total needs approach
IMSA
advisor responsibilities
professionalism
misrepresentation
compliance
errors and omissions insurance

Review Questions

2-1. List and explain the five steps in the buying cycle.

2-2. List and explain the 8 steps in the selling/planning process.

2-3. List the six steps of the financial planning general model.

2-4. What elements should be included in a comprehensive financial plan?

2-5. Outline the five parts of the sale.

2-6. Describe the concepts and principles of the client-focused sales approach.

2-7. Describe the total-needs approach to selling.

2-8. Summarize advisor obligations regarding the client, the profession, the company, and the public.

The following questions concern the case on Dr. Robinson and Relationship Selling.

2-9. How did Robert approach Dr. Robinson?

2-10. How did Robert establish rapport with Dr. Robinson?

2-11. What principles of client-focused selling did Robert demonstrate with Dr. Robinson?

Self-Test Questions

Instructions: Read Chapter 2, then answer the following questions to test your knowledge. There are 10 questions. Circle the correct answer. When finished with the test, check your answers with the answer key in the back of the book.

2-1. The last step of the five-step buyer's cycle is

(A) make the purchase
(B) buyer's satisfaction
(C) take delivery
(D) continuously monitor the plan

2-2. The first step in the buying cycle is

(A) desire a solution
(B) recognize a need
(C) make the purchase
(D) decide on the best available choice

2-3. Which of the following statements concerning the Insurance Marketplace Standards Association (IMSA) is correct?

(A) It is sponsored by the federal government and regulates insurance activity.
(B) It is a voluntary organization of the life insurance industry designed to promote ethical standards.
(C) It is an organization which provides compliance-approved sales materials to insurance companies.
(D) It is a membership organization that requires annual membership renewal.

2-4. The client-focused approach is designed to allow an agent to

(A) obtain referrals
(B) determine how to sell the insurance product solutions
(C) separate the prospect's problems from the symptoms
(D) discuss the prospect's present situation and help the prospect establish goals

2-5. The client-focused approach means

(A) helping people discover what they need to know
(B) advising on all legal, tax, and insurance issues
(C) consulting with your client before taking action
(D) reaching a consensus about which policy to purchase

2-6. Telling a prospect that a policy has features that are not included in the written contract is known as

(A) rebating
(B) twisting
(C) churning
(D) misrepresentation

2-7. To sell equity-based products, an agent must be registered with

(A) the Investment Advisors Associations
(B) the National Association of Securities Dealers
(C) the Insurance Marketplace Standards Association
(D) the National Association of Insurance Commissioners

2-8. All of the following are steps in the financial planning process EXCEPT

(A) Establish financial goals
(B) Analyze the data
(C) Recognize the problem or need
(D) Implement of the program

2-9. Which of the following is the first step in the general model of financial planning?

(A) Establish financial goals
(B) Gather relevant data
(C) Analyze the data
(D) Develop a plan to achieve goals

2-10. Burke A. Christensen, JD, CLU, former general counsel and vice president of the Society of Financial Service Professionals, suggests that "a professional is a person engaged in a field that requires all of the following EXCEPT

(A) knowledge generally understood by the public
(B) a threshold entrance exam requirement
(C) a sense of altruism
(D) a code of ethics

3

Meeting With the Prospect

Overview and Learning Objectives

In this chapter we pick up the sales/planning process where the advisor meets with the prospect or client in a face-to-face setting. The objectives of the initial interview are the focus of the first section of the chapter. Methods of establishing rapport and trust are discussed in order to enhance the value of this initial meeting. Following the introduction of the total needs approach in the last chapter, the benefits of the total needs approach for both the advisor and the prospect are described. Next, the benefits and factors involved in conducting single or multiple interviews are explained. Lastly, the actual procedures of the initial interview are discussed, suggesting effective things an advisor can do when meeting with the prospect for the first time.

By reading this chapter and answering the questions, you should be able to:

3-1. Describe the initial interview from both the buyer and advisor's perspective.

3-2. List and explain the objectives of the initial interview.

3-3. Explain the benefits of total needs selling for the advisor and the client.

3-4. Recognize and describe a dominant needs versus a total needs sales situation.

3-5. Compare and contrast a single versus multiple interview sales situations.

Chapter Outline

The Initial Interview

This section examines the initial meeting with the prospect in the selling/planning process. The objective of the advisor is to establish rapport and get the client's agreement to do fact-finding and continue the sales/planning process. In this chapter we will also discuss different sales situations involving total needs and dominant needs approaches and methods, and single and multiple interview selling techniques.

In the sales/planning process to this point you have carefully qualified a suspect and prepared that person for your approach. Your approach was made, generating interest in your services and ideas, and your request for an interview was accepted. In this section we will discuss the five objectives of the initial interview and how to prepare for and conduct this opening interview.

In the sales process the advisor must help the prospect understand the nature and extent of the problems that exists without life insurance. The potential problems must be clearly identified and understood by the buyer before he or she will be motivated to take action. The buyer must have a strong desire to solve these problems and the advisor must present compelling reasons to act now rather than later if the sale is to be made and the problems resolved.

Though the sales/planning process may be completed in one interview or in two or more interviews, the steps followed by the advisor are the same. The real difference is the time required and the depth of fact-finding and background information involved in the planning process. The client and his or her situation often dictate the time allotted to the planning process. The sale could be completed in an hour or it could take weeks or months. There is no right or wrong time frame. The circumstances of the client's needs and goals, the nature of their assets, and the complexity of their personal and financial situation will determine how quickly the sales/planning process is completed.

Five Initial Interview Objectives

There are five basic objectives to the initial interview. Whether you use a sales track supplied by your company or create your own compliance-approved presentation, the purposes are essentially the same. Your objectives are to

1. create a sense of rapport and credibility, and build trust
2. uncover insurance and other financial needs and determine priorities
3. Establish your ability to help
4. obtain the prospect's permission to proceed, and a commitment to work with you
5. build an ongoing relationship

Let's look at each one of these objectives separately.

1. Create a Sense of Rapport and Credibility

The first objective is to begin building a strong sense of rapport and credibility with your prospect. If you fail to establish your credibility in the initial interview, you may not have another chance. People want to do business with people they feel understand them, with whom they share something in common, who are competent, and whom they can believe and trust. It is important to establish this as quickly and as early as possible in the relationship. Having something in common increases the prospect's level of comfort about doing business with you and allows the relationship to develop.

When you meet the prospect, introduce yourself and chat for a few moments. As you do this you can begin with things you know you have in common. You want to expand on this as much as possible, since people feel comfortable with those whom they have things in common. You may notice something familiar in the room or remark on a common interest. If this prospect is a referral, you want to refer to the person who gave you the prospect's name with sincerity and appreciation. The referrer might have told you some of the prospect's interests to help you find common ground. You want to engage the client in conversation that builds warm, positive feelings of trust and rapport.

Your manners, appearance, and confidence will create an immediate impression. They will say much about your attitude toward yourself, your business, and the prospect. Do you look like you know what you are doing? Are you dressed appropriately? You need to communicate your intention to be helpful and competent. Your words must match your body language and tone of voice.

Make sure you know your presentation and are comfortable using it. The only way to prepare for the interview is to practice what you plan to say. It helps to practice with other people who can respond to your questions and offer helpful suggestions.

The prospect's time is as important as your own. Be prepared to move right into an explanation of the services you and your company provide once rapport is established. When you first meet with a prospect, what you are really doing is interviewing for a "job" to do insurance and financial planning. It is your responsibility to establish rapport, not his or hers. It is a good idea to prepare a resume or brochure to support your personal qualifications and to outline the services and products you offer. An effective piece will help to establish yourself as a professional who offers value to the prospect through a comprehensive planning process. You may include introductions and testimonials from others with whom you have worked. You must clearly communicate that you can be trusted to do the job.

Building Rapport and Credibility—There are four important areas that a person uses to determine if they will trust an advisor and allow rapport to develop. A client-focused advisor is well aware of this and plans ways to communicate credibility. By anticipating a prospect's expectations, listening carefully to the prospect, and observing the prospect's behavior, the advisor can attempt to overcome negative responses from the prospect, improve credibility, and hasten the development of rapport.

These four factors build upon one another and culminate in establishing the advisor's credibility:

Propriety—There are many adjectives to describe this factor: appropriateness, correct appearance, proper image, suitability, correctness, and "fit." It centers on meeting the expectations of what the prospect considers proper business customs, dress, and behavior; looking the part, appearance, manners, protocol (greetings, shaking hands, recognition of the prospect's status), and appropriate speech. First impressions matter, although they play a relatively small role in long-term relationships. The prospect will be asking herself, "Does he walk, talk, and look like a competent advisor?" This factor could be considered initial screening by the prospect. Propriety avoids a negative assessment and dismissal before you can show your stuff. Arriving on time, looking the part, being well groomed, and dressing professionally are good ways to get started.

> **I'm a Great Closer**
>
> Selling isn't about being a great closer. Selling is about being a great opener. It's about creating opportunities. It's about discovering what people want and need and then giving them a solution to their problem. Selling is about making the client's life better and easier. When you're not opening cases, you have nothing to close.

Commonality—This factor includes: shared experience, having things in common, harmony, agreement, comfort level, camaraderie, companionship, comradeship, friendship, and a good "gut" feeling.

Commonality represents the foundation of trust and rapport. The prospect asks him or herself, "Is this the kind of person I want to do business with?" Often a common understanding and respect for one another's attitudes and values is present, either initially or over time, through sharing and disclosure. This is the basis and value of a third-party referral: you come well regarded and respected. It is natural that people feel more comfortable with people like themselves.

Competence—Words that capture this factor include: skillful, knows what he/she is doing, inspires confidence, experienced, capable, able, expert, and puts my mind at ease.

Competence is the foundation of trust and rapport based on awareness and judgment. Developing a prospect's perception of your competence involves providing information about yourself and knowledge of the prospect's situation. Can you do the job?

Credentials are certainly one thing that people look for in a professional, since they are a method of establishing professional competence. Credentials establish that you are a knowledgeable person. In the financial services, such designations as CLU, ChFC, CFP, and LUTCF show the public that our competence comes from experience, knowledge, and education.

This is also a place where a professional brochure can help to establish your competence. By listing your educational background, designations, areas of specialization, awards, business philosophy, and other such information that can be placed in a brochure, you can communicate your ability to do the job.

You do not need to claim expertise in every area. You can also establish competence by explaining that your colleagues are available to provide technical support or work with you on subjects that require a specialist, including meetings with the prospect.

Intent—Intent involves the prospect's perception of the advisor's motives and the advisor's interest in helping and benefiting the client. Does the advisor have the prospect's best interest before his or her own? The prospect must decide whether the advisor has a true problem-solving attitude, or is just trying to make a sale for his or her benefit. Intention is perceived in more than words. It is perceived through the advisor's body language, tone of voice and follow-through on commitments.

This is perhaps the most important factor in developing credibility. As the saying goes, the prospect does not care what you know until he or she knows that you care. Stating your purpose in a clear and understandable manner, then backing it up with words and actions help to establish your intent and the prospect's ability to believe and trust you.

Your level of confidence, enthusiasm and openness will affect how you are perceived. Be positive and do not apologize. Avoid statements like, "I'm new at this" or "I'm not really too good at this." If you are not enthusiastic about your work, how can your prospects be convinced to rely on you? If you don't think you can do the job, why should they? Demonstrate your enthusiasm through your voice, body language, and speech. Carry yourself with assuredness. Openness means you are genuine, that you don't try to fake expertise. There is no façade, no role-playing of what a professional advisor is considered to be. You are yourself, and what you see is what you get. If you don't know something, admit it and find the answer. Following through on a promise is another way to establish your credibility.

Just by Listening

Some people listen, while others merely wait to speak. When a customer complains about a salesperson, it is often that he/she does not listen, but forces the sales agenda on the customer. This is not marketing (or good selling, either). Learn to listen by focusing on what the customer has to say.

—John Melchinger
www.melchinger.com

Empathy—Trust equals empathy plus credibility. Credibility is only part of building trust. The other part is empathy, the ability to see things from the prospect's point of view. You understand how the other person feels, although you may not necessarily feel the same way.

As an advisor, empathy refers to the way you demonstrate focus on solving the prospect's problems. Empathy involves allowing the prospect to see that you see things from his or her point of view, that you understand their problems and feel their pain, by accurately expressing a problem that need to be fixed. It involves the capacity to lay aside your own set of experiences in favor of those of your clients. It also involves skillful listening to hear not only the obvious, but also the subtleties of which even the client may be unaware. Communicate your understanding by sharing with the prospect what you have been thinking. Confirm that your perceptions are accurate before proceeding.

The Time/Tension Model—What happens to you, or anyone, when you are in a new or unfamiliar situation? We find it stressful and demanding, making us uncomfortable, tense, and anxious. We may be defensive and guarded, or feel threatened and insecure. This may be expressed as a reluctance to talk, with folded arms, lack of eye contact, and general body language that is closed and defensive. Remember that this is a common experience and that your prospect is most probably feeling the same or in a similar way. To create a receptive environment for conducting an interview, you are looking for a relaxed and open expression, eye contact, and more warm and open body language from your prospect.

The time/tension model looks at the interaction of interpersonal relationship or rapport and the accomplishment of a task. The uneasiness at a personal level is called relationship tension, and the ability to work on business (or any task) is known as task tension. You can help the rapport-building process by doing what you can to reduce relationship tension, discomfort caused by an unfamiliar situation or unfamiliar people. If the prospect remains uncomfortable, he or she will be much less willing or able to provide serious information about his or her financial and personal situation. Little can be done to move forward with the sales/planning process unless attention is paid to relieving this initial discomfort.

As we become familiar with the situation and the people in it, we begin to relax and feel at ease, and eventually comfortable. We gain an increasing ability to focus on the task at hand and what needs to be done to accomplish it. The advisor should pay attention to the comfort level developing between himself or herself and the prospect, and attempt to lower the relationship tension before raising task tension (business issues). At the beginning of the interview, we use small talk (light conversation) and seek things in common with each other that can further the development of a comfortable social situation. By being aware of these relationship issues at the beginning of the initial interview, the advisor can reduce this relationship tension and hasten the development of a comfort level, and begin discussing business matters sooner. The advisor can also be more sensitive to the timing and introduction of more serious and personal information and topics into the interview (task tension).

2. Uncover Insurance Needs and Establish Priorities

Your second objective is to identify needs. Your use of open-ended questions, designed to elicit the prospect's goals, attitudes, and feelings, is the best route to uncovering needs. The needs are not yours, but those of your prospect. As you ask a question and get a response, pay attention to which topics seem more important to the prospect. Comment on how those issues of particular interest are expertly handled by you, your agency, and your company for many people who have faced the same or similar problems. Discuss problems common to people in the prospect's situation, such as survivor income, saving for college and retirement, and so on, to see how the prospect feels about these issues. This may be more formally addressed in the data-gathering session that may follow this initial interview, or at another time in the future.

3. Establish Your Ability to Help

As you are identifying needs, you will accomplish your third objective, which is to let the prospects know how you can help them find solutions for their needs. Explain what you do, how you do it, and the scope of your business. This establishes in your prospect's mind that you can help, and most importantly, that you are the one who should help. Explain that you are in the business of helping people achieve their financial goals. You are a problem solver.

The key to becoming a successful financial services professional in a highly competitive market is to make yourself appealing to prospects by setting yourself apart from your competition. You should ask yourself, "Why should a client want to work with me rather than hundreds of other professionals in my marketplace?" If you cannot answer that question yourself, how can you expect your prospect to know the difference and choose you? You must understand what you offer, how it is different and better than what your competition offers, and why people should want to work with you. Determine your strengths and match them to the needs of your potential clients. Look at your background, past work experience, education, personal philosophies, values, and attitudes to find strong points. Talk to your manager and other advisors about ways you can promote yourself professionally. This is not all about you; it is about how you can help the client. To be a success, you must develop an engaging, client-centered message that differentiates you from your competition.

4. Obtain Prospect's Permission to Proceed

Finally, you must get the prospect's permission to proceed. You cannot ask sensitive questions of someone who is not prepared to answer them. Explain why gathering personal information is important: you have to understand his or her full financial and personal situation to make intelligent recommendations. You must obtain agreement on what you and your prospect will do together. This is the first commitment you make to each other. This must be a mutual commitment; the prospect must be serious about participating in the process, and in a position to seriously consider acting on any need that is uncovered. He or she must also be willing to make the time commitment necessary to complete the process. By taking this step, you begin to build an advisor-client relationship that should continue long after the sale is completed. It will also go a long way toward preventing the possibility of future lapse or cancellation.

Until now, you have been busy building rapport and trying to establish the need for further life insurance planning. Now is the time to find out if your efforts have succeeded. You must be willing to disengage and leave if the prospect is unwilling to give complete information or make a commitment. Your time is valuable and shouldn't be spent on people who are not real prospects.

How much will this cost?

One question often asked is "How much is this going to cost?" There are a number of ways to answer. Here is one example:

"It is too soon to tell exactly how much additional insurance you might need, and therefore also the cost. However, I am prepared to analyze your situation and make recommendations at no cost to you. If it turns out that you do need more life insurance, I will be able to recommend a plan and products that will fit your budget. The main thing is for us jointly to determine exactly your situation, for me to design a plan to provide for any needs you may have, and for you to commit yourself to carrying it out. Does that sound reasonable?"

Throughout the interview you have asked questions to determine if the prospect agrees in principle with your ideas ("Does this sound good to you?"). You may have collected some personal information, asked poignant questions, and uncovered some general needs. The need for further planning should be clear, and you can close on an agreement to proceed by asking, "Would you like to continue this process?" The prospect will either voice their concerns or agree to proceed.

If the prospect has time to do information gathering on the first appointment, and you do also, then you may proceed. If not, then schedule another appointment to begin data gathering.

Establish Expectations—After you have agreement to proceed, you can then describe the next step in the process and what you and the prospect should expect from each other. Fact gathering is the next important part of the process, and you should explain what information you will need, why you will need it, how you will get it, what you will do with it, and how it will contribute to the analysis and recommendation phases of the planning process.

Point out that you expect your prospect to be frank and open with you in providing this information. Then add that any personal or financial data you receive will be held in confidence by the company and by you. Explain clearly that the release of any information, and any subsequent inquiries about the prospect with outside parties, will only be undertaken after getting the prospect's consent.

This is also a good time to introduce the idea of referrals. Explain to your prospect that the way you do business is through personal recommendation, since most people prefer this method of selecting services. Ask the prospect to introduce you to people they value, people like them, and people who may also benefit from your services.

5. Building the Relationship

Image, rapport, and trust are the major elements of the relationship you are trying to build with your prospects. They are part of the developing relationship that makes everything you do important, including mannerisms, listening skills, dress, speaking style, and nonverbal expression. Keep in mind that the objectives are to build credibility through establishing needs and demonstrating how you can help fulfill those needs.

At the initial meeting, trust is a serious issue for the prospect if they do not know the advisor. Many people behave defensively and guarded in new situations; they may feel threatened and insecure. Some of this may be seen in nonverbal behavior such as tone of voice, folded arms, quietness, and so on. You want to be aware of this and work to reduce this tension. Small talk and finding topics of common interest are a starting points. Asking questions that encourage prospects to think about their most important needs builds trust and shows that you are concerned about their future.

Planning the Interview

Now let's look at the planning that will make your first meeting with your prospects comfortable and productive for everyone involved. You have an opportunity when you make your appointment to set the stage for what you wish to happen. First, you want all the decision makers to be present. Offer to reschedule the meeting if someone will be missing. Rarely can a prospect effectively present the advisor's ideas; The missing person loses the benefit of listening to you. It also forces you to repeat your presentation when the group reconvenes, slowing the momentum of the process.

Preparing the Prospect

Just as you prepare for the interview, you may ask your prospect to prepare as well. The client's preparation depends upon his or her situation.

Simple situations require little or no preparation from a client. In dominant needs situations (covered later in this chapter) such as a mortgage insurance need, details on existing life insurance policies and the mortgage will suffice.

For a total needs analysis or a more complex case, many documents may be required. You may need to schedule an appointment with the prospect's other advisers, such as an attorney or accountant. Ask that insurance policies be available for review, including medical, disability, and group benefits booklets from employment, and other family members' coverage. Request that any other papers such as trusts or wills that will have bearing on the planning process also be available to review. Many advisors prepare a list to help prospects gather family papers that should be considered.

If you don not see all of the family's documents, ask about them. Some of the documents you should ask about include:

- life insurance policies on all members of the family
- disability income and health insurance policies
- all coverage from an employer (life, health, retirement)

- bank account statements, CDs
- credit union accounts
- brokerage account statements
- mutual fund statements
- a copy of the latest Will and Living Will or Health Care Directive
- mortgage(s) statements with some explanation of the terms and status for each
- trusts and any other legal instruments for managing money
- pension and profit sharing plan statements
- IRA accounts, 401(k) or 403(b) statements
- loans, pledges, notes, or other liabilities indicating money owed to others

This preparation allows you to begin the business discussion without delay since everyone is prepared to talk about the prearranged topics. Your attitude and approach demonstrate your professionalism. The time you spend with the prospect will be much more valuable if the prospect is prepared to discuss the documents and data you request.

Preparing Yourself

Prepare carefully for your interviews. Arrange resource papers and forms neatly in your briefcase, where you can reach them as they are needed. Be ready to conduct your business meeting professionally and in a reasonable amount of time.

Your company or agency should provide forms for information gathering. Fact-finders are valuable for working with prospects in developing their total needs. A good fact-finder asks the routine questions about mortgage and age of family members, and will also inquire about the prospect's attitudes and feelings. Shorter forms are available to help determine single needs for such concerns as mortgage insurance.

Use a sales presentation book for visual illustration of the points you are making if your company permits. Your company probably provides useful marketing brochures. Plan each interview thoroughly, including the presentation of sales aids. It is most important that you know how to use them with ease, so practice and master your interviews ahead of time. This is the only way to build your self-confidence and polish your performance.

Before you meet, review your material and go over all the information you have about the prospect. The more you know, the easier it will be to plan the meeting. Review your objectives. Collect sales literature and prospectuses that may be relevant. Plan an agenda. Know what outcome you expect from this meeting. Is it an application for mortgage insurance on a new house? Is it a completed fact-finder that you will use to analyze all of the insurance needs of the prospect? Establish your goals before you sit with the prospect, so that everything you say leads the conversation towards accomplishing them. The meeting will not falter because you are prepared. Preparation is the key to success.

A few comments are needed about the following fact-finding policy review questions. Some questions contain jargon that may be too technical for the general public. It is normally undesirable to use jargon with prospects and clients because it gives a negative, authoritarian character to the practitioner's intent. Secondly, the questions may confuse, mystify, or frighten the prospect, which is also undesirable. If used honestly and genuinely with a helping attitude, this language is fine. By using these questions you may begin to determine the knowledge and sophistication of the prospects regarding their insurance program and overall financial situation, past experiences and attitudes about it, features contained or not contain in their current policies, areas of interest, and objectives you may pursue in your interview.

Fact-Finding—Policy Review Questions

Look over the list below. It is designed to serve as a background to help you prepare for an interview. Pick several questions that will help focus your interview and questions you may want to ask the prospect about their existing life insurance and overall planning.

1. When desired, can you obtain from the policy's cash values an income for yourself?
2. Have you planned for the distribution of your estate?
3. If your children are beneficiaries, have arrangements been made for their minority?
4. Why did you buy this policy and what do you expect it to accomplish?
5. Would a common disaster jeopardize your children's interests?
6. Are all beneficiary designations correct and complete?

7. Should your beneficiaries be changed due to new family circumstances?
8. Will the proceeds of your life insurance be subject to probate delays and expense?
9. Will your estate expenses be properly and speedily liquidated if your children are minors?
10. Will your grandchildren share in your estate?
11. Have your Social Security benefits been coordinated with your life insurance?
12. Have you planned the extent to which your life insurance will provide income for your survivors?
13. Can your spouse outlive the income provided?
14. Have your policies been arranged to guarantee an income for your children's college education?
15. Is a cash fund provided for your spouse's last expenses?
16. Have you made your policies lapse-proof insofar as possible?
17. What nonforfeiture option is now provided? Would a change be beneficial?
18. Might the proceeds of your life insurance be subject to double taxation if you predecease your spouse?
19. Is the plan of distribution of your life insurance coordinated with that of your general property?
20. Do you now own a substandard policy? If so, do the conditions that caused the extra rating still exist?

Summary of the Initial Interview

- Make a statement of your intentions—the purpose of your meeting with the prospect.
- Include what will happen and why—what is the benefit of this meeting to the prospect?
- Ask permission to ask questions.
- Ask open-ended questions designed to obtain information and feelings about the prospect's financial situation and goals.
- Ask more specific questions about needs and desired solutions.
- Address how your products and services may apply to the prospect's situation.
- Make a summary statement of how the prospect sees the situation. Ask checking questions (solicit feedback) to be certain that what you understand is accurate.

Conducting the Initial Interview

Your Purpose

Begin the meeting by stating your purpose. Let the prospects know why you are making the call, and how much time you need. Get confirmation that the time you need is available now. If you sense that interruptions may occur, ask that they not be allowed to intrude on your conversation. In your opening comments, introduce yourself and your services and products. Explain briefly how they might be beneficial to your prospects and why the time you spend with your prospects will be profitable for all concerned.

Explain that, as a financial services professional, the service you offer is the review and analysis of your clients' financial goals and needs in relationship to the family's current income and budget. Add that your objective is to determine the appropriate types and amounts of protection suggested by your clients' personal and financial situation. Describe the process you will be using with the prospect (both the format and subject matter), which is fact-finding and conversation about their financial situation and goals. Explain that this process is essential in order to discover the current financial and personal situation and future goals and needs, and that everything discussed will be held in the strictest of confidence.

You should explain how your clients would benefit from these services. You want to give some predictions of what type of outcomes the prospect might reasonably expect. You will be dealing with many important concerns, such as the immediate and long-term financial consequences of an income earner's death, the adequacy of the family's life insurance planning, the need to budget for financial security protection, and the importance of having up-to-date wills, topics to which most people have not given enough consideration. There is no obligation for these services, of course, yet the information and analysis you will provide will be valuable whether there is a need for additional insurance or not, and whether or not the prospects act on your recommendations.

As you describe your services and products, ask questions such as "how does this sound to you?" or "would that be of interest to you?" The answers will help the prospects to participate in the interview. If the answers are positive, it will mean that you have agreement to continue. Ask this type of question frequently throughout the meeting.

This structuring, or setting the stage for what will take place, need not be lengthy and cumbersome; in fact, it is far better to structure the interview in a clear, straightforward, succinct fashion. Consider the following example of structuring your initial comments:

> "In order for me to be able to provide the best possible service for you, we'll probably need to see each other on several separate occasions, although I want you to know that I'm available to you as often as you need me. Today, I thought we would start by defining your financial situation. To do this, we will use the fact-finder pages, which will remain confidential between the two of us. As we continue working together, I expect that we will develop a sensible financial plan to help you meet your goals. Do you have any questions?"

Time Commitment

You must plan to spend enough time with prospects so that you can communicate easily without pressure. I'm sure you have noticed how some people seem to take forever to move through a point of discussion. They need to fill you in on everything in their lives from Aunt Millie's illness and her health insurance problems to the children's schoolwork. Others are businesslike, reach conclusions quickly, and need minimal explanations. Interacting with others' personal social style is discussed later in this chapter.

You may want to ask a new prospect "a few simple questions" to get an idea of how much time you might need to do your job right. You may be restricted by your prospect's need to use less time than you would like to have. If the time restriction imposed by your prospect is more than you can accept to complete your work, you must communicate this and negotiate for more time, perhaps on another occasion. Simply by asking this, you communicate that you are a professional who cares about your clients.

Until you learn to read the amount of time your prospect requires to communicate effectively, you will struggle for success with those who do not exactly match your own natural style. An advisor's success in relating positively to a prospect rises sharply when the advisor succeeds in matching the behavior patterns of the prospect.

Test this theory on yourself. Look through your own files of clients and see what you find. How similar to your own personality are your current group of clients and policyowners? Next, think about a sale you did not close or are currently having difficulty closing. Can you learn anything from this line of thought? The art of communication is really your ability to address the behavior styles of the prospect as you go through the steps of the selling/planning process. As terrific as a phrase may sound to you, it will be useless, perhaps damaging, if uttered for your benefit rather than that of the client. Never lose your focus on the prospect.

Establishing an Agenda

Follow a set agenda for each interview session. This tells prospects what is expected of them and reduces anxiety and discomfort concerning what will happen during the meeting. Whenever possible, involve your prospects in setting the agenda.

Setting proper expectations for the meeting helps establish rapport and gets the initial interview off to a positive start. You can reduce any initial tension that exists in an interview with a prospect whom you have never met before by outlining the steps involved in your approach to planning. The highlights to be covered involve explaining the steps of the planning process, which are to

1. assist the prospect in forming goals and objectives
2. help the prospect identify existing resources for meeting goals and objectives
3. analyze the gap between goals, objectives, and existing resources
4. devise a plan for bridging the resource gap
5. implement the plan
6. monitor the plan

You should have an agenda for every sales meeting. In presenting the agenda you should

- communicate what you intend to accomplish during the meeting
- explain how you will work with the prospect
- state the benefit for the prospect
- check for acceptance

In the initial planning session, you might propose the agenda by saying something like this to the prospect:

Purpose	**What You Say**
Communicate what you intend to accomplish during the meeting.	During this meeting, we will discuss some life planning issues that may be of concern to you.
Explain how you will work with the prospect.	First, I will tell you a little about who I am and the company I represent.
	Then we will talk about your concerns, goals, and desires regarding your financial planning.
	Next, we will look at how your financial status currently stands in regard to your net worth, cash flow, and budget.
	Finally, I will identify any problems or gaps in your current long-term plan.
State the benefit for the prospect.	That way you can determine whether it will be valuable for us to move ahead and develop a planning strategy tailored for you.
Check for acceptance	How does that sound?

By proposing the agenda in this way, stating the benefit to the prospect, and checking for acceptance, you are sharing control of the interview with your prospect, which helps you to establish rapport.

Also, as an afterthought, it may be advisable to reassure the prospect of your continuing commitment to the process by adding the following:

"If in the course of our work together we should discover that you have a need for a product I offer, I will assist you in devising a customized plan that addresses your individual concerns. I will then help you to implement that plan and promise to monitor and service that plan in the future."

After you present your agenda, ask for any other concerns that your prospect wishes to discuss. Write them down and be sure to cover these concerns in your discussion. Do so even if the concerns fall under categories you had on your agenda. Your prospect's input is an important first step in the open exchange of data and feelings.

Establishing Rapport and Credibility

Client building begins with establishing rapport. People want to work with professionals who build meaningful relationships with them and listen to what they want to accomplish. If rapport and credibility are developed in the process of exchanging information, then the product options and amounts you recommend will more likely be reflective of their real insurance needs and values. In order for prospects to buy from you, they must first trust you. Trust is the intangible aspect of selling that must be gradually cultivated and earned. You must prove that you are there to help them, not simply to sell them something.

A professional way to establish credibility is to assemble a single page or a brochure with some basic information about yourself, your agency, and your company. The information may actually be less important to the average prospect than the fact that you have created a professional sales piece to communicate your intent. This helps make a favorable initial impression, and removes any doubt about your promises to serve the prospect well. Check to see what your company or agency provides.

The newer you are to the business, the more difficult it may be to establish credibility. You simply do not have enough experience in the life insurance business and your résumé is too incomplete to stand on its own. However, you can borrow some credibility from your agency and company through the use of brochures and company sales materials.

It is likely that your company or agency has already put together information like this in a sales promotion piece. You may want to use that piece as it is, or transfer the information you want to highlight to your letterhead or personal brochure to create a more personal approach. If you create your own materials, follow your company's compliance procedures before you take it into the field, since it has to be approved before use. Use it to help establish your credibility at the beginning of the interview. Make a point of leaving it with your prospect. You may even want to use it again later to write down the names of references. Your prospect may want to know the names of people you have done business with in the past. If used properly, this summary background information of your professional qualifications and services can become a powerful sales tool, especially at the critical stage of establishing credibility and building rapport.

When a sale does not close, or problems develop along the way, it may be traced back to this initial meeting. Perhaps the proper groundwork was not done; you did not establish your ability to help, you were not at ease with each other, or you did not establish an open, candid means of communication. Think about this as you evaluate yourself after you have met with the prospect. Of course, sometimes, even with our best efforts nothing can be done about this. No one is 100-percent successful in developing relationships.

Developing Relationship Skills

The following ideas should help you improve your ability to develop rapport in a positive relationship with your prospects.

- *Relax and be yourself.* When preparing to meet a new prospect, feeling the pressure to make a sale will make it difficult to be relaxed. If you are relaxed, the prospect will follow your lead.
- *Show the prospect respect and consideration.* Ask if this is a good time to talk. Ask permission to ask fact- and feeling-type questions. By asking, "May I ask you a few questions about your financial situation and goals," you show respect for the personal nature of the questions and focus attention on your interest in their needs.
- *Take time to know your prospect.* You didn't ask your spouse to marry you on your first date, did you? You took time to know him or her, listen to his/her opinions and life priorities, and then decided if that was the right person for you. Selling is based on a similar process. Focus on making a new friend and learning about his or her needs and priorities. Take the time to get to know your prospect, and for him or her to know you. Focus on a potentially long-term relationship rather than a quick sale. See the prospect as a person, not as a sale.
- *Bring value to your meeting by showing how you can help.*
- *Look for connections and common ground.* Do not assume you know what interests them. Be genuinely interested in them and what they say.
- *Listen and do very little talking.* Be warm, friendly, and inviting to find their needs. Insincerity based on pressure to get the sale and being too focused on closing the sale, rather than focusing on the individual as a person, will turn prospects off. When you listen to the prospect, they will be more interested in listening to you. That helps build trust and a meaningful relationship, the basis for sales.

- *Think of yourself as the prospect.* How would you want to be treated?
- *Listening sounds easy and we take it for granted.* But active listening is really hard work and requires constant concentration on the prospect. You must be totally in the moment with the other person, not distracted or thinking about anything other than what that person is saying.
- *Active listening is aided by paraphrasing and questioning.* Summarize, repeat, and highlight what the prospect says. Ask clarifying questions. Take notes. Make good eye contact and show positive body language, such as nodding, leaning forward and giving feedback. These techniques will show the prospect you are interested in them, and rapport will be enhanced.

Alleviating the Prospects' Concerns

Various barriers that can create tension between you and your prospects during an initial meeting must be removed if rapport is to be established. These barriers can be divided into four major categories:

Distrust of Salespeople—Many people have a negative image of salespeople and avoid meeting with them for fear of being talked into buying something they do not want or need.

Fear of Making a Decision—Decisions involve risk, and many people avoid risk, especially when money is involved. Also, fear of making the wrong decision or potential buyer's remorse can cause avoidance of stressful decision-making situations.

Need for Status Quo—Many people are complacent and resistant to change because they prefer familiarity.

Time Constraints—At today's increasingly hectic pace of life, busy prospects are reluctant to commit their time.

Being aware of prospect stress can help you identify opportunities to alleviate it and to establish rapport. Here are some tips.

- *Do not impose.* Schedule your initial meeting at times that are convenient for the prospects.
- *Watch your verbal pace.* Talk in an unhurried, businesslike manner. Never interrupt when prospects speak. Listen carefully

to what they say. As we will discuss shortly, listening is your best tool.

- *Remember nonverbal behavior.* You might be surprised to learn that as little as 7 percent of a first impression is based on what is actually said. The remaining 93 percent is based on nonverbal and vocal behaviors, such as physical appearance, body language, voice quality, and tone.
- *Encourage prospects to talk.* Having prospects talk is not only a great tool for getting feedback, but it is also a common way for them to relieve stress. Encourage prospects to do most of the talking.
- *Control your anxiety.* Several studies have shown that a person who is already anxious becomes even more so when talking with someone who displays nervousness or anxiety.

Responding to the Social Style of Prospects

Establishing rapport is your responsibility. This means you should be able to detect what each prospect wants in a sales relationship, and to use your versatility to shape the discussion and your responses to his or her respective needs. Social style is a characteristic way a person behaves and reacts in different situations.

Psychologist Dr. David Merrill described the characteristics of four different social styles:

- Driver
- Expressive
- Amiable
- Analytical

When you adapt to a prospect's social style, you make him or her feel at home and less threatened. Listening closely and observing carefully during the first few minutes of the initial interview gives you an idea of how to treat the prospect. The chart titled "Responding to Prospects' Social Styles" summarizes the characteristics of each social style and indicates how you can best establish rapport with a person who has that style. Listen carefully and observe your prospect to determine which set of characteristics most closely describes him or her and then establish rapport by responding in an appropriate manner throughout the interview.

EXAMPLE 1: If your prospect, Jane Weston, enthusiastically talks at length about the plans she has for the new business she is starting, she would be classified as an Expressive. To establish rapport, respond to her by taking time to listen and ask about her plans.

EXAMPLE 2: If your prospect, Ben Hammer, tells you where to sit when you enter his office and looks at his watch when you ask about the photograph of the sailboat on his wall, he would be classified as a Driver. To establish rapport, respond to him by immediately getting down to business and explaining the purpose, process, and benefits of the appointment.

What would happen if you responded to Jane Weston by going directly into an outline of the agenda for your meeting? What would happen if you tried to share your sailing exploits with Ben Hammer?

Here are two more examples to review.

EXAMPLE 3: If your prospect, Bob Hinds, greets you with a worried smile, apologizes for being 15 minutes late, and says that he could not get away from his last meeting where they were planning a retirement party for his administrative assistant—a wonderful woman who has been with him since he started the company—he would be classified as an Amiable. To establish rapport, respond to him by taking time to ask about his retiring administrative assistant.

EXAMPLE 4: If your prospect, Dr. Patricia Gibbons, stands to greet you from behind her desk when you are ushered into her office, waits for you to take a seat, and immediately asks you what the maximum gift is that she can give tax-free to each of her grandchildren, she would be classified as an Analytical. To establish rapport, respond to her by taking the time to answer her question with a detailed and documented reply.

What would happen if you responded to Bob Hinds by launching into a discussion of gift taxes? How would Bob Hinds respond if you took a few moments to tell him about seeing old friends at your high school reunion last weekend? What would happen if you tried to tell Dr. Gibbons about your high school reunion?

If you are able to identify and respond appropriately to a person's social style in a sales situation, you will be able to establish rapport more quickly and will facilitate the relationship-building process.

Responding to Prospects' Social Styles

Social Style	The Prospect's Style Characteristics	Your Best Response
Driver	Forceful, direct	Focus on objectives
	Will not waste time on small talk	Move right along
	Wants to be in control	To get decisions, provide options
Expressive	Outgoing, enthusiastic	Focus on dreams
	Enjoys telling about personal projects and dreams	Take time to listen
	Wants to be recognized	To get decisions, provide incentives
Amiable	Easy-going, dependent	Focus on relationships
	Enjoys telling about personal relationships	Be personal
	Wants to be accepted	To get decisions, provide personal assurances
Analytical	Logical, quiet	Focus on principles and thinking
	Is uncomfortable with small talk	To get decisions, provide evidence
	Wants to be accurate	Be accurate

The Interview Setting

Where you meet your prospect is very important. You want a private and quiet place where you can talk about confidential subjects. It must be convenient and comfortable for the prospect. If you need equipment to make your presentation, space and the proper facilities need to be available.

New advisors are often reluctant about asking prospects to compromise on where they will meet. The traditional expectation for personal insurance has always been that the advisor goes to the prospect's home, often in the evening. This is often not the only place where you can meet, nor the only time of day when you can see each other. Ask yourself where you want to hold your interviews. If this matters to you, begin to figure out how you are going to control the setting of your meetings with prospects and clients.

Most personal sales appointments are conducted in the prospect's home. This has one advantage; the advisor is more likely to meet all of the family and see the home. It will give you a better opportunity to get a sense of the life style and standard of living of the prospect and make sure that all of the decision makers are present for your interview. It never works well to have one marriage partner tell the other what you discussed. It delays the sale and can damage your rapport with the family. Make sure everyone who should be there is present when you meet. You need to meet with all of the decision makers.

You should sit with the prospects at their kitchen or dining room table. It is difficult to work off a long table in front of the sofa. Ask to sit where you will be able to conduct business. As you are seated, ask if the chair you are choosing is acceptable. If you are asked to sit at the end of the table with prospects flanking you on either side, you will have a difficult time. Ask to shift the table seating around so that they are side by side and can share your presentation pages. You will have better success facing both so that you can look at them and they can look at you and not to each other. If this is the first of a series of meetings, you may have a difficult time changing the site or even the seating arrangements in the future. Make sure you can work comfortably with your initial choices.

Your prospect's office could be another choice for your meeting site. You might find that the flow of office business will interrupt your meetings. Make sure the telephone will be answered outside of the office and that the prospect still has the same amount of time to visit with you that was agreed upon.

Interruptions within a home are as disruptive as those in an office. If there are interruptions from children, the television, or the radio, you will have a difficult time competing for your prospect's attention. You can guard against this by setting your meeting time after young children will be in bed or before or after regular business hours in an office. Do not compete with children for their parent's attention. It is better to leave and return at another hour or another day.

Your best choice for having the ideal interview environment is to conduct it in your own office. You can ask the prospect to come to your office when you make the appointment. Everyone is used to keeping appointments in the offices of those with whom they do business, from the accountant to the dentist. It should come as no shock that a financial services representative should make the same request.

Whether or not the prospect will agree to meeting in your office depends on how you ask. If you ask with confidence, indicating that this is routine and a benefit to your client, you will probably have more office appointments. It is the cautious request that implies a favor that will suggest to the prospect that his dining room table should be the setting for your meeting. Explain that all the material you will need is in the office and that you conduct most of your business in your office.

Sales Presentation Book

Your sales presentation book or other visuals help you to guide a prospect through the series of topics and questions you wish to cover. You should ask your prospect's approval to use the piece as a way to stay on track and to insure that you cover everything. Tell the prospect that there are several topics to consider and the book helps keep you on track. Be careful, though, because some prospects will not like being led through a book. They may feel that they are being treated impersonally or immaturely, being plugged into a formula to sell insurance. You have to decide when it is appropriate to use a presentation book to conduct an interview, based on your assessment of the prospect's needs and wants. You may want only to use the presentation book approach in the early part of your career, until you thoroughly know its contents. At that point you may want to pull sections or single pages from it to enhance your presentation in the same way you would use a policy ledger illustration. This will allow you to make highly individualized presentations and personalize each interview. Make sure your company approves all the material in the presentation book.

Yellow Pad

Many advisors like to draw concepts, pictures, or graphs to educate a prospect on a particular point. You must be sure that both your drawing and writing are clear and legible. Leaving a visual of an important point or concept with your prospect is a negative if the prospect cannot make sense of it later or does not understand it. Make sure that anything you leave with the client is approved and in compliance.

As an example, you may wish to describe how you market your services to people in a few targeted groups, rather than trying to be all things to all people. You may wish to represent all people by a large circle and, as you speak, simply draw a few smaller circles within the larger one to identify the few smaller groups you concentrate on. This demonstrates to the prospect or client how you define your markets, and insures his or her understanding that you do not go after everyone's business. Just five or six circles on a page will suggest the scope of your business.

This will be valuable later when you ask for referrals. It is a good visual technique to use with centers of influence, too, when asking for referrals within your definition of target markets.

Game Plan

Just as sports team approaches a game with a plan on how to win, you should enter the interview with a general game plan. Here is a simple overall strategy of what you want to accomplish with the prospect.

1. **Generate Awareness**—The first step is to help educate the prospect about the needs that you can address. Many prospects have no idea what they need or what you can do. Discuss financial and insurance problems and issues in general.

2. **Probe the problem**—People buy products because they have a problem that they believe the product can solve. You often need to help them understand the problem and how you can help them solve it.

3. **Solve the problem**—After you have exposed the problem or problems, you must deliver a satisfactory solution that solves the problem. If you neglect to identify the problem, solve the problem insufficiently, or solve the wrong problem, your solution will not be purchased or maintained.

4. **Take action**—If you have progressed successfully through the sales/planning process, the prospect should be ready to take action on your recommendations. Do not assume they will take action on their own; you must ask for the business. By failing to ask the prospect to take action, you risk that he or she will do nothing, buy from a competitor or put off the decision to implement a solution to their problem.

Uncovering Needs

Open the general conversation of the prospect's needs by asking a series of open-ended questions to get the prospect thinking and participating in the discussion. Open-ended questions are the type that draw out thinking and explanations from the prospect. Open-ended questions solicit opinions, thoughts, ideas, values, and feelings. You will bring forth goals and objectives. You may uncover gaps that the prospect feels uneasy about, sensing inadequate protection or unfulfilled goals.

Your questions allow you to steer the conversation without having to make awkward observations about inadequate protection. With well-directed questioning, your prospects will discover that they may not be meeting their objectives. As you examine the goals and needs of your prospects, you may encounter areas in which the steps taken to date by your prospects are insufficient to meet their goals and needs. When this occurs, simply ask if they would like to consider doing something about these matters. This is how a series of small commitments builds into a sale.

Take the time to care. When you ask your open-ended questions, make sure that you listen to the answers. Let the prospect know that you are really listening. Summarize what you have heard and check for accuracy. Rephrase important points and demonstrate that you understand. Take notes.

Open-ended Questions to Use in the Initial or Fact-finding Interview

- How do you feel about your savings plan to date?
- Tell me about your most important personal goals.
- How do you feel about your life insurance program?
- What are your most important financial goals?
- How do you feel about saving for your children's college education?

The questions are really limitless. Get the prospect to talk about what is important to them, and get a sense of their financial situation and how they feel about it.

Self-Evaluation

After your initial interview, as well as any time you are with a prospect or client, take some time after the appointment to review what was said and how the interaction progressed. Be sure to look at positives as well as areas needing improvement. Note things the prospect said that were interesting, ideas you could use again, areas of confusion, times when the interview went smoothly, and times when things were collapsing and you did not know what to do. Noting these observations will help you to identify areas of your presentation to improve, or areas of knowledge to expand.

The first interview with the prospect sets the stage for your future relationship. Your objective is to establish rapport and gain permission to gather personal information in order to develop a plan or a set of alternatives. Keep refining what you do. Your objective is to create relationships from which you can develop and expand your clientele.

Many advisors like to take their prospects to breakfast or lunch and begin their business relationship over a nice meal. There are always those prospects that may feel it makes them obligated to take an advisor's gift of the meal's check. Do not be offended when someone suggests an alternative. Your invitation may be accepted and appreciated more when the two of you have become better acquainted.

Total and Dominant Needs Approach

So far in this book we have discussed a variety of needs answered by life insurance products. These have included maintaining the survivors' lifestyle, liquidating the mortgage on a home, funding a child's college education, providing an emergency fund, and others. Let's now look at dealing with all of these life values and needs at the same time. This is called the total needs approach to insurance planning.

Done properly, you will see that working with your prospects to solve their total needs can be of great value to them, as well as very profitable to you, especially as we deal with the prospect's long-range, total life situation.

Total Needs Approach—Benefits to You

Multiple Needs = More Sales Opportunities—Most people do not want to put small patches on big problems. They may fail to recognize all of their insurance needs. Even if entire plans cannot be completed now, if you work with your prospects to identify all of their goals and the ways to achieve them, they will have a clearer picture of where they stand. This ability to see the big picture will make it easier for your prospects to appreciate each of its pieces. This approach to total needs will motivate your clients to coordinate all of their protection for their families' interests. It will help them acquire the insurance they need when they can afford to do so.

Professionalism and Ethics—Prospects expect professional behavior, which certainly includes thoroughness. If you don't discuss their total situations and work to help solve all of their needs, you will be falling short of the prospects' expectations and your own professional standards. You will not be able to make meaningful recommendations without understanding the full situation.

There are legal considerations to be observed as we think about the ethics of our business. These include the standards for professional behavior that we impose upon ourselves such as the impulse to not leave someone inadequately protected. We must try to sell adequate amounts of the right kinds of protection.

This requires us to do more than sell just the mortgage policy or college funding program. It means talking about all of the prospect's needs, understanding all of the prospect's financial goals, and examining how far along the prospect is in meeting his or her objectives. We should not be satisfied to sell piecemeal, leaving clients only partially protected. We should offer each prospect the opportunity to make his or her decision based on full knowledge of the consequences.

Higher Closing Ratios—Solving total needs does mean the advisor will need to do more work up front. A more thorough understanding of the situation, however, gives you the leverage you may need to close the sale. There should be a clear understanding of and agreement on goals when the decision to buy is requested. The logic of the sale is complete, and the emotional reasons for making the purchase are crystallized. The prospect has had ample opportunity to identify and define personal needs, so concerns will be minimized. The information has come from the prospect working through the planning process with you.

Thoroughness leads your prospect to a feeling of appreciation and positive regard toward you, for you have taken the time to care, to educate, to explain, and to support your prospect in making the right choices. The professional-client relationship is fixed more firmly in the total needs approach than in any other sales method. You more easily gain client loyalty, and this can help you make the next sale to your new client.

Better Markets—The best prospects for complete planning of total insurance needs are those people who have more complex financial situations and incomes in the higher brackets, and who have the willingness and desire to address them. Your services should be tailored to the needs of markets that not only want but also can afford the products you offer.

Persistency from Selling a Comprehensive Plan—People who have bought policies think about policies as commodities. They are the ones who most often shop for the better deal. People who buy a plan of insurance, however, buy the concepts of the plan and recognize that the policies are only vehicles to achieve the protection they want. With the big picture in place, they are not confused by loose pieces of the puzzle. They tend to keep their coverage intact, to make premium payments on time, and are less likely to accept any recommendations from someone who does not understand their total needs. They understand and appreciate the value of their protection. Seasoned advisors estimate that it costs five times more to win a new client than it costs to keep an existing client, so this client is a valuable part of your business. You want to keep clients.

The creation of the plan makes it more than an important insurance document. Clients will refer to it anytime someone suggests that they buy additional coverage. They will want to know how the suggestion fits into their personally tailored plan. The plan has been designed to offer complete security and they do not want to tamper with its purpose. They bought a concept—financial security.

You want to sell solutions, not products. People lapse policies; typically they do not lapse solutions. The carpenter does not really want a drill; he wants a hole. He buys the drill as a solution to his problem, needing a hole.

Prospecting Boost—Prospecting is easier with the total needs approach. First, referrals are stronger. You have provided a valuable service and your clients will want to share you as good news to friends and family. Think how much easier it is for them to tell a friend, "Bob helped me a great deal by carefully working through all the details," than it is to say, "you should see Bob. I really like the new mortgage coverage."

Second, you will get a better response from the referrals when asking for appointments. You offer a service that will explore and review an individual's financial goals and objectives thoroughly. Based on that review, you will recommend a plan of action for achieving those goals. This blueprint will be custom designed to the client's needs, not simply a formula for selling insurance. When you understand how valuable this service is, you will be able to convey this to your prospects.

Inviting Repeat Sales—When you do a thorough job for your clients, they will not want to work with anyone else. They will return your phone calls and expect annual reviews of their existing plans. You become their trusted advisor, rather than just someone who sells them insurance. As their situations change, their needs for coverage often increase. You will be the natural person to take care of this for them in the future.

Your Own Pride and Satisfaction—Your efforts are as important to you as to your clients. Planning a total needs program is a big effort, but it is also a complete effort. You know you have done everything you could to help your prospects and clients, and this should bring you considerable satisfaction. You are a professional doing what a professional is expected to do. You protect families and businesses from ruin. You can look your prospect in the eye and accept with satisfaction and pride the appreciation when he or she says, "Thanks for all you have done. You have been a wonderful help."

Total Needs Approach—Benefits to Your Prospects

Your prospects face a variety of challenges every day of their lives, and their finances are not exempt. The accumulation, management, and distribution of assets to assure security for themselves, their families, and their businesses are primary concerns. Proper application of the total needs approach assures your prospects the best opportunity to solve challenging problems in a changing environment.

Client Understands their Needs—Your approach to providing complete insurance planning helps prospects understand the needs they want to fulfill. They will no longer be satisfied considering just the mortgage or education fund. They will insist on working out the consequences of every change or new product idea offered. Everything will have to dovetail into their overall plan. They will have a much better grasp of their total life value after you have helped them work through all of the details of a well-conceived program.

Work From a Plan—The sheer number of issues to consider makes insurance planning complex. Add to this the changing circumstances in the prospect's life and the need for a plan is evident. You have the opportunity to find solutions that can benefit your client. The plan can also be to your benefit, since the sale of insurance becomes easier when the insurance becomes part of the solution, rather than the only solution you can offer.

Your suggestion might be a simple rearrangement of settlement options in present life insurance policies, or it might be to develop a complex estate plan. In every case, no matter how simple or complex, your job is to help your client use his or her assets in ways that will satisfy as many financial needs as possible.

At the death of the insured, many decisions need to be made. Should the children be kept in private schools? Should the mortgage be paid off? Should liquid assets, such as savings accounts or certificates of deposit, be drawn upon for immediate cash? Should non-liquid assets, such as stocks and rental property, be placed in a trust?

No Threat: Calling a Referral for an Appointment

"(Prospect), I recently did an analysis of insurance needs for your friends, the Charleses. They suggested that since the analysis was so valuable, I should offer the same service to you and some of their other friends as well. The purpose of my call is to follow up on Bob Charles' letter and see if we can get together. Did you receive the letter Bob sent? (Wait for a response.) Good. As I mentioned, I would like to arrange a mutually convenient time for us to meet so that I can show you what I do and how I go about my business. This will take no more than 30 minutes, and I make three promises that should appeal to you: First, the only purpose of this meeting will be to get acquainted. I will merely describe the services I offer. Second, I will not call again unless you invite me back. Finally, I will leave with you at least one valuable idea, whether we continue to do business or not. Is that fair enough?" (Wait for a positive response, then set the appointment date.)

Professionally Monitored and Serviced—The policyowner with an insurance plan recognizes the planner not only as a salesperson, but also as a trusted and respected professional advisor. When your competitors call, your clients can say, "my insurance is taken care of by Kim Martin with ABC Life. I have a very comprehensive plan."

Some decisions will be based on the availability of funds provided by Social Security or employee benefit plans. In total needs planning, mere assumptions cannot be relied on. You must get at the facts as they apply to each case. Your knowledge of the dreams and realities of a family's life will help you in the services you may be called upon to provide someday in the future. These are services that will make a difference.

Customized Solutions—Perhaps the greatest benefit of total needs planning is the satisfaction the client feels knowing that the plan was professionally prepared and implemented, was custom made to the client's needs and goals, and can be referred to when needed as a basis of an ongoing planning process.

When the need for more life insurance is recognized by the prospect, the next decision is how much and what kind to buy. Your recommendations hinge on the answers to questions such as:

- What are the total needs?
- What policy will best satisfy those needs?
- What is the premium cost?
- How much can the prospect afford?

If there is a substantial need for family income, as well as for retirement income, you might propose a permanent plan of insurance. This plan would create an immediate estate at death as well as build cash to supplement income for retirement. If the premium is too high, perhaps term, or a combination of term and permanent protection, should be purchased now and the term converted to permanent coverage later as premium payments can be increased. The client may have preferences, either for permanent or term insurance, which will dictate the buying decision. This topic will be discussed in the coming chapters.

Educating the Client

Your clients might want a permanent policy to satisfy just the major needs now, planning to buy additional, permanent coverage later to cover the less-pressing needs. Your clients will not begin to understand these insurance options unless you help them plan. You must educate your clients in the process. Informed consumers are better buyers. Their decisions will be based on their recognition of needs, the order of priority, and the costs of the various options. The insurance plan decided upon today will be the basis for deciding when, how much, and what kinds of life insurance will be needed in the future.

Buying a Policy or a Plan

People who have bought policies think about policies. People who buy a plan buy concepts and recognize that the policies are just the vehicles to achieve the plan.

Motives to Planning

The insurance you sell is not bought on a lark, without good reasons. There are motives for buying insurance and reasons for holding on to it, although they may not be immediately obvious to your prospects. The more you understand what influences your prospects, the better equipped you will be to motivate them to implement your recommendations. The more they understand about the purpose of their plan, the more likely they are to appreciate and keep it.

Security Needs—Many prospects are compelled to provide those basic types of coverage that will minimize the risk of being sued, protect against loss of property, minimize medical and health expenses, insure that basic living needs will continue to be met in the event of disability, and insure that survivors are cared for until death. Additional security needs are satisfied when the life insurance purchased also provides cash accumulations that are available for emergencies and retirement income.

Prospect Wishes—Although some of their concerns may appear less important to you than to your prospects, you cannot afford to discount or dismiss what your prospects wish to accomplish. There may be a strong desire to insure that a child does not miss any educational opportunities. There may be some special wish to liquidate the mortgage, although the client may be better advised, in your judgment, to have the survivors fund the payments for a few years. Sometimes there are overriding emotional or other issues that will take a dominant position in an individual or family's planning, even though it may not be the best decision from a financial perspective.

> **You Can't Get It When You Really Need It**
>
> Only life insurance can make money available to the people who need it, at the very moment when it is needed most: at the death of the family breadwinner.

Perhaps the prospect's parents lost their home because they could not make mortgage payments. Experiences like these are truly motivating events, and although the actions may not be "needed," the client's desire makes them almost imperative. Learn to recognize that these wants and wishes often override needs, and that you must be ready to work with your clients, not against them, as you plan their insurance. Always remember that it is their plan you are designing, not yours. You should provide them with information that can assist them in making a good decision, and give them your opinion or interpretation, but realize that ultimately it is their decision.

Fear—Fear can provide a strong motivation, especially if established through a personal experience. You may meet a prospect that has made a series of random, almost desperate, life insurance purchases because a parent died and left the family destitute. That experience motivates clients through fear of having their own loved ones suffer a similar experience.

Others may have an intense fear of reaching old age penniless, with no one to rely on and no money to allow them to maintain their self-respect and independence. You must recognize these fears and help your clients put them in perspective. You must recommend purchasing the appropriate amounts and right types of insurance coverage to protect them in these situations.

Consumer's Need for Information

Today's consumers want to be informed, according to a LIMRA (Life Insurance Marketing Research Association) report. The advice LIMRA offers is useful as we consider the advantages of selling insurance to provide for all of the buyer's needs, not just the dominant ones. Buyers are not confident buying something they know nothing about. But, once they have acquired the knowledge, they want to do business and develop a relationship with the insurance advisor. Buyers prefer to work with one professional insurance representative when they can. They're looking for someone who offers competent, consistent, frequent, and patient concern, according to LIMRA. The advisor must be able to answer a buyer's questions. The advisor must establish a service standard and never deviate.

Total needs selling can turn customers into clients. Consumers do not want our products to be sold to them; they want to buy the products they need. Most consumers realize they are not knowledgeable about insurance and financial products, so they need to find someone who is knowledgeable and whom they can trust. They are looking for unbiased advice, which is why they may be reluctant to ask the most knowledgeable person—the insurance advisor. Consumers trust advisors when they feel their own interests are put before the advisor's interests in selling to them.

> **Malpractice**
>
> In selling life insurance, as in the practice of medicine, prescribing before diagnosis can be considered malpractice.

Advisors need to realize that relationships do not develop quickly, and few sales are made after one approach. The buyer wants to buy on his or her own time schedule. They do not like to be pushed. Most of all, they want to consider everything the advisor has to suggest about their needs. Don't underestimate your prospects.

Dominant Needs Selling/Planning

Let's look at dominant needs selling to see how it can fit into insurance planning. Providing life insurance for the most apparent need the prospect may have is not unusual. This is a common way to prospect. When we call or write to people who have recently purchased a house and ask them for an appointment to talk about mortgage liquidation insurance, we use the dominant needs approach. We sell them the policy that would pay the mortgage should a breadwinner die. We find a hot button. It gets the advisor in the door.

What the Advisor Does Next

What the advisor does next determines the future of the relationship with the policyowner. The advisor can walk away, content with having sold the policy and looking for the next new homebuyer. This is the process we earlier called transactional selling. In the long run it is very difficult and unfulfilling. You are constantly trying to find new prospects.

The advisor can ask the policyowner if buying the house hasn't created other new needs for the family that also should be considered. The advisor offers his or her services to review the new homeowner's entire insurance program and see where they stand. When the advisor offers to help the homeowner develop a master plan for the future, he or she is offering to do a total needs analysis. It is important to remember that the benefits you sell are sufficient when they are needed. The same approach to every prospect may not always be the best approach. You must be able to identify when to sell to dominant needs and when to sell to total needs. Your key to success rests with your ability to identify your prospect's needs and motivations, evaluate the situation, and proceed according to the wishes of the prospect and the approach that will accomplish the most in that situation.

The key objective of the dominant needs sale should be initially to make a sale to obtain a client, but longer-term objectives should be to win the client's confidence, develop a strong, positive relationship, and work toward a total needs analysis approach when the client is ready.

Dominant Needs as the Total-needs Approach

Below are listed many of the needs that are sold as a dominant need to prospects. As you look them over, think of them as a whole—the total family needs of a typical family. Could dominant needs selling be just a part of total-needs selling? You be the judge.

- Final expenses
- Mortgage liquidation
- Spousal insurance
- Educational expenses
- Juvenile insurance
- Dependency period income
- Disability income insurance
- Long-term care insurance
- Individual health insurance
- Retirement income
- Medical supplement insurance
- Estate settlement fund

Single- and Multiple-Interview Selling/Planning

There are many different points of view on how much time and what content should be covered in the initial meeting. Some advisors prefer to conduct a single meeting process where the initial meeting completes the sales process, walking away form the initial meeting with an application. Others follow a system that requires two or more interviews in virtually all circumstances. Sometimes the length and timing of the sales planning process is determined by the preferences of the prospect or the degree of simplicity or complexity involved in the prospect's personal and financial situation. In this section we will discuss these variables, and the benefits and appropriateness of different strategies for the initial meeting with the prospect.

Single-Interview Selling

As our economic opportunities and choices have become more complex, people find it increasingly necessary to consider their total financial picture when buying life insurance. This means that now it usually takes more than one interview to make a sale. As a result, many financial advisors have come to accept the multi-interview approach as the normal way of doing business. This is also largely due to a total needs selling approach and tendency to move toward a comprehensive financial planning approach.

There are still times when you can close a sale and give your prospect good service in one interview. Much of this will depend upon the market in which the advisor operates and the objectives and needs of the prospect. Some advisors regularly complete the sale with a single interview, particularly where a dominant need is the prospect's primary concern and his or her financial situation is not complicated. With your cost of business going up, it pays to know how to recognize a single-interview sales opportunity when one is presented.

A particular need may be so prominent and in need of immediate attention that the total needs assessment will be postponed for another day. The prospect may be concerned about a single need and wish to address it, so only one interview may be required to complete the sale. This would be also true if the client does not wish to divulge personal information for a total needs analysis. Such situations may include:

- To fulfill an obligation, such as a condition for a loan or a divorce decree, where the client must have life insurance immediately. This does not mean that this is the prospect's only need; only that it is prominent and requires immediate attention.
- Where the prospect cannot afford to take care of all life insurance needs at once, as is often the case with a young family or a new business. Many prospects may have to delay the start of a complete plan now, but are prepared to focus on one or two of the most pressing, or dominant, needs. Your job in this situation is to help your prospects identify their total life insurance needs, set priorities for solving them, and acquire solutions for the ones at the top of the list.
- Specific needs selling, often as a result of a prospecting campaign for products such as mortgage insurance, disability income, or juvenile insurance. Although there may be other

needs, the prospect does not wish to take a total needs approach and is only interested in addressing this primary concern.

Begin now to establish the long-term relationship you want to create with these clients as you close on the priority needs in the first interview. In the future, you want your role as their financial advisor to become even more important. You will be needed to help reevaluate your clients' total needs, to reestablish their priorities, and to reconfirm their commitment to executing the plan. At first, however, your role is to help your clients act now to meet their most important needs.

Your Preparation—Since all calculations and analyses take place in one interview, it is important to prepare to conduct a thorough analysis. You may not always know prior to meeting that a single-interview sale will be appropriate, so ask in advance that the necessary information and documents that will allow you to complete your analysis be available. To assure that the information you need is on hand, provide your prospect with a complete list of documents you will need. Send a note in advance of your meeting to outline the information you need, or tell your prospect on the phone when you arrange the appointment.

Multiple-Interview Selling

Multiple-interview selling simply means that a sales process is begun and completed over more than one interview with the prospect. Some advisors will tell you that it is unnecessary and inefficient to meet with the prospect more than once to close a sale. In some cases, these advisors are right. Any advisor can give evidence of sales that are completed in a single appointment. However, a second interview, or even a third, does not necessarily reflect poor sales skills on the part of the advisor. If you take a good look at effectiveness, particularly in regard to the demands of the prospect and the complexity of the situation, you should see many instances where it is appropriate to conduct a sale in more than one interview. Multiple interviews may be needed in a sales situation for a variety of reasons. Let's consider the ones that are most prevalent in the life insurance marketplace today.

Complex Situations—First, the sales situation may be complex. As you have seen in our treatment of total needs, there is often more to do than can be accomplished in a single sitting. It takes time to explain your concept of service and the relationship you wish to have as a professional with your clients. After initial trust is developed, you may have to gather a great deal of information. Often, this process takes more time than can be allotted in one interview. You must analyze the case, present your suggestions, and recommend a plan. You may need to get information, additional work such as a will or trust, or agreement from the prospect's other professional advisors. Complexity alone may require that more than one interview to complete the sale.

Prospect Expectations—The prospect may consider his or her personal situation rather sophisticated. Today, there are many people who are reaching financial levels that are higher than any they have ever experienced. This leads them to want to be treated in a sophisticated and thorough manner. If you obtained an interview with a prospect by promising to be professional and thorough, that prospect may feel that you should conduct more than one interview.

It is entirely possible that you could be referred to an individual who heard from your client that you are thorough and, in fact, conducted several thoughtful interviews. On the strength of the referral, it may be advantageous to conduct a two-interview sale, even if the new prospect's situation might not require it. You should always think of your prospect's expectations.

Not Prepared—On occasion, you will find that either you or the prospect is not prepared for the initial interview. There may be interruptions, necessary documents may be unavailable, or a spouse who should be part of the discussion may not be available. You need more time to do your job professionally. You will find in selling that whenever you take a shortcut, it can come back to haunt you.

You Need Help—You may be new to the business, or uncover a situation where you need help. In this case, you need to take information back to your office in order to analyze the case and gather more information and advice. Do not hesitate to use a multiple-interview process to learn. Especially important here is using a mentor or experienced person with whom you can do joint work. This will be time well spent if you prepare between interviews with those who are more experienced and knowledgeable to develop the case. This time of analysis and preparation will help you develop finely honed skills in all aspects of the selling process. You will learn new ways to analyze a case and learn about ways of dealing with various financial situations. As your skills increase you will find it easier to conduct multiple-interview sales involving increasingly complex situations and more advanced analyses and solutions.

Establishing Rapport—Developing a good relationship with a prospect may take time, more with some than others. As you conduct the initial interview, you should be alert to signals that show your prospects need more time to develop trust and confidence with you than one meeting will allow. Be aware of their feelings about the complexity of their situation, even if it may seem simple to you. Plan your time accordingly. At this point, you may do no more than begin to establish the relationship, do some preliminary questioning, and set the date and time for the information-gathering interview.

Information Gathering—In the process of helping the client establish goals and discuss assets, liabilities, and any other pertinent information, you may find that the time required to conduct this portion of the selling/planning process fills one interview. It may be that even though a case seemed simple on the phone when you first contacted the prospect, when you sit down and talk you discover many more complexities than were anticipated. In this situation, it is important to take the time to conduct as thorough an information-gathering interview as possible, even if a second interview is required to close the sale.

Case Analysis—In most total needs situations and other cases that require some kind of complex analysis, it is advantageous to take information back to your office to review and think about it. For example, you may encounter a prospect with several life insurance policies already in force. In this case, you would certainly want to examine each policy for premium paid; cash values; dividends, if available; current beneficiary designations; ownership; and other pertinent information.

You might want to record all this information in a client data folder, on a computer, or on a spreadsheet, where you can list policy values to study the policies as a group. In addition to examining the policies, you may want to get written authorization from the prospect to contact the insurance company or companies that wrote the policies. You may need to obtain current information regarding premium payments, beneficiaries, cash values, dividends, and anything else that will aid your analysis. All this takes time.

Whether you use a computer, a clerical assistant, technical materials from a library, or simply your own expertise, proper analysis of a complex insurance situation does require time. Most sales to people in complex financial situations require more than one interview. Not only is this time required for you to do your job properly, it is also very helpful for preparing a well-conceived and expertly executed sales presentation.

Presentation

The skills of taking the information from your case analysis and putting it into a professional presentation will be discussed in a future chapter. For now, simply consider that the presentation you make in a multiple-interview situation will probably be the primary topic of one of the interviews. This means that both you and your prospect anticipate meeting on one occasion solely for the purpose of presenting your findings. During this presentation, you will be reviewing your prospect's needs and desires, goals and expectations, priorities, and reasons for acting now.

Closing

There may be more than one meeting required to close the sale in a multiple interview or total needs situation. Although you may satisfy the needs of an individual with your thorough and expert proposal, your prospect may need time to think about it. He or she may want to discuss your ideas with an accountant, attorney, or trusted friend or relative. Even though you may be able to overcome the hesitation to start the plan now and may actually get the prospect to sign the application, the complete implementation of the plan may, in fact, depend upon the concurrence of one of these other people who has influence over your prospect.

You may take an application and a check to your company, and schedule a medical examination, but the insurance will only remain in force if it is understood as a necessary part of a plan. In this regard, a plan implies some degree of complexity, so your prospect may seek additional advice to satisfy the need to know that your suggestion is the best way to answer his or her problem. Legal work, such as Wills and trusts may need to be drafted. You should ask to be present when your prospect discusses the plan with other advisers, so that you can answer any questions or concerns that come up.

One advantage to using a multiple interview situation is often overlooked by many advisors. When you show that you are willing to conduct your sales process over time by using more than one interview, you demonstrate a belief in yourself and your approach to your business. This further allows you to understand and answer real objections that your prospect might have regarding your proposal. The more attentive you are to answering the questions that your prospect has, even encouraging your prospect to ask questions, the more competence you demonstrate and the more successful you will be. On the other hand, if you demonstrate a need and desire to end the sale quickly, perhaps before your prospect is ready, your prospect may help you do that. The price you pay, however, is often the loss of the sale.

Service

By conducting your sale in more than one interview, you also imply that you will be providing ongoing service. Whether you promise or simply imply it, using multiple interviews to conduct your sale demonstrates your willingness to use whatever time is necessary to support the products and services you provide. Clients may come to expect this same time commitment after the policy is sold. For example, you may offend a client by encouraging brevity when servicing policies you have sold or promised to help with, if during the sales interview you demonstrated or promised a sincere desire to take the time to do everything right. This action would imply to your client that as long as you were in the process of selling something you were attentive and patient, but in the process of doing just service work, you lose your patience and are inattentive to your clients. This is an inconsistent image and should be avoided. For this reason, keep your interviews crisp, lively, and on a professional business level. Respect both your client's time and your own when in sales situations and conducting service work.

Financial Problem Solver

Your job as a financial advisor is best described as a healer—not a snake oil salesman or mystical type of healer, but a provider of good medicine to ensure that people attain their fundamental financial goals. This means you must make a thorough examination of your "patients" and not miss or willfully ignore symptoms that should be considered. This is the most compelling reason for learning and doing insurance planning for total needs, not just selling to one need or another. Your clients need planning and they want it. Planning has become part of the meaning of the term "professional" when people talk about life insurance and financial advisors. Make the most of your opportunities and do the best, most complete job you can for all of your clients. If you do, they will come back to you again and again, and they will also recommend you as a problem solver to many qualified referred leads.

Service Pays

One thing is clear. Prospects, the American public, want their needs answered in a plan, not haphazardly. Many policyowners complain that advisors sell insurance without examining needs, and that they do not provide adequate service afterwards. The advisors, they say, are "just out to sell more policies." Only one prospect out of three expressed disagreement with this view.

People who had insurance plans were better satisfied with what they bought, and they were more likely to give their advisors credit for rendering "good service." When the client's needs have been carefully planned, the resulting advice is not a guess. When you make your recommendation and complete the sale, you do it in full confidence that you are serving the best interests of your client, for today and tomorrow. You are doing the best possible job that can be done. Learn to do it the right way.

Case History

Unlimited Prospects

Jeff Renner, LUTCF, is 31, single, and has been in the life insurance business for about 5 years. He went into insurance sales right out of college. Jeff obtained his LUTCF 3 years later and is well along today with the courses for the CLU designation. He is a past moderator for the Disability Income Course and the Meeting Client Needs Course. He is a three-time MDRT agent and has a full-time assistant who handles much of his business.

Prospecting Methods—"I started my seminar approach 3 years ago when I became frustrated with prospecting," Jeff told the LUTC program. "I was tired of always approaching my friends and people I knew. Frankly, I was also running out of prospecting avenues. It was necessity that forced me to put on my first couple seminars. I now run two or three seminars a month and teach retirement courses at a local community college. The seminars, quite honestly, have allowed me find an unlimited number of older, motivated prospects. I can easily make 10 to 15 appointments each week with four to five closes from them."

The Prospect—"I met Shelly when I conducted my second seminar. She was a teacher at the community college. At the end of the seminar, Shelly signed up for a complimentary retirement consultation. I called. We set up an appointment for the next weekend when her husband could sit down with us."

The Approach—"That weekend I completed the fact-finder. The three of us got along well. When I brought back proposals for $100,000 each for universal life insurance plans to supplement their pensions, they completed the applications. Shelly also filled out an application to begin a tax-deferred annuity by payroll deduction at the community college. She applied for the maximum the formula would allow. Underwriting went without a hitch and they were obviously pleased with our work together when I delivered the policies."

"I counted them as the ideal type of clients that my new seminar approach to prospecting could produce. They became the carrot in front of my nose. Every time I met committed prospects and made a good sale, I'd say, 'they're just like Shelly and Ernie. How can I find more of these people?' "

The Call—"Everything went well with my ideal case and perfect clients until I got the phone call. My first impression when I heard Shelly had called was that they wanted to drop their insurance. As I learned later, you should always expect good things when a client calls and not have negative thoughts about the worst. I called her back with great anxiety. I even felt short of breath when I dialed. I had allowed these people to grow to mean too much to me.

"Was I in for a surprise! Shelly answered my ring and proceeded to tell me of about a serious accident her parents had in a rental car. There was a clear possibility of a $2,000,000 settlement in a lawsuit that could be paid anytime. Obviously, I was very distressed by the severity of the accident suffered by her retired parents and I felt great sympathy for her and the whole family. Shelly's parents are still in a nursing home. Her father will have no recovery from his paraplegic condition. Her mother's condition has its ups and downs and she too may well spend the rest of her life in a wheelchair in the home."

The Settlement—"As time went on, I was able to meet with the attorney involved. Representing my clients, I helped them invest the proceeds of the auto insurance settlement. After fees and expenses there was a little over one million dollars left to invest. Our investment objective was safety of principal and tax deferral. I was able to help my clients by setting them up with $900,000 in single premium deferred annuities using two companies. We used fixed annuities because of the guaranty of principle and the fact that they could take out 10 percent a year from each contract without penalty. Guarantees are very important to Shelly. Her parents' retirement income was adequate to take care of the nursing home expenses. This settlement represented emergency money to be held in reserve.

"The remaining $100,000 plus we put in a municipal bond mutual fund. Last year we withdrew part of the fund. Shelly and Ernie were distressed when the fund value went down. We bought an additional fixed annuity with the best performing of our two companies. We also bought a second-to-die policy. Again, I worked with their attorney, this time to fund the new trust that will protect the insurance settlement for grandchildren and great grandchildren after them.

"You know how I felt. This was a big case and I wanted to do the right thing. It's still the largest case I have ever handled.

"Shelly and Ernie are still my carrots as I look forward to each new prospect."

Seminars—"Although this is my best example of a case coming out of one of my seminars, I firmly believe that you treat every client like your best client. When something like this happens the prospect or client will call you and not someone else. It's such a shock to find a client who has more confidence in the agent than the agent himself. I no longer fear client calls. With better prospects who need my services, I have more respect for my recommendations and confidence in our relationships.

"Since this case, I've opened up a number of big cases through my seminars, but the small, average clients are the ones who keep me in business. My seminar system has allowed me to have unlimited prospects who usually are motivated to review their retirement goals and concerns. Referrals are becoming easier. Also, I'm really excited now that I have no prospecting problems anymore! Seminars, I am convinced, for me, are the best way to prospect."

Case History

My Alma Mater

K.C. Peters is a third-year agent in a Kansas college town, selling mostly to college seniors, graduate students, and local people. K.C. averages about 100 new cases each year.

Situation—Lynn Mathers is a 24-year-old graduate student, about to complete the masters curriculum in geology. I got his name from the student directory, and observed that Lynn's permanent address and student address were the same. Suspecting that Lynn might be going to summer school to complete courses as soon as possible, I saved this lead to make a call in the summer months. This is a slower time for me as undergraduates are away. I did not know Lynn, so I called on the phone and asked to meet. We agreed to meet and talk about Lynn's financial future.

One Interview—College students live in a one hour culture, focused on class time, and usually don't have very complex present-time financial needs. The most efficient and economical approach is to conduct a single interview sale. Since their attention span is also limited, it is necessary to conduct a crisp sales interview within the time they are generally willing to give full attention to the topics discussed. I feel that if you cannot complete your business in one hour, you will lose the sale.

Topics—What I want to do is to help each student envision today the financial responsibilities to be faced 15 years from now. Once this vision becomes clear, I want to help the prospect decide to act now to satisfy what we know will be important needs in the future, establishing a plan that will save a lot of dollars over time. Another cost of waiting that I point out is the possibility of becoming uninsurable. Both of these are very important factors when selling to college students and young people.

The Interview—My office is near the campus and convenient to get to, so Lynn agreed to meet me there after class one afternoon. It was a hot summer day and Lynn was dressed pretty casually. I always work in proper business attire to demonstrate a truly professional approach to my work. This is one case where dressing like the customer is not an effective way to demonstrate rapport. Students are pleased to be treated as adults, and it is often the first time that anyone professional sits down to listen seriously and talk with them.

I opened the interview by thanking Lynn for spending time with me. I asked how school was going and found out that Lynn was really ready and anxious to finish school in January and find a job in geology. Employment with an oil company looked like a good start, but only for enough years to establish a track record and eventually become a consultant to oil exploration companies. Lynn obviously had high goals, but they were not unrealistic given the opportunities available in this line of work.

I set the standard for the interview by saying, "Lynn, in financial matters, there are three basic considerations: the person you do business with; the company you do business with; and most importantly, your needs and what planning can do for you. In order for my services to be of any value to you, I need to know more about you: your goals, your plans for the future, what you want and why you want it. Therefore, may I get your answers to a few questions?"

Now's the time to have some fun with Lynn and explore what he really wants out of life and how he sees success coming in the future. This may be the first time Lynn has had the opportunity to envision really winning in life, on his terms. I always enjoy this part of the interview.

Lynn's Vision—On the basis of conservative assumptions, Lynn sees a salary in 15 years of about $100,000. Home ownership is a high priority, and a mortgage balance of about $150,000 to start is estimated. There is a possibility of Lynn's having a family with two children, and although there is no plan for that now, he wants to make that assumption.

Besides these topics, we also discussed interest rates for earning money, general savings and investment strategies, general and personal inflation rates over the next 10 years, and the family history in health and finances. In all, we established that Lynn came from a family that always respected money and the power of long-term accumulations. They were also fairly healthy over the generations, with only one known case of premature death from heart disease.

This conversation set the tone for Lynn to understand the enormous amount of capital and cash flow that would be required between now and 15 years from now when Lynn is self-employed, a homeowner and parent. Even with the most conservative assumptions, it was easy to see that the need for financial protection from premature death would require several hundred thousand dollars of capital. I assured Lynn that this was "normal" because we were looking ahead 15 years. The opportunity to act now would be an act of foresight and financial maturity.

Proposal—I offered Lynn the opportunity to start a program of personal financial security today. By purchasing $100,000 face value of permanent insurance, Lynn could establish both a capital account for death protection and an account for accumulations. He responded well to the concept, especially to the $8,000 of additional accumulations available by acting now rather than waiting just a few years.

Thanks to my laptop computer, I could enter Lynn's personal data and create a typed proposal for the illustration in just a few minutes. The laptop can be very effective when used properly in front of the prospect.

One Objection—Lynn's only objection was a very common one for students, even graduate students. Lynn said, "I want to discuss this with my Dad." I responded simply by asking why. The answer was predictable. Like so many other students whose parents had made or helped make all their decisions for so many years, Lynn was in the habit of discussing important issues with one or both parents.

I asked, "considering the clarity of your goals and the things we've already discussed about your future, all based on extremely conservative estimates, why do you feel it necessary to consult your father now? What more can he add to help you reach an informed decision? Isn't this really your first decision about your future that you can make successfully on your own?"

As in so many cases like Lynn's, the reality of the situation took hold. This is the first time a decision can be made successfully without consulting parents or others. For many students, this is the first step to financial independence. Lynn was no exception, and although the feeling of being alone in the decision-making process was there, Lynn also felt really happy about making a decision without parental aid. In less than an hour we completed the approach, interview, presentation, and applications. Lynn and I were both happy with the outcome. He even voiced appreciation for the feeling of independence gained, and I supported this first step to personal financial maturity.

Follow-up—As you can imagine, the lapse ratio for sales to students is higher than the national average. I am particularly proud of my low lapse ratio in the college market, which I attribute directly to follow-up and service. In the 15 months following every sale to a college senior or final year graduate student, each client gets no less than eight letters and four phone calls from me about items of interest regarding basic finances, friendly reminders that I am available for servicing their plan, or just calls to say, "hi."

This is done almost effortlessly, thanks to the client file system and word processing capabilities of the agency computer. As a result of this intensive but low-key approach to service, I have not only a much better lapse ratio than other agents, but I also get more than three times the referred leads that other agents get from their clients.

My Future—Now that I've been in the college market a few years, I have well over 300 clients to service. They are all college educated and beginning to make a lot of money. As long as I continue to grow personally and professionally, the future looks very bright for me in this business. The college market has been very good for me, and I think it will be good for a few more years, but I am excited about growing into new markets and learning more about our business as I do. I expect to take all the LUTC program courses offered, as well as to earn other professional credentials. I know that over the next several years my clients will need full-service financial planning support, and I want them to be able to count on me to provide it. With luck, hard work, and a clear path to the future, I look forward to growing in this remarkable business.

Chapter Three Review

Key terms and concepts are explained in the Glossary. Answers to the Review Questions and Self-Test Questions are found in the back of the book, following the Glossary.

Key Terms and Concepts

rapport
propriety
time/tension model
empathy
single-interview selling
social style
multiple-interview selling
dominant needs approach

Review Questions

3-1. List and explain the five objectives of the initial interview.

3-2. What types of documents should a prospect should have ready for the initial interview?

3-3. What should an advisor do to prepare for the interview?

3-4. What are four elements important in developing rapport?

3-5. What are the benefits of total-needs selling to the advisor?

3-6. What are the benefits of total-needs selling to the prospect?

3-7. List some dominant-needs sales situations.

3-8. What are reasons for conducting a single-interview sale?

3-9. What are reasons for conducting a multiple-interview sale?

The following questions concern the case histories titled "Unlimited Prospects" and "My Alma Mater."

3-10. What can Jeff's experience in the "Unlimited Prospects" case teach us?

3-11. What are the reasons for needing life insurance for the prospect, and the benefits for the prospect of purchasing life insurance in the youth market?

3-12. What sales points did the advisor use in the "My Alma Mater" case?

Self-Test Questions

Instructions: Read Chapter 3, then answer the following questions to test your knowledge. There are 10 questions. Circle the correct answer. When you are finished, check your answers with the answer key in the back of the book.

3-1. Which of the following statements is correct regarding the time/tension model?

(A) The advisor should attempt to lower the relationship tension before raising task tension.
(B) Uneasiness at a personal level is called task tension.
(C) You can improve your interview and build rapport by reducing task tension.
(D) You should avoid small talk and seek things in common with the prospect because your prospect will not appreciate diverging from the task.

3-2. Empathy involves one's capacity to:

(A) lay aside our own experiences in favor of others
(B) feel sorry for other people
(C) be real and not play roles
(D) make assumptions about others' feelings

3-3. Having a professional designation will help establish rapport with the prospect because

(A) your manners, appearance, and confidence will create an immediate impression
(B) the prospect will be more likely to view you as competent
(C) you will more likely have unquestionable ethics
(D) the prospect will be confident in your interest in helping the prospect

3-4. Which of the following is an example of propriety in the initial interview?

(A) Respect for one another's attitudes and values is present.
(B) Credentials establish that you are a knowledgeable person.
(C) You arrive on time, are well groomed, and dress in an appropriate way.
(D) Does the advisor have the prospect's best interest before his or her interest?

3-5. Which of the following statements about social style is (are) correct?

I. A driver is forceful and direct, will not waste time on small talk, and wants to be in control.
II. An amiable person is easy-going and dependent, enjoys personal relations and wants to be accepted.

(A) I only
(B) II only
(C) Both I and II
(D) Neither I nor II

3-6. Which of the following statements concerning rapport-building is (are) correct?

I. Propriety involves the perception of one's motives, the prospect's perception of an advisor's interest in helping and benefiting the client.
II. Intent centers the expectations of what the prospect considers proper business customs, dress, and behavior.

(A) I only
(B) II only
(C) Both I and II
(D) Neither I nor II

3-7. Which of the following is (are) reasons to use a multiple-interview approach?

I. The prospect may consider his or her personal situation rather sophisticated.
II. You find that either you or the prospect is not prepared for the initial interview.

(A) I only
(B) II only
(C) Both I and II
(D) Neither I nor II

3-8. All of the following are reasons why an interview may be a single meeting EXCEPT

(A) The prospect needs to fill an obligation such as a condition for a loan or a divorce decree.
(B) You find that either you or the prospect is not prepared for the initial interview.
(C) The prospect cannot afford to take care of all life insurance needs at once but wants to focus on dominant needs.
(D) The prospect wants to focus on a dominant need or does not want a total needs analysis.

3-9. In the initial interview, you should try to achieve all of the following EXCEPT

(A) Establish yourself as a person who can help.
(B) Uncover insurance needs and establish priorities.
(C) Create a sense of rapport and credibility.
(D) Analyze the client's situation and propose solutions.

3-10. All of the following are important factors in building credibility and rapport EXCEPT

(A) notoriety
(B) commonality
(C) competence
(D) intent

4

Gather Information and Establish Goals

Overview and Learning Objectives

Chapter 4 discusses the techniques and strategies necessary to conduct an effective information-gathering interview with prospects. Conducting meaningful fact- and feeling-finding sessions that explore the prospect's current situation, determine goals and needs, and reinforce the continuation of the sales/planning process and the development of the advisor/client relationship are the focus of this chapter. The chapter also places emphasis on effectively communicating with prospects. Techniques and concepts of good communication are reviewed.

By reading this chapter and answering the questions, you should be able to

4-1. Identify and explain the objectives of the information-gathering interview.

4-2. Identify and describe skills and techniques used in the fact-finding interview

4-3. Describe the process of qualifying a prospect and characteristics of a qualified prospect.

4-4. Explain the principles of communication that affect the selling/planning process.

4-5. List the benefits to the advisor and client resulting from conducting a fact-finder.

4-6. Explain how an understanding of nonverbal behavior can improve the sales/planning process.

4-7. Describe how active listening techniques can be used in the interview process.

4-8. Explain questioning techniques and how they are used in the fact-finding interview.

4-9. Explain the discovery agreement and why it is important to the sales/planning process.

Chapter Outline

Gathering Information

The Information-Gathering Interview

The objective of the information-gathering process is to uncover meaningful information about the prospect by asking questions. This will enable the advisor to have a discussion about the prospect's goals, attitudes, priorities, current situation, and any changes anticipated for the future. As a result, recommendations can be made from an informed exchange of ideas.

Objectives of the Information-Gathering Interview

The following are the objectives of the information-gathering interview for the advisor:

1. Gather relevant factual and objective information about the client's current situation, including important personal and employment information, assets and liabilities, financial information, and other related data.
2. Gather subjective data, including important values, feelings, and attitudes toward financial issues. Most importantly, determine client goals, objectives, and needs. This includes a prioritizing of goals in terms of importance and completion target date(s). One important piece of information is risk tolerance, the client's attitude towards risk. Another would be the client's expectations for the process.
3. Gain a dollar commitment for the amount the client is willing and able to spend to accomplish the identified goals.

Outline of the Information Gathering Interview

The following is a brief outline of the actions taken by the advisor in the information-gathering interview:

1. **Communicate the process to the client.** This includes explaining the purpose, the process itself, and the potential benefits derived from the information-gathering interview. A

time commitment to the process should also be agreed upon. The role of the advisor should be defined and the expectations of the advisor and prospect discussed and established.

2. **Completion of fact-finding and feeling-finding information gathering**. This involves the gathering and recording of the information, normally through the use of a structured fact-finder form. As we will discuss in this chapter, this includes understanding the subjective rationale (attitudes, values, and feelings) behind the objective facts.

3. **Identify and prioritize goals, needs, and objectives**. Goal setting is fundamental and primary to the planning process. Goals should be quantifiable, measurable, and have time horizons. Rather than stating a goal as "living comfortably in retirement," it is much better to define the goal more precisely. For example, "We want to retire in 20 years with an after-tax income of $60,000 per year in current dollars, and continue that income for as long as we live, with increases of 3 percent per year for inflation, without depleting the principle" would be an ideal goal statement. The more precisely the goal is defined, the more clear it is, and the more accurately we can establish programs to accomplish it.

    Prioritizing the prospect's goals involves ranking them by order of importance and completion date. These two dimensions can be managed as necessary, depending on client resources and other factors. Through the information-gathering process we wish to determine where the prospect is now and where he or she wants to be. Our solutions will help the client close the gap between the two. In this way, the recommendations that ultimately emerge will be in line with the client's goals, their importance, when we need to achieve them, and what resources need to be committed to attain them. Finally, summarize your findings and ask the prospect to confirm that your understanding of their problems and goals is accurate.

4. **Get a dollar commitment.** Obtaining a dollar amount that the client can afford and is committed to spend is an important step toward accomplishing satisfactory results for both the client and the advisor. This commitment must be realistic and genuine. The client must be able to maintain the plan for it to be successful, and the advisor must know what he or she has to work with to accomplish the client's objectives and/or solve his or her problems.

Using the Fact-finder

The following is a summary and overview of fact-finding skills. As we cover this topic we will develop the key ideas behind these skills and ways to effectively implement them.

- **Questioning**—Ask open-ended questions to probe for feelings and goals. Ask confirming questions to ensure understanding.
- **Listening**—Actively listen. Restate or rephrase the prospect's statements to confirm that your understanding is accurate.
- **Motivating**—Ask open-ended questions designed to help the prospect see the reality of the situation and the necessity of taking action to accomplish their goals.
- **Note-taking**—Write down important numbers, facts, goals, needs, priorities, and feelings.
- **Summarizing**—Ensure understanding before proposing next steps.
- **Proposing**—Propose next steps based on a consensus (discovery agreement) between the prospect and the advisor.

Questioning and Listening

Effective information gathering requires the advisor to listen actively and pose relevant questions. You must demonstrate your genuine interest in the prospect's responses by giving feedback. Clarify your understanding of the prospect's experiences, behavior, and feelings by rephrasing, summarizing, and asking clarifying questions.

The prospect must be serious about his or her financial future, and the advisor must have established enough trust for the information-gathering process to proceed. If this is not the case, it is best for the advisor to reestablish the purpose for and value in conducting the needs analysis. If trust is the problem, the advisor should reconfirm the purpose of the fact-finding interview (determining needs and goals to improve the financial security of the prospect). The advisor could also review his credentials, his company's services and reputation, his planning philosophy, and so on, to put the prospect at ease.

The problem solving that will result from the interview requires complete and accurate information about the prospect's financial situation, including current income, accumulated assets, investments, pensions, and other qualified plan holdings. In addition, it is important to develop an outline of the prospect's priorities and objectives. A fair amount of time and energy is often spent in gathering the necessary information before any steps can be taken toward analysis and recommendation.

Motivating

The information-gathering interview is normally where the sale is discovered, based on the foundation established during the initial interview. Your success depends on your ability to establish rapport and to conduct interviews that help the buyer to identify, understand, and want to satisfy his or her needs. Questions can be designed to motivate the prospect into thinking about and acting on his or her needs. The need for empathy is critical. Demonstrate your understanding of their prospect's needs and values without judgment.

Many advisors help the prospect determine a human life value or perform a needs analysis during the information-gathering interview. The goal is to determine the prospect's total financial need for family security, should the breadwinner die. Your company may provide you with such a fact-finder. The text includes a fact-finder that may prove useful to you as well. When you sell to the prospect's total needs and implement an ongoing program to complete the plan you help the prospect develop, you have achieved the ideal of serving the public and professionalism.

Taking Notes

When you record information, you want to get as much down on paper as possible without missing anything that is important. In order to accomplish this, you may find it beneficial to record data you already have on the form before the interview and to review and fill-in information after the interview.

For example, if you have the opportunity to collect old policies, benefit books, and other documents, you do not need to take time in the interview to transfer this data to the form you are using. You do not need to spend time asking questions about them either, if the information is already documented. Use the interview to ask the questions that uncover needs and concerns. Pay attention to what the prospect tells you, and use the form to jot down notes about only those things that need attention. You can use the form as a guideline for your discussion, because it provides a good outline of the topics to be worked through. This is especially true in total-needs situations and multiple-interview sales in which the information-gathering session is longer and in greater depth.

After the interview you can take the time to fill in your notes. Many advisors find it useful to write a summary of the meeting. While your thoughts are fresh you can record impressions and points of view that you may not have recorded during the interview. They will be invaluable later, when you analyze the prospect's situation. A copy can be sent to the prospect or incorporated into the discovery agreement, which is defined below.

Summarizing and Proposing

When the fact-finding interview is concluded, there are a few things you should do before you leave.

- Briefly **review and summarize** the prospect's goals and priorities. Make sure you know what the prospect wants. These initial results will be further developed in the analysis step into a *discovery agreement.* A discovery agreement is a written or verbal acknowledgment of the facts, feelings, values, and attitudes uncovered in the process. It states the prospect's present situation and what they want to accomplish financially, and it outlines the commitment to work together cooperatively to achieve these objectives.
- Get a **dollar commitment.** You cannot make a sale unless the prospect agrees to spend money. Your ability to design a plan based on the prospect's needs and goals depends on knowing what the prospect is able and willing to commit to the solution.
- If appropriate, **schedule** a follow-up meeting.

Feeling-Finding Questions

If a financial consultant were to look at your situation today, how would it be summarized?

- What do you most want to accomplish?
- What are your aspirations for the future?
- How far along are you toward meeting your goals?
- Are you satisfied with the amount of money you have saved so far?
- Are you on schedule?
- Do you work hard to make your life better, or does it seem that you live to make your work better?
- What do you want for your family now? Next year? In 5 years? In 10 years?
- How do you picture your life during retirement?
- Have you, or has anyone close to you, ever suffered a long disability? What were the effects?
- How much insurance do you own? Why did you buy that amount? When did you buy your last policy?
- What is your number one financial priority?

Fact-finding and Feeling-finding

One point needs to be emphasized. The information-gathering process involves asking questions of a factual and objective nature about things such as income, saving and investment amounts, and similar pieces of information. Of equal, or possibly more importance, are questions of a subjective, emotional, and more personal nature. This involves the reasons why people have made certain decisions and what factors go into their decision-making process. Feeling finding involves identifying the goals, attitudes, and values that are the rationale and background for the factual data. It is extremely important to understand the subjective aspect of the prospect's life as well as possible.

For example, he or she owns a whole life policy for $25,000 purchased 10 years ago. This is an objective fact. The subjective or feeling aspect of this fact includes the reason it was bought, what this purchase was intended to accomplish, and how the prospect feels about it now. To the extent practical, this subjective information should be gathered about most, if not all, of the factual information you gather.

The Non-Interview

The non-interview is a technique designed to visit with another person that does not look or feel like a formal interview. It is an informal get-together to just be yourself and allow your prospect to just be him or herself, to get acquainted, to become familiar with each other, and to start that important relationship.

Most sales are influenced by the interpersonal relationship established before the business interview begins. When meeting a new person, this technique involves simply becoming involved in interpersonal communication that leads to establishing a comfortable rapport with the other person. The advisor should initiate non-threatening conversation with warm, smiling, and friendly communicative techniques accompanied by consistent body language and charisma.

Norman G. Levine, "A Passion for Compassion"

Qualifying the Prospect

Qualified prospects display certain characteristics that make them potential customers. Prospects for life insurance are people who

- need protection from loss of life or health
- can afford to pay the premiums for the protection
- can be approached by you
- are insurable

As you get to know the people you choose to contact, you will begin to qualify them in these four areas. You have already done much of this in the selling/planning process to arrive at this point. But qualifying the prospect is not an event; not something that happens and then is done and the prospect is qualified forever. Instead, it is a process that starts at the first contact in the prospecting stage and continues through the delivery of the policy, and even beyond into the servicing stage as your prospect becomes a prospect for another product or service. There is always room for more qualifying. It is an ongoing process.

Much qualifying is done in the fact-finding stage as we collect information regarding facts and feelings about key financial issues and situations. It is not a separate step or action, but is intertwined with the entire sales/planning process. We want to learn what it will take to move the prospect from a possible (and eligible) buyer to a probable buyer to an eager buyer. We learn what the prospect is likely to buy, and when and why he or she will buy it.

From a sales point of view, we want to know if this prospect is saleable. Ask yourself the following questions about the prospect: If he recognizes that a financial problem exists that insurance best solves, is he likely to accept the insurance solution and buy? If he will buy, will he buy from me? Are we compatible? Do I have reasonable chance for his business? Will he buy enough to make it worthwhile? Is he financially able to do so? Is he likely to keep what he buys? Can we build a working relationship in the future? Will he invite me back for annual reviews and buy more for his family or business? Are his needs within my range of experience and expertise? Does he have a reasonable expectation of performance of both the product and me?

One goal for the advisor is to foresee that the prospect is not likely to buy, or unable to buy, and uncovering this fact as early in the process as possible. There may be only one reason or several reasons. Immediately, stop the sales process and address the issue(s). If the issue cannot be resolved, and there may be a valid reason for it, be ready to discontinue the sales/planning process.

Qualifying is not always accomplished by a deliberate effort. Instead, a prospect will sometimes volunteer a piece of qualifying information as time goes on and rapport develops or the prospect begins to see the importance of revealing this information. Remember, much of the information you are seeking is personal and it may take time—weeks, months, even years—for the prospect to feel comfortable telling you and understanding the reasons for revealing certain personal information.

The goals of qualifying include determining:

- How much time, energy and money should I spend to make him a prospect? How much do I really want him as a prospect?
- What does the prospect see as his needs?
- How does the prospect feel about his responsibility to his family?
- What does he know about insurance, investments and taxes, and where did he learn it? Current advisors may be strong competition if he is knowledgeable.
- What is his relationship with his current advisors. Are they any good? Does anyone control him? What have they done for him lately?
- Where do I stand in the sales process? Can I succeed with this prospect or should I let him go?

Determining the Best Policy

The policy was a 10-year modified deposit term, convertible to 25-pay endowment at age 65, with triple protection to age 100, written on a split life basis, a 10-year family income rider, a family policy rider, double indemnity in case of accidental death, $400 monthly indemnity for 10 years and lifetime waiver of premiums in the event of total disability, a return of premium rider, a guaranteed insurability rider, an accelerated death benefit rider, and a cost of living rider.

Whether this is the best policy is difficult to say. However, without a doubt it is the most nearly complete dictionary of life insurance terms ever seen in one policy. Are you buying insurance or collecting policies? If you were collecting policies, you should buy this one, because it is a rarity and will become a collector's item. If you are buying life insurance, then no one can look at a policy and tell you it is the 'best.' Instead, one must look at you.

Determining the best policy starts with an analysis of the buyer, not the policy. First, one must determine the problems he or she intends to solve with life insurance and whether life insurance provides the most effective solution. If so, the next step is to find the most efficient life insurance solution. The term *best* has meaning only when used in comparisons, as no best policy exists in an absolute sense. The question "Best for what need?" must be asked. The best policy is the one most suitable for accomplishing the desired objectives.

Let's briefly look at each characteristic of a qualified prospect.

Need—Rarely will you meet a person who has no need for your products and services. Just the same, few will readily acknowledge a need. You must help uncover the importance of the needs for each individual you meet. This is your job. It can be difficult when the prospect realizes that he or she will have to spend money and meet the company's underwriting standards in order to satisfy that need.

You must ask questions of the prospect that may lead to the discovery of possibly undefined or unrecognized needs. You might ask your prospects if they have purchased a new home, have recently married, had any major financial changes in their lives in the past few months, have a new baby, or have a child graduating from college. You can also ask questions about the presence of adequate funds for retirement or the need for health insurance or disability income insurance.

Ability to Pay—Often, simply on the basis of what you know about the prospect or can personally observe, you can generally determine whether or not he or she can pay the premiums for insurance. Until you start gathering information about finances you will not know whether there is sufficient income. The background you have from observation will be enough to get you started, however. It is sad to say that many of the people who can least afford to buy insurance need it the most. You must spend your time working with those who can afford to buy. This is no different from any salesperson's work. You should confine your work to qualified people.

Ability to Approach the Prospect—It would be a wonderful world if advisors could approach everyone they meet. It is not easy to determine whether or not you can approach a prospect. The only way to find out is to ask. The person you can approach and sell to may have chosen not to work with the last advisor who called. A good prospect for you may be a bad prospect for someone else. Or, it can work the other way too. The person you call may not recognize that you are the person who can help. You may plant an idea in her mind and the next advisor who calls will get the appointment. Timing is often important.

When you fail to get an appointment and you think the prospect is a good one, ask if you can call again in the future. Do not discard the name. Put it aside for a few months in a tickler system for a callback. Next time you call you may be pleased to find a more receptive voice on the phone. Use the information you got in the first call to increase your chances in the callback.

It is important to learn whom you can see on a regular, favorable basis. When you do, you will find your prospecting work more profitable and enjoyable. You seek those you find rapport with, those with whom you share common attitudes, interests, income levels, education, and similar lifestyles. Most insurance advisors sell to people who are like themselves and because of this they build a clientele with whom they have things in common. This is your natural market. Make an effort to qualify prospects by selecting those with whom you have something in common. These are the people you will generally have a better chance of interviewing on a favorable basis and subsequently selling to.

Insurability—You may not know whether your prospect is insurable until you begin working together on the insurance program. Sometimes health problems are not discovered until the application is taken. Some people you will talk to know they have had insurability problems in the past and may still have them. By seeing you they are displaying wishful thinking. If you do find out that your prospect will not qualify for insurance because of health or another reason, all is not wasted. Save the person's name. This person may be a prospect for other products, such as retirement annuities, that do not require medical underwriting. This person may become a powerful referral source. Often when a person wants to buy life insurance and can not, he or she will realize how important it is to have. Keep your relationship open by calling them again and always ask for referrals. Who knows, you may establish a new center of influence.

Success Formula

Work eight hours; sleep eight hours; just make sure it isn't the same eight.

John Savage,
"High Touch Selling"

The Prospect's Financial Responsibilities

The fact-finder typically provides a section for needs analysis, which includes some or all of the family breadwinner's financial responsibilities listed below. To determine the prospect's need for life insurance, a financial needs or capital needs analysis, discussed in the next chapter, identify the amount of money needed today to maintain the family's lifestyle in the future. The financial needs and capital needs analyses determine the total needs resulting from the prospect's financial responsibilities and goals.

The following are a typical list of a breadwinner's responsibilities to his or her family:

- to replace the spouse's income contribution to the family
- to provide funds for child care and other expenses for a work-at-home spouse
- for rent or to pay off the mortgage
- to complete the children's education
- to liquidate debt
- for an emergency fund
- to care for a disabled child or adult
- to pay for young children's home care
- to pay for uninsured medical costs
- for nursing home/long-term care expenses
- for funeral expenses

- for attorney/executor fees
- for federal estate taxes
- for inheritance taxes
- for probate court costs
- to handle inflation and at what rate
- to satisfy income needs
- to support one or more charities
- to provide funds for relatives and friends
- for other reasons of an individual or personal nature

Sample Fact-Finding Form

The following form is a typical fact-finding form. The first page collects general information about the prospect. The second page represents a financial needs analysis or insurance needs assessment, as an example. The next chapter will go into this process in great detail.

Brief-Fact-Finding Form

Personal Data

NAME ______________________DOB ___________________SS# ________
SPOUSE ____________________DOB ___________________SS# ________
HOME ADDRESS ____
CITY _______________________STATE ____________ZIP ____________
PHONE CELL _________________PHONE ___________EMAIL __________
TOBACCO USE Y/N _________SPOUSE Y/N _________

MEDICAL HISTORY/MEDICATION

JOB TITLE/DUTIES ____
EMPLOYER ____
ADDRESS ____
CITY ______________________________STATE ____________ZIP ________
PHONE ____

SPOUSE ____
TITLE/DUTIES ____
EMPLOYER ____
ADDRESS ____
CITY ______________________________STATE ____________ZIP ________
PHONE

CHILDREN
NAME ____________DOB ________SS# ______________Child of whom? ______
NAME ____________DOB ________SS# ______________Child of whom? ______
NAME ____________DOB________SS# ______________Child of whom? ______
OTHER DEPENDENTS (SIBLINGS, PARENTS, ETC.)

	PROSPECT	SPOUSE
DO YOU HAVE A WILL?	____________________	____________________
ADVISORS	____________________	____________________
ATTORNEY	____________________	____________________
ACCOUNTANT	____________________	____________________
OTHER	____________________	____________________

Insurance Needs Assessment—Cash Needs

If you were to die today, would your family have the money it will need to maintain its current standard of living? What bills would you want them to pay?

	Prospect	Spouse
CASH NEEDS	________	________
FINAL EXPENSES/BURIAL FUND	________	________
MORTGAGE PAYMENT FUND	________	________
DEBT PAYMENT FUND	________	________
EDUCATION FUND	________	________
OTHER/EMERGENCY FUND	________	________
OTHER IMMEDIATE CASH NEEDS	________	________
TOTAL IMMEDIATE NEED	________	________

Would they be able to keep the standard of living you have been working for, or would they have to make major sacrifices? Would they need some or all of the income you earn to keep living the way you want them to? For how long will they need that help?

CURRENT ANNUAL INCOME	________	________
AMOUNT TO BE REPLACED ANNUALLY	________	________
FOR HOW MANY YEARS	X ________	X ________
TOTAL FAMILY INCOME NEED	________	________

Will your savings be enough? Will your employer take care of them? Will they count on family and friends? Will your life insurance be enough?

SAVINGS AND INVESTMENTS	________	________
COMPANY BENEFITS	________	________
FAMILY AND FRIENDS	________	________
OTHER ASSETS	________	________
CURRENT LIFE INSURANCE	________	________
TOTAL AVAILABLE RESOURCES	________	________
TOTAL IMMEDIATE & INCOME NEEDS	– ________	– ________
minus TOTAL AVAILABLE RESOURCES	________	________
DEFICIENCY/SURPLUS	________	________

HOW MUCH ARE YOU ABLE TO COMMIT TO MEET THESE NEEDS? ________

Client-focused Selling/Planning Approach Is Based on Data Gathering

Client-focused selling concentrates on helping people discover what they need to know to make informed decisions. Fact-finding is the basis for accomplishing this in client-focused selling. It requires that the advisor know a great deal about what the prospect wants to achieve and the resources that are available to that prospect. In the financial services, this means asking your prospects and clients about what they would like to accomplish financially, what their attitudes are towards the vast array of financial opportunities available to them, and how they view their present situation regarding personal assets and liabilities.

The client-focused approach to selling includes many of the themes we have discussed in this and other chapters. The need for empathy, demonstrating your understanding of the client's needs and values, is significant. Explaining the process you are going through is also helpful. This keeps everything in a perspective the prospect can understand. Support the developing relationship by helping the buyer understand why you are asking certain questions. There will be details about personally intimate topics such as their present financial situation, family relationships, and family and business goals. It is important that you and the prospect understand why you are asking these questions and that you are committed to the importance of their answers.

Problem-Solving Attitude

Problem solving, instead of product selling, is the key to successful selling in financial services. Regardless of the quality of the product, it is likely that someone else has something cheaper. Advisors who are trying to sell solely on the basis of product or price are likely to find competition costing them a great many sales.

Present yourself as a problem-solver, not a salesperson. People do not like to be sold. If they suspect someone is trying to sell them something, their conditioned response is to become defensive and negative. The prospect must see you as a problem-solver rather than someone trying to sell them something.

Help the prospect identify and accept their problem. The prospect must believe there is a problem, otherwise there is no reason to do business with you. This is the importance of the fact-finding process, where a problem is uncovered and clarified.

Explain how your recommendations will solve their problems. This may seem obvious, but many advisors do not clearly explain how the solution they are recommending will solve their prospect's problem. The product is a merely a way of solving the problem. Sell the benefits of the solution, not the product.

Summary of the Information-Gathering Interview

Just like a doctor trying to treat a child's cough, you must gather pertinent history, obtain impressions of the nature and location of the problem, perform an analysis, pinpoint the potential cause of the problem, and prescribe a solution. The only way you can do the job for your prospects and clients, recommending the best solutions for their situations, is to gather all the pertinent information before you formulate your opinion. This makes your recommendations informed and timely, and allows the prospect to make a sound decision.

The result of good information gathering is that you find the prospect's motivation upon which to position the solution (sale). Remember that you do not create the need; you merely discover it. Through this discovery process, the most apparent and meaningful need(s) becomes isolated and established as a financial problem in the mind of the prospect. When the problem is recognized and understood, the prospect should desire a solution.

Think about one or two of your recent sales. Did your client's interest change at some point during your discussion? Think back and see if you can pinpoint the conversation and what triggered the prospect's increased interest in your insurance solution. When you can recognize the increased interest your prospect suddenly displays, you are well on the way to easier closes. You will find it often hinges on uncovering the motivating need and helping the prospect recognize it.

Establishing rapport and trust is the key to successful interaction. When your prospect senses that you have a genuine concern for helping them, not primarily yourself, they will begin to trust you and allow the relationship to continue and build.

Effective Communication

Communication Principles

Many people take communication for granted. Communication is something we have done since we were young children, so why not assume we do it well? Sadly, all of us are ineffective communicators at times. We assume we have mastered this critical skill in our roles as financial advisors. Communication is far too important a skill, especially in financial advising to treat lightly. It is the single most critical skill that an advisor brings to client relationship.

> **One of the best ways to persuade others is with your ears—by listening to them.**
>
> **—Dean Rusk**

The purpose of this section is to review important aspects of effective communication, provide you with useful techniques, and make suggestions for how to improve your communication with prospects and clients, thereby improving your skill as a financial advisor.

Communication has a Purpose

Communication always has a purpose. Often, especially in the sales situation, the purpose of communication is to understand the other person and to help them act in ways that are beneficial to them. Whatever your purpose, you should have a clear idea of why you are saying and doing the things you say and do—a desired objective or outcome. The first principle of effective communication is to have a goal.

How many times can you recall going through a sales situation without having a clear goal, direction, or objective? Did you "wing it" or try to muddle through? Many advisors do this and suffer as a result. If you don't know where you are going, any road will get you there.

Empathy and Trust

Relationship building is based on good and effective communication. It is the basis for increasing the trust and rapport necessary to gain the confidence of prospects. You will usually find that the best way to understand your prospect is to ask relevant questions. Until you get enough information from the prospect, you really do not know how to help them. In effective communication, assumptions should not be made about our understanding or perceptions of others. We must clarify and confirm our understanding by asking questions.

The need for empathy is critical. Demonstrating your understanding of the client's needs, goals, and values is the basis for establishing rapport and trust in the developing relationship. Make an effort to see things from your prospects' perspective. This will help you understand how and why they view things the way they do, and will help you help them. We want clients to feel that we are in touch with them, that we are closely following and understanding them.

Empathy involves the capacity to lay aside your own set of experiences in favor of those of your clients, as seen through their eyes, not yours. This will enable the relationship to grow because you can understand prospects' motives, goals, and backgrounds, the things that influence their thinking, values, and decision-making processes.

Qualities that contribute to building rapport between the advisor and the prospect include friendly and interested concern; an unhurried, leisurely pace; an accepting and non-judgmental attitude; attentive, active listening; and an equal and open relationship. In this climate, prospects feel free to be themselves, since they do not have to be afraid that what they say may be evaluated in a negative way by the advisor. They should also begin to realize, if they have not before, that the ultimate responsibility for setting goals, planning, and taking action rests with them and not the advisor.

Another trait that is important to establishing effective communication is genuineness. The financial counselor should be "real," that is, not playing a role or hiding behind a façade. This entails being aware of your feelings, attitudes, values, and thoughts. It means expressing yourself openly and honestly. However, your own needs should not interfere with your understanding of the feelings and concerns of your prospect. It is important to recognize your feelings and thoughts so that you can focus on the feelings and thoughts of the other person. This is important in communication since ultimately we want to help a prospect make decisions based on their own values and judgments, not ours. The more we know about ourselves and can interpret, evaluate, and control our own behavior, the better able we are to focus our attention on our clients.

Be a good counselor and help-giver in your sales efforts, seeking ways to understand your prospects, and developing versatility in helping them to understand themselves. By understanding your behavior and your prospect's behavior you will be able to improve your sales efforts. Even though this may sound like a simple process, it is not. It is usually a long-term process, characterized by struggles, setbacks, and insights that lead to changes in the client's behavior that help them live happier and more fulfilling lives. You will gain success that is lasting and a clientele that respects you as a professional and as a trusted adviser.

Before a prospect buys from you ... He has to buy you

You must sell yourself to the prospect before you sell your ideas or products. What is the "you" he buys? He buys the advisor he thinks will do right by him. He must believe you are a person of integrity, that you are sincere in wanting to help him, and that you know your business.

We will now focus our attention on ways we can improve our understanding and communication with others.

Nonverbal Behavior—Body Language

Picture yourself in front of a prospect, just having made a major point in your sales presentation. The prospect leans back in the chair, crosses his arms over his chest, and looks up at the ceiling. Do you notice and understand what this means? Would you know what to do about the message this behavior is sending? In the heat of selling, even the best-trained salespeople sometimes miss signals as clear as this, or they get the signal but fail to understand it.

Nonverbal behavior is the aspect of communication that is influenced by culture and personal habit. It has two main sources, the body and the voice. It is expressed through body position and movement, gestures, facial expressions, eye contact, voice pitch and voice tone. Most sociological research claims that non-verbal channels communicate about two-thirds of the total message, especially where emotions are concerned. Much of this message cannot be clearly understood unless you ask about it. As "experts," we often out-think ourselves, trying to translate rather than simply asking our prospects for clarification.

Insanity

Change is not easy, but it is necessary if you want to work less and/or earn more. One definition of insanity is doing the same things over and over and expecting different results. Think about that.

Recognizing Nonverbal Cues

Your attention in an interview should focus on nonverbal cues as much as verbal cues. You must recognize signals from your prospect and understand what they mean. All impressions of meaning and the significance of any body language must be checked out against other clues given by the client. Do not assume that you know what a given behavior means. Often, only your prospect can explain. Do not hesitate; just ask. It is better to ask rather than make assumptions.

For example, consider our original illustration of your prospect leaning back at a critical point, folding arms over chest, and breaking eye contact by looking up. What does this behavior mean? We could argue and guess for hours about it, or make the smart move and ask the source. All we know for sure is that your prospect's behavior changed at this point, and that the prospect suddenly appeared to back away from the situation. You want the prospect to be involved, so you must do something to support continued involvement.

Was it something you said? Was it something else the prospect just thought about, like the next appointment, a sick friend, or taxes due? Was it something beyond your presentation? Was it something as simple as heartburn? Who knows? Only your prospect knows for sure; so ask. In this case, your best approach would be to assume there could be a problem. You could ask something like, "What's the problem?" or "I notice your seem distracted. Is something bothering you?" Give your prospect the opportunity to reenter the conversation by refocusing on it. Try asking something: "Did I make that clear enough?" In answering, your prospect must respond to you by focusing on the topic at hand, your topic.

Remember that you exhibit nonverbal behavior to the prospect as well; it goes both ways. What you do with your eyes, face, hands, arms, legs, and posture sends out signals as to whether you are or are not listening to and understanding what the other person is saying. If you are talking and the other person yawns, glances away, looks at the ceiling, cleans their fingernails, or sighs, what would you think? You would quickly get the message that they have very little interest in what you have to say. Conversely, if they look into your eyes, smile, raise eyebrows, or lean toward you, you feel you have their interest and attention. Be attentive to your own nonverbal behavior as well as that of your prospect. It is a way of getting feedback on how your message is being received.

To help you better understand and deal with the dynamics of nonverbal behavior, a list of behaviors and what they might indicate is included below. There are also suggestions on how to get clarification from your prospect or client. You will notice in the chart that your reaction to the prospect's thought process could call for questions from you to close, to seek an opinion, or to ask for attention or agreement. Being alert to a prospect's posture and facial expression can smooth your presentation and help develop trust between the two of you in a non-threatening manner.

Examples of Nonverbal Behavior

We get information from others nonverbally from their body positions, body movements, gestures, facial expressions, eye contact, and voice tone and pitch. For example, what would you think if you noticed someone you were talking to doing the following: glancing sideways, sighing, yawning, frowning, cracking knuckles, looking at the ceiling, or fidgeting in their chair? Conversely, what might the following mannerisms indicate: looking into your eyes, smiling frequently, raising eyebrows periodically, grinning at appropriate moments, using expressive hand gestures when speaking, or keeping their eyes wide open.

The following chart gives examples of various nonverbal behaviors, what they suggest, and what you might do in response.

Nonverbal Behavior		
Prospect Behavior	**Suggests**	**Your Action**
1. Leans forward	Increasing interest	Lean forward/ask closing question "Do you feel this idea is appealing?"
2. Leans back	Decreasing interest	Pause/ask involving question "What would you like to see happen here?
3. Makes eye contact	Increasing interest	Ask closing question
4. Breaks eye contact	Decreasing interest	Pause/ask involving question
5. Crosses arms	Blocking/disagreement	Make eye contact, smile, lean forward, ask opinion question to draw out feeling "What do you think about . . .?"
6. Pushes away	Concern/disagreement	Do not pause/do not ask involving question
7. Stands up	Made conclusion/tired of sitting	Stop presenting, make eye contact, quietly wait for prospect to speak
8. Changes seating, moves closer	Interested/wants to be more involved	Lean towards prospect/involve in illustrations, images, graphs, ideas, and so on.
9. Allows interruptions, answers telephone	Not involved/not high enough priority	Ask for attention without interruption, ask to hold calls if possible, make another appointment
10. Looks at watch	Pressed for time/disinterested	Ask how much time remains
11. Nods head "yes"	involved and interested	Ask agreement questions "Isn't that right?"
12. Opens eyes more	More interested	Ask agreement questions
13. Rubs chin	Sign of interest	Ask agreement questions

Active Listening Techniques

Since useful information gathering requires skilled questioning, it must also require active listening. You must demonstrate that you are truly interested in your prospects' responses. Unless you do, it will appear that your questions are not really important, or that you are not really interested in the answers. Either way, your business will suffer unless you learn to listen well.

Active listening introduces a psychological involvement into listening or attending to others. It adds personal involvement in the message, putting the nonverbal behavior, the voice, the words, and the meaning of the message together. An active listener is an understanding listener, one who attempts to see the world from the other person's frame of reference. Active listening means involving yourself in the inner world of another person, while, at the same time, maintaining your own identity and being able to respond meaningfully to the messages of that other person. Attentive listening involves the art of being alert, perceptive, and creative in searching out what your prospects feel or think about their needs and desires.

> **Oops! I did it again.**
>
> Most of the things that can go wrong in sales happen when the salesperson's mouth is open.

Here are a few techniques for sharpening your listening skills. Some are especially helpful for those evening interviews when you may be tired, sitting in a warm living room, and wishing you could go home. These suggestions will help keep everyone awake and involved.

- *Ask good questions, then wait for an answer.* This is not just polite; it shows that you respect your question and your prospect's answer to it enough to hear the answer. Put aside your personal issues and concentrate on hearing what the speaker has to say.
- *Give feedback.* Repeat the essence of what you just heard, using the same or similar words, paraphrasing or restating what the prospect said. Example: The prospect says that the present coverage was purchased 4 years ago. You might say, "I understand that the coverage was bought in a plan of insurance designed 4 years ago. Have you talked to a company representative about it within the last 6 months? Are all the interest-return projections still current?" This shows active listening and concern. If you comment meaningfully, the prospect will know you are listening and may offer more information.

- *Check for experiences, behaviors, and feelings.* Ask for examples of anything your prospects say that you are not sure you understand. "I'm not sure I know what you mean. Is there an experience you had in this area that makes you feel this way?" You show empathy as you respond to human issues and feelings. Ask questions to clarify information; this helps you better understand and is also an indication to the prospect that you wish to understand better.
- *Use your own examples to clarify, if necessary.* If your prospect is having difficulty articulating an idea, give a brief example from your own experience and ask if his or her experience is the same. If it is not, ask how it is different from the idea or feeling the prospect was trying to share. This may help prospects focus on what they are trying to express.
- *Take a break and change your tack if you detect interest is wandering.* The prospect might be fidgeting or ruffling papers. Ask your prospects if they are comfortable with this part of the interview process. The answer may be a simple yes, or it may be one that shows the need for you to move faster, slower, or with more deliberation and explanation. Make sure that you and your prospects are on the same course, moving at the same pace.
- *Check nonverbal clues.* When people lean forward and make eye contact they are often demonstrating interest and involvement. Leaning back, crossing arms over the chest, propping feet up on the table, and losing eye contact are all signs that interest is waning. This is not to be confused with an abrupt break in eye contact when your question is especially poignant or disturbing. This may happen when you ask, "What would your family be doing today if you had died last night? What would you like them to be doing?" When a disturbing question does bring on an abrupt break in eye contact, let the prospect think about the answer in silence.
- *Give good physical attention.* Face the other person in an open posture. Lean toward them. Maintain good eye contact and be relaxed. Listening is communication, too. When we listen carefully, with understanding, and respond relevantly, we are communicating to the speaker, "I care about you and what you are saying."

- *Respond to the last answer or comment.* Do not simply go through a list of questions that you have prepared. Make sure the next question you ask, if at all possible, is related to or follows logically from the last answer (not your last question). Keep the questioning in your prospect's perspective and line of thought as much as possible. Learn to use transition phrases to return to your menu.
- *Ask yourself what the prospect really means.* If you do not know what the prospect really said, make sure you ask for clarification. You may ask, "Just to make sure I understand what you mean, would you explain it again? Is there an example that you can use to demonstrate your point?" Clarifying techniques are extremely important, and we will cover them more thoroughly later in this discussion.

Talking and Listening

Many sales professionals talk too much, and listen too little. We don't learn by talking, but we can bore people by talking. The least we need say, to achieve our end, is the most we should ever say.

One of my favorite expressions is that "most of my prospects want to buy my product but they don't know it." My job, therefore, isn't to sell products, but to find out what they want. Until I find something they want that can be best achieved by using my products, I can't make a sale. Sales professionals can't find out what prospects want by talking; they can only find out by listening. The trick, then, is to get people to talk about what you want to hear.

Norman G. Levine, "A Passion for Compassion," Le Gesse Stevens Publishing, 2000. Reprinted with permission.

Questioning Techniques

Effective Questioning

The information-gathering interview is often where the sale is discovered. Some salespeople believe that the sale is made in the closing interview, while others believe that it is actually made during the process of gathering information. Regardless of where it occurs, this process of uncovering and discovering goals, objectives, assets, liabilities, fears, lifestyle dreams, and concerns certainly has a profound impact on every sale. Your success in selling will depend upon your ability to conduct interviews that not only gather information, but help the buyer to identify, understand, and desire to solve his or her needs now.

Asking questions is an art. Success is dependent upon the questions asked, their timing, and their style. Let us take time to explore some of the principles of asking questions effectively, stressing style, timing, and the construction of the actual questions.

It is important that the prospect understand why you are asking certain questions. Fact-finding involves the sharing of private personal information, including financial matters, family relationships, business issues, attitudes, values, and goals that are normally kept to oneself. Disclosing these matters requires a good reason and a lot of trust. Be prepared to answer the question, "Why do you need to know that?" If you do not know why you need to know something, or cannot clearly state a reason why you need to know, you probably should not be asking for that information.

To create an active exchange of ideas and information, give your own examples in rephrasing the prospect's statements. Change the pace when you feel the prospect's attention is lagging. Continually check for any non-verbal cues the prospect gives. Respond to the last comment or answer from the prospect to clarify the conversation. Ask yourself what the prospect really means. If you are unsure, ask clarifying questions, such as "I didn't understand you when you said your were confused about saving for retirement. Can you make that more clear for me?"

Talking and Listening

Whenever you lose control of an interview, or when you seem to be losing ground in developing the sale, turn the interview around, or buy some time for mentally re-grouping, by asking questions.

Norman Levine

Open-ended Questions versus Closed-ended Questions

Open-ended questions are the type that allows the prospect to answer with something other than a simple yes or no. They elicit thinking and explanations from the prospect. Open-ended questions solicit opinions, thoughts, ideas, values, and feelings. Here are several good examples that work effectively in many situations.

- Why did you purchase your last insurance policy?
- In your opinion, how much insurance should you have?
- Why is your will set up the way it is?

- How do you make financial decisions in your household?
- What is your most important financial goal?
- How did you get into this business?
- What ideas do you take to your attorney, what ideas does your attorney bring to you?
- In what ways do you direct the efforts of your accountant, and in what ways does your accountant direct you?

You may find this type of question the best way to begin an interview, focusing on needs and issues important to the prospects rather than just beginning this important discussion with routine questions like proper name, date of birth, and the like. If you begin with open-ended questions you will give your prospects the opportunity to express themselves. This establishes that you are interested in them, not just their data, and that they have something important to convey that you find interesting.

Closed-ended questions limit the prospect to a specific, narrow response, often yes-or-no or short answers of just a few words. Closed-ended questions are usually used to solicit factual answers.

Talking Versus Listening

When you talk there is only one thing you learn. The things you already know! That's great if you're a teacher, lecturer or dispenser of information. That's not so good if you're a salesperson.

What is the information you want to glean from your prospect? Remember, the more information you have, the better chance you have of prescribing a solution that is right on target for helping your customer to get what he or she wants from your product or service. What is the specific information you're after?

- What they will buy
- When they will buy
- How they will buy
- Under what conditions they will buy

Unfortunately, gathering this information is much easier than most salespeople make it. Sometimes they don't know where to find it, how to find it or even how to ask the right questions to uncover it. The single biggest problem, though? They simply don't take the time. Why is that?

Perhaps they underestimate its importance. Maybe they are in such a hurry to tell and sell that they don't stop to listen and ask. They are so busy worrying about giving an effective presentation that they give the wrong presentation.

Salespeople tend to be so focused on their own product, meeting a quota, earning a commission, winning a contest, staying ahead of the competition, pleasing a sales manager or keeping their job that they tend to forget the key to achieving all these things. It is simply paying attention to—listening to—the prospect or existing customers.

1. Do you ever present your product or service and then have to "course correct" your presentation?
2. Do you receive frequent objections?
3. Do you find yourself having to rewrite proposals or action plans?
4. Do you ever interrupt a prospect?
5. Do you talk more than listen in a typical sales call?
6. Do you say things in your presentation that don't add direct value to your prospect?
7. Do your prospects ever appear overwhelmed or confused by your presentation?
8. Do you find you have to make last-minute changes to presentations?

Consider the following suggestions carefully.

- Allow your prospect to do at least 50% of the talking in any sales interaction. In some cases it should be as much as 80%.
- Invest time in pre-call planning to better understand the dynamics, needs and direction of the prospect. Use this information to ask the right questions.
- Learn to ask questions. Master the art of empowering your prospect to tell you those things that are most essential to them and their buying decision.
- Listen more than you talk. Remember, when your prospect is talking they will tell you the things you need to know. Again, if you talk, you will only tell them what you know—which may or may not have anything to do with their decision to buy your product or service.
- Monitor yourself harshly. On your next sales call observe yourself. Be your own worst critic. Analyze the quality of your questions. Monitor the amount of time you're talking and the prospect is listening to you instead of you listening to them.

There is little doubt that many salespeople still believe that the "gift of gab" is what makes a great salesperson. Just like old beliefs about lots of things, they are wrong. About as wrong as they can be.

Bill Brooks, www.billbrooks.com. Reprinted with permission.

Combining Questions

Combining an open-ended question occasionally with a closed-ended question is a natural process in the interview situation. It can help you direct the interview and keep the prospect from lingering on one topic past the stage where you have obtained all the information that you need. You can follow the yes answer with another question that probes for the prospect's feelings about this new topic. For example, ask the prospect a closed-ended question, such as, "what is your mortgage/rent payment?" You can follow this with a feeling-finding question, such as, "how do you feel about owning your own home?" Think about one of your recent interviews and visualize your conversation with the prospect. You will see how naturally this can occur. If you develop this as a deliberate technique, you may find that you have better control during your interviews.

Another example of this process would be in the fact-finding interview regarding family needs. By moving back and forth between closed-ended and open-ended questions, you can collect the facts and the feelings behind them. This keeps the information moving, it is more interesting for both parties, and you get a much fuller and meaning understanding of the prospect's situation. For example:

- "Does the family have a mortgage payment?" (closed)
- "How much is it?" (closed)
- "What are your future plans regarding staying in this house?" (open)
- "Do you want to cover the cost of higher education with insurance?" (closed)
- "What are your hopes and dreams for your children's education?" (open)
- "How much do you think college will cost when your kids are ready to go?" (closed)
- "Are your parents alive?" (closed)
- "Do you think any of them will be needing extra attention or care in the future?" (closed)
- "What plans have you made for that situation?" (open)

Clarifying Questions

Proper questioning techniques can help you get the right information. Developing good questioning techniques is important because the prospect may be thinking about the topic for the first time. You must help the prospect by probing and discussing these issues until the prospect's position is clarified, not just for you but for the prospect as well.

One effective technique is to rephrase what the prospect said, and then ask if what you said is correct. Listen to what the prospect says, and then say, "I think what I hear you saying is... (rephrase what you heard). Is that correct?" Another variation is to say, "Do you mean... (rephrase)?" This gives the prospect another chance to think about the original answer and to make adjustments if necessary, or to confirm the position. This reassures the prospect that you are listening, that you understand, and that you care. It also assures you that you have the correct information or have uncovered the real attitude.

Another clarifying technique is to follow a simple model. It is often difficult for a prospect to give you clear responses. He or she does not know you well enough to be comfortable sharing sensitive information, and may not have had ample opportunity to think through a particular question. Here is a rule to apply to any similar situation.

Avoidance = Question and probe (gently)
Agreement = Expand and rephrase
Resistance = Qualify the reason

If the prospect appears to avoid any question or issue, ask about it in another way. Question your prospect again, and probe gently for an opening that will allow the prospect to give an answer. You may be treading on a topic that is controversial if, for example, a prospect avoids your question, "does one person write all the checks for your family?" You might probe a little by asking if there is more than one checking account, or if there is a joint account. After that fact is established, go back to the original question and ask how these accounts are managed.

When there is immediate agreement to something you have said, take a moment to expand on the topic. If your prospect readily agrees to your statement that life insurance is the foundation of financial security, either by nodding or saying something like "absolutely," don't just accept it as a positive sign, and continue on. Pause a moment to ask the prospect to expand on that. You can get clarification by saying, "I'm pleased that we both are in agreement on that, but could you expand a little on why you feel that way?" This will not only clarify what the prospect agreed to, it will also give you more information about why the prospect has made purchases in the past.

There are times when you will encounter resistance on the part of a prospect. These may appear as comments like "all insurance is a rip-off" and "you have to die to win." In some cases people may refuse to take a physical examination by anyone other than their own doctor, if at all. Other people may be adamant about buying only mutual funds or only one type of life insurance. You must qualify just what the prospect means so that you have solid information with which to work. You must inquire as to why the person feels this way, ask for examples or experiences that led to this attitude, and encourage discussion about the matter. Many times the simple act of articulating and explaining the details of a problem will help the prospect eliminate or dilute its importance.

A similar technique for probing and getting the prospect to discuss his or her needs, interests, goals and other personal information, is to ask questions that can help you learn more about the reasons behind what they say initially. Resist the temptation to continue with your presentation. For example, when a prospect makes an important statement, say something like:

- "Tell me more"
- "What do you mean?"
- "I believe I can help you with that, Tell me more about . . . (your past experiences)."
- "Please go on.
- "I'd like to know more about that."
- "Please continue."

When the prospect reveals an important point, clarify it, highlight it, and draw it out. When they touch on a need, amplify and quantify it. These are the points that will build your eventual sale.

Stop Selling

Too many salespeople become overly focused on making the sale happen. Many motivational speakers, sales managers, and seminars stress "making things happen," which results in selling for the salesperson's reasons, not the prospect's.

Instead of forcing the sale to happen, stop selling and become genuinely interested in your prospect's activities, needs and wants. Get your prospects talking about themselves.

To keep your prospects talking, ask them questions that will get them to open up. The goal is to get them to tell you exactly what they want and need from you. Get them to detail how they envision you helping them. You can then use that information to highlight your product or service to best show how it will solve their problem.

By paraphrasing, or restating in your own words what the prospect has just said and posing it as a clarifying question, you can convey your understanding of what the prospect has told you, and confirms more fully his or her position.

Motivating Questions

Motivating questions are designed to make the prospect think about situations that need fixing. They uncover problems that the prospect must think about and act on. Here is a list of motivating questions that have proven themselves to be extremely useful when talking with anyone about life insurance. You may already know some of them. What is important is that you practice them and learn to use those with which you are personally comfortable.

- Who would suffer if you were not here?
- What would your family be doing today if you had died last night? What would you like them to be doing?
- Does your will do what you want it to do? What is that?
- Who would pay your household and grocery bills if you were too sick or hurt to work?
- How successful have you been in saving money in your lifetime?
- How much cash is available for emergencies?
- What would happen to you financially if your spouse died?
- What would the situation be for your spouse if you died?
- What will happen to your children if one or both parents die or become severely disabled?
- When was the last time you and your spouse looked at the problems that would arise in the event of premature death? What did you conclude?

As you look closely at these questions, say them out loud. After you have spoken them each a few times, think about how you would respond if someone asked you the question. If you find some that disturb you a bit, that is good. If you consider a few of the topics raised by these questions and begin to put priorities to your concerns, that is good, too. You are experiencing the influence and importance of questions that clarify priorities and motivate people to act now to solve needs.

Listening

Top MDRT professionals have discovered that the key to successful selling in not primarily the result of their talking but a direct result of how well they listen....

Unless they already trust and respect you, there are many things in people's lives they will avoid talking about. Most people in an impersonal situation will tell you what they think you want to hear or simply not say anything. If you can't get prospects to open up, they probably will not buy you as their sales advisor. You will be disadvantaged because they will not completely share why they really do, or don't want your product and/or service.

So what is listening? It is not hearing alone but rather learning what the prospect thinks and feels. To do that effectively you must use your ears, eyes, and sometimes your heart. Eye contact is important. Body language can tell you as much about prospects as their verbalization. Are they comfortable? Are they telling the truth? Are they emotionally involved? Is there something left out? It's always a two-way communication vehicle. Are your eyes darting all over the place, or do you really care about them, and are concentrating on them? Is there a comfortable relationship between the two of you?

Another sign of good listening is when the answer to your questions is significantly longer than the question. Successful sales professionals can ask good questions that get the prospect not only to answer the question, not only to expand on the question, but also to extend their answers to relevant thoughts way beyond the scope of the original question....

The bottom line of this concept is that you must learn to get prospect's to talk freely and with trust. You must learn when the prospect's observations are relevant, and when they are, learn to keep your mouth shut and listen sincerely. In the early part of sales interviews, you must learn to use questions to get the prospect talking. The most important part of a sales interview is the first part, when you are selling yourself. This is when the prospect must be encouraged to do most of the talking and you most of the listening.

Norman G. Levine, "A Passion for Compassion"
Le Gesse Stevens Publishing, 2000. Reprinted with permission.

TALKING

His arguments were well received.
His point had, clearly, been achieved.
And his sincerity had quelled
All reservations that I held.
I would have signed the order, then,
If he had just produced the pen.
But he kept right on talking.

Couldn't he see he'd raised my hopes;
That I was hanging on the ropes?
He had sold and, man alive,
The time to close had now arrived.
I wanted desperately to sign
If he would just point out the line;
But he kept right on talking.
And then my mind began to stray
To pressing matters of the day.
His voice, now growing even higher
In his enthusiastic fire,
Became distraction, then a bore.
I couldn't take it any more.
But he kept right on talking.

I stood, to bring it to an end;
"My time is limited, my friend."
"But, sir, I thought. . . ," he numbly said.
"You thought that I was interested?
Perhaps I was, but not today."
I didn't have the heart to say,
He'd killed his sale by talking.

It is a paradox, but true;
Though talk can bring success to you,
Oh, what a tragic thing to see
The source of failure it can be.
So, if you want the winner's cup,
You'll make your point and then shut up. . .
And not keep right on talking.

—Anonymous

Leading Questions

Leading questions can be ineffective and manipulative. These questions usually begin with, "Don't you think..." or "Do you really feel that…." They are usually designed to lead the prospect toward the conclusion that the advisor has already formulated, so there is an element of dishonesty in even asking the question. It is more effective, and honest, to rephrase the question into a declarative statement in the form of sharing a perception or opinion with the prospect. Consider the following leading questions:

"Do you think that you should start an investment program now?"

"Do you really feel that $100 a month is enough?"

"Are you sure you have considered all the possibilities?"

With a bit of reflection, we can see that the advisor is really saying:

"I think you should start an investment program now."

"I do not feel that $100 a month will be enough."

"There are other possibilities that you have not considered."

The latter statements are more honest, genuine, and to the point than the leading questions. Generally, declarative statements communicate more clearly than leading questions. Save questions for honest information seeking. Most importantly, if you are trying to establish trust, rapport, credibility, and a good relationship with the prospect, manipulative questions have no place in the process.

Questions and the Selling/Planning Process

Client-centered selling focuses on what matters to the prospect and client. You build sales momentum by showing that you are delivering an important solution to an important problem. Asking the right questions can guide you and your prospect through the sales/planning process, creating a message that sounds right to the prospect.

Ask yourself and the prospect the following questions:

1. What is the prospect's problem?
2. Why is it a problem?
3. What are the prospect's objectives for a successful solution to the problem?
4. Which of those objectives are most important?
5. What are the ways we can solve the prospect's problem?
6. What are the probable outcomes of each possible solution?
7. Which solution is best?

Talking versus Listening

Talking is important, but the key is to let the prospect do as much of it as possible. To listen productively you must first discipline yourself to let the prospect do the talking. Your job is to ask questions and listen. In the client-focused sales method, the importance of asking questions and listening cannot be overstated. The stereotype of the fast-talking salesman is the opposite of what we want.

If you want information, you have to listen. If you feel you need to find a way to limit your tendency to talk, to have an answer to everything your prospect says, remember this: the person in control is the one who asks the questions. As an old Chinese aphorism points out, "while fools speak on, the wise listen."

We should, however, take this one step farther. You can become more effective in your sales by listening to the way you talk when conducting an interview. You give out clues to your prospects from your first telephone call about your own confidence, sincerity, depth of knowledge, and belief in your products by how you talk about them.

Feelings reflected through your voice increase the authority and conviction of what you are saying. Speech becomes habit with all of us. We forget that we can adjust our voice to match what we say. Your voice

To Bat .500

Here's a way to make sure your comments are remembered. One prominent psychologist claims your chances increase by as much as 50 percent with this simple act. As you make your point, look your prospect directly in the eye. Hold contact for a moment. With this technique, you have the prospect's full attention!

should be warm, friendly, and unthreatening. The best tone is the one you use when talking to a favorite family member.

Voice experts say that accents do not bother people unless they cannot understand what you are saying. The aim should be to achieve a lively tone of voice and a concise manner of presenting your ideas, letting your prospect respond as often as possible.

Here are a couple of tips:

- Slow your rate of speech. Nervousness and fear cause us to take shorter breaths and tense our chests, causing our pace of speech to quicken.
- Relax your upper body when you are speaking. You can do this by taking a breath, rotating your shoulders and neck.
- Finally, breathe deliberately from your stomach area. It slows you down and lowers the pitch of your voice. This will ultimately calm the people you are speaking to also.

Your Audience

Two truths we have all heard before also apply to selling life insurance: everyone is different; everyone is the same. As individuals, you will meet prospects of many different styles, interests, and behaviors. As people who need life insurance protection, you will find that most of those you will meet are similar or the same. People buy because they love somebody. You must know how to treat people as individuals without losing sight of the common objectives that make them candidates to buy additional protection from you.

You do this by asking effective questions, ones that are open-ended and will reveal the prospect's feelings and attitudes. Remember you are asking very personal questions of your prospect. Sometimes the answers are difficult to share, are embarrassing, or have never been expressed before, at least to someone outside close family members or friends.

Your prospect may not wish to express feelings that you might not understand or approve of. The prospect does not know how you will react to what he or she says. Never assume your questions don't affect the prospect. They always do. Just because they become routine to you does not mean a prospect might not wonder about your motives, or even your good taste.

Appropriateness

Appropriateness should be the key to the questions you might ask at any point in the selling/planning process. Your style of asking is very important. For example, if your prospect is soft-spoken or needs reassurance along the way, and your normal style is clear and comparatively loud, you may want to soften your approach simply by lowering the tone and volume of your voice.

A question like "Just to clarify my thinking, why is that important at this particular time?" may be inappropriate if it is asked in a manner that does not fit the audience. It could, however, be successful if said firmly or softly, depending on the intended receiver. You will have to choose how to say a particular phrase or question, and you should practice a few variations of every line, question, or power phrase you use. As you practice, try each phrase on for size by varying the tone and pitch of your voice. Sometimes something as simple as ending with a rising tone or falling inflection can make a sentence either appropriate and appealing or arrogant and challenging.

Create Images in the Prospect's Mind

Another way to facilitate communication is to create images in the prospect's mind. You can do this by using experiences, analogies, examples, statistics, and facts.

Experience: actual involvement with the idea or situation.
- **Example:** a loved one died.

Analogy: something similar but not actually the same.
- **Example:** retiring without money is like being disabled without income.

Example: someone observed in the same situation.
- **Example:** the person down the street who lives well.

Statistic: numerical support or evidence.
- **Example:** 6 percent of the population earns more than $75,000 annually.

10 Tips on How to Ask the Right Questions

1. ***Prepare some of your questions in advance.***
   Certain basic questions that come up in every interview can be planned in advance. By carefully planning them, you can make sure you cover all bases and that your wording is precise.

2. ***Ask open-ended and indirect questions.***
   Closed questions that call for a "yes" or "no" answer tend to discourage people from talking. Ask open-ended questions that require prospects to tell you how they feel, what they want, or what they think.

3. ***Ask need development questions.***
   You want to get your prospect to tell you what he or she needs. Therefore, frame questions that will give you insights into how prospects perceive their needs.

4. ***Ask questions that help you identify dominant needs.***
   Usually there is an overriding need in the prospect's mind, a need you can pinpoint by asking the right questions.

5. ***Ask questions that help you pinpoint the dominant buying motivations.***
   Buying motivations and needs are not always the same. Buying motivations have to do with desires, feelings, tastes, and so on.

6. ***Avoid offensive questions or asking questions in an insensitive way.***
   Some questions can offend prospects and cause them to distance themselves from you.

7. ***Start with broad questions, then move toward questions with a narrower focus.***
   Broad questions can help you get things rolling and steer you in the right direction.

8. ***Ask questions that are easy to answer.***
   Questions that require knowledge the prospect doesn't have can often make a person feel stupid.

9. ***Use questions to guide the interview and keep it positive in tone.***
   Some people love to ramble on and on, but by skillfully using questions you can keep the interview focused and moving in the right direction.

10. ***Ask...then shut up and listen!***
    The prospect can't talk while you're talking. More importantly, you can't learn while you're talking.

Bill Brooks is CEO of The Brooks Group, an international sales training and business growth firm based in Greensboro, N.C. For more information visit www.thebrooksgroup.com.

Fact: known situation that can be verified.

- **Example:** There will be less than $12,000 cash available at death without additional life insurance protection.

Use illustrative images liberally to vary your presentations. You are painting a picture in your prospect's mind. Brighten the image with an experience or analogy and your point will be remembered.

> **Needs and Wants**
>
> You need to motivate the prospect because needs and wants are not the same thing. Most people need life insurance, but they do not want it. Most people want a new fancy car but they do not need it. You have to bring the need out, so that the prospect can turn it into a want.

The Discovery Agreement

To get a preliminary commitment from the prospect regarding the results of the initial and fact-finding interviews, the advisor can take some time after the information-gathering session to create a discovery agreement. A *discovery agreement* is a written or verbal acknowledgment of the facts, feelings, values, and attitudes uncovered in the sales/planning process to this point. It states the prospect's present situation and what they want to accomplish financially, and it outlines the commitment to work together cooperatively to achieve these objectives. It confirms that you and the prospect understand his or her problems. This serves as a basis for proceeding forward to the next steps of the process. The discovery agreement acknowledges an understanding between the advisor and the prospect regarding the objectives and/or needs of the prospect that will be addressed by the advisor in the analysis of the prospect's current situation and the eventual proposed solutions.

Following the fact-finding, draft a letter to your prospect restating that person's goals and the information that you have found that is pertinent to working towards them. Ask for your prospect's agreement that this information is correct, so that you can proceed to study the situation and develop your recommendations. Included in this letter would be:

1. The purpose of the letter and introductory remarks
2. The prospect's current status: facts and observations about his/her situation, including attitudes, values and relevant issues
3. The prospect's goals and their desired status

4. Request for the prospect's agreement/corrections/clarifications of these statements. They can sign the letter and return it to you. When they agree and/or correct any errors, you can proceed.
5. Recommendations for the next step

When the prospect sees the discovery agreement he or she shuld know whether to agree, reconsider goals and priorities, or offer additional facts or other relevant information. This process helps clarify the advisor/client relationship and the commitment necessary to complete the planning process. It helps the advisor and prospect come to a mutual understanding of the current situation and what the client wants to accomplish.

The discovery agreement lays the groundwork for the analysis and recommendations you will perform next. When the prospect agrees that the discovery agreement accurately reflects the current status, his or her objectives and needs, and the causes or obstacles, you have succeeded in establishing a reason for the prospect to take action.

Discovery Agreement Checklist	
Current Status	1. What are the individual's financial strengths? 2. How are they currently handling their financial plan? 3. Summarized personal data 4. What is their planning philosophy? 5. What major problems and obstacles does the individual face? 6. The main problem to be solved is:
Goals &Desired Status	1. Summarized objectives and goals 2. What do they think they need to do to reach these goals? 3. What would be the perfect situation? 4. What would be gained if the perfect situation is achieved? 5. Who cares about and who is responsible for achieving these goals?
The People Involved	1. What is the process for making decisions? 2. Who gets involved? What is the role of each player? 3. Where is the money coming from? 4. What do you expect of me? 5. What is the timetable for implementation? 6. What is the next step?

Planning Considerations

Distinctions among Planning Processes

Before we begin to discuss analyzing the information, developing and presenting financial solutions in the next few chapters, some distinctions should be made between insurance planning, estate planning, retirement planning and financial planning.

Insurance Planning

Insurance planning is the process of examining all of the client's needs, comparing needs with means, and selling, where appropriate, the types of policies and the amounts of insurance that best suit the client's purposes. Insurance is an appropriate technique for treating many of the pure risks facing most individuals and families. In this regard an advisor should understand what different insurance contracts provide and how they may be used to a client's identified risks.

When considering the risk of death, the client is not concerned only with specific needs, such as children's' education or mortgage liquidation. He or she is concerned with providing capital in the case of death, in order to provide for many possible cash and income needs. There are many possible problem areas and there are many financial goals to be achieved. Chapter 5 develops how this process is applied to life insurance.

Estate Planning

Estate planning is the process of examining all the goals of the client regarding fulfilling their wishes upon their death. It encompasses the accumulation, conservation, and distribution of an estate and involves their financial desires in the context of their personal desires. Estate planning involves calculating the financial consequences of dying, such as probate and estate administration expenses, estate taxes, and liquidity needs. It requires knowledge and experience in estate law and taxation. It may also include a determination of life income needs for the survivors and a disposition of business and personal assets.

One important piece of estate planning advice you can give is the importance of a will. So many people have not undertaken this relatively simple procedure, which if left undone, can cause many problems for survivors. Dying intestate (without a will) leaves distribution of one's assets to the state, through the probate court. This can cause unnecessary delay, extra cost, and family conflict. Of even greater importance, the will can provide for guardians for minor children in the case of the death of both parents. In this way the parents' wishes can be carried out for the care of their children. Be aware that you may not render legal advice unless you are an attorney, so refrain from specific legal advice.

If a prospect may have or expect to have in the future an estate of over a million dollars, he or she may be a candidate for estate tax planning. All prospects, even those with less than a million dollars of assets, may be interested in and benefit from estate planning, which involves the satisfactory accumulation and distribution of worldly possessions after death. Under current law, only those who die in 2004 and 2005 with estates over a million and a half dollars are subject to estate tax. This will increase to 2 million in 2006 through 2008.

Remember that at death an estate is comprised of all the assets that the decedent owns, or has any incidents of ownership in the property. For this reason, if you write a large amount of insurance on someone, to avoid inclusion of the face amount of that policy in that person's estate, he or she should not be the owner or have any rights of ownership in the policy. Some other family member or a trust should have ownership control.

Retirement Planning

Retirement planning primarily involves determining the desired amount of money one needs to accumulate to retire. But today, retirement is no simple process. Changing lifestyles, increased longevity, and a new perception of retirement as an active and vibrant period and as the reward phase of life has dramatically altered the nature of retirement. Key issues in retirement are what amount of income is needed (the retirement income objective), at what age can one retire, or at what age does one want to retire, and the number of years until that retirement date. To calculate the amount needed to fund the retirement income objective, the advisor needs to record all sources of income available, such as company pensions, Social Security, and personal retirement savings, and investigate their provisions. By recording current values and projected additional deposits and accumulations, the income projected to be available is determined. If a shortfall exists from the retirement income objective, additional amounts would need to be provided that would fill the income gap by implementing new products or accumulation amounts, or reevaluating the income objective.

Retirement planning is expanding into lifestyle areas and many other insurance and financial issues. Medicare and medical insurance planning are important topics. Living arrangements, such as retirement communities and relocating, are becoming more common. Long-term care coverage is another very important topic as longevity and the cost of nursing care increase. This is another area that is appropriate to review in the total needs approach.

Financial Planning

Financial planning is the process of examining all the client's goals and objectives, doing a comprehensive analysis of all present aspects of the client's financial position (insurance, investments, savings, pending inheritances, and so on), assessing appropriate risk levels for investments, and planning redistribution and acquisition of assets to fulfill those needs and objectives. This requires a working knowledge of investments, insurance and taxation. When done for a fee, financial planning is regulated by the rules of the Securities and Exchange Commission regarding investment advice. The rules and regulations on practicing financial planning are in the process of becoming stricter and the licensing tests much more comprehensive. Do not call yourself a financial planner unless you have the proper credentials, and the company you represent, and the state(s) where you do business permit it.

One important area covered by financial planners that we can review, as an example of financial planning, is budgeting, or cash flow management. Budgeting is a process of creating and following a detailed plan for spending and investing the resources available. By establishing a budget, a person can compare expected and actual results to adjust spending and investing towards a desired level and can recognize and even anticipate problems. Budgeting is financial self-evaluation.

Some hints for establishing a budget. It should be

- flexible enough to deal with emergencies and the unexpected
- long enough to employ a strategy, typically a year
- simple and brief

- tailored to specific goals and objectives
- adjusted as results indicate that revisions are necessary and realistic
- capable of anticipating changing income and expenditures in advance

Creating a budget involves five steps:

1. Estimate the family's annual income.
2. Develop estimates for fixed and discretionary expenses.
3. Determine the excess or shortfall of income within the budget period.
4. Consider available methods for increasing income or decreasing expenses.
5. Calculate income as a percentage of the total to determine a better allocation of resources.

The best way to determine a prospect's ability to pay for a product is to compare income and expenses. You can do this by using a simple income statement, and simply by subtracting expenses from income you will have the prospect's current disposable income. This provides you with a picture of the person's financial stability. It can tell you if the premium payment commitment you have discussed is realistic by measuring the prospect's ability to pay for the sale.

The Effects of Inflation

What inflation does to life insurance and other savings and investment programs can be severe. The $100,000 life insurance policy of today may be only worth $60,000 10 years from now in terms of buying power because of inflation. Yet many people do not take simple actions to increase their life insurance to compensate for inflation.

Even today's low inflation rates cut into the value of your clients' life insurance. Your clients may not realize they have additional needs brought on by inflation, but you should. Your annual policy reviews can demonstrate this. When you talk about new needs you should also talk about the damaging effect of inflation. An adjustment in the amount of coverage may have to be made based on the lost purchasing power of the existing insurance, as well as any changes in the client's life situation or financial goals and needs.

The Rule of 72

A very important, yet simple, financial tool you can use to measure the effect of inflation as well as the effects of interest on investments is the rule of 72. To apply the Rule of 72 to inflation, divide 72 by an assumed rate of inflation to determine the number of years it takes to reduce a life insurance program to 50 percent of its current value.

The Rule of 72 is a handy mathematical rule which helps in estimating approximately how many years it may take for the life insurance policy, due to inflation, to be cut to half its buying power at a particular rate of inflation. It also approximates what twice the face value purchased today will be halved to in the same number of years. For example, if a policyowner has an $80,000 policy and the rate of inflation is expected to average 8 percent, by dividing 72 by 8 (72 divided by 8 = 9), it can be determined that the $80,000 will be worth half, or $40,000, in 9 years. Conversely, the policyowner needs $160,000 of life insurance today to have the equivalent of $80,000 9 years from now.

The Rule of 72 suggests that a prospect should buy more insurance than is currently needed, in anticipation that the cost of living will soon catch up. One way to make this idea work in situations where the prospect cannot afford to buy permanent insurance is to sell renewable, convertible term to partially fund the plan. In that way, a conversion schedule can be established so the term is gradually converted to permanent protection as the client is able to afford it.

Prospects may object to this approach on the grounds that they can add more protection as they need it in the future, rather than buying it all now. Buying more insurance periodically will work, if one remains insurable or purchases a guaranteed insurability option. In fact, one of the appealing features of products such as universal life is that coverage can be increased without having to buy a new policy, although evidence of insurability would need to be furnished.

The rule of 72 is also a commonly used tool to apply in many situations where the effect of interest, called the present or future values of money, need to be estimated. The rule of 72 estimates how long it will take for an amount to double in value at various compound interest rates. The number 72 is divided by the applicable interest rate and the result is the number of periods until the amount doubles. For example, if I have $10,000 and it can earn 10-percent interest per year, it will double, or be worth $20,000 in 7.2 years. Accumulation objectives, such as education or retirement money, can be quickly estimated by applying this rule.

Rule of 72 Assumed Inflation Rate—6%		
After:	$100,000 is reduced to:	The equivalent of the initial need:
12 years 24 years 36 years	$50,000 25,000 12,500	$200,000 400,000 800,000

The Rule of 72														
Rate of Return (%)	1	2	3	4	5	6	7	8	9	10	11	12	13	14
Years to Double or Half	72	36	24	18	14.4	12	10.3	9	8	7.2	6.5	6	5.5	5.1

Measuring What Inflation Does To Life Insurance

Many prospects quickly see what inflation does to their life insurance programs by figuring what percentage of their incomes they spent on premiums in the past and comparing that to the percentage they are spending now. Just as the Consumer Price Index increases, so too do wages and salaries. This means that people's ability to increase their insurance protection through higher premium commitments also increases.

The federal government measures inflation through the Consumer Price Index (CPI). There are several different measures used by the Bureau of Labor Statistics to establish changes to the base of each testing period. The reference base here is for 1983 to show the effects of inflation on purchasing power over the illustrated period of time.

The accompanying chart illustrates what inflation has done to the purchasing power of a 1983 dollar by the year 2000. This is a handy reference to measure the comparative value of today's dollar to the past. Column two illustrates what it costs today to purchase $1.00 worth of 1983 goods. The next column of the chart shows what this percentage increase represents over the base year. The final column illustrates the dwindling value of the 1983 dollar.

What Inflation Does to Life Insurance			
The Consumer Price Index (CPI) is the government's statistical measure of the changes in prices of goods and services bought by urban wage earners and clerical workers. It is commonly used to measure the rate of inflation.			
Year	**Index***	**Percent Increase**	**Purchasing Power of the Dollar**
1983 (base)	100	—	$1.00
1984	105	4.3%	.95
1985	108.05	3.6%	.91
1986	110.1	1.9%	.90
1987	114.06	3.6%	.86
1988	118.73	4.1%	.83
1989	124.43	4.8%	.79
1990	131.15	5.4%	.75
1991	136.66	4.2%	.72
1992	140.76	3.0%	.69
1993	144.98	3.0%	.66
1994	148.75	2.6%	.65
1995	152.92	2.8%	.64
1996	157.20	3.0%	.62
1997	161.13	2.3%	.60
1998	163.70	1.8%	.59
1999	167.31	2.2%	.58
2000	172.83	3.3%	.56

U.S. Bureau of Labor Statistics purchasing power of the dollar is rounded off to the nearest cent. U.S. City average. Urban wage earners and clerical workers: Base year index of 100 is divided by the index for the year in question.

* Rounded to the nearest whole number.

To illustrate how to use it, assume your client has a policy purchased in 1983 for $10,000. Today you wish to reevaluate the face amount for inflation. You would use the 1983 base year index of 100 and the 2000 index of 173. (Rounding makes these numbers approximations.)

173 (2000) ÷ 100 (1983) = 1.73

Then, by multiplying the prospect's current coverage ($10,000) by the index figure of 1.73, you determine the additional amount. The calculation below indicates that $7,300 of new life insurance will be needed to adjust your client's insurance policy for inflation today.

$10,000 ÷ 1.73= $17,300
$17,300 – $10,000 = $7,300

This does nothing more than restore the $10,000 buying power of the 1983 life insurance policy. It does not address the new insurance needs. Neither does it take into account the fact that the insured could well have bought additional insurance since then or had other changes in financial circumstances.

You might want to use these calculations when you review old policies that your clients purchased in the past. When new prospects ask you to evaluate their insurance portfolios, make use of this calculation to illustrate the eroding effect of inflation. It can be a revelation and can open the door to additional purchases.

As with the Rule of 72, the opposite outcome can be illustrated here as well. Using the same chart, look at the last column and you will notice that the dollar value of a 1983 purchase shrank to 56 cents in 2000 because of inflation. It will take more than $1.73 today to buy what $1.00 did in 1983. This clearly illustrates what we all know—a dollar isn't worth what it used to be.

Case History
Clean Sweep

Kirby Buckner, age 28, married, with two children, entered the life insurance business after 3 years as a sales advisor for a small firm that sells automated cleaning equipment for swimming pools. A Navy veteran, Kirby was among the company's leading new advisors.

Prospect—A year or so ago, I had an appointment with Dana Spencer, with whom I had worked for 18 months at my former company. Dana had joined the firm after I had been there about a year and a half, but had quickly shown considerable promise as a sales person; in fact, we had vied for the top sales spot for the last year I was there. Dana is a college graduate and is related to the family that owns the pool equipment company we worked for. They make an ingenious gadget that keeps swimming pools clean automatically. It's just what a working family needs, or anyone who doesn't want to spend an hour or so a week doing the job by hand.

My friend is in line for a partial ownership of the company some day, which I learned after trying to interest him in a career in life insurance selling. Dana wants to move up to management and product development with the company. No matter what line of work he chooses, it will be a success.

I had spoken with Dana about life insurance several times in the last year in connection with my efforts to interest him in joining our agency, but this was the first time we had met specifically to discuss his insurance needs. We had the interview in the living room of his condominium apartment on the northwest side of town.

Interview—Dana is single, but is engaged and plans to be married within the year. Since we've both had a lot of sales skills training, I kept things light by announcing each time I went from one part of the sales process to the next. "Now that we've established rapport and explained the purpose for my visit," I said, "let's gather pertinent information about your personal situation. Is that okay with you, prospect?"

This seemed to lessen the slight discomfort we both felt at this new situation. You know it's always tough to try to sell to a former colleague and competitor. Once we were into the fact-gathering process we both got serious about what we were doing and it seemed perfectly natural. Dana is a fairly typical young person with a good background and education, and a drive to do well in business. Although still single, he was buying the condominium we were in and had used family funds to pay for the first 2 years of college, along with some government loan money. Dana needed about $100,000 of protection now, but could be expected to need a great deal more in the coming months and years. Another factor in the current equation was that Dana's income was well below what it would be once he had learned the business from the ground up and moved into a management job, or achieved an ownership position with the company in another 2 or 3 years.

Recommendation—I showed Dana a prepared illustration of an adjustable life policy that I felt would meet current needs as well as offer the flexibility of changing the policy as his needs and circumstances changed. In this policy we would be able to adjust premium, type of insurance, and face value in the future. I explained that by starting out with a $750 annual premium—which fit the premium commitment he had suggested would be appropriate—we could provide the $100,000 coverage that was needed now. In this case, the initial plan of insurance would be term to age 65. After Dana married and needed more protection, however, the face amount and plan could be changed, to perhaps, $125,000 of term to age 57, without changing the premium. This would make sense because Dana's income would not increase that much in the next few months, and additional expenses would be expected after marriage. "By the time you're 30, Dana, maybe you will have started a family and will be making more money. If so, you will be able to increase your protection. If you bump it up to $150,000, the premium would probably go up to about $1,500."

"At any time, though, you could put more money into the policy and change the plan to permanent insurance to build cash values at current investment yields. The plan is just what its name says: 'adjustable.' That means you can change the premium amount or the death benefit (subject to evidence of insurability, of course) as your needs and financial situation change. You can also make a lump-sum payment into the policy that will extend the protection or shorten the premium payment period. For instance, a large enough payment would change a term to age 55 to term to age 65, or change a life paid-up at 70 to a life paid-up at 60 policy."

"Further, if you change the policy to permanent insurance, you'll be able to use the cash accumulations and dividends if you need money for the business, for some other opportunity, or in case of an emergency.

"All in all, Dana, this plan is going to take care of you today and it's going to be with you tomorrow. It is going to simplify your life insurance planning a great deal because each year when we review your situation, you can make whatever adjustments are necessary. There is no need to buy additional policies every time your needs increase or you want to increase your premium commitment to keep pace with inflation. If you want to put additional money into the plan to build more cash value, you can. This policy is a contract that permits you to do it all."

Conclusion—Dana took my recommendation, although the initial premium was dropped to $600 annually. Later, after he was married, Dana increased the premium to $900. I've stayed in contact with Dana both socially and as his insurance adviser. I have also sold another adjustable life policy to his wife. At our next review, I intend to recommend that they both increase their coverage to protect some additional short-term debt they have taken on. Now that Dana has moved into sales management and the business has expanded, I'd like to discuss a mass marketing/payroll deductible life insurance plan my company offers. It's just the thing for a small firm like his. As in many small businesses, the current employee benefit package is not very competitive.

I think the future is bright for this client relationship, both in terms of providing Dana's personal life insurance needs and for getting a foot in the door of a business that is on the move. They can use some additional help with their business insurance and employee benefit planning.

Case History

Double-Duty Dollars

Corey Combs was a retail salesperson at a local department store until entering the life insurance business 5 years ago. Corey made MDRT after 2 years and is involved in the personal market in a medium-sized city.

Prospect—Since I started in the business I've made it a habit to send out at least 50 direct mail letters a week. This has helped supplement my prospecting activity very effectively.

One letter I especially like to use is the mortgage protection letter. It's a standard company letter. I find most people are interested in guaranteeing a debt-free home for their families in the event of death.

Pre-approach—After receiving a reply card from Tim and Mildred Ford, I phoned and spoke with Mildred. I said that I had received the card and was calling to arrange the appointment. Mildred was very interested in meeting with me and suggested that they come to my office during one of Tim's lunch hours. Was I surprised! Not about the appointment, but at the suggestion of their coming to my office.

I asked for some preliminary information, such as ages, smoking history, mortgage amount, and interest rate so that I could prepare some preliminary suggestions that would fit their needs. Tim was 35, a nonsmoker, and a junior high principal, and Mildred a housewife.

Approach—My office has a welcome board in the waiting area, so I made certain that the Fords' name were on the board when they arrived.

I had made arrangements to use the agency conference room. This was necessary for my presentation since I feel it's important to use visuals to help the prospect understand the concepts that I propose in my mortgage presentation.

I began by spending a few minutes in general conversation with Tim and Mildred. This helped me get a better idea of how best to communicate with the two of them. Since time was limited, however, I started my presentation without too much of this warm-up.

Information Gathering—Since I had taken some preliminary information over the telephone, this portion of the interview was short. I confirmed the information that I had and found it was correct. I also laid the groundwork for further work with the Fords.

"Tim and Mildred," I said, "this meeting will take care of one of the needs for insurance you have now. Once we have taken care of the mortgage protection, it's important for us to review your overall program to be certain that this insurance for your mortgage won't have to be used for income, education, or other debts that may someday become priorities."

Both agreed to discuss other needs later, but their major concern was having insurance on their new home. Tim said they had seen the program they wanted. They were looking for a level premium with a declining death benefit that approximated the declining mortgage. Tim's comment gave me the opportunity to make my suggestions.

Close—I spent a few minutes illustrating on the flip chart how different insurance plans worked, concentrating on decreasing term and ordinary life. I used diagrams to explain the products.

Then I reviewed the Ford's mortgage information. The mortgage was for $125,000 at 8 percent on a 30-year fixed loan. I showed Tim and Mildred that their actual payments would exceed $330,000 over that 30-year period. That surprised them. Neither had realized just how much interest would have to be paid and what $920 a month really added up to.

"If I could show you how to save some interest costs on your new home by using a particular type of insurance program, would this be of interest to you?" Both were a little confused when I asked this but were interested in hearing my idea.

I showed them two of the computer runs I had made. The first was an amortization schedule on their home. This illustration showed the outstanding mortgage balance at the end of each year. The second was an ordinary life illustration for $125,000 on Tim's life. I focused their attention on the policy's cash values, taking special care to point out the twenty-third year's cash value. This year-end cash value was a few thousand more than the outstanding mortgage balance in year 23. To complete the concept, I showed them the money they would save if they paid off the mortgage in the twenty-third year. It would be over $77,000! My final illustration was a rough drawing on the flip chart of the cash value growth of the insurance plan intersecting with the Ford's declining mortgage.

Now, back to my plan. It was making sense. If Tim were to die prematurely, the death benefit would be available to pay off the mortgage immediately. But, if Tim lived until a ripe old age, the cash value 23 years from now could be used to cancel the mortgage and save over $77,000 in payments. This added opportunity to save money really adds sizzle to the mortgage cancellation sale for me.

Incidentally, I always add waiver of premium. It's the insurance on the insurance. That's how I sell it. When the extra premium for this permanent insurance plan I was suggesting was related to this mortgage cancellation program, with more than $77,000 in expense saved, it was easy to close the sale. The Fords did not mention the decreasing term insurance idea they brought to our meeting again. The application was completed, a prepayment made—and Tim made it back to school in plenty of time.

Comment—Not everyone will buy cash value life insurance to cover the need to liquidate a mortgage. Not everyone can or will afford the higher initial premiums. Our primary goal is to cover the needs of our prospects from whatever source is necessary. For those who do, however, the security of equity in both the home and its insurance protection are quite comforting. The dollars saved eventually create a long-term benefit that greatly exceeds the short-term sacrifice needed to put it in place. There is nothing ordinary about this application of ordinary life!

On another point in this sale, this was the first time a prospect had come to my office for an appointment. I had heard other advisors talk about it but had never felt confident enough of myself to suggest it. Since then, one of my first questions after setting the date of the first appointment is to ask, "do you know the way to my office?" Then we can negotiate what will be easiest for the prospect. Many times I find the prospect has no objection to coming to me.

Chapter Four Review

Key terms and concepts are explained in the Glossary. Answers to the Review Questions and Self-Test Questions are found in the back of the book, following the Glossary.

Key Terms and Concepts

fact finding
close-ended questions
feeling finding
discovery agreement
insurance planning
nonverbal behavior
rule of 72
Consumer Price Index (CPI)
open-ended questions
clarifying questions
active listening
qualifying prospects
motivating questions
estate planning
financial planning
leading questions

Review Questions

4-1. What are the objectives of the information-gathering interview?

4-2. Identify and describe skills and techniques used in the fact-finding interview.

4-3. What are benefits do the advisor and client receive from conducting a fact-finder?

4-4. How would you describe the process of qualifying a prospect and characteristics of a qualified prospect?

4-5. What are the principles of communication that affect the selling/planning process?

4-6. How can an understanding of nonverbal behavior improve the sales/planning process?

4-7. How can active listening techniques be used in the interview process?

4-8. How are questioning techniques used in the fact-finding interview.

4-9. What is the discovery agreement and why is it important to the sales/planning process?

4-10. What are the distinguishing characteristics of insurance planning, retirement planning, estate planning, and financial planning?

4-11. What are the effects of inflation on the value of a life insurance policy, and how can the rule of 72 be used to determine these effects?

Self-Test Questions

Instructions: Read Chapter 4, then answer the following questions to test your knowledge. There are 10 questions. Circle the correct answer. When you are finished, check your answers with the answer key in the back of the book.

4-1. A statement created by the advisor after the fact-finding process that outlines the prospect's current situation, needs, and objectives is known as the

(A) discovery agreement
(B) financial plan
(C) fact-finder
(D) financial priority schedule

4-2. According to the rule of 72, if the inflation rate is 6 percent, a life insurance policy will lose half of its value in how many years?

(A) 6
(B) 8
(C) 10
(D) 12

4-3. The best way to understand a prospect's nonverbal behavior is to

(A) ask the prospect about it
(B) assume you understand it and listen for verbal clues
(C) mirror their behavior by doing it yourself
(D) ask yourself what it would mean if you did that behavior

4-4. You will give your prospects the opportunity to express themselves by starting an interview with a question that is

(A) leading
(B) open-ended
(C) motivating
(D) closed-ended

4-5. Which of the following is the first principle of effective communication?

(A) Speak clearly.
(B) Match your vocabulary to the prospect's level of understanding.
(C) Have a goal.
(D) Spend enough time so that prospects and clients can react without undo pressure.

4-6. "I think what I hear you say is . . . (rephrase what you heard). Is that correct?" is an example of which of the following types of questions?

(A) combining question
(B) motivating question
(C) clarifying question
(D) leading question

4-7. Which of the following statements is (are) goals of the fact-finding interview?

I. Build trust and credibility with the prospect.
II. Obtain at least three referrals.

(A) I only
(B) II only
(C) Both I and II
(D) Neither I nor II

4-8. Which of the following documents should the prospect typically have ready for your review?

I. birth certificate, passport, and Social Security information.
II. wills, insurance policies, and employee benefit information.

(A) I only
(B) II only
(C) Both I and II
(D) Neither I nor II

4-9. All of the following are criteria for qualifying prospects for life insurance EXCEPT

(A) ability to pay premiums for the protection
(B) clear awareness of their insurance needs
(C) approachability
(D) insurability

4-10. In the fact-finding interview, you want to achieve all of the following EXCEPT

(A) establish yourself as a person who can help
(B) differentiate yourself from the competition
(C) get a dollar commitment for an amount that can solve the problem
(D) analyze the client's situation and offer preliminary solutions

5

Analyze the Information

Overview and Learning Objectives

Chapter 5 discusses how to analyze a prospect's need for life insurance, based on the fact-finding process just completed. An extensive discussion of the capital and income needs analysis process is provided as a foundation for establishing the prospect's needs. To complete the analysis, a thorough review of the prospect's employee benefits and social security benefits is necessary and the chapter examines the content of these benefits.

By reading this chapter and answering the questions, you should be able to

5-1. Identify the key factors in analyzing the client's current situation in light of his or her financial goals.

5-2. Explain an income and cash needs analysis.

5-3. Describe the life insurance planning process using the capital conservation and capital distribution methods.

5-4. Explain how employee benefits and social security fit into the total-needs analysis.

Chapter Outline

Analyzing the Information

This chapter will discuss the task of analyzing the information gathered in the fact-finding interview to determine the client's current financial situation and propose solutions to achieve the desired goals. Skills relating to this step of the selling/planning process will be discussed. Employee Benefits and Social Security will also be reviewed, since they make up a large part of the overall insurance and financial plan for most prospects and therefore must be included in the overall planning process.

Determining the Client's Situation

To this point in the selling/planning process, you have gathered the facts and figures, goals and priorities, and attitudes and values that constitute a profile of your prospect. Now that you have a reasonably complete picture of the prospect, what do you do with it? You examine the situation to pinpoint real problems and needs that you can solve with your products and services. This brings us to the next step in the sales/planning process: analyzing the information.

Basic Questions

You will need to ask yourself several questions as you analyze a case after a data-gathering interview.

1. What are the desires, concerns, objectives, and needs to be considered?
2. Where is the prospect now in relation to established goals?
3. How is the prospect's situation likely to change in the future?
4. How far will existing life insurance and other benefit sources go toward meeting these needs?
5. What additional life insurance or other recommendations are needed to make up the shortfall or to complete the plan?
6. What are the goal priorities of the prospect?
7. What possible product solution(s) may fit in this situation?
8. How much can the prospect reasonably be expected to pay for the protection?

9. What objections can I anticipate?
10. Who are the decision-makers in this sale?

Review the Facts

Compile and categorize the answers to the key questions listed above. This process determines the facts of the client's current financial situation. Next, review the client's goals. You will then be in a position to calculate the amount of any additional insurance or investments needed to close the gap between their present situation and their desired situation. Finally, you will design a solution, and alternatives, to present to your prospective client to achieve this task. Let us briefly examine each of the main areas you will consider in your analysis.

Needs

The list of your prospect's needs, concerns, and desires identified in the information-gathering interview represents your sales opportunities. You should be able to attach both a monetary value and a priority to each of them. List any foreseeable changes that are likely to occur in the prospect's personal or business life, such as marriage, birth, inheritance, or promotion. These should be incorporated into any current insurance planning.

Remember that most people don't buy what they need—they buy what they want. Listen carefully to what the prospect is telling you he or she wants and what he or she needs. Do not transfer your own standards and values in determining the prospect's motives.

Existing Program

Some people are already well protected, while others need extensive additional planning and protection. You should know or be able to determine the eligibility, amount, and duration of any employer- or government-provided benefits, as well as present life, disability, and health insurance coverage. You should also know the present beneficiary, ownership, and payout arrangements for each of your prospect's existing policies. You want to evaluate and take into account the strengths and weaknesses of the current plan in designing the proposed plan.

Additional Protection

There are several techniques used in measuring the need for additional protection and personal life insurance planning. Simpler techniques can calculate needs manually or with a simple calculator. The more sophisticated and complex techniques will require a computer and printouts. These are covered in the discussion of planning methods in this chapter.

Product Solutions

At this point you may be considering possible product solutions that may apply to this prospect's situation. A final decision of a product or products should not take place until the completion of your analysis. But you can make some initial "ballpark-type" generalizations to assist you in considering what may help the prospect.

The number and variety of life insurance products available to meet consumer needs are enormous. The level of knowledge you have about the products you sell is of primary importance in analyzing your prospect's needs and designing appropriate solutions. A general treatment cannot take the place of a thorough, detailed study of your company's product line. Know the features and benefits of your products and how to present them to prospects. Know what your products can and cannot do, whom they are designed for, and what the requirements are for selling them. As any experienced salesperson will tell you, "there's no substitute for product knowledge." Knowledge is power. Just because you shouldn't tell each prospect everything you know doesn't mean you shouldn't know it.

The Choice of Product

After needs and amounts are agreed upon, you should then help the prospect consider the types of policies that best fit his or her needs. With numerous policies, options, and riders available, the possibilities are almost unlimited.

The Best Policy

No valid generalizations can be made with regard to the best life insurance policy. The best policy is the policy that most effectively meets your client's needs. Thus, emphasis in planning must be placed on your individual prospect's needs, and not on the relative merits of a particular kind of policy.

This decision requires a high degree of familiarity with the products you offer. You must know what they can do, what their inherent risks are, and what trade-offs are involved in selecting one product versus another. This also requires broad knowledge of your client's situation and an awareness of existing client resources and objectives so they can be matched with the proper product. You must have sensitivity to client risk-taking propensity and a feel for client views regarding such things as guarantees, premium levels, and policy flexibility. Only then should you evaluate alternatives and make recommendations. Here are some questions you and your client should consider before deciding on a form of insurance.

Will It Be There When Needed?

It is apparent and without argument that the best life insurance policy is the one that is in force when the insured dies, if there is a need for it then. All of the arguments, pros and cons, strengths and weaknesses, and whatever else one could say about a policy are meaningless if the needed insurance is not in force at death.

The most important question to ask about any insurance is, "will it be there when it is needed?" A chief difference between life insurance and other forms of insurance is the degree of certainty about whether the peril will occur. Many perils never happen; death always does. The only question is, "when?" As years pass, the likelihood of death increases. Logically then, if a life insurance policy is to do its job, it must be in force at death—at whatever age—in the right amount.

How Will the Prospect Pay for It?

An inescapable companion question is how to pay for life insurance in old age, when it is most needed, because death is nearer and insurance is most expensive for the same reason. While some forms of insurance have higher premiums in early years, such policies have lower or no premium payments in old age. Other policies have lower early-year premiums that increase over time. A person's inability to pay increasingly steeper premiums may jeopardize their ability to maintain coverage in force.

You should have walked away from the fact-gathering interview with a budget commitment and a considerable amount of financial and personal information about your prospect. This will be valuable in helping you determine the type and amounts of coverage to recommend.

For example, from this information you will know how much the prospect can afford to pay, or if there are ways the prospect can generate additional premium dollars. You have an agreed amount of coverage desired, or information that can be used to determine that amount. You have information about goals, desires, needs, and wants that can be used to design a plan.

Risk Tolerance and Suitability

Many of today's policies have transferred some of the risks from the insurance company to the policyowner. No discussion of policy selection would be complete without a consideration of risk tolerance.

Risk tolerance is the degree of a client's willingness or reluctance to accept the risk that his investment may decline in value and that the premium may increase over time. You need to ask questions concerning your client's past investment decisions, investment experience, total assets, asset allocation and diversification, time horizon, liquidity needs, investment objectives, and so on. Your company should have a questionnaire and guidelines for this process, especially when selecting variable products. A product recommendation must always be suitable and in the client's best interest, regardless of type. *Suitability* deals with the appropriateness of the product for the client based on their overall need, financial situation, ability to pay the premium, and risk tolerance, as discussed above.

Calculations

After you have itemized and reviewed the prospect's personal and financial information and answered the key questions discussed, you are ready to begin the number-crunching part of your analysis. Your objective is to arrive at the specific amount of coverage your prospect needs now to be fully protected. There is more than one way to do these calculations. Although your company or agency may endorse one method or another, you should be aware of the various alternatives.

Anticipating Client Concerns

The finished product should provide a comparison of the results anticipated from the current plan, those anticipated from the proposed plan, and its alternatives. Each plan will contain certain strengths and weaknesses, which should be explained and discussed with the prospect. In the final analysis, the plan must be the client's plan, not the advisor's plan.

Life Insurance Planning

How Much Life Insurance Is Enough?

How much life insurance should a person have? This can be a difficult question to answer and requires a detailed analysis of the person' life circumstances. There is no blanket formula to determine this. The traditional approach is to look at the present and future financial needs of the family developed through a financial needs analysis. Hopefully, the prospect will be able to afford the premium to pay for the entire need. A plan should be developed that can satisfy the agreed-upon need within the family budget. Sometimes a combination of permanent and term is needed to complete the need. Sometimes we are able to sell only part of the needed protection, aiming to supplement the plan with additional purchases in the future, if insurability permits. It may take years to build towards completion of the program. Often it is never completed, but any insurance in force is better than little or none.

Human Life Value

As discussed in Chapter 1, the human life value concept is important to the determination of the life insurance need. Human life value is the foundation for the life insurance need, although as we will see below, there are also other methods for determining life insurance amount based on specific needs. Without establishing needs or human life value, the prospect is left with simply a suggested amount of insurance that may sound high or nonsensical if there is no rationale for determining that amount. To someone with less than $1,000 in the bank at any one time, a $250,000 life insurance policy sounds enormous. It is simply a large amount of money without any context, even though the individual in question may have a human life value to his or her family in excess of one million dollars.

One method of determining how much life insurance a person should carry is called the *human life value approach*. It is based on the proposition that a person should carry life insurance in an amount equal to the *capitalized value* of his or her net earnings. Under this theory, a person should capitalize this economic value at an amount large enough to yield, at a reasonable rate of interest, an income equal to the family's share of those earnings. In an attempt to obtain the same general result, others have recommended that a person capitalize this value at a figure large enough to yield an annual income equal to a specified percentage, such as 50 percent of those personal earnings at the time of the provider's death. In response to the significant inflation in recent decades, some suggest capitalizing the worker's full income (or more) so that the income portion that would otherwise have gone to income taxes and the insured's self-maintenance can be used to offset general price inflation.

These approaches are based on the assumption that the income from an income producer should not end at death. All would preserve the capitalized value of a portion of those earnings into perpetuity. Such an assumption is theoretically invalid. Personal earnings are subject to termination at any time by the producer's death or disability and, in any case, will generally not continue beyond the date of retirement. Therefore, in capitalizing the earnings of an individual, their terminable nature should be taken into account.

The technically accurate method of computing the monetary value of a person involves an estimate of the individual's personal earnings for each year from his or her present age to the date of retirement, taking into account the normal trend of earnings and inflation. From each year's income the cost of self-maintenance, life insurance premiums, and personal income taxes is deducted. The residual income for each year is then discounted at an assumed rate of interest and against the possibility of its not being earned. In the latter calculation, the three contingencies of death, disability, and unemployment have to be considered. The sum of the discounted values for each year of potential income is the *present value* of future earnings or the monetary value of the life in question. That is, the present value is what some money to be received in the future is worth today. It is equivalent to the given sum to be received in the future, discounted (reduced) by an interest rate that represents the interest that could be earned on that money if it was received today instead on in the future.

When determining the economic value of a human life for purposes of insuring that value against loss by death, one should consider the projected flow of income to the family rather than the probability of the provider's death. The objective is to determine the present value of the income flow to the family if the family provider survives to the end of his or her income-producing period. Ideally insurance will be sufficient to permit the family to enjoy the same standard of living that it would have enjoyed had the provider(s) not died.

Financial Needs Analysis

Cash and Income Needs Analysis

There are several different approaches to determining the amount of life insurance appropriate for any given client. Financial journalists tend to prefer simplistic rules of thumb, such as some multiple of annual income, because it is short and easy to explain. However, there is a trap in this seductive simplicity. The thing that is most interesting about this approach is the large variation in the multiple to be used, commonly ranging from three times to 10 times (or more) annual income.

An attempt to determine life insurance needs that does not rely upon a fair amount of client information is of questionable worth. The rule-of-thumb approach ignores information about how much the client has already accumulated and any external sources of finance such as trusts and inheritances. The rule-of-thumb approach can err in either direction; that is, it can overinsure or underinsure the client. Simplistic rules of thumb may perform a positive function if they are the only approach that motivates the client to purchase needed insurance. Sometimes clients resist providing the information necessary for a thorough analysis of their needs.

> **Plan for Life by Planning for Death**
>
> Plan for life as though you will live forever; plan for death as though it will come tomorrow.

The analysis of post-death financial needs is separated into two main categories.

Cash Needs—an analysis of the amount of funding that would have to be set aside to pay expenses that the deceased would otherwise have paid. *Cash needs* at death include final expenses such as funeral, burial, or cremation, if applicable; estate taxes; probate expenses; attorney fees; unpaid costs of a last illness; and operating expenses for the survivors' household. An emergency fund and a child-care and educational fund can also be provided in this category.

Income Needs—an analysis of the needs for income for survivors and sources of income available to fund those needs. If there is a shortfall of income, this method determines the amount of life insurance needed to cover the shortfall, using a capital conservation or capital distribution method. This amount, together with the amount from the cash needs analysis, will provide the funding for the lifestyle that the survivors will have in the future.

The need for survivor income becomes evident at the moment of death. These needs will continue until those dependents can become self-supporting. In some family situations this can be a short time, or it can last decades. In some families the surviving spouse may never become self-sufficient, and there is no intent that he or she do so.

It is common to classify the survivors' ongoing *income needs* into four categories:

- income for the readjustment period immediately after death
- income for the dependency period, until the youngest child becomes self-sufficient
- income, if needed, for the surviving spouse for the *blackout period*, after the children have become self-sufficient. The blackout period, discussed later, is the period in which a spouse will not be eligible to receive Social Security income.
- income, if needed, for the surviving spouse after eligibility for social security and any private pension benefits

Because the purpose of life insurance is to fund the unfunded portion of these objectives, it is important to consider any and all existing funds that can provide part or all of these needs. Most planners suggest about 70 percent of the pre-death income to carry on after death, based on a decrease in living costs, commuting costs, and other work-related expenses from the death of the income provider. Any shortfall between the intended goals and objectives and the current financial sources is usually a candidate for life insurance. Life insurance provides a means for completing the financing of family goals that individuals work toward during their lifetime.

The following Guidelines for the Insurance Needs Assessment can be reviewed with the Fact-finding Form found in Chapter 4.

Guidelines for the Insurance Needs Assessment

Cash Needs

Final Expenses/Burial Fund—These are the costs of funeral expenses plus other costs that are associated with death, such as medical expenses for a last illness, estate settlement costs, property transfer costs, and so on.

Questions for Final Expenses: Have you ever thought about what it costs for a funeral? Are you aware of all of the costs that might arise immediately in the case of your death? How much do you think that would require?

Mortgage Payment Fund—This is the amount required to pay off the balance of the mortgage on the family home to allow the family to keep the home. If the family rents a home, calculate the annual rent times the number of years the fund will be needed.

Questions for Mortgage Payment Fund: If you were to die tonight, would you want your family to be able to keep the house? How much do you think that would require?

Debt Payment Fund—This is the amount required to pay existing debts that may become due immediately like car loans, credit cards, personal loans, and so on.

Questions for Debt Payment Fund: Would you want your family to be able to pay off all your outstanding debts if you were to die tonight? How much do you think that would require?

Education Fund—This is the amount that would be needed in the future to help fund the children's higher education.

Questions for Education Fund: How do you feel about education for your children? Is providing an education for your children a priority for you? How much do you think that would require? Where do you see them going to school? If you or your spouse were to die, do you think it would be harder for the remaining spouse to save for college?

Other/Emergency Fund—This is a fund set aside to meet the routine emergencies of daily living like car repairs that are currently met with the help of the wage earner.

Questions for Emergency Fund: Would your family be able to handle other emergencies, like major car repairs or home repairs, without you here to help? How much do you think should be set aside for emergencies?

Other Immediate Cash Needs—List any other special needs identified by the prospect.

Questions for Other Immediate Cash Needs: Are there any other obligations that you can think of that your family might have difficulty meeting if you were to die tonight?

Annual Income Fund—For both the prospect and spouse, enter the amount of annual earned income from salaries, wages and regular bonuses.

Questions for Annual Income Fund: If you were to die tonight, your family would lose your earning power, wouldn't they? How much of what you earn would they need to maintain their current lifestyle? How long would they need it? Your income probably increases annually. Would you want your family's income to increase as well? By what percentage?

Total Family Income Need—The annual amount needed is the amount of the prospect's income that would be needed by the family to maintain its current lifestyle. Replacement income from other sources, like Social Security, can be taken into consideration in determining the amount needed. The annual amount needed is multiplied by the number of years the amount is to be provided.

Savings And Investments—Include all savings and investment programs including personal retirement plans (IRAs) that would be available.

Questions for Savings and Investments: If you were to die tonight, your family would be faced with all of the needs you just identified, wouldn't they? Let me ask you, would your current resources meet those needs?

Company Benefits—Include company-sponsored life insurance plans that would be available in the event of death. Also include any pension or other benefits the employer provides that would be available at death.

Family and Friends—Include the amount that would be provided by other family members or friends.

Current Life Insurance—Include the total of all existing life insurance in force excluding that provided through employment that was included above.

Other—Include any other sources of cash that the prospect thinks would be available.

Calculation—Total all the available resources. Total the immediate cash needs and the family income need. Subtract the available resource figure from the combined needs figure.

Capital Needs Analysis

There are many ways to calculate the amount of additional insurance needed, ranging from simple to complex and from exact policy-by-policy allocation to an aggregate approach. Some planning techniques can be done by hand and some can be done on notebook or desktop computers. Keep in mind, however, that one method is not necessarily better than another. Your choice should be based on such factors as how accurate and in-depth the program needs to be for the prospect, whether the sale is to be made on the first or a subsequent interview, and whether the prospect wants to preserve or consume capital. When calculations for determining the amount of insurance a person should have are made following the methods discussed in the next section, the capital needs analysis and financial needs analysis, this process is traditionally called *insurance programming.*

The *capital needs analysis* method

1) identifies the needs a family would most likely want to satisfy when death stops part or all of a family income
2) estimates the funds necessary to cover the identified needs
3) identifies existing sources of funds available to cover those needs
4) subtracts those existing resources from the total needs
5) creates a capital sum through life insurance to produce enough income the meet the identified needs of the family after a breadwinner's death

How Much Do I Need?—You may get this question from a prospect. You could answer in the following way:

> "This is not an easy question to answer spontaneously because insurance needs are complex and they differ from person to person. But I'm sure we can come up with the amount you want your family to have if you will tell me what you would like to accomplish for your family."

Mr. Prospect, Is Your Group Protection Enough

How much life insurance does your company have for you? Ask yourself, "How much of your total life insurance need is that going to cover?" For instance, will it provide enough income for your family for more than a year or two—even on top of Social Security survivor benefits? Would it pay off your mortgage if you died today? Would it send your children to college? Would it provide any cash accumulation for your retirement years?

If you don't know or are uncertain about the answers to those questions—and, believe me, you wouldn't be alone in not knowing those kinds of things—I can help. By reviewing your employee benefit package and eligibility under Social Security, we can determine how these benefits measure up to the financial security objectives you have for your family. Don't you agree that this would be good information to have?

Assume Death Occurs Today—The cardinal rule in insurance planning is the assumption that the insured will die today. If there is no assumption of immediate death, it will be impossible to pinpoint the need for or the sources of the available income. It would be a rough estimate only. You must plan for the circumstances as they exist today. In presenting your analysis, it is not too difficult to imagine using the words: "(Prospect), had you died today, this would be your situation . . ." This is not intimidation. It allows the prospect to be realistic and focus on the present.

Dual-Income Families—Today, most families have more than one income earner. When planning methods were first developed, most families had only one primary wage earner and the needs were more easily determined. Today, we need to consider both incomes and a variety of possibilities. Total-needs planning becomes more urgent when the circumstances are complicated by a variety of needs: income, disability, and retirement planning. The result is often two programs, each satisfying the appropriate share of the total needs.

Considering Social Security—The handling of anticipated Social Security benefits gives the advisor another planning tool. Social Security is either fully or partially calculated into the program, or set aside as a future inflation hedge. People have opinions about the future soundness of the program in general. Almost everyone still believes that they will have a Social Security income after paying the FICA taxes on their earned income over the years. But many are suspicious about what that amount will be when they retire.

When choosing the planning method to be used, the inclusion or exclusion of Social Security income must be considered. People who prefer not to use Social Security as part of their total-needs planning will probably consider the conservation methods more attractive for their programs. This is the most conservative approach to take, for all future income needs with be provided through the client's own resources. Social Security can be figured into dependency income through the survivor's benefits and in retirement income calculations. Each step can be considered individually. But clients should decide this based on their own individual preference, not simply on what is the traditional way of handling this. Some prefer to include Social Security, feeling confident in the program, while others do not, preferring to allow Social Security to serve as a hedge against inflation, future reductions in benefits, and other unforeseen events.

There are two basic approaches to planning for capital needs, the amount of money necessary to fund future financial needs for survivors of an insured person. They are the capital distribution method and the capital conservation method.

The Capital Distribution Method

In this method, both principal and interest are used to provide income for a certain period of time into the future, at which point the total capital is spent. This is also known as the liquidating approach, since all funds are expected to be distributed over time. Since the principal is used as income, this method requires a smaller amount of initial principal to provide the desired income than in the capital conservation method. The serious, and potentially severe shortcoming of this method is that at some point in the future the entire capital sum is consumed. This may be unacceptable if the income is expected to last indefinitely, or at least for the lifetime of a designated beneficiary. This method, although requiring a smaller amount of principal, would leave no room for contingencies, adjustment for inflation, or for any balance of principal to be passed on to other beneficiaries.

Capital Distribution Example—Let's take a look at an example of how the capital distribution approach would work. This method determines the income need of the family by identifying specific amounts of cash that would be needed during specific time periods, namely the readjustment period, the dependency period, the blackout period, and the retirement period. The sum of the differences between desired income and available income would be used to calculate the amount of life insurance needed to cover the capital shortfall. One would then find the present value of this amount, meaning we would discount the dollar value by an assumed interest rate from the time in the future that we would expect to use that money. This can get very complicated and is speculative at best. Some suggest we should not discount the future need, since the calculation is an estimate and the full projected value will give some room for inflation and unfavorable events. Inflation should be addressed with the client, and an inflation-adjusted rate of return should be considered in calculating the need if inflation is a concern to the client.

A simple example will illustrate the procedure. Fred and Mary Baker are a young couple with a 4-year-old daughter, Laura. Fred is a 31-year-old bank executive earning $48,000 per year. Mary, age 27, is a schoolteacher earning $28,000.

A fact-finding interview yielded the following information:

- Cash needs at Fred's Death

Estate clearance fund	$ 10,000
Mortgage retirement fund	$ 140,000
Emergency fund	$ 15,000
Education fund for Laura	$ 100,000
Total	$ 265,000

- Income Needs after Fred's Death

Readjustment period income for one year	$ 65,000
Dependency period income per year for 17 years	$ 50,000
Life income per year for Mary after Laura finishes college	$ 40,000

Collecting Fred and Mary's sources of funds already in place for meeting the above needs results in the following:

• Group term life insurance on Fred from work (face amount)	$ 96,000
• Individual universal life insurance on Fred (face amount)	$ 50,000
• Investments (mutual funds, 401(k) plan, market value)	$ 20,000
• Checking account (average balance)	$ 2,045
• Social Security lump sum death benefit	$ 255
• Social Security survivorship benefits (Laura until she finishes high school at age 18)	$ 6,000/yr.
• Mary's income	$ 28,000/yr.
• Mary's combined Social Security retirement benefits and miscellaneous income at age 65 for life	$ 15,000/yr.

No specific amount of Social Security survivorship benefits are identified for Mary because her income will cause her to forfeit benefits while she is working. For simplicity her income is projected to remain level. Also notice that the retirement income of $15,000 is combined from her pension, Social Security retirement benefits, and miscellaneous sources. She will not be eligible for full Social Security benefits until age 67, the normal retirement age for someone of her age.

At Fred's death, a cash need of $265,000 was noted above. The present sources of funds to meet this need are only $166,000 (group insurance $96,000; individual insurance $50,000; investments $20,000). The checking account and Social Security death benefit are ignored here. This leaves an immediate need for $99,000 of life insurance to meet cash needs ($265,000 minus $166,000).

The income needs for the family show the following gaps:

> $65,000 minus $34,000, or $31,000 for one year; followed by
> $50,000 minus $34,000, or $16,000 for 13 years; followed by
> $50,000 minus $28,000, or $22,000 for 4 years; followed by
> $40,000 minus $28,000, or $12,000 for 20 years; followed by
> $40,000 minus $15,000, or $25,000 for life (20 years assumption)

The amount of life insurance proceeds needed to fill the income gap is the present value of each of the separate gaps. If discounted at an assumed after-tax rate of return of 6 percent per year, the total present value using a financial calculator net present value (NPV) function is approximately $293,000.

The total amount of insurance in Fred's case to provide cash needs of $99,000 and income needs of $293,000 is $392,000. There are two difficulties with this amount of insurance.

- It does not provide Mary with income that she cannot outlive. The assumption is that she would die at age 85. The insurance needed to increase to age 100 would be merely $8,000. This small amount of additional insurance is due to Mary's young age.
- It does not provide for any inflationary increase in the income to the survivors.

A possible solution to the above can be provided by additional life insurance on Fred at a later date (if he does not die or become uninsurable). Two other possibilities would be a life income settlement option or immediate life annuity for a portion of the life insurance proceeds.

Several approaches may be taken regarding inflation. Social Security has an automatic adjustment for inflation. A rate lower than 6 percent could be used as a rate of return to provide a higher face amount needed. Another approach could be to add insurance in the future through the use of a guaranteed insurability rider on the policy. One more possibility is for Fred to buy a variable type life policy, although the Bakers' do not appear to be in a position to properly fund the policy, in light of their present income and the large amount of life insurance needed.

Mary's life insurance needs would be determined using the same approach.

The Capital Conservation Method

The premise for the capital conservation method is that capital is preserved rather than spent. This method uses only interest generated from an investment to provide the desired income and thus is also referred to as the non-liquidating or capital retention method. Capital is not invaded, so there is an investment amount that basically does not vary, if invested conservatively. Conversely, if the client can tolerate risk, the money could be invested more aggressively for potential growth. The money would be placed in a well-allocated and diversified portfolio, depending on risk/return characteristics suitable to that client. The goal is to produce an after-tax income from the interest to meet the beneficiary's need. The principal remains intact to be used as a hedge against inflation or other contingencies, or to be passed on to the beneficiary's heirs.

For this technique, a simple financial statement is prepared which lists the prospect's goals, assets, and liabilities. From this is determined the need for additional life insurance using a calculation that conserves, rather than consumes, principal. In this case it might look something like the box that follows. You will note the prospect has existing life insurance of $100,000. In our illustration the net interest assumption (the effective interest rate after tax) is 6 percent. A realistic look at the economic future in a discussion with the prospect will help you determine a rate of return that will be acceptable to him or her.

The insurance need generated by capital conservation exceeds that generated by the capital distribution technique illustrated earlier. The gap is often not so wide as to put this method of calculation beyond the means of most people. The flexibility and the added advantage of preserving capital make the capital conservation concept appealing to many prospects. It is widely endorsed by insurance practitioners and is the basis for many of the computerized needs analysis programs.

Most companies have computer software that can do these calculations for you, often presenting them in an attractive proposal format. Become familiar with these concepts and use them with your prospects.

Capital Conservation Example—A family needs additional annual income of $5,000 (net after taxes) beyond Social Security and all other income sources. Assuming that 5 percent after taxes can be earned on the income producing assets, the amount of insurance required can be determined by dividing $5,000 by .05.

$$\$5{,}000 \div .05 = \$100{,}000$$

In other words, $100,000 earning 5 percent annually will produce $5,000 in interest income. The $100,000 in principal will not be used. It will be preserved to provide annual interest income into the future.

Financial Statement for the Prospect
Capital Conservation Approach

Goals:	
Mortgage liquidation	$ 45,000
Final expense	15,000
Cash fund for emergency	8,000
Education guarantee fund	60,000
	$ 128,000
Income replacement (33 percent) at current rate of $833 per month without touching principal (6 percent return)	$ 166,600
($833 x 12 mos. = $9,996 ÷.06 = $166,600)	
Total needed to complete goals	$ 294,600
Assets:	
Non-liquid assets (home, auto, furniture) are not considered working capital and will not be considered for investment. Liquid assets include:	
Life insurance	$ 100,000
Savings	
Liabilities:	
There are no outstanding debts except the mortgage.	
There is a capital shortfall of $194,600.	capital shortfall
($294,600 – $100,000 = $194,600)	$ 194,600
Recommendations:	
Make up the capital shortfall with additional life insurance.	
Start a savings program now for the future.	

Interest Rate

One of the attractions of the capital conservation technique is the use of current interest rates instead of the more conservative guaranteed rates in settlement options that may or may not pay a current rate of return. Many advisors suggest the use of a fairly conservative interest assumption, usually between 4 percent and 6 percent, because it is a reliable long-term rate of return after taxes, and can provide a degree of inflation protection for the client's life insurance.

A prospect may object, however, arguing that if a higher interest rate were assumed, less insurance would be needed. You can answer this objection by explaining that you are assuming an interest rate after taxes. By using a lower rate, the prospect can be fairly certain that the family will always have the necessary income to meet its needs.

For example, if inflation increases, it is likely that rates will also rise. With adequate insurance, the increased earnings from higher interest rates will meet the family's greater income needs during periods of inflation. If these explanations do not produce agreement on an estimated interest rate, ask what interest rate after taxes the prospect would like to use. Work with that figure. If your calculations are based on a rate that your prospect does not agree to, your likelihood for success in the sale will be reduced.

It may be that the prospect's figure is extremely inflated. Rather than ignoring the figure as unreasonable, ask the following question: "You've asked me to use a 12-percent after-tax rate to make these calculations. Tell me, what investment did you have in mind that would currently provide you 12-percent income after tax?" By asking this type of question, the prospect is encouraged to determine a reasonable rate for your calculations. If, however, the prospect continues to insist on an inflated interest rate, you should use that rate for the insurance need calculation. To do otherwise will likely reduce your value as an advisor in the prospect's eyes.

Advantages of Capital Conservation

An insurance program built on the capital conservation concept has several advantages.

- First, it suggests the possibility of investing life insurance proceeds at current interest rates, rather than placing them under more conservative contractual guaranteed rates normally found in settlement options.
- Second, capital conservation provides an opportunity to hedge the client's life insurance program against inflation. Income-producing principal is preserved and can be passed on to the prospect's heirs or used for other investment or business opportunities that may arise in the future.

- Third, it guarantees that a beneficiary will not outlive the benefits of the insurance proceeds and other capital if the principal is not invaded or if the assumed interest rate is achieved.

Despite its advantages, however, capital conservation is not appropriate for all prospects. Since it assumes current, not guaranteed, interest rates, capital conservation offers no assurance that the prospect's precise economic goals will be accomplished.

Capital Conservation Method

IF...
- client needs/wants long-term security
- inflation is a primary concern
- survivors are young and dependent
- flexibility (liquidity) is needed
- Social Security is not to be used in determining needs

THEN... create interest-only income from a fixed pool of capital.

DO...
1. determine present unfunded cash needs
2. determine unfunded annual income needs
3. agree on assumed net interest rate
4. establish new capital required to solve income need (divide unfunded annual income by assumed net interest rate)
5. add item 1 and item 4 totals

RESULT life insurance amount required to create a capital pool to fund immediate cash needs and ongoing income needs without depleting capital

Case Study—The following case study demonstrates capital conservation in the context of a more fully developed total-needs situation. It is the case of Dave and Jean Woodley. Dave is 40 and Jean is 38 years old. They have two children, a boy age 7 and a girl age 9. Dave earns $50,000 per year as a bank officer of a medium-sized bank and Jean earns $30,000 as a secondary school teacher. During the information-gathering portion of the interview, you have determined that Dave and Jean would like to concentrate on the financial consequences of Jean's death. They believe they have taken adequate precautions in the event that Dave dies.

The couple decided that $20,000 is the amount needed to meet Jean's final expenses. Final expenses consist of funeral costs, administration costs, last medical bills, and one month's income to cover the time needed to file the necessary Social Security forms. Their outstanding debt is $12,000 and consists primarily of an auto loan and balances due on credit cards.

Their home mortgage balance is $70,000. Although Dave and Jean do not feel it would be financially prudent to liquidate the mortgage at death due to a favorable interest rate, they believe it is appropriate to establish a mortgage fund. If economic conditions change, this fund would have the flexibility to pay off the debt. Both think that a $15,000 emergency fund would be adequate and that $80,000 would meet their objectives for their children's educations.

Jean has $60,000 of group term life insurance from employment (two-times salary), but has no personally owned coverage. Their joint bank account has a balance of $3,000. In addition, they own $2,000 of common stock, and Jean's TDA account is currently $5,000. This means that $70,000 will be available if Jean dies.

You discuss in detail the family income needs in the event of Jean's death. Both Jean and Dave agree that 70 percent of their income would be appropriate. In the event of Jean's death, $1,750 (.70 x $30,000 ÷ 12 = $1,750) per month is needed to replace her income. When you are sure that the financial data is accurate and that there is a clear understanding of the goals the Woodleys have set for themselves, you can perform the following financial analysis.

I. First, determine if there is a surplus or deficit between the cash needs that Dave and Jean have set for themselves and the total assets available at Jean's death. If there is a surplus, this money can be used to provide income. If there is a deficit, additional capital will be required to offset it. In this case, the Woodley's have decided that $197,000 (the sum of the Woodleys' needs) is necessary to meet their financial goals. However, only $70,000 will be available at Jean's death. This leaves a $127,000 deficit.

$197,000 – $70,000 = $127,000 shortfall

II. Second, focus on the income requirement of the family. To do this, the income period should be broken into two distinct areas. First is the dependency period: that period of time from the date of death to the youngest child's age 16. The second period, or *blackout period*, is the time from the youngest child's 16th birthday to the surviving spouse's age 60, during which no survivor income benefits are available from Social Security. Since the surviving spouse will continue to be employed, you may wish to use his normal retirement age of 67, ignoring the end of the blackout period. To determine if there is a deficit or surplus of income, review all other income sources that may include the spouse's separate property, pension benefits, or government survivor benefit programs.

A. First, examine the dependency period in the Woodleys' case. The income objective to replace Jean's income was $1,750. This was 70 percent of Jean's current monthly gross income. On the basis of Jean's employment record, the family would receive $1,040 per month in Social Security benefits during the dependency period. Jean has no other income source.

Step 1: Subtract from the monthly objective of $1,750 the income available from all sources (in our case $1,040). This produces a deficit of $710 per month. To determine the annual amount of income necessary, multiply $710 x 12 for a total of $8,520 per year.

Next, determine the amount of capital necessary to produce $8,520 a year at a given interest rate. To determine this amount, use a 6-percent interest assumption as a rate representative of what they can expect to receive. After some discussion Dave and Jean agree that 6 percent is appropriate. Take the deficit of $8,520 and divide it by .06, equaling $142,000. That is, $142,000 invested at 6 percent net after taxes will provide $8,520 per year to meet their monthly deficit.

$$\$8{,}520 \div .06 = \$142{,}000$$

B Next, examine the blackout period. In most cases, the income necessary during the blackout period is less than the amount required during the dependency period as it assumes the children are no longer living at home. Jean and Dave agree that this would probably be true in their case as well. They decide that instead of $1,750 to replace Jean's income, $1,000 per month would be enough.

If your clients have problems determining the amount of money necessary during the blackout period, a good rule of thumb to use would be between 45 percent and 60 percent of current income. Since Dave will be receiving no Social Security benefits during this period and there are no other sources of income available, Dave's deficit will be $1,000 per month. However, the $142,000 that was provided to meet the dependency period continues to produce $710 per month, making the actual deficit $290 per month.

$$\$1,000 - \$710 = \$290$$

To continue, calculate the amount of capital required to offset the income deficit during the blackout period. First, multiply the $290 monthly deficit times 12 to find the annual deficit.

$$\$290 \text{ x } 12 = \$3,480$$

Divide this annual deficit by the same interest rate assumption used in the previous calculation.

$$\$3,480 \div .06 = \$58,000$$

Because this capital will not be necessary for income until the youngest child age 7 is 16, the $58,000 can be discounted for 9 years. $58,000 discounted for 9 years is:

$$\$58,000 \text{ x } .5919 = \$34,330$$

To find the appropriate discount factor refer to a discounted value or compound discount table.

Note: This capital conservation example does not take into consideration the Social Security benefits that the surviving spouse would receive at retirement. In this case, Social Security retirement benefits would become a hedge against inflation.

III. To determine the amount of additional capital required to meet the Woodleys' goals, take the cash need of $127,000 and add it to the income needs of $34,330 for the blackout period and

$142,000 for the dependency period. The insurance need is $303,330.

$$\$127,000 + \$34,330 + \$142,000 = \$303,330$$

In cases where a prospect cannot purchase the total amount of life insurance needed, even on an all-term basis, encourage the prospect to begin a program that will fulfill at least some of the family's needs. This may mean funding current income needs now and making additional purchases later to meet some of the discretionary cash needs of education or mortgage. When a family is able to purchase only enough insurance to meet dominant needs, make it clear that this is simply an initial purchase, the first in a series of regularly scheduled purchases to ultimately achieve the family goals.

Dave and Jean Woodley
Financial Analysis

I.	**Cash Requirements:**		
	Total Cash Resources	$ 70,000	
	Total Cash Obligations	–197,000	
	Surplus or (Deficit)		($ 127,000)
II.	**Income Requirements:**		
	A. Dependency Period:		
	Income Objective (70% of Annual Income, $30,000)	$ 21,000	
	Social Security ($1,040 per month x 12 months)	$ 12,480	
	Income Produced by Cash Surplus at 6% Rate	–NONE	
	Surplus or Deficit	($ 8,520)	
	Capital Needed to Offset Deficit at 6% Rate ($8,520 divided by .06)		$ 142,000
	B. Blackout Period:		
	Income Objective	$ 12,000	
	Social Security	NONE	
	Other Income	NONE	
	Annual Shortage Already Provided For	8,520	
	Surplus or Deficit	($ 3,480)	
	Capital Needed to Offset Deficit at 6% Rate ($3,480 ÷ .06 = $58,000), Discounted for 9 Years, Capital Needed Today ($58,000 x .5919)		$ 34,330
III.	**Capital Required:**		
	Cash Requirements Deficit	$ 127,000	
	Capital Needed for Dependency Period Income	142,000	
	Capital Needed for Blackout Period Income	34,330	
	Total Additional Capital Needed:		$ 303,330

Footnote: *This calculation does not consider inflation. A 6-percent net after tax rate, at 3-percent inflation, would result in a net after tax of 3 percent. In this example, the insurance need would double by including the effects of inflation.*

Selecting a Method

When and how to use the capital conservation method will be determined by the prospect's situation, objectives, and feelings. In the discussion that follows, look at factors that qualify prospects for capital conservation and suggest how you can present this method in your sales interviews.

The main feature of capital conservation, of course, is that it conserves the capital used to provide the desired income. If there is a clear reason not to deplete the capital, the prospect will probably favor the capital conservation method regardless of income level or need for life insurance protection.

What are some of the reasons a prospect would have for not depleting capital? Perhaps the most common would be the desire to bequeath the money to someone else. Anyone with a family or someone with a favorite charity would be a prospect for capital conservation. Other reasons involve wanting a hedge against some turn of events that could change the basic assumptions of the plan. A sharp increase in inflation or a decrease in Social Security benefits are two such examples. In either event, keeping the capital intact would mean that funds would be available to make up any shortfall in income to the beneficiary. Capital conservation could mean the difference between success and failure in planning for an uncertain future.

Offer A Choice

In most situations you will want to give prospects a choice—capital conservation or capital distribution. In others, however, you should strongly recommend capital conservation. These situations include young couples with several children, little or no cash savings, and a plan that may include a large percentage of term insurance. Preserving the capital could be very important for them, especially if the insured parent dies early. Other capital conservation situations are those in which the prospects clearly feel that it would be unthinkable for the surviving spouse to remarry, or if they reveal by the way they talk about their finances that they are highly conservative and would not want to tamper with the family's "Pot of Gold."

Presentation Language

In approaching prospects such as Dave and Jean Woodley with the capital conservation method, you might wish to explain in this way how it works and why it will benefit them:

"There are a couple of ways to determine how much capital you will need today to provide the income you want for your family if one or both of you dies. With both approaches, life insurance can make the money available when it's needed; but how to calculate the amount of insurance you will need to meet your objectives is a decision you may want to think about.

One method takes the life insurance proceeds and provides income for the beneficiary in a way that uses up both the principal and the interest by the end of a certain period. It is a plan to deplete the pool of money.

The other method generates income by using only the interest earned on the principal. The pool is never spent, except in emergencies. It is your hedge against inflation. The principal remains intact; it's never touched and can be part of your legacy to your family or used as a gift to your favorite charity—whatever is most appropriate at the time.

As with most things, though, there is a trade-off between the so-called capital distribution and capital conservation methods. The capital distribution method generates income from a smaller pool of money, since it draws on both principal and interest to produce income. This means that if we calculate the amount of life insurance you need under this method, the figure is going to be less than it would be if we used the capital conservation approach. To conserve your capital, you would have to have enough to produce needed income using only the interest."

However, you do not want to take the chance that your income will run out while it is still needed—something that is possible if the principal is used to make up part of your income. Keep in mind, too, that the life insurance used to create additional capital is also going to build cash values and other guaranteed benefits. You will be accumulating greater cash values that you will have available for retirement income or to borrow against in an emergency. Either way, you will be dollars ahead with the capital conservation approach. I suggest that we use it in making our calculations."

Two Quick, Rough Calculation Formulas

An experienced advisor will tell you there are two quick formulas that can come within a few thousand dollars of any fact-finder or computer program. When calculating a prospect's insurance needs, accuracy and individual goals should always be the basis of any recommendations that the advisor makes. Practicality, though, will dictate occasions when on-the-scene projections are necessary to open the more thoughtful discussion with the prospect that will lead to the correct sale. Try these formulas:

1. 10 x gross income
2. 5 x gross income + mortgage + debts (+ final expenses + college fund)*

* The expenses in parentheses give some room to individualize the rough calculation. These could include the mortgage on a second home or anything else that might be important to the prospect.

Understanding Employee Benefits

The Role of Employee Benefit Programs

It is important when asking applicable fact-finding questions to be familiar with employer-sponsored employee benefit and retirement plans. Employee benefits normally play a significant role in an employee's overall financial situation. Good data gathering must address the prospect's benefit plans through current and previous employers. Find out what type of group life insurance and retirement plan balances the prospect has that may be included in the insurance analysis. Most people want the insurance they have from work to be included in their personal planning. It is important to determine the job history and future of the client and spouse. It would be regrettable to count on job-related benefits if the prospect or spouse does not plan to stay with his or her company, or if either's job or company is unstable.

Employee benefits have gone from being "fringe" to making up about 40 percent of an employee's total compensation. Today, salary alone is not a sufficient reason for people to take and keep a job. Good benefits are a critical part of the total employment package. Most people depend on employee benefits as the foundation of their financial welfare and a major component of their financial plan. Unfortunately, although most people depend on these benefits, they have a vague or poor understanding of what benefits they have and lack understanding of important details about how these benefits work. It is helpful to ask them to bring their employee benefit handbooks to the initial interview or fact-finding interview so you can review and evaluate their benefit packages. This will be important information when developing an overall plan.

Employee benefits generally fall into the following five categories:

- Legally required programs for government programs, including Social Security, Medicare, unemployment compensation insurance, workers' compensation insurance, and temporary disability insurance

- Payments for private insurance and retirement plans, including the cost of establishing and maintaining such plans, such as pensions and profit-sharing plans, life, disability, medical, and dental insurance
- Payments for time not worked, including paid vacations, holidays, jury service, family and maternity leave, and National Guard duty
- Extra cash payments, such as educational assistance, moving expenses, motivational awards and bonuses
- Cost of services to employees, including day care, financial planning programs, subsidized meals, wellness programs, counseling services, company parties and picnics, and free parking

Eligibility for Benefits

Covered Classifications—An employee's benefits pertain to his or her job classification. Some benefits may include all employees, while others may apply to specific job classes or have other requirements, such as length of service.

Contributory versus Noncontributory Plans—The cost of employee benefits programs is not always totally paid by the employer. If the company offers benefits on a *contributory* basis, the employee and employer typically share the cost. The employee must pay some part of the premium, normally through payroll deduction. An employer may offer such benefits as group term life insurance for dependents, health coverage, or some pension benefits on a contributory basis. Other benefits, such as group term life for employees, may be *noncontributory*, where the employer pays the entire cost.

A typical example is where the employer pays the cost of the employee's medical insurance, but the employee would have to pay some or the entire premium for dependents. Employer contributions are generally tax-deductible to the company. Generally noncontributory plans must be made available to all eligible employees. Contributory plans must be offered to all eligible employees, but participation is optional.

Full-Time Employment—Most types of employee benefits limit eligibility to full-time employees. Some benefits may be provided to part-time employees, although these are usually smaller or more limited than those provided to full-time employees.

Probationary Periods—Employee benefits plans may contain a probationary period that must be satisfied before an employee is eligible for coverage. Such probationary periods are usually 1 or 3 months and rarely exceed 6 months.

Insurability—While most employee benefits are issued without individual evidence of insurability, in some instances underwriting practices require evidence of insurability. This commonly occurs when an employee fails to elect coverage under a contributory plan and later wants coverage (referred to as a late entrant) or when an employee is eligible for and elects a large amount of coverage. Evidence of insurability is also frequently required in voluntary benefit plans.

Termination of Coverage—Employee benefit plans specify when coverage for an employee (or dependent) terminates. The coverage for any covered person terminates automatically (subject to any provisions for a continuation or conversion of coverage) when

- the employee terminates employment, including retirement
- the employee ceases to be eligible (for example, employee becomes part-time or changes job classification)
- the policyowner (employer) or insurance company terminates a group insurance contract
- any required contribution by the employee has not been made (generally because the employee has notified the employer to cease the required payroll deduction)

Insurance Benefits

Group Life Insurance

A Bureau of Labor Statistics survey showed that some form of group term insurance covered about 85 percent of all surveyed employees. Regrettably, this is the only life insurance that many people have. Many think it is adequate, when it is not. This is where an insurance advisor can provide a valuable service.

The most prevalent plan is group term life insurance. Group term is one-year renewable term insurance, which may be extended to cover the employee's spouse and eligible children. The widespread use of group term is due to its ability to provide employers with low-cost death benefits for the protection of the employees and dependents. This type of coverage, however, has limited guarantees, no permanence, and little flexibility. Benefits for group life may be based on a multiple of earnings schedule or a specified dollar amount. The coverage ends when the employee discontinues employment, and it is often reduced or eliminated when an active employee reaches certain ages, such as 65 or 70, or in retirement. Group term insurance contracts often provide additional insurance benefits in the form of supplemental life insurance (employee can purchase additional amounts of term life insurance), accidental death and dismemberment, and dependent life insurance.

Section 79 of the Internal Revenue Code gives favorable tax treatment to group term life insurance plans. Under Section 79, the cost of the first $50,000 Of employer-provided coverage is not taxed to the employee. The cost of coverage in excess of $50,000, minus any employee contributions for the entire amount of coverage, represents taxable income to the employee, determined by a government table called the Uniform Premium Table I.

Voluntary Payroll Deduction Insurance Plans

The employer may offer, on a voluntary basis, a term or permanent life insurance plan that employees can pay for through *payroll deduction*. Benefit providers may offer, in addition to life insurance, a menu of insurance plans such as disability, cancer, dental, long-term care, deferred annuities and mutual funds. The key advantages of these plans is the convenience of payroll deduction for premium payments, liberalized underwriting compared to similar coverage in the individual marketplace, often lower costs than in the individual market for similar coverage, and portability of coverage (employees can take the coverage when they leave their employment).

Group Accidental Death and Dismemberment (AD&D)

In the event of an accidental death, this coverage would provide a benefit in addition to the group insurance plan, or as an alternative if there were no group life. This coverage is often referred to as "double indemnity" since the amount is usually in the same amount and in addition to the base group coverage.

AD&D also provides defined dismemberment benefits. For example, the loss of a hand by severance at or above the wrist, or the loss of a foot by severance at or above the ankle, and so on, would pay a certain dollar amount. This type of protection has limitations similar to those found in individual AD&D plans. Many in the insurance field suggest that because of the accidental cause and means provisions of this coverage, it should not be considered life insurance and should not be considered in the insurance needs analysis.

Disability Income

Group disability income protection provides for the partial replacement of earnings lost during disability caused by accident or illness. Benefits are determined by the income earner's normal pay. A weekly or monthly benefit is provided. Income benefits start after a fixed number of days absent from work due to injury or sickness and continue during disability up to a maximum time period. Generally, short-term policies have a benefit limit of 10, 13, or 26 weeks, often designed to coordinate with Social Security eligibility rules. Long-term disability policies generally begin after 6 months and may provide benefits until age 65. In some cases, lifetime benefits are available when disability results from an accident. If the employer pays the premium, the benefits are taxable to the employee. If the employee pays the premiums, the benefits are tax-free.

Long-term Care

In 1996, Congress passed several acts of major importance to those who market or purchase long-term care insurance. Long-term care became a tax-qualified product. As a result, long-term care contract provisions were required to meet certain specifications.

To be considered a tax-qualified product, a long-term care contract

- must be guaranteed renewable
- can not have any cash surrender value except for specified refunds of premiums or dividends
- may not duplicate Medicare benefits
- may only cover long-term care services that include necessary and rehabilitative services and maintenance or personal care services required by a chronically ill individual
- must also meet the requirements of the Consumer Protection Provisions

If these conditions are met, then the business may deduct the premiums it pays for qualified long-term care insurance. If the employee pays the premiums, then he or she may deduct them as unreimbursed medical expenses. In order to do this, the employee must itemize his or her medical expenses and meet the 7.5 percent threshold for the medical expense deduction.

Medical Expense Insurance

Medical expense insurance is arguably the most important type of insurance protection to most Americans and the type of protection that causes the most anxiety if it is lost or unaffordable. Group medical expense coverage is not as standardized as other types of group insurance. Coverage may be provided through Blue Cross and Blue Shield plans, health maintenance organizations (HMOs), and preferred-provider organizations. Skyrocketing costs of providing medical expense benefits over the last few decades has led to changes in coverage and plan design aimed at controlling costs. This has led to the continued shift to managed care plans and provisions, and a blending of traditional services into the managed care model.

Medical expense coverage is offered under two basic models: service and indemnity. Service plans operate essentially on a prepaid basis for covered benefits. Traditional health plans indemnify or reimburse the insured for paid covered expenses. From the insured's viewpoint there is often little difference in the two in terms of benefits because most providers will accept an assignment to the doctor or hospital and the insurer will pay the provider directly. The insured then would have to pay only the excess of the bill not covered by insurance. Physicians and hospitals that participate in service plans agree to the standards established by plan, usually at a prescribed fee level. Participants may be allowed to see only physicians in the plan to qualify for their coverage use and payment.

Employer contributions for an employee's or dependent's medical expense coverage do not create any income tax liability for an employee. Benefits are not taxable to an employee except when they exceed any medical expenses incurred, an extremely unlikely event. If the employee pays the premiums, then he or she may deduct them as unreimbursed medical expenses, itemized on Schedule A of Form 1040, subject to the 7.5 percent threshold for the medical expense deduction.

Blue Cross/Blue Shield—These geographical organizations typically specialize in providing medical coverage through service and managed care plans. Traditional Blue Cross provides hospital expense coverage while Blue Shield provides coverage for surgical expenses and physicians visits. They offer two types of contracts. In one, the more traditional plan, specific services are provided to a participant who has paid a premium. The participant can then go to a hospital or physician who participates in the Blues plan. In the other type, the Blues contract with physicians and hospitals and reimburse them for services provided. The expenses are usually paid directly to the providers.

Managed Care Plans

True managed care plans have five basic characteristics:

1. controlled access to providers and specialist
2. comprehensive case management, including utilization review
3. encouragement of preventative care and healthy lifestyles
4. sharing by the medical care providers in the financial consequences of medical decisions
5. the careful selection and monitoring of medical providers

Health Maintenance Organizations—HMOs hire physicians who agree to provide health care to patients who enroll in the HMO. There are two types. In one the physician is an employee of the HMO. In the other type, independent practice physicians are reimbursed for treating HMO patients based on a capitation fee (set fee to provide services for each member using that doctor as a primary care physician (PCP) and/or a fee-for-service basis. HMOs emphasize treatment by primary care physicians (PCPs) who provide family medicine and serve as gatekeepers to medical care and control access to specialists. HMOs emphasize control of medical expenses.

Preferred Provider Organizations—PPOs are similar in concept to HMOs. They differ in that they provide service on a fee-for-service basis subject to a payment schedule, not by prepaid (capitation) agreement. PPOs are groups of physicians and hospitals that contract with employers, insurance companies, or third-party administrators to provide health care services at reduced fees. Enrollees do not have to use the PPO physicians or facilities. They can alternatively go outside the PPO network or use the plan's regular group medical providers. They can make a choice each time health care is necessary. The PPO offers a lower deductible and co-payment, giving participants an incentive to use the PPO providers. However, broader types of care may be available outside the group insurance plan.

Point-of-Service Plans—POSs are really a combination of HMO and PPO plans. Participants in the plan elect, at the time medical treatment is needed, whether to receive treatment within the plan's tightly managed network, usually an HMO, or outside of the network. PPOs and POSs are very similar, but POSs offer a higher degree of managed care than found in most PPOs.

Dental Expense Insurance

One of the fastest-growing forms of employer-sponsored benefits is dental expense insurance. In 2000, it was estimated that more than 175 million individuals were covered by workplace-based dental benefit plans. To a large extent, dental insurance plans have been patterned after medical expense plans, and they contain similar, if not identical, provisions. For example, as dental plans adopt more managed care provisions, a greater emphasis is given and greater benefits are provided for preventative care. This has resulted in a greater percentage of persons receiving preventive care, and a decrease in the number of persons requiring care for more serious dental problems.

These plans typically provide coverage for most routine diagnostic (oral exams and X-rays) and preventative (teeth cleaning and fluoride treatment) dental procedures. Most other types of dental treatments are covered in varying degrees. Orthodontics, if offered, is usually a limited benefit and may even be available only to the employee.

Additional Health Coverage from Carve-out Plans

The use of specialty providers, using managed care techniques, is becoming more common, as health benefit plans realize they cannot provide the quality of care or manage costs to the degree of specialty providers. Such benefits as vision care, prescription drugs, mental health insurance, and substance abuse treatment are on the list of health coverage provided in recent years to an increasing number of workers, as is health coverage for retirees. This latter protection is especially valuable in view of the trend toward early retirement and the fact that Medicare does not begin until age 65.

Other Employee Benefits

Employee Stock Options

Employee stock options are another form of employee benefit, replacing the annual cash bonus approach in many organizations. Under an employee stock option, the employee is able to pay today's market price for shares in the company at a future date. Thus, if the price per share is higher when the option is exercised, the employee pays the original option amount. If the plan is qualified, no income tax is due on the transaction until the shares are sold. In a nonqualified employee stock option plan, the employee would realize taxable income when the option is exercised.

Salary Continuation and Deferred Compensation Plans

These are two other popular forms of employer-sponsored benefits. Under a *salary continuation* plan, the employee's salary is continued at retirement, at death, or at disability, and the employee is not taxed on the income until it is received.

Under a *deferred compensation* plan, a portion of the employee's current or future compensation is postponed until the time of death, disability, or retirement. This arrangement shelters income until the money is received.

These two plans are nonqualified, which means an employer's contribution dollars do not create a tax deduction for the company. Later, when the benefits are paid out to the employee or family there would be a tax deduction to the employer as the money is dispersed. Because the plans are nonqualified, the employer has some latitude and may be selective in deciding which employees will be offered these plans.

Work/Life Benefits

With the many demographic changes over the last few decades, employee benefits have changed to meet the changing attitudes and needs of the changing workforce. Much of this has to do with more women in the workforce, with career goals, and with a changing mindset of employees towards family and quality of life issues. As the workforce becomes more diverse, work/life issues become broader and more complex. Some benefits that are becoming increasingly common are

- family and medical leave
- flexible work hours
- telecommuting
- dependent care (child and elder care)
- educational assistance
- group legal services
- financial planning

Cafeteria Plans

The employee benefit picture has been changing in recent years. One major fact that employers have had to deal with is that yesterday's benefit packages do not fit the lifestyle situations or meet the needs of today's workers. Consider the effect that the increase in two-income families has had on benefit plans. Typically, under traditional fixed-benefit plans, many married wage earners have almost exactly the same benefits as their spouses. Generally, to prevent duplication of group health coverage, only one plan will pay benefits, with the other acting as a secondary plan.

Further, the increasing frequency of divorces, second marriages, delayed parenthood, and a growing acceptance of alternative lifestyles have all combined to make many traditional benefit plans inefficient and obsolete. Flexibility is needed in arranging benefits to suit the changing needs of employees. For example, a single parent or a family with a large mortgage and other long-term debts needs more life insurance than might a worker who is approaching retirement and is concerned with either continuing medical coverage or creating additional retirement income. One answer to this complex situation has been found in the development of cafeteria plans.

These plans let employees decide which benefits they want and in what proportions, based on their current needs and circumstances. Within certain limits, they are able to spend their benefit dollars in whatever way makes sense to them at the time, and to revise their benefit packages as their needs change. This enables working spouses to coordinate their benefits, thus eliminating overlap or duplication of coverage. Many plans allow employees to purchase additional benefits on a payroll deduction basis.

Flexible Spending Accounts are a type of cafeteria plan commonly used among smaller employers. The participating employees elect to have their salaries reduced each month. The employer then uses these funds to pay for employee benefits that otherwise would be purchased with after-tax dollars. The typical benefits include health insurance, medical expenses not otherwise covered, and dependent-care expenses. This is a way for employees to pay for noncovered medical expenses on a pretax basis.

One of the chief concerns employers have with cafeteria plans is with the cost of installing and administrating complicated, individually tailored benefit packages. The cafeteria plan is an expensive process and so, generally, only larger companies have introduced it to date. They are finding, however, that if carefully planned and maintained, cafeteria plans can live up to their potential.

Sales Opportunities in Employee Benefits

A concern that employers share about their employee benefit plans is communicating the value of these benefits to their employees. In many instances, this is an area in which life insurance advisors have an opportunity to provide valuable service and open new markets. By offering to explain the benefit program to employees, advisors may have an opportunity to discuss insurance and financial planning with a potentially large audience of prospects. This could provide a reason to discuss with the business owner many possible personal and business planning ideas.

An employer can undermine his own efforts if he fails to let the employees know the full extent of the benefits available to them. Most employees are not only surprised, but also more appreciative when made aware of the employer's cost for these plans. Many will realize how much these benefits would cost if they had to pay for them out of their own pockets. The better the communication of employee benefits in the company, the more useful the benefit package will be as an incentive for employee loyalty and high morale.

In larger companies, employee benefit managers, trained in this specialized field, are able to develop effective employee benefit communication programs. These companies often present annual reports that outline medical protection, current and future retirement benefits, and the other benefits offered to employees, including sick leave, paid holidays, and vacation time.

Smaller companies do not have the ability to provide this type of program on a regular basis. In these cases, the life insurance advisor has the opportunity to sell his communication services to the business owner. Advisors often conduct meetings with groups of employees to explain a plan and answer questions. Employers are grateful for the help.

Such a step could be a path into a new market for you, the business market. A well-informed and ambitious advisor would be able to use his or her services to gain the confidence of the businessowner and be offered the opportunity to become an advisor for the company's insurance programs. Let us explore in more detail some of the personal insurance sales opportunities that may develop from your knowledge of an employee benefit program.

The Recommended Approach to Employees

"Through your company-sponsored plan and Social Security benefits, you have the foundation of a solid financial security program including life and health insurance and retirement benefits.

(Prospect), it is possible to build on that foundation, to add individual protection that provides security and comfort for your family. For most of us, in fact, it is only by adding this personal, guaranteed protection available through life insurance, disability income protection, and retirement savings that our financial security is fully completed."

Personal Insurance Sales

By becoming familiar with a prospect's employer-sponsored benefits, you can coordinate the benefits revealed in your life insurance planning with the family's Social Security benefits, present life insurance, and any new protection they may need.

If one or both income-earning spouses are covered under a cafeteria plan, you can review their respective benefits to be certain that they are being used in the most efficient way to avoid possible waste or overlapping coverage.

Once you are knowledgeable about the benefit packages available from these prospects' employers, you will have information that may be valuable to other employees of those companies. Ask your prospects, "Whom else in your company should I be speaking with about these benefits?" You can then begin targeting your marketing activities to other employees of that firm.

If you are successful in developing a market among a company's employees, you may want to approach the employer directly to offer to work with the other employees. This enables you to assist the employer in a couple of ways: first, you provide an answer to the common problem of providing clear, consolidated benefit information to the firm's employees; and, second, you help the employer add one more item to the employee benefit package: professional life insurance planning for each employee.

What if I leave this company?

"Yes, most of us have some life insurance under our company's group policies. Like our medical protection, sick leave, and vacations, these are valuable benefits provided by our employers. But, did you realize that unless you are guaranteed continued employment with your present employer, you really cannot count on your group life insurance being there when you need it? Do you have any guarantees like that?

If you were to leave your job today and start your own business, or if you were laid off, or if the company went under, you would have the option of converting your group policy to permanent, individual insurance during a limited period. If that happens 15 years from now, you would have to pay the premium at your age then—I'll show you what that might be . . ."

Work Site Marketing Sales

Working with businesses this way can also lead to the sale of life insurance through the mass marketing/payroll deduction method. Many insurance companies offer a special mass-marketed individual permanent life product, as whole life or universal life, for this purpose. These plans typically feature simplified underwriting, level premiums and face amounts, and inexpensive dependent coverage. The employee personally owns them, so upon leaving that employer or retiring the employee may continue them. Most are sold on a money-purchase basis; that is, the insured employees decide how much to set aside each week from their paychecks for life insurance. The amount of insurance these premium increments purchase depends on the insured's age.

After the initial sale to the employer to offer the plan, mass marketed policies are made available to the employees through individual (preferably) or group sessions. Each employee is asked to sign up for the plan, or decline it, using special enrollment cards. The plan is then administered by the employer, who makes the deductions from the participants' pay and forwards the money to the insurance company in one check on a periodic statement bill.

This is a highly effective, cost-efficient way to sell life insurance. It also builds solid relationships with the employer and enables you to do further life insurance planning with the employees on a selective basis.

Group Insurance/Cross-Selling

Many advisors approach businessowners initially about their group life and health insurance plans. They find that employers are often more willing to discuss group coverage than they are to go into their other personal insurance needs, especially if they are not familiar with the advisor. Group insurance is a price-sensitive product and employers frequently shop their group plans. Switching from one plan to another is not uncommon, even on an annual basis for some companies.

Businesses employing fewer than 50 people will probably be your best prospects if you are working primarily in the personal market. In dealing with small groups it will be easier to see the decision-makers. They will be more used to dealing with individual advisors rather than with home offices or brokerage managers of insurance companies. Your present clients who are employed by smaller companies may be able to refer you to their employers if you have not made a direct approach by mail and phone.

Your objective in approaching small business owners about group insurance is two-fold: you want to sell the group case; but more importantly, you want to make a crossover sale of personal life insurance planning to the owners (and employees). This can be the way to build solid relationships with these clients. But be prepared to provide good service, as this is a demanding product.

As you develop rapport and trust with businessowner clients, you can lay the foundation for helping them in the future with their business insurance needs. These needs include the orderly disposition of a business interest at the owner's death (buy-sell agreements), key executive coverage and other employee incentive plans, salary continuation and deferred compensation, and the company's pension or profit-sharing plan. You will, of course, need to acquire the necessary knowledge before approaching your businessowner client about business insurance needs. Along the way, you can work with experienced advisors and your company's staff as you gain expertise in these areas.

Workers' Compensation

Workers' compensation provides weekly cash benefits and necessary medical care to a worker who is disabled because of accidental injury arising out of, or in the book of, employment, or because of an occupational disease. When death results from such injury or disease, weekly cash benefits are also payable to dependents as a survivor's income payment. Workers' compensation is regulated on a state-by-state basis, and the benefits and rules vary.

The employer or the workers' compensation insurance company pays all benefits, including cash benefit and bills for medical, osteopathic, surgical, hospital, dental, and chiropractic care. Weekly cash benefits for total disability are usually two-thirds of wages lost (minimums and maximums are stipulated in each state). No compensation is payable for the first 7 days unless the disability exceeds 14 days. There is no maximum on the aggregate amount of benefits. Death benefits as survivor benefits may be payable to a dependent spouse and children up to a stipulated maximum per week for a disabled worker who dies of a covered injury. The state workers' compensation board usually provides for a rehabilitation program for disabled workers to reduce disability as much as possible and to help the worker return to work as soon as possible.

Employee Retirement Plans

As with employee benefits, employer-sponsored retirement plans typically make up a major part of an employee's retirement plan. Knowledge of this area and its benefits will help you in creating an overall plan for your client.

Qualified Retirement Plans

Qualified retirement plans are employer-sponsored plans that meet federal tax regulations to qualify for tax-deductible contributions and tax-deferred growth. Retirement plans can be grouped into the two major categories discussed below.

Defined-benefit Pensions—Under a defined-benefit plan, retirement benefits are determined by a formula. A contribution is calculated requiring annual deposits based on the benefits promised and the number of years in the accumulation period. Defined-benefit plans are not as common as they once were. If the company goes out of business, an organization called the Pension Benefit Guarantee Corporation ensures benefits up to $1,500 a month. Generally, most plans today base benefits on the worker's final average pay. Benefit payments are calculated by using a proportion of income earned during the worker's final years of service, then averaging that figure and multiplying it by the number of years of service. Typically, most plans average only the last 5 years of service.

Defined-contribution Pensions—Under defined-contribution plans, annual contributions are determined by a contribution formula applied to an employee's earnings. The future benefits paid to a participant depend on the size of the contributions made and the length of service under the plan. Defined-contribution plans make no guarantees about the size of the participant's monthly pension benefit, but will accumulate based on the contribution amount and earning on those deposits.

Profit Sharing—In one type of defined-contribution plan, a profit sharing plan, the employer agrees to contribute part of the company's profits for the benefit of its employees. Contributions are limited to an amount equal to 15 percent of participating payroll. Typically, the contributions will be held in a trust fund for distribution at death, disability, or retirement. This amount or percentage can change annually.

401(k) Plans—The 401(k) plan has been perhaps the most popular retirement savings idea in recent times. Typically, employees contribute to their own retirement accounts with before-tax dollars. The use of tax-deferred salary can lower an employee's current income tax. It allows employees to shelter part of their income and accumulate earnings tax-deferred until retirement. In some 401(k) plans, the employer also contributes to the employee's fund, thus significantly increasing the amount saved.

SIMPLE Accounts—The most recent vehicle used for qualified retirement plans is the SIMPLE (Savings Incentive Match Plan for Employees) Account. SIMPLE Accounts can be established only on a qualified salary reduction basis. This means that the employees elect to have contributions made to the plan or to receive the contribution in cash.

Like other qualified plans, there are certain vesting, participation, and administrative provisions that must be met. The amount of the election cannot exceed $6,000 per year. The employer must make matching contributions or certain nonelective contributions. If the employer chooses to match the contribution, the match is generally up to 3 percent of the employees' compensation. There are special requirements if a lower match is desired. If the nonelective contribution formula is chosen, the employer may simply contribute 2 percent of each eligible employee's compensation.

All contributions must be fully vested. Contributions are not subject to income tax, and are subject to penalties for early withdrawal. This plan is available to all businesses with less than 100 employees and every employee must be allowed to make the salary reduction election or to receive nonelective contributions. A SIMPLE Account may be set up in the form of an IRA or a 401(k).

Simplified Employee Pension—A SEP is a retirement plan that uses an IRA as a receptacle for contributions. This plan is simple and very inexpensive to administer, so it is attractive to small employers. No trust accounting is needed, because individual IRAs are set up for each employee in the plan. The contributions are fully vested immediately and the benefit is the IRA account balance. All eligible employees must be covered. Employer contributions are determined year to year, but must apply to all employees as a level percentage of compensation.

403(b) Tax Sheltered Annuity—A 403(b) can only be sold to nonprofit 501(c)(3) organizations, such as tax-exempt organizations and schools. Also referred to as a tax-deferred annuity (TDA), or tax-sheltered annuity (TSA), these plans are similar to 401(k) plans. They permit employees to defer tax on income by allowing before-tax contributions to an individual's account. Employers may make matching contributions.

Social Security

Americans have come to rely on Social Security as the pillar of support for their retirement years. The program was designed so workers use the earnings from their working years to provide income when they retire for themselves and their families. Other benefits of the program provide for survivor benefits of those participating workers who die and leave dependent families. The disability income benefits protect those who are severely incapacitated by providing an ongoing income.

Social Security provides a minimum "foundation of protection" or "safety net" for retired workers, and for workers and their families who face a loss of income due to disability or the death of a family wage earner. About 150 million workers, over 90 percent of the U.S. workforce, are covered by Social Security and almost 45 million people receive benefits from Social Security.

Social Security is important to financial advisors because it forms the foundation on which employee benefit programs and individual insurance plans are built. It is impossible to do a proper job of personal insurance planning or financial planning, without taking Social Security into consideration.

General Characteristics of Social Security

Payroll Taxes Fund Program

All the benefits of the Social Security program and Part A of Medicare are financed through a system of payroll and self-employment taxes paid by all workers covered under these programs. The tax for each eligible employee is shared fifty-fifty by the worker and the employer. These taxes are often referred to as *FICA* taxes because they are imposed under the Federal Insurance Contributions Act. For self-employed persons, the tax is the combined rate for employers and employees.

Two taxes provide the funds necessary to meet present commitments. The old age, survivors, and disability portion (*OASDI*), the Social Security tax, is separate from the health insurance (HI-Medicare Part A) portion of the tax. OASDI has a maximum contribution based on income limits (in 2004, this amount was the first $87,900 of an employee's wages), and this amount is indexed for inflation annually. The Social Security tax amount is currently 6.2 percent of income paid by the employee and matched by the employer. Workers and employers pay a current 1.45 percent of earned income into the HI program regardless of the worker's earnings. Part B of Medicare is financed by a combination of monthly premiums paid by persons eligible for benefits and contributions from the federal government. These payments represent the most significant insurance expense for most individual Americans, and nearly one-quarter of the dollars employers spend on benefits for their employees is used to make legally required payments to these programs.

Political Pressure

Social Security's problem is that there is a large "baby boom" generation preparing to retire and a smaller 'baby bust" generation following them. It is important to note that today's workers are supporting today's retirees. When the program was devised, there were 42 American taxpaying workers for every covered retiree. Now the ratio is 3-1, and it will be 2-1 in a decade or so.

Additionally, we are living longer and healthier lives. When Social Security was created in 1935, a 65-year-old had a life expectancy of 12.5 more years; today, it is 17.5 years and rising.

Social Security is now taking in more in taxes than it is paying out in benefits, and the excess funds are credited to the Social Security's trust funds. But it is projected (estimates vary) that benefit payments will begin to exceed taxes paid in 2015, and the trust funds will be exhausted in 2037. Social Security will only be able to pay about 72 percent of benefits owed if nothing is changed before then.

Paying for Social Security and Medicare

Social Security—Employees pay 6.2 percent of the first $87,900 (2004) earnings. Employers pay the same. Self-employed persons pay 12.4 percent of the first $87,900 (2004) of self-employment income.
Medicare Part A—Employees pay 1.45 percent of all earnings. Employers pay the same. Self-employed persons pay 12.9 percent of all self-employment income.
Medicare Part B—Covered persons pay a $66.60 (2004) monthly premium. General revenues of the federal government cover the remainder (about 75 percent) of the program's cost.

Political pressures by the public on the federal government have sent a message in the past not to tamper with Social Security. Congress meanwhile has continued to struggle with ways to balance the federal budget and leave entitlement programs such as Social Security in place. So complete is public dependence on the Society Security System that any question of the system's soundness or any suggestion that benefit levels or eligibility may be open to review can have severe political repercussions. Suggesting the curtailing of benefits is political suicide, so politicians avoid the apparently inevitable need to act to control the spiraling costs of Social Security. Still, the public worries that after years of paying into the system, there will be no benefits available to them when they become eligible and income is needed.

Adjustments apparently will need to be made in the decades to come. Actuaries argue that the program will not be able to support the programs as they now stand, although there is much disagreement on this point.

Normal Retirement Age Change

Some adjustments have already been made. The normal retirement age, now referred to as *full retirement age* to receive the full old-age benefit, is being pushed ahead to older ages. For those recipients born in 1938 and later, a 65th birthday will no longer be the point where this calculation is made. Each later year of birth will push that age up by 2 months until it reaches age 67 for those born in 1960 and later. Regardless of the age at which full retirement benefits may be taken, a worker can continue to take reduced benefits at age 62. The percentage of reduction will be greater for those retiring in younger age groups.

Eligibility

As you work and pay taxes, you earn credits that count toward eligibility for future Social Security benefits. This credit is based on *quarters of coverage.* For 2004, a worker receives credit for one quarter of coverage for each $900 in annual earnings on which Social Security taxes were paid. You can earn a maximum of four each calendar year, and the amount of earnings necessary to earn a quarter of coverage is adjusted annually for changes in the national level of wages.

A *fully insured worker*, who has 40 quarters of coverage, is eligible for the full range of disability, survivor, and retirement benefits. Once a person acquires fully insured status, he or she is fully insured for life even if covered employment under Social Security ceases. Under a second test, a person who has credit for a minimum of 6 quarters of coverage is fully insured if he or she has credit for at least as many quarters of coverage as there are years elapsing since 1950 (or after the year in which age 21 is reached, if later) and before the year in which he or she dies, becomes disabled, or reaches age 62, whichever occurs first. Therefore, a worker who reached age 21 in 1992 and who died in 2004 would need credit for only 11 quarters of coverage for his or her family to be eligible for survivor benefits.

A *currently insured* worker who has at least six quarters of covered work during the previous 13 quarters, ending with the quarter in which his or her death occurs, would qualify but his/her survivors would receive fewer benefits.

A *disability insured* status is required to receive disability benefits. A disability insured status requires that a worker (1) be fully insured and (2) have a minimum amount of work under Social Security within a recent time period. For example, workers aged 31 or older must have credit for at least 20 of the last 40 quarters, ending with the quarter in which the disability occurs.

The benefits themselves are calculated in a complicated manner. Many needs analysis computer software programs provide Social Security calculations so you can estimate approximate benefits based on current income. The Social Security Administration also mails annual notices to workers, detailing benefits earned and projections at retirement age. Final calculations for an eligible beneficiary are completed when application is being made.

Types of Benefits

There are five major categories of benefits paid for through Social Security and Health Insurance taxes: survivor, retirement, disability, family, and Medicare.

Your benefit is a percentage of your earnings over most of your working lifetime. Social Security was never intended to be your only source of income when you retire or become disabled, or your family's only income if you die. It is intended to supplement other income you have through pension plans, savings, investments, insurance policies, etc. Low-income workers receive a higher percentage of their earnings than do those in higher income brackets, but a worker with average earnings can expect to receive about 40 percent of his or her average lifetime earnings.

Survivor Benefits

In addition to a $255 lump-sum death benefit, eligible family members of a fully or currently insured worker receive income benefits during the period when children are the most dependent. Surviving spouses are eligible to receive income benefits as long as the spouse is caring for children of the deceased worker under age 16 or disabled (before age 22). Each dependent, unmarried child under age 18, or age 19 if a student in elementary or secondary school, may also receive a monthly benefit. Disabled children of any age are eligible for benefits as long as they were disabled before age 22.

The period between the last child's benefit and retirement eligibility for the surviving spouse is called the *blackout period* because no benefits are paid before age 60 to a widow or widower if there are no qualifying children. Benefits are reduced if taken prior to full retirement age. If you are divorced, your ex-spouse could be eligible for widow(er)'s benefit on your record if the marriage lasted at least 10 years. Also eligible is a parent age 62 or over that was a dependent of a deceased fully insured worker at the time of death.

Most presentation software programs or paper versions of these products have reference charts for approximate social security benefits that can used in determining income sources after an eligible worker's death.

What You Need to Report to Social Security

You should notify the Social Security administration when something happens that might affect your Social Security benefits. Here are some examples

- if you move
- if you get married or divorced
- if you change your name
- if your income or earnings change
- if you become a parent or adoptive parent
- if you are imprisoned
- if you leave the United States
- if a Social Security beneficiary dies or becomes unable to manage his or her funds

Retirement Benefits

A worker who is fully insured under Social security is eligible to receive monthly retirement benefits as early as age 62. The amount of the lifetime permanently reduced benefit depends on how soon the worker retires before age 65 (measured in months) and ranges in months beginning with a 20-percent reduction at age 62. The chart provided below details the changes in full retirement age. Full retirement benefits are payable when a participant attains *full retirement age*.

The spouse aged 62 or older is eligible but has the same reductions for early benefits (prior to full retirement age). This benefit is also available to a divorced spouse if the marriage lasted at least 10 years. An uninsured nonworking spouse's benefit is 50 percent of the working spouse's benefit.

A spouse of any age caring for a child of the worker under age 16 or disabled is entitled to a child's benefit. A child's benefit is for those dependent, unmarried children under 18. This benefit continues until the child is age 19 as long as the child is a full-time student in elementary or secondary school. In addition, disabled children of any age are eligible for benefits as long as they were disabled before reaching age 22. In situations where someone is eligible for dual benefits, only an amount equal to the higher benefit is paid.

Disability Benefits

A disabled worker under age 65, and dependent family members, may qualify for benefits if the worker is disability insured and meets the definition of disability for Social Security. The definition of disability is very rigid and the disability must prevent the worker from engaging in a substantially gainful activity ($810 per month in 2004) and must be expected to result in death or to last for at least 12 months. The waiting period for application is 5 months.

The benefit would generally equal the normal retirement benefit. Children and spouses are eligible while the children are young enough to meet the standard Social Security age test. These rules and benefit eligibility requirements are the same as those described under retirement benefits.

Changes in Social Security Retirement Benefits for Those Born After 1937				
Year of Birth	**Attainment of Age 62**		**Normal Retirement Age—year/month***	**Benefit Age 62 as % of PIA****
1938	2000	65/2	79.2	
1939	2001	65/4	78.3	
1940	2002	65/6	77.5	
1941	2003	65/8	76.7	
1942	2004	65/10	75.8	
1943-54	2005-16	66/0	66/0	75.0
1955	2017	66/2	74.2	
1956	2018	66/4	73.3	
1957	2019	66/6	72.5	
1958	2020	66/8	71.7	
1959	2021	66/10	70.8	
1960 & later	2022 & later	67/0	67/0	70.0

** The normal retirement age formula applies to both the worker and spouse benefits.*
*** For this calculation, when you apply the percent of PIA benefit to early retirement, the old pre-1938 date of birth reduction factor of 5/9 of 1 percent per month is used to calculate the first 36 months' receipt of early retirement benefits and the new reduction factor of 5/12 of 1 percent per month is used for each additional month.*

What Social Security Does Not Cover

Final Expenses

Topping the list are final expenses. Social Security does pay a very small, lump-sum death benefit to the families of deceased workers. The benefit is $255—virtually nothing, considering that final expenses typically range from $5,000 to $10,000. Similarly, Social Security does not provide funds to cover the emergency cash needs we all face from time to time, and which are more acute when incurred by a surviving spouse. Whatever amount your prospects plan to make available to cover cash needs at death will have to come from life insurance or some other source. Social Security is not designed to cover them or to help in this area.

What Social Security Does Not Cover

There are no benefits for the following personal and family needs from the income coverage offered through the Social Security system:

- Only a $255 maximum payment for final expenses to the insured. No payment for other family members who do not meet employment qualifications.
- No funds for emergency cash needs.
- No mortgage or rent protection for the family's home.
- No higher education funds for children or the surviving spouse.
- No income payments to the surviving spouse after children have reached the Social Security maximum age during the blackout period.
- No coverage for family members who may die or become disabled. Limited qualification restrictions for the insured.

Mortgage Protection

Mortgage protection is another major need not covered by Social Security. The purpose of this protection is to give the surviving families the choice of paying off the mortgage and owning their own homes debt-free, or having the money available to continue the mortgage payments. This is a decision that may depend on the interest rate of the loan and the need to retain the mortgage interest tax deduction. The main purpose, however, is giving the family the choice. Social Security provides nothing in this area of family planning. Life insurance will create enough money to make either decision exactly when it is needed.

Plug into the Social Security Web Site for Information

You and your prospects can use a computer to explore possible retirement benefits. The Social Security Administration maintains an extensive Web site: http://www.ssa.gov. The site includes extensive explanations of how the system works, and allows you to file an online request for a Personal Earnings and Benefit Estimate Statement. If you have questions about Medicare or Medicaid, log into the Health Care Financing Administration at http://www.hcfa.gov.

Education Fund

Social Security pays nothing past a young person's eighteenth birthday, or to the 19-year-old if still in elementary or high school. As a result, all new life insurance plans that use Social Security in their calculations have to include provisions for cash or income to pay potential college costs. Also, a number of existing plans should be revised to make up for the shortfall created by the elimination of the education benefit.

Blackout Period Funds

No benefits are payable for the surviving spouse of a deceased covered worker from the time the youngest child reaches age 16 (or is no longer disabled in certain cases) until the surviving spouse is eligible to receive his or her own benefit at age 60. This may represent many years without income. Providing the income replacement for surviving spouses during this period is an important function of family life insurance planning. Without adequate life insurance protection during the blackout period, a surviving spouse could face reduced income.

If the surviving spouse is working, the question becomes how well the family's lifestyle can be maintained on one income? It may be that with the children grown, expenses will be reduced to the point at which the spouse can get along fairly well without additional income. This will most likely occur when life insurance has been used to pay the remaining mortgage balance and if an educational fund was established to pay tuition. Retirement income should be considered here, as well. If the couple had been basing their retirement plans around two pensions and two IRAs or other investments to which both were contributing, the resulting reduction may lead to funding and income problems. Remember when doing life insurance planning for two-income couples that consideration of the blackout period in the overall plan is essential. Depending on individual circumstances, additional income protection may be needed.

If a spouse has not had a job, the situation may be more acute. Spouses with little or no income-earning capacity, or whose job skills have not kept up with the demands of today's workplace, can be highly vulnerable during the blackout period. Without life insurance to provide adequate income, the surviving spouse will probably have little choice but to try to enter or reenter the workforce. Competing with younger, more recently trained workers could make this a difficult transition. Remarriage is another possibility, but not one that most people will want to have to count on in their planning.

Discuss these issues with your prospects and clients. Find out how they feel about them and, most importantly, how they want to prepare to meet them in their life insurance planning. Setting income objectives for the blackout period is an important part of your work with families. Be sure they understand the situation, their options, and how life insurance can help them to make the best choices.

Family Members Not Covered Under System

Social Security provides no benefits to cover the economic loss resulting from the death of a nonworking spouse or child. Final expenses and last illnesses can be costly to the surviving family members in either situation. The financial hardship caused by a nonworking spouse's death can be especially severe. That person's economic contribution to the home is as real as if it were paid employment. Replacing this contribution can result in a severe drain on the family's resources. It is estimated that the cost of hiring a housekeeper runs anywhere from $400 to $2,400 per month or more, depending on the area of the country, number of hours worked, and duties assigned.

Clearly, there are a number of expensive needs for which Social Security provides no protection. These cash and income needs are relatively easy to identify and can result in your recommending substantial life insurance purchases.

Determining Benefits

While eligibility status determines who may receive benefits and when they become eligible to receive them, it does not determine the dollar amount of the benefit.

Your Social Security Statement

Each year the Social Security Administration sends to all entitled persons, an updated Statement of their Social Security earnings record, as required by law. This statement, mailed about 3 months before the taxpayer's birthday, gives estimated benefits based on actual credits earned through working, and projects future benefits based on average earnings over your lifetime.

Since future benefits can be lost if Social Security records are inaccurate, every wage earner has an opportunity to correct his or her earnings record. It is important that these records are accurate, for future benefits are based on the Social Security Administration's records for each account.

When you look at your own Social Security earnings record and begin to apply the process of determining your personal retirement and survivor benefits, you will find it easier to use with your prospects and clients. Many insurance sales would never happen without both the limitations and the benefits of Social Security. Your personal Statement will serve as a very real background reference for your own knowledge, as well as a tool to familiarize yourself with benefits that you can explain to prospects and clients.

Primary Insurance Amount (PIA)

The benefit is determined by a worker's *primary insurance amount* (PIA). This is the basic unit used to calculate the amount of each monthly benefit payment. It is determined by the amount of contribution a worker makes during years of work through Social Security withholding taxes. A complicated wage index is applied each year and an individual calculation is made. In 2004, the average PIA for a retired worker is $922. A worker who has continually earned the maximum income subject to Social Security taxes can expect to have a PIA for retirement purposes of $1,825 if he or she retires at age 65 and 4 months in 2004. The maximum PIA in 2004 for purposes of disability and survivors benefits ranges from approximately $1,825 to $2,100. The higher PIA results for workers who are disabled or who die at younger ages.

When a worker is fully insured and delays receipt of benefit payment after full retirement age because of continuation of work, the worker will receive special credit as a percentage added to benefits. It will vary depending on the worker's date of birth.

Dependent and survivor benefits as well as retirement and disability benefits for members of the insured worker's family are all figured as a percentage of the worker's PIA. The total amount is limited by the maximum family benefit for the worker's PIA eligibility. See the following tables for these amounts.

Benefits for Family Members of a Disabled or Retired Worker	
Family member	Percentage of Worker's PIA
Spouse at full retirement age	50%
Spouse caring for disabled child or child under 16	50%
Child under 18 or disabled	50% each

Benefits for Survivors of a Deceased Worker	
Family member	**Percentage of Worker's PIA**
Spouse at full retirement age	100%
Spouse caring for disabled child or child under 16	75%
Child under 18 or disabled	75% each
Dependent parent	82.5% for one, 75% each for two

The full benefits described in the table above may not be payable because of a limitation imposed on the total benefits that may be paid to a family. This family maximum is determined by formula and is usually reached if three or more family members, including a retired or disabled worker, are eligible for benefits. If the total amount of benefits payable to the family exceeds the family maximum, the worker's benefit is not affected, but the benefits of the other family members are reduced proportionately.

Social Security has an *earnings test* that applies to beneficiaries under full retirement age. We referred earlier to the surviving spouse who could lose benefits by working. This applies to retirement benefits as well. Retired workers under full retirement age have an annual limit that changes each year, penalizing them with a cut of $1 for every $2 in excess earnings. In 2004, they are allowed earnings of up to $11,640. Retiring workers age 65 who exceed the dollar figure of eligible earnings ($31, 080 in 2004) will lose $1 for every $3 in excess earnings in the months of that calendar year prior to retirement. Retired workers aged 65 and over have no earned income ceiling and have no excess earnings penalty.

If a worker elects to receive retirement benefits prior to full retirement age, benefits are permanently reduced by 5/9 of one percent for each of the first 36 months that the early retirement precedes full retirement age and 5/12 of one percent for each month in excess of 36. For example, for a worker who retires 3 years before full retirement age, the monthly benefit is only 80 percent of that worker's PIA. A spouse who elects retirement benefits prior to full retirement age has benefits reduced by 25/36 of one percent per month, for each of the first 36 months and 5/12 of one percent for each month in excess of 36. A widow or widower has benefits reduced proportionately from 100 percent at full retirement age to 71.5 percent at age 60. If the widow or widower elects benefits prior to age 60 because of disability, there is no further reduction.

Workers who delay applying for benefits until after full retirement age are eligible for an increased benefit. Benefits are increased for each month of late retirement until age 70. Benefits can increase from ¼ of one percent per month, which is equal to a 3 percent annual increase for older workers. This percentage increases to 2/3 of one percent per month, for an annual increase of 8 percent, for workers born in 1943 and after.

Income Tax Limits

Social Security benefits may be subject to annual income tax. Up to one-half of the amount received may be taxed when it exceeds base amounts. The figures are different for single and married filers and are subject to change each year.

For individuals whose modified adjusted gross income plus one-half of Social Security benefits received during the taxable year exceeds a stipulated base amount ($25,000 to$34,000 for single taxpayers, $32,000 to $44,000 for married filing jointly taxpayers), there will be a Tier 1: 50 percent rule, meaning income tax will be imposed on 50 percent of Social Security benefits. This threshold can change from year to year.

Percentage of Final Pay Replaced by Social Security Retirement Benefits

	Beginning at Age			
Current Pay	**65**	**64**	**63**	**62**
$10,000	55%	52%	48%	44%
20,000	42	40	37	34
30,000	37	34	32	30
40,000	29	27	25	23
50,000	24	23	21	20

A more stringent percentage is applied to those who have a higher threshold of income with a Tier 2: 85 percent rule. These excess base amounts of modified adjusted gross income will have up to 85 percent of the Social Security benefit subject to income tax.

Case History

The "Reserved" Agent

Sue Stanley entered her insurance career after 8 years in the Air Force. After separation from active duty, she entered the Reserves as a public affairs officer. Her duties included writing articles for the local news media and escorting visitors at her base of assignment. She remained in touch with many of her military friends and made many new contacts both on active duty and in the Reserves. A growing number have become insurance clients over the last couple of years. This is the story of her experience with one client on the base. She related this story when she was taking the LUTC Program's Meeting Client Needs course.

Prospect—One friend, Peter Mitchell, asked her about saving money for retirement through an annuity advertised in a military magazine. Although she was careful not to reveal her true feelings about the ad she'd seen before, she suggested that an annuity might be a good idea, but it would be better first to review his entire financial program to coordinate his military benefits with his personal savings, investments, and life insurance. She also recommended that Pete's wife Diana be part of the review. Pete readily agreed. They set a time to get together at Sue's office in town off the base. She asked Pete to have copies of all insurance policies, savings and investment statements, Wills, and payroll statements available for review when they met the first time.

The First Appointment—At the meeting one evening the next week, Sue took a few minutes to explain to the Mitchells how she worked. She informed them that she would ask a lot of questions, and that all information would be held in strictest confidence. It turned out that Sue began working with this couple at an important point in their lives. During the discussion, Pete said he planned to retire within the next 2 years and would return to school to complete his degree and obtain a teaching certificate to teach high school. Diana was already working full time as a teacher's aid in a school district near the base. At the time, their two children were 9 and 6. They lived in base housing and were planning to buy or build a home in the next year in the $150,000 range. This would prepare them for the transition to civilian life. They had saved $32,000 for their home purchase and had an additional $8,000 in U.S. Savings Bonds.

Diana had a tax-sheltered annuity (TSA or TDA as it is often called) with an account balance of $12,000. Pete owned a $50,000 universal life policy and had Servicemen's Group Life (SGLI) coverage of $200,000. Diana had a $25,000 universal life policy and group insurance of $20,000 through her school. Pete is a Senior Master Sergeant (E-8), and earns approximately $30,000 per year. Diana's salary is $15,000 per year. If one were to die, they feel they would need about 60 percent of their combined income to protect their lifestyle. They had been saving $800 per month in the credit union and $100 in savings bonds.

The Second Meeting—Sue moved the location of the next meeting to the Mitchell's home. She said she finds this an effective device to establish a closer relationship.

To illustrate their current financial status, Sue used a simple net worth statement and listed their goals. These were reviewed at this meeting. A copy of it is in the following box. At this second meeting, Sue showed that if Pete died, the current amount of coverage would cover the net liability with money to spare ($250,000 – $168,000 = $82,000). In addition, there would be $3,000 payable by the Air Force, plus a payment for outstanding leave. If Diana died, there would be a shortage of $128,000 necessary to take care of the home purchase and education funding.

For family income, Pete's current income would suffice if Diana dies as long as he remains in the Air Force. But this will soon change when he retires because his income will be reduced, and he will return to school. Pete and Diana elected to discount his expected income to his retirement level ($1,200 per month).

Their current income is $45,000 ($3,750 per month), and desired income is 60 percent of that ($2,250), leaving a shortfall of $1,050 per month. They felt this would be necessary for a period of 5 years, until Pete was able to work full time as a teacher. Total coverage needed: $1,050 x 12 x 5 = $63,000.

If Pete died, Diana would need the same level of income per month ($2,250). From his military benefits, Diana would receive $861 Dependency and Indemnity Compensations, and the children $75 each until age 18. If Pete died after retirement, Diana's survivor benefit would depend upon the level of survivor benefits elected under the Survivor

Benefit Plan (SBP). Pete and Diana elected to accept the level of benefits currently provided and look at the retirement problems closer to Pete's actual date of separation.

Talking It Over—In summary, they felt the amount of coverage on Pete's life ($250,000) was adequate for the present. They agreed to purchase additional coverage of $186,000 for Diana. They spent some time discussing various kinds of life insurance with Sue, pointing out both advantages and disadvantages of each. They liked the concept of lifetime coverage and equity of the permanent plans, but were unsure that it was totally right for them with so many changes in their life coming up in the next few years. Sue recommended universal life since they had experience with this type of protection that was flexible and still offered the option of tax-deferred savings for the children's future college expenses and their own retirement.

Peter and Diana Mitchell

	LIABILITIES	ASSETS
Lost Expenses	$ 10,000	
Home Purchase	150,000	
College Fund (2 ¥ $30,000)	60,000	
Savings		$32,000
Bonds		8,000
TDA		12,000
TOTALS	$ 220,000	$52,000
Net Liability	$ 168,000	

Goals and Priorities

1. Home purchase if either dies
2. College education for children
3. Survivor income if either dies
4. Accumulation of money for (a second) retirement

An Unusual Recommendation—Sue did not look closely at the savings for retirement issue that had originally brought them together through the magazine advertisement. She suggested they use Diana's TDA at school and invest up to her legal maximum before buying another annuity. She told them nothing else could match its tax advantages now and in the future.

Conclusion—Sue described how much this sale meant to her. It opened what will be a long-term business relationship. The Mitchells have become occasional social friends as well. Diana introduced her to faculty members at her school and she made additional sales and obtained other referrals. Sue says her endorsement of the TDA was what got her in the door. Early on Sue has learned the lesson of generosity in praising the good decisions that clients have already made.

Pete, on the other hand, considered his own future professional plans confidential and was unwilling to refer Sue to others he knew on the base. It was tough to hide her disappointment but she said she understood. Sue said she was surprised over the next few months when Pete stopped her on two occasions to suggest she call someone. She followed up and did so, armed with Pete's reasons why the person might be a prospect. She got an appointment each time. When she told the LUTC program about her experience with Pete, she laughed and said he has put a whole new spin on the definition of "suggesting referrals" for her.

Case History

A Legacy for Life

Emilio Ortero was born and raised in Argentina. He became an American citizen many years ago, and worked as an engineer. After signing an application for insurance, Emilio asked the agent to arrange an interview with the agency manager and in no time was out in the field persuading others to put their estates in order. Emilio calls it "falling in love with life insurance."

Prospecting—In approaching the educational and juvenile insurance market, I look for people with three qualifications.

1. a good income
2. an awareness of the value of life insurance, to the extent that it is a definite part of their own financial pictures
3. one or more children or grandchildren

Pre-approach—Most of my prospects in this market are clients or referred leads. Before approaching them, I already have considerable information on their backgrounds and circumstances. I use no letters but find the telephone invaluable for making appointments.

I try to control the sale from the very beginning. The initial step is to tell my prospect that I am going to come by between 9:00 and 10:00 the next morning. The technique is telling—not asking—the prospect that I'll be calling. Also, I never state a precise time. By estimating the approximate time of arrival, I allow myself a little leeway. If the time suggested is inconvenient, the prospect won't hesitate to say so. When this happens, he or she is likely to concentrate on convincing me that there really is a conflict and goes on to arrange a mutually convenient time. By being definite and affirmative during this telephone contact, I build more prestige and am accorded a better reception at the interview.

Approach—If the interview is with prospects who have children, my opening remark is, "Mr. and Ms. (Prospect), would you surrender your life insurance today?" Invariably the answer is no. "Why not?" This question puts them on my side immediately. Since they don't feel they should drop their insurance, they must think highly of it. Then I point out that their children will feel the same way in 25 or 35 years, and doubly so if their insurance had been purchased at a younger age. Reactions to this approach are always favorable.

I follow by stressing that their children will reach certain stages in life when they will need money in varying amounts. After they agree to this generalization, I turn the tables and ask the prospects to estimate the amounts that will be needed, and when. My recommendation is determined by their responses.

Interview—"Of course, you would do anything in your power to help your children, wouldn't you? Right now they're at the threshold of life, dependent on you for everything they have, and they will be for a long time—not only for all the material things, but for the building of character, the forming of habits, the knowledge of what to do and what not to do.

"No other human beings, as long as your children live, will ever have as much influence as you on the kind of people they become. As the years pass they will stand more and more on their own feet. Whether you are around to guide those footsteps or not, your influence will be felt by them for many years.

"I have an idea for their benefit that I am sure will interest you. Let me explain it with the help of this chart. Assume that we arrange an umbrella of life insurance to cover each of them throughout their lives. For the sake of an example, let's say $25,000 of whole life insurance—the same kind as you own.

"Perhaps the wonders of life insurance are never so clearly portrayed as when it starts at so young an age. It stands behind the children, through their lifetimes, ready to help in the emergencies they will face."

At this point I draw my prospect's attention to a chart showing cash values, at various ages from 18 to 65.

"For instance, when the children are about 18 years old they will be ready to start college. Am I correct in assuming that you want them to have this opportunity? In that case there will be a financial demand. Of course, if you are around, this problem will not be too serious; and if you are not, your own insurance program may provide enough. But if cash should be scarce then, they are going to be hit hard. If all other sources fail, these contracts you have arranged for them as little ones stand ready to serve. They will make money available to start your children on their way so they will have a chance to help themselves as they go along.

"Later, when they marry, they will be thinking about life insurance for the benefit of their own families, just as you and I did. Perhaps they will be able to meet the requirements of good health, but perhaps not. In either case, don't you think they'll be mighty glad to have the $25,000 of insurance provided by their parents, and won't they be particularly grateful about the accumulated cash reserve? If you had been so fortunate when you married, wouldn't it have been a great contribution toward solving your own problems?

"It won't be long before they will have the age-old desire for a home of their own. Again your plan comes to the rescue by making money available to finance their homes. They'll certainly appreciate the privilege of using the cash value as collateral—at an interest rate that is likely to be substantially lower than the market rate.

"At age 65, if they want to take it easy, as I am sure we'll want to at that age, this plan which has been available for emergencies through all the past years can provide a guaranteed monthly income that will be paid for the rest of their lives.

"The great advantage in arranging this lifetime program for your children now lies not only in the tremendous savings in cost, but in the assurance that they will have something that may not be available to them later. There is no way to be sure that they could qualify for life insurance when they're older. Even if they could, here is what it would cost to delay this plan until later ages."

At this point, I show a second chart illustrating the total of all premium payments for starting ages from 2 to 45, extending to age 65 and retirement. Of course, the lowest total occurs at the youngest starting age.

"Would you like to pay the premium annually, or would you prefer paying through our automatic monthly bank-o-matic withdrawal service?"

Details—Usually I recommend ordinary life for children and, sometimes, limited payment plans. Although the latter calls for a higher premium, the cash values are proportionately higher. Every family is different in their approach to premium payment periods for insurance on their children.

Comment—It is a peculiar thing, but I find a superstition among many people who should know better. Some feel that the purchase of insurance on a child's life is bad luck—sort of a death omen. Fortunately, this idea has greatly diminished in the past few years, thanks largely to the fact that tax legislation favors juvenile insurance. Wealthy parents and grandparents have found it especially attractive as a means of making gifts to potential heirs, thereby reducing tax liabilities on their estates. Both annual premium and single premium plans are used for this purpose. The policy serves as a depository for the funds until the child is ready for college or is off on his or her own.

Obviously, safeguarding insurability is another, and probably more important, buying motive. Guaranteed issue options are an extra incentive not only for today's sale but for repeats in the future. By keeping in touch with children through birthday greetings, graduation cards and so forth, I have developed a fine nest of future prospects. Some of my young policyowners will be leaders in business not too many years from now.

The importance of insurability to a successful businessperson is becoming increasingly evident to the public. This has made the market more receptive than ever to juvenile insurance. As a result, I have great success in obtaining interviews using this approach. Best of all, my records show that three out of five prospects approached with this idea buy more insurance on their own lives.

Chapter Five Review

Key terms and concepts are explained in the Glossary. Answers to the Review Questions and Self-Test Questions are found in the back of the book following the Glossary.

Key Terms and Concepts

risk tolerance
human life value approach
suitability
insurance programming
financial needs analysis
capital needs analysis
capital liquidation/distribution
defined benefit pensions
capital conservation
OASHDI
fully insured
currently insured
disability insured
full retirement age
quarters of coverage
primary insurance amount (PIA)
earnings test
employee benefit plans
contributory/noncontributory
Section 79 (IRC)
voluntary payroll deduction plans
accidental death and dismemberment (AD&D)
managed care plans (HMO, PPO, POS)
qualified retirement plans
defined contribution pensions
profit-sharing plans
401(k) plans
403(b)- TSA or TDA
Simple Plans
SEP plans
cafeteria plans
FICA
salary continuation
deferred compensation

Review Questions

5-1. What are the key factors in analyzing the client's current situation in light of their financial goals?

5-2. What are some considerations in the choice of a product solution for the prospect?

5-3. Explain an income and cash needs analysis in the financial needs analysis method.

5-4. Explain the capital needs analysis method of determining a life insurance need.

5-5. Describe the life insurance planning process using the capital distribution and capital conservation methods.

5-6. What are the key components of the major types of employee benefit programs?

5-7. What are the major types of employer-sponsored retirement plans, and how to they work?

5-8. What types of social security benefits are available to workers and their dependents, and what do they provide?

5-9. What types of life insurance needs does Social Security not cover?

5-10. How are Social Security benefits determined?

Self-Test Questions

Instructions: Read Chapter 5, then answer the following questions to test your knowledge. Circle the correct answer for each of the 10 questions. When finished with the test, check your answers with the answer key in the back of the book.

5-1. When planning an insurance calculation for a prospect based upon the use of both principal and interest from the proceeds of a life insurance policy, the approach used is called

(A) a settlement option
(B) capital conservation
(C) capital distribution
(D) capital needs analysis

5-2. The capital conservation method assumes that in the calculations

(A) principal is sacrificed to decrease dependency on interest rates
(B) both principal and interest will be drawn upon to generate the income needed by the beneficiary
(C) the after-tax interest generated by the principal will be enough to provide income without using the principal
(D) the cost of protection will equal the principal

5-3. The Social Security "blackout period" is best described as the period

(A) between a surviving spouse's last child's benefit payment and his or her first Social Security survivor benefit check at age 60
(B) between a surviving spouse's 60th and 62nd birthdays, during which no Social Security payments will be made
(C) between a dependent's graduation from school and finding a job, during which Social Security pays no benefits
(D) when dependent surviving children are too young to collect Social Security retirement benefits but are too old to work

5-4. The Primary Insurance Amount (PIA) of Social Security is the

(A) eligibility rule for receiving benefits
(B) basic unit used to determine the amount of each monthly benefit payment
(C) basic unit used to determine the amount of social security tax for each worker
(D) the wage index applied to each year of eligible wages used to determine monthly benefits

5-5. The lump-sum death benefit from Social Security will provide an insured's eligible beneficiaries with

(A) $1,000
(B) $500
(C) $255
(D) There is no longer such a benefit.

5-6. Which of the following statements is true about contributory employee benefit plans?

(A) In contributory plans the employer "contributes" the total cost of the plan for the employee.
(B) The amounts paid by employees to contributory plans are usually taken out of the worker's pay by payroll deduction.
(C) The employer's contribution to a contributory plan is not tax deductible to the company.
(D) Contributory plans are often provided for a select group of key employees to provide "golden handcuffs."

5-7. Which of the following statements is (are) true regarding the capital conservation planning approach?

I. Income-producing principal is preserved and can be passed on to the prospect's heirs.
II. It guarantees that a beneficiary will not outlive the benefits of the insurance proceeds if the assumed interest rate is achieved.

(A) I only
(B) II only
(C) Both I and II
(D) Neither I nor II

5-8. Which of the following statements about Social Security eligibility is (are) correct?

I. A currently insured worker who has at least eight quarters of covered work during the previous 12 quarters is eligible for the full range of disability, survivor, and retirement benefits.
II. A fully insured worker with 40 quarters of coverage is eligible for the full range of disability, survivor, and retirement benefits.

(A) I only
(B) II only
(C) Both I and II
(D) Neither I nor II

5-9. All of the following are qualified retirement plans EXCEPT

(A) Deferred Compensation plan
(B) Defined Benefit plan
(C) Profit Sharing plan
(D) Defined Contribution plan

5-10. Suitability for a product selection for a prospect involves all of the following considerations EXCEPT

(A) the appropriateness of the product for the client
(B) the ability of the prospect to tolerate fluctuations in cash value
(C) the prospect's ability to pay the premium
(D) the product recommendation must be in the advisor's best interest

6

Develop and Present the Plan

Overview and Learning Objectives

Chapter 6 examines the process of developing and presenting your recommendations and solutions to meet the prospect's needs and goals. These recommendations and proposed solutions are based on the planning steps that have taken place up to this point. The chapter then reviews life insurance products and their features and benefits that are available to the advisor to design these solutions. It also examines life insurance policy illustrations, and offers points to consider in their construction and presentation to prospects. We will also look at the cost indexes and ways of fairly comparing policy costs.

By reading this chapter and answering the questions, you should be able to

6-1. Develop the solution to the prospect's needs and present it to the prospect.

6-2. Explain the difference between term and permanent insurance policies and riders.

6-3. Describe the economic living values of the various types of permanent life insurance.

6-4. Describe the different types of term and permanent insurance.

6-5 Discuss the assumptions made in policy illustrations and their shortcomings.

6-6. Explain the cost-adjusted indexes and how they are used to compare policy costs.

Chapter Outline

Developing and Presenting the Solution

In the last chapter, we reviewed the process of analyzing the client's current situation. It is now time to develop a plan to meet the client's needs and goals. If the development of needs from the data gathering and analysis steps revealed the need for a product you provide, it is time to offer your recommendations to your prospect. This chapter will review life insurance products, their features and benefits, and discuss how to develop plans and present them as solutions to your client's needs and goals. It will also emphasize the design and proper use of policy illustrations, and keys to understanding their strengths and weaknesses. We will also look at how to fairly compare the costs of life insurance policies using the cost-adjusted indexes.

Developing the Solution

Review of Fact-finding Highlights

The analysis of the prospect's situation involves taking the relevant information gathered from the fact-finder and designing a plan that reflects the prospect's needs, goals, and premium commitment. Creating a solution to meet the prospect's needs depends heavily on the quality of the information gathered during the fact-finding process. The solution must be based on the prospect's circumstances and preferences. Thus, the importance of a thorough fact finder cannot be overemphasized.

Price versus Value

Price can be bartered, but value must be explained.
The best value is the policy that is in force when you die.
Do you want the lowest initial premium, or the best value?
Usually you get what you pay for.

Designing the Solution

Your objective is to help the prospect get the best value for his or her money through an effective plan design. Plan design is a balancing act between the prioritized coverage needs of the prospect and his or her premium commitment. One way to approach this task is to begin with the basic coverage design, creating an "ideal plan." Then, using the premium commitment and the prospect's priorities, begin adjusting the plan to create an optimal solution that will best meet his or her priorities within the specific premium commitment.

Decisions can be made about each aspect of the coverage by referring to the information gathered from the fact-finding process. For example, the fact finder will provide information about the existing and projected resources, preferences for types of coverage, coordination with other assets, and so forth. Unfortunately, there may be many variables to account for, and objectives in conflict. Furthermore, there may be a long period between the purchase of the coverage and the eventual occurrence of a claim. As a result, the advisor and prospect must make some assumptions about future events.

In analyzing the information, you review the data collected and design a plan. You should prepare a few alternatives in order to give the prospect choices based on the features and benefits of each option. Having choices is something that most buyers appreciate. The advisor is an expert, a counselor and consultant, who educates the buyer on the key advantages and differences between product solution choices. The buyer is then free to buy, to be in control and make the decision.

As you design the plan, it is important to work within the premium commitment as determined in the fact-finding interview. While a policy with all the features that anyone would like to have is desirable, if its premium is beyond what a prospect can or will pay, then presenting this solution may be a formula for losing the sale. Instead, develop some alternative policy designs that reflect the prospect's priorities and fall within his or her premium commitment. Limit your choices to just a few so that you do not confuse the prospect. You can always customize further by using a few basic designs and illustrations as a starting point and introducing modifications (within cost parameters) by adding or subtracting certain features and benefits.

> **The Mind Rehearsal**
>
> Before you meet with the prospect to conclude the sale, visualize what will happen in your presentation. How will the prospect answer your questions? How will you reply if the prospect asks a difficult question or voices an objection that makes you hesitate? What papers will you need? How will you handle all the forms? Where will you sit when making the presentation? What will be the expression on the prospect's face when he or she signs the application?
>
> This is a mind rehearsal for the sales interview. Sit quietly and let your imagination take over the process of making the sale. When you can see the sale in progress and visualize the prospect saying yes, then you have the necessary confidence and are prepared to meet. Visualization prepares you for the close.

In preparing your recommendations, review the prospect's key issues discovered in the fact-finding.

- How long will they need the coverage?
- What level of premium will they be paying?
- Is premium flexibility important?
- What are the prospect's financial priorities, goals, and budget constraints

Preparing for the Presentation

The key to an effective presentation is preparation. Take the time to prepare material for your sales presentation. You may want to organize it in a binder or portfolio. As in cooking, presentation is everything. The appearance and organization of your materials will go a long way toward the acceptance of your presentation.

The amount of time needed to prepare will decrease as you gain more experience, but initially you will want to create a detailed presentation outline for each closing interview. Here are some examples of ways for you to prepare for this interview:

- *Analyze your prospect.* What were his or her attitudes toward life insurance? Does he or she appear to recognize and accept the risk of death? What are the prospect's probable motives for buying? What are the barriers?
- *Create a summary* of the *fact-finding* interview that you can use as an outline when you re-establish the need. Use the discovery

agreement or a simple outine of the main points established from fact-finding.

- Check your *suggested plan alternatives.* How do they reflect the prospect's needs, priorities, and budget? What are the pros and cons to each alternative? Which do you feel is the best alternative and why?
- Collect any *company-approved sales material* you will use in the presentation. If you have a series of such items, put them in order in your sales presentation binder.
- *Create policy illustrations* for all of your recommendations ahead of time. Check the prospect information (name, age, and so forth) for accuracy.
- Put together any *written proposals* you will use with your presentation.
- *Confirm the appointment* time and location with the prospect.

The better prepared you are, the more you can focus on the prospect and his or her reaction to your presentation, and handle any objections or concerns. Furthermore, you will present a professional image to the prospect if everything you need is available, organized, and persuasive.

Presentation Checklist

Review the following items in preparing to deliver your solution presentation:

- Determine your purpose: What are the prospect's financial objectives, goals, and needs, that you will help him or her solve?
- Who is your prospect, and what decision-makers will be present?
- What are the buying motives of the prospect and/or the decision-makers?
- What is the prospect's current situation?
- What is the prospect's desired situation?
- What are the specific buying conditions, such as budget (premium commitment), other resources, desired policy features, start date, parameters of coverage, and so on?
- Does the prospect agree with your assessment of the problem?
- Develop your solution and statements to support it. This may involve a few alternative plans.
- Review specific factual and feeling-finding information collected.
- Anticipate any objections or concerns and prepare responses to these.
- Rehearse your presentation and answers to objections or any other anticipated verbal exchanges.
- Visualize a successful presentation as you would like it to proceed.

Presenting Solutions

Elements of the Presentation

Although the specifics of an effective presentation will vary from advisor to advisor, there are two main components to every presentation. The first component is to reestablish the prospect's need for life insurance; the second is to present possible solutions.

Re-establish the Need—In a one-interview sale, you simply have to review points regarding the prospect's needs and goals that were established from the fact-finding portion of the interview. In a two-interview sale, some time will elapse between the first and second interviews. Therefore, it is important to reestablish the prospect's interest in and need for life insurance by summarizing the relevant points from the first interview. The best way to rekindle the prospect's interest is to review the gap between his or her desired outcome and the projected outcome without life insurance.

Fundamentally, this should involve nothing more than reviewing the key points of the fact-finding interview, including how the prospect felt about them. You want the prospect not only to recognize the financial gap again, but also to feel it. Here is one method for accomplishing this goal:

> **Establishing the Need**
>
> One advisor shares her insights into the importance of establishing the need:
>
> "Don't be anxious to make a sale. Instead, focus on listening to prospects and understanding their needs. People can tell when you're trying to sell them something.
>
> This is a need-based sale, so you have to explain the need. If people don't know what they want, you have to educate them. They are not stupid and will not buy something they don't need or consider valuable. If there is no need, price is irrelevant. Would you pay even $10 a month, let alone hundreds, for something you don't think you need?"

- *Review the facts and planning assumptions*—What assumptions were incorporated into planning? Has anything changed since the fact-finding interview? Would the prospect like to change any of the assumptions?
- *List the prospect's objectives*—Review and confirm the prospect's objectives, concerns, and priorities. Essentially you are summarizing the prospect's answers to the following questions.

  - What does the prospect want to provide for the family?
  - What does the prospect want to leave to his or her heirs and to charity?

- What priorities does the prospect have for the family's lifestyle ?
- What is the prospect's premium commitment?

It is extremely important to match policy benefits with a prospect's objectives and priorities. These will vary for each prospect depending on his or her age and circumstances. In many cases the sales presentation will be built around a "hot button" or primary concern of the prospect.

- *Outline the expected need for life insurance*—While reestablishing the prospect's need for life insurance, you should also refresh his or her understanding of just how expensive it will be for the family to live without his or her income.
- *Summarize the prospect's current plan*—This is a review of what may happen if the prospect does not buy life insurance. Recap the information from the fact-finding interview. Give the prospect your professional assessment of the current plan's ability to achieve his or her stated objectives considering his or her current situation.

Steps in Presenting Possible Solutions

Once you have re-established the prospect's need for life insurance, you are now ready to present possible solutions to the prospect. Here are some suggested steps.

Summarize your observations—Summarize your observations about the current plan's inability to accomplish the prospect's objectives. These observations should paint a picture of the gaps you found in the current plan, demonstrating just how important it is that the prospect implement the recommendations you are about to make if he or she wants to achieve his or her stated objectives for meeting income and cash needs. Ask confirming questions to get agreement on what is important to the prospect. You may wish to summarize the main types of insurance and their features, advantages, and benefits.

Make your recommendations—Outline your recommendations, including both insurance and non-insurance solutions. If you are working with very affluent prospects, present your recommendations in a proposal that you give them. You should have a recommendation for each observation.

In the interview, present your recommendations beginning with the non-insurance solutions that are the easiest to implement. For example, if you notice the prospect does not have a living will, you can recommend that he or she see an attorney and have one drafted. Starting with an insurance recommendation might make the prospect cynical, raising his or her fears that you are only interested in making a sale.

During your presentation, you want to focus the discussion around the plan alternatives you are recommending. You want the prospect to pick the alternative that suits his or her needs, priorities, and budget. Discussion creates a sense of involvement on the part of the prospect and reinforces in his or her mind the selected alternative's ability to meet the objectives.

If at this point in time your prospect still has some reservations about purchasing life insurance, you may find it necessary to review the relevant financing alternatives so you can eliminate them as possibilities. Since you do not want to muddy the waters, review only those alternatives that the prospect is considering using instead of life insurance. With these alternatives are questions that highlight some of the reasons why they may not be sufficient by themselves to cover the projected needs, or may need to be part of a more comprehensive plan that includes life insurance.

Presenting Solutions

Here is one advisor's advice for presenting solutions to prospects.

- Summarize the discovery agreement, including a self-assessment of the prospect's current situation, expected needs, desired changes, and goals.
- Summarize the benefits and possible shortcomings of each alternative solution.
- Ask checking questions (trial closes) to confirm the prospect's position, such as "How does that sound to you?" or "Could this help your situation?"
- Make your presentation and reinforce how the solution addresses the problem. Present alternatives if the prospect requests comparisons.
- Ask a summarizing question, such as " Has everything been addressed?" or "Do you have any further questions about this?"
- If all issues are resolved, ask the prospect to buy.

Outline the implementation plan—The implementation plan provides you with a way to review your recommendations while providing the prospect with the action steps necessary to complete them. It should identify who is responsible for implementing each step and establish deadlines for the implementation.

Presentation Techniques and Tips

No matter how well you have prepared, or how good your recommendations, presenting them is still the critical element. There are a few things you can do to enhance the effectiveness of your presentation.

Focus on Relevant Features and Benefits—One mistake advisors make is to think that the purpose of the presentation is to educate the prospect about the technical, legal, tax, and product aspects of insurance. While an advisor should discuss these aspects, they should be discussed in light of the features and corresponding benefits that are relevant to the prospect and are the basis for your recommendations.

It is important to stress the difference between product features, advantages, and benefits. Features are characteristics of the product itself—what it is. A feature is a fact about the product. Features are descriptive, and are not given values. Advantages are what the product does, or how it works. Conversely, a *benefit* is what the prospect gets as a result of the feature, or the advantage of owning the product. It is what the product does for the prospect and the reason he or she wants it. Benefits are value-laden and subjective. They are the features desired by the individual.

A feature may not have a benefit to one prospect, while it will to another. If you are selling group insurance to a group of young single males, maternity and dependent coverage may not have a benefit, whereas to a group of young, married men with families these features may be of enormous benefit.

When presenting a recommendation, you want to explain what it is, how it solves the problem, and what it does for the prospect. The benefit aspect is very important. Is the benefit worth the price? Is it the best option? Will it save money? How well will it work for the prospect? These and other, similar questions must be answered if the prospect is to buy your solution. Thus, the benefits for the prospect must be clearly communicated.

An effective way to present features and benefits is to

- state the feature
- follow it with the words, "what this means to you is..."
- state the benefit as it relates to a need, value, or objective the client has stated

For example, in presenting the waiver of premium rider, you may say

"Prospect, this policy contains the waiver of premium rider. What this means to you is, should you become disabled, the company

- will pay the premium for you. This will give you the peace of mind of knowing that if you cannot work
- because of a disability, your premium will be paid and your life insurance
- coverage will remain in effect, protecting your family in the event of your death."

Sample Benefit Statements

Whole Life coverage—"This means you can feel comfortable knowing that you can never outlive your benefits."
Increasing Death Benefit—"This feature increases your policy's face amount to help keep up with the increasing cost of inflation."
Life Insurance—"This coverage is a wise decision because it protects the estate you have worked so hard to create."

Be sure to show how the features of your solution benefit the prospect. People buy benefits and solutions. Features and advantages produce the benefits. For example, you buy a drill because you need a hole. People often buy on emotion and justify the decision with logic and facts. They buy because it makes them feel good or secure. In selling benefits, we want to eliminate a negative feeling (something missing), create a positive feeling (need satisfied), and present a measurable benefit (I feel good).

To effectively sell benefits, you should go through a mental review before the sales call. Put yourself in the other person's shoes to see things from his or her perspective. See how your solution and the benefits of your product help the prospect get what he or she wants.

In summary, when you explain a feature of a policy, stress the benefits that the prospect will receive. Prospects respond to benefits. How a feature provides a benefit is not the point. Focus your presentation on the benefits—what a feature will do for a prospect is what he or she cares about. Concentrate on the benefits that matter most to your prospect—those you uncovered in the fact-finding process.

Keep the Prospect Involved—It is important to have the prospect's participation and involvement in the sales process for several reasons:

- It helps prospects feel responsible for solving their own problems.
- It helps you know whether you are on target with your presentation.
- It builds agreement one step at a time.
- It helps clarify any misunderstanding by either party.
- It helps lead to a logical and successful close—a conclusion to buy.
- It provides opportunities to deal with objections before asking prospects to buy.

The simplest and most effective way to keep the prospect involved is to ask questions throughout the presentation. Use questions to help the prospect express his or her feelings and to confirm that he or she understands what you are saying. For example, after explaining the waiver of premium benefit to the prospect you could ask, "What would a waiver of premium benefit mean to you?" This will reveal not only if the prospect understands the concept of a waiver of premium benefit, but also how he or she feels about it.

Insist on All Decision-Makers Being Present—If applicable, both spouses should be present at the interviews. Experienced advisors know they need to have all decision-makers present for a positive outcome.

Be Alert for Buying Signals—Sometimes advisors find that they have talked themselves out of a sale. The prospect was ready to buy but the advisor continued explaining details that confused and bored the prospect. To avoid this situation, monitor the prospect for buying signals. Many people who show a desire to fulfill their unmet needs are ready to

Selling the Solution

Instinctively, the typical sales professional believes that the solution to every problem must be a product he or she sells. Nothing could be further from the truth. Typical prospects do not care a bit about my product or which particular product they should buy. What they want to know is if the purchase they make will solve their problems and satisfy their wants. The sales professional should speak of the solution in terms of benefits, not features.

For example, it is not uncommon for a life insurance agent to say, "Mr. Prospect, the solution to your problem is an ordinary life policy with a term rider attached. We can add a guaranteed insurability rider, plus disability waiver or premium, and additional indemnity." Though the insurance agent fully understands what has just been said, it doesn't mean a thing to the prospect. The agent has been expressing the solution in terms of product features. Most prospects won't understand how these features will solve their problems.

A sale would be more likely if the agent would say, "(Prospect's name)", the solution I am about to recommend will provide an income to your wife and children, will keep them in their own world; will accumulate cash for yourself as a future source of capital like a savings account; and will cost you very little in comparison with the security it will provide. If you are disabled you won't have to continue payments—they will be paid for you. And, if you should die as a result of an accident, I have arranged for substantial additional benefits for your spouse and children."

Both statements describe fairly accurately the recommended solution. The difference is the first one concerned itself totally with the product (features) while the second expressed how the product could satisfy the wants of the prospect (the benefits). Clients identify with the benefits, so the benefits are what the sales professional must sell. This is where the expression "sell the sizzle, not the steak" came from. Unfortunately, the instinct of most sales professionals is to sell the steak (the product) and the instinct of most prospects is to buy the sizzle (the benefit).

Regardless of the product you are trying to sell, be sure to spend significant time on the benefits and advantages, from the prospect's perspective, and only as much time as is absolutely necessary on the technical features of the product

Norman G. Levine, "A Passion for Compassion," pp. 174-175. Reprinted with permission.

buy long before they ever say so. From the prospect's comments, you should be able to distinguish some fairly obvious verbal and nonverbal signals that indicate acceptance or rejection. Some examples are:

Verbal signals:

- "It would feel good knowing we had this kind of coverage."
- "I see what you mean."
- "Can we include that benefit with what I can afford to spend?"
- "Do you need a physical to get this insurance?"
- "I appreciate the thoroughness of your presentation."
- "When would the coverage start (if I sign an application)?"

Nonverbal Signals:

- Leaning forward
- Listening attentively
- Good eye contact
- Nodding, showing appreciation
- Speaking up, participating

Paying attention to the verbal and nonverbal clues will alert you that you should attempt to close the sale. Simply acknowledge the signal, whether verbal or nonverbal, and proceed with your close. For example, if the prospect says, "When would the coverage start?" You could reply, "It starts as soon as I have collected the first premium. We can get started with an application right now, if you would like." Or if they give you good eye contact you could say, "It looks like you might be ready to proceed with an application. Do you have any questions before we do that?"

What are you buying? Features and Benefits

You don't buy coal, you buy heat
You don't buy circus tickets, you buy thrills
You don't buy a paper, you buy news
You don't buy spectacles, you buy vision

The Life Insurance Product

Our next step in the selling/planning process will be to identify how life insurance products can provide a solution to the needs uncovered in the information-gathering step. This section will review the basic types of life insurance products. The chapter will conclude with ideas on sales illustrations and how to present these products to your prospect.

Choosing a Company

Insurance companies are classified as stock or mutual. They offer the policies as either nonparticipating or participating, reflecting the type of ownership rights available to their policyowners. Each type of company may offer contracts that reflect aspects of the other. For instance, a stock company can offer participating life insurance, usually thought of as the domain of mutual companies, in many states.

Choosing a company is done through the analysis of its financial strength, its products, its general reputation, and its ability to pay claims and offer quality service. Cost, policy features, and types of insurance offered will also certainly come into play. Rating organizations publish the financial history, ratings and analyses of individual insurers. These organizations include A.M. Best Co., Fitch Ratings, Moody's Investors Services, Standard and Poor's, and Weiss Ratings. Although each of these companies differ in the criteria and methods used to evaluate insurers, a company that has very high ratings from several of them should be a good choice.

Stock Company—A stock life insurance company is organized for the purpose of making profits for its stockholders. As in other corporations, the company is organized with outside ownership. Stock is sold to the general public to raise capital for the operation of the company. The stockholders elect the members of the company's board of directors and vote on major issues facing the company such as mergers and acquisitions.

The insurance plans of such a company are referred to as nonparticipating since the policyowner shares neither in any profits or savings nor in any losses that may arise in the business operations of the company. Since they will usually not receive dividends, the policyowner's fixed premiums represent both the initial and the final cost to them for their insurance policy coverage.

Mutual Company—Also organized as a corporation, a mutual life insurance company is organized and owned by the policyowners. The capital resources come entirely from the policyowners, who are both customers and, in a broad sense, owners. The policyowner is a member of the corporation and has a right to vote for the company's board of directors, who in turn select the management of the company.

The policyowner in a mutual company is a contractual creditor. The company's assets are held for the benefit and protection of all policyowners and beneficiaries as reserves, surplus, or contingency funds. Surplus funds are distributed to policyowners as dividends to the extent that management deems appropriate and are based on the company's experience and profits.

> **What is a Dividend?**
>
> The return to the policyowner of part of the premium paid for a policy issued on a participating basis. It represents an excess of collected premiums over expenses, actual mortality, and investment experience during a period of time.

The mutual company policyowner pays a fixed premium as stated in the policy (usually higher than the premium for a similar nonparticipating contract in a stock company). The actual or net cost to the policyowner will depend on the dividends allocated each year to the policy by the board of directors. The fixed premium is the initial cost and represents a maximum charge but the final actual cost is less by the amount of dividends paid. Thus, the policy is called a participating contract.

Many companies in recent years have been "*demutualizing*," that is, changing their organization from a mutual to stock company. This gives the company more opportunities for raising capital through issuance of stock, and more opportunities to acquire other companies through purchases and mergers.

Fraternal insurance companies—*Fraternal* companies are similar to mutual companies in that there are no stockholders. They are organized to serve the members of beneficial, not-for-profit organizations. Originally, fraternals operated on a pure assessment system. That is, when a member died, the other members of the organization were assessed (charged) enough to pay the claim.

Today, while still marketing to their own members, the fraternal companies operate much like nonfraternal companies. They are regulated in all state jurisdictions and, like other insurers, maintain cash reserves to protect their policyowners.

Product Innovations

Most of the product development activity that has taken place over the past three decades has involved the introduction of interest-sensitive, variable and flexible premium life insurance policies. Beginning in the early 1970s, a period of high interest rates and soaring inflation, the industry responded to consumer demand for life insurance products that were more flexible and offered a better rate of return than traditional, permanent life insurance. Additionally, increased competition from other financial service organizations, such as banks, securities firms, and financial conglomerates, caused insurance companies to become aggressive in protecting their market share, and creating a constant flow of product innovations.

Flexibility—a new model for life insurance—The result was the development of products such as universal life (flexible premium adjustable life), variable life, and variable universal life that not only provided the growth characteristics and flexibility the market was calling for, but also met the competition head-on. While these innovative new products were being introduced and marketed enthusiastically, companies were also modernizing their existing product portfolios. More attractive dividend schedules were issued, for example, and new variations of traditional products, such as modified life, graded premium life, and joint and survivor life were introduced.

New Policy Riders—We have seen a constant introduction of policy riders that offer benefits that people seek to solve financial problems they face today. For example, the "living benefits" provision idea was extended to existing policies by a growing number of insurance companies. Many more are offering the concept, sometimes called *accelerated death benefits*, through riders that can be purchased with new applications. Living benefit provisions provide a percentage of the death proceeds of a policy to those insureds that are terminally ill, have been diagnosed with a dread disease, or are confined to a nursing home. These riders provide a prepayment of the death benefit by taking terminal benefits while still living. Each company making this offer has its own requirements and means of payment. The taxation of the life insurance proceeds paid as accelerated benefits are excluded from gross income.

Another innovation responding to current needs is the *long-term care rider*. As people live longer and have an increased need for assisted living and nursing home care, and as the cost of these services continues to escalate, providing this coverage within a life insurance policy is an attractive benefit to the consumer.

Some long-term care riders allow direct access to the policy face amount at a stipulated percentage each year. Typically, the rider pays two percent of the face amount of the policy each month for long-term care expenses. Another version of this rider works like a stand-alone individual long-term care policy, paying a separate daily benefit with an elimination period and benefit period.

Each new product and each new variation meets a consumer need or responds to a challenge posed by a competing financial service provider. All of these product innovations have one thing in common, representing a creative way of providing life insurance protection to individuals, families, and businesses.

As you study this often-confusing array of products, one fact remains: the sale of life insurance is to secure the financial well being of families and individuals. The availability of both traditional and interest-sensitive products gives you more versatility in meeting the special needs of your prospects than ever before.

The Two Basic Types of Life Insurance

Despite all of the recent product development, there are still only two basic types of individual life insurance on the market: permanent insurance and term insurance. They both provide protection, that once purchased and accepted, can only be canceled at the policyowner's option. Permanent insurance is intended to be for life; term is designed to provide protection for specific periods of time. Most permanent policies provide guaranteed cash value accumulation and nonforfeiture benefits that represent the policyowner's equity in the policy. With term, there is normally no cash value buildup. The insured is buying "pure" life insurance protection for a stated time.

While premiums for permanent insurance are initially higher than they are for the same amount of term coverage, permanent premiums usually remain level while term premiums generally increase as the insured ages. Term premiums can be higher in the later years than permanent premiums.

The distinction between the two types of insurance can be summed up by analogy; owning a permanent policy is like buying a house; owning a term policy is like renting. By owning you build up equity in the home. With renting, you have no equity. In reviewing the several policies available of each type, the reason why the rent/buy analogy is still a good one will become clear.

Let us now turn our attention to term life insurance plans.

The Concept of Term Insurance

Term insurance policies provide a death benefit if death occurs during the period of time that the policy is in force. The policy period in term life insurance is expressed as a number of years (such as 1, 5 or 30) or until a certain age of the insured (such as 65 or 70). If the insured dies during the policy period, the specified amount (normally the face amount of the policy) will be paid to the designated recipient (beneficiary). If the insured survives until the end of the policy period, or term, the insurance company pays no benefit and the coverage ends.

Term insurance is tied directly to the cost of mortality, which increases as the individual grows older. The premium is initially relatively low and increases periodically in most types of term insurance, to reflect the increased mortality of the insured. The older a person is, and the longer the period of coverage, the higher the premium and mortality costs will be.

Term life insurance has great value to those who need large amounts of protection but have little cash to pay premiums. If a need is short term, as it may be in business or in some personal situations, term insurance is the most economical way to purchase the protection. For example, a person lending a large sum of money might want the borrower to guarantee the repayment of the loan if the borrower were to die. Term insurance works well in this case. In another situation, a court may require life insurance coverage on a parent who is getting divorced and will be paying child support, to guarantee the financial security of the children until they reach adulthood. A young family with dependent children, but with limited funds, may be best served by 1- or 5-year term with a renewability option to provide the large amount of life insurance needed to protect the spouse and children in the event of the premature death of the breadwinner spouse. If this need is only for a few years, term coverage may be the best type of insurance.

Term insurance has an important place in solving some needs. You must be careful, however, to make sure that your recommendations to use term or permanent insurance truly reflect the needs of your clients. Additionally, term can serve to protect one's future insurability. A young doctor or businessperson may need a large amount of life insurance, but can only afford a relatively small premium at the present time. If there is a need expected in the future, this person can purchase term insurance with a conversion provision, which will allow an insured to exchange the term policy for a permanent policy at a later time.

Types of Term Insurance

Level Term—Until now we have been talking about term insurance that provides a level death benefit at an increasing premium. In long-term contracts, the premium is averaged over the years to achieve a level rate. The premium remains level but builds up a reserve in the earlier, low mortality years to offset the higher mortality risk in the later years of the term. As a result, a term contract can be designed to provide both a level premium and level protection for a set period of time.

Decreasing Term—Under decreasing term, the premium is level, but the face amount decreases over the policy period. A company usually will establish its own scale or let the insured coordinate it with the amortization of a mortgage. While the premium is level, it is generally higher than for the same initial amount for level or annual renewable term insurance.

Decreasing term is often used to protect long-term, decreasing debts or to track some other type of diminishing financial obligation. For example, decreasing term is an extremely popular form of mortgage life insurance. It is often inexpensive and usually well suited to the purpose. As the mortgage balance decreases so does the face amount, which is what makes it attractive to the buyer. Many mortgage policies can plug in the mortgage interest rate to control its decreasing dollars to reflect the life of the mortgage. Families can purchase decreasing term when they need additional, economical income protection for a limited number of years—for instance, when the children are in college.

Reentry Term—With all insurance pricing, the anticipated mortality experience of an insurer is better in the early policy years than it is in the later years. This is because of recently obtained and evaluated underwriting information. The resulting rates are called *select mortality* *rates*. Over the years, people have changes in health, habits, occupations, and generally mortality experience worsens. Mortality rates associated with the latter are called *ultimate rates*. It is this difference in rates (select versus ultimate mortality) that led to the development reentry term.

Reentry term is a yearly renewable and convertible level death benefit term product. Periodically (every fourth, fifth, or tenth year, for example) the policy renews and the premium is subject to two schedules. As the initial underwriting period ends, the insured is allowed to reapply at company expense for a lower rate, subject to new evidence of insurability. Thus, the insured may be eligible for a new "select" rate at a substantially reduced premium. If the insured does not submit evidence of insurability, or does not meet the underwriting requirements for the lower rates, the existing policy is continued at the higher "ultimate" rates guaranteed in the contract.

Reentry term is attractive because of its low initial cost. It is sold when there is a need for large amounts of term insurance and the individual is a standard risk. However, the insured must accept the risk that premium rates may be very high at a future date.

Term Insurance Features

Renewable Term—For insurance needs that are of shorter periods of time, *renewable term* is often used. Whether the term is 1, 5, 10 or more years, the contract allows renewal at the end of the period. The death benefit remains level but the premium for the new term will increase. Yearly Renewable Term (YRT), commonly called Annual Renewable Term (ART), is very popular and is often renewable to ages exceeding 70. Many people who can afford permanent insurance also buy renewable term for long periods—for instance, for those years when children are at home or for a mortgage cancellation. There has been a growing sales trend in renewable level term of 10 and 20 years. Despite this, overall figures show that most ART policies remain in force less than 2 years.

When a term policy is renewable, it means that renewal can take place within the renewable period at the policyowners option by simply paying the renewal premium. No *evidence of insurability* is required, meaning no questions can be asked or information gathered by the company concerning the insured's health, occupation, habits, avocations, or any other underwriting issues.

Conversion Provision—The *conversion provision* is an option contained in a term policy that gives the owner the right to change to a plan of permanent insurance within defined company limits, without providing evidence of insurability. The policy will define the time period in which a conversion may be exercised; it may be limited to a number of years after policy issue, such as 5 or 10 years, or to a certain age, such as age 65. This time limitation is to minimize *adverse selection*, which is always present in term renewals and conversions. Those policyowners in poor health at the time of renewal, or as the conversion period ends, are more likely to use these policy provisions and pay a higher premium than those who believe themselves to be in good health.

The conversion may be on an *attained age* (current) or *original age* (or retroactive) basis. Attained age is the most common type of conversion. The premium rate of this conversion is based on the insured's age today. Original age term conversions, permitted in some plans, allow the new policy to be issued at the age of the originally issued term policy. Home office calculations must be made to determine the amount of premium due, since credit is given for past term premiums paid. The back premiums for the permanent insurance must be calculated and the balance due paid. This can become complicated because a discount factor is applied to past premiums to discount for interest. Good judgment must be applied if policy loans are proposed to pay some or the entire back premium because this can have a dramatic effect on policy costs and death benefits over longer periods of time.

Term Insurance as a Rider—Term insurance is also sold as an optional rider, which can be added to a permanent policy. Most companies make this rider available for a modest extra premium with permanent policies that are over certain minimum face amounts, such as $10,000 or $25,000. Although the same coverage is usually available as a separate term policy, the convenience of this form of protection, and the advantages of combining different types of protection under one contract, have earned term riders a lasting place in insurance portfolios. Because the policy fee (flat administrative cost) is charged for the contract as a whole, the term rider cuts the cost of the policy by the amount of the policy fee for most company plans.

Term riders are useful tools that can help you customize your prospects' protection to their changing needs. You can do some very creative life insurance planning using term riders in combination with permanent base policies. To understand how term insurance can be used this way, we will look at two typical term riders: the level term rider and the decreasing term rider.

Level Term Rider—The level term rider is used to provide temporary additional term protection for a specified number of years. For example, income earners may wish to have extra income protection during their peak earning years. A 10- or 15-year level term rider added to a base policy would meet that objective.

Level term riders that offer both the renewal and conversion provisions are also available. An advantage to having term coverage is that it protects insurability for the amount of the coverage, and can be converted, if desired, in the future regardless of health, occupation, and other underwriting factors.

Term Riders for Family Protection—In addition to providing protection for the person insured under the base policy, level term riders are also used to insure other family members. The spouse and children of the primary insured may be covered individually under a spouse or children's term rider, or collectively under a family term rider.

Spouse Riders—Spouse insurance riders offer level term protection for the insured's spouse. Typically sold in $1,000 or $2,000 units, the maximum protection available depends traditionally on the amount of the base policy. The rider's insurance continues to the spouse's age (or primary insured's age) of 60 or 65, but may be converted to a separate, permanent policy at any time during the term period, without proof of insurability. This coverage is not used much today and would more commonly be seen on older policies in force.

Children's Riders—Children's term riders provide level term insurance on the children of the insured parent. Purchase is available through age 18 in most cases. Premiums are based on a set rate per thousand. Protection is available in $1,000 or $2,000 units, and maximum amounts are determined by the base policy. The coverage continues until the child reaches a certain age, such as 18, 20, or 25, or until the insured parent reaches age 60 or 65. The rider is convertible to permanent insurance while in force. Some are convertible at the child's age of maturity and offer protection to the child for up to five times the original face amount. This is known as a *jumping juvenile policy*.

Another advantage of the children's rider is that it insures the offspring as a group instead of individually. It offers protection to a growing family without additional underwriting as each child is born. It could very well provide insurance for a child who might be uninsurable as an individual. Premiums are charged for all children at one rate, whether there is one child or five.

Family Riders—The family term rider combines the best of both the spouse and children's term riders. It is a unique package plan that covers each member of a family under a single contract. Most family term riders are sold in units, geared to the amount of the base policy. For example, a minimum $10,000 base policy may enable the insured to add one unit of family term rider protection. This might provide for $5,000 of coverage on the spouse and $2,000 or $2,500 on each child. Larger base policies enable the insured to buy additional units of coverage, up to a maximum amount. Premiums for this type of protection are determined by the insured's age when the rider is added to the base policy and are unaffected by the number or ages of the children to be covered. Coverage is automatic after a waiting period of 0 to 15 days for each child born or adopted after the rider is issued, and there is no increase in premium. Coverage under a family term rider is convertible. It continues for spouses for 20 or so years, or until the insured is 65, and for the children until each is 18, 20, or 25 years of age, depending on the insurer.

Family term riders are extremely useful to young, growing families whose insurance needs usually exceed their ability to pay premiums. This protection, when added to a base permanent policy, can provide a solid footing on which the family can build its life insurance program. When you consider the low cost of term insurance and the conversion features that enhance its flexibility, it is easy to see why these plans are practical and popular.

Decreasing Term Rider—This rider works the same way as the decreasing term plan described earlier. As mortgage protection, it can track a decreasing mortgage balance for 10, 20, or 30 years. When used as family income protection, it can provide a guaranteed amount of income to a surviving family member for a certain period of time if the insured dies prematurely.

Let us say, for example, that your client bought the $25,000 permanent policy with a $100,000 uniform annual 30-year decreasing term rider to provide extra coverage while the family was young and growing. If the insured dies in the fifteenth year, the surviving beneficiary would be paid the $25,000 death benefit from the base policy and $50,000 from the rider. Depending on company practice, or on how the policy's settlement options were arranged, the full $75,000 benefit could be paid as a lump sum, entirely as regular income payments, or some combination of both.

The Concept of Permanent Insurance

Permanent insurance is designed to be in force for the whole of a person's life (therefore the name "whole life"). Traditionally, permanent insurance ends or endows at age 100. At that time, the insured would receive the death benefit proceeds as a living benefit. Some companies now allow the proceeds to remain with the company as a certificate, earning interest to be ultimately paid out, since more and more people today live past age 100. The new mortality tables for CSO 2001 extend to age 120, evidence of this longevity trend.

The primary disadvantage of term insurance is its ever-increasing premium. Permanent insurance solves this problem by leveling and guaranteeing premiums over the life of the contract. The premium is higher than term insurance in the early years but substantially lower than term insurance in later years. This occurs because the extra amount paid in the early years accumulates in the policy with interest and offsets the increasing cost of insurance in later policy years.

The cash values in permanent insurance policies are guaranteed. They are available for borrowing and provide a financial foundation for many clients. This element frequently is the reason insureds maintain their life insurance programs even when circumstances require them to cut back on other expenditures.

Life Insurance Product Lines Annualized Premium Market Share

	2002	2003
Universal Life	28%	35%
Variable Life	1	1
Variable Universal Life	21	15
Term	23	22
Whole Life	27	27

Source: U.S. Individual Life Sales, 2003, LIMRA International, Windsor, Conn. Reprinted with permission.

The Economic Values of Permanent Life Insurance

Permanent life insurance is property. In fact, it is special in ways that other forms of property and investments are not. It is important for you to understand this concept so you can share it with your prospects and clients.

A permanent life insurance policy is property in much the same way a stock certificate or bond is property. The paper it is printed on has only negligible value, but it is evidence of a right to value. Rights of control or disposition are ownership rights, and ownership rights—not the objects themselves—are what constitute property in the legal sense of the word.

Ownership Rights

The ownership rights provided by traditional permanent life insurance illustrate why a policy is valuable property. These include

- a guaranteed schedule of cash values
- guaranteed optional nonforfeiture values
- nonguaranteed total cash surrender values
- tax-deferred growth of policy values until the maturity of the contract
- a guaranteed ready buyer, the insurance company, and a guaranteed predetermined price if it becomes necessary to sell the policy
- a guaranteed amount of annual income for life to either the owner or heirs through the policy settlement options
- loan interest rates that have specified limitations in the policy
- the borrower's privilege to determine the time and amount of repayment of a loan on the policy
- the insurance company's guarantee to honor the contract
- the right to name a beneficiary or beneficiaries

No other property provides all of these features. Finally, and perhaps most importantly, only life insurance provides a greater value at death than during the insured's lifetime.

Lifetime Values

One of the most valuable features of permanent life insurance is the guaranteed level premium. Without this ability to keep payments level for the course of a lifetime, the increasing chance of death as the insured gets older would create premiums generally impossible to pay. The rising costs of term insurance in the later years demonstrate this. After about age 40–45, term insurance premiums accelerate quickly to almost prohibitive amounts for most people approaching life expectancy. Permanent insurance avoids this problem.

If a person has a long-term need for insurance, permanent insurance guarantees coverage for the rest of life at a predictable cost. If their estate is large enough to create an estate tax bill, heirs can use the death benefit to pay the IRS or other final expenses, providing estate liquidity. If a person wishes to leave a legacy to grandchildren or a charity, permanent insurance can provide a guarantee for accomplishing this. Providing a lifetime income to a surviving spouse can also be guaranteed.

Accumulating Cash Values

In the early years of a permanent policy the premiums exceed the amount necessary to provide the face amount of protection. A cash *reserve* is accumulated to offset the increasing cost of protection in later years, and to pay other future obligations of the insurer. These cash values are available to the policyowner to borrow, or may be left to accumulate for future needs such as retirement.

The value of level premiums and accumulating cash values is visible in other ways. Level premiums allow people to maintain life insurance protection beyond the ages when the cost of term insurance protection would be prohibitive, assuring the continuance of protection into their 70s and 80s, if needed, at premiums that they can afford. It may, in some cases, even provide the cash reserve to pay its own premiums. This is one of the miracles of life insurance: You do not have to die to win; you win by living too.

At any time during the life of the contract the policyowner may surrender the policy for the cash value, or may borrow against it at an interest rate stated in the policy. Surrendering the policy automatically cancels the contract and ends the protection. Borrowing against the cash value does not cancel the contract unless the loan amount and accumulated interest exceed the cash value. If the insured were to die during the period of a loan against the cash value in the policy, the beneficiary would receive the face value less any loan and its accumulated interest. Borrowing against cash value decreases the death benefit of an ordinary life policy.

Net Amount at Risk

The difference between the face amount and the reserve (cash value) at any given time is called the *net amount at risk.* This is the actual insurance, or risk amount. This is the amount of money the insurance company must produce from the policy reserves in the event that an insured dies. As the reserve increases, the net amount at risk decreases if the face amount remains constant. The face amount is composed of the cash value and amount at risk. When the insured dies, the beneficiary does not receive the cash value of the policy, because it is already included in the face amount payable upon the death of the insured.

Permanent insurance is a combination of protection and cash accumulation. The level premium concept allows the policyowner to prefund the policy so that premiums do not become higher and excessive as the insured ages. This is also the basis for the nonforfeiture and policy loan features of cash value insurance.

Permanent Coverage

If a policyowner should stop paying premiums, he or she has some attractive options in a permanent insurance policy. First, the policy may automatically pay the unpaid premiums from its cash values, if available. This option, the *automatic premium loan provision*, is used to keep policies in force if premiums are missed due to an unintended lapse.

The policy may also be annuitized to produce an income. This is one of several settlement options, which is another way to continue the values in the policy, either during the life, or at the death of the insured. Settlement options will be discussed in detail in Chapter 8.

If the need to stop paying premiums arises from disability, then the disability waiver-of-premium rider, if in force at the time of the disability, would provide the funds to pay the entire premium or the cost of coverage, depending on the type of contract. The policy would allow the accumulation of cash values to continue as long as the disability lasted, even for life.

For this reason, permanent life insurance is referred to as *self-completing*. That is, in the event of death, the insured's financial goals for his or her survivor's can be realized. If a person survives, but becomes permanently disabled, the waiver of premium provision can continue the policy. Should the insured live a long life, cash values can supplement the established financial goals.

Nonforfeiture Values

If the policyowner decides to stop paying premiums, and cash values have accumulated, he or she may convert the policy to a paid-up policy at a reduced face amount or continue the policy at the same original face amount as extended term coverage. The policyowner could also surrender the policy for its accumulated cash value. These options give the permanent insurance contract a degree of flexibility unavailable in any other financial vehicle a person might own.

Loan Values

A remarkable feature of permanent insurance is that policyowners may borrow accumulated cash values from the contract. The amount that may be borrowed at any time is stipulated by contract. The money is always available without question. In some cases, a loan form with the policyowner's signature is required to complete the transaction.

The insurance company does not ask why the policyowner wants to borrow. There are no credit references, background investigations, or cosigners involved. Installment repayments are not required, and the loan may be repaid (or not repaid) at the convenience of the policyowner. An interest rate—either fixed or variable depending on the state and company rules—is charged annually. The owner may choose never to repay the principal, although if the loan remains outstanding it would be deducted from the proceeds payable at death, maturity, or cash surrender. Loan interest may have to be paid to keep the policy in force if the cash value is heavily borrowed against.

This contractual right to borrow may cause confusion for some people who object to "borrowing their own money." Although a policy loan is termed a "loan," it is not a loan in the usual sense of the word. It is an advance against the sum the insurer ultimately must pay upon death. An ordinary debtor-creditor relationship is not created. The policyowner does not borrow from a savings fund that has been created through the payment of premiums. No such fund exists. The policyowner is borrowing the company's money, using the cash value of the policy as collateral.

Meanwhile, the policy cash values continue to increase at the same rate as if the loan had not been taken. The reserves continue to build because they are untouched until the policy is surrendered or matures. As a result, the interest credited in the cash value accumulation grows because the loan still earns interest.

Naturally, clients should be advised to save the use of this right for emergencies. Like other emergency funds, life insurance equity should be conserved. Additionally, loans existing in the case of death will reduce the amount payable by the policy, because this money has already been paid.

Why Should I Borrow My Own Money?

"(Prospect), I can understand why you asked this question. Perhaps an example can clarify what happens when you take advantage of your death benefit.

If a homeowner has accumulated equity, perhaps $25,000 in a home, we could agree that the equity is the property of the homeowner. However, there are only two ways that homeowner can get at the $25,000: sell the property or take a loan against the equity.

Surely you would not surrender the policy to free your cash value, since this would mean losing the protection that is so important to you and your family. By taking an advance, you can have the needed cash and still protect your family. Unlike the home equity loan, you will not be faced with a required repayment schedule. You can choose to repay the loan or not. I'm sure you can see the benefit of using a product that builds equity this way."

Life Insurance as Collateral

Collateral created by the equity of permanent life insurance can be very useful to its owners. The contract combines several desirable aspects of collateral, each valuable even when standing alone. When combined, these elements create a product that is wholly unique in its usefulness as the basis of credit. This superiority of life insurance as collateral arises from the fact that

- the cash value is unconditionally guaranteed
- the policy is readily and effectively assignable
- the cash value is an increasing value
- protection is afforded the lender in the event of the borrower's death

We can see how all this works in reality if we request a loan from the loan officer of our local bank where we usually do business. If we ask for a mere $10,000, backed by collateral of 200 shares of Eastern Shores common stock selling at $50 1/4 currently, with a good dividend history and steady growth, we will probably be turned down. Although the value of that stock today is about $10,000, it is a volatile and risky asset. To the banker, the stock is not strong collateral, and the amount of the loan backed by that collateral will often be less than half the present value. With permanent life insurance, a policyowner can go to the bank and pledge the cash values of the policy as collateral for the loan. The cash value is guaranteed cash, so the banker will consider it dollar-for-dollar collateral.

Summary of Permanent Insurance

Permanent life insurance has unique properties that benefit the owner in life and at death. It offers a disciplined method of accumulation through manageable installment payments. It offers safety of principal, the accumulation of cash values at a guaranteed or current interest rate, and the possibility of significant appreciation in value. It is readily marketable and fully liquid, free from the need for managerial care. Life insurance has unexcelled collateral values, making it highly resistant to disruption for unexpected emergencies. The importance of life insurance in a family's financial security plan has even earned its cash values special tax treatment. Not only does it protect the family, it keeps society and government from having to support survivors who lack the capital to take care of themselves. As Supreme Court Justice Oliver Wendell Holmes declared, "...life insurance has become in our day one of the best recognized forms of investment and self-compelled saving."

Types of Permanent Insurance

Traditional Plans

Ordinary Life (Whole Life)—The basic form of permanent life insurance is ordinary life. It is the standard policy design upon which all other permanent products are based. Like level term insurance, ordinary life provides level death benefit protection for a level premium. But unlike any term policy, ordinary life's coverage and premiums are paid to age 100, and the policy builds guaranteed cash values which equal the face amount at age 100. At that time, if the insured is still alive and has paid all the premiums, the policy will mature (be completed). The cash value will equal the face value of the original policy. The cash value will be paid to the policyowner and the protection will end. When this happens, the policy is said to endow. It is assumed under the 1980 CSO Tables that every insured will be dead by age 100. The 2001 Mortality Tables extend to age 120.

Issuing and underwriting expenses (including sales commissions) are taken out of the policy for the first few years, so there is little, if any, cash value build up in most ordinary life policies in the early years. The company also has to establish the policy reserve for future claims, cash values, loans, surrenders, and withdrawals.

Ordinary Life Marketing Applications—Of all the traditional permanent products, ordinary life offers the most permanent protection for the least premium. For this reason, more people have bought ordinary life to meet their individual, family, and business life insurance needs than any other type of permanent policy.

Ordinary life provides a guaranteed lifetime benefit for a guaranteed level cost. This is why so many people at all ages use it to provide protection for long-term needs such as final expenses, income protection, estate conservation, and estate creation, or for a number of business life insurance needs. Business insurance applications are studied in depth in the Financial Advisor Series *Essentials of Business Insurance* course.

Flexibility—Since ordinary life builds cash values while at the same time providing a guaranteed insurance amount, many people use this product to accumulate funds for retirement in addition to providing adequate death benefit coverage. It is useful for younger people who are just getting started. They can take advantage of the low premium schedules at younger ages.

Ordinary life's cash and nonforfeiture values give policyowners considerable flexibility. Of course, policyowners can continue paying premiums but, if they need to, they can surrender the policy or borrow against the cash value. They can stop paying premiums and take either reduced paid-up or extended term protection, or just simply let the policy be paid by using the policy's automatic premium loan provision. If the policy pays dividends, this provides a great deal of additional flexibility in structuring coverage and premium financing.

Limited Pay Life—Variations of the basic ordinary life policy are designed for people who need permanent protection but who want accelerated cash accumulation, or who prefer not to pay premiums to age 100. With limited pay plans, insurance protection extends to age 100, when the policy endows as it would with ordinary life. The differences are that the premium payments stop before age 100, resulting in higher premiums and cash values that build up at a faster rate. Generally, the shorter the premium payment period, the higher the premium and the faster the cash value accumulation.

To show how this works, we have a diagram comparing three plans. These plans are 20-pay life, life paid-up at 65, and whole life.

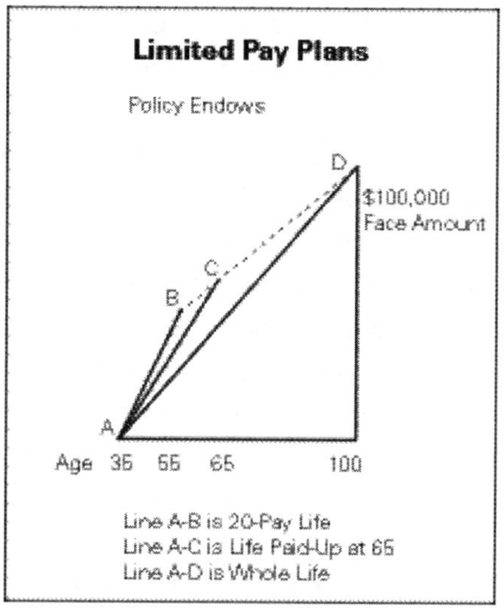

In each of the three policy plans illustrated here, the policyowner's premium payment period is represented by the solid lines (A-B, A-C, A-D). The shorter the line, the higher the premium and the faster the cash value build-up. In each plan, the cash values continue to increase after the premiums stop until they equal face amount (endowment) at age 100. Of course, the ultimate limited pay plan is the single pay life policy in which, at issue, the policyowner pays the full amount of premiums due on the policy in one payment (*net single premium*).

Limited Pay Life Marketing Applications—Many people want to arrange their life insurance programs so that the protection continues as long as they live but their premiums are completely paid up before retirement. In this way, they can enjoy full insurance protection for as long as it is needed without having to pay for it out of their retirement resources.

These plans are also attractive to individuals who want to emphasize cash accumulation in addition to protection. Limited pay plans make larger amounts of cash available sooner, which can be used to supplement funds for college tuition, retirement planning, emergencies, or opportunities such as the down payment on a home or business.

Single Premium Whole Life—Single premium whole life is the ultimate limited pay plan. The entire premium for the policy is paid in a lump sum at issue. Prior to 1988, when tax laws changed, this policy had a great surge in popularity because it was perceived as a life insurance policy that acted like a tax-advantaged investment. The bulk of the premium goes to the cash value rather than to the cost of protection. The insurance is paid from the current earnings of the cash value.

7-Pay Premium Test—With the enactment of TAMRA (Technical and Miscellaneous Revenue Act of 1988), policies that have premiums that exceed the government-established "7-pay premium test" are classified as Modified Endowment Contracts (MECs). With a MEC, the taxation rules change for distributions other than death proceeds. Distributions, which represent money coming out of the policy, are subject to a 10-percent penalty tax prior to age 59½ to the extent there is gain in the policy. The gain is treated as taxable income. Distributions may occur through dividend surrenders, partial policy surrenders, loans, or withdrawals.

MECs are not necessarily bad. There are two points to be made, however. First, MEC distributions will be treated the same as distributions from a nonqualified annuity. Second, of the three great advantages of life insurance, tax-deferred growth, income-tax-free death benefits, and tax-free withdrawals to the cost basis of payments, MECs enjoy the first two only. Tax-free withdrawals to cost basis are not available with MECs.

Before TAMRA, single premium whole life (SPWL) was an ideal plan to fund future cash needs because the money in the plan grew without current taxation and was available for borrowing from the policy at a low interest rate. TAMRA changed this: SPWL is still a valuable product if its being a Modified Endowment Contract is not a concern and an income tax-free life insurance death benefit is the primary purpose for buying the insurance.

Two other common forms of traditional permanent policies that you should know about are modified life and graded-premium life. Both differ in significant ways from the plans just described and both provide additional marketing flexibility.

Modified Life—The distinctive feature of modified life is the way the premiums are structured. For the first several years, modified life premiums are lower than they would be for the same amount of ordinary life (and higher than for comparable term insurance). After the initial period, typically 3 to 5 years (but that can be almost any number of years), the premiums increase to a level higher than ordinary life would have been at the issue age but less than the premium would be at the attained age at the end of the modified premium period. Modified life premiums are the *actuarial equivalent* of regular ordinary life. Premiums stay at this ultimate level amount to age 100. Cash values and other nonforfeiture values accumulate to age 100 in proportion to the premiums paid at each level, and at this point the policy operates exactly like ordinary life.

As with universal life insurance, the low entry-level premium in modified life makes it especially useful to younger people who need the full amount of permanent protection now but will not be able to pay the full premium for it for a few years. Young professionals are often good modified life prospects, since their income should rise substantially as they get established in their careers. Modified premium prospects also include people who want permanent level premium insurance but do not have cash value accumulation as an objective.

Graded-premium Life

The graded-premium life plan operates on the same principal as modified life. Instead of having only two premium levels (an entry-level and ultimate level), however, graded-premium life usually has a series of increasing premium levels over 5, 10, or 20 years. At the end of the period of graded premiums, the policyowner pays the ultimate, level premium amount until age 100.

Alternatives to Term—Modified Life and Graded-premium Life are attractive to prospects whose incomes are expected to increase and who want to establish permanent insurance programs in anticipation of their higher earnings. These policies are useful compromises between ordinary life and term insurance plans with a conversion provision. Policyowners get the protection needed without having to pay the full ordinary life premium. While they pay more than they would for term insurance in the early policy years, these lower payment plans give them the benefit of cash value accumulation and other nonforfeiture benefits from the start. The premium increase is not as severe with these modified permanent plans as it is in converting term insurance. Finally, because much term insurance is never converted as originally planned, the policyowner may ultimately be safer with either modified or graded-premium life.

Adjustable Life Insurance

Families changing needs for life insurance over long durations prompted some insurers to introduce whole life insurance that can be adjusted when needed to accommodate life cycle shifts.

Adjustable life insurance is a product that contains all of the same guarantees regarding cash values, mortality and expenses as traditional cash value insurance, but has the flexibility to allow the policyowner to adjust the plan of insurance, the premiums, and/or the face amount after it is in force. Adjustable life can be configured anywhere along the spectrum from short-duration term insurance through single-premium whole life insurance. The policyowner can request a reconfiguration of the policy at specified intervals. This allows changes to be made within the original policy instead of issuing a new policy each time needs change. Most changes can be made without evidence of insurability, but increases in face amount—except guaranteed increases—require such evidence.

The introduction of adjustable life marked the first major change in the insurance industry toward the development of flexible products. The sales thrust is to coordinate current life insurance needs and premium-paying ability. As either of these factors change, the plan of insurance can be adjusted. Interest in adjustable life waned after the success of universal life, which broadened the concept of flexibility originally introduced through adjustable life.

One important aspect of adjustable life is that it is a whole life policy with fixed premiums. Although premiums can be changed, such a change requires a formal adjustment agreed to by both the insurer and the policyowner before it can be made. The premium remains fixed and inflexible between formal adjustments.

Adjustable life can be changed, within limits. The policyowner may

- increase or decrease the premium
- increase or decrease the face amount
- lengthen or shorten the protection period
- lengthen or shorten the premium payment period

To summarize, the basic policy features of adjustable life are:

- Premiums may be flexible but are designed to be level and fixed for a chosen period of time between policy changes. The policyowner may change the premium amount as desired within policy boundary limits.
- Death benefits are flexible at the option of the insured. Increases in the death benefit may be subject to evidence of insurability.
- Cash values depend on premium and face amount.
- Policy loans are available as with traditional insurance.
- Withdrawals of dividends can be made without impairing the base policy.
- Dividends reflect current experience and can be paid in cash, used to reduce premiums, accumulated at interest, or added to the policy values, thus either increasing the death benefit or lengthening the protection period. Once applied under this last option, dividends become a part of the guaranteed value and may not be surrendered separately.
- Like many other products on the market today, adjustable life uses a current investment yield pricing method, and generally uses current mortality.

One of the significant sales appeals of adjustable life is that it is billed as the last or only policy a client will ever have to purchase. As insurance needs or premium-paying ability change, adjustments can be made within the framework of the single policy. A further example of this flexibility is the unscheduled premium privilege. This feature allows policyowners to make lump-sum payments, which will lengthen the protection period or shorten the premium-paying period. For example, a large enough payment might change a plan from term to age 43 to term to age 56, or from a life paid-up at 75 to a life paid-up at 68. In selling this feature, advisors should remember and remind prospects about exposure to the MEC rules. (Some companies restrict the availability of this feature during the early years of the contract.)

The premium for adjustable life is usually somewhat more than that for a comparable conventional life insurance policy. Part of this difference is due to the flexibility of making adjustments within the policy. However, the policyowner may end up paying less in the long run than by buying new policies or exchanging existing ones every time changes are needed. To help policyowners keep track of what they have, a report showing current benefits is sent every year from the company.

Interest-Sensitive Plans

Universal Life—The advent of universal life has had a tremendous impact on sales of life insurance products. For the first time, clients can actually see the costs of the contract, because the component parts of earnings, protection costs, and expenses are separately identified. This is referred to as "unbundled" life insurance and has had great consumer interest because the cost and return features are identifiable. At the end of every policy year, policyowners are sent an annual report on their universal life policies. This statement details the activity and status of the policy for the preceding year. The publication of the annual report is an excellent opportunity to review the policy and make any necessary changes or additions. Like adjustable life, it is an insurance plan that requires the technology of the computer to individualize the performance possibilities of a contract for a prospect.

Universal life combines the features of renewable term insurance with a tax-deferred cash value account that earns competitive current interest rates. Policyowners can pay premiums on a flexible, nonscheduled basis. The current interest rate is applied to all premium deposits in the cash value account. The policy is designed as back-end loaded, meaning there are surrender charges typically during the first 10 to 15 years that are intended to recover company acquisition costs through charges to policies surrendered or lapsed during the earlier years. The policyowner can increase or decrease the amount of death benefit protection under the policy at any time within company and IRS rules.

Universal life was the first variation of whole life to offer truly flexible premiums as well as adjustment provisions like those in adjustable life. These policies shift some of the investment risk from the company to the policyowner. Two other features initiated with universal life policies are the policyowner's ability to withdrawal part of the cash and not be treated as a loan, and the choice of either a level death benefit design or an increasing death benefit design.

Flexible Premiums—The true innovation of universal life insurance was the introduction of completely flexible premiums after the first policy year, the only time a minimum level of premium payments for a universal life policy is rigidly required. As usual, the first year's premium can be arranged on a monthly, quarterly, semiannual, or annual basis. The insurance company requires only that a minimum specified level of first-year premium payments be equaled or exceeded. After the first policy year, it is completely up to the policyowner as to how much premium to pay and even whether or not to pay premiums. The status of the policy depends on the amount and frequency of the premiums paid, as well as the interest earned and the death benefit option chosen. As long as there is enough money in the cash value account to pay for the term insurance each month, the policy remains in force.

Nevertheless, the aggregate premiums paid, regardless of their timing, must be adequate to cover the costs of maintaining the policy. If the policy cash value is allowed to drop too low (for example, the cash value is inadequate to cover the next 60 days of expense and mortality charges), the policy will lapse. If an additional premium payment is made soon enough, the policy may be restarted without a formal reinstatement process. However, if an injection of additional funds comes after the end of the grace period, the insurance company may force the policyowner to request a formal reinstatement before accepting any further premium payments.

Premium Funding—Universal life coverage is generally more costly than term but less costly than traditional whole life coverage. If the client's objective is to provide pure protection on a permanent basis and the client is not interested in accumulating significant cash values, then the cost can be relatively inexpensive. If the client wishes to use the product as an accumulation vehicle where cash values are important, then higher premiums will be needed to meet the client's objective.

The policyowner selects an initial amount of life insurance protection (known as the specified amount) and a premium level, which must meet a minimum amount. The premium, reduced by premium loads or expense charges, is deposited into the cash value account. Each month the costs of term insurance and administrative expenses are deducted. The mortality charge is based on the amount at risk. The mortality charge can vary at each attained age, and the guaranteed maximum charge for mortality is set forth in the policy contract. After deductions for expenses and mortality, interest is credited to the cash account, based on current crediting posted by the insurance company, not to drop below a guaranteed contractual rate.

Interest crediting rates are usually the focal point of competition among companies, with little emphasis on mortality rates and expense charges levied against incoming premiums. In reality all three factors constitute the total cost of insurance. The overall value of a policy and its ultimate performance will depend on all three factors taken together, and a very inaccurate portrayal of the policy can result in focusing only on interest crediting rates.

Target Premium—The target premium is the suggested premium to be paid on a level basis throughout the contract's duration. This amount is merely a suggestion and carries no liability if it is inadequate to maintain the contract to any duration, much less to the end of life. In some companies the target premium is sufficient to keep the policy in force under conservative investment return and mortality assumptions through age 95 or 100 and to pay the cash value equal to the face amount if the insured survives to that age. On the other hand, some companies with a more aggressive marketing stance have chosen lower target premiums, which are not adequate to carry the policy in force to advance ages, even under more generous assumptions of higher investment returns and lower mortality costs over future policy years.

If the actual investment return credited to the cash value falls short of the amounts assumed in deriving the target premium, the policyowner is faced with two options: 1) to increase the premium level or (2) to reduce the death benefit amount.

Some insurance companies have introduced a secondary guarantee associated with their target premium. These companies have pledged contractually to keep the policy in force for, say, 15 or 20 years and to pay the full death benefit as long as the premium has been paid in an amount equal to or greater than the required premium amount at each premium-payment interval. These provisions guarantee that the required premium will provide coverage at least as long as the guarantee period. Probably the best indication of whether or not the target premium is adequate to keep the policy in force up through age 95 or 100 is to compare it with premiums for a traditional whole life policy of a similar face amount and issue age. Universal life policy target premiums less than premiums for a comparable whole life policy should be suspect; they may be intentionally low by design because the insurance company does not expect the policy to remain in force until the very end of life in the majority of cases. The only people who will ever really find out whether or not their policy target premiums are adequate are those who pay the premiums religiously throughout the duration of the contract and live to be an age that is old enough to test the target premium.

Prefunding—The policyowner can pay maximum premiums and maintain a very high cash value (keeping the automobile gas tank full at all times). On the other hand, the policyowner can pay minimal premiums and just barely cover the mortality and expense charges because there is little or no prefunding (constantly running near empty).

The higher the amount or proportion of prefunding, the more investment earnings will be used to cover policy expenses. This follows the adage that there are two sources of money: people at work and money at work. By putting money into the policy early, the money starts earning money and therefore reduces the amount of premium payments needed from people at work at later policy durations. The ultimate extreme of prefunding is the single-premium approach, where an adequate fund is created at the inception of the policy to cover all future costs. The more common approach is a level premium structure in which partial prefunding creates an ever-increasing cash value that in turn generates increasing investment returns to offset mortality and administrative costs.

All premium suggestions are based on some assumed level of investment earnings and the policyowner bears the risk that actual investment earnings will be less than that necessary to support the suggested premium. Even though investment earnings cannot go below the guaranteed rate, a long-term shortfall may necessitate either an increase in premiums or a reduction in coverage at some future point.

At the other end of the spectrum is the minimum-premium approach, which is virtually synonymous with annual renewal term insurance. There is minimal, if any, prefunding, and premium payments barely cover the current mortality and expense charges. Under this approach the premiums must increase as the insured ages since mortality rates increase with the age of the insured. Premiums increase rapidly at advanced ages because there is still a maximum amount at risk (the cash value is very low, and the mortality rate must be applied to nearly the full death benefit amount). Under the partial prefunding approach, however, cash value increases make the amount at risk decrease as the insured ages, and the increasing mortality rate is applied to a smaller at-risk amount.

Under traditional whole life insurance policies insurance companies design a wide range of level premium contracts, each with a different level of fixed premiums. Contracts with a higher-level premium develop larger cash values at earlier policy durations. When the policy cash value is adequate to prefund the policy totally, the policy can be converted to a guaranteed paid-up status. Under participating designs, dividends can exceed the premiums after the policy has developed a large enough cash value to prefund all future policy elements. The flexible premium nature of universal life allows the policyowner to do this on his or her own.

Under the traditional contracts with cash values, the only mechanism for returning any policy overfunding in the early years was policyowner dividends. With universal life policies, however, the accumulations from prefunding are credited to the policy's cash value and are quite visible to the policyowner. The earnings rates applied to those accumulations are also clearly visible as they fluctuate with current economic conditions. This open disclosure for universal life policies eliminates some of the doubts about fair treatment often directed at whole life insurance.

Additional Premium Payments—The flexible features of universal life premiums allow policyowners to make additional premium payments above any target premium amount at any time the policyowner desires without prior negotiation or agreement with the insurance company. (The only limitation on paying excess premiums is associated with the income tax definition of life insurance.) However, the insurance company reserves the right to refuse additional premium payments under a universal life policy if the policy's cash value is large enough to encroach upon the upper limit for cash values relative to the level of death benefit granted in the policy.

Withdrawal Feature—As noted above, another new feature introduced with universal life policies is the policyowner's ability to make partial withdrawals (surrenders) from the policy's cash value without incurring any indebtedness. Money can be taken out of the policy cash value just like a withdrawal from a savings bank, and there is no obligation to repay those funds; nor is there any incurring interest on the amount withdrawn. Of course, enough must be left to pay the cost of insurance. Withdrawals affect the policy's future earnings because the cash value earning interest is reduced by the amount of the withdrawal. Its effect on the death benefit depends on the type of death benefit in force. Depending on company policy, the death benefit may or may not be reduced by the amount of the partial surrender, and the partial surrender may be subject to surrender charges, if applicable.

Death Benefit Type—Two death benefit options are available to the policyowner with universal life: the Level Option and the Increasing Option.

Level Option—The Level Option emphasizes cash accumulation. The amount payable upon death is the policy face amount (adjusted by any loans or withdrawals). The amount of protection, or net amount at risk, decreases as the cash value account increases, much like a conventional whole life policy. If the cash value approaches the face amount, which may happen in later years, an additional amount of insurance, called a corridor, is added and maintained in addition to the initial face amount. This is necessary to keep the policy from endowing and from disqualifying the policy as a life insurance contract under the federal income tax definition of life insurance.

Increasing Option—An innovation introduced with universal life, the Increasing Option, allows policyowners to emphasize insurance protection. The death benefit payable is the level risk amount (face amount) plus the cash value. The risk amount remains level, and the increasing cash value account results in an increasing (or fluctuating) death benefit. To comply with the definition of life insurance, the cash value cannot be disproportionately larger than the term insurance portion (amount at risk). Excess premium payments that threaten the policy's tax-advantaged status will be returned to the policyowner. Policies with an increasing death benefit design overcome the criticism of whole life policies that the death benefit is partially made up of the contract's cash value portion. The increasing death benefit option ensures that the death benefit will be made up of the cash value and an at-risk portion equal to the face amount of the policy. A higher amount of premium is needed for the larger amount at risk under this design.

There are similarities between the increasing death benefit design for universal life and the paid-up additions option under a participating whole life policy. Under a whole life policy, dividends are used to purchase single-premium additions to the base policy. In both types of policies the excess investment earnings are used to increase the cash value and the death benefit.

The choice of death benefits depends on the prospect's situation and objectives, and can be changed as often as necessary. For example, a young single person with few responsibilities may select the Level Option in order to build the cash account at the fastest rate. Once married and with a family, a switch to the Increasing Option would increase the protection element. This option is also an effective way to help keep the death benefit in pace with inflation. The company may require evidence of insurability when changing from the Level Option to the Increasing

Option because the cash value will be added to the policy's death benefit. Any increase in face amount starts a new 7-pay period and will be retested. Caution must be taken here, because a policy that was not a MEC could become one as a change is made. Because of the increased insurance the premium may also increase to meet the increased amount at risk.
Coverage can be adjusted up or down in a universal life policy. For example, the policyowner can increase coverage after the first policy year as long as the increase meets company guidelines and there is enough accumulation in the cash value account to pay for it. Evidence of insurability is also usually required. Decreases in coverage can be made as long as the amount of death benefit remains at or above minimum policy issue standards set by the company and the IRS.

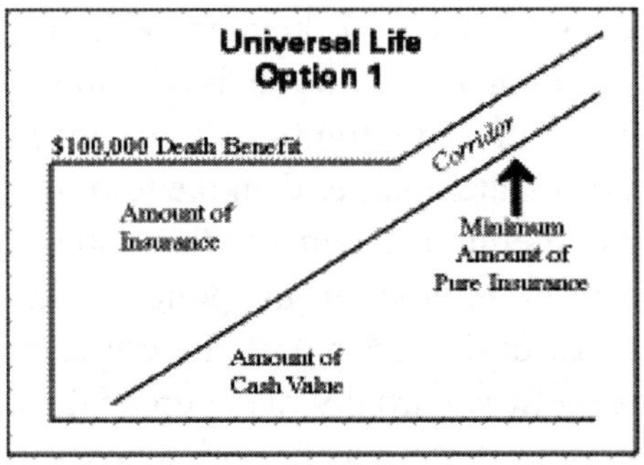

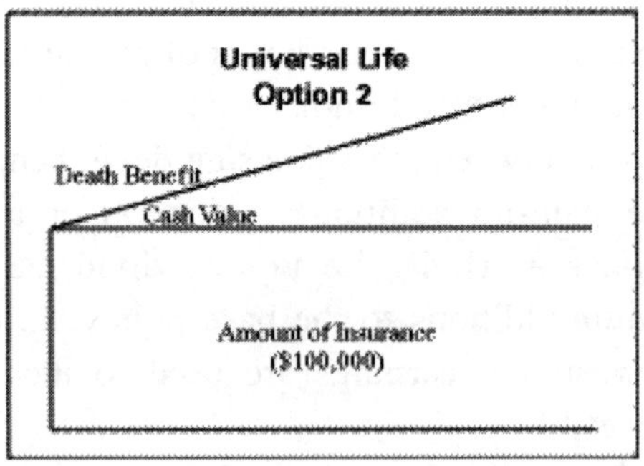

Policyowners can also borrow from the policy's cash value account. Depending on the company, the maximum loan amount may be as much as 90 percent of the cash value. Like any other cash value policy, outstanding loans at the time of death will reduce the death benefit by the amount of the loan plus any unpaid interest on the loan.

The policy may be surrendered for cash at any time; however, a surrender charge may be incurred unless the policy has been in force a certain number of years. Any surrender could be subject to taxation if there is a gain in the contract.

Most universal life policies offer the full range of additional benefit riders available with other permanent policies. A monthly deduction from the cash value is made to pay for this additional protection.

In explaining how this plan fulfills the prospect's needs, a computer-produced ledger (illustration) tailored to the prospect is generally used. Various interest rate projections of cash value are shown for future years. As will be discussed later in this chapter, it is very important that advisors use this computer capability and the policy illustrations carefully. The guaranteed rate of a plan must always be shown, as well as the current rate that the company is offering to be sure the prospect understands that cash value growth can and will change over the years. During times of high interest return on cash values, flexible permanent policies illustrate incredible growth in cash values. As returns decrease future projections change, sometimes even needing additional premium deposits. Much has been learned in the product's 20-year existence about the need to be realistic and conservative with policy performance projections.

Universal Life Marketing Applications—Universal life's flexibility makes it a useful and highly marketable product. Individuals and their families are attracted by the ability to tailor premium payments and coverage to changing circumstances.

As with any life insurance plan, young, single people who buy a universal life policy create an immediate life insurance estate. At the same time, they are able to pay into the cash value account, which grows at a current interest rate on a tax-deferred basis. These accumulations can grow even more rapidly as the insured's earnings improve and discretionary premium payments are increased.

When children enter the picture, universal life can show its flexibility. Changed to the Increasing Option, the policy can provide the additional death benefit protection that families with children should have. Optional additional benefits may be available by using family insurance riders with the policy. If financial circumstances change, premiums on that policy can be decreased, or even stopped for a period of time, possibly without having to reduce the amount of protection. Premium payments can be resumed or increased at any time.

As the insured's income grows, their life insurance protection and cash accumulation in their policies can track their career success. When the children are ready for college, premiums may be temporarily discontinued and funds withdrawn from the cash value account to pay college costs either through partial surrender or by loans. Advisors should check carefully and explain every consequence to the client when money is taken from a policy.

After graduation, the premium payments can resume and the family can begin preparing in earnest for retirement. At that time, their premium payments can be increased significantly to make the most of the tax-deferred cash buildup in the policy within policy limitations.

The juvenile market also offers excellent opportunities for universal life sales. Many parents and grandparents find this product an ideal way to start life insurance programs that can generate meaningful cash accumulation for their children and grandchildren.

Universal life can also be a versatile form of mortgage life insurance. Coverage already in force before the mortgage is acquired can be increased to compensate for the additional need for protection. There may be no need to buy a separate policy, but evidence of insurability may be required. The cash accumulation can be used to pay off the mortgage early, thus saving a considerable amount in future interest payments. The policy adds the dimension of a rapid-pay mortgage plan: establish a premium schedule that will generate the cash value needed to prepay the mortgage balance at a certain future date. If the insured dies prematurely, the policy's death benefit can pay the outstanding mortgage balance or provide the means to continue the mortgage payments if the survivors find this to be advantageous.

Universal life is a highly adaptable policy that will meet the needs and circumstances of many of your prospects. While it has proven to be a popular product for all of the reasons given here, it is not for everyone. The term cost per thousand increases as the insured ages, so the monthly deductions for this coverage will become increasingly larger.

The flexible premium schedule can prove to be a mixed blessing. Not everyone has the self-discipline to make the payments to keep the policy in force. Without the semi-compulsory nature of premium notices or authorized bank drafts from the company, many people would end up uninsured. Not everyone is comfortable with the idea of life insurance without the familiar guarantees. They may not be comfortable with life insurance that is not the simple, conservative product they have come to know.

Current Assumption and Interest-Sensitive Whole Life

Current assumption whole life is a variation of whole life that lies somewhere between adjustable life and universal life. It uses current mortality and interest earnings based on current yields rather than overall investment portfolio yields. Current rates reflect interest rates that can be obtained today. Portfolio rates represent the collective rate being earned on all the funds of the insurer that are invested at different rates at different times with different maturities. In all other respects, it is identical to conventional whole life. Current assumptions are reflected in different ways, depending on whether the company is a stock or a mutual company. Mutual companies generally reflect their current assumptions through the dividend formula, stock companies through the cash value formulas and/or through premiums.

This policy has many of the guarantees found in traditional whole life. There is a guaranteed death benefit and a minimum guaranteed interest rate to be credited on policy cash values. Some companies guarantee the mortality charge and the expense charge. When mortality and expense charges are guaranteed, the policy is often referred to as *interest-sensitive whole life,* because excess interest (credited interest minus guaranteed interest) credited to the cash value becomes the only non-guaranteed element in the contract. Because many of these designs periodically reformulate the premium based on recent experience, some of these policies are referred to as *indeterminate premium whole life.* There is a guaranteed maximum possible premium that could be charged, but actual mortality, interest, and expense result in lower premiums as a result of favorable experience in the policy.

Current assumption whole life has a redetermination feature that essentially recalculates the premium amount, and in some instances the death benefit, in reaction to the most recent interval of experience. The level of premiums influences the frequency of redetermination. Some companies use a low and/or high premium design. Adjustments are made to lower or raise the premium and/or the death benefit level, very much like what can be done with a universal life policy design. The lower the premium design, the more frequent the policy's redetermination dates. They may be annual, or every 2 or every 5 years. The policyowner selects how he or she prefers to adjust the policy. For example, if redetermination results in a potentially lower premium, the policyowner has three options:

- continue the past premium level and have the favorable results applied to enhance the policy's cash value
- increase the face amount (assuming satisfactory evidence of insurability)
- lower the premium amount

When past experience is less favorable than expected, the policyowner has a number of options, including lowering the death benefit, increasing the premium, or maintaining the status quo and allowing the policy accumulations to offset mortality and expense charges that exceed the investment earnings, within limits.

Here, briefly, are some of the significant features of this product:

- Current assumption whole life design lies somewhere between adjustable life and universal life.
- Premiums are basically fixed, but may change based on company experience. A policyowner does not have as much control of premium levels as with universal life.
- Death benefits do not fluctuate except when interest rates fluctuate and cause cash values to increase beyond the cash accumulation test limits. This is the level death benefit option "corridor" test in universal life, that is, the required amount of insurance in relation to cash values at various ages.
- Cash value minimums are guaranteed, although company experience may enhance the cash value.
- Policy loans are available as they are with traditional insurance.
- Withdrawals can be made from dividends without impairing the base policy. With nonparticipating policies, excess accumulation value can be withdrawn, subject to any surrender charges, usually without impairing the base policy.

Variable Life

Another type of interest-sensitive product, variable life, offers a combination of permanent life insurance protection and the growth potential of variable fund investments. Its unique feature is that the policy's cash value is invested in an account made up of separate account funds of equities, money markets, and bonds. The policyowner decides which separate account to invest the money, and periodically, within contract limits, may transfer funds from one fund to another. Although the policyowner chooses among the offered funds, he or she has no control over the assets purchased and sold by the individual funds. The policy guarantees a minimum death benefit, but the actual death benefit paid may be much higher if the investments perform well.

There is also risk with this type of contract. The investment risk of the policy is shifted from the company to the policyowners. The cash values are not guaranteed and fluctuate daily with investment performance. If the investments to which they are linked perform poorly, the variable life cash values may grow at a lower rate than in traditional products or not at all.

One unique benefit of a variable life policy is that it does guarantee a death benefit equal to the original face amount of the contract, regardless of how badly the investment performance is, if all required premiums are paid. The fixed-premium variable life policy provides more guarantees to the policyowner than universal life and variable universal life.

Variable life policyowners pay a level premium for the duration of the policy. There are no flexible premium payments with this product as there are with universal life. Variable life offers traditional product provisions such as loan privileges and the usual variety of optional additional benefit riders. The product is entitled to tax-free death benefits and tax-deferred cash value accumulations. Variable life is both a life insurance and equity product. For this reason, *advisors who sell it must be licensed and registered with the National Association of Securities Dealers (NASD) and the state where the product is sold.*

The product is regulated by both state law, where applicable, and by the Securities and Exchange Commission. Advisors who sell variable life insurance policies must be licensed as both life insurance agents and securities agents. The company selling variable life must provide a prospectus, which the advisor must give to prospects prior to or during the initial sales interview. The prospectus provides thorough and accurate information to the prospective purchaser concerning the company issuing the life insurance contract as well as a full disclosure of all material facts concerning the contract.

Variable Life Marketing Applications—The market for variable life is with mid- to upper-income prospects who need permanent life insurance protection, but who also have these points and objectives in common:

- They should have a basic understanding of investments and believe they are capable of making good investment decisions.

- They must have a relatively high risk tolerance. If the sometimes uncertain, nonguaranteed nature of this product makes an individual uncomfortable, this is not the product to buy.
- Variable life insurance contracts are life insurance policies, not exclusively investments. They contain mortality charges for the death benefits they provide, so the prospect should have a life insurance need.
- For the same reason, variable life insurance should not be purchased as a short-term investment vehicle. It will typically only make sense to purchase for a long-term duration, for investment performance in the short run, sales loads, mortality charges, and surrender charges will all work against any potential gains in the policy's early years.

Variable Universal Life

Variable universal life (VUL) combines the investment features of variable life and the premium flexibility and adjustment features of universal life products. Most all of the features of those two products are combined into variable universal life. There are no interest rate or cash value guarantees in this policy.

Policyowners select an initial insurance amount and premium level. Premium dollars can be directed to investment funds and switched from one fund to another, as they can in variable life. Policyowners also decide the amount of premium to pay into the policy, within company and IRS limits, and when to pay it, just as in universal life. As in universal life, the cash account must always be large enough to pay the monthly cost of term coverage and monthly expense charges. Within certain limits, policyowners can adjust the combination of cash value and term insurance in the policy by making larger or smaller premium payments.

VUL adopts the death benefit options of universal life (level and increasing). Under the level option, the death benefit does not change, regardless of how positive or negative the investment performance. If the policyowner wants the death benefit tied to investment performance, he or she must choose the increasing death benefit option. Generally the equity based investments available and the increasing death benefit option will provide an automatic hedge against inflation.

Variable universal life is regulated by applicable state law and the SEC. Sales representatives must be life insurance licensed and NASD registered, and companies must prepare a prospectus, copies of which must be given to prospects before discussing a variable product.

Variable Universal Life Marketing Applications—The market for variable universal life is typically the financially sophisticated, upscale individual who wishes to maintain maximum control over the policy. The product can be useful in personal estate planning and business insurance situations but, clearly, the policyowner must first accept the risks and responsibilities of owning this type of product.

The risks are those associated with the speculative nature of the cash value investment account. If the investments perform well, the policy performs well. If the investments perform poorly, the policy performs poorly. The policyowner must be knowledgeable enough to make the right investment decisions and must be able to accept the risk if the investments fail to live up to expectations. This caveat also applies to variable life policyowners, as previously mentioned.

The flexible premium feature means that the policyowner has full responsibility for keeping the protection in force. As with universal life, the absence of fixed premiums and regular premium notices removes the semi-compulsory nature of traditional life insurance. Policyowners must accept responsibility for guaranteeing that their life insurance will be in force when they need it.

Variable universal life is unquestionably an attractive product. It offers maximum control, investment potential, and tax-deferred cash accumulation. It is a life insurance product and should be sold for its death benefit. More importantly, it must be sold that way to qualified prospects that fully understand what they are buying.

Term versus Permanent: The Age Old Argument

This age-old question, whether term or permanent is the better product, can only be answered if we know when the insured will die. If you knew the answer to that question, you could design a policy that exactly meets your time frame. We need that type of insurance that best meets our ability to pay premiums, over our lifetimes, so that the policy will be in force when death occurs or the need for insurance protection ends.

Did you know that only 2 or 3 percent of term policies result in death claims? This is because the great majority of term policies are not in force when death occurs. Term insurance is designed to expire one day before you do. While people intend to keep term policies in force, they often change their minds when situations change. This occurs especially after retirement. Term insurance premiums become increasingly higher, no cash reserves are accumulating, and an expiration day is rapidly approaching. The insured's only option is to convert if a need still exists, at a premium well beyond what the insured can afford or wants to pay.

Which is better? What is more appropriate? It is not for you to say, although many clients will seek your opinion. The client will have to live with whatever decision he or she makes. All clients can do is take into consideration all factors which could influence their situation, make realistic projections, and monitor the performance of their plan, being aware of changes in their life and how these effect their insurance needs.

Buy Term and Invest the Difference

There are those who argue that people can do better with their money by buying term and investing the amount they would save by not paying the higher permanent premiums. The side investment would eventually be large enough to more than offset the steadily increasing term premium and, in the end, the insured would be many dollars ahead. This could be a reasonable idea, in theory, but it can run into trouble in practice. Here is why.

First, many of us do not have the discipline to make regular deposits to an investment account. Fewer still have the skill or time needed to manage a crucial investment program continuously. We use "crucial" deliberately, because the funds involved are neither discretionary nor speculative investment monies. They represent the foundation of a family's financial security. Any mistakes or mismanagement could be disastrous.

Further, even though the investments may do well enough, the difference between the term and permanent premiums that is left to invest is going to become ever smaller with passing time. The term premium will continue to increase, and commissions and fees will have to be paid to investment brokers.

Permanent policy cash values grow income tax deferred, which is not the case with earnings in most noninsurance investments such as stocks or savings accounts. They are taxed annually on the growth or distributions. The investment "side fund" is going to have to show consistently good performance to live up to its billing and offset the effect of taxes and fees. Conversely, life insurance values are guaranteed.

Any investment fund that will yield the returns needed to make this plan succeed will also bring with it an additional amount of risk. Depending on what happens and the risk philosophy of the investor, this risk may or may not have been worth taking.

Term: Least Expensive or Most Expensive?

Term insurance offers maximum protection with minimum outlay. It is the best source of temporary protection to solve temporary needs. We emphasize "temporary," however, because when term is used as a permanent solution to permanent needs, it may no longer be either efficient or effective. In fact, if the insured dies one day after the term insurance expires, it is probably the most expensive and inefficient protection that could have been purchased. Otherwise, for short and medium range needs, term is a perfectly good solution.

Much is made of the low premium outlay of term insurance. It is undeniably appealing, and rightly so, to people who may not be able to afford permanent insurance premiums but who realize that their needs are clearly long term. Term insurance can be very helpful to these people in providing the protection they need right away. If they continue to rely on term protection, however, serious consequences may result if their need is permanent. First, unless the term is converted to permanent protection some time earlier, the insurance will be discontinued by the company if the insured lives to the end of the contract term, which may be short of life expectancy age. But well before then, the term premiums that were once so attractively low will have risen to prohibitively high levels. Additionally, if the insured's insurability changes negatively during the term of coverage, it may be difficult or impossible to buy insurance at the end of the term contract.

It is said that with term you have to die to "win." Term insurance provides a death benefit only, for a specified period of time. When the term coverage terminates, so does the protection. Also, if you stop paying premiums, the coverage ends. Period. Nothing remains or can be recovered from the contract.

Check your company's rates. Compare the premium for $100,000 of permanent insurance at age 30 to the same amount of term protection to age 60 (purchased at age 30). Then consider the fact that the term premiums all went to buy "pure insurance." In other words, they were "pure" cost, just like a rented apartment. See how that compares to the cash value that has accumulated in the permanent policy by the time the insured is 60. Which would you rather have been paying for all that time?

The main thing to remember about selling term insurance is that it has a job to do: providing low-cost, temporary protection. It does that job very well. As with most products, however, it has its advantages and its drawbacks. Term, for instance, should not be used to solve permanent needs or to meet long-term insurance objectives. It is not designed to do that, and it usually does not do it very effectively. Term is, however, a valuable addition to your product portfolio. If properly sold, it can be a flexible, important part of your clients' life insurance programs. The real argument centers around what needs are long term, or if long-term needs are best addressed with life insurance.

Joint Life Plans

In recent years there has been great growth of interest in joint life policies. A joint or joint-and-survivor life contract is one that is written on more than one life. They are used in a variety of situations with different triggers for payment of the policy proceeds.

Survivorship Life Policies—Survivorship life, also referred to as second-to-die, or last-to-die, insures two or more lives and pays the death proceeds upon the death of the second or last insured to die. Some survivorship policies are traditional or interest-sensitive permanent designs, while others are term.

This is a policy that is priced and based on the probability of having to pay benefits at the death of someone other than the first to die. Since it is a form of joint life insurance, it has premiums that are less than the cost of separate policies on each of the insureds. Premiums normally continue after the first death, but some products provide that premiums cease at the first death, or offer this feature as a rider.

With some permanent policies, cash values increase dramatically at the first death. The basic reason is that the policy is designed to pay benefits following the occurrence of two events—two deaths. The reserves (cash values are a function of reserves) required by the insurance company are minimal when payment of the face amount is contingent upon two deaths rather than one. However, when the first insured dies, the death benefit will become payable upon the occurrence of only one death, so the reserve requirements for this contingency become much greater. As a result, the cash value increases substantially after the first death.

Survivorship Life's Market Application—This product is attractive in estate planning situations in which the unlimited marital deduction is used. The unlimited marital deduction allows 100 percent of assets to be passed from one spouse to another at death or by gift without paying estate taxes. Upon the death of the surviving spouse, taxes may be due. The second death triggers payment of the insurance policy benefit and the proceeds may be used to pay the taxes. It can also be used in many business and family situations. Aside from estate taxes, it is particularly attractive in those situations where a business or family could survive financially after one death, but not after a second death.

Underwriting benefits come from combining two insureds within one policy. It is even possible to get coverage for a person who would be considered uninsurable under individual underwriting standards. One version of this product will insure as many as five lives, and at the time of issue, the policyowner can elect at which death(s) proceeds will be paid.

First-to-Die Policies—The trigger for the benefit payment in a joint life policy that is designed as a first-to-die plan is the first death of those insured. It could be two people, such as a husband and wife, or it could be more. This product is used in business situations when all the partners are insured for a buy-sell agreement. It is used for pension maximization needs where retirement income is lost when the first spouse dies, for college planning, for retirement planning, and for joint mortgage redemption needs.

First-to-Die Plan's Marketing Application—It is an insurance solution for the dual-income couple when insurance is needed only as family protection at the death of the first parent. It can help meet long-range financial needs in a cost-effective manner. A LIMRA study indicates that only 65 percent of all working wives have life insurance. Providing an even greater invitation for the advisor, half of all respondents to the study said they believed that the working wife needed the same amount of life insurance as the husband.

There are a growing number of insurance companies that offer first-to-die riders that are attached to survivorship life plans. In this arrangement, a death benefit is paid at both the first and last death. There are term riders that can be used with the first-to-die plan that will pay additional benefits when the survivor dies.

Policy Illustrations

Life insurance sales usually rely on multiple-year and multiple-page policy illustrations. Prospects and clients typically do not always understand the differences between guaranteed, illustrative, and current values typically found in life insurance policy illustrations. If the differences are not clearly explained, a prospect can easily be mislead into believing that the policy promises significantly greater values than those guaranteed in the contract. Allowing this misconception to exist, or actually fostering it, is a serious form of misrepresentation.

In recent years more emphasis has been placed by insurance regulators and insurers on proper formats of illustrations and a clear distinction of what is guaranteed in the contract and what is not. As a result of the NAIC Life Insurance Illustrations Model Regulations (discussed later) insurers and state insurance departments require a full illustration, including all footnotes and explanation pages, of a product purchased by an individual to be signed by the prospect. The signature indicates that the prospect has read and understands the guaranteed and non-guaranteed elements in the illustration.

As will be discussed in detail later in this section, it is important to keep in mind that policy illustrations are based on a variety of assumptions that may or may not occur in the future. It is an estimate of what may happen based on past performance and projections of what may happen as time unfolds. Although some of these projections may be accurate some of the time, the chance that all of these factors will interact consistently as proposed is almost impossible. In fact, the only real thing we can guarantee about a policy illustration, other than those features that are guaranteed, is that what is projected will most likely not happen.

Presenting Illustrations

Life insurance illustrations are typically used in the sales presentation to show the prospect how life insurance works. They display the key policy values: the premium, guaranteed cash values, and guaranteed death benefits. Illustrations also show hypothetical future values based on certain performance assumptions such as interest rates, mortality charges, or dividend scales. This can be especially problematic when the cash value accumulation depends on variable interest rates and the value of underlying equity investments.

In your presentation, be sure that prospects understand the difference between guaranteed values and the illustrated values shown in the illustration. Describe the assumptions and variables that affect policy performance, both positively and negatively. A complete illustration will clearly explain which values are guaranteed and which are not.

The full explanation of the illustration is especially important when focusing on the projected cash values, dividends or interest accumulations in the future. It is critical to show the client that the premium will still be required if the illustrated values are not achieved. Lower credited interest rates or dividends, and increases in administrative expense or mortality charges can all negatively affect the illustrated cash values. This should be explained to the client.

The life insurance policy illustration is a tool designed to assist the advisor explain an intangible, abstract, and in many cases highly complex and sophisticated financial product. In the past few decades, with the advent of the personal computer and financial software, many advisors have turned to "illustration" selling. Illustration selling involves an emphasis on the product "looking for a need," rather than a need looking for a solution (product). Illustration selling focuses the appealing numerical values on the printed illustration, rather than conducting a fundamental financial planning process, uncovering the client's needs based on sound fact-finding, and designing real solutions to real financial problems and concerns. Avoid the trap of "illustration selling" instead of selling insurance. The temptation to leave these preferable procedures and dwell on the columns of numbers must be avoided.

As we have discussed throughout this course, you need to stay focused on the prospect's needs and how to solve them. If you don't, the columns of numbers will take on a life of their own, and soon you will drift away from solving problems toward a discussion of the life insurance illustration.

Cost Comparison

The NAIC developed a Model Regulation to give consumers a way to compare the relative costs of different policies and to improve the quality of the cost information provided to consumers. The policy summary that you are required to deliver to your client must contain two cost indexes for the issued policy. In determining the cost of the life insurance, these indexes reflect the time value of money (interest), recognizing that money paid and received at different points in time has different values.

The Model Regulation also endorses the use of a 5 percent interest rate, so that the costs of different policies can be better compared by using a specified interest assumption.

Premiums alone do not always reflect the true cost of a life insurance policy. This is especially true with permanent insurance. The public perception typically is that the premium is the price of the contract, so that the higher the premium, the higher the cost of the policy. This is too simplified and is not always or necessarily true.

The cost comparison methods described here apply to all life insurance policies. Where dividends are paid to the policy, there are provisions to properly account for their effect on the cost of the policy.

In reality, several factors (premiums, cash values and dividends, if applicable) determine the ultimate cost of insurance. We say "ultimate" because until we know how long a policy will stay in force, we cannot know for certain what the final, true cost will be. Although you cannot tell prospects the exact cost of the policy they bought today, there is a way of estimating what a policy will cost in different situations. This is done with special measures that show what the annual cost per $1,000 of insurance would be if the insured died or surrendered the policy in a certain number of years, for example 10 or 20.

Net Payment Index

This index represents the annual cost per $1,000 of insurance, adjusted for interest, if the policy remains in force over a given period of time. It considers the amount of premiums paid, less dividends received, if any, but disregards the cash value. This index is useful in comparing costs when death benefit protection is emphasized.

Surrender Cost Index

This index represents the annual cost per $1,000 of insurance, adjusted for interest, if the policy is surrendered for its cash value. Unlike the net payment index, this index takes the cash value into consideration. It is most useful in comparing costs when cash accumulation is of primary interest.

Calculation Example

In most cases, you can find a policy's interest-adjusted indexes on its policy summary or in commercial publications. However, the calculation procedure is illustrated here so you can better understand the concept or should you ever need to make the calculations yourself. Following are the calculations and, for this example, the assumptions used.

Net Payment Index Computation

To compute the net payment index:

1. Accumulate the premiums at the desired interest rate (5%).
2. Accumulate the dividends (if applicable) at the desired interest rate (5%).
3. Subtract step 2 from step 1.
4. Divide step 3 by the amount to which one dollar paid each year will accumulate for the period selected (20 years) at the desired interest rate (5%). This amount is the future value of an annuity due factor for 20 years at 5 percent (the factor is 34.7193). The result represents the estimated level annual cost of the policy.
5. Reduce the result of step 4 to a cost per $1,000 of coverage by dividing it by the number of thousands of dollars in the policy's death benefit. The result is the estimated level annual cost per $1,000 of coverage.

Assumptions

Accumulated value of $1 per year for
20 years at 5 percent $34.72

Per $1,000 Values

Annual premium $21.00
20th year accumulation of cash value $370.00
20th year accumulation of dividends at 5 percent $211.00

Calculation

1. Accumulation of premiums
   $21.00 x $34.72..$729.12

2. Accumulation of dividends*............................–$211.00
   $518.12

3. Net Payment Index:

$$\frac{\$518.12}{\$34.72} = \$14.92$$

4. Surrender Cost Index:

$$\frac{\$518.12-\$370}{\$34.72} = \$4.27$$

*Omit this step for nonparticipating or guaranteed cost policies that do not pay dividends.

Surrender Cost Index Computation

To compute the surrender cost index:

1. Accumulate the premiums at the desired interest rate (5 percent).
2. Accumulate the dividends (if applicable) at the desired interest rate (5 percent).
3. Subtract step 2 from step 1.
4. Subtract the cash value at the end of the period from step 3 and divide by the amount to which one dollar paid each year will accumulate for the period (20 years) selected at the desired interest rate (5 percent). This amount is the future value of an annuity due factor for 20 years at 5 percent (the factor is 34.7193). The result represents the estimated level annual cost of the policy.
5. Reduce the result of step 4 to a cost per $1,000 of coverage by dividing it by the number of thousands of dollars in the policy's death benefit. The result is the estimated level annual cost per $1,000 of coverage.

Notice that the steps are the same for the net payment and the surrender cost indices, except that there is no subtraction of the 20th-year cash value in the net payment cost index.

Policies whose net payment and surrender costs indexes are lower than these would generally be better buys. Policies with higher index figures would probably be less favorable buys, all other things being equal.

A simple way to explain these indexes to your prospect or client is to treat the policy's premium as being split into three parts: the dividend, the cash value, and the company's share. Even though the premium remains level throughout the life of the policy, the size of these three parts varies through the years. In the early years, dividends and cash value accumulations are small and the company's share large, but as time passes, dividends and cash values increase and the company's proportional share decreases.

Assume that the annual premium of $21 per thousand can be broken down into the average dividend of $6.08, the average cash value increment—coming directly from the premium, not from earned interest—of $10.65, and the average company share of $4.27. These averages take into consideration the time value of money.

This concept can be diagrammed as follows:

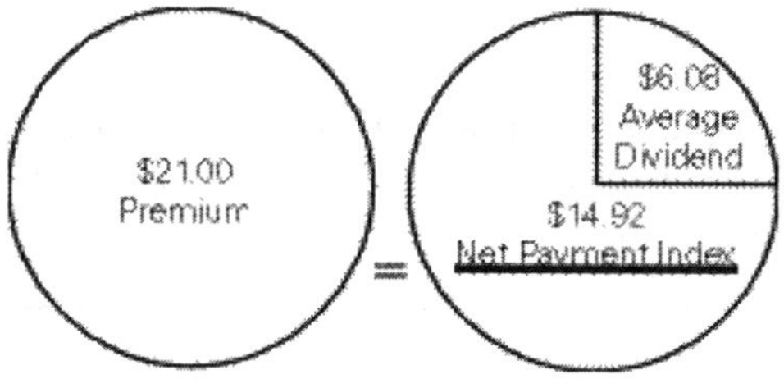

Subtracting the average dividend from the premium leaves the net payment index of $14.92. This is the policyholder's average yearly cost, assuming the policy is still in force 20 years from date of issue.

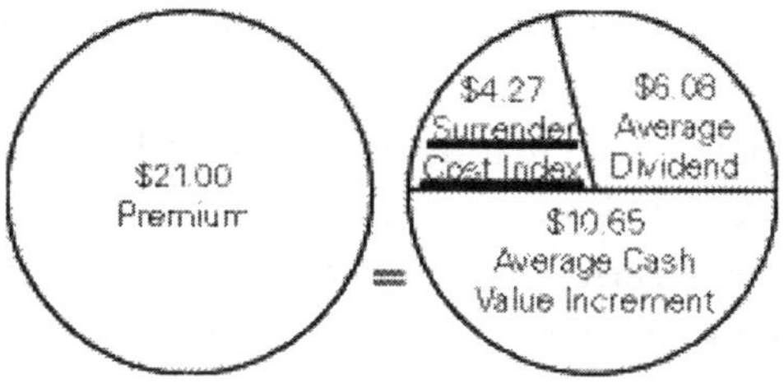

Subtracting the average dividend and the average cash value increment from the premium leaves the surrender cost index of $4.27. This is the yearly cost—that portion of the premium the policyowner does not get back—assuming that the policy is surrendered for its cash value in the 20th year.

Equivalent Level Annual Dividend

A third index that might appear on the Policy Summary is the equivalent level annual dividend. This is a measure of the part that dividends play in the cost of a participating policy. This index—which is labeled the average dividend in the diagram we just illustrated—is an average of the total dividends with interest over the 20 years. It is found by dividing the 20th year accumulation of dividends by the appropriate accumulation of one dollar per year factor. Referring to our previous calculation example, this index would be $6.08, found by dividing $211 by $34.72.

No More Virtual Strangers

"(Policyowner), as you can imagine, it's always somewhat awkward approaching virtual strangers about a subject not many people are terribly anxious to talk about. But if I can get a good word in advance from someone I've worked with and who appreciates the value of what I've done, it makes the approach so much easier..."

Guidelines and Regulations for Policy Illustrations

The proliferation of illustrations in the early 1980's prompted calls for standards or guidelines to standardize illustrations. Computerized illustrations and software evolved rapidly, yet there were no regulations to monitor and control illustrations. Competitive pressures pushed companies to become more creative in producing the best-illustrated policies.

This led to companies creating assumptions for their illustrations that might be considered misleading, irresponsible, and unrealistic. Projecting values for interest earnings, mortality improvements and expense reductions that might not be possible, let alone sustainable, became a part of the cat-and-mouse game of "out-illustrating" the competition.

Professional Practice Guidelines

To bring some sense to the "illustration game," the Society of Financial Service Professionals took the initiative and adopted the *Professional Practice Guideline*, a checklist of guidelines for sales material and presentations.

The principal items addressed in the checklist were interest rates, mortality expenses, dividends, benefit changes, surrender charges, waiver-of-premium benefits, policy comparisons, and issues concerning replacement. The *Professional Practice Guideline* was intended to serve as a checklist of information to be evaluated before a prospect or client was asked to make a buying decision. This checklist could be shared with prospects to see if they feel that all of their questions have been answered and that they understand all of the issues.

It is important for advisors to understand and be able to explain to their clients how changes in interest rates, investment gains, mortality experience, cost of insurance, persistency, and expenses can affect the future performance of a life insurance policy and the policy illustration. Understanding how the figures are derived and what they represent will help advisors communicate the risks as well as the benefits of a life insurance contract to their clients. Advisors can provide details on guaranteed and non-guaranteed elements in the contract and help avoid disappointment in the future.

Many life insurance products sold today are adjustable, either as a traditional "participating" product or as one of the family of products referred to as "interest sensitive." While adjustable products incorporate guarantees, sales illustrations are designed to convey to the prospect the benefits and costs under a set of optimistic assumptions. Since the insurance company generally limits its responsibility to the guarantees, risks associated with the development of a higher benefit or lower cost than that generated by the guarantees are borne by the policyowner.

The following guidelines for sales materials and presentations using policy illustrations are excerpted from the Society of Financial Services Professional's *Professional Practice Guide* (The Society Page, June 1988, a publication of the Society of Financial Service Professionals, Bryn Mawr, PA 19010). Though this document is no longer supported by the Society, the concepts are still valid and important.

As you will see as you review these guidelines, many aspects and assumptions behind illustrations, not normally revealed by the company to advisors or their clients, have a tremendous impact on the resulting policy illustrations. To properly understand the illustration being presented, an advisor and his or her client must understand how the following factors impact the illustration being presented.

For example, in looking at mortality assumptions, you can see that a company may use recent mortality experience, or assume mortality improvements in the future. Looking at interest, the policy illustration may assume that investment experience will improve, or use rates from an index not actually tied to company results. Some companies assume that lapse rates will improve, or take some other assumption that may be unrealistic, yet impact the illustration in most favorable ways.

Excerpts from the Professional Practice Guideline

I. Mortality—The mortality expense used in an illustration may reflect
   1. the company's actual current or recent mortality experience
   2. actual current or recent mortality experience modified at an assumed rate of increase or decrease
   3. a combination of mortality and other expenses
   4. zero mortality

   Which of the above is used in the illustration?

II. Interest Rate—The interest assumption used in an illustration may be based upon
   1. interest rates earned by the company on
      a. all investments now held
      b. new investments
      c. new investments over a certain number of past years
      d. other combinations of actual investments
   2. an independent index such as
      a. Treasury bills
      b. Moody's long-term bond index
      c. other indexes
   3. another basis not tied to company results or an index
   4. Interest rates may be the gross interest rate resulting from investments, indexes or other measures, or the gross interest rate reduced by
      - investment expenses
      - investment expenses and other expenses
      - expenses and profit
      - a fixed amount or percentage
   5. Interest assumptions may be constant or they may be assumed to change over future years.

   Which of the above is used in the illustration?

III. Basis of illustration
   1. Is the policy of the traditional participating variety, or does it contain nonguaranteed pricing elements using a means other than dividends?
   2. If the policy is not participating, describe the nonguaranteed elements involved (such as nonguaranteed interest crediting rates, mortality charges, loadings, and so on)
   3. If the policy is participating, does the company state that the contribution principle** is being followed in the illustrative dividend scale? If it is not, how does it differ? (The contribution principle states that aggregate divisible surplus should be distributed in the same proportion as the policies are considered to have contributed to the divisible surplus.)

4. If the policy is not participating, what is the company's policy with respect to determination and redetermination of nonguaranteed pricing elements, with particular reference to (a) the degree of discretion reserved by the company and (b) whether any of the elements are guaranteed to follow an outside index?
5. Basis of dividends or nonguaranteed factors
    1. Are any of the underlying experience factors different from current experience? If so, describe how and for what factor(s).
    2. If the policy is participating, is there a substantial probability that the current illustrative dividend scale cannot be continued if current experience continues?
    3. If the policy is not participating, is there a substantial probability that current illustrations cannot be supported by currently anticipated experience?

IV. Special Considerations

A. Some contracts provide for future benefit increases. Are such increases subject to evidence of insurability?

B. Some Disability Premium Waiver provisions waive a term cost of insurance and some waive a level (permanent) cost. Specifically what is waived?

C. Are any surrender charges illustrated? Are surrender charges fixed or determined at company discretion?

D. Comparisons for replacement transactions:

1. Is the current experience of the product to be replaced being used and have all available amendments which might improve the performance of the product been taken into consideration?
2. Will suicide and incontestable provisions be extended by the replacement?
3. Are there any differences in assumptions of the old and new product that will affect the comparison?
4. Will the replacement produce a short-term loss? How long will it take any superior performance of the replacing product to offset any short-term loss?
5. Are any assumptions of either product contradicted by either carrier's past experience?
6. Is the replacement clearly to the advantage of the policy owner?

Life Insurance Illustration Questionnaire

The Society took further initiative regarding policy illustrations in 1992 by adopting the *Life Insurance Illustration Questionnaire*. It was intended to stimulate advisors to question and more thoroughly understand the intricacies of illustrations, so they could better explain them to prospects. The questions were directed to the insurance company regarding the assumptions underlying the responding insurer's illustrations. The questionnaire has been since abandoned by the Society because of the labor-intensive nature of checking and compiling the reports coming from the life insurance companies, who are constantly changing their product portfolios. But the nature and types of questions asked in the questionnaire are still valid and useful to advisors.

It is generally acknowledged that policy illustrations work well to educate clients in the mechanics of how policies work. But policy illustrations are not an adequate tool for comparing costs of policies from different insurance companies. Illustrations do not create accurate projections of future performance because of differences in assumptions made by insurance companies and the actual future performance of the company and the economy.

The Life Insurance Illustration Questionnaire is designed very much like the Professional Practice Guideline. It asks similar questions and has a similar purpose, which is to uncover the assumptions that make up the design of a life insurance policy illustration. The key factors examined by the Illustration Questionnaire are: the general nature of the policy, mortality, interest or crediting rates, expenses and persistency. A summary of some of the questions from the Illustration Questionnaire (IQ) follows:

I. General

1. Is the policy participating or non-participating?
2. Describe the non-guaranteed elements. How does the company re-determine non-guaranteed pricing elements?
3. Do any experience factors(s) underlying the dividend scale or other non-guaranteed elements used in the illustration differ from recent historical experience?
4. Is there a substantial probability that the current illustrative values will change if actual recent historical experience continues unchanged?

5. Is it company policy to treat new and existing policyholders of the same class the same or consistently with respect to the underlying factors in pricing?
6. Describe all the effects of the first death on the policy and riders in joint and survivor policies.

II. Mortality

1. Do the mortality rates underlying the scale used in the illustration differ from actual recent historical experience?
2. Does the illustration assume mortality improvements in the future?
3. Do the mortality or cost of insurance charges used in the illustration include some expense charge?
4. Do the underlying mortality rates vary by product?
5. Indicate the approximate duration, if any, when all underlying mortality rates vary only by attained age. (For example, when does select become ultimate?)

III. Interest or Crediting Rates

1. What is the interest rate used in the dividend scale or credited in the illustration? The portfolio rate, new Money Rate, gross rate, or net rate?
2. Does the absence of interest rates reflect the earnings on all invested assets, a portion of assets, or just new investments?
3. Does the interest rate used in the illustration vary between new and existing policies?
4. Do the interest rates used in the illustration reflect actual recent historical earnings rates? At any point in the illustration do the interest rates used exceed the actual recent historical earnings?
5. Do the interest rates used in the illustration vary by policy duration, policy type, class or otherwise?
6. How does individual policy loan activity affect the illustrated interest rates?

IV. Expenses

1. Do the expense factors used in the illustration reflect actual recent historical company experience?

2. Are the expense charges used in the illustration adequate to cover the expenses in sales and administration? If not, how are remaining expenses covered?
3. How are investment expenses and all taxes assessed?
4. Are expense factors used in the illustration different for new and existing policies? Do they vary by product type, class, policy duration or otherwise?

V. Persistency

1. If the actual persistency was better than assumed, would that negatively affect illustrated values?
2. Does the illustration involve a persistency bonus (to policyholders who pay premiums for a specified number of years)? Is it guaranteed?
3. Is there any limitation or company discretion in deciding to pay the bonus?
4. What conditions must be met to pay the bonus?
5. What is the form of the bonus (cash, additional interest, refund of mortality and/ or loading charges)?
6. Does the company set aside any reserve or other liability earmarked for future bonuses?

As you can see, there are many assumptions behind the numbers on a policy illustration. In a way, without knowing these assumptions, the illustration is totally worthless because these assumptions have such a significant impact on the illustrative values. How is the interest rate determined in the illustration? Are mortality improvements assumed? These and the other questions on the IQ should be understood if the illustration is to have any value.

NAIC Life Insurance Illustrations Model Regulation

In 1996 the National Association of Insurance Commissioners (NAIC) adopted a model regulation pertaining to life insurance illustrations. The stated purpose was to provide rules for life insurance policy illustrations that will protect consumers and foster consumer education. Its goals were to ensure that policy illustrations do not mislead purchasers of life insurance and to make illustrations more understandable and standardized. A key strategy in the regulation was to clearly define and distinguish for the consumer what is and what is not guaranteed in the contract.

There were some basic similarities among policy illustrations, such as a listing of the annual premium and the policy's cash value for each policy year. However, despite the similarities, there were no uniform standards applicable to policy illustrations prior to the introduction of this NAIC Model Regulation. The organization of information within a single illustration varied drastically from one insurance company to another, even if the same information was contained in the report. Rogue insurance companies could publish illustrations with any assumptions they wished without regulatory consequence.

The model regulation has had a tremendous impact on illustrations in all states because life insurance companies moved toward using the same illustrations in all states. By making all their illustrations conform to the most stringent state's requirements, insurers could meet the regulatory requirements as well as the NAIC Model Regulations.

The life insurance illustrations model regulation does not apply to variable life, credit life, or life insurance with a face amount of less than $10,000. It does not apply to either individual or group annuity contracts. The regulation applies to all non-variable group and individual life insurance policies and certificates for more than $10,000 of death benefit.

The regulation requires the insurance company to declare to the state insurance department for each policy form it files whether or not it intends to use illustrations to market that form of coverage. A copy of each illustration the insurer intends to use must be forwarded to the state insurance department. The regulation contains significant minimum standards dealing with the format and content of any information provided in the illustration. Both the producer and the client must sign the initial illustration, with a copy provided to the insurance company and the client. If the issued policy differs in any way from the originally issued illustration, a revised illustration must be submitted, following the same procedures.

Each illustration used in the sale of a life insurance policy covered by the regulation must be clearly labeled "life insurance illustration" and must include the following:

1. the name of the insurance company
2. the name and business address of the insurer's agent
3. the name, age, and sex of the proposed insured
4. the underwriting or rating classification upon which the illustration is based

5. the generic name of the policy (for example, whole life, universal life, and so on)
6. the initial death benefit amount
7. the dividend option election or application of nonguaranteed elements, if applicable

The NAIC Model regulation prohibits insurers and their advisors from the following:

1. representing the policy as anything other than a life insurance policy
2. using or describing nonguaranteed elements in a manner that is misleading or has the capacity or tendency to mislead. The nonguaranteed elements must be labeled as nonguaranteed.
3. stating or implying that the payment or amount of nonguaranteed elements is guaranteed. It must clearly be stated that these elements are subject to change and that the actual results may be more or less favorable.
4. using an illustration that does not comply with the illustration regulation
5. using an illustration that is more favorable to the policyowner than the illustration based on the illustrated scale of the insurer
6. providing an applicant with an incomplete illustration
7. representing in any way that premium payments will not be required for each year of the policy in order to maintain the illustrated death benefits, unless that is the fact
8. using the term "vanish," "vanishing premium," or a similar term that implies the policy becomes paid up, to describe a plan for using nonguaranteed elements to pay a portion of future premiums
9. using an illustration that is not "self-supporting." The illustration must include actuarial assumptions of self-sustaining profitability.

The NAIC model illustration regulation specifies that all illustrations must be dated as of the date prepared. All pages must be marked to indicate both the individual page number and the total number of pages in the illustration (for example, "page 3 of 7"). The illustration must clearly indicate which elements are guaranteed and which are not. Any amount available upon surrender shall be the amount after deduction of surrender charges. Items presented in illustrations can be in the form of charts, graphs, or tabular values.

Each illustration must be accompanied by a narrative summary that describes the policy, premiums, and features, and defines column headings used in the illustration. The summary should also state that actual results might be more or less favorable than those shown in the illustration.

Case History

Variable Universal Life

Tony Tyler entered the insurance field after spending 8 years as a real estate loan officer. Tony had met several insurance advisors at the mortgage company and saw the career opportunities. With a year in the business, Tony has no regrets and is eager to learn more.

Prospect—E. Francis Mindlin was a member of our town's Chamber of Commerce when we first met. At our monthly luncheon meeting we had shared the same table. During lunch I found that Fran was an associate attorney at one of the larger law firms in town.

When given the opportunity to talk about my background, Fran expressed some interest in insurance. Fran remarked that she had many clients ask for advice, but really didn't know much about the product. We scheduled an appointment at Fran's office for later that week so I could explain the different products. I knew a center of influence in Fran's position would be helpful.

The Interview—When we met, I suggested that I explain the different programs by using Fran's situation as an example. Fran was a little embarrassed by this, and said that someone who didn't have a family really didn't need insurance.

I told her that many of my clients were in this position when I first met them, but that with today's products, insurance could be useful to almost everyone. Besides, the uses and examples of life insurance I was about to show her would be more real if we used her as the insured.

I asked if she could design a perfect program, what would it be? Fran thought for a long time, and it was tough for me to keep quiet. After what seemed like an eternity, Fran said, "I would want a policy that could grow in equity; it would have to keep pace with inflation. I would want control over the equity."

I asked if the plan should feature tax-deferred growth and flexibility in payments. Fran asked for an explanation about the premium. I said I was suggesting a premium, which within certain guidelines, could be raised or lowered.

"I don't believe it! If you have an insurance program that lets me set a premium, invest the money, and control the equity, I may buy it today," Fran said with a laugh.

"There is such a policy," I said. "It's called variable universal life. If you are really interested, I would suggest a meeting tomorrow at my office to see what we can build."

Fran agreed and the appointment was set.

Close—I decided to make my presentation on the assumption that Fran had become a prospect. I made arrangements to have a computer available for the meeting.

Together we began to look at the different alternatives and played out the assumptions on the computer. After we had run four alternatives, Fran sat back in her chair and said, "I'm really impressed. I didn't realize life insurance was so flexible."

"Does this policy meet your criteria of what your perfect policy would accomplish?"

When she answered yes, I brought up the previous day's remark, took out an application, and started to complete it. I fully expected Fran to stop me, but to my surprise each question was answered as I asked it. Fran decided on a $50,000 death benefit to complete the process.

Summary—I was taught a valuable lesson. First, I learned that everyone I speak to is a prospect, even when you are not more than luncheon seatmates at a Chamber luncheon. My second lesson was that if you can meet a person's needs, the sale is a natural event. No struggle at all.

Chapter Six Review

Key terms and concepts are explained in the Glossary. Answers to the Review Questions and Self-Test Questions are found in the back of the book following the Glossary.

Key Concepts and Terms

feature/benefit
stock company
demutualization
fraternal insurance company
accelerated death benefit
term insurance
permanent insurance
reentry term
select/ultimate mortality
renewable term
conversion privilege
reserve
net amount at risk
NAIC Model Regulation
net payment index
illustration selling
ordinary life
mutual company
limited pay life
modified life
graded premium life
adjustable life
universal life
current assumption whole life
interest-sensitive whole life
variable life
variable universal life
joint life
survivorship life
cost-adjusted indexes
surrender cost index

Review Questions

6-1. Discuss the key factors in developing the solution to the prospect's needs.

6-2. Explain the key points you should review when preparing to present the solution.

6-3. Discuss the key steps in presenting the solution to the prospect.

6-4. Explain the key differences between term and permanent insurance.

6-5. Briefly describe the different types of term insurance.

6-6. Summarize the economic living values of permanent life insurance.

6-7. Briefly describe the different types of traditional permanent insurance.

6-8. Briefly describe the different types of interest-sensitive permanent insurance.

6-9. Discuss the assumptions made in policy illustrations and their shortcomings.

6-10. Explain cost-adjusted indexes and their importance.

Self-Test Questions

Instructions: Read Chapter 6, then answer the following 10 questions to test your knowledge. Circle the correct answer. When you are finished, check your answers with the answer key in the back of the book.

6-1. In a level premium ordinary life (whole life) policy, the net amount at risk

(A) increases each year
(B) decreases each year
(C) remains the same over time
(D) could increase or decrease based on investment returns

6-2. Which of the following statements best describes a benefit?

(A) Benefits are characteristics of the product itself.
(B) Benefits are descriptive, and are not given values.
(C) Benefits are value-free and objective.
(D) A benefit is what the prospect gets as a result of the feature.

6-3. Which of the following is a characteristic of an ordinary life policy?

(A) It is the most expensive form of cash value insurance.
(B) It matures at age 65.
(C) It has an increasing cash value and a decreasing risk amount.
(D) Both the cash value and amount at risk increase annually.

6-4. Bruce, age 40, is interested in accumulating cash value in a permanent life insurance policy as rapidly as possible to have funds to supplement his retirement 20 years from now. Which of the following policies would best achieve his goal?

(A) 20 Payment Life
(B) Endowment at Age 100
(C) Life Paid-up at 65
(D) Ordinary life

6-5. The interest-adjusted index method of comparing policies is

(A) very well suited for evaluating policy replacements
(B) well suited for comparing dissimilar polices such as term and whole life
(C) basically a buy-term-and-invest-the-difference approach
(D) indicating that a policy with smaller numerical values (indexes) is preferable to a policy with higher indexes

6-6. Which of the following statements concerning policy illustrations is (are) correct?

I. The NAIC model regulation does not apply to variable life, credit life, or life polices with a face amount of less than $10,000.
II. The NAIC model applies to non-variable life and individual life policies for face amounts over $10,000.

(A) I only
(B) II only
(C) Both I and II
(D) Neither I nor II

6-7. Which of the following statements regarding developing a plan is (are) correct?

I. Take the relevant information gathered from the fact-finder and design a plan that reflects the prospect's needs, goals, and premium commitment.
II. It is best to present only one solution because presenting more will confuse the prospect and probably make closing more difficult.

(A) I only
(B) II only
(C) Both I and II
(D) Neither I nor II

6-8. Re-entry term may be a good choice for a person who is in good health and remains insurable. Which of the following statements concerning re-entry term insurance is (are) correct?

I. The initial premium is based on an ultimate mortality table if the insured's health is better than average.
II. Future premiums will be based on a select mortality table if satisfactory evidence of insurability is periodically provided as required by the insurer.

(A) I only
(B) II only
(C) Both I and II
(D) Neither I nor II

6-9. All of the following statements concerning universal life insurance policies are correct EXCEPT

(A) Under the increasing death benefit option the total death benefit equals the stated face amount plus the amount at risk.
(B) The component parts of earnings, protection costs, and expenses are "unbundled."
(C) Withdrawals effect future earnings because the fund that remains intact to earn interest is reduced by the amount of the withdrawal.
(D) The target premium amount is merely a suggestion and carries no liability if it is inadequate to maintain the contract to any duration.

6-10. All of the following statements are correct regarding adjustable life insurance EXCEPT

(A) It is a good choice for the individual who wants to assume the investment risk for potentially increased returns.
(B) The insurer can request evidence of insurability if a policy change increases the risk.
(C) It is a type of whole life policy with fixed premiums and policy guarantees.
(D) The policyowner can request a reconfiguration of the policy at specific intervals.

7

Implement the Plan

Overview and Learning Objectives

Chapter 7 focuses on implementing the plan as a solution for the prospect's financial needs and goals. Included in this discussion is the process of obtaining the prospect's approval and agreement to take action on the advisor's recommendations, techniques for putting these recommendations into action, and suggestions on responding to prospect concerns, resistance and objections. Another important aspect of the selling/planning process when life insurance is a solution is the underwriting process. The chapter will review what is involved in underwriting, and the advisor's role in getting the contract issued in the most expedient and favorable way.

By reading the text and answering the questions, you should be able to:

7-1. Know when and how to ask the prospect to buy.

7-2. Explain how to clarify and respond to objections.

7-3. List and explain four categories of objections.

7-4. List and describe closing techniques and how to implement them.

7-5 Define the underwriting process and the information that is used in underwriting.

7-6. Describe the advisor's role in field underwriting and facilitating the underwriting process.

7-7. Describe substandard policy issue, types of substandard ratings, and the criteria and rationale used in assigning them.

7-8. Explain the importance of explaining the underwriting process to the client.

Chapter Outline

The Closing Interview

This chapter will cover the next step in the selling/planning process: Implement the Plan. We will review traditional closing techniques and ways to answer prospects' concerns and objections. In the client-focused approach and financial planning process this step is called "implementing the plan" and "supporting the decision to buy." This terminology is used by some financial services companies and advisors to avoid traditional sales terms such as "objections" and "closing," which have a negative connotation, and support the trend toward the financial planning model and client-focused selling. Many training materials today use words and phrases such as "implementing the plan," and "getting commitment" for closing, and "managing resistance" and "answering client concerns" for answering objections. For some companies the word planning has replaced selling. This demonstrates a general trend away from transactional sales approaches and techniques.

The text will continue to use traditional sales terms, but it must be made clear that "hard-sell," transactional, and manipulative techniques are not conveyed in these terms. This textbook adheres to a client-focused selling philosophy. This is partly based on the perception that the "close" is not a separate, distinct event or step in the sales process, as traditionally thought, but an integral part of the entire presentation. There is no magical or "drum roll, please" moment that is the close; no bells, no whistles, no silence. The close is simply the culmination of the entire sales/planning process.

The term closing has many meanings: to stop, suspend, terminate, but also more positive meanings such as to make complete, to come together, to come to an end, to conclude, finish, or culminate. Although closing comes at the end of the sales/planning process, it really signals the beginning of a new account and a new relationship, as the prospect becomes a client. Closing should not be hard to do and should not be a negative experience for the advisor or the prospect, if it is viewed simply as the culmination of the process, as securing commitment to your proposed recommendations by asking the prospect for a decision.

The Mind Rehearsal

Before you meet your prospect again to conclude your sale, visualize what will happen in your presentation. How will the prospect answer your questions? How will you reply if the prospect asks a difficult question or voices an objection that makes you hesitate? What papers will you need? How will you handle all the forms? Where will you sit when you talk together? What will be the expression on his or her face when the application is signed?

This is a mind rehearsal for the sales interview. Sit quietly and imagine completing your sale. This will give you confidence for the actual meeting. When you can see the sale in progress and visualize your prospect saying yes, then you are prepared to meet. Visualization prepares you for the close.

Preparing for the Closing Interview

In preparing for the closing interview, you should review the information gathered previously and highlight key areas. Refresh your memory on the details discussed, so that you are very familiar with the client's information when you meet again. Review their needs, goals, and priorities, making note of factual and subjective information. Refresh your conversation about issues and concerns of the client. You are now ready to prepare your closing presentation.

Review your recommendations and the reasoning behind the decisions you have made regarding the solutions you have designed. Analyze the alternative plans you may have prepared, and be ready to discuss the benefits and drawbacks of each option. This will give your client the information they need to decide what is best for them.

Mentally walk through the presentation, anticipating objections, concerns, and points of resistance that the client may present. This will sharpen your focus on the important points of each option and the pros and cons of each. Be sure you have any presentation materials you wish to show ready to go. Review these so everything you plan to discuss is fresh in your mind. Check your briefcase to be sure all application materials are in adequate supply. You are ready to go!

Asking for the Sale

Closing means carrying the interview to its natural conclusion, which is asking for the sale. The advisor must develop the skill of knowing when and how to ask the question that leads the prospect to make the decision to buy. It is a matter of commitment for the client to accept the product recommendation, the company, and the advisor. For the advisor it means

Closing Statement

(Prospect's Name), as I understand it, you want to achieve certain goals which we have identified (restate those goals) and I think you agree these goals cannot be achieved unless you make some changes. Now if I could show you a way to accomplish precisely what it is you want to do, at a cost that you could afford, am I correct in assuming that you would be interested in implementing such a plan?

—*Norman G. Levine, "A Passion for Compassion"*

being skilled at asking the question in a way that demonstrates sincerity and integrity, avoiding any perception that you are a stereotypical life insurance salesperson just "turning a sale."

If you have completed all the previous steps of the selling/planning process with honesty and thoroughness, your attempts at closing will be accepted as professional and be expected as a natural part of the sales/planning process. In the initial prospecting step, you qualified the prospect. In the initial interview, you introduced yourself, explained your services, continued to qualify the prospect, and began to establish rapport and expectations for the relationship. The prospect was accepting of this or the relationship would have most probably ended. You got commitment from the prospect to engage in the fact-finding process, and established and prioritized client goals. You got a dollar commitment and mutual agreement on the needs to be addressed. You developed solutions and alternatives and presented them to the client. After all, you are there to help the prospect. Once the prospect knows you believe you are offering the best possible solution to his or her individual needs, the close is a natural, not a forced, event.

The Real Villain

Don't permit your prospect to make insurance the villain when the objection is his or her own problem with funding. Life insurance is not the problem; it is the solution. The premium is not the problem; it is the cost of the solution.

When to Close (Confirm the Sale)

At the beginning of this step in the sales/planning process, you review with the client their needs, concerns, and objectives. Reconfirm the dollar commitment, the amount he or she is willing to spend. Arriving at this step should in itself express the prospect's commitment to address his or her needs. You have or will present a solution and possibly alternative solutions. You present a benefit summary that reviews all of the relevant features and the benefits in which the client is interested.

You can now ask an open-ended question, such as "where do we go from here?" "How would you like to proceed?" or "What's our next step?" You can also be more direct with a closed ended question like, "Would you like to start this plan today?" or "Is there any reason why you would not want to get this started?" Essentially, closing is simply seeking agreement from the prospect that the solution proposed is a proper and acceptable plan to address the need or needs uncovered in the process.

Watch your client's interest level and buying signals. If the client is acting and speaking in ways that indicate they are ready to buy, stop talking and confirm the sale. Observe nonverbal cues; leaning forward, listening carefully, open arms, and relaxed posture all indicate interest. If the nonverbal communication is negative, such as crossed arms, negative expression, tense posture, or gazing off into space, ask an open-ended question such as, "Do you have a question about that?" or "Is there something on your mind?"

On the other hand, a prospect may want more information before making a decision. Any attempt to get confirmation too soon would be seen as sales pressure and may close off communication and damage rapport.

If you encounter resistance, it may be that one of the earlier parts of the sales process was done incompletely, improperly, or was skipped. Mentally review the earlier parts of the sales process. You may have failed to sell yourself, or failed to find an unfulfilled dream or want, or convince the prospect of your ability to provide a solution to his or her problem. You must take charge and be enthusiastic. Your self-confidence, positive mental attitude, knowledge, belief, and communication skills are an important requirement for sales success.

Once you have presented your solution, the prospect may have questions, express concerns, or raise objections to what is proposed. One important thing to keep in mind is that closing should not involve a bag of tricks, a series of maneuvers to outwit the prospect. Closing methods are designed and should be used as a way of helping the prospect make the buying decision. Even if everything is going well and the prospect appears ready to buy, sales skills are necessary and you may want to employ techniques to help the prospect commit to the solution and buy.

Confirming the Sale

Making it easy for your prospect to say yes is important. Many of the objections that are raised are just the prospect's need to participate in the thinking process, test your ideas, and be assured that your proposal is the best answer to the needs you have clarified. If you have addressed the objections properly, you will have your sale and a new client. To do this, encourage questions.

Questions to Increase Understanding

You may want to stop occasionally during your presentation to elicit questions from your prospect, or even to ask a few questions yourself. In this way you can continually check what your prospect is thinking and feeling, and manage your sales approach to tune into the prospect's increasing understanding. This is empathy in action. Here are a few examples of checking-typequestions or trial closes that will work well to keep you in tune with prospects during a sales interview. Be careful that some of your questions require more than a yes or no. Hearing yes too often will lull you into complacency.

- "Is what I am saying making sense so far?"
- "Can you see where we are headed with this line of reasoning?"
- "While I am presenting my recommendations, if there is anything at all that is not perfectly clear, please interrupt. I really encourage you not to leave questions until later, unless we know that one will be answered in the course of my presentation. Is that agreeable?"
- "What do you think so far?"
- "Did the point I just made raise an issue?" This works well as a response to a frown or facial expression that demonstrates a reaction other than understanding or agreement.
- "Wouldn't you agree?" This is one of the most powerful questions you could pose during your presentation. It asks the

Client-Focused Selling—Getting Commitment to the Solution

The client-focused sales/planning process is not designed to put pressure on your prospects or clients. It is designed to solve their problems or help them take advantage of opportunities. It's what you have done up to the presentation that will make or break the sale. If your customer isn't sold by now, more sales pressure won't do it. What's needed is more specific communication about what they need and what you have to offer. That's why we ask open-ended questions like "where do we go from here? " or "how should we proceed?" and "what do you see as our next step?" You're asking your customer to tell you what else he needs in order to move the process forward so you can implement the solution you've created together.

The sales/planning process should be a natural process of two or more people working together and communicating to develop a solution to a problem or a need. It requires trust, respect, and open communication on both sides. You can't work as partners through all the stages of the sale and then at the end try to use a manipulative closing technique to clinch the deal. It doesn't make sense.

One of the reasons traditional closing sometimes works is that the sales pressure on the client forces him to tell you what's really holding up the sale. But you can get this same information by communicating openly and honestly.

For the professional salesperson, the confirmation (purchase) is a mutual commitment to an ongoing business relationship. The emphasis is not solely on the confirmation of the sale but on the entire process. Professional salespeople, who sincerely match customer needs with products or services, can be much more relaxed once they reach the commitment stage, If you've been conscientious all along the way in working with your prospect, the two of you will *naturally* progress into the commitment stage.

In collaborative selling, the separation between 'selling' and 'closing' is barely perceptible. If the sales/planning process has been done well up to this point, the client has clearly specified needs and problems and knows how your product or services will solve them.

—Tony Alessandro, "Non-Manipulative Selling," 1975. Reprinted with permission.

prospect to make a judgment about what you have said. By asking this and similar checking questions like "Isn't that right?" and "Is that the way you see it?" and "Does that coincide with your thinking?" you continually keep pace with your prospect and help your prospect stay on track with your recommendations.

- "If this was not a concern, would there be any other reason why we could not put this program in force today?" This final testing question is designed to find out what the true objection is. Once known, it can be handled.

It's All in the Attitude

Inexperienced advisors hope to close without objection. Experienced advisors look for objections. They seek them out. Experienced advisors know that once the objection is known, the sale has advanced considerably and the chances of closing are excellent. If you detect apprehension in the prospect's voice, realize he or she may be saying "convince me further and I'll buy."

The Progressive Yes

By getting prospects to say yes this way at several points during the interview, it will be easier for them to say yes again when it comes to signing the application and writing a check to bind the application. Through progressive agreement on the small points that support your ideas, you will lead your prospect logically to the big decision. Through this approach, the sale or close will come naturally; you will not have to force it. It will be the natural conclusion of your meeting.

With some exceptions, a general rule states the harder you have to work to make the sale, the worse your persistency will be on the case. The better way to the sale is to ask the prospect about his or her financial goals to provide for loved ones. What has been done so far to reach the goals, and what could be done now to assure their achievement in the provider's absence? Objections, then, arise mostly to test your line of reasoning. Satisfy the objection and your reasoning is accepted, supporting your credibility as a thorough, thoughtful, and professional advisor.

Implementing the Solution

Not all sales are closed with one question in the so-called "closing interview." In meetings with the prospect, the advisor can tell by the questions asked and the ebb and flow of interest how the sale is going. Often the seemingly small question, the trial close or checking question asked by the advisor, such as "How does this fit in with your financial goals?" and the response by the prospect becomes part of the final close at a later time. At the point of closing, the advisor can refer back to the earlier question and point out the prospect's response on how important this benefit is to the prospect's financial goals because it will do what the prospect needs or wants it to do.

Asking a Prospect to Buy is How You Make the Sale

By Bill Brooks

What happens when you fail to ask someone to buy your product or service? The short version is that you don't get the sale. The longer version is that they buy from someone else, don't buy at all, or defer their decision. In any of these cases you have failed in your role as a salesperson. After all, aren't you paid to make sales?

One of the most intriguing and elusive sales questions of all time is simply this: Why do salespeople spend a great deal of time, effort, energy and commitment to get in front of a prospect only to let the opportunity to sell their product or service slip away from them?

Why does that happen? Is it a sense of caution that is driven by a desire not to offend—or to avoid being offended yourself when your prospect says "No?" Is it an inability to create such value in the mind of the prospect that the salesperson never really knows when, precisely, to ask someone to make a purchase decision? Could it be a simple lack of knowledge when it comes to knowing precisely how to ask someone to buy?

It's probably a little bit of all of these things. The truth is that the answer is not an easy one. Let's look at some of the real causes:

- A lack of results orientation on the part of the salesperson
- A lack of assertiveness on the part of the salesperson
- A lack of sales skills on the part of the salesperson
- A lack of confidence or self-worth on the part of the salesperson
- A lack of belief in a product or service on the part of the salesperson
- A lack of a sales process that leads to the sale on the part of the salesperson

There are probably a lot of other reasons too! But the real fact is this: whenever a sale is not made, it is generally the fault of the salesperson. So stop blaming poor marketing, pricing, product management, sales management, geography or territory, product failures or everything else for your own failure. It's you...not them, who has failed.

That being said, how do you fix the problem? Let me provide eight specific ideas or strategies to help you begin finalizing transactions immediately:

- Understand what your real job is. It is not public relations, customer service, technical support or anything else. It is making sales. Period.
- Learn how to use feedback questions ("how does this look") to be sure you're on target with your presentations.
- Learn how to listen and observe better. Listen to what prospects say. Better yet, listen to what they really mean. Be sensitive to non-verbal behavior.
- Master the art of value-added selling so you can provide your product or service in a way that makes it virtually irresistible.
- Be sure you're in front of qualified buyers who really do have the authority to say yes.

- Believe in yourself, your sales process, organization, and product or service so much that you badly want others to become a part of it - and ask them to do so.
- Learn, apply and master no more than 2 well-applied, non-heavy handed ways to finalize a transaction and use them consistently.
- Learn the fundamentals of negotiation and learn how to ask people to buy after agreeing on terms.

If you are a straight commission salesperson your lack of bringing sales to closure can lead to lots of things including a lack of income and all the bad things that that can create. If you are a salary-based salesperson it eventually leads to plateaued income, failure to progress in your career and a tiny, quiet voice that says to you "you're not really selling...who are you kidding?"

The bottom line is this. A failure to ask for the order on the part of salespeople is like an athletic team that loses every game in the final seconds. Or a bus driver who never reaches the final destination...or a hair stylist who only cuts half the hair...or a fast food server who gives you the bun with no hamburger! The job is only half done...and never completed to the point that it even comes close to accomplishing the intent of entire activity.

I am struck by another strong analogy. We recently tried to have some custom software designed for our company. The well-intentioned programmer who designed it kept telling me "we're 90% done," then it was "95% done," then "99% completed." He never completed it. I sent him away with this statement, "Whether it is 1% or 99% done, I can't use it unless it's 100% completed." That's true for software—it either works or it doesn't. The same is true for a sale. You either make it or you don't. Even if it's 99% done, it's of no value unless it's 100% sold. Think about it.

Bill Brooks is CEO of The Brooks Group, an international sales training and business growth firm based in Greensboro NC. For more information visit www.thebrooksgroup.com. Reprinted with permission of the author.

There are several important factors in closing. The advisor must make a closing attempt, because it is he or she who logically is leading the conversation and in control of the process. But we must be cautious of "sales pressure," which largely results from a premature attempt to ask the client to buy: something is still hanging, an objection not answered, confidence and rapport not completely solid. Something is missing. Possibly the need has not been firmly established. The following are points about properly asking for the sale:

Timing—Your teacher is experience. Many sales people who are learning how to close often ask how to learn the particular skill of timing. The answer is really pretty simple: you learn by mistakenly trying to

> **Solutions Cost Money**
>
> "(Prospect), you say this protection costs a lot of money, and it does. But how much does it cost compared to guaranteeing the accomplishment of your goals? What do you really want? Getting these benefits to insure your goals will cost you money."

close too soon and too often. It is a skill that is learned by experience; you will need to determine what is excessive in an interview with particular types of prospects and clients. Then you should back off until you have clarified the line between doing the job right and putting too much pressure on the prospect, which could force a "no" response.

Buying Signals—There are signals that you should learn to recognize. These are the signs that your prospects will make when it is time for you to take action. Buying signals are like traffic lights; they can be red (negative), yellow (neutral), or green (positive). By the end of your presentation you should have a good feel for the overall color projected by the prospect, generally indicating the type of question and direction you should choose. When the signals are red, ask an open question to get feedback on what concerns the prospect has. When you get yellow, offer a benefit summary and ask an open question. When green, the person is saying, "I'm sold." Proceed with implied consent or confirm with a closed question.

Consider the following signals:

- The prospect hesitates, asks for further clarification or explanation of a point you just covered. (Yellow)
- The prospect's tone of voice, including inflections with rising and falling tones, indicates high interest. (Green)
- The prospect makes negative remark, indicating internal struggle ("I like the plan, but I really shouldn't . . ."). (Yellow or Red)
- The prospect nods his head, showing interest and agreement. (Green)
- The prospect asks a specific question, such as "How much does it cost?" or "Is there a blood test?" or "When would the coverage start?" (Green)
- The prospect leans toward you. (Green)

Body language is important. Positive gestures and movements may indicate interest and nonverbal signs of approval. Trust your intuition. Eventually you will just know from experience when to ask for the sale.

Trial Closes and Checking Questions

When you have made your presentation, discussed it, and answered all of the concerns and questions of your prospect, it is time to ask the prospect to buy. Some advisors like to use checking questions, or trial closes, as they move through the presentation, before they have even reached the close. Trial closes are questions designed to receive feedback from the prospect regarding a specific aspect of a plan or some feature of your presentation. This enables the advisor to find the "hot buttons" to close upon, or to get feedback from the prospect about what is important and meaningful to him or her. Examples may be

> **"We'll Wait Until Our Vacation Bills are Cleared Up"**
>
> "(Prospect), I know it's hard to think about starting a major plan of this type when you have a trip coming up and bills to face when it's over. But we've uncovered a fairly substantial need to protect income. If I could show you a way to start this plan now, at a price you could afford, wouldn't you feel better going away on your vacation knowing the protection was in force?"

- What interests you most in this proposal?
- Do you think that this figure still represents the correct amount of protection?
- I figured the premiums on a monthly basis. Would you prefer them on an annual basis? There is a slight premium savings annually.
- We can still add accidental death (or whatever else you may have discussed). Would you like for me to do this?
- How does this look so far?

Using checking questions as one moves through the presentation, you can get a feel for how a person is thinking, as well as making little or trial closes. It might involve getting a feel for a person's hot buttons, the features and benefits they really seek. Getting the prospect's feedback helps to provide the advisor with valuable information about what the prospect wants from and likes about the plan. It also eases into the final request to buy by asking for many small decisions, rather than one momentous one. Repeating or summarizing prospect responses to trial closes can be used to get final agreement on implementing the plan.

Using trial closes and observing buying signals go hand in hand. If you observe a buying signal, ask a trial close question to confirm the observation. You can also get feedback from a trial close by observing nonverbal cues and body language as well as specific answers to determine the course of the sale.

Using Circles to Get the Point Across

The famous John Savage, whose reputation for savvy sales ideas and platform speaking expertise is admired far and wide, was responsible for this sales idea. You may even recognize it. It is widely known and is used by many to close sales.

The idea is to draw two circles on a piece of paper. At the top of the first circle, draw a horizontal line one-fourth of the way down. On the second circle, draw a line three-fourths of the way down.

Explain to the prospect that the second circle represents people who spend first and save second. The first circle represents people who save first and spend second. Then ask: "to which group of people do you belong, Circle One or Circle Two? The people in Circle One accumulate and usually own things. The people in Circle Two always are in debt and can't get ahead." Next, ask the prospect to which group he or she wants to belong. The answer is usually Circle One, which sets the stage for a commitment to save. When you recommend that 10 percent of his or her income should be saved, you can recommend a savings and insurance plan that meets those needs to build for the future.

Supporting the Decision to Buy

It is important for you to understand where empathy is most important. Of all the steps in the selling process that require an acute awareness of what your prospect may be feeling and thinking, information gathering and closing the sale are the most important. The greatest test in your relationship with your prospect or client is here. Your level of professional behavior has its greatest test here as well.

It takes time and practice to develop the skills of effective listening and the professional problem solving, counselor style, but this development is well worth the effort. The net effect is the time it allows you in the sales/planning situation to think through each idea your prospect wants to discuss. You can calmly isolate the real issues from the stalls, alibis, untruths, and excuses that may be raised. It will give you the skill to successfully encourage the buyer to make the right purchase for the right reasons, and to make the decision now. Once you reach this point—using all of your sales/planning skills to convince your prospect to make the right decisions—you will have achieved sales/planning maturity.

Many studies have shown that people approach buying decisions with anxiety and often have very mixed emotions. You have probably felt this when you have made an important buying decision. The buyer asks himself or herself, “Is this the right purchase? Can I afford it? Should I spend this much on this purchase? Is there a better solution elsewhere? Those same studies show that many prospects regularly look to salespeople to help them make up their minds.

If a prospect asks you, How much is it?” they may be looking for an excuse or justifying not buying something they need or desire because it costs “too much.” This may indicate mixed emotions based on confusion and anxiety. The question of costs often scares salespeople. Do not be intimidated. It does not necessarily mean that price alone is the final determinant in the decision, but that the prospect may be having difficulty justifying spending the money on the purchase, based on their perception of their overall financial situation and their confidence in your recommendations.

Continue to focus on how you can be of service, how you can offer and build value for them, how you and your product and services can be the best solution. Sometimes people need reassurance that they are doing the right thing, making the right decision. Confidently give them reassurance, and back it up by repeating the benefits (and not just blowing smoke) that they are making a good decision to buy, and they can afford it.

Welcome Your Prospect's Objections

Expect and welcome objections. Not all objections are negative. Most advisors say the worst appointment they could imagine is the one without objections. The prospect who sits listening straight-faced with a dull demeanor is impossible to communicate with, experienced advisors claim. You need the feedback of your prospect's opinions. You need both the positive and negative reactions to the ideas you are presenting if the sale is to be made. Be sure your prospects don't let you down.

Understanding Objections and Client Resistance

All Advisors Get Objections

The sales/planning process is one of give and take, a sharing of information and ideas. Communication is a two-way street. You respond to the information the prospect gives you. You form opinions about the person. You analyze financial data and make recommendations based on your opinions and expertise.

Prospects are doing the same thing with the information you give them. They are in the process of making a decision about matters that are very important to them. They are evaluating you and your product, as well as analyzing your ideas and recommendations. It is only natural, then, for them to respond to you in some way, either during or after your presentation. If they do not respond, you should ask them for feedback on how they view your presentation. These responses, and how well you deal with them, are important because they determine the course the sale will take from that point onwards.

Identifying Real Objections and Concerns

Being able to resolve a prospect's comments and concerns is a matter of realizing that some of them are a genuine reaction to your proposal. Others are excuses not to act. Recognizing the difference between an excuse and a real objection, and knowing how to respond to real objections with real answers is the key.

It's Going to Be Paid for Anyway

"(Prospect), the values you have put on your life are all tied directly to the goals you have set for yourself and your family. Whether or not you buy this protection today, those goals are real. Your present situation is real. In the event you are no longer able to meet your goals yourself, your family must try to live the best it can. They will pay the price, one way or another. The costs they will pay without this protection will far exceed the cost of the payments to provide it."

An excuse is often a smoke screen put up by prospects to delay a decision, to feel they are in charge of the situation, or appear knowledgeable enough to ask good, tough questions. Excuses express a lack of "buy-in," a lack of interest or commitment to the process at this time. Also in this category are minor points of interest or even legitimate questions that have relatively obvious answers. You can see that excuses are comments or questions that may seem important at first, but which turn out to be of little consequence. If this is happening at this point in the process, something is missing. You need to go back to get commitment to the process and the solution of needs.

An objection, on the other hand, is a real issue. To the prospect, objections are fundamental concerns that the insurance is not needed, that the solution is not right, that it is too expensive or that it is too much to be troubled with just now. These concerns or questions must be resolved before the sale can proceed.

Whether you are dealing with an excuse or a genuine objection, remember that you are asking prospects to make a substantial long-term commitment. Your job is to give the information and perspective they need to make an informed choice. When prospects interrupt your presentation, they are often telling you that they want more or clearer information. Do not be so intent on sticking to your sales track that you fail to respond intelligently to your prospects' questions and concerns.

Empathy

Selling without empathy means forced sales, lower persistency, and lost opportunities. Selling with empathy does not mean, however, that you do not work hard or be persistent in the sales/planning interview. You must stay strong, especially if your prospect wants to take the easy way out—to avoid facing the problem and acting now to solve it. For this reason, you must remember that empathy is understanding without judgment.

In client-focused selling, we want to accept the viewpoint of the prospect. But when we feel the prospect is not facing up to the reality of what needs to be done to accomplish his or her stated goals or meet his needs, we should address this and give the prospect our honest opinion. You must understand how they think and feel, but you must also work to help them accept and act on their need. There is a delicate balance between being empathetic and being persistent about what you think is the right course for the prospect to take. The prospect's basic trust in the advisor is the critical factor in just how delicate this balance will be.

> **Age Change Close**
>
> "Prospect, do you know what's going to happen at the stroke of midnight 2 weeks from tomorrow? "The premiums on all the life insurance that you're ever going to buy, but have not gotten around to buying, are going to go up for the thirty-sixth time."
>
> You guessed it. This 35-year-old has a birthday age-change in 2 weeks.

Do Not Take Objections Personally

Objections are responses to the proposal or idea you are presenting. They are normally not directed at you as a person. You must be able to distinguish this aspect of selling or you will not like it or be able to tolerate the resistance and rejection that is a natural part of the job.

We will now look specifically at objections or concerns, and how to handle or manage them. Although this section of the course deals with closing the sale specifically, this discussion will pertain to objections or concerns that may appear at any time in the selling/planning process.

Categories of Objections

Although it would seem that people could come up with an almost unlimited list of reasons not to buy life insurance, most objections can be grouped according to four main categories.

- No Need
- No Trust
- No Hurry
- No Money

> **Why Not Today?**
>
> "(Prospect), you are asking if I can come by again next week. There is a saying, 'you cannot do a kindness too soon, for you never know how soon it will be too late.' Doesn't this apply to your situation today? Why not start planning today?"

Even though each objection must be addressed individually, it is reassuring to know that most can be identified and treated in ways that will soon become second nature to you. Further, by categorizing objections this way, you are able to organize your thoughts, see objections as less threatening than they may seem otherwise, and respond to them with more confidence and from a position of strength.

Keep in mind that some objections can fall in more than one category. For example, someone who tells you, "I want to shop around," may be giving you a "no trust" objection, as well as a "no money" objection, with some "no hurry" thrown in for good measure. When you understand the basics of each category, you will be able to develop the response that best fits the situation.

Of course, people will usually be more inventive than to say, simply, "I have no trust in this recommendation," or "There is really no hurry for doing this." When they tell you, for example, "I want to talk it over with my spouse," or "See me later, I want to wait," that is really the message. Being able to interpret objections is the first step in categorizing them. As we discuss the different categories, you will get a better feel for the kinds of comments and concerns that go in each. As you gain firsthand experience with these objections, you will become an expert in automatically categorizing them and coming up with the response appropriate to each situation.

No Need

The "no need" objection is often expressed by people who truly believe they do not need the protection offered by life insurance. You will find people, for example, who plan to accumulate adequate security for their families through various savings or investment programs. The problem, of course, is that these alternate investment programs may not work out as planned—there is no guarantee that they will, or even that they will be available to provide an adequate benefit when needed.

Rather than trying to marshal reams of documentation to reeducate the prospect, your main purpose should be simply to determine with the prospect if the accumulation plan in force now would provide the income needed if the prospect were to die today. Has the prospect even started it? If so, ask for the details and work the numbers with him or her. Will the plan accomplish what the prospect wants, if he or she were to die today? If it will, you do not have a prospect. If it will not, life insurance is the logical solution. Other "no need" objections you will hear are:

- "I'm too old to buy life insurance."
- "I have too much insurance now. I'm worth more dead than alive."
- "I have my money in real estate."
- "I'm single. Whom do I need to protect?"
- "My company pension and Social Security will take care of me."
- "I'm going to live a long, long time."

It's Too Expensive

"(Prospect), you said it seems very expensive. What I think I hear you saying is that it costs too much. Is that right?" *(Usually the prospect will agree, "it costs too much.")*

"How much too much does it cost?"

(Now, focus on the difference in the figure your prospect suggests. What does the difference buy in terms of benefit to the family's financial security?)

People who claim they have no need, but do, should be shown that they do have a need. By illustrating the risks associated with their present situations, simply and graphically, you can shake prospects out of their complacency.

No Trust

A "no trust" objection may refer to you, your agency, your product, your company or to life insurance in general. You are asking the prospect to make a major financial commitment based on your recommendations. A lack of trust on the prospect's part is a serious matter, which can stop the sale if it is not addressed.

Among the objections you may hear that indicate a lack of trust are the following:

- "I want to talk it over with my spouse."
- "My attorney advises me on these matters."
- "I want to see what other companies (or advisors) are offering."
- "I put all of my money into securities."
- "I don't believe in life insurance."

> **How Much Do I Own?**
>
> "(Prospect), I'm glad you asked me about my personal coverage. So many times salespeople offer products they do not really believe in. The fact that I own what I sell should demonstrate my convictions about the products. Here are my latest two life insurance policies, which I carry with me just to show that I buy the products I sell and that I update my plan on a regular basis, just as I have recommended to you."

In each case, lack of information is often the basic problem. Someone who says "I don't believe in life insurance," may not be well informed about the product. They may be admitting that they just do not understand life insurance. Maybe they really haven't thought about it seriously, or someone they respect once told them not to buy it. They may be unaware of its purpose and what it can do. If they believe in human dignity, in financial security, and in the responsibility of one person to another, they should believe in life insurance.

To carry your message and to help this type of individual discover the purpose of life insurance, you should ask questions relating to the things that life insurance will do. If a person loves and cares for a family, nothing can protect its future security as life insurance can. The person who puts all available money into securities is making a fundamentally misinformed financial decision.

If the objection is, "I want to see what other companies or advisors are offering," you should advise your prospect that price and cost alone are not the only criteria on which to base buying decisions. Someone who objects on the basis of needing to discuss the matter with an attorney, spouse, or parent may be saying, "I don't trust myself to make this decision alone," or perhaps they do not trust you. By patiently reviewing how the plan meets the prospect's needs and objectives, you can overcome this reluctance to act independently. If not, ask to meet with the other person and the prospect to discuss the proposal and your answer to the need.

No Hurry

The "no hurry" objection flies in the face of logic. The prospect may agree that the insurance is needed, but wants to wait to put the protection in force. The "no hurry" objection is often evidence of procrastination. Procrastination is commonly associated with a fear of making the wrong decision, or "buyer's remorse."

It is not unusual for "no hurry" objections to be a sign of an "immortality" complex. Nothing is going to happen to these people, or so they think, so why rush into buying life insurance? They will get around to it one of these days. In general, the approach to take here is to give the prospect a few examples of people who proved to be all too mortal—much to their family's misfortune. Then discuss the prospect's situation in terms that show how unrealistic the "no hurry" objection actually is.

Examples of "no hurry" objections include:

- "Leave a copy of your proposal. I'll consider it over the weekend."
- "We'll do something after the first of the year (or after vacation, or when our tax refund check comes)."

Family Guarantees

Prospect:	"I can't really afford this insurance plan right now."
Advisor:	"Why is that, (Prospect)? "
Prospect:	"For one thing, we're paying off the installments on this dining room furniture we're sitting on."
Advisor:	"Look at it this way, (Prospect), with this life insurance you will be guaranteeing that your family can keep this table and the chairs."

No Money

If people waited until they had plenty of money to spare, no one would buy life insurance. In dealing with the "no money" objection, it is important to decide if the person is objecting to buying the plan or really cannot afford the premium you have quoted. The time to explore the money issue is early in the fact-finding. If it is settled early, what you suggest later should not stop the selling process.

If the prospect really would be getting in too deeply with the plan you have suggested, revise the premium or protection level to better suit the prospect's finances. If, however, by clarifying the concern as we did earlier ("You say this plan costs too much. How much too much does it cost, $50, $100?"), you find that there really is no money problem, your job is to show that life insurance is a major purchase which should be budgeted along with the other necessities of life. After all, the proceeds of a life insurance policy could well be what provides the necessities of life if the prospect dies too soon.

Examples of "no money" objections include:

- "I can't afford it."
- "I'm putting my money into my business."
- "My taxes are too high this year to take on any more expenses."
- "I need to pay off some debts first."
- "We're saving for a new car and the down payment on a house."
- "This is just too big a commitment for us to make right now."
- "Our budget is way overloaded as it is."
- "It's too expensive."

Be sure that you have a money commitment before you leave the fact-finding portion of your interview or you may hear one of the above.

If you have done a good job of qualifying your prospects, selling yourself and your expertise, fact gathering, establishing needs, obtained a premium commitment, and presented an appropriate solution, many of the objections we have covered here should not come up. If they do come up, they should not be hard to deal with. Simply remind the prospects of the information they gave you earlier in the interview. For instance, people who told you that $175 a month was a reasonable amount to commit would be hard pressed, 20 minutes later, to say that the plan involving that amount would not fit their budget.

A "No" Means More Questions

When your prospects tells you no, that means it is time for you to start asking more questions! In other words, get clarification for what you or the client needs to understand to complete the sales process.

Overcoming Objections and Managing Resistance

The first step in answering an objection is to listen to the prospect. No one likes to be interrupted or feel they are not being listened to. Listening to what the prospect has to say will help you understand the objection. Encourage the prospect to explain and tell you more about how he or she feels about the issue.

Give yourself and the prospect the opportunity to confirm your understanding of the objection by restating or rephrasing it. This gives you an opportunity to learn more about the exact nature of the objection. This also puts you in a better position to overcome it.

As you talk with your prospect, use trial closes, such as, "Other than affordability, is this the product you think will best suit your needs?" or "Is this a feature you would definitely like in your plan?" Because overcoming objections takes practice and experience, it is important not to get discouraged if at first you are not successful.

The sales/planning process should build logically to the inescapable conclusion that the prospect needs the protection and there is no reason it should not be put in force at once. Each step in the process supports the one that follows, so that by the time you get to the point where prospects can raise issues and concerns, you should know enough about their personal and financial situations, their attitudes, and their feelings to respond directly, honestly, and convincingly.

The Problem-Solving Approach

In general, you should take a problem-solving approach to objections, focused on three things:

- building trust and rapport with the prospect
- dealing with needs, not personalities
- instilling a sense of urgency

You can build trust and rapport by demonstrating, with your professionalism and forthrightness, that you care about answering the prospects' concerns with real answers. Be empathetic. Reassure prospects that by keeping their objectives in mind and reviewing the various alternatives available, they can move toward their goal. You can work together to resolve the issues that are causing the concerns.

You can deal with needs rather than personalities by focusing on the issues, not on winning debate points, getting the upper hand, or having the last word. It also means that when a prospect raises a difficult objection, you do not imply that unless the insurance is purchased as recommended, the prospect really does not love his or her family. That surely is not the issue. The real concern may be money or timing; it is best to stick to the problem. Another related piece of advice is to avoid arguing with prospects. Pointing out to a potential client that an objection is not valid is sales suicide. You may win the argument, but you will surely end up losing the sale. That is not a smart trade-off.

You can instill a sense of urgency by not being so intent on overcoming the objection with facts that you forget perhaps the most convincing point: the risk of taking no action at all. The need to act should be continually stressed. Postponing decisions is not recommended when it comes to a family's financial security needs.

Five Steps to Handle Objections and Concerns

The process for handling objections involves five steps:

1. **Listen** to the prospect.
2. **Summarize** or rephrase what the prospect tells you.
3. **Wait** for the prospect to respond.
4. **Clarify** and categorize the response.
5. **Deal** with it directly, honestly and completely; then resume your presentation.

Let's examine each step in this process to see how it can help you become more comfortable and proficient in dealing with your prospects' questions, comments, and concerns.

1. **Listen**—In order to be able to deal with a question or concern, you must be very sure you understand it. This means that when your presentation is interrupted, listen carefully to what the prospect has to say. Do not to take a glib, "yes, but" approach to every objection the prospect offers. Listening carefully reassures prospects about their concerns. It tacitly acknowledges that they may be nervous and prone to make excuses for the sake of making excuses, while it treats as legitimate those concerns and objections that are genuine. In short,

this process deals with prospects' questions and concerns the way you would want yours treated if you were the prospect.

2. **Rephrase What You Heard**—The next step in the process is to repeat what the prospect told you to make sure you heard it correctly. This means restating what the prospect said, using key phrases, as a summary. This may seem pointless, but it is not. Communication is a tricky process. The message sent by one person is not necessarily the one received by the other. By repeating what the prospect said, you are making sure that you received the message correctly. The more you practice the art of listening, the better you will be at it. You are also communicating that you are interested in the prospect and concerned about correctly understanding what they think and how they feel.

   Part of your goal in repeating the prospect's comment or question is breaking it down into its main parts. For instance, a prospect might tell you, "We are planning a very expensive vacation this summer. It will tie up our cash for several months. I like what you've told me here, but it isn't something we can handle financially until after we get back and our bills are paid."

   Does this mean that prospects will be ready to start the plan soon after they return from their trip? Or does it mean that it may be several months before they will be able to afford it? That would certainly be a major consideration in how you approach their situation: a 3-week delay is one thing; a 6-month postponement is quite another.

Questions Can Defuse the Objection

Here's a favorite technique for overcoming objections. Rephrase the objection as a question and then answer it. You then have an inquiry in search of a reasonable answer, not an offensive move that puts the advisor on the defensive. Now, with an answer to the question, the sales process can continue and the advisor is back on track.

The advisor says, "If I understand you correctly, your concern—or I should say question—is . . ." (Rephrase the prospect's statement.) "Am I correct?" "Yes" is the reply. Now the advisor answers the question and moves on.

By repeating the comment, you make sure you get the right message. In this case, you would say something like this, "Let me make sure I understood what you just said. You mentioned that you liked these recommendations (always restate the most positive part of the comment or question first), but that you were planning a rather expensive trip this summer and would not be able to begin this plan until after you return and your vacation bills are paid." Now that you have repeated what you thought you heard, let the prospect confirm that the message was correctly or incorrectly received. This shows the prospect that you are an attentive listener interested in understanding the prospect's side of the story.

Another technique for doing this is to rephrase the objection in the form of a question. Rephrase what the prospect just told you, ask the prospecting the prospect to give you more information or clarify their concern. Encourage your prospect to expand and tell you more. When the objection has been precisely defined, you will be in a better position to respond to it.

3. **Wait For a Response**—By asking for confirmation or correction, you keep the prospect talking. Giving your prospect the chance to respond to your version of their objection will bring amplification of the part that is of greatest concern. For example, what the prospect might really be saying above is that it is not so much the vacation that is preventing the implementation of the plan as it is a cash flow problem. In fact, the situation may not be corrected even after the travel expenses are paid. This information is critical and needs to be discussed further. This is why the next step is so important.

4. **Clarify and Categorize the Response**—Rephrase the question or comment to clarify it. Explore the meaning of the response. In our example, you might be able to clear up the matter of when, specifically, the plan can be implemented by saying, "Does that mean you will be able to begin the plan within a week or two after your return? Or do you feel it will take longer than that for your finances to get back in shape?" If the prospect says that it is really just a temporary situation that will be resolved within a week or two after the vacation ends, you can treat the matter lightly. Reassure the prospect that there is no problem and go on with your closing attempts. If, on the other hand, the prospect tells you that it will be a matter of several months before the plan can begin, you may be facing an objection that will stop the sale unless it is satisfactorily resolved.

The Shopper

"(Prospect), if you feel you want to 'shop,' that's fine. You might find a bargain policy and the 'best' company if you have the time, the inclination, and the perseverance.

May I make a suggestion? Rather than shop for a bargain policy and the 'best' company, find the best advisor—one in whom you can have complete faith and confidence.

I would like to be considered for that job as your insurance advisor. May I show you the kind of work I do so that you will be in a position to judge?"

If, when you attempt to close, the prospect tells you that it is "too expensive," ask how much too expensive it is. "Is it $50 a month too expensive? Is it $100 a month too expensive? If we were to make it less expensive by $50 a month, would you be able to commit to it?" If the prospect says yes, you have a sale; if the prospect says no, you have identified an objection that you may or may not be able to overcome. If you got a dollar commitment earlier, this should not happen. Otherwise it may indicate that the prospect is not serious about or ready to make a commitment to a plan.

By rephrasing the comments and waiting for a response, you isolate either a "yes" or a "no" answer. Get prospects to talk out whatever it is that is really bothering them, enable your prospects to withdraw the comment gracefully, or pinpoint specific information you need about the question or comment to deal with it effectively.

Remember the value of silence. After you have paraphrased the prospect's remarks, do not say anything until the prospect has responded. If you break the silence first, you will probably lose the intended result.

5. **Reassure and Resume**—You can reassure the prospect in one of several ways. You may be able to use a motivating story or anecdote. You may chose to do it with a sales visual appropriate to the situation or go back to one of the supporting materials you used in the presentation. You are deliberately treating the comment or question directly, honestly, and completely.

Acknowledge, Clarify, Resolve

Another common technique for responding to client resistance is to take the following steps.

1. *Acknowledge* a concern. You should validate the prospect's thoughts and feelings on the topic. If you do not acknowledge the concern, but instead take it head on and try to wrestle it down, all you succeed in doing is putting more distance between you and the prospect. Responses such as, "I understand how you feel," or "I can appreciate that," show your prospect that you are listening to them and care about what they say.
2. It is often necessary to *clarify* a vague or negative response from the prospect before it can be effectively resolved. Any statement that is too global, vague, or over-reaching should be clarified. Clarification can take many forms, such as "Could you please explain that," or "I don't understand what you mean."
3. *Resolve* the concern by making appropriate recommendations.

Feel, Felt, Found

An excellent technique to respond to a concern by the prospect is "feel, felt, found."

- "I understand exactly how you *feel*."
- "Many of my prospects *felt* the same way..."
- "...until they *found* that this plan was a good solution for their situation."

> **Another Way to Handle Objections**
>
> Some say that the best way to handle objections is not to get any. Easier said than done. But anyone who listens carefully in the fact-finding interview can cut down on the objections heard later if attention is paid to the points the prospect makes. If the prospect has told you that money for the premium is a problem, bring it up immediately in your presentation interview. "(Prospect), this is what we can do . . . " Keep track of the types of objections you receive. They may show a pattern that you can correct. So, at least sometimes, it may be a matter of bringing up the objection yourself before your prospect does in the presentation interview.

Notice that this technique begins by using the acknowledgment step. You then put the prospect at ease by reassuring him or her that this is a common feeling. You finally point out that once others have been introduced to this new idea, they often found it really was okay. This neutralizes the situation and gives you an opportunity to address their concern. People like to do what other people do. It gives reassurance to know that others have already done this, having gone through a similar process or faced a similar problem. For many people, the "herd instinct" is very powerful in unfamiliar situations.

Some things that look like objections often turn out to be nothing more than excuses. The process for distinguishing between objections and excuses is easy to follow. It involves the prospects by having them talk through their questions and concerns. Sometimes these issues collapse under their own weight; when they do not, you know you have a real objection on your hands. Objections, although phrased in many different ways, all fall into the four categories discussed earlier: no need, no trust, no hurry, and no money. There are proven ways to overcome each type of objection after you have categorized them and understand what problems or misconceptions are behind them.

The Advisor's Three Rs

A simple formula may help keep you on track the next time you are having a difficult time closing a sale. In proper order, it can be called "the insurance advisor's three Rs.

1. Restate the objective
2. Reassure
3. Resume

Closing Techniques

Methods of Asking for the Sale

After you have isolated and answered the prospect's concerns or objections, and perhaps even before you have dealt with objections at all, you will want to try to complete the sale if the prospect appears interested. There are a number of techniques to do this, but as mentioned earlier, a word of caution is necessary. Any technique that is presented before the prospect is ready to buy will appear as sales pressure. If the prospect is not ready, he or she will let you know and you will have to reinforce those areas of concern that are preventing him or her from taking action.

Also remember that the close really started at the beginning of the first interview. Although closing is considered the culmination of the sale, every step along the way was a part of the whole represented by the prospect's decision to buy.

Assumed or Implied Consent—With this technique, the decision to buy is assumed or implied; it is not directly asked or confronted. It presumes the prospect has decided to buy. In fact, many prospects have decided to buy, and saying anything else will more likely hurt the sale than help it. At this point many prospects will simply need a gentle nudge to agree to buy.

One strategy is for the advisor simply to take action. For example, begin completing the application form without permission to proceed; it is assumed. Then consent is obtained by the prospect's willingness to continue, and to eventually sign the application. Or if a check is needed, hand the prospect a pen and tell him or her you need a check for a specific amount. Put the ball in their court and see what they do. Miraculously, they will often comply with your request. If not, they will state their objection and you will know where you stand.

This is considered by many to be the most powerful closing method, because it forces the natural conclusion to the process without being forceful. It allows the buying decision to happen easily, with gentle persuasion, with finesse, never with aggressive force. Some feel every closing attempt should begin with implied consent. In a closing interview you can return to one of many techniques employing it, as a response after dealing with an objection.

The Assumed Close: It's Only a Matter of Choice

"(Prospect), I've come up with two solutions that should help cover your needs." (Present both solutions.) "Which one do you feel would do the best job for you." The prospect makes the choice and you fill in the proper application blank.

Alternative Choice—Instead of asking the prospect to say yes or no to a proposal, present two or three options. Ask them which one they would prefer. This is a variation on the implied consent technique. Now the only choice is which one to choose.

"(Prospect), I have come up with two proposals which will meet your needs. Which one do you prefer?" or "Which one do you feel would do the best job for you?"

Fatal Alternatives or Forced Choice—This is an implied consent technique following the basic sales principle that the one asking the questions is on offense and the one answering the questions is on defense. A fatal alternative question is one that offers two or more alternatives, none of which can be answered with a "yes" or "no," and all of which would mean the prospect has agreed to buy. Sample fatal alternative questions could be any of the following:

"Would you rather pay for the whole year now or just give me a deposit?"

"Do you want just 50 or would you prefer to have 100 because it's cheaper that way?"

"Would you rather be examined in your home or your office?"

Silence—Whenever you have asked a closing question, do not speak again. Wait in silence until your prospect reacts. Deal with the prospect's reaction to you and your idea—your call to action.

Do not allow yourself to give up the impact of the process by reacting to yourself. Whenever you ask a closing question—the answer to which confirms that the prospect has bought—wait for the prospect's decision. If you do not, you will delay the close of your sale. You can see how this can work in the assumed consent closing technique when you ask, "which do you prefer, annual or monthly premiums?" The answer to that will tell you if your prospect has agreed to the sale or not.

Direct Question—Perhaps the most obvious method is the direct question, asking the person if they have made up their mind and wish to start the plan. Simply asking the prospect, "Are you ready to start this plan?" or "What do you think?" or "How does this sound to you?" or any other direct question that gets to the heart of the matter. Waiting for a prospect to take the initiative to decide or take action is usually not going to happen. The advisor often needs to make it clear that it is time to decide, to give a gentle nudge to the prospect sitting on the fence. Other possible questions that will accomplish this include:

- Do you have enough information to make a decision or would you like to review anything we have discussed?
- What would you like the next step to be?
- If you don't have any other questions, I will go ahead and begin the paperwork.

- You seem positive about this plan. Why don't we take the next step and schedule the medical exam?
- Do you have any questions or are you ready to take the next step?

It is good to review how you plan to do this before your interview. Write down what you will say and practice it. This way you can say it with confidence and conviction. It is easier for a prospect to say no to someone who is winging it. Asking for the sale is no time to be improvising.

Why?—Actually, "Why" is just one of many questions that can be asked when the advisor feels he or she is losing the sale. By asking this powerful question, you are shifting the pressure back on the prospect to regain control of the interview, or to go on the offense by asking questions. You do want to get into a debate, but sincerely listen to the response and determine if you are dealing with an excuse or an objection. This technique should produce a direct reply from the prospect.

The Last Paycheck

For many who buy life insurance for income replacement to support their surviving families, the proceeds from their life insurance policies will be their last paycheck.

Ben Franklin's Balance Sheet—Ben Franklin used this technique for making difficult decisions. Simply draw a "T" on a paper and on the left side write "pro" and on the right write "con." Under "pro" write all the positive reasons favoring the decision and on the right, under con, list those reasons against the decision. After listing all the reasons, weight the arguments for and against each. If possible, give weigh to each one in terms of degree of importance. By identifying the points, writing them down, and being able to study them in one place, often a decision becomes easier to make.

The advisor can help the prospect, but caution should be taken not to manipulate or bias the process. To try to influence the prospect by encouraging positive reasons and discouraging negative ones only jeopardizes the trust and credibility of the advisor. Also, do not debate the "con" answers. In a relationship of trust you must be the prospect's ally and trusted advisor.

Use Transitions to Give New Power to Your Presentations

A poorly presented proposal can wreak havoc on the most compelling ideas in a close. Your clients gain confidence in you when they sense you know where you are going to go and how you are going to get there. You can't just present all of your ideas in an interview and expect to accomplish your mission unless you can lead your prospects to the close. Your speech must show control of your ideas and purpose. You must have transitions to work with in your speech that make smooth passage from one idea to the next.

Here are six transitions that are easy and effective:

1. Use bridge words. These are words that alert the listener that you are moving on to a new thought. Examples include words such as: furthermore, meanwhile, however, in addition, nevertheless, therefore, consequently, and finally.
2. A question can serve as a good transition. It can be broad or quite specific. For instance, "what are your feelings about this?"
3. A flashback doesn't have to be far into the past to create a clear connector with your presentation. You can transition with a comment like, "you remember a few moments ago when I mentioned how the cash value in this policy you bought in 1980. . . Well, here is how this proposal will. . ."
4. A point-by-point transition can also work, but don't have too many points. By saying, "there are three important reasons this policy is right for you" and then listing them gets you quickly to the specifics of your proposal.
5. Pausing is a nonverbal transition that helps your prospect shift with you. Good use of the pause—if used sparingly—helps everyone focus on what you are about to say.
6. Physical movement can act as a transition. One advisor takes off her glasses once or twice during a sales presentation to emphasize her key points. The objective is to change the pattern of the presentation. Stand up if you have been sitting. Change your sitting position. Whatever move you make will draw attention to what is about to come next. This is the essence of any good transition.

Women Life Underwriters Confederation (WLUC) News Bulletin, 1995. Reprinted with permission

Similar Situation—This technique requires a personal decision to apply it fairly. It has often been misnamed "backing the hearse up to the door," which is really an unfair and misguided notion. This is not intended to be threatening. What you really want to do is to relate to your prospect a similar situation so that he or she can reflect on the possible consequences of not taking action now. The only rule is to be honest. Tell only true stories, whether they are your own experiences or not. Using specific emotional stories (something bad happened because someone did not take action, or something good happened because someone did) is often all you need to complete a sale. Just remember: this technique can easily be seen as manipulative and high pressure.

Medical Close—There are a few ways to use this concept. One is where the person has had some medical history that can be used to raise some concern in the prospect about insurability. In this case there may be special underwriting procedures and information needed, so the person should submit an application to see what underwriting decision will be made. Check your company's underwriting rules to avoid submitting an application that is not acceptable to that company.

The other common use is to bring up the fact that medical underwriting is required and we can let the insurance company think it over as the prospect does, but cash with the application initiates conditional coverage. You might say, "Prospect, why don't we let the company think it over while you think it over?"

"Let me think it over"—Perhaps one of the most common responses at the end of a sales presentation, the advisor must determine if this response is a genuine need to think about their situation and your proposal, or simply an excuse to get you out the door and the sales process ended or deferred. If it must be thought over, you must determine that this is exactly what the prospect means. You must try, at least once, to test the "need to think it over" response, to see if it is a genuine need or simply an excuse to end the sales process or procrastinate and not commit to a decision.

This is a normal human reaction to making a major purchase decision. A good sales professional will recognize that the person must have interest, or they would give the advisor an outright rejection. Answering all the objections may not really get to the core of the concern; the prospect is stalling for time. Procrastination is natural. Nevertheless, you need to push through the excuses and work toward getting a commitment. You might say something like the following:

"That's fine. Obviously you wouldn't take your time thinking this over unless you were really interested, would you? So, may I assume that you will give it very careful consideration?"

"Just to clarify my thinking, what phase of the plan do you want to think over? Is it the expense? The benefits it provides? (If they say "the whole thing," try to narrow it down, because it is most probably only one or a few specific aspects that need to be thought over.)"

Just move to another close, like the medical close, and try to get agreement to start the plan, or a definite time when a decision will be made. At this point you are walking a fine line between trying to help them to take a positive action and being seen as exerting high-pressure sales techniques. When you get together again, go right back to your close after you have a warm-up conversation. Review the presentation and topics discussed. Do not ask if the prospect thought it over, for this might invite another postponement. If you can get an appointment after a postponement, your chances are better for making a sale.

"I Want To Think About It" is a common and difficult response from a prospect. Many initial objections or prospect concerns are just delaying tactics, or excuses not to deal with an issue. Have you ever gone to a store looking for something, and when a sales clerk approaches you and asks if he or she can help you, you say, "No thanks, I'm just looking?" We all do it. It is a reflexive response to preserve our freedom and control of the situation, and prevent the salesperson from altering our agenda.

Many objections are automatic responses, defensive comebacks, or knee-jerk reactions that are more about preserving privacy than a real response to an action request. Remembering this, give the prospect an opportunity to equalize the situation, taking the initiative in pursuit of his or her goals.

To effectively deal with this response (objection) we need to understand where this response is coming from. There are five primary sources:

1. For some reason, the prospect truly needs to think about it.
2. The prospect is concerned with the price or is unsure about the value.
3. The prospect is a procrastinator or is analytical and never makes a fast decision.
4. The prospect has no interest in buying and wants you to go away.
5. The prospect needs someone else's input to make a decision.

Addressing these possibilities in reverse order, you should have discovered reason five in the qualifying process, asking "Who else, besides yourself, will be involved in making the final decision." If number four is in play, you need to decide if you can gain the prospect's interest, or drop him or her from your efforts. If you push too hard with reason three, the prospect may become a reason four.

Concerning reasons one and two, you need to determine what the person needs to think about. You need to ask and find their real concern. Acknowledge the objection with empathy by saying, "I understand how you feel. If I were in your shoes, I would probably want to think about it myself." Then ask if they are primarily concerned with the cost. If this is the concern, you will need to review the benefits or add value, or you will not have a sale.

If the prospect's reason for wanting to think about it stems from some hidden concern, you need to get that concern out into the open where you can respond to it and do something about it. Ask "May I ask what concerns you still have?" or "May I ask what is causing you to hesitate?" or "What questions have I left unanswered?"

One technique you can use is to have the prospect restate the perceived benefits of taking action to you. You can say something like this: "What part of the proposal do you like best?" or "How do you see yourself benefiting from this plan?" or "What benefits do you feel are most important to you?" In this way you can try to build momentum for the prospect to make a decision now.

The Cost of Waiting—Another effective sales idea designed to emphasize the need and advantage of beginning a life insurance program today is called the "cost of waiting." A comparison between the costs and values of a plan started today and one started 5 or 10 years from now can show a dramatic difference in the face amount of protection a given premium can purchase as well as the cash value that can accumulate over the years. By waiting, the premium will grow increasingly higher, the cash value growth over the prospect's life will be smaller, they will be without the protection by delaying, and they could lose their insurability in the interim. These are all good reasons to buy today.

Try This Before You Give Up Hope

If there seems little hope to close the sale after repeated attempts to do so, try this: "(Prospect), you have a level of interest in more life insurance. Perhaps, the timing is not right. Is this correct?"

When the prospect says yes to your question, establish a future time when you will call. Then make the call. A successful advisor says that 40 percent of these people will see you at a later date. You can then reopen the sale and have a chance of closing it then.

Getting Cash with the Application

One of the final things you will do in most sales interviews is ask the prospect for money. Paying for goods and services when we buy them is normal procedure, and so it should be with life insurance. It is not unusual, though, for people to try to put off paying the first premium. Reasons are varied for this reluctance to part with their funds; some are, no doubt, more valid than others. They may range from the commonplace (for example, a temporary shortage of cash) to the inventive (the prospect is shopping with several companies to compare costs).

A good case can be made, however, for getting the prospect to give you the premium money, not the next day or the next week, not when the policy is issued nor when the first premium notice arrives from the home office, but at the time of application. Prepayment shows that the prospect is completely serious about wanting the life insurance. It also offers several compelling advantages to the client.

Immediate Protection—The most compelling reason for getting cash with the application is the matter of putting the insurance in force. If you are able to take the initial premium at the time of application, and if the company eventually approves the policy, the protection will have been in force from the date of application. This, obviously, is a vital consideration for the applicant and the beneficiary because the applicant has no guarantee that he or she will survive long enough to see the policy issued.

Insurance company records are full of examples of applicants who died between the dates of application and issue; some were covered, some were not. Few situations so dramatically illustrate the protection value of life insurance as do these prepayment cases. They show, tragically, what could have been, had the applicant paid the first premium at the time of application.

Conditional or Binding Receipts—In some companies, a conditional receipt is given in return for the applicant's first premium check. This is an acknowledgment that the insurance is in force from the date of the receipt (or medical examination, if later), assuming that the applicant is insurable at standard rates. Other companies use binding receipts, which provide temporary protection from the date of the receipt (or medical examination) but enable the company to terminate the coverage if the applicant does not meet underwriting standards.

Read the receipt attached to your company's applications carefully. It is your responsibility to understand what it covers and what it does not cover. You are obligated to explain the conditions accurately to your prospect when you take the check with the application.

Also, find out how your company handles claims that occur between the time of application and date of issue. Sometimes, the receipt is worded more restrictively than the procedures that the company actually follows. This is valuable information for you to have.

You must be accurate in the promises or representations you make to your prospects. Any statement you make before, during, or after a sales interview that materially misrepresents the policy can be damaging to all concerned. The situation of prepayment of insurance and the wording of conditional and binding receipts are good examples of this, similar to quoting the guaranteed versus projected cash values or dividends of a proposal. Again, it is your obligation and responsibility as a representative of your company not to make any misrepresentations, even inadvertently, for which your company or you could be held liable.

Insurance companies are in business to pay legitimate claims. If a person applies for insurance in good faith, meets all the underwriting rules and pays an initial premium, the company will want to honor the claim.

It's Just a Month's Checking Account Interest

It is not an unfamiliar situation to most of us. You have filled out the application and your heartbeat quickens as you ask your next question: "Would you like to write a check for $250 to put the insurance in force now?"

Not surprisingly the client replies, "I'd like to think it over."

One advisor turns around and asks the applicant if he or she earns interest on a checking account. The usual reply is "Yes, about 4 percent."

Then the advisor explains the refundable deposit for the conditional insurance agreement of $250, or whatever the figure may be, will cost only 4 percent for the month it takes to underwrite the application.

The cost of interest lost would be $10 a year or 83 cents a month on the $250. That 83 cents in interest is taxable, so the real cost to the applicant is close to 50 cents. "Would it be worth a 50-cent gamble on your insurability for this lifetime opportunity for protection?" With the situation reduced to these terms, refusing seems trivial and the advisor almost always gets the prepaid application before she leaves.

Premium Payment Completes the Contract—If no premium is paid, however, the situation is completely different. There is no contract. The contract is not completed until the customer pays for it. If no premium is paid, it is just an offer to the customer by your company, at its approval, to purchase the contract. Your prospect completes the obligation, not with a signature, but with his or her premium payment.

In this case, not only could the claim be legitimately denied, it must be denied. If companies began paying claims in these situations, they would set a legal precedent that could keep them from ever denying such claims in the future. The result could be the undermining of the entire application and underwriting process designed to protect both insurer and applicant.

For business and legal reasons, then, insurers may not hesitate if they can legitimately avoid paying a death claim under those circumstances when the policy is unbound. For the prospect, the prospect's family, and for you, a claim denied because no premium had been received can be very bad news, indeed. The beneficiaries may even blame you. Remember this next time you are tempted to submit an application without the premium.

Protects Insurability—By prepaying the insurance premium, the prospect is protected in case there are any changes in health before the policy is issued. This is not so when the first premium collected at delivery. If no premium is collected at application, the applicant must still be in insurable, good health at delivery when the first premium is paid. If not, the company may cancel the policy, or additional premiums may be charged. Cash with the application protects the applicant's insurability for the time that it takes to underwrite the case, usually several weeks.

What happens in cases where no prepayment is made and the proposed insured does not reveal an interim medical problem? The answer is that the insurance will not be in force during the contestable period, even if the policy is issued and the insured pays renewal premiums. If, under these circumstances, a claim is made during the contestable period, it can be denied.

It is in the prospect's interest and ultimately in your own interest to get cash with the application. This is something you should be personally committed to each time you close a sale and take an application.

False Start

"(Prospect), this plan will be one of the best you've ever created. "Yet, if we merely discuss how you can use your accumulations later and how your family will benefit—without getting the life insurance plan started—wouldn't this be about the same as opening a bank account without making a deposit?"

Advantages to the Advisor—In selling, you must realize that no sale is made until the customer pays for the product. This means that when a prospect postpones paying the first premium, you have actually sold nothing except a second interview. This not only exposes the applicant to unnecessary risks, it doubles your sales costs and it means that you must resell the case during the follow-up delivery interview. You have invested a lot of time. No commissions have been paid, and you are forced to go through the whole process twice.

A Down Payment on Life

"I see what you mean, (Prospect). Probably money will be easier for you after (insert excuse). However, if you die before a premium is paid, this plan will not help unless it is in force. I realize the chances of this happening are much less than 1 percent, but if you are the one to die, the loss to your family is 100 percent. Death does not happen at anyone's convenience. Don't you want to make a down payment on your life?"

In fact, the sale may be harder the second time around. The urgency may be lost. The prospect may have thought of other ways to spend the premium dollars, or new reasons not to buy right now. Worse, another advisor, taking advantage of the need you have established, may have been able to prepare a competitive proposal and closed the sale behind you.

Experienced advisors will tell you that nothing invites competition like a C.O.D. case; nothing cements a sale like cash with the application. Statistics show that persistency is better with prepaid policies. Similarly, weak cases are more easily identified. Applicants who will not submit cash with the application are often not serious about wanting the protection.

Finally, policy delivery will be easier. The number of "not taken" policies is reduced. The rated cases are more likely to be placed if only a small additional premium to cover the rating needs to be collected.

Expect Cash with the Application—Getting cash with the application is an important part of the close—and a mark of professional competence in the advisor. Ask for the money directly and confidently. If you treat prepayment as normal procedure, the prospect will be more likely to do so also.

The best approach is to be confident and assume consent. If you have led the prospect through each decision-making step of the sale and have instilled a sense of urgency about the need for additional protection, you have every reason to expect payment with the application.

"I Want to Think It Over"

"Of course, I want you to think it over, too. In fact, I want you to take at least 2 weeks. It's going to take the company that long to think it over also. You see, it isn't up to me to offer you this plan. The company must decide if you qualify. So you have that time to make up your mind, too."

(Go on to complete the application.)

"Assuming the company approves your application, do you know any reason why you wouldn't want your family to get this money if anything happened to you?"

"Then give me a check for a one-month premium; you can start your semiannual or annual premiums in 30 days after both you and the company have thought it over."

Assume consent by asking, "do you wish to pay the first premium by check for an annual payment or do you plan to make premium payments more frequently?" You will have to explain the other premium models offered by your company such as the semiannual, quarterly, and monthly payments. If you want the prospect to use the automatic check payment mode, ask, "do you have a checking account? If so, why not pay the first premium now and set up subsequent premiums to be paid automatically from your account."

If asked if it's necessary to pay now, simply say, "Yes. It's customary."

The Life Insurance Application Process

Your best means of communicating with the underwriting department is through the application. Doing a good job with each application you submit can, over the years, save weeks and months of additional underwriting time and expense and help you receive your issued policies and commission checks that much sooner. Treat the application as the important document it is. Make sure you fully explain each question to the applicant and allow plenty of time for complete answers.

Your Role

By spreading the risk of an individual's death among a larger group of insureds, the economic loss caused by death is shared by many instead of a few, specifically, the insured's surviving family. A life insurance company's underwriting process must strike a balance. It must be flexible enough to allow people to become members of the large group of insureds at standard rates. However, it must remain selective enough to reject clearly unacceptable risks, while still accepting others who are substandard.

If underwriting or selection is too severe, the company's advisors will lose their share of the market to the competition and may abandon that insurer. If selection is too liberal, mortality costsare likely to be excessive and the financial strength of that company may be threatened. For these reasons, deciding who will and who will not be insured, and at what rates, is a critical function.

The Application Form

After your initial selection through your prospecting, your next role in the underwriting process is to provide the information the home office underwriters need to decide whether or not the risk is acceptable and what the appropriate premium will be. The information you gather and submit to the home office is contained in the application. This important document is used by the underwriting department and becomes a formal part of the contract between the company and the insured.

The underwriters in the home office depend on you to make sure the information on the application is complete, detailed, and accurate, and that other relevant information about the applicant's situation is provided, even though it may not be called for specifically on the application.

If you wish to clarify a situation or give the underwriter additional information about a client, a cover letter is an excellent way to communicate with the underwriter. Remember, to the underwriter the applicant is just a collection of facts, test results, medical reports, and other pieces of information on a paper or computer screen. If you have information that will give a more complete picture of the person, or give a favorable impression, do not hesitate to submit it. For example, if the applicant is involved in the community, has a stellar reputation, or is a hard-working family man, let the underwriter know. It can only help.

It is in your client's interest, as well as in the interest of the company, to give complete and accurate information on the application. Your responsibility in these matters—to your company as well as for your client—is to present as accurate a picture as possible of the individual's personal, moral, and financial circumstances. In this way, you help to see that your company is fairly informed.

Explain the Process to the Proposed Insured

One of the things you can do for your prospect when taking the application is to explain what goes on in the underwriting process. You are asking the prospect to give you a lot of highly personal information. It is up to you to assure the prospect that the information you receive will be held in confidence by you and the company and that it is necessary to the underwriting process.

Explain to your prospects that the underwriting decision is based on a number of factors, including financial, lifestyle, and medical requirements that must be satisfactorily met by anyone applying for life insurance. There must be an insurable relationship for the amount of insurance applied for and the personal income, net worth, and insurance need of the proposed insured. Lifestyle factors would include the nature of one's job, hobbies, use of alcohol or drugs, driving and arrest record, and so on. Medical requirements are discussed elsewhere. The information that will be requested on the application and which, with the prospect's consent, may be gathered from other sources, is designed to provide the company with a thorough, objective view of the prospect.

As you fill out applications, tell your prospects why risk analysis is important and how factors such as age, health, occupation, or hobbies determine an individual's rating as a standard, substandard, or preferred risk. Discuss the possibility of an inspection report being requested. Discuss why they are necessary and the kinds of information typically gathered as well as the methods used to obtain it. Emphasize that these are purely routine, done with the utmost discretion, and that the results are held in strictest confidence. Explain the function of the Attending Physician's Statement (APS), (which may or may not be necessary) and the Medical Information Bureau (MIB) report. If your state or company has information access requirements, review them fully, explaining how your prospect can look at information obtained by the company on the case and correct any errors. If a medical requirement is needed, fully explain what is involved in the process and reassure the prospect that it is a simple procedure.

Because of the potential legal liability involved, both during and after policy issue, all applications and other life insurance-related paperwork must be legally perfect to stand up in court. Home office underwriters are trained to treat paperwork that way, and so should you.

Fully Answer Questions

When we recommended giving complete information, we meant making sure each question on the application is fully answered. Some situations will require a separate memo or letter to be submitted with the application. You need to anticipate when more complete information will be needed. For instance, if your applicant's financial situation is unusual and a large amount of insurance is being applied for, you should prepare a supplement to the application providing net worth and other pertinent details. Most companies have special financial data forms to use for applications of large amounts of insurance.

Document Avocations

Similarly, if your prospect has a hobby such as hang gliding, which may place the individual in a higher risk category, send a memo to the underwriting department giving full details on your prospect's aeronautic activities and training and where this sport is practiced. An avocation questionnaire may be required.

Names

Be sure full legal names are given and that spellings, addresses, and dates of birth are correct. This will help assure that the right person is the subject of the company's analysis and that the beneficiary designation is accurate. If your prospect has other insurance with your company, see to it that the insured's name, and the beneficiary's name are spelled the same way on all company records. For example, a beneficiary listed as B. Scott Thomas on one policy should not appear as Bradley S. Thomas on another. It is confusing and can lead to mistakes. If you get it right the first time, the underwriting department will not have to spend additional time checking to determine which information is correct.

Further, if the client is simultaneously applying for insurance from other companies, give full details as to companies and amounts. If you do not, your underwriter will have to ask you for the information when routine checking discovers other applications.

Insurable Interest

When someone other than the insured is buying the life insurance, acceptable *insurable interest* must be present before a company will issue a policy. This means that a family, economic, or commercial relationship is required of the person who purchases the policy, establishing an interest in the continued longevity of the insured. Again a precaution: In situations in which insurable interest is not obvious, you should provide a full explanation in a memo along with the application.

Insurance Age

The insured's insurance age is usually the age at issue. Some companies use the insured's age at last birthday, while some use age at nearest birthday in determining insurance age. Some companies allow policies to be backdated a certain number of months to pick up a lower insurance age. Be sure you follow the rules of your company in these matters.

Policy Date

Unless the premium is prepaid, the policy will be dated when it is issued or approved. Many companies will honor a request to date a policy ahead up to 30 days from the date of application. This can be another sales/planning point for you to use. The policy date can be amended to a current date on some plans if company rules allow it.

Correct Policy Titles and Amounts

Take care that the right policy title and face amount are listed on the application. Any error here can lead to the wrong policy being issued, which will then have to be corrected or amended at the needless cost of time and paperwork.

Signatures

The applicant's signature is needed on the first part of the application and on the medical portion. If the insured is to be someone other than the applicant, you will need the signatures of both the applicant and the insured. If the insured is a minor, you will need the signature of a parent or guardian. If the applicant is a corporation, the corporate name should be used, followed by the signature of an authorized executive other than the insured. Your signature should appear as witness to the signing of the application, along with the date and location where it was signed. Make sure that you witness every signature on your applications. It is the proper way and will save you from potential problems later.

Medical Information

The second part of the application is the medical background section. Most companies will issue smaller policies on a non-medical basis in which no automatic examination is required; the insured simply answers a series of medical questions. If the answers to the questions are all satisfactory, the policy will probably be issued without further medical investigation. If not, medical background checks or a physical examination, or both, may be required.

Advisor's Role on Nonmedical Applications

If you are able to write nonmedical applications, understand the responsibility you have in being certain that all questions on the application are answered and that all the responses are recorded in the presence of the applicant. None of the questions should be left blank to be filled in later by someone else. Here your role as the field underwriter becomes essential to the approval process for your applicant.

This section of the application is the one that typically causes the most delays in underwriting and issuing policies. All information requested must be provided, and it must be accurate, complete, and clear. If any of those criteria are not met, the underwriting department either will ask you to go back to the applicant for information or it will request an attending physicians statement (APS) from your applicant's physician for clarification or amplification of the points in question.

Without complete information about a condition or treatment, a policy that could have been issued in a few days may take 3 or 4 weeks to go through the underwriting process. In many cases, doctors are slow to return their statements to the home office. In fact, you may need to call the doctor's office to verify that a request for information has been received and that it will soon receive attention.

Medical Questioning Tips

Here are some suggestions for asking medical questions that can save everyone time.

Ask probing questions—If the prospect hesitates in answering one of the questions, ask some more questions to find out why. For instance, a prospect that has had chronic chest colds over the years may wonder how to answer your question about respiratory disorders. If you sense this, inquire about the frequency of the condition, how long it usually lasts, what treatment has been given, and by whom. It is often best to check the yes block, give details in the space provided, and let the underwriting department decide whether to pursue the matter.

Use concrete terms—Do not use loose phrases such as, "applicant was sick for several days last year." Be specific: "applicant had severe nausea and stomach cramps May 2 through May 5, 2003, following a picnic. Did not consult physician, but self-medicated. Condition has not reoccurred."

Provide details of all treatment—Give dates and reasons for all medical treatment in the past 5 years. If, for example, the applicant last saw a doctor for a routine physical exam in December, put it down, and indicate the results of the examination. If there were none, say so. Do not leave any vague or unanswered questions for which the underwriters will have to find answers.

Write legibly; use black ink—Take your time and print the information you enter on the application. If it cannot be read, you will be asked to decipher your writing and may have to rewrite the application and get all new signatures. Remember, the application becomes a permanent part of the contract and you will want your client to be able to read it in the future, too.

List physicians' full names and addresses—If the underwriters need to contact your prospect's doctors for more information, they will need full names and mailing addresses. Many include the phone number as well. If a person has seen several doctors for a condition, list the names of each physician; often, complete records are not kept by any one of them. This alone can cut underwriting time by weeks.

When Not to Take Cash

Normally for younger ages and lower amounts of coverage, you can submit the application nonmedically (and get cash with the application) even if you have listed several conditions that may need further investigation. If your questions reveal that the prospective insured appears to have a serious medical problem, do not accept an initial premium payment. Your agency can suggest where to draw this line. Obvious conditions would include recent recovery from heart surgery or diagnosis of cancer. The underwriting department will let you know if a medical examination is required with your normally bound application. Be sure to tell your prospect that the health questions on the application are a first step in the medical underwriting of the policy. Further information may be needed from the prospect's doctor, from the Medical Information Bureau, or in the form of a physical examination.

The exception here is the person who has been declined or rated by another company. Do not submit the application nonmedically or accept prepayment without authorization from the home office in such a case.

Finally, the same rules of completeness, accuracy, and legibility apply to the final section of the application, the advisor's report. This section varies from company to company, just as there are variations in the first two parts. In all cases, follow your company's guidelines in these areas.

Other Sources of Information

The information provided on the application may or may not result in the company's requesting further background on the individual. An APS, the MIB, the inspection report, a Personal Health Interview (PHI) and/or a medical exam may provide additional information.

Most companies require some sort of financial balance sheet from applicants of large face value policies. Find out what your company requires and what forms are used.

Medical Exam

In some cases, the company may request that the applicant take a medical examination, given at the company's expense, by a doctor or paramedic. This gives the company a better, more immediate understanding of the applicant's condition and the extent to which any health problems may increase the risk involved.

The more life insurance applied for, the more medical data the company will require. In some companies, the nonmedical limits are \$100,000 or even \$250,000 with a blood or oral fluid test up to age 30, less at older ages. For larger amounts of insurance, most companies require that applicants take a medical examination in order for the application to be considered. Be sure you know the nonmedical limits of your company. It can save you time and grief.

If a medical exam is necessary, explain why it is being requested (again, it may be routine at certain ages, or when larger amounts of insurance are involved). You can help your prospect be in top form for the medical exam by making the following suggestions.

Usually the best time for an insurance physical is early in the morning, when most people are more relaxed than they are later in the day. Your prospect should be at ease and confidant, not pushed to squeeze the examination into a busy schedule. It may be better to postpone the examination than to have your prospect uptight from a hard day at work.

It is best not to eat for 10 or 12 hours before the exam. That is another reason why morning is a good time for insurance physicals; the person will not have eaten since dinner and can wait until after the examination to eat breakfast.

Runners and other aerobic athletes can have much lower pulse rates than other people and produce what may seem like abnormalities in their urine specimens. If this could be a possibility, advise your prospect to let the examiners know of these activities in advance. People who have borderline weight problems should know that the examiners would weigh them fully clothed. Underwriting scales account for clothing and shoes.

Blood Profiles

It is very important to note that since the advent of AIDS in our society, we are finding a greater use of blood profiles in the underwriting process. Companies are now able to screen for such things as prescription drugs that treat high blood pressure, diabetes, and heart disease as well as the human immune deficiency virus (HIV) that causes AIDS. Applicant urine samples are tested for indications of nicotine or illegal drugs, albumin, glucose, and certain medications. With this additional information, underwriters can more accurately and fairly evaluate proposed risks. More recently, oral fluid testing has been introduced which eliminates the need for blood or urine testing.

Attending Physician's Statement (APS)

The *Attending Physician's Statement* is a form sent by the insurance company to the applicant's doctor(s) listed on the application as having provided either preventative medical care or treatment for specific ailments or injuries. An APS is typically used when additional information is needed to determine the nature or extent of a particular medical problem. It might also be requested for verification of information or simply because of the age of client or the amount of insurance sought. You may need to call a physician, or ask the applicant to do so, to expedite the completion of an Attending Physicians' Statement.

Medical Information Bureau (MIB)

One of the sources of additional health information is the *Medical Information Bureau.* The MIB is an independent, not-for-profit association of life insurance companies that pool and exchange medical information on applicants who have applied for coverage elsewhere in the past. No detailed medical histories are involved, simply numbered codes signifying health conditions and dates and related factors that may be significant to underwriting departments.

Information is found on file in only about 15 percent of the applications submitted to the MIB. They usually provide background on only two or three conditions that have previously been reported to the Bureau. Identifying details on the individual in question are provided so that it is certain that the person in the report is the one about whom the company is inquiring.

Personal History Interview (PHI)

Some companies are obtaining additional data or confirming the application with a *Personal History Interview*. Companies use it for intermediate amounts in specific age groupings. The applicant is telephoned from the home office underwriting department or an independent company performing this function. The PHI requests the same type of information found in an inspection report and replaces it for an increasing number of applications. Occasionally an additional APS may be ordered based on information discovered in a PHI.

You should prepare your applicant for the PHI call. Explain what type of applications it is used for and what questions are asked. Find out when the applicant will be available, in the evening or in the morning, at home or at the office. The questions are personal and you want your applicants to be prepared for them. Check back with your applicant after the call to make sure it went smoothly. Your agency can give you a general time frame of when underwriting will telephone.

Inspection Report

Sources are also used to verify nonmedical information provided by the prospect on the application, as well as to add other background data to what is already known. A valuable source of information on applicants, the *inspection report* provides extensive information on subjects such as credit rating, lifestyle, smoking and drinking habits, neighborhood conditions, hobbies, occupations and workplace conditions, criminal and driving records, employment, and military service information. These reports are prepared through personal interviews by professional investigators who determine, by referring to the applicant's past and present circumstances, who the most logical people are to interview. The name of the insurance company is not mentioned in most cases, and the inspector, using other sources, verifies any adverse information obtained. Once completed, an inspector's report is evaluated for thoroughness and accuracy before being submitted to the insurance company.

International Residents' Applications

Today's global economy will create situations where sooner or later most advisors will submit an application on a prospect that is a citizen of another country. It is best to clarify the legal issues with your company before you submit paperwork on a non-citizen to see what the requirements are. A state's insurance laws may be more liberal than the insurer's underwriting rules. Most insurers will require proof of intent to establish permanent residency with a green card if the applicant is an immigrant. Many U.S. insurers will find applicants who are in the country temporarily unacceptable risks because of the difficulty of investigating claims in areas of the world where they do not do business already or have local contacts.

If the prospect is a foreign national who works for an American company, the advisor should request a formal letter from the employer verifying salary and other forms of payment. Signed verification from U.S. banks regarding the applicant's depositor status may be needed. All the verification that the advisor can provide about the assets and liabilities will help the underwriter evaluate the case.

How Underwriting Gets Delayed

Naturally, some cases take longer than others, especially where there are medical problems to sort through. Small things that could be avoided if more attention is paid to filling out the application correctly and completely can hold up underwriting. All too often, though, when this happens, it costs the company more to issue the policy, you do not get paid as soon as you would like and, worse, your prospect is left wondering, "what's going on with my insurance?" In the next section, we will look at underwriting, your role, the underwriting department's role, and how you can facilitate the process by developing your skills with the application.

Underwriting Concepts and Processes

The purpose of this section is to review the major components of underwriting to ensure that advisors understand the terminology and components of underwriting and the importance of their role in the process. We will also clarify the importance of explaining the underwriting process to the client.

The underlying principle of insurance is a sharing of a loss by those exposed to a common hazard through the creation of a common fund. If the plan is to be valid and equitable, each participant must pay into the fund a fair amount determined for people in the same risk classification.

Underwriting is the process by which insurance companies analyze risks to decide if they want to insure them, and at what rates. It is also designed to reject clearly unacceptable risks. The home office underwriting department does much of the work, but the first step in the process is the gathering of prospect information on the insurance application. Making sure that this information is complete and accurate is a part of your job. If it is accurate, and no attending physician's statement is required, your prospects' application will make its way through the underwriting process faster. If it is inaccurate, you can probably count on delays of several weeks in getting your business on the books.

The Underwriting Process

If underwriting is the selection of people who may share in the risk of the larger group and the setting of the appropriate premium for these individuals, then the first question underwriters must ask is, "how long is the applicant likely to live?" The answer, of course, depends on the individual's age, health, and other factors. The underwriters examine the information they have on the applicant, provided by the application you submit and other sources, and then compare it with statistics of the general population. The company must be able to counteract the tendencies of adverse selection. *Adverse selection* is the natural tendency for those who know they are highly vulnerable to a specific risk to be most inclined to acquire and retain insurance to cover that loss.

As you know from earlier in this book, a key factor in underwriting is the mortality experience for people of the same age. Mortality tables, such as the 2001 Commissioners' Standard Ordinary (CSO) table, are used to determine the chances of a person of any given age dying in a given year. Most insurance companies have their own mortality tables based on information they have collected from their own applicant pool over time.

Major Considerations in Underwriting

Health is a major consideration, but underwriters also consider other factors in their determination of a rating classification. The underwriters take into account not only the medical experience of the applicant, but also the health histories of members of the applicant's family. They want to know, for example, if there is a history of heart failure, cancer, diabetes, or other conditions that could be hereditary.

Occupation, hobbies, and lifestyles are also of concern. A person who is a weekend pilot or who works in construction of high-rise office buildings is more of a risk than a college professor or office worker. Similarly, a recreational pilot or motorcycle rider is generally considered to be at higher risk than a chess player or golfer. An applicant's drinking habits, use of drugs, and possible criminal records are also of concern in underwriting.

Three Classifications of Risk

The underwriting department needs to evaluate this type of information in order to tell whether the applicant falls in one of three general risk classifications: *standard*; *substandard*; or *above standard*, also called a *preferred* classification. A person who has, statistically, no greater a risk of dying than anyone else in that age group, is considered a standard risk. A person who does have a statistically greater risk of death is usually considered to be a substandard risk. A person who is above standard has a statistically lower chance of death than people in the same age group. The criteria for determining these ratings vary greatly from one company to another, so it is sometimes difficult to compare and justify a rating from one company to another.

Standard Risks—Most applicants are insured at standard rates. In fact, according to the American Council of Life Insurance (ACLI), 95 percent of all cases are standard or better. How is this determined? After the company knows how many individuals in a given age group will die each year, it can determine how much to charge each person in that group who is a standard risk. The premiums that the policyowners pay provide the funds needed to pay the beneficiaries of the people in the group who die during the year. For example, let us say that out of a group of 1,000 insureds, two people age 35 are expected to die this year. If each person in this group has a $10,000 policy, we know that the company needs at least $20,000 to pay the beneficiaries of the two who will die. By dividing the number of people in the group (1,000) by the amount of money needed to pay the anticipated death claims ($20,000) the mortality expense for each person in the group can be determined. In this case, the amount needed would be $20 per person. The same calculation applies for all other amounts of insurance.

Naturally, the company needs to factor other costs into the premiums it charges, such as salaries and overhead expenses, commissions, and projected policy lapses. Basically, though, that is how standard risk premiums are structured.

Mortality Classes

Table or Chapter Designation	Average Mortality Assumed	Mortality Range
1 or A	125%	120%–139%
2 or B	150%	140%–165%
3 or C	175%	166%–189%
4 or D	200%	190%–215%
5 or E	225%	216%–239%
6 or F	250%	240%–265%

Substandard Risks—People who are considered substandard risks usually pay premiums that are rated upwards according to certain factors. In reality, the group is a small percentage of this type of insurance sale. It is reported that only 3 percent of issued policies are rated, while only another 2 percent are declined. The selection process is concerned with the isolation of impairments and hazards that are not common to all insurance applicants. Impairments that are common to all applicants in a group will tend to increase the general mortality level. Companies must constantly strive to keep the risk factors of their underwriting in balance and also in line with what other companies are doing. Insurance companies use a variety of ways to classify substandard mortality risks.

Multiple Table Extra Premium—The most common pricing method used for impaired or substandard risks is called the multiple table extra premium method. For each age and plan of insurance, a number of premium rates are established. The standard risk is assumed to have 100-percent mortality and pays the normal, standard premium. Risks that are assumed to have a mortality of above 100 percent pay higher premiums. In fact, multiple tables provide extra premium rates for assumed mortality percentages of up to 1,000 percent or higher.

Flat Extra Premium—Another means of measuring the extra risk is by use of a flat extra premium. The regular premium is charged but an extra premium is also charged for the expected increased mortality. It is often used for occupational and avocational risks since the increased risk is accidental and not tied to the age of the applicant. It is most commonly used in situations where the amount at risk by the company is constant, as in level term insurance. Where permanent insurance is used, the net amount at risk decreases each year for the company as the growing cash value offsets the risk. The same applies to decreasing term insurance designed to have a smaller face value over time. Therefore, with this type of substandard rating system the company could charge a smaller extra premium for a 20-year endowment policy than for a whole life policy.

Rated-Up Age Plan—Under a third type of substandard rating, the rated-up age plan, the applicant is assumed to be a specific number of years older than his or her actual age. In other words, the applicant's condition predicts a shorter life span. By adding to the age at issue of a policy, the company can equalize life expectancy for all risks. The extra age is figured by adding the net premium of actual age to an amount that will provide for the extra risk of the impairment in question. This is then compared to the company's standard table and a new and greater age is calculated for the applicant. For instance, in this type of rating system the applicant might be charged the premium for a 32-year-old male instead of that of a 26-year-old.

Understanding how your company establishes substandard ratings strengthens your position in the sales process. You want to be able to answer questions about a rating with authority and to possess the knowledge to reassure the insured that the rating is accurate and should be accepted.

Guaranteed Authenticity

"(Prospect), in purchasing the policy, you have everything you need to understand it fully. There will be no provisions hidden from you; everything will be aboveboard and complete.

"You will have in writing all the things my company promises. Attached to the policy will be a copy of this application which we will examine together to make sure that everything is just as you wanted."

Reconsideration—In many cases, companies will consider removing a substandard rating under certain future conditions. A rating that has been assigned because of occupation will probably be removed if the insured no longer works in that occupation. Ratings assigned for medical problems may be evaluated periodically. If the condition improves or is eliminated over a period of time, such as a year, the rating may be reduced or removed.

You should ask your underwriter if there might be a chance to have a rating changed in the future if this information is not provided with the issued policy. If so, find out when and what the procedure would be. Your client will find this possibility good news. Be sure to note it in your client's file and remember to contact the client at the appropriate time. Your concern for a client's premium dollars and improving health will always be appreciated.

Preferred Risks—A person who is classified above standard may be eligible for reduced or preferred premiums. Companies vary in the terms they use for this category of risk. Applicants may be considered as above standard by some companies if they have not smoked cigarettes, a pipe, or cigars for a year or more, or if their weight-height ratio is within the range of special tables designed for the preferred risk group. Companies use many different criteria to determine preferred ratings. Preferred premiums are generally used to lower the standard premium, the same way substandard premiums are used to raise the standard premiums.

Reinsurance

Reinsurance is a device by which one insurance company or insurer transfers all or a portion of its risk under an insurance policy or policies to another company or insurer. There are a number of reasons this is done. They include: transferring a company's liabilities, achieving objectives, achieving favorable underwriting results, reducing drain on surplus from writing new business, limiting the amount of insurance on one life (retention limits), using the reinsurer's expertise, and transferring substandard business.

When the application is for a very large sum of life insurance, your company may use a reinsurer to take some of the risk. Companies routinely limit the amount of risk they accept on an individual life. This may be for amounts ranging from $100,000 to about $5 million or more per life. It varies from company to company. An *automatic reinsurance* limit would be a mutually acceptable amount to the direct writer, your company where the application was submitted, and its reinsurer. When the reinsurer looks at all of the application papers and evidence of insurability before accepting its portion of the risk, the reinsurance is called a *facultative agreement*. You may not even be aware of this type of process during the underwriting of your application.

On the other hand, if the reinsurer evaluates your applicant's risk differently than the direct insurer, additional requirements may be requested for underwriting the application. This is done in an attempt to allow the reinsurer to price the risk at the same rate as your company, the direct insurer. The direct insurer also may send the application to another reinsurer with whom it maintains a treaty, an agreement to do business together.

Advisors should be aware of the reinsurance process and help the applicant understand the purpose and the advantages of cooperating when additional requirements, such as specialized tests, are requested during underwriting. The advisor should ask questions through the agency about the status of underwriting on applications. You should stay aware of everything that is happening with all of your applications. Your applicant is concerned and you must be too. All of this is done to help the advisor place the business at the best premium. This is another reason for doing a thorough job when taking an application. Ask questions about everything.

Home Office Relationships

Both you and the home office underwriting department have the same objective: putting quality business on the books. A case that lapses after one or two premiums because the insured really could not afford the coverage is not quality business; in fact, it is costly business to you and to the company. A case issued to someone who deliberately misrepresented a health condition, or which is applied for by someone of questionable character is, again, not quality business. It can become costly to the company and to you.

Clearly, both field and home office underwriters have pivotal roles in seeing that only quality business is submitted and issued. In order to carry out their roles, there must be a good cooperative relationship between the field and the home office. In many ways, you set the tone of this relationship, since it is you who initiates most of the contacts with the underwriting department. As in any successful business venture, three qualities are needed to establish good relationships with members of the underwriting department: trust, candor, and communication.

Mutual Trust—The underwriters must be able to depend on your judgment in submitting only qualified risks. In turn, you must be able to trust the underwriter's evaluation of the cases that you submit (and be able to count on their fast follow-up). Trust is built on consistency. If the cases you submit are consistently well documented, your reputation for trustworthiness will be assured.

For most underwriters, any discovery of dishonesty by the applicant in response to the application creates an aura of suspicion. Unfortunately, if the information was so obvious that the advisor could not possibly have been unaware of it, the advisor's reputation will suffer as well. For instance, if the applicant's weight on a nonmed application is written as 190 pounds and it is later discovered to be more than 300 pounds, then underwriting will wonder about the advisor's judgment. An advisor's reputation is very difficult to repair after any obvious lack of candor involving such acts of advisor complicity. After investigation, some companies will terminate advisor contracts for application fraud.

The Advisor's Responsibility

Every advisor should remember that the difference between being insurable and being uninsurable, or being issued a risk rating, may mean the difference between financial stability and insolvency to a family when a breadwinner dies. Do your part in underwriting with submission of only well documented applications. The advisor must take the process seriously, be responsible and submit complete, legible, and accurate applications.

Well-documented Applications—What does well-documented mean? It means that

- your applications provide complete, accurate information and are legibly written
- if there are any unusual circumstances connected with the applicant's background or present situation, medically or otherwise, they are clearly documented
- appropriate amounts of insurance are applied for by responsible and financially stable individuals

It is only natural for you to want to picture your prospective clients in the most favorable light. This can and should be done in such a way that any potential problem areas are also candidly brought to the underwriter's attention. Not only will this bolster the underwriting department's confidence in you, it will usually help to speed up the underwriting process. It is also much better to ask your prospects probing questions and to discuss potential problem areas at the time of application than to have adverse information discovered later.

Professional Communication: Cover Letters—Communicate with the underwriting department in an open, professional manner. If it is appropriate, send a cover memo with an application, giving any additional details or describing special circumstances that you wish to be considered in underwriting the case. This communication should be in a typed, formal business memo format. In some instances, you may want to follow up by phone to discuss special situations with the underwriting department, if your company encourages this.

This direct, professional approach will help you establish your credibility. Underwriters expect advisors to go to bat for their applicants, but they will put a lot more stock in your requests for special consideration of certain cases if you are equally forthcoming in pointing out areas of potential concern to them.

Writing Senior Citizens

The fastest growing segment of the U.S. population is the age group over 65. They also represent a substantial life insurance market. National Underwriter estimates that most geriatric applicants have 3.5 chronic diseases. This is because most major diseases become more prevalent with advancing age. Some conditions such as osteoarthritis may have little impact on insurability, while other diseases make the purchase of insurance impossible. Company underwriting is naturally more conservative with the older the applicant.

How to Avoid Problems—Helpful hints include the following:

1. The medical history is often long and complicated on older applicants. Take a preliminary medical history during the fact-finding interview so that you can discuss any unusual impairments with your underwriter before putting the case together. Use cover letters as discussed earlier that include statements of amplification where appropriate and are signed by your applicant. Make your case accurately and fully.

2. Attending Physician's Statements may be the key to successful underwriting for applications on older prospects. Make sure records from specialists seen by your applicant are submitted along with those from the primary physician. Encourage more detail about a condition, not less. Copies of test reports, biopsy pathology reports, and other documents are essential. Without these reports underwriting is delayed and your case can be

weakened as additional requests are made of the physicians who are concerned.

3. During the fact-finding interview, discuss medications taken by the prospect. You need to know about the over-the-counter medications as well as prescription medications. Everything needs to be fully disclosed, even vitamin tablets and alternative medical treatment such as the use of herbs and herbal supplements. Everything has implications in the underwriting process.

4. Electrocardiograms (ECGs) are commonly required on older applicants. Since the significance of an ECG abnormality may be determined by how long it has been present, a more favorable outcome is more likely if the advisor can obtain prior readings for home office review. If you know that a prior ECG has been made, let the underwriter know about it when you submit the application.

Cover Letters Move Business

Cover letters move business. Successful advisors whose business seems to breeze through underwriting are usually chronic cover letter writers. Frustrated advisors who blame underwriting for everything from lost sales to global warming typically have never heard of them. Try using a cover letter with your next application that needs extra explanation. It will help the underwriter and may speed up approval of the case.

—Hank George and John J. Krinik, "Getting It Issued," published by National Underwriter.

Market Conduct Issues with Older Applicants

In recent years, both companies and public interest groups have been concerned about the vulnerability of older people. Older buyers are more susceptible to financial scams involving telephone and door-to-door solicitors. It is very important for every selling contact with an elderly person to be fully documented by the advisor. The advisor has a great responsibility to the elderly buyer to do everything possible to make sure that any purchase is fully understood and a suitable product for that person is sold.

Case History

A Millionaire Prospect

Kim Lewis is age 26, married, and has completed 2 years of college. At the time of this case, Kim was in the process of finishing the Meeting Client Needs course, and had been in the life insurance business a little over 3 years.

Prospect

During a policy delivery recently, a policyowner gave me the name of this prospect, Ann, who was a fourth-year medical student. I like to focus on referrals at delivery because I feel I am in my strongest position in the eyes of the client at that time. Ann's husband Jerry was also a medical student. Both had allowances from their families, so they were financially comfortable. They lived in a nice but simple apartment near the medical school and hospital. Their only life insurance was made up of small juvenile policies owned by their parents.

Pre-approach

The day after I got the referral, I telephoned my prospect. "Doctor, my name is Kim Lewis of the ABC Life Insurance Company. You don't know me, but I'm a friend of Karen Lincoln. Karen suggested I go over some of the ideas we discussed regarding Karen's future life insurance program. Karen is very pleased with the work I've done and offered to talk to you if you wanted to find out what she thought of our work together. Would it be convenient for us to get together tomorrow night at 7:00 or would Thursday night at 8:00 be better for you?"

Ann replied that they were not in the market for life insurance. Because of heavy tuition and living expenses, they did not want to do anything about starting a program at this time.

"Doctor, all I will be doing is giving you some ideas for your future life insurance program so that when and if you decide to do something, you might consider me as your agent."

Ann said that would be fair enough and that they would let me know. I said that I would be working at the hospital in 2 days, and that I'd like to stop in and say hello. Possibly we could make a future appointment then. Ann agreed.

Approach

When I went to the hospital 2 days later, I had Ann paged on the public address system. We met in the main lobby. I tried to arrange an appointment for that same week, but Ann said they were too busy. Possibly we could get together the following week.

I looked for Ann on my next visit to the hospital. We met in one of the corridors. Ann told me they thought they would wait until they returned to Jerry's hometown before they did anything about their life insurance program. I replied that I was still interested in talking to them because I could give them some ideas about the use of life insurance that would be helpful. Again I pressed for an appointment at their home when both Ann and Jerry would be present. I had decided that both prospects definitely should be in on the conversation. Finally, an "OK" and we set a time for 3 nights later.

As soon as I walked into their apartment, the whole atmosphere of our relationship seemed to change. Until then Ann had been rather cold and distant, but now she was cordial. I think probably Jerry can be given the primary credit for this. The coffeepot was perking, and they were both quite friendly. There was no indication that they were going to buy, however.

Seniors in medical school are frequently called "Doctor," so I addressed them both by this title until they asked me to call them Ann and Jerry. When they did, I had a clear indication that I was making progress. We became better acquainted as we visited for 10 or 15 minutes about the rigors of their education and the internships and residency appointments they were hoping to get after graduation.

Presentation

My first mention of life insurance was in saying that I had done a good bit of work for many of their classmates and other doctors who were in circumstances similar to theirs. I added that I didn't know whether I could be of any help to them at the moment, but I wanted to give them some ideas at least. If and when they bought in the future, they would be in a better position to make a decision and, hopefully, they would contact me.

I briefly outlined my credentials and told them a little bit about my insurance company, stressing its size and national scope.

They said “Fine,” and I started my variation of “You’ll Earn a Fortune.” Using a large piece of plain white paper and a pencil to illustrate the main points, I began like this:

“Ann, Jerry, have you ever thought how much you will earn in the next 40 years? Provided you keep your health and assuming you work at least until you are 65, you each have about 40 years of great earning power ahead of you. The average physician in 40 years time will probably earn at least $4 million—maybe more.

“It is also safe to assume that you will eventually own at least $500,000 to $1 million worth of protection through life insurance. Physicians eventually buy at least this much because they need it to protect their families and finance their retirements. Aside from Social Security, doctors in private practice generally have no benefits of any kind to supplement the government plan. The primary source of money for your old age will be what you begin setting aside now while you are young. You will have to do your own planning.”

They were surprised and seemed to be impressed with these figures. Neither had given much thought about earning several million dollars. Nor had it ever occurred to them that they would need at least as much life insurance as I showed them.

“Ann and Jerry, your problem is no different than that of any other young couple today. You must build and create an estate. You must start to conserve, to save something. It has greater magnitude for you—and greater opportunity—because you’re going to earn more money than the average person.”

Then I mentioned one of my favorite analogies: a trash-truck driver enjoys as much financial security as does a young physician. Even if the truck driver has no other employee benefits, the Social Security benefits will be at least as much as the doctor’s. In fact, the family of a young physician could be even worse off because of the relatively small income earned during internship and residency in the early years; under the Social Security income-averaging rules, the doctor’s average wage could be less than the truck driver’s.

When I tell this story to young physicians, it’s usually quite a blow to their ego. I’ve already spent time telling them how much money they are going to make, thereby building their sense of self-importance. Then I proceed to shatter it, showing that a person of very modest means and training could leave a family more secure.

They agreed with everything I said, but gave no indication that they were going to do anything about it. Then they began to ask questions. I had the impression that they were very concerned about what would happen if they started a life insurance program and had to stop it in the middle because they could not afford the premiums. They were curious about the different types of policies available, and very interested in learning what their classmates were doing about their insurance.

I told them I never mentioned names, but I could give them an idea of the types of plans their friends were buying. "A permanent insurance policy with a term rider is the most popular plan. They buy the term rider with the idea of converting it as soon as possible. In a young physician's program, there is definitely a place for term insurance because the needs are so great and usually funds are limited. Like everyone else, physicians run the risk of becoming uninsurable, and term covers this risk as well as providing a lot of protection."

Then Jerry suggested building a future estate by acquiring stocks and bonds. I replied, "Yes, that is possible, but if we were to draw a circle (I drew one on a piece of paper), and put the business world here, and the physicians were all here, they would be exactly 180 degrees apart from each other. Your patients expect their doctor to know a great deal about healing, not about buying and selling stocks. In turn, this means that physicians must spend almost all their time concentrating on their practices and studying new medical developments. This explains why physicians can be among the biggest losers in the stock market."

Next, Ann brought up the question of real estate. I talked about some of the common hazards of owning real estate, that it is easy to buy and oftentimes hard to sell. I turned the subject to life insurance, pointing out that insurance is the only form of guaranteed accumulations that could be counted on to create an estate whatever else might happen. No other vehicle could do this. They understood and seemed interested.

Then Jerry wanted to know about the guarantees offered by a life insurance company. I highlighted the major points, adding that my company had been in business for the better part of a century, and was well known for its prompt payment of claims. I then showed them a simple ledger statement illustrating the results of what could be accomplished. It was apparent that they were becoming more impressed, and I was moving closer and closer to success.

Close

I have one effective close I use in almost all my cases: "Jerry, Ann, doesn't it make sense to get started on a program now?"

"It does, but we don't have the money to do anything about it."

I laid my rate book on the table, and said, "I've got a book full of ideas here, but there's nothing I can do until you tell me how much you can set aside each month. I realize that you might not be able to solve the whole problem tonight, but half a pie is better than none. Ann, can you save $200 a month?"

"Of course not!"

"Well, can you save $50 a month?" When Ann answered yes, I continued, "Well, somewhere between $50 and $200 is a figure you can save, isn't that right?" So I started counting down until I arrived at a figure that we agreed they could save. "Can you save $150? Can you save $100?"

This is when I found out that they had been holding something back from me. It appears that just a week before, Jerry's father suggested to Ann that they buy life insurance. This was the first indication that they had even thought of it. I commented, "Well, Jerry, if you've been giving this any thought, you must have some figure in mind that you can save each month without too much of a problem."

They agreed that they had, and that they felt they could save $100 a month.

After I had figured the coverage of whole life and term and the applications were signed and they had given me a check, I asked Ann and Jerry, "Why did you buy this insurance?"

"Frankly, I have talked to a few life insurance agents. But you were the only one who came right out and told me from the very beginning that you were interested in selling me insurance, and making me a client of yours." Jerry added that they were pleased about the way I had explained everything so thoroughly.

Delivery

When their policies came down from underwriting, I made up a summary sheet showing face amount, premium, beneficiaries, and so forth, and I added a few suggestions about making a Will and having a power of attorney for each spouse. I reviewed the policy for accuracy and prepared a policy wallet with my business card. I also included company-produced materials about Wills and the benefits of life insurance, as well as the policy summary and buyer's guide. I prepared an NAIC illustration and delivery receipt to be signed as is required by my company. At this time I also set up a client file containing my fact-finding information, notes about our conversations, and the sales materials and illustrations of the policies sold.

When I saw them again at their apartment I went through the major parts of the contract paragraph by paragraph, to be sure each provision was understood. I reaffirmed their reasons for buying and what these policies could do for them.

Ann and Jerry have moved out of town. However, I have kept in touch with them by mail and I have made two sales from the referred leads they gave me.

Comments

As this case illustrates, I think that we sometimes make a mistake in trying to give the impression that all we want to do is "stop by" and give prospects an idea. It is a definite mistake to give them the impression that we aren't trying to sell anything. In the long run, you never lose by being straightforward with people.

It is also important to remember that a lot of students do have money to buy life insurance. Often they plead poverty, but this young couple who became my clients were anything but impoverished. You won't find all students as well off as Ann and Jerry, but in many cases one of them will be working and they are perfectly capable of affording at least a start on a life insurance program.

Chapter Seven Review

Key terms and concepts are explained in the Glossary. Answers to the Review Questions and Self-Test Questions are found in the back of the book, following the Glossary.

Key Concepts and Terms

closing	objections
buying signals	trial close
implied consent	conditional receipt
risk classification	reinsurance
standard risk	substandard risk
multiple table extra premium	flat extra premium
preferred risk	insurable interest
policy date	Attending Physician's Statement (APS)
Medical Information Bureau (MIB)	Personal History Interview (PHI)
Inspection report	adverse selection

Review Questions

7-1. Describe what the advisor should do to prepare to ask the prospect to implement his or her recommendation(s). When and how do you ask the prospect to buy?

7-2. List and explain four categories of objections.

7-3. Explain how to clarify and respond to objections.

7-4. List and describe closing techniques and how to implement them.

7-5. Discuss the advantages to the applicant and the advisor of taking cash with the application.

7-6. Describe the advisor's role in field underwriting and facilitating the underwriting process.

7-7. Describe the underwriting process and the information that is used in underwriting.

7-8. Describe underwriting classification in general. Then explain substandard policy issue, types of substandard ratings and the criteria and rationale used in assigning them.

Self-Test Questions

Instructions: Read Chapter 7, then answer the following 10 questions to test your knowledge. Circle the correct answer. When you are finished, check your answers with the answer key in the back of the book.

7-1. "Leave me a copy of your proposal. I'll think about it over the weekend." This is an example of which type of objection?

(A) No need
(B) No trust
(C) No hurry
(D) No money

7-2. If a prospect does not respond to your presentation, which of the following actions should you take?

(A) Pack your briefcase and leave as quickly as possible.
(B) Ask for feedback from the prospect on how he or she views your proposal.
(C) Try to employ a closing technique.
(D) Take this as a buying signal and use the implied consent technique.

7-3. The first step in answering a prospect's objection is to

(A) listen to the prospect
(B) think of ways to answer the objection
(C) consider it a buying signal and close
(D) ignore it since it is probably an excuse

7-4. "What interests you most about this proposal?" This is an example of what type of question?

(A) progressive "yes"
(B) closed-ended
(C) disturbing
(D) checking

7-5. When someone applies to be the owner of a life insurance policy on another person's life, the insurance company will require

(A) insurable interest
(B) relationship by blood or marriage
(C) underwriting of the premium payer
(D) pre-payment of the annual premium

7-6. A sales idea comparing the cost and values of a plan started today and one to be started 5 or 10 years from now is an example of

(A) premium maximization
(B) the cost of waiting
(C) assumed consent
(D) the alternate choice

7-7. An insurance application is completed when the

(A) prospect signs the application
(B) prospect makes a premium payment
(C) beneficiary receives the policy proceeds
(D) policy is recorded in the insurer's home office

7-8. What should your reaction be to your prospect if she hesitates, leans forward, and asks you for further explanation of a point you just covered?

(A) This is an example of a checking question.
(B) Recognize her body language as expressing a lack of active listening.
(C) Understand that this may be a buying signal.
(D) The Ben Franklin close could be used in this situation.

7-9. Which of the following statements regarding closing techniques is (are) correct?

I. The implied consent technique presumes the prospect has decided to buy.
II. The direct question asks the prospect if they have made up their mind and wish to start the plan.

(A) I only
(B) II only
(C) Both I and II
(D) Neither I nor II

7-10. All of the following are examples of buying signals EXCEPT:

(A) The prospect hesitates, asking for clarification or explanation of a point you just covered.
(B) The prospect nods his head, showing interest.
(C) The prospect asks a specific question, such as "When does coverage start?" or "Do I need to get a blood test or physical?"
(D) The prospect leans back in her chair, folds her arms and looks at the ceiling.

8

Service the Plan

Overview and Learning Objectives

Chapter 8 wraps up the selling/planning process with the very important and undoubtedly longest portion of the advisor/client relationship: service. The chapter makes recommendations regarding how the advisor can maximize his or her efforts in continuing and strengthening the long-term relationship with the client. The chapter also reviews contract features which typically come into play in the servicing phase, such as delivery requirements, beneficiary designations, supplementary contracts, and death claims.

By reading this chapter and answering the questions, you should be able to

8-1. Discuss the objectives of the delivery interview and how to achieve them.

8-2. Explain what should you do to properly prepare for the delivery interview.

8-3. Discuss the common state and company requirements for policy delivery.

8-4. Explain how to provide high-quality policy service and how this can enhance your business.

8-5. List and explain beneficiary types and issues relating to beneficiary designation.

8-6. List and explain five types of supplementary contracts used to pay claims.

8-7. Describe a life settlement and why it is gaining popularity today.

8-8. List and explain what is needed to file a death claim.

Chapter Outline

Policy Delivery

A good policy delivery interview goes a long way toward keeping your policy *persistency* rate high (and lapse ratio low) and strengthening your client base with each new sale. Your persistency rate measures the number of policies that remain in force over a given time period, normally measured in years. Selling a policy is your first challenge; keeping it on the books is the next, and policy service plays a key role in maintaining a high persistency rate.

The delivery of the policy confirms for the client their decision to buy and completes the sales process in the their eyes. This is why it is so important to meet with your new policyowner to deliver the contract in person. You establish a pattern of service for the future and you demonstrate and reinforce your personal approach and philosophy of selling and service. Explain the kinds of service the client can expect and reinforce the systems you have in place to accomplish that service. Set an appointment for an annual review to express your commitment to these service goals. Then, of course, deliver on your promises.

The purpose of this section is to demonstrate that the policy delivery is a key part of a sale and should not be taken lightly. It confirms for the buyer their decision to buy, and it completes the selling process. For the salesperson it represents the satisfaction of completing the sale, opening new opportunities to work with that client, and moving on to new sales opportunities. The delivery interview is a strategic event to set the stage for the future with this client.

Everything that you do at the policy delivery will have a profound effect on your subsequent relationship with clients. Throughout the sales process you have been carefully building and enhancing the level of trust between yourself and your clients. You are delivering on your promise to continue to meet and emphasizing your ongoing interest in your client. The buyer should realize that he or she means more to you than just another sale.

Customers versus Clients

All clients are customers, but not all customers are clients. Clients are people who have bought from you, but also someone with whom you have developed, or are developing, a strong interpersonal business relationship. Because of this relationship, if the client has any problems in areas relevant to your expertise, he or she will look to you for direction. An advisor finds comfort in knowing that he or she can call or visit the client for a private meeting at almost any time.

How does a customer become a client? Most consumers buy products and never develop an interpersonal relationship with the sales person. They might not even recognize the advisor after they made the purchase. For advisors representing products and services that depend on client relationships, time spent developing those relationships is very important. To build a lifetime career on client relationships, it is essential to convert customers to clients.

Developing client relationships is mutually beneficial for the advisor and the client, because the client knows the advisor will deliver promised services and will be available when he or she is needed. For the advisor the relationship is a building block in the development of a long-term career.

In client building, the sale is not the end; it is the beginning. All of the promises of service made during the sales/planning process and at the delivery interview must be fulfilled. Client expectations and advisor promises should be exceeded, if at all possible. Frequent contact and updates should be made. This entails more work than servicing a customer, but it is more rewarding. As clients grow, the advisor grows, and more doors are opened through referrals and the development of clients' other financial needs and wants.

Your clients are your most valuable business inventory. You can achieve total success in the financial services business when your established client base and the referrals and repeat business they provide enable you to reach your personal sales goals.

Just because someone purchased a product from you does not make that person a client. Without developing a personal relationship, that person is as likely to go to another advisor as much as they may turn to you in the future. What can you do to cement that relationship and protect your customers from competition as you develop them into customers? Doing the following should help you to develop clients.

- Try to broaden the product portfolio you can offer to customers, and develop strategic alliances with other producers and professionals who offer products and services you do not. This would especially be true for contacts with attorneys, accountants, bankers, and specialists in other lines of insurance in which you are not involved.
- Broaden your areas of expertise. Pursue professional designations, add additional licenses, and generally improve your expertise and skills that make you more valuable to clients.
- Be sure to frequently tell your prospects and clients, through mail and personal contact, about your total product and service portfolio.
- Go back to every client, as least for regular review, and explain your total portfolio, particularly in areas you may not have previously addressed.

Customer or Client

Many advisors use the terms "client" and "customer" interchangeably, failing to make a distinction. Others use the term "client" to refer to all their accounts, believing it is a sign of professionalism. Actually, every advisor has some customers and some clients and should be aware of the difference.

According to the Merriam-Webster dictionary, a customer is one who purchases a commodity or service. A client, on the other hand, is defined as one who is under the protection of another, a person who engages the professional advice or services of another.

What do people insured with you say? Do they consider themselves customers or clients? What do people working in your agency say? Are they busy getting customers or committed to developing clients?

A customer buys a policy from you, but a client is different. A client seeks your advice on coverage. A client respects your time. A client responds promptly to your request for information. A client may occasionally take quotes, but, when he gets a lower price, he asks you why. A client does not expect you to personally attend to all the details of his or her account. A client values your opinion. A client pays bills on time. A client sends you referrals.

There is a big difference between a customer and a client. Every advisor must recognize the difference and find ways to turn customers into clients. The rewards are a stable book of business and quality referrals.

Delivery Interview Objectives

Often the policy delivery is your first return visit with the client after the sale. To a world accustomed to a "take the money and run" approach to selling, the *delivery interview* can be your chance to excel and stand apart from other salespeople. Conducting an effective and thorough delivery interview and providing ongoing client service will be critical to your long-term success.

A polished policy delivery accomplishes the following:

- **Reinforces the buying decision**: Time has elapsed since you wrote the application. It may be many weeks since you last met. Your policyowner remembers saying yes to your proposal, but may not remember exactly why. You have the opportunity to reemphasize the needs and reasons the prospect bought the policy. It is essential that the client understand why he or she bought the product, the solutions it provides, and the benefits he or she will derive from keeping it.
- **Builds trust**: Here you sell the future. By promising future service on this policy and ensuring that the policy and your continued service will meet the client's future needs, you offer your expertise as a true financial services professional. Tell the client of your continued support through periodic reviews. The timing of these should be based on a mutually agreeable time interval.
- **Reopens the selling/planning process**: At policy delivery you can set the stage for addressing the needs and remaining objectives of the buyer. If a total needs analysis was not done, then an attempt to schedule this type of planning could be made. If the total needs analysis has been performed, additional needs can be addressed.
- **Obtains referred leads**: Some feel that the delivery interview is the best time to ask for referrals because the buyer's interest is highest at that point. With the purchase completed, the buyer feels that the goals he or she set out to accomplish have been addressed. A satisfied buyer can be your best source of referrals. What better source to ask for names of people for whom your services and products might also be of value?
- **Prevents lapses**: There should be nothing casual about policy delivery. The advisor must treat it seriously. Industry statistics show that half of all policy lapses occur during the first 6 months

after policy issue. The only way to effectively reduce the chances of this customer becoming one of these statistics is to deliver in person every policy you sell. Of equal importance is the need to do it in a way that reinforces the buyer's confidence that the purchase was made for the right reasons. Only the advisor can take this step for the policyowner.

Service is Your Business

When customers buy your product or service, they receive an extra bonus—*you*. As a salesperson, you have a professional obligation to ensure your client's satisfaction as long as the account is active. Your value to the customer takes many forms.

1. **You are a person, not a company, for the client to contact.** People prefer to relate to individuals instead of large customer service departments.
2. **You are an open, concerned person who listens and understands.** You can be reached for even the smallest questions.
3. **You have a depth of knowledge that can be helpful in solving specific problems.** You also have the means to obtain further information inside and outside your company to save your customer time.
4. **You are accessible and make your company accessible.** You act as a conduit through which clients can reach other people in your company. If a client wishes to consult an engineer, for example, he or she can arrange to do so through you.
5. **You represent security.** Clients know you have a vested interest in their business. They also know you are reliable and consistent. You are a known entity, whereas a competitive salesperson is not.

Develop an attitude of friendship, respect, and concern. The more you give of these, the more you receive from your clients. The working relationship that grows from this is a strong one that resists destruction. Clients who return these feelings are extremely hesitant to change to a competitive product or service.

Tony Alessandra, "Service is your Business." Reprinted with permission.

How to Achieve Delivery Objectives

- **Reinforcing the buying decision:** Any symptoms of buyer's remorse must be handled. At this meeting, you can deal with objections up front and face-to-face, instead of months later when you hear the policy is about to lapse. Send the client a thank you letter for his or her confidence in you, expressed through the purchase. In the letter, summarize the reasons for the purchase and the benefits provided by the plan. Some advisors include this letter with their policy delivery package so the client can easily see and review it, or they send it shortly after the sale is made.

- **Building trust:** Promise a lot and deliver more. If you told the policyowner you would do something (for example, get an attorney's name, check on another policy, or bring an agency calendar) be sure to follow through and do it in a timely fashion. Not fulfilling expectations can lead to immediate customer dissatisfaction and introduce difficulty in the relationship. Trust is not built in a day. It is nurtured over time. When you deliver what you promise after the sale, clients begin to trust you.
- **Reopening Selling/planning process:** Be sure that the client knows about all the products and services you offer. Even if you have already presented this information, review what you can do again. If you have a personal brochure or resume, be sure that the client has one. Periodically send compliance-approved articles, brochures, or reports based on what you know about the client's interests, business, or company. This will build rapport as well as generate or develop interest in further cross-selling opportunities.
- **Obtaining Referred Leads:** Help the client by sharing the specifics on the types of referrals that would be most helpful. Ask the client if he or she would be willing to be a reference for you. If appropriate, socialize with the client, building the relationship and sharing in a common interest (golf, community activities, and so on). Volunteer to provide an added value to the client, such as speaking at meetings, providing services to the client's organization, or introducing him or her to other clients whom they may benefit from knowing.
- **Preventing Lapses:** You must keep a customer satisfied in order to fight off competition. You are naive if you think that your competitors use different prospecting and relationship building techniques from you. The reason for diligence in maintaining customer satisfaction is to protect your investment from your competitors.

It is said that people lapse products, not solutions. The emphasis in this course on problem solving and relationship selling methods and the selling/planning process is to help you make good sales and keep them on the books. Nobody benefits from early policy lapses.

Educate the policyowner about the policy. Do not assume they do not care, or that they feel intimidated by it. They are paying hard-earned dollars for this product and you should want to be sure that they understand and value it. One key reason why people lapse policies is that they do not understand the policy because the advisor did not explain it to them.

Preparing for the Delivery

The policy delivery should not be an afterthought or a casually dismissed step in the sales process. This interview should be taken as seriously as any other part of the selling/planning process. You must prepare and practice for the interview as you would with any other sales technique, or it will not be as effective as it could be. Work to accomplish all the objectives discussed in this chapter to maximize your effectiveness and efficiency. After the interview, as with any other client contact, you should debrief yourself, reviewing and evaluating the highlights of your time with the client. What went well, what needs improvement, and what can you do to make your delivery presentation better?

In preparing for the delivery, the following topics must be covered. State and company compliance requirements involved in policy delivery must be followed and completed. Techniques designed to reinforce the client's decision to purchase your solution should be prepared. Efforts toward establishing a solid, long-term business relationship and making the new policy less susceptible to lapse should be initiated.

The first step of policy service and delivery actually starts with the first meeting with the prospect and carries through each meeting in the sales/planning process. This is because you deliver all the themes and processes outlined in this book in every meeting.

The importance of the relationship escalates when the prospect completes an application. Call your applicant from time to time during the underwriting period of policy issue. Let the buyer know the status of the application, why there are delays, if any, and any other information that might be requested during underwriting. Make the applicant feel part of the process. This shows that your interest continues on the buyer's behalf. It also begins to develop a pattern of your service, and an expectation in the client that you will be contacting him or her regularly.

Alert the client to future contact points at the delivery interview. If you use a client newsletter, show the client a sample or deliver an issue. Set the expectation of a mutually agreed-upon review timetable, and inform the buyer of other typical times when you routinely contact your clients.

Check the Policy

Check the policy when you receive it, before you call the applicant for delivery. Make sure it is exactly as applied for. Is the policyowner information correct? Does the policy outline the selected mode of premium payment and does it quote the same figure you and the buyer discussed? Are all the beneficiary names correct? Are the optional benefits you applied for included? Have you included a current policy illustration?

If there are any problems with the finished policy, you want to discover them before you sit down with the insured. Having these errors surface when you are delivering the policy can be embarrassing, and can erode the confidence of your new client in you and your company. If you discover something when reviewing the policy, it must be returned to underwriting for reissue, or the modifications will need to be explained to the buyer.

Take My Name and Number

"(Prospect), most of my clients like to enter my name, address and telephone number in the family telephone directory. Do you keep a book like this?" While the book is out, begin by saying: "By the way, who do you know that might be interested in the services that I provide? All of the client's friends and family members are probably listed in this book.

If you discover an error or that the policy has been issued differently than applied for, call the client as soon as possible. Explain what has happened: either why the policy is being returned for reissue, or the reasons the policy was issued differently than originally requested. Provide a time frame of when it will be ready and promise to stay on top of the situation and to call the buyer regularly.

If the policy changes concern such things as a rated premium or excluded rider, be sure you can explain the situation accurately. Understandably, the buyer may question you in detail about changes in coverage so you must be prepared with honest and accurate answers.

When you are ready to deliver the policy, call the policyowner for an appointment to deliver the policy when you know he or she will not be distracted by other pressures of the day. Set the stage for your valuable delivery interview.

Plan Enough Time for the Interview

Ask for an appointment time that will give you plenty of time to review the contract, ask for referrals, and set the stage for your continuing relationship with this client.

This meeting will reinforce the benefits of this purchase, so do not allow yourself to be rushed through it. You want to review all of the ideas you talked about in the past. It may take more time than a policyowner thinks. You are not planning to hand deliver your policy to the front door like a package from UPS. Calculate the block of time you want. Later, if it is too much, admit it as you close the meeting. Compliment the buyer on efficiency and leave.

The necessary meeting time that each client requires will vary. Sometimes you will find the client is reluctant to talk, while at others the client wants to talk about things other than your business together. This latter situation is the way people build strong relationships, so do not run out on the opportunities that present themselves. However, do not impose on your clients either. The answer is to be sensitive to each relationship.

The Compliment and the Questions

"Any business relationship is much more satisfying when the people involved like and respect each other. I feel we've gotten along well together—I hope you feel the same way. Naturally, in order for my business to grow, I need to be able to find people who need my services and products. Personally, I'd like my business to grow with people such as you. I would appreciate it if you could recommend me to other families like yourselves, whom you feel would benefit from a similar relationship."

Policy Wallet

Give your policy a professional appearance by delivering it in an attractive policy wallet. It need not be expensive to give prestige and a professional touch to your delivery. It is important to have a cover and a place for your business card for future reference. Some portfolios provide space for several policies, sales literature, or other important documents. Carefully prepare the delivery package before the delivery appointment. It is important to your client and it should be to you as well.

Advisors develop and include company pieces in the delivery package. Policy review checklists can be typed on your letterhead or may be provided by your company, and can be inserted in the wallet. You may include a copy of the computer sales illustration of the policy. The Buyer's Guide and Policy Summary should also be included. Some advisors have letters explaining the purpose of the insurance and the benefits it provides. Check with your agency to see what support materials are available, and find out what other advisors are using. They know the value of making every policyowner feel special and appreciated.

All these additions will become useful in the future when the policy is reviewed. They reinforce the purpose of the insurance, the benefits, and the needs that led to the purchase.

Obtaining Feedback

When you have completed a sale or when you have finished delivering a policy, you may want to use the positive critique format and review your performance with your new client. Do this by asking three simple questions.

First, "Obviously we are both pleased with how this worked out. May I ask, though, what you particularly liked about the work I did?" This will tell you what worked.

Second, "If we were to go through this again, but differently, how would you change it, and why do you feel that would work better?" This will spotlight what could be improved in the future.

Finally, you may or may not want to rate the overall situation by asking, "Overall, how would you think we did together, say, on a scale of one to 10?" This will keep the overall outcome in perspective.

If a sale fails and you really want to know why, the same type of questions will elicit valuable feedback to help you improve your future performances.

You will know how well you are communicating during the sales process when people tell you they like you because "you make them think" and "you ask important questions." When you start getting feedback like this and hear people pointing out that you are a good listener, you know you are on target, communicating effectively, and building credibility and rapport with your prospects and clients.

> **A New Advertising Campaign**
>
> "(Prospect), for me, the best and most economical advertising I can find anywhere is when one satisfied client refers me to another. Would you be able to do some 'advertising' for me?"

Company and State Requirements at Policy Delivery

The number and complexity of delivery requirements from state insurance departments and companies has grown over the last few decades as regulators and insurers respond to marketing and producer conduct issues, and the public's desire to feel protected from fraudulent and unethical practices. The following are a summary of the most common policy delivery requirements.

Buyer's Guide—Generally a Buyer's Guide is required to be delivered to the consumer with the policy. Some states require it to be delivered with the application, and there are state variations in the forms themselves and state-specific requirements that must be followed. The Buyer's Guide is designed to give the consumer and prospective purchaser a clear explanation of products and how to shop for them.

Policy Summary—Most states require that a Policy Summary be delivered with the policy. This form, normally produced by the home office with your policy, defines the main features of the currently issued policy and includes specific information on the policy values (guaranteed and non-guaranteed) of the contract, including the premium, guaranteed cash values, guaranteed death benefit, and the policy's loan interest rate.

Signed Illustration—The National Association of Insurance Commissioners (NAIC) Model Illustration Regulation has become law in most states and policy in many companies. This regulation establishes guidelines for companies and advisors regarding the content and presentations of sales illustrations. The regulation covers all life insurance products except face amounts under $10,000 and variable life. It requires that an illustration matching the issued policy be presented to the policyowner. The advisor and policyowner must sign this illustration; one copy is given to the policyowner, one is returned to the company, and one is retained in the advisor's client file.

Delivery Receipt—Most companies and some states require that the advisor and policyowner sign policy delivery receipts upon policy delivery. This form typically contains information regarding guaranteed and non-guaranteed elements in the policy and information regarding proper policy delivery. The client and advisor sign and retain a copy, with a copy being returned to the insurer.

Client File—A client file must be kept as long as a policy is in force. Once a policy is no longer in force because it lapsed, was surrendered, or a claim was paid, a file must be kept for 5 to 8 years, depending on jurisdiction. Where litigation or other disputes exist, files should be kept even longer if necessary. Inactive files must normally be kept for 2 years. Individual companies and states may have their own rules for documents to be maintained in files, but these are the typical general guidelines:

- complete illustrations, including signed NAIC illustration
- any sales materials used in solicitation of the sale
- fact-finder and suitability related materials
- replacement forms and related materials, if appropriate to sale
- copy of policy delivery receipts
- contact sheet used to keep records of date and content of all client contacts
- substantive correspondence concerning contractual changes or concerns of the client
- Check with your company for its specific requirements.

Rated Case Delivery

One type of policy delivery that needs special attention is delivering a rated case. An advisor may feel uneasy because the policy does not have a standard premium and he or she is bringing bad news to the policyowner about health, or life and death. In truth, most applicants know in advance that they may have a problem getting standard premiums. Their doctors have already told them about their health. You may have discussed the difference between standard and substandard ratings during a previous interview or at the time of application when you filled out the medical history section. Some advisors say this type of delivery is actually easier than many other deliveries. The insured often feels grateful to be able to buy any life insurance.

You should expect to occasionally have a rated case. Standard issue is only available to those who can qualify. In a recent year, only 4 percent of all ordinary life insurance issued and paid for was extra-risk issue. You may not have many rated case clients, but it is reasonable to expect that some insureds will have more difficulty qualifying than others. Companies are issuing rated policies and people are taking them and paying for them.

The best way to deliver a rated policy is to resell the need. The need is even greater in view of the increased risk. Acceptance of the policy transfers the risk from the insured and the insured's family to the insurance company, where it belongs.

Let the insured know that you feel the company's action was correct. Do not sympathize or condemn your company's underwriting department; have confidence that they properly classified the insured. Keep in mind that if the policy was issued, the policyowner is insurable, and the company and you provided the coverage.

Reviewing the Life Insurance Contract

Once you have resold the need and explained the value of the policy at delivery, you will want to review the policy contract, pointing out its key features. Few people take the time to read their life insurance policies cover to cover. Even if they did, they would not understand everything they read. They depend on you to explain their policies to them in a way that is understandable and makes sense. Not only do you need to understand policy provisions and language, but you must be able to explain them thoroughly, carefully and, above all, accurately to your policyowners.

Servicing the Client

Good client service separates the best businesses from those that fail. The successful businessperson recognizes that each service opportunity is a marketing opportunity, a chance to demonstrate to clients that he or she is reliable, responsive, trustworthy, and empathetic to their needs. When servicing opportunities are seen as marketing opportunities, referrals and more sales follow.

This section will review briefly some key elements of good client service. We will then look at common service opportunities, such as beneficiary considerations, selecting settlement options and supplementary contracts, and death claims.

As your career as an advisor progresses, you will have more and more opportunities to provide service to your clients. Some advisors incorrectly view client service as something that takes time away from their selling activities. However, successful advisors know that providing good client service increases both client retention and sales productivity.

In every industry, businesses that have demonstrated the greatest success are those that deliver the best customer service. People return year after year to Disney World because it is clean, the employees are polite to customers, the entertainment is reliably good, and large crowds are managed with dignity. The sale occurs when the first ticket is purchased at the gate, but it is the quality service that brings the customer to the gate again and again thereafter.

The same is true in the financial services business. The best advisors realize that in the client's eyes, they are the company. They also realize, just like the employees at Disney, that every service request is an opportunity to build a reputation for caring about clients. The sale is made when the application is completed and the check is signed, but it is the service that leads to repeat sales and referrals to new prospects.

There are many ways to build trust and rapport throughout your relationship with clients. You can begin to express your interest in a new policyowner the day after policy delivery by sending a letter of thanks, if you have not already done so. Return phone calls and letters promptly. Contact the client whenever there is an opportunity to exercise a contractual option. Remember birthdays, promotions, and other events and dates that matter to people. Most of all, you should schedule annual policy reviews with each policyowner. Be there to provide the service you promised. Have an attitude that you will exceed client expectations of service.

A Lesson in Handling the Competition—Outstanding Service is the Key

Mr. Tracy had been my client for 10 years. I am a very successful advisor from the capital city of a western state. I have a highly trained office staff that knows how to get the most out of my computerized client files. It is a sophisticated operation that has been carefully tuned over the years, as you will see by the developments in this case.

My client, Mr. Tracy participated in the computerized service system developed in my insurance office. He had increased his insurance twice and referred several family members to me. Any advisor would want to retain a client like Mr. Tracy.

Mr. Tracy called to say he was considering changing his insurance to a plan where he would buy term insurance and invest the difference. Mr. Tracy said that he thought he should talk with me before making a change because I had worked with him and his family for so long.

When we met, we discussed the fact that he had an insurance program consisting of 30 percent whole life and 70 percent term insurance. We also discussed my motivation for wanting to keep his coverage with me. Once he understood his current situation, he and his wife decided to maintain their insurance with me.

My contact sheet shows that I completed two routine service calls over a period of 14 months after the visit about the policy surrenders. Then I had a call from Mr. Tracy saying that he wanted to transfer his insurance from whole life to universal life. I recommended that he not do this but that any additional insurance he purchased should be universal life. He said he had already signed up with a new company that offered him twice as much coverage.

He was calling to say that he wanted me to expedite the surrender of his policies so that he could give the money to the new company. I must admit I was a little hot under the collar when I told him that I thought he was making a mistake and that the only reason he was getting twice as much insurance the first year was that the new advisor would get a full commission on the entire cash value transferred from my company. He said he wanted to go ahead. I told him that we would speed the surrender process as much as we could.

I also asked Mr. Tracy if it would be all right if I kept in touch with him, just in case he ever had any questions or I had some new ideas for him. I added that I still considered him to be my client. He said he did not mind me keeping in touch.

I maintained Mr. Tracy's name in our automatic service contact system. About 12 months later I called to touch base. He said everything was fine. I told him I would continue to keep in touch when he said he was surprised to hear from me.

I was out of town about a year later when he called the office. He told my assistant that he had made a mistake and wanted me to be his advisor again. From the beginning, he said that his wife had been upset about transferring their insurance. One of Mrs. Tracy's complaints was that they never heard from the new advisor after they had bought from him. Mr. Tracy said that he thought all advisors contacted their clients the way I did, but he found out the hard way that some do not.

My assistant scheduled an appointment and I drove out to the Tracy's house on my return to the city. I ended up that day writing an increased amount of insurance on the family. I explained how they would lose some of the cash value in the transfer, as they would have to pay a surrender charge to end the universal life plan. Mrs. Tracy said, "I don't care what it costs! I want you to be our advisor. Do whatever it takes."

I felt good about continuing to provide service to these clients, even though they did not want it or expect it after surrendering their policies. This situation made me realize that I am really on the right track with my service program.

The lesson: call clients at regular intervals. You need not always have the next sale in mind. Be patient with your clients. They are human and they will make mistakes like everyone else. Be loyal to the people who trust you enough to buy from you. The personal service that the thoughtful advisor can provide separates the shotgun artist from the professional. In my mind, the Tracy family proved to me that I was the professional I have long considered myself to be.

You are trying to create clients rather than customers. A customer is someone who buys from you once; a client is someone who will buy from you, and perhaps only you, again and again.

Satisfaction with the Purchase

In the buying cycle we established that the psychological process is similar for the buyer whether he or she is buying a life insurance policy or a new car. The buyer must go through the same process for each purchase before arriving at the decision to buy. These steps are:

1. recognizing the problem or need
2. desiring a solution
3. deciding on the best available choice
4. making the purchase
5. taking delivery

At this point, after policy delivery, the buyer moves on to other concerns. In most purchases, there is no need to wait to consider satisfaction. The buyer begins to use what was purchased and the product either works well or it does not. In the case of purchasing life insurance, satisfaction with the purchase may be elusive. The client pays for something they cannot use or see except for the continual reminder of the premium payments. They may well wonder at some future date why they should even keep paying them. Since the buying cycle has no step to measure satisfaction with the purchase, it is up to the advisor to make sure the buyer remains satisfied.

Dissatisfaction with a purchase is a common experience with an easily recognizable name: buyer's remorse. *Buyer's remorse* is general dissatisfaction with a purchase, usually not long after the purchase has been made. It is a feeling that "I should have shopped around more," or "I could have gotten a better deal, a better product, better features, better salesperson, etcetera." For some life insurance buyers this remorse can be traced to the intangible nature of the product; there is nothing to hold, except the paper of the policy, to remind you of the promises you have received for the future.

Continued satisfaction of the customer is the insurance advisor's challenge in selling. It is so important that every advisor spends a great deal of time servicing sales already made. The difference in experience between the buyer and the advisor is something that every advisor should continue to think about. At the very moment you are closing the policyowner's file after successfully delivering the contract and anticipating your well-earned commission check for the sale, your new policyowner may be opening his or her new policy, reflecting on how you sold the policy. Even satisfaction with the personal benefits provided by the policy may not always be enough to stave off buyer's remorse. The wise advisor always remembers that all efforts must center on the buyer's peace of mind.

Servicing the Plan

As a step of the selling/planning process, servicing the plan has a number of responsibilities. It also presents a number of opportunities for building the advisor/client relationship and developing the client as a source of continued business opportunities and mutually profitable benefits.

The advisor and the client need to mutually agree on the extent and frequency of service and review activities. Servicing and monitoring activities may include, but are not limited to:

- identifying changes in conditions that would impact the current plan and recommendations made by the advisor
- obtaining information from the client to determine changes in personal circumstances
- reviewing work done by other professionals and providers of financial services
- reviewing the client's progress toward financial goals

After the plan is implemented, the advisor should periodically monitor and evaluate the soundness of recommendations, review the progress of the plan toward stated goals, and the appropriateness of insurance coverages. Normally the advisor would meet with the client annually, or more frequently if circumstances warrant. The advisor should discuss and evaluate changes in the client's personal circumstances such as family births or deaths, illness, divorce, job status or retirement. Any relevant changes in tax laws and the legal and economic environment should be reviewed and evaluated before the advisor makes recommendations to accommodate new or changing circumstances.

Brochures, Newsletters, and Cards

Most successful advisors have an automated system to assure regular contact and communication with clients and prospects on a year-round basis. This is very personal and individualistic, with much freedom to fit an advisor's personality, his or her clientele, budget, manner of doing business and a variety of other factors. There is no right or wrong way to do this, but all advisors should devote some attention to this broad area of communications.

Resistance to Reviews

Often a customer may display resistance to scheduling annual reviews, or even hearing from the advisor. Responses such as "Why are you calling me?" or "I'm not ready to buy anything else right now" can be disappointing and unnerving to the advisor who is sincerely trying to provide good service for its own sake. The reason for that kind of response is that such customers identify every visit or contact from the advisor as another attempt to make a sale. They perceive that the advisor's sole motive is to make a sale and another commission. Regardless of the advisor's true motives, perception is reality. You must change their perception.

You should contact your clients at least annually, with a purpose only to touch base, keep in touch, say hi and wish the client a happy birthday or anniversary, or some other reason that is totally unrelated to the financial services business. Some successful advisors who do this refuse to discuss business, even if the client raises the topic, so that the message is clearly that this is a relationship call, not a business call.

The client's perception should be that you care about them, you like them as a person, and your contact is sincere. As you plan your day, week, month and year, see to it that every client you have has contacts from you for no other purpose than to build the relationship and show you care.

Of course, besides these social visits or contacts there should be occasional reviews to make sure that their plans and any products you sold them are still effective and see if there is a need for any other sales. So each year you should schedule two kinds of visits, one geared towards sales and service, and one specifically geared for strengthening interpersonal relationships.

Norman G. Levine, "A Passion for Compassion." Reprinted with permission.

Keeping in touch by various methods is an important part of the client-service process. Newsletters, birthday and anniversary phone calls, and periodic mailings about topics of interest continue to put you in front of the client, build prestige, and foster the agent-client relationship.

Brochures—A brochure can be like a simple resume or can be created as a beautiful, multi-colored piece with graphics and high-quality paper. Many companies provide a template that you can complete with your own personal information. There are many business services and printers who also do this type of work, for a wide range of charges. In addition to your business card, you should have a descriptive piece that promotes your expertise, products, services, education, business philosophy, community involvement, personal background and any other combination of information that help build your relationship with clients. The brochure can be used as part of an initial contact, a handout at your first meeting, or used at policy delivery.

Newsletters—Newsletter are a good way to keep in contact with your clients, keep your name in front of them, and provide interesting items of financial interest which may also serve as prospecting ideas. You can write your own. Some companies provide subscription services that offer options on a continuum from full-service direct delivery to clients to do-it-yourself delivery of the newsletters. There are also numerous industry services and associations that offer them. The newsletter should have your name, address, and phone number, with your photo as optional.

Greeting Cards—Birthday cards are a way of saying "I'm thinking of you and I care about you." Calendars and greeting cards at the holidays also help you to stand out and also bring your name in front of the prospect or client. Many advisors use other gifts like calendars, pocket diaries, pen sets, and so on as a technique to keep in contact with clientele.

A hand-written note is an especially "high-touch" (meaningful personal contact) technique in this day of technology and rapid-paced life. It is such a rare occasion that we receive something someone has cared enough to write in his or her hand that it creates an impression as being something special.

Maintaining Records

Insurance companies today have file inspection and maintenance requirements as a routine part of the compliance process. In all cases follow your company procedures, which may require that you keep records of

- fact-finding forms
- written notes describing the basic events and discussions with the client
- contact log with dates and topics discussed
- copies of quotes or illustrations
- copies of applications and related materials
- copies of correspondence with the client

Normally no original documents or blank, signed documents should be stored in a file. Original documents should be submitted to the company and blank, signed documents are strictly forbidden. You should keep good and compliant files, not for compliance only, but to build a good servicing system that helps you to develop satisfied clients.

Periodic Reviews

The periodic review covers many objectives of the agent-client relationship. Relationship building is fostered by regular contact, which should lead to policy persistency, cross-selling, networking and referral opportunities. Proper service is based on timely reviews and contacts, and prompt response to client requests. Changes in coverage should be made to conform to changes in the client's situation. Although annually is the traditional review period, a mutually agreed-upon interval should be established based on the client's circumstances and needs.

Retaining clients can have a huge effect on your bottom line. Research shows that profits can grow by 100 percent from a 10 percent increase in retention. U.S. businesses lose from 10 to 30 percent of their customers each year, yet most of those customers would not have changed if they would have received more responsive attitudes and a passion to make things right. How can you sustain significant growth when you have to replace 20 percent of your customers each year just to stay even? The cost of acquiring a new client is five to seven times higher than retaining a current one. It is cheaper and easier to sell more to existing clients than it is to win new ones. Here are some strategies to consider:

Relate one-to-one—Realize that all business is personal and no relationship is static.

Reinforce relationships—Seize every opportunity to learn about your client's needs, dreams and realities. Communicate and reinforce the reason your client chose you. People do business with people, not companies.

Exceed expectations—Meeting clients' expectations is the price of admission into today's market. Strive to exceed expectations to create customer commitment and loyalty. Expect to lose business if you deliver merely what the customer needs, since they probably have many avenues to get it. Instead, discover and deliver what they want. If you do not add value, you are no longer necessary.

Be an expert listener—Demonstrate your knowledge and gain customer loyalty by asking the right questions and listening closely to the answers.

Differentiate yourself—Do not compete on price, but rather on policy benefits and the value of your expertise and your products. Differentiate your services in clients' minds by adding choice, specialization, research, responsiveness, technology and knowledge. Most clients do not buy on price alone. Your job is to offer the best overall value, not the lowest price. Educate clients about the value of your products.

Establish strategic alliances—Look to suppliers, clients and even competitors for joint opportunities that will add value to your clients. Introduce clients to each other,to those who can build value in their situation.

Become referable—To get referrals you need to be referable. That means you must offer more than a product. You have to offer a process and even better, a memorable experience. *You have to earn the trust of your clients.*

The Role of Beneficiaries

The designation of the beneficiary of a life insurance policy is one of the most important decisions the policyowner makes because the death benefit of a policy is the primary reason for its purchase. It reflects the insured's decisions concerning the disposition of his or her human life value. The beneficiary is the person, trust, or other entity named in the life insurance contract to receive all or a portion of the proceeds to be paid from the policy.

At the time of application, care should be taken in helping your prospects and clients make beneficiary choices that will accomplish what is intended. It is very important for the advisor to check for the continued accuracy of the beneficiary designations at each annual policy review. It is through this type of service that you can help see that the intentions of the insured are carried out at death.

Naming the Beneficiary

Who then should be the beneficiary of a life insurance policy? The answer is the person whom the insured wants to protect. Caution should be taken in naming a beneficiary. For example, parents who wish their children to benefit from their life insurance may be ill advised to name the youngsters as their beneficiaries. A minor's capacity to receive and give a valid receipt for the proceeds of a life insurance contract is limited by many laws and circumstances. Similarly, it may be wise, for estate tax purposes, to have a trust own and be the beneficiary of the insurance, rather than having it paid directly to the spouse, children, or to the estate. If a policyowner names another person as beneficiary, gift taxes may result when the proceeds are paid to that person.

As simple and straightforward as beneficiary selections can be in the personal insurance markets, many of the problems arising after the death of an insured can be traced to mistakes made in naming the beneficiary. The goal of the policyowner is to see that the proceeds will be distributed in the desired manner. The goal of the insurance company is to pay the proceeds in a simple and timely manner without any legal problems. Clarity in the wording of the designation should be uppermost in the advisor's mind.

In this section we examine beneficiary designations. We will look at the various types of beneficiaries, as well as the rights of beneficiaries, the rights of creditors, and how to know when beneficiary designations should be changed. When we are through, you will be better prepared to advise your prospects and clients in this important part of life insurance ownership.

Beneficiary Designations

Generally, there are five types of beneficiary designations:

- the estate of the insured
- a specifically named person or persons
- a class or classes of persons
- a business organization
- a trust

Let's review each type of beneficiary designation.

Estate of the Insured—Naming the insured's estate as beneficiary of life insurance is generally unwise, unless the proceeds are to be used by the executor to cover debts, taxes, funeral expenses, and other estate settlement costs. The drawback is that such a designation will increase the probate assets of the estate by the amount of the insurance proceeds, thus exposing the proceeds to possible estate and inheritance taxes and to higher estate administration costs that can otherwise be avoided.

Additionally, a surviving spouse may be unable to use an appropriate payout option for long-term income if the proceeds are tied to estate settlement. The proceeds would also be available to the claims of creditors of the estate under these circumstances. These consequences can be avoided by designating a named beneficiary, such as the insured's spouse, to receive the entire proceeds.

Specific Persons—The most common beneficiary designation is to name a person or persons. For instance, "Lynn W. Smith, wife of the insured," or "Jamie T. Smith, Casie T. Smith, and Fran J. Smith, children of the insured," are examples of single- and multiple-beneficiary designations. It is also advisable to include the beneficiary's date of birth. Many companies currently require the submission of the beneficiary's Social Security number.

This is usually the simplest approach and the one least likely to be a problem at the insured's death, unless the designation is improperly worded or there is some other form of ambiguity in the way the person or persons are named. By naming "Lynn W. Smith, wife of the insured, DOB 9-20-55" there is little doubt about the identity of the intended beneficiary. It will be unlikely, for example, that a Lynn R. Smith who may have been in business with the insured would be confused with the insured's wife of approximately the same name.

A problem could rise, however, if Lynn W. Smith is no longer married to the insured at the time of his death, and the insured has remarried but forgotten to change the beneficiary designation. In such a case, some state laws provide that all funds will be paid to the insured's estate. In other states, the proceeds will be paid to the divorced spouse as the named beneficiary.

Multiple Designations—With multiple designations involving children, problems can develop if additional children are born or adopted by the insured after the designation has been made. In our example regarding the Smiths, a fourth child would not be included as a beneficiary as the designation is now worded, even though the insured may have intended to have all his children share equally in the proceeds of the policy. Also, if one of the children dies before the insured, the beneficiary designation will have to be revised in order to avoid confusion at the insured's death. In this situation, it might be better to name the children as a class of persons, a form of beneficiary designation we will cover next.

In naming specific beneficiaries, be sure to give the individual's complete name, date of birth and relationship to the insured. Avoid designations that may cause confusion at the insured's death because of wording. As with all forms of designations, periodically review the beneficiary designation of a policy to be sure it continues to reflect the insured's intentions.

Class Designations—One way to avoid the problems inherent in naming multiple beneficiaries mentioned above is to use a class beneficiary designation instead of listing specific individuals by name. For example, the insured may simply designate "children of the insured," "children of this marriage," or "grandchildren, and brothers or sisters" without naming them specifically.

In the situation of a young, growing family it is common practice to make a designation such as "any child or children born of or adopted by the marriage of my wife Tracey M. Jones and myself." This wording includes any unborn children and protects against the claims made on behalf of an illegitimate child when the insured is no longer living or incapable of acknowledging or denying paternity. Many companies require their own specific wording. When in doubt check with your company as to how the designation should be worded.

Per Stirpes or Per Capita—One interesting complication that can arise is how to pay proceeds to the heirs of deceased beneficiaries. For example, suppose your client, Judith Hanna, wants the proceeds of her life insurance to be paid to her children, Robert, Susan, and John, or to the surviving heirs of a deceased child. Further suppose that Robert and John both die before their mother, and that John has four children. Robert has none. The question is: How should the proceeds be distributed when Judith dies? The answer lies in Judith's wishes in this matter and spelling out the correct procedure in the beneficiary designation. There are two ways of going about this: using a per stirpes distribution or a per capita distribution.

Per stirpes, which means "by branch," gives the share of the deceased child to his or her heirs. The distribution at death is to the descendants who take the share of the deceased, as it would be distributed if he or she survived. In this example, Susan would take 50 percent of the proceeds; John's surviving heirs would divide the other half among themselves.

Per capita means "by head." Under this arrangement, the proceeds would be divided equally among the surviving beneficiaries. In our example, Susan would be the only beneficiary named, but would share the proceeds, with 20 percent going to Susan and each of John's children because of the wording, "to the surviving heirs of a deceased child." If the phrase "or to the surviving heirs of a deceased child" were deleted, Susan would be the sole beneficiary in the example and would receive the entire proceeds.

Per stirpes arrangements are used more frequently than per capita distributions. However, it is important to determine which approach your policyowners wish to adopt. Your company's procedures may dictate how this type of designation is to be worded and you should be familiar with what your company recommends in these situations.

If a beneficiary designation is complicated or unusual you will wish to contact the legal department of your company to be sure that it is worded correctly so there will be no future question about it. Many advisors urge the policyowner to inform all beneficiaries that they have been named.

Business Organizations—The uses of life insurance in business situations are many and varied. In all applications, correct arrangement of policy ownership, and beneficiary designations can mean the difference between a successfully executed business insurance plan and one leading to more problems than it was designed to solve. For instance, when the insurance is to be used to stabilize the business at the death of a key employee, the firm would apply for, own, and be the beneficiary of the policy on the employee's life.

"*Golden Handcuffs*"—In cases where insurance is designed to provide "golden handcuffs" for top performers, the employee would normally be able to designate the beneficiary, as in group coverage or a pension plan. *"Golden handcuffs"* normally refers to executive or key person benefits that are designed to keep the employee with the firm. Typically arranged as deferred compensation, the employee will receive additional benefits if he or she stays with the company for a stipulated period of time.

In business buyout plans, the ownership and beneficiary arrangements vary according to whether the company is a corporate or unincorporated organization and the type of purchase agreement used. In some cases, the people involved own the insurance and are beneficiaries of policies on each other's lives (cross-purchase plans). In others, the business owns and is the beneficiary of the policies (entity plans). In these situations, improper handling of beneficiary designations can lead to unfortunate and costly consequences to all concerned.

These matters are covered in more detail in *Essentials of Business Insurance* in the Financial Advisor Series. If you become involved in business situations, your role is to be able to advise prospects and clients on how life insurance can help them meet their objectives. Part of accomplishing this is to be able to recommend the correct arrangement of policy ownership and beneficiary designations. Ask your agency or home office for assistance if you are not well versed on the proper designation to use.

Life Insurance Trusts—Frequently, life insurance is put in trust to be managed by a specialist (a trustee) for the benefit of another person. Trusts may be established during the insured's (the grantor's) lifetime, called an *inter vivos trust*, or at death under the terms of a will, called a *testamentary trust*. These life insurance trusts are either funded or unfunded at their creation. If the trust is funded, it is provided with the cash and securities to create an income to pay the premiums on the policies held in the trust. If it is unfunded, someone other than the trust pays the premiums. This type of trust is created to take effect at the death of the grantor when the trust becomes the beneficiary of the insurance proceeds.

A typical beneficiary designation involving a lifetime trust might be worded this way: "Harold W. Gray and the ABC Trust Company, as trustees, their successor or successors in Trust, under the Trust arrangement dated _____." Your company will have established language for the wording of the beneficiary designation of a trust on any application you write. Your applicant can obtain the information you need from the attorney who wrote the agreement.

Some trust agreements name the grantor's spouse as an individual co-trustee. In other situations, the spouse is named as primary beneficiary of the proceeds with a trust as contingent or secondary beneficiary.

Purpose of Trusts—Life insurance trusts are typically used for estate management, tax reasons, or both. For example, where direct payment of life insurance proceeds to a spouse or to children of the insured would be impractical or unwise, a trust can be established to receive the funds—typically in a lump sum—and manage them according to the wishes of the insured. *Revocable* (recoverable) *trusts* are common. In them, the trust owner, known as the grantor in income tax law, can revoke or change the terms of the agreement in the future.

In an *irrevocable trust,* the agreement is permanent and final on the day it is created. The grantor has no power to alter, modify, amend, or revoke this type of trust. The testamentary trust mentioned earlier is by its nature an irrevocable trust, as it comes into existence only upon the death of the insured.

Tax advantages of naming a trust as beneficiary of life insurance depend on how the trust is arranged, specifically, as revocable or irrevocable.

Insurable Interest

Insurable interest is the requirement that insurance applied for has a legitimate reason for being written—an interest in the insured that is clear and apparent—to assure that the contract is not really a wager about the insured's longevity. The insurable interest must be clearly established in the interest of seeing that the insured lives longer, not in the profit of the insured's death. Consequently, the requirement of insurable interest safeguards against the possible misuse of life insurance.

Insurable interest for life insurance must exist at the time of application, but not necessarily at the time of a claim. Where the insured is the applicant, there is generally no question about having an insurable interest. Individuals are recognized as having unlimited interest in their own lives, unless they intend to later assign the contract to someone with no legitimate insurable interest. Generally, then, an application in good faith on one's own life will not raise the issue of insurable interest. In situations where a third party applies for insurance on the life of the insured, the applicant-owner must have an insurable interest in the insured. Of course the applicant may not always be the beneficiary of the policy. An example would be the father who applies for life insurance on his son-in-law's life and names his daughter as the beneficiary. At the time of application an insurable interest must be established between the insured, the applicant, and the beneficiary. Caution must be taken in the case where the policyowner names a third party as beneficiary because the life insurance proceeds may become a gift to the beneficiary and create gift tax consequences to the policyowner.

Types of Relationships—Relationships by blood or marriage, and business relationships in which the loss of the insured's life would mean serious financial loss to the survivor, constitute insurable interests. Creditor-debtor relationships usually create insurable interests, to the extent of indebtedness, for the creditor on the debtor's life, to assure recovery of monies owed but left unpaid by the debtor's death.

Generally speaking, you must assure that you establish the insurable interest for each life insurance application you write. In cases of doubt, help your underwriting department understand why the insurance is being applied for. A cover letter with the application outlining the reason will help establish the policy's purpose.

Rights of Beneficiaries

The extent to which beneficiaries have rights in a policy depends on whether the beneficiary designation is revocable or irrevocable. In the nine community property states (Arizona, California, Idaho, Louisiana, Nevada, New Mexico, Texas, Washington, and Wisconsin) a spouse's rights in a life insurance policy are influenced by whether or not the premiums were paid with community funds. In Mississippi, marital property is divided according to which spouse has legal title to the property. In the remaining 40 states, assets and earnings accumulated during marriage are distributed "equitably."

Revocable Beneficiaries—Most beneficiary designations are made revocable so the policyowners can change them if necessary and the policyowner retains full control of the policy, including the right to borrow the cash value, surrender the policy, or name a new beneficiary. Under this arrangement, the beneficiary has only a mere expectation in the policy that will not materialize until the insured dies, assuming that the beneficiary designation has not been changed by then.

Irrevocable Beneficiaries—In only a limited number of situations—generally involving divorce or separation—are beneficiary designations made irrevocably. Under this arrangement, the policyowner generally gives up all rights in the policy, yet is still responsible for paying the premiums. For example, under most irrevocable beneficiary designations the beneficiary must give consent before a policy loan can be made, before the policy can be surrendered, or before the beneficiary designation can be changed. The beneficiary, therefore, has a vested interest, a right, in the policy even during the lifetime of the insured. This restrictive approach seldom serves a useful purpose, except that of complying with a court order. If it were intended that the beneficiary control the policy, a better way to accomplish this would be to designate that person as policyowner. This will give full control of the policy to the beneficiary, without the complications.

Most insurance policies provide that if the irrevocable beneficiary precedes the insured in death the owner designates a new beneficiary.

Community Property—In the nine *community property* states noted above, the rules covering life insurance policies paid for with community funds tend to be more restrictive. These states view the earnings of each spouse as being the joint property of both. Thus, if one spouse saves and successfully invests, one-half of the resulting property interest belongs to the other spouse.

If either spouse owned property prior to the marriage, it would not be considered community property. Full title remains vested in the prenuptial owner, as long as one does not taint the ownership by using community property funds to maintain it, making it community property. Similarly, property of one spouse received by gift or inheritance during marriage does not become community property. Generally, only property that is traceable to the earnings of one of the spouses during their marriage is considered community property.

While community property states look upon property holdings as belonging to both spouses, the husband is usually viewed as the manager of the "partnership." Consequently, the wife is bound by most of the decisions he makes, provided he does not give away her property without her consent.

A life insurance policy is a piece of property. Since it is normally paid for out of income, it will usually be considered as community property. As manager, the husband may ordinarily surrender it without his wife's consent. However, even though the beneficiary designation may be revocable according to the policy, the wife's concurrence will usually be required in a community property state to make the change totally binding. In these states, either beneficiary-spouse must consent to a change that would deprive the spouse to that part of the proceeds to which he or she otherwise would be entitled.

For example, in California if a husband designates someone other than his wife as beneficiary without her consent, the wife may recover at least half the proceeds at his death, regardless of whether she was ever mentioned in the policy. In the state of Washington, the wife could recover the entire proceeds.

Minor Beneficiaries—Although it is generally not advisable to name children as beneficiaries of life insurance unless they have reached the age of maturity, under some circumstances it is the correct thing to do. The difficulties are created by the legal procedures designed to protect the property of minor children. They are so complex and rigid that it is often impossible for the child's surviving parent or guardian to carry out the deceased parent's intentions. For example, the court will require conclusive proof that policy proceeds are being spent for the child's benefit and that the expenditure is necessary in the court's judgment.

Ironically, after having taken all these precautions during the child's minority, frequently making the management of insurance proceeds exceedingly cumbersome for the surviving parent, the court will turn over full control of the money and other property to the child at the age of majority—age 18 or 21, depending on the state. Naturally, the child may be no better equipped to manage the funds wisely at that time than in the past and the money may be foolishly spent.

You may find parents who have no plan of who the guardian or trustee of their young children would be if they were both to die before the children are grown. This is a good time to help your applicants think through this difficult choice.

If a grandparent is selected you should ask about age, interest, and health. If a brother or sister, or even a friend is selected, the same questions should be asked with the additional questions of responsibility in the trust of the proceeds for the exclusive use of your applicant's children. The applicant would not wish to name any person to this responsible role who had not enthusiastically agreed.

Unless the insured parent's wishes cannot be carried out any other way, children should not be named beneficiaries of a policy. In most cases, it is advisable for the surviving parent or a trustee to have full control of the proceeds for the child's support during the child's minority.

Where the financial welfare of minor children is concerned, many feel that a trust arranged to take effect at the death of the insured or surviving parent is the safest answer. You may wish to ask your company for a specimen agreement to study and discuss this in your agency.

Contingent Beneficiaries—Where policy proceeds are left in a lump sum, the designation of a contingent beneficiary becomes especially important in the event of simultaneous death. For example, assume that your client's primary beneficiary is his wife. They are both killed in a car accident. If it can be established that she outlived him, the proceeds would, in most states, become her property and pass to her estate upon her death. Thus, the contingent beneficiary would probably receive nothing if the wife survives her husband by any amount of time.

Common Disasters—If an insured policyowner and his beneficiary are killed in a common accident, and it cannot be established by medical evidence who was the last to die, the insured policyowner is presumed by law to have survived and the proceeds will go to the contingent beneficiary. Without the contingent beneficiary, proceeds would be payable to the insured's estate. So, if spouses both owned insurance on their own lives with the other named as primary beneficiary, a policy owned by the husband would go to his contingent beneficiary, and the wife's policy would go to her contingent beneficiary or to the individual estates if the circumstances so demanded.

This discussion applies to insurance payable in cash. Where a settlement option has been designated, any undistributed proceeds remaining at the death of the primary beneficiary pass to the contingent beneficiary, regardless of the time elapsed between the two deaths. This applies even where the proceeds are left at interest with the primary beneficiary given full withdrawal privileges. If these withdrawal privileges are not exercised, these rights are forfeited at the subsequent death of the beneficiary and the funds are passed to the contingent beneficiary.

It is not unusual for accidents to take the lives of both spouses, and sometimes their children, simultaneously. It is generally a good practice to provide for this contingency.

The problem that can develop in these situations can be illustrated as follows. Suppose you have two clients, Hank and Blair Desmond, who are a childless couple. If the Desmonds are killed in an accident and Blair survives Hank by a few hours, how will the insurance proceeds be distributed? Even though Hank's parents were named as contingent beneficiaries, unless a settlement option has been designated, the proceeds would go to Blair's estate and probably then to Blair's family. This may not be Hank's intent.

Common Disaster Clause—One way this problem can be prevented is by adding a short-term survivorship clause, referred to as a *common disaster clause*, which requires the primary beneficiary to survive the insured by a specified number of days or months in order to qualify. If the beneficiary's death occurs sooner, the beneficiary is considered to have predeceased the insured and another selection is made. However, if the beneficiary dies even one day after the stated period, this solution will have failed to prevent the common accident problem.

Using a Settlement Option—Another solution is for the insured to designate a settlement option, which will protect the contingent beneficiary in the event of a common accident. If an insured wants a spouse to have complete flexibility, the interest option with full right of withdrawal can be used. This gives the spouse the freedom of a cash settlement and enables the spouse to decide whether to withdraw all or part of the proceeds. Any funds not withdrawn at the second spouse's death go to the contingent beneficiary.

Rights of Creditors

In most states, creditors have no rights to life insurance proceeds the way they do to other property of the deceased. In order to achieve this status, the policy must have a named beneficiary other than the estate. In some states, the beneficiary must be the spouse or children of the insured if the policy proceeds are to be protected from creditors.

In general, when insureds designate their spouses as beneficiary, creditors cannot attach the proceeds at death. During the insured's lifetime most states will also regard the cash values of a permanent life insurance contract as exempt from creditors' claims. Of course, if the insured executed a valid assignment of the policy to a particular creditor, the assignment cannot be defeated by the laws, nor will these laws protect an insured that misuses them with the aim of defrauding creditors.

These exemptions for life insurance are not motivated by a desire to frustrate creditors or provide a means whereby an individual can avoid an obligation. Rather, they are recognition of the fact that life insurance ownership contributes greatly to the well being and security of society. It is deemed socially desirable that a family not lose the protection which life insurance affords. This being the case, a protective arm has been thrown around life insurance to preserve it for the family's benefit.

A major exception to these general rules exists when the federal government is the creditor. State laws protecting proceeds from creditors do not block satisfaction for unpaid federal taxes. Most states recognize spendthrift clauses where a general creditor or even the state itself is involved, but the federal government does not allow a taxpayer to evade taxes, even if it means taking the insurance.

A Promise of Service

One successful advisor includes a beneficiary change letter addressed to herself in every policy delivery she makes. This extra reminder that a change in the insured's family will probably call for a change in the policy's beneficiaries is her first step in servicing her new client. Also it provides an automatic opportunity to propose the next sale.

Spendthrift Clause

The above discussion refers to the qualifications of the rights of creditors of the insured policyowner. The majority of states will also give similar protection against creditors of the beneficiary when the policyowner requests the addition of a spendthrift provision in the policy, and the insurance proceeds have been left under a settlement arrangement with the company.

A *spendthrift clause* states that the proceeds will be free from attachment or seizure by the beneficiary's creditors. Without a spendthrift provision it would be possible for a creditor of the beneficiary (but not a creditor of the insured) to obtain a court order requiring the insurance company to withhold each settlement option payment from the beneficiary, and to pay it over instead to the beneficiary's creditor until the claim has been fully met.

Changing Beneficiaries

Fortunately, unless the beneficiary is named irrevocably, the insured is able to change beneficiary designations easily, and as often as necessary. The first beneficiary designation usually appears on the application, while subsequent changes are usually made on a policy service form provided by the insurance company, signed, registered, and returned to the policyowner for inclusion in the policy. If there is ever any doubt as to how beneficiary designations read, they may and should be checked with the company.

Your Role

Your role in these matters is to advise the client in making the initial beneficiary designation, which should be fairly routine in personal life insurance applications unless some special circumstances arise. From then on, include a check of beneficiary designations as a normal part of your annual policy review with your clients. Be sure beneficiary designations are up-to-date and meet the policyowner's current objectives at each review.

When to Change Beneficiaries

Policy beneficiary changes should be considered in several situations. Consider this a brief list of things to watch for in policy reviews:

- the insured has married or remarried
- the insured is separated or divorced
- the insured's parent(s) died
- the beneficiary died or is terminally ill
- a child of the insured died or reached the age of majority
- the insured has become a business owner, or incorporated an existing business
- the insured adopts a child or gains custody of children from a previous marriage
- the insured takes out a substantial loan
- the insured inherits a large sum of money, establishes a trust, or both

Remember, these are just indications that a beneficiary change may be needed; whether or not the change should actually be made depends on the circumstances.

Making Beneficiary Changes

Use a change of beneficiary form supplied by your company to make any changes of beneficiary designations that may be required. For instance, you have a policyowner who you would like to do more work with but who has been resisting your approaches. If, during a routine service call, you determine the need to change the beneficiary designation on the insured's policy with your company, you can suggest that the policyowner let you handle the beneficiary changes with other companies with whom the insured has life insurance. This will let you perform a professional service for which the person should be appreciative, but it will also give you an opportunity to determine the full extent of the individual's coverage. You will be in a good position to make recommendations for additional protection if it is needed. Most importantly, you will have done so before advisors from the insured's other companies will have had a chance to become involved. You may have taken an important step in turning that policyowner into a client, at the same time demonstrating your interest in the client's well being.

Changes must be made in writing and may require that the actual policy be submitted to the company for endorsement. However, in situations where the policy cannot be submitted or where the insured policyowner dies before the form has been processed, most companies will deem the change to have been made, assuming they are assured that the insured did all that could be reasonably expected to comply with the change of beneficiary procedures. The courts have not looked kindly on the use of wills or their codicils to change beneficiaries to a policy. However, this form of testamentary disposition of proceeds is allowed for Government Life Insurance and National Service Life Insurance policies issued to active members of the armed services and veterans.

The Service Call to the Beneficiary

Obviously, the advisor should follow his or her own instincts and be sensitive to the emotional state of the beneficiary, but the service call should be made as soon as the beneficiary will allow it. When you meet, the bereaved should be encouraged to talk. The advisor should be prepared to listen. It is not necessary to be worried about what you will say. The advisor's objective is to listen with genuine interest.

When the time is appropriate, the advisor should offer assistance in submitting insurance claims to other companies, as well as assistance with Social Security.

Tact is important in filling out the claim form. A death certificate usually is needed and provided by the survivor. Many of the claim form questions will be found on it such as the dates of birth and death and the cause of death. Use the death certificate to answer as many questions as you can. Candor is important. Explain the claim process.

On the first visit, the advisor may wish to handle only those matters that are absolutely essential. Grief often prevents absorption of too many things during a first visit.

The most important impression the advisor can leave on the first service call is assurance of a sincere desire to be of help. Later, the advisor should remind the survivor of a number of things that should be addressed: the need of a new Will, Social Security and other possible benefits, the need to change the titles on cars, the house, investments, bank accounts, and insurance policies.

Some survivors expect the insurance advisor to be only a conduit for claim forms. Others look for guidance and care. It is this opportunity to provide unselfish service that will show the real character of the truly concerned advisor.

Settlement Options

Supplementary Contract

When proceeds are to be paid under one of the *settlement options* other than the cash settlement, a new contract called a *supplementary contract* is issued. Insurance companies guarantee the safety of the funds and keep them invested at a contractual rate of return. When the proceeds of a life insurance policy are payable in a lump sum, the company's liability under the policy is fully discharged with the payment of that sum. If the company retains the proceeds under one of the optional modes of settlement, its liability continues beyond the maturity of the policy and must be evidenced by a legal document called the *settlement agreement.*

Letters of Condolence

Letters of condolence or servicing the claim of a policyowner's beneficiary should be attended to immediately upon learning of the death.

The letter need not be eloquent or long. It should express what the heart feels. The degree of emotional content will be determined by one's relationship with the bereaved.

The condolence letter should not be written by someone else for it must contain the individual's own personality and sincerity. Below are some general phrases that might be used:

- "I am sorry to hear about your loss."
- "You are very much in our thoughts and hearts."
- "We were saddened to learn of your loss."

A kind observation or memory of the deceased is always appreciated. It is not considered appropriate by most to use the words "death," "died, or "killed" in this type of letter. Seek approval from your company before you send out material.

The typical settlement agreement is one entered into between the insurance company and the insured, or policyowner, to control the distribution of the policy proceeds to third-party beneficiaries after the insured's death. Depending on company practice, the agreement may be a basic part of the insurance policy, or it may be separate and distinct from the policy. It can be drawn up at the time the policy goes into effect or at any time prior to the insured's death. Although the policyowner can revoke the agreement at any time and substitute a new agreement, he or she can revoke the beneficiary designation only if such right has been specifically reserved. The policyowner may or may not give the primary beneficiary the right to set aside the prior agreement after the insured dies. Upon the insured's death, the insurance company's obligation under the original contract terminates, and it assumes a new obligation, which is defined by the terms of the settlement agreement.

The insured may also enter into a settlement agreement with the insurer to provide payments to himself or herself from a surrendered policy's cash value. If the agreement relates to the proceeds of an endowment policy, it can be entered into at the policy's inception or at any time prior to the policy's maturity.

If the insured did not elect a deferred settlement or did elect one but gave the primary beneficiary the right to set it aside, under the rules of most companies the beneficiary may elect a settlement option and enter into an agreement with the company to govern the distribution of the proceeds. The beneficiary is usually given 6 months after the insured's death in which to elect a settlement option, provided the check offered by the insurer in full settlement of the death claim has not been cashed. Insurers pay interest on the portion of proceeds still held by the insurer after the insured dies. The interest starts accruing from the date of death (even if the election of the specific option is made long after the insured dies) and continues accruing until the underlying proceeds are distributed to the beneficiary.

Parties to Settlement Agreements
Insurance company Policyowner Beneficiary may have the option of becoming a contracting party after the insured dies (if so provided by the policyowner)

The insurance company can prepare illustrations and figures for any of the settlement options you may wish to discuss with a client or beneficiary. A list of the most common arrangements follows. Most companies permit arrangements not specifically granted in the contract, but are generally more liberal in working out different settlement plans adopted by the policyowner before death than for unusual requests by a beneficiary after death. The first payment choice, lump sum or cash, is *not an option* in the strictest sense because life insurance contracts usually provide for lump-sum payment in the absence of any other direction from the policyowner or beneficiary. The company's liability is fully discharged when proceeds are paid in a lump sum.

Lump-Sum or Cash Proceeds

All of the contract proceeds under this arrangement are paid to the named beneficiary in a cash payment by check. In deciding whether the proceeds should be paid in a lump sum, it should be remembered that this option offers no protection against the creditors of the beneficiary. The choice of the interest-income option can provide protection against creditor rights of proceeds.

Lump-sum distributions allow the beneficiary to manage the money, either reinvesting it at a higher rate, using it to pay estate settlement costs or debts, or using it for whatever he or she chooses. Many life insurers now make the lump-sum death benefit payable through an interest-bearing checking account. These accounts work in way similar to a money market fund. The beneficiary can withdraw the total proceeds in one transaction or make partial withdrawals as funds are needed, merely by writing checks. The balance in the account continues to earn interest until withdrawn. Even though the beneficiary can leave the benefits in the account and earn more interest income, over 90 percent of beneficiaries still choose the lump-sum withdrawal and take possession of all the proceeds.

For many beneficiaries, however, especially those who are relatively inexperienced in money management, receiving guaranteed payments in installments may be more desirable. Many times, survivors have received lump-sum distributions in cash amounts larger than they have ever experienced, and within months have lost it all through ill-advised purchases and poor investing. Other settlement options can help avoid this common risk.

Interest Income

Under this settlement option the insurance company holds the proceeds and will make regular interest-income payments to the beneficiary based on a guaranteed rate of return for life. This selection preserves the capital for the future. The option can also be set up to enable the beneficiary to make cash withdrawals from the proceeds. The most flexible of all available settlement options, the interest option is also the only one in which income is fully taxable to the recipient (with the other options, income is made up of principal and interest; only the interest portion is taxed).

Fixed-period Income

Under this option the company pays out both policy proceeds and interest earned in installments over a specified period. If the insured or the beneficiary wants the assurance of some income, however small, over a specified period, he or she should select the fixed-period option. The income received depends on the amount of proceeds and the period selected. The fixed period payout for insurance proceeds offers no flexibility to the beneficiary and is not used unless a clearly defined purpose and time frame for need can be established.

Specified (Fixed) Amount

With this option, policy proceeds, plus interest, are used to pay out a specified amount of income at regular intervals for as long as the proceeds last. The larger the payment, the shorter the period of income. This option is similar to the fixed-period settlement choice except that excess interest above the return guaranteed by the company would extend the length of time for the payout. If the need is for a certain amount of income, and its duration is secondary, the insured or the beneficiary should choose the fixed-amount option.

Life Income

This is a settlement choice unique to the insurance industry. The promise is to pay a stated income for as long as the beneficiary lives. The contract ends at death, whether the beneficiary lives many years or dies within the year. This is a *pure no-refund immediate annuity*, also known as a *pure* or *straight life annuity*. Any settlement option based on a life contingency is known as a *life income option*. A life income option is simply the annuity principle applied to the liquidation of insurance proceeds (each payment is composed partly of principal and partly of income on the unliquidated principal). Hence, there are as many variations of the life income option as there are types of immediate annuities.

The life income option is extremely inflexible. Benefits are calculated on the basis of the age and sex of the primary beneficiary, and once the payments have begun, no other person can be substituted for the designated beneficiary, even with an adjustment in the benefits. Typically no right of withdrawal is available and no discounted lump-sum privilege exists for benefits payable under a life income annuity. Otherwise, persons in poor health would be inclined to withdraw the proceeds. When the benefits are guaranteed for a specified period of time, however, a few companies will permit the proceeds payable under the fixed-period installment option to be taken as a lump sum.

For most people, even though it may offer the highest return in income to the beneficiary during life, it would prove unsatisfactory without a guarantee of return built into the annuity. Because of this, a more popular and commonly used life income settlement builds in a refund or period-certain guarantee.

Life Income with Refund

The life-income with refund option guarantees payments for the life of the annuitant. If the annuitant should die before all the proceeds have been distributed, the balance of payments would be paid, either in a lump sum or installments, to the annuitant's beneficiary or even a third beneficiary, until all proceeds have been depleted. The annuitant is assured through this method that all proceeds will be paid out.

Life Income with Period Certain

Under this payout option, the annuitant receives payments for his or her entire life. In addition, he or she is given a guarantee that if he or she should die within a certain period of time (such as 10, 15, 20, 25, or 30 years) the payment will be paid to a beneficiary for the balance of the time selected. For example, John Doe selects a life-income option with a 10-year period certain. He dies 3 years later. His designated beneficiary would receive payments for 7 years, the balance of the period certain. If John Doe should live longer than the 10-year period, he will have income for the rest of his life under the life-income portion of the payout.

Joint and Survivor Life Income

Under this settlement option, income is provided for two people. It is most commonly used by married couples for the payment of retirement benefits from a pension or some other source. It can be set up to expire at the second death or to have the refund or period-certain guarantees built into the settlement. The joint income may be set up so that the survivor's income continues at 100 percent of the amount paid when both annuitants were alive. This is called a joint and 100-percent survivor income. This can be varied so that survivor income is reduced to a percentage of the full amount. The common arrangements are joint and two-thirds or joint and one-half. The income varies under the joint arrangements per $1,000 of proceeds depending on the difference in age of the recipients and their gender. The survivor payout percentage can be used to leverage more income during the joint payout if less is taken at the survivor payout.

Taxation of Settlement Options

The death proceeds of a life insurance contract generally become the property of the beneficiary without any income tax obligation. This income tax exclusion does not extend in full to all money paid to the beneficiary under a settlement option, since the payment would normally include both principal and interest. While the principal is not subject to income tax, the interest element of each settlement option payment is reportable for federal income tax purposes.

Interest Option—When life insurance proceeds are placed under the interest option, the interest received is taxable in full. This is because the money received is an extra benefit and not the actual death proceeds. There is no tax advantage whatsoever. Both the guaranteed interest and any excess interest are fully reported, whether withdrawn or not, each tax year.

Fixed Options—When life insurance proceeds are placed under the fixed-period or fixed-amount option, the monthly installments are taxed under a special rule.

First, the total amount of guaranteed payments is computed. From this figure the amount of insurance proceeds is deducted. The difference is divided by the number of years for which benefits are guaranteed. The resulting amount must be reported as income for tax purposes each year.

Example: An insured dies, leaving a $50,000 life insurance policy. The beneficiary places the proceeds under the fixed-period option for 20 years. The guaranteed option factor in this case is $5.76 per month per thousand.

Total Guaranteed Payment..............$69,120 (50 x 5.76 x 12 x 20)
Policy Proceeds 50,000
Difference (interest)...........................19,120 ($69,120 – $50,000)
Amount reportable each year ....956 ($19,120 divided by 20)

The $956 interest income must be reported each year. This calculation assumes guaranteed interest. Any interest paid above the guaranteed rate during a particular year must be reported in the year received. Let us assume excess interest in our example is $623 the first year. The total reportable income that year will be $1,579 ($956 + $623).

If the beneficiary elected the fixed-amount option to provide $250 a month ($3,000 a year) as long as it would last, the guaranteed payments would continue for about 25 years under the policy. The reportable portion of each year's $3,000 of income would be computed as follows:

Total Guaranteed Payment ....$75,000 ($250 x 12 x 25)
Policy Proceeds.. $50,000
Difference (interest)...................... $25,000 ($75,000 – $50,000)
Amount Reportable Each Year ... $1,000 ($25,000 divided by 25)

On the fixed-amount option, excess interest is normally paid at the end of the guaranteed period rather than year-to-year. Therefore the taxable portion of the $3,000 benefit would be $1,000 per year under the fixed-amount option for 25 years, and additional payments would be fully taxable thereafter.

The computations shown above are simply methods of determining the amount of reportable income for tax purposes. The important thing to remember is that the death benefits as such are not taxed, but interest earned on those proceeds will be subject to taxation as income. Whatever method is used, the purpose is the same: to determine what portion of each year's payment represents proceeds and what represents interest.

Life Income No Refund—If the option selected is a no-refund life-income option, the proceeds are taxed in a manner very similar to that used for the fixed-period option. However, since we do not know how long the beneficiary will live, we do not know the period for which payments are guaranteed. To overcome this problem, the Internal Revenue Service prepared a life expectancy table, which serves as the basis for computing the tax. The life expectancy of the beneficiary when this option is selected is assumed to be the period for which payments are guaranteed.

To determine the taxable portion of any income received each year, multiply the monthly income times 12, times the beneficiary's life expectancy at the time the option is selected. This is the total expected return. From this figure subtract the amount of proceeds from the life insurance that is placed under the option. The difference is divided by the life expectancy when the option is selected. Only the interest portion of the monthly income payments is taxed. The portion of each payment attributable to the life insurance proceeds is prorated over the beneficiary's life expectancy and is not subject to income tax. This portion of each payment is referred to as the excludable amount, since it represents a payment of the death proceeds over time. This excludable amount is not subject to income tax for the life of the beneficiary, even if the beneficiary lives beyond life expectancy and receives the total amount of insurance proceeds. If the beneficiary lives beyond life expectancy, the excludable amount will continue to be free from income tax.

This tax treatment is different from the tax treatment for life income payments from an annuity funded by money other than life insurance proceeds. Once basis is recovered, all amount received are fully taxable. This offers a distinct tax advantage to settlement options funded with life insurance proceeds.

Example: A female beneficiary age 63 places the $35,000 proceeds of a life insurance policy on a no-refund life-income settlement guaranteeing $5.50 per month per thousand. The IRS life expectancy table indicates a life expectancy of 19.6 years.

Total Expected Return .... $45,276 ($5.50 x 35 x 12 x 19.6)
Policy Proceeds..$35,000
Difference ....$10,276 ($45,276 - $35,000)
Approximate Amount Reportable
Each Year... $524 ($10,276 divided by 19.6)

Life Income Period Certain—A period-certain life-income option means that the proceeds of the policy will be paid out (or refunded) over a specified (certain) period of time even if the initial beneficiary dies before the end of that period. When using the period-certain life-income option, an additional calculation is required to determine the taxable portion of each payment. The value of the refund feature must be determined by referencing the Internal Revenue Service tables.

Percentage Value of Refund Features (IRS)					
Age		Years Certain			
Male	Female	5	10	15	20
55	60	3%	8%	13%	18%
56	61	4	8	13	20
57	62	4	9	14	21
58	63	4	9	15	22
59	64	5	10	16	24
60	65	5	11	18	25
61	66	5	12	19	27
62	67	6	12	20	28

These tables show the percentages of the proceeds that are the value of the refund feature. The value of the refund is deducted from the proceeds to determine the value of the annuity feature. The annuity value is then deducted from the total expected return. (The total expected return is monthly income times 12 months, times life expectancy.) The difference between the total expected return and the value of the annuity is then divided by the life expectancy to determine the reportable income. The following example will help illustrate this calculation.

Example: A female beneficiary receives the proceeds of a $100,000 life insurance policy at age 62. The proceeds are placed on a 15-year certain life-income option guaranteeing $4.60 per month per thousand. The beneficiary's life expectancy at age 62 is approximately 20.3 years according to IRS tables. The value of the refund feature shown is 14 percent for a 15-year certain life income based on the table shown here.

Insurance Proceeds	$100,000	
Less Value of Refund Feature (14%)	14,000	
Value of Annuity Feature	86,000	($100,000 – $14,000)
Total Expected Payments	112,056	($4.60 x 100 x 12 x 20.3)
Value of Annuity Feature	86,000	
Difference	26,056	($112,056 – $86,000)
Approximate Amount Reportable Each Year	$1,284	($26,056 divided by 20.3)

The beneficiary receives a total income of $460 per month, or $5,520 a year (4.60 x 100 x 12). Of this amount, $1,284 is reportable for tax purposes.

Life Settlements

An industry that is rapidly growing and has become a new financial tool is the life settlement market. Typically used by senior clients, it is a way to release dormant cash values in a life insurance policy that is no longer needed or wanted. Seniors who need cash to pay for living expenses, long-term care expenses or other needs, may find this an attractive alternative. Through a life settlement a policyowner can obtain a higher value for their policies than to lapse, surrender, or borrow from them.

A *life settlement* is a transaction of selling an existing life insurance policy by its owner to a third party. In exchange for a cash settlement, the policyowner transfers ownership and all other rights of the policy to that third party. The sale of the life insurance policy is completed through a broker or financial advisor to a settlement company or other provider, to obtain a sum of money that exceeds the policy's cash value. The provider keeps the policy in force by making subsequent premium payments, and collects the proceeds at the policy's maturity (the earlier of the maturity date or the death of the insured). All types of policies, as long as they are out of contestability, are life settlement candidates.

Companies use a variety of criteria to calculate an offering price for a policy:

- face amount
- anticipated premiums to maintain the policy until maturity
- the insured's age
- health status and health conditions
- the client's overall situation
- life expectancy
- policy structure
- loans and money drawn against the policy
- the insurance company's rating

The broker's compensation is usually based on a percentage of the policy's face amount or a percentage of the amount paid out to the policyowner. Life settlements deal with a wide variety of clients with life expectancies generally of less than 10 years, whereas viatical settlements require that the insured be terminally ill, typically with a life expectancy of less than 2 years.

Because there are so many potential problem areas for this type of contract involving fraud, ethical treatment, questionable sources of funds, and lack of insurable interest, it is important to carefully evaluate and perform due diligence in the selection of a settlement company. A reputable and financially sound institutional investor, such as a bank or insurance company, treats settlements much the same way as an insurer underwrites new business, creating a portfolio using the law of large numbers, pooling together settlement contracts. The provider performs medical and financial underwriting, just like an insurer. Funding is derived from capital markets by major institutions. Like individually issued policies, there is no individual interest in any one policy. Private or individual investors may provide unreliable funding, and create a potential problem with privacy concerns where individuals have a financial stake in the insured's health and longevity.

While reputable life settlement providers exist, this business has been largely unsupervised and unregulated, so both the selling policyowner and the financial advisor must be on guard against those having dishonorable practices and methods. Additionally, 16 states require a broker to be licensed as a life settlement broker, and with the rapid growth of this business, more states will follow.

The life settlement is an asset and should be viewed like any other. As with any other recommendation you may make, proper fact-finding must be done and suitability issues addressed. The need, the product, and the prospect must be correctly matched.

Death Claims

Among the many considerations for policyowners at the time of a life insurance purchase is the manner in which any death proceeds will be paid. Failure to do so may defeat the very purpose for which the insurance was intended.

When the death benefits of a life insurance policy are being considered for the most appropriate payout options, one special consideration does not apply to other situations: You will be dealing with a beneficiary instead of the insured policyowner who worked with you to design the coverage and keep it in force. When a life insurance death benefit has been paid to a beneficiary, the proceeds are the sole property of the beneficiary. The insurance company gives up control at distribution.

The insurance advisor should offer to help a beneficiary who receives life insurance proceeds. All too often, no effort is made to forge new counseling ties with the beneficiary. This can alter the wishes of the insured and can impede the purposes for which the insured purchased the insurance policy.

The loss of a loved one will make current decisions emotionally charged, and immediate concerns may appear to be unrealistically more important than long-term needs at this difficult time. It can be an awkward time to talk about money with some people. Doing nothing may be better than taking action. You must advise your clients carefully. You may be well advised to suggest leaving the cash proceeds with the insurance company at interest for 6 months or so.

Later, after the initial adjustment to the loss of the loved one, you can help suggest a course of action that will assure the proceeds will be used in the most advantageous way to meet long-term goals. You can bring in additional expertise if it seems appropriate. Your influence in the situation will be easier to handle after a period of time. This does not mean that the advisor should ignore beneficiaries and not care about their concerns and interests. Just as the family was of professional concern to the advisor during the years of work with the client, that same interest should continue and intensify through the new bond of common sorrow that has emerged.

Handling Claims

Since this may be such an emotional time for the beneficiary, you may find yourself offering services that you normally would not. You may have to call the funeral director and help make the arrangements for the funeral. You may have to contact the deceased's other financial advisers or attorney. You may have to help in locating and procuring important papers, like certified copies of the death certificate or a copy of the most recent will.

Contacts may have to be made with the local Veterans' and/or Social Security office and you may have to be the one who starts the process. The beneficiary may be entitled to Civil Service or employer benefits and may not even think about this aspect of the claims process. As the deceased's insurance advisor, you may have to contact several life insurance companies and help the beneficiaries file claims. You may find it helpful to have the following information on hand before contacting the companies involved:

- policy number(s) and face amount(s)
- Social Security number of the deceased
- full legal name and address of the deceased
- deceased's occupation, last day worked, employer's name, address, and telephone number
- deceased's date and place of birth
- date, place, and cause of death
- beneficiary's name, age, address, and Social Security number
- several certified copies of the death certificate

In any case, you need to be prepared to handle or find a resource for any matter that may cross your path in regard to the deceased. The advisor's job is not complete when death occurs; in many cases it is just beginning.

Always remember that when you help your clients' beneficiaries select the most appropriate payout options for their circumstances, you will be doing the right thing and earning a reputation as a trustworthy professional who sticks with your clients and their families in good times and bad.

What Do You Say to Someone in Mourning?

Shortly before his 63rd birthday, my father-in-law died suddenly. The shock, pain, and anger we experienced from this intrusive event proved instructive to my family and me. We came together in a bonding of love, shared grief, and focused memories.

Quite a few people spoke with me upon learning of our loss. Their most common response was: I don't know what to say. This made me think. What do you say to someone who has just lost a loved one?

We who mold our careers around the important business of delivering dollars to widows, orphans, business associates, and charities need to know what to say and do in times of grief. We make ourselves vulnerable. We earn the right to be present at these sad moments, precisely because we help people focus on the priorities in their lives that need addressing while they are alive and able to take care of them.

Why is it then when a client, friend, or relative dies we have such difficulty expressing ourselves appropriately? If you apply the following techniques, you will never again be unsure of what to say.

- During times of tragedy, people's emotions are raw and on edge. They are susceptible to additional hurt and manipulation, but also open and responsive to a caring, concerned touch, word, or gesture. What you say is less important than how you say it. Nonetheless, be aware of the impact of what you say or do.
- If you know the person who has died, focus your thoughts on some pleasant memory you shared. Let the family know that you share their loss because of that shared moment. You will be able to offer consoling words because your grief is real.
- Perhaps you know only one of the surviving family members, but did not know the deceased at all. Your personal grief may not be deep, yet you share the sadness that has stricken your friend. Try to remember what your friend has told you about the deceased. Remind him of that memory, and say, "I know you will miss going to the theater with her. Maybe you and I can do that together soon in honor of her."
- If you don't know of any personal events between your friend and his deceased relative, what should you say? Reflect on the good qualities of your friend, imagining that they are inherited. Tell him this. Let him know that you would like to spend some time with him soon to learn more about the deceased.
- Finally, there's a situation where you must deliver a check to a client who is beneficiary. In all likelihood you are not particularly close to the family, yet you represent the financial linchpin that will hold that family or business together for years to come.

Feel proud about what you were able to accomplish while your client was alive. Congratulate the surviving spouse or partner on the soundness of that prior decision. Remind the survivors of how thoughtful your client was in making certain premiums were paid.

Tell them, "My company and I understand that this check will not bring him back, but his foresight in planning for this event will free you from financial worries, allowing you to dwell positively on his memory. And, besides, don't you remember that when we were setting up this life insurance program, I told you that this contract was unique and wonderful precisely because the event that creates the need provides the solution? Here, now, is proof of that. I am pleased to be able to hand you this check at this difficult time."

These suggestions should help you get through a trying time. Plan now to be more consoling the next time you are faced with someone grieving.

As professional life underwriters, we, more often than other professionals, will find ourselves facing grieving people. We must know how to respond with compassion.

David P. Dashner, CLU, ChFC, "What Do You Say to Someone in Mourning?" Life Association News *(Volume 84, Number 4), April 1989, p. 154. Reprinted with permission.*

Case History

Temporary Help

B. Tracey Gunter had been an accountant for 6 years before giving up tax forms for insurance applications 3 years ago. Tracey is happy about the career change. The clientele Tracey has worked hard to develop is mostly of the two-income family category. Many were initially Tracey's tax clients. It has been a natural extension for many clients to continue to work with Tracey.

Prospect—After 2 years in the business, I was beginning to spend more time servicing my clients. At first I thought it was nothing more than busy work, but I soon found that a service call could be profitable. Like any other aspect of this business, I wanted to plan to be profitable, so I designed my approach to service to create additional sales opportunities. I made such a call on the Murphys.

Pre-approach—Every year, 2 weeks before each policy anniversary date, I send a letter to my clients to arrange a service appointment. This letter informs them of the upcoming anniversary and says that I will be calling. This way, I am certain to make the call for the appointment within a week after sending the letter.

"Hank, this is Tracey. Did you receive my letter? . . .Great. As I noted in the letter, your life insurance policy is a year older now, and I think it is important for us to review it together. I will be in your area next Thursday and Friday. Which day is best for you?"

Hank said they could both meet me Thursday evening at home. This was acceptable to me. I have personally begun to enjoy doing service work in the evenings when I can relax a little with clients with whom I have already established a good relationship.

Approach—I arrived Thursday evening and spent a few minutes with Hank and Sue talking about things that had happened in their lives since I last saw them 6 months earlier. It was during this conversation I learned that their oldest child, Ronnie, had recently started a business. Sue and

Hank had taken a second mortgage on their home to help get the business started.

The Interview—I reviewed the policies that Hank and Sue had purchased from me and brought them up to date on their other policies as best I could. When we had finished, I asked for more information about the loan to Ronnie.

Sue told me that Ronnie had been interested in starting a small business for some time. A good opportunity had presented itself, but Ronnie needed some financial help from them to take advantage of it. They were proud of their first-born, so Hank and Sue had decided to loan Ronnie the money. To accomplish this, they had to take out a $40,000, 7-year second mortgage on their home. This represented about half their total equity.

Close—I asked Hank and Sue, "What have you done to protect yourselves and insure your equity against sudden loss?"

Sue said that they had not really thought about it, and Hank added he did not consider that additional insurance necessary. After all, they had loaned the money to their son. I asked if additional insurance had not been considered because of cost. They agreed it was the primary concern.

I explained to them that although I was sure Ronnie would repay the loan, if something happened to Hank in the meantime, and there was a downturn in business causing difficulty for Ronnie to meet the loan obligation, Sue would have to use personal income sources to repay the loan. I could tell that I had disturbed them so I went right to a trial close.

"Hank and Sue, if I could show you a low-cost insurance program that will protect the other income sources you have, would it interest you?" They said if it is affordable they would be interested.

I then showed them a $40,000 yearly renewable term policy. I explained this program was meant to be used for short term, temporary situations only, and carried only for the protection of the death benefit. Hank and Sue were pleased at the low premium cost and thanked me for bringing the option to their attention. We completed the application and Hank gave me a check for the full annual premium.

Dividend—Proud parents that they were, the Murphys also shared a concern for Ronnie's security and protection, not just relying on the business blossoming for the future. They asked me to meet with Ronnie to find out the details of the situation, and give him some counseling and advice. Of course, I agreed. I had a good referral even before asking for any. Using my standard "Who else might need my help?" talk, I also received four more qualified referred leads!

Summary—The commissions on this case did not add up to very much money, but the situation provided other nice rewards. The most important thing, however, is that through the service I was able to provide, more protection was put in force and more qualified people were made available for me to meet. The needs of my clients were satisfied first, and then I reaped the benefits.

Chapter Eight Review

Key terms and concepts are explained in the Glossary. Answers to the Review Questions and Self-Test Questions are found in the back of the book, following the Glossary.

Key Terms and Concepts

policy service
delivery interview
buyer's guide
policy summary
NAIC Model Illustration Regulation
persistency
client satisfaction
beneficiary designations
common disaster clause
per stirpes
per capita
settlement options
taxation of settlement option
trusts
inter vivos
testamentary
revocable
irrevocable
claims of creditors
community property
"golden handcuffs"
spendthrift clause
supplementary contract
life settlement
life income option

Review Questions

8.1 Discuss the objectives of the delivery interview and how to achieve them

8-2. Explain what should you do to properly prepare for the delivery interview

8-3. Discuss the common state and company requirements for policy delivery.

8-4. Explain how to provide high-quality policy service and how this can enhance your business.

8-5. List and explain beneficiary types and issues relating to beneficiary designation.

8-6. List and explain five types of supplementary contracts (settlement options) used to pay claims.

8-7. Briefly summarize the tax treatment of the settlement options.

8-8. Describe a life settlement and why it is gaining popularity today.

8-9. List and explain what is needed to file a death claim.

Self-Test Questions

Instructions: Read Chapter 8 first, and then answer the following questions to test your knowledge. There are 10 questions. Circle the correct answer. When finished with the test, check your answers with the answer key in the back of the book.

8-1. The document given to the buyer at policy delivery that illustrates the premiums, the guaranteed death benefit, and the policy's loan interest rate is called the

(A) policy summary
(B) buyer's guide
(C) policy receipt
(D) prospectus

8-2. A life insurance trust which becomes effective at the death of the insured (grantor) is called a(n) __________ trust

(A) inter vivos
(B) testamentary
(C) irrevocable
(D) revocable

8-3. The right to change a revocable beneficiary belongs to the

(A) beneficiary
(B) insurance company
(C) owner of the policy
(D) insured and beneficiary jointly

8-4. Mary elects to take her deceased husband's proceeds as "life with 10 years certain." What does this mean?

(A) A lifetime income will be paid to Mary, but only if she lives 10 years or less.
(B) Interest will be paid to Mary over a 10-year period and the principal will be paid out at the end.
(C) A maximum of 10 years of income will be paid to Mary or, if she dies before that time, then to her beneficiary until the original 10 years are completed.
(D) A lifetime income will be paid Mary, but if she dies in less than 10 years, her beneficiary will continue to receive her payments until a total of 10 years are completed.

8-5. The spendthrift clause is intended to protect life insurance

(A) against attachment of proceeds by the insured's creditors
(B) policies against attachment by both the insured's and beneficiary's creditors
(C) proceeds against attachment by the beneficiary's creditors, excluding the IRS
(D) proceeds against attachment by the surviving spouse's creditors, including the IRS

8-6. The booklet prepared by the National Association of Insurance Commissioners that provides objective advice and comprehensive cost comparison for those purchasing life insurance is called

(A) The Insurance Guide
(B) The Consumer's Resource Book
(C) The Buyer's Guide
(D) Choosing the Policy that Fits

8-7. If your client Benny Marchetti wants his insurance proceeds to be paid to his children, Carmine, Enrico, and Lisa or their surviving heirs, how would you suggest that he designate the beneficiaries of the policy?

(A) Name Benny's estate as the beneficiary.
(B) Name each of the three children as beneficiaries.
(C) Name each of the three children as a beneficiary under a per capita arrangement.
(D) Name each of the three children as a beneficiary under a per stirpes arrangement.

8-8. Which of the following statements concerning life settlement options is (are) correct?

I. A life income option and an immediate annuity are based on the same principle.
II. The life income option is flexible, and once payments have begun, changes can be made to the income amount and the recipient(s).

(A) I only
(B) II only
(C) Both I and II
(D) Neither I nor II

8-9. All of the following are objectives of the delivery interview, EXCEPT

(A) reinforce the buying decision
(B) obtain a premium commitment
(C) reopen the sales/planning cycle
(D) build trust

8-10. All of the following are one of the five general types of beneficiary designations EXCEPT

(A) a class or classes of persons
(B) a business organization
(C) the estate of the insured
(D) immediate family

Glossary

Absolute Assignment—the irrevocable transfer of complete ownership of a life insurance policy from one party to another.

Accelerated Death Benefit—a life insurance policy provision that allows death benefits to be paid to the policyowner prior to the insured's death when the insured is terminally ill and has a limited life expectancy.

Accidental Death and Dismemberment Benefit—a life insurance policy provision that provides an additional amount—usually equal to the policy face value—if the insured is killed in an accident. Also known as *double indemnity*. The dismemberment benefit, if included, pays a set percentage for the loss of eyesight and loss of hands or feet at or above the wrist or ankle.

Active Listening—the process of listening to the responses of others while giving feedback, demonstrating that you are, in fact, listening.

Actuary—a highly specialized mathematician, professionally trained in the risk aspects of insurance and related fields, who calculates the premiums, reserves, and other values in policies.

Adjustable Life Insurance—a variety of whole life insurance allowing the policyowner to change the type of insurance, raise or lower the face amount of the policy, increase or decrease the premium, and lengthen or shorten the protection period of the policy at specified intervals.

Administrator—the person appointed by the court to manage and settle the estate of a deceased person, usually because the deceased person left no will. See also: *Executor*.

Adverse Selection—a tendency of poorer risks to continue insurance to a greater extent than normal risks, producing an abnormal increase in mortality rates for those less-healthy members still in the plan. It also includes the tendency for poorer risks to seek out insurance to a greater extent than normal risks. See also: *Anti-selection*.

Advisor Responsibilities—An advisor has responsibilities to his or her client, company, the general public, and the industry. These include, but are not limited to acting ethically, professionally, honestly, and in the best interest of others. Some responsibilities are legal and are regulated by the state and federal departments or imposed by companies, whereas others are promulgated by industry and professional associations.

Age Change—the date at which an individual's age increases for insurance underwriting purposes. Companies use one of two methods in determining age change: age at last birthday; or the date between birthdays, with the age being set at the closer of the two birthdays.

Age Limits—stipulated minimum or maximum ages below and above which the company will not accept applications or may not renew policies.

Age of Majority—the age at which a person has the legal capacity to enter into and be bound by a contract. It differs from state to state.

Agent—a sales and service representative of an insurance company licensed by the state to solicit the sale of insurance. In this text we refer to all types of producers as advisors. An agent represents the company and is given powers by the company to act in its behalf.

Agent of Record—the agent or broker recognized by the insurer as the person to whom the commission is to be paid on a sale.

Agent's Statement—a part of the application form where the agent reports anything about the proposed insured that is not recorded elsewhere on the application.

Aleatory Contract—a contract in which the values exchanged are not necessarily equal. In an insurance policy a small amount of premium may result in a large payment of death benefits, or a large amount of premium may result in no payment of death benefits.

Altruism—unselfish regard for the welfare of others; acting unselfishly; taking others' needs and concerns into account before your own.

Amended Policy—a policy on which a change has been made in rates, values, benefits, or any policy provision either before or after delivery with the acceptance by the insured.

Amendment—the formal document changing the provisions of an insurance policy.

Amortization—the liquidation of a financial obligation, such as a mortgage, on an installment basis.

Amount-at-risk—the difference between the face amount of a policy and the reserve or policy value at a given time. It is the amount over and above what the policyowner has contributed toward the payment of his claims. Amount-at-risk is the true insurance amount, or the amount the company is responsible for paying from the reserve.

Anniversary—the yearly anniversary of the issue date. Premiums, cash values, dividends and other policy benefits are determined as of anniversary dates.

Annuitant—the person during whose life an annuity is payable, and usually the person who receives the annuity income.

Annuity—a contract that provides a periodic income at regular intervals for a specific period of time, such as for a number of years, or for life.

Annuity Certain—a contract that provides an income for a specified number of years, regardless of life or death. The payments are not linked to the duration of a specified human life.

Annuity Consideration—the payment, or one of the regular periodic payments, made to an insurance company to purchase an annuity.

Anti-selection—also called *adverse selection*. It refers to the tendency of people with a greater than average likelihood of loss to apply for or continue insurance to a greater extent than other people.

Applicant—the person who applies for insurance by signing a written application. The applicant need not be the insured but must have a clear insurable interest in the person to be insured.

Application—a statement of information made by a person applying for insurance. It is used by the life insurance company to assess the acceptability of risk and issue the policy. A copy of the application is usually made a part of the policy when it is issued.

Assignee—the person or business institution eligible to receive the benefits of the insurance contract when assigned by the policyowner.

Assignment—the signed transfer by the policyowner of some or all of the rights under the policy to another person or entity. After assignment the policy can no longer be changed without approval of assignee.

Assignor—the policyowner who assigns and transfers his or her rights under an insurance policy to another.

Attained Age—the age the insured has reached on a certain date, based on nearest birthday or last birthday, depending on the company. Sometimes referred to as *insurance age.*

Attending Physician's Statement (APS)—a statement of medical history and treatment by a physician who has treated the insured or proposed insured.

Automatic Premium Loan (APL)—an elective policy feature wherein any premium not paid by the end of the grace period is paid by the insurance company by making a loan equal to the premium from policy cash values.

Average Indexed Monthly Earnings (AIME)—a Social Security calculation to determine the amount of benefits for which a worker is eligible, based on the money the worker earned and contributed into social security during the years of covered employment according to formula.

Aviation Clause—a clause limiting the liability of the insurer if death is related to aviation, to a specified degree. This may be used if the insured is a crewmember or pilot.

Back Date—establishing the policy issue date prior to the date of application, usually to give the insured the benefit of a lower premium rate for a younger-than-current age.

Beneficiary—any person, class of people, institution, or trust specifically named in a life or annuity contract to receive the policy benefits at the death of the insured.

Beneficiary Change—The named beneficiary may be changed only if the policy gives such right to the policyowner and law permits the change. Most policies allow such change with the formal request and signature of the owner.

Beneficiary, Contingent—the person(s) designated in the policy to receive the benefit if the primary beneficiary dies while the insured is living.

Beneficiary, Primary—the person(s) designated in the policy to receive the benefit at the death of the insured.

Ben Franklin Close—also known as the *T close* because of its construction. The advisor and/or prospect list the reasons for buying on the left of a vertical line and the reasons for not buying on the right. The number and importance of the reasons in each column help determine the outcome.

Binding Receipt—a receipt provided to indicate temporary protection of the applicant from the date of the receipt of the medical examination, but enabling the company to terminate the coverage if the applicant does not meet underwriting standards.

Blackout Period—the name of the period of time between a surviving spouse's last child's benefit payment and eligibility for the first retirement income check at age 60, under the rules of Social Security.

Blue Cross—an independent, nonprofit membership corporation providing protection on a service basis against the cost of hospital care in a limited geographical area.

Blue Shield—an independent, nonprofit membership corporation providing protection on a service basis against the cost of surgical and medical care in a limited geographical area.

Branch Office Distribution System—Under this system for selling life insurance, the soliciting agents assigned to a branch office are under contract to the insurance company, not to the branch manager. The agents receive commission directly from the insurance company. The branch office manager, supervisors, and clerical employees in the field office are employees of the company and are treated as any other employee of a company would be.

Broker—a sales and service representative who handles insurance for clients and represents the client, not the insurance company. They generally sell insurance of various kinds and for several companies.

Brokerage—a field office operation in which a general agent is contracted with a number of insurance companies to sell their products.

Brokerage Distribution System—a distribution system that licenses and relies on commissioned producers, called *brokers*, who sell the products of more than one company.

Bundled Insurance Product—a life insurance product in which the mortality, investment, and expense factors used to calculate premium rates and cash values are not identified as such, as in traditional whole life insurance.

Business Insurance—a policy that primarily provides coverage of benefits to a business, as contrasted to an individual. It is issued to indemnify a business for the loss of services of a key employee or a partner who becomes disabled or dies.

Business Life Insurance—life insurance purchased by a business enterprise on the life of a member of the firm. It is often bought by partnerships to protect the surviving partners against loss caused by the death of a partner, or by a corporation to reimburse it for loss caused by the death of a key employee.

Buyer's Guide—a publication required by many states to be given to the applicant of life insurance by the insurance company before an application is taken, or at the time of policy delivery. It is designed to help the buyer make a more informed decision.

Buying Cycle—the five-step process an individual goes through in making the decision to purchase. The steps are: (1) recognizing the problem; (2) the desire for a solution; (3) choosing the best solution, (4) making the purchase, and (5) taking delivery.

Buying Signals—the signs your prospects will make when it is time for you to take action. They indicate readiness to buy, or express interest in the ideas or proposals you are presenting.

Cafeteria Plan—an employee benefit plan under which an employee can use a specified amount of employer funds and/or salary deductions to design his or her own benefit package from an array of available benefits.

Capital Conservation—the use of interest income alone to provide income for a beneficiary over time without depleting the principal providing the interest.

Capital Distribution—the use of both interest and principal to provide income to a beneficiary for a certain period of time. Both will be depleted at a predetermined date in the future.

Capital Needs Analysis—a system for determining how much life insurance a prospect needs if the principal sum is to be preserved in the process of meeting the financial objectives for his or her survivors.

Capitalized Value—the amount of money that must be set aside to replace the income of an income producer. The monetary value of the future earnings and total economic values of a human life that can be created to replace the economic value of that life to that person's dependents.

Cash Needs—part of the needs-based or financial needs analysis approach, cash needs at death represent lump-sum amounts of money that can liquidate expenses that the family will face at the death of an income producer, such as final expenses, debt repayment, mortgage cancellation or a rent fund, emergency fund, or education fund.

Cash Surrender Value—the amount available in cash upon voluntary termination of a policy by its owner before it becomes payable by death or maturity.

Cash Value—the cash fund within a permanent life insurance policy that is part of the death benefit and is owned by the policyowner for purposes of cash surrender or policy loans.

Cede—to transfer all or part of a risk written by an insurer to a reinsurer.

Center of Influence—from the advisor's point of view, an influential person you know, who knows you favorably, and who agrees to introduce or refer you to others.

Certificate of Insurance—a statement of coverage issued to an individual insured under a group insurance contract, outlining the insurance benefits and principal provisions applicable to the member.

Children's Rider—unit(s) of term insurance attached to a parent's life policy to provide a death benefit for all eligible children. Age limitations for coverage usually extend from 14 days to 22 or 25 years.

Claims of Creditors—Generally the cash values during lifetime, and the death benefits afforded the beneficiary at death, are free from the claims of the creditors of the insured and the beneficiary. The only exception to this is that the federal government can exercise tax liens against the cash value.

Clarifying Questions—a type of response during active listening that enhances communication, where the advisor asks the prospect to restate or clarify a statement, or the advisor repeats the statement to translate or clarify the meaning of a statement by the prospect.

Classification—combining insurance applicants into groups with the same general characteristics so that the various groups' inherent differences in exposure to loss can be isolated for rating and underwriting.

Client—a person who has bought from you, but also someone with whom you have developed, or are developing, a strong interpersonal business relationship. Because of this relationship, if the client has any problems in areas relevant to your expertise, he or she will look to you for direction.

Client-Focused Sales/Planning Approach—emphasizes helping clients by providing solutions to their insurance and financial needs and helping them achieve their objectives with a genuine agenda of helping in an open, honest, and forthright manner. The client's satisfaction is central. The advisor's role is helping people recognize and understand their financial needs, providing needed information, removing obstacles to financial success, and assisting in taking positive action to achieve their goals.

Close—the term applied to the part of the selling process where the prospect is asked to make the decision to buy.

Close-ended question—a type of question that solicits singular facts or one-word replies.

Collateral Assignment—the assignment of a policy as security for a loan; the creditor receives proceeds or values to the extent of his interest in the agreement.

Commercial Insurance or Lines—various kinds of insurance written for businesses and organizations. This contrasts with personal lines, which covers individuals. Both types primarily provide property and liability insurance.

Commissioner of Insurance—the state official charged with the enforcement of the laws or regulations pertaining to insurance in the respective states. This post is normally appointed by the Governor, but in some sates is an elected official.

Commissioners Standard Ordinary Mortality Table (CSO Table)—mortality tables based on inter-company experience during a particular period of time. The 1980 CSO Table is widely used today, although newer tables based on more recent mortality for 2001 are being introduced and will be considered for approval in the various states over the next few years.

Common Disaster Clause—a clause sometimes added to a policy that defines the method of payment of proceeds from policies when the insured and named beneficiary die simultaneously (by legal definition) in a common disaster. It states the insured will be deemed to have survived the beneficiary and policy proceeds will be paid accordingly if the insured dies within a certain period after the beneficiary.

Community Property—property acquired during marriage in which both husband and wife have an undivided one-half interest. Not more than half can be disposed of by either party individually by will. There are presently nine community property states: Arizona, California, Idaho, Louisiana, New Mexico, Nevada, Texas, Washington, and Wisconsin.

Compliance—following the laws and regulations, including company rules, that apply to the sales of insurance and financial products. These are the minimum standards.

Conditional Receipt—a receipt given in return for the application's first premium payment, acknowledging that the insurance is in force from date of the receipt (or medical examination, if later) before the policy is issued, but under the condition that the proposed insured is found to be insurable at standard rates.

Conservation—the process of keeping issued business in force, including the reinstatement of lapsed policies, and the efforts by a company and advisor to prevent a replacement of in-force business.

Consumer Price Index (CPI)—a measure of the changing costs of goods and services in the USA from year to year.

Contestable Period—a period (normally 2 years) after a policy is issued during which the company has the right to cancel the policy because of the insured's material misrepresentation or fraud. Normally after 2 years from the policy date the policy becomes incontestable.

Contract—a binding agreement between two or more parties, legally enforceable to do certain things. An insurance policy is a contract. The "Law of Contracts" specifies four requirements for the formation of a contract: (1) parties of legal capacity; (2) expression of mutual consent of the parties to a promise, or set of promises; (3) a valid consideration; (4) the absence of any statute or other rule declaring such agreement void (having a legal purpose).

Contract of Adhesion—a legally binding agreement that is prepared by one party and must be accepted or rejected as a whole by the other party, without bargaining between the parties to the content of the contract. An insurance contract is a contract of adhesion.

Contract of Indemnity—in this contract the amount of the paid benefit is based on the actual amount of financial loss as determined at the time of loss. Many hospital expense contracts are contracts of indemnity. Indemnity is a principle of insurance whereby the insurance seeks to reimburse the insured for approximately the amount lost, no more or no less.

Contributory—a plan of insurance in which part of the premium is paid by the employee and part is paid by the employer.

Conversion Privilege—the right of the insured to change the type of plan of coverage within defined company limitations without evidence of medical insurability.

Convertible Term Insurance—term insurance that can be exchanged, at the option of the policyowner and without evidence of insurability, for another plan of insurance.

Cost Basis—the investment in a contract that determines the amount of the proceeds from the disposition of a contract can be recovered tax-free.

Cost-of-Living Adjustment (COLA)—an increase in an insurance contract to compensate for an increase in the cost of living, such as disability income benefit or a life income benefit.

Credit Life Insurance—term life insurance issued through a lender or lending agency to cover payment of a loan, installment purchase, or other obligation, in case of the death of a borrower.

CSO Table—see Commissioners Standard Ordinary Mortality Table. The new 2001 CSO mortality tables will reflect a higher life expectancy and generally lower mortality rates.

Current Assumption Whole Life—uses current mortality and interest earnings based on current yields rather than overall investment portfolio yields. Current rates reflect today's interest rates. Portfolio rates represent the collective rate being earned on all the funds of the insurer that are invested at different rates at different times with different maturities. In all other respects, it is identical to conventional whole life.

Currently Insured—an insured status under Social Security that requires a person to have credit for at least 6 quarters of coverage out of the 13-quarter period ending with the quarter in which death occurs.

Current Settlement Option Rates—settlement option rates that reflect the interest rates currently earned by the insurer.

Date of Issue—the date (day, month, year) on which the policy was issued. Normally controls contestibility and suicide provisions dates.

Death Benefit—the amount payable to a beneficiary according to the policy terms upon the death of the insured.

Death Claim—when the insured dies, the person(s) entitled to the proceeds must complete certain insurance company death claim forms giving proof of death and establishing the claimant's right to policy proceeds.

Declarations—the part of the policy describing the named insured, address, effective date, term of the policy, applicable coverage, amount of insurance, and premium. Normally associated with property and liability coverage.

Decreasing Term Insurance—term life insurance with a face value that will decrease each year over a stated period of time. It may be purchased as a single contract or as a rider to another type of policy.

Deferred Annuity—an annuity contract providing for the income payments to begin at some future date.

Deferred Compensation Plan—an employer-sponsored plan to provide benefits to an employee at a later date, usually at retirement. May be funded with life insurance.

Deferred Group Annuity—a type of annuity providing for the purchase each year of a paid-up deferred annuity for each member of an employee group. The amount received by an employee at retirement is based on the sum of these deferred annuities.

Defined Benefit Plan—a pension plan stating either (1) the benefits to be received by employees after retirement or (2) the method of determining such benefits. Employer contributions are actuarially determined.

Defined Contribution Plan—a plan in which the contribution rate is fixed and benefits that will be received by employees after retirement depend to some extent upon the contributions and their earnings.

Demutualization—the process of converting a mutual insurance company into a stock company.

Dependency Period—the period during which there are dependent children. This period extends from the date of the insured's death until the youngest child is self-sufficient or completes the desired level of education.

Deposit Term Insurance—a form of term insurance in which the first year's premium is larger than subsequent premiums (the deposit). Typically, a partial endowment is paid at the end of the term period. In many cases the partial endowment can be applied toward the purchase of a new term or whole life policy.

Disability Insured—the insured status under Social Security necessary to receive disability benefits. It requires a worker to be fully insured and have a minimum amount of work under Social Security within a recent period.

Disability Waiver of Premium—a policy rider providing for the automatic payment of premium by the company should the insured become totally physically incapacitated. It extends through the period of disability only and usually is offered to age 60.

Discovery Agreement—a written or verbal acknowledgment of the facts, feelings, values, and attitudes uncovered in the selling process. It states the prospect's present situation and financial and personal goals, and outlines the commitment to work together cooperatively to achieve these goals.

Dividend—the return to the policyowner of part of the premium paid for a policy issued on a participating basis by the insurer. It represents an excess of collected premiums over expenses, actual mortality and investment experience during a period of time. Dividends may be used by the policyowner (1) as cash refunds, (2) to reduce the next premium, (3) to be kept at interest by the insurer, (4) to purchase paid-up life insurance, and (5) to purchase one-year term up to the amount of cash value in the policy.

Dividend Accumulations—a policy dividend option representing the amounts of money resulting from the accumulation of dividends, and interest earned on those dividends in the policy when the policyowner leaves the money with the insurer.

Dividend Addition—an amount of paid-up insurance purchased with a policy dividend and added to the face amount of the policy.

Domestic Insurer or Company—a term used for an insurance company in the state where it is organized or incorporated under state law.

Dominant-Needs Approach—based on immediately addressing a key concern of the prospect, with the intention to analyze total needs, if warranted, at a future date.

Double Indemnity—See: *Accidental Death and Dismemberment.*

Earned Premium—that portion of a policy's premium payment for which the protection of the policy has already been given. For example, an insurance company is considered to have earned 75 percent of an annual premium after a period of 9 months of an annual term has elapsed.

Earnings Test—the process of determining whether income benefits of Social Security beneficiaries under age 65 should be reduced because of wages that exceed a specified amount that is subject to annual indexing.

Eligibility Date—the date on which an individual member of a specified group becomes eligible to apply for insurance under the group insurance plan.

Eligibility Period—a specified length of time, frequently 31 days, following the eligibility date during which an individual member of a particular group will be eligible to apply for insurance under a group life or health insurance policy without evidence of insurability.

Eligible Employees—those members of a group who have met the eligibility requirements under a group life or health insurance plan.

Elimination Period—the number of days after a disability occurs before policy benefits become payable.

Emergency Fund—one of the basic uses of life insurance to protect the family of the insured against sudden, large, unbudgeted expenses at the death of the insured.

Empathy—the ability to recognize and understand how others think and feel about their problems without making judgments.

Employee Benefits—those programs in addition to salary offered to an employee. In the area of insurance they include mainly life and health insurance and pension plans.

Employee Retirement Income Security Act (ERISA)—ERISA is a federal law enacted in 1974 that set minimum standards of information disclosure and fiduciary responsibilities in the establishment, operation, and administration of employee benefit plans, including group life, pension, and health plans.

Employee Stock Ownership Plan (ESOP)—a defined contribution pension plan that is designed to invest primarily in employer securities.

Endorsement—a change made to an existing policy. Usually additional coverage is added or some part of the existing coverage is eliminated, clarified, restricted, or enlarged. The endorsement becomes part of the policy.

Endorsement Method—a method of changing a provision of a life insurance policy. It may be done by (1) the policyowner returning the policy to the insurance company and the insurer attaching an endorsement changing a provision, or (2) the policyowner requesting the change by letter or phone without the policy and the insurer sending a form to be attached to the policy with the endorsement change. In split-dollar life insurance, the employer owns the policy, pays the premium, and endorses part of the death benefit to an employee's beneficiary.

Endowment—cash from a life insurance policy payable to the policyowner, if living, at the policy maturity date, normally equal to the face amount. If death occurs prior to the maturity date, the face amount is paid. Some partial endowments will pay some portion of the face amount at maturity.

Entire Contract Provision—a life insurance policy provision that states that the policy itself, along with a copy of the application for insurance, if attached, constitutes the entire agreement between the insurer and the policyowner.

Errors and Omissions Insurance—a type of professional liability insurance that indemnifies professionals for losses caused by their errors or oversights in the conduct of their business.

Estate Planning—a program designed to accumulate, conserve, and distribute the personal assets of an individual at death.

Estate Tax—a tax imposed upon the right of a person to transfer property at death. This tax is imposed not only by the federal government but also by a number of states.

Ethics—behaving according to the principles of right and wrong that are accepted by your profession. Behaving ethically requires putting the prospect's best interest before your own, maintaining the highest possible standard in all your business dealings.

Evidence of Insurability—any statement of proof of a person's physical condition and/or other factual information required for the person's acceptance for insurance.

Excess Interest—the difference between the rate of interest the company guarantees to pay and the interest actually credited on such funds by the company.

Exclusion—specified conditions or circumstances for which the policy does not provide benefits, usually applied to health insurance coverage.

Executor—the person or corporation appointed by the court to carry into effect (execute) the provisions of a will. The court will normally appoint the person named in the will of the deceased as executor, provided that the person consents and qualifies. See: *Administrator*.

Executrix—a female executor.

Experience—a term used to describe the relationship, usually expressed as a percent or ratio of premium to claims for a plan, coverage, or benefits for a stated period.

Experience Rating—the method used by actuaries to determine the premium levels for a select group of insureds that uses actual loss ratios to determine the group's premium rate. This method is one of segmenting the market into smaller groups to ensure profitability.

Experience Refund—amount of premium returned by an insurer to a group policyowner when the financial experience of a particular group has been more favorable than the premiums collected from the group anticipated.

Expiration Date—the date shown on the declarations page of the policy when coverage will stop. In property and casualty insurance it may be a specific date or a statement that coverage is continuous until cancelled.

Expiry—a policy or benefit rider that has reached the end of its specified period of coverage. This is sometimes used to refer to the end of the premium payment period.

Exposure—in the insurance field, exposure may have several meanings: (1) possibility of loss, (2) loss potential as measured by type of construction, area, or values, (3) possibility of a loss being communicated to an insurance risk from its surroundings, and (4) a unit of measure of the amount of risk a company assumes.

Extended Term Insurance—a nonforfeiture value of a permanent life policy providing term insurance equaling the face value for the period of time into the future that the existing cash value of the policy will purchase as a net single premium at the attained age of the insured.

Face Amount—the sum of money as stated on the face of the policy that will be paid in case of death of the insured or at the maturity of the policy. It does not include additional amounts payable under accidental death or other special provisions, or acquired through the application of policy dividends. It will be reduced at payment by an outstanding policy loan.

Face of Policy—the first page of the insurance policy containing the essential elements of an insuring agreement between the insurer and the insured.

Fact-Finding—gathering of all relevant prospect information regarding financial resources and obligations, personal information, needs, concerns and goals, and personal values, attitudes, and expectations in order to determine financial strategies to meet personal and financial goals.

Family Income Policy—a life insurance policy combining ordinary life and decreasing term insurance. The beneficiary receives income payments to the end of a specified period if the insured dies prior to the end of the stated period plus the face amount of the policy. The face amount is paid either at the beginning or end of the income period.

Family Policy—a life insurance policy providing insurance on all or several family members in one contract, generally whole life insurance on the principal insured and smaller amounts of term insurance on the spouse and children, including those born after the policy is issued.

Feature/Benefit—Features are characteristics of the product itself, or facts about the product. Features are descriptive, and are not given values. A benefit is what the prospect gets as a result of the feature, or what the product does for the prospect and why he or she wants it. Benefits are value-laden and subjective. They are features wanted by that individual.

Feeling-Finding—gathering relevant prospect information regarding the personal values, attitudes, and expectations that are behind a prospect's financial resources and obligations, needs, concerns and goals, and in order to determine financial strategies to meet personal and financial goals.

Field—the group set up to sell and service insurance. They represent the operations of the company that take place outside of the home office.

Field Underwriting—field underwriting occurs when an advisor selects the prospect and then gathers pertinent information about the proposed insured to report on the application for the company's underwriting department to make the final decision.

FICA—taxes imposed under the Federal Insurance Contributions Act. All the benefits of the Social Security program and Part A of Medicare are financed through a system of payroll and self-employment taxes paid by all workers covered under these programs. The tax for each eligible employee is shared 50/50 by the worker and the employer. For self-employed persons, the tax is the combined rate for employers and employees.

FIFO/LIFO—First In, First Out (FIFO) and Last In, First Out (LIFO) represent the cost recovery rules, or the methods for determining cost basis that are used to determine gain upon disposing of an asset. First In represents one's investment or cost basis, and Last In represents cost recovery, or what you get out of the investment. Life insurance is taxed on a FIFO basis, and annuities are taxed on a LIFO basis.

Fifth Dividend Option—using a part or the whole of the policy dividend to purchase one-year term insurance equal to the cash value amount as of the next policy anniversary.

Final Expenses—the financial costs related to dying. Typically included are funeral expenses, debts, medical expenses, taxes, administrative expenses, and so on.

Financial Needs Analysis—a system for determining how much life insurance a prospect needs if the principal sum is to be liquidated in the process of meeting the prospect's financial objectives for his or her survivors.

Financial Planning—must consider all aspects of the client's financial position, which include the client's total financial needs and objectives, and develop strategies for fulfilling those needs and objectives. It is very similar to the total needs analysis view of life insurance planning. This approach sees the personal and financial situation as an integrated whole, with each part potentially impacting on any other. It encompasses all the personal and financial situations of clients to the extent that they can be uncovered, clarified, and addressed.

Financial Planning Process—The general model specifies six steps to the process: (1) establish financial goals, (2) gather relevant data, (3) analyze the data, (4) develop a plan for achieving goals, (5) implement the plan, and (6) monitor the plan.

First Year Commission—the amount paid to an insurance advisor after a sale based on the contract sold, the amount of the policy premium, and the company's commission rate for that contract.

529 Plan—a tax-advantaged savings vehicle that can be used for qualified post-secondary education expenses. There is also a provision for special needs education regardless of level. EGTRRA 2001 made qualified distributions tax-free. 529 plans are sponsored by individual states and can either be pre-paid tuition plans or freestanding savings accounts.

Five-Year Renewable Term Insurance—a policy that provides term insurance to a stated age, normally 65 or 70, with the premiums increasing every 5 years. Although it has no cash values, it may contain a provision that allows the insured to convert the policy to a permanent plan.

Fixed Amount Option—a life insurance settlement option under which the insurer pays the beneficiary the policy proceeds plus interest in a series of installment payments for as long as the money lasts. This is also referred to as the *fixed payment option*.

Fixed Period Option—a life insurance settlement option under which the insurer pays the beneficiary the policy proceeds plus interest in a series of installment payments for a specified length of time.

Flat Extra Premium Method—a method used to rate substandard risks when an insurer considers the extra risk to be constant and ongoing by charging a specified extra premium per $1,000 of insurance regardless of age.

Flat Schedule—a type of schedule in group insurance under which everyone is insured for the same benefits regardless of salary, position, or other circumstances.

401(k) Plan—a salary reduction qualified retirement plan that allows employees to contribute a portion of their salaries on a tax-deferred basis.

403(b) Plan—tax favored vehicle for deferring compensation exclusively for an employee of a public school or nonprofit organization exempt from taxes under IRC (Internal Revenue Code) sections 501(c)(3) or 403(b). These plans are also called *Tax Sheltered Annuities (TSA)*.

Foreign Insurance Company—designation for any insurance company in any state or country other than the one in which it is chartered.

Franchise Insurance—individual insurance contracts issued to members of a specific group (examples include members of an association or employees of a common employer) under group-like arrangements in which the employer or association collects and remits the premiums.

Fraternal Life Insurance—life insurance that is provided by fraternal benefit orders or societies, organized without capital stock and as not-for-profits, and maintaining lodge systems.

Fraud—intentional concealment or misrepresentation with the objective of forcing an insurer to provide a benefit which otherwise would not be provided.

Free Look—a notice written in the contract to the policyowner that the company provides a given period of time (usually 10 days) to examine the policy after delivery and return it for a refund of premium if dissatisfied.

Front-Loaded Policy—usually found in a universal life insurance policy where most of the expense charges are deductions from each premium payment that may continue throughout the premium payment period. In a back-loaded policy, the expense charges are usually applied for a stated number of years and will be charged to the policy for a surrender occurring before that time period expires.

Fully Insured—an insured status under Social Security requiring one of the following: (1) 40 quarters of coverage, (2) credit for at least as many quarters of coverage as there are years since 1950 (or after the year in which age 21 is reached) and before the year in which the person dies, becomes disabled, or reaches age 62, whichever occurs first.

Full Retirement Age—the age at which a worker can retire under Social Security and receive non-reduced benefits equal to his or her primary insurance amount (PIA).

General Agency Distribution System—in the general agency system, each field office is headed by a general agent under contract to the insurer and considered an independent entrepreneur. Typically, the GA employs the field staff and agents that report to the GA rather than the company. Traditionally, all commissions are paid to the GA who keeps an override expense commission and then pays the selling agents. Some insurers pay agents directly with separate payment to the GA.

"Golden Handcuffs"—refers to executive or key person benefits that are designed to keep the employee with the firm. Typically arranged as deferred compensation, the employee will receive additional benefits if he or she stays with the company for a stipulated period of time.

Government Allotment—payroll deduction of insurance premiums by members of the armed services or federal government. Can apply to group insurance or to individually owned plans.

Grace Period—the period of time, usually 31 days following the premium due date, during which the insurance policy remains at full benefit and payment of the premium may be made without penalty.

Graded Premium by Policy Size—a method of premium computation recognizing savings in the cost of issue of larger policies by providing a step reduction in the premium rate per thousand as the amount of insurance increases by specified amount groupings. This is also called *banding*.

Graded Premium Life—a policy type offering a series of increasing premium levels over 5, 10, or 20 years. At the end of the period of graded premiums, the policyowner pays the ultimate, level premium amount until age 100.

Gross Premium—the actual amount that a policyowner pays in premium. This is the net premium plus loading.

Group Annuity—a contract providing retirement annuity benefits to a group of persons under a master policy, usually issued to an employer.

Group Contract—a contract of insurance made with an employer or other entity that covers a group of persons identified as individuals by reference to their relationship to the entity.

Group Insurance—insurance written on a group of people under a single master policy, issued to their employer or another entity, usually providing life and health insurance.

Guaranteed Convertible—the promise that a policy may continue at the current face value under another form of insurance at the new premium without underwriting by the company. Usually conversion is offered in term policies for permanent insurance.

Guaranteed Insurability Option—a provision or rider to a policy allowing the purchase of additional insurance at specified future dates at attained age without evidence of insurability.

Guaranteed Issue Insurance—insurance coverage for which there is usually no individual underwriting for its issue. Underwriting approval is undertaken at the group level.

Guaranteed Renewable—a life or health policy issued with the promise that it may be continued beyond the current contract period by the insured with the future payment of premiums when due. The premium may be raised on a class basis.

Guardian—one appointed by the court to administer the estate of a minor. Also a person named to represent the interest of minor children or disabled or incapacitated individuals.

Hazard—a condition that could increase the likelihood or severity of a loss or injury to property or persons.

Home Office—the principal office of an insurance company where the chief executive and general supervisory departments are located.

Home Service Distribution System—a method by which premiums are collected. Usually the commissioned agent collects the insured's premium at the home or place of business on a monthly or sometimes weekly basis. The home service agent sells in a defined geographical territory. This was formerly called *debit insurance*. Some companies specialize in this type of client service, although its costliness makes it a rarity in the insurance market.

Hospice—a health care facility providing medical care and support services such as counseling to terminally ill persons and their families.

Human Life Value—the capitalized value of an individual's earning ability into the future. The present value of that portion of a person's estimated future earnings that will be used to support dependents.

Implied Consent—With this technique, the decision to buy is assumed or implied, not directly requested. It presumes the prospect has decided to buy. The advisor proceeds with closing the sale unless or until the prospect objects.

IMSA—the Insurance Marketplace Standards Association is a voluntary organization of life insurance companies seeking to promote ethical marketplace conduct. Adoption and implementation of IMSA's Principles of Ethical Marketplace Conduct and the Code of Life Insurance Ethical Market Conduct is required for membership.

Income Needs—the family's ongoing need for income formerly provided by the deceased. Money must be found to provide readjustment income, dependency period income, and income for the surviving dependent spouse.

Incontestable Clause—a policy provision preventing the insurance company from declaring the contract invalid after a certain date, usually 2 years, as established by the individual states.

Increasing Term Insurance—a type of term life insurance in which the face amount increases during the term of the coverage.

Indemnity—benefits of an insurance contract paid in an amount approximating or equal to the amount lost, no more, no less.

Indexed Life Insurance—a whole life insurance policy that provides for the face amount, and consequently the premium, to increase automatically each year, based upon the Consumer Price Index.

Individual Insurance—policies that provide protection to the policyowner and/or his or her family. This is sometimes called *personal insurance*, as distinct from group and blanket insurance.

Individual Retirement Account (IRA)—a popular tax-deferred, individual retirement plan that can be established by anyone with earned income.

Industrial Life Insurance—life insurance issued in small amounts (usually less than $1,000) with premiums payable weekly or monthly. Premiums are usually collected at the home or place of business by the agent. This was formerly called *debit insurance*.

Illustration Selling—focuses the numerical values on the printed illustration, rather than conducting a fundamental financial planning process, uncovering the client's needs based on sound fact-finding, and designing real solutions to real financial problems and concerns.

Inflation—the persistent increase in the price levels of goods and services, caused by a number of complex economic and social factors within the economy of the country.

In Force—a policy on which premium payments are either up to date or not in arrears beyond the grace period.

Inspection Report—the report a company receives from an independent investigator giving general information on the health history, occupation, financial status, and moral problems of an applicant.

Insurability—qualifications of age, health, occupation, and other factors that enable the proposed insured to meet the requirements of a company for the issuance of insurance.

Insurable Interest—the condition that must exist at issue of a life insurance policy calling for the person applying for the insurance and the person who is to receive the policy benefits to share a common insurable interest in the potential loss. This means that these are persons who would suffer an emotional or financial loss in the event of the death of the insured.

Insurable Risk—the conditions that make a risk insurable are (1) the peril insured against must produce a definite loss not under the control of the insured, (2) there must be a large number of homogeneous exposures subject to the same perils, (3) the loss must be calculable and the cost of insuring it must be economically feasible, (4) the peril must be unlikely to affect all insureds simultaneously, and (5) the loss produced by a risk must be definite and have a potential to be financially serious.

Insurance—insurance is a contractual arrangement in which a customer pays a specified sum (the insurance premium) in return for which the insurer will pay compensation if specific conditions or events affect the customer. Generally, it is a formal social device for reducing the individual's risk of losses by spreading the risk over a group of people.

Insurance Planning—the process of examining all of the client's needs, comparing needs with means, and selling, where appropriate, the types of policies and the amounts of insurance that best suit the client's purposes.

Insurance Age—an age upon which current premium rates may be established. It is commonly based on age at last birthday, age at next birthday, or age at nearest birthday.

Insurance Agent—a representative of an insurance company who sells insurance.

Insurance Commissioner—the state official who enforces the state government's regulations and codes governing the operations of both companies and agents licensed to do business in the jurisdiction.

Insurance Company—any corporation primarily engaged in the business of furnishing insurance protection to the public. Also called an *insurer*.

Insurance Department—a government department in each state or territory charged with the supervision and licensing of insurance companies and agents and the general administration of insurance laws or codes.

Insurance Examiner—the representative of a state insurance department assigned to participate in the official audit and examination of the affairs of an insurance company.

Insurance Policy—a written legal document issued by an insurer setting forth the terms of the coverage and the rights and obligations of each party under the contract.

Insurance Programming—this process of calculating the amount of insurance a person should have following the capital needs analysis and/or financial needs analysis methods.

Insurance Rating—insurance rating is the process of determining rates (or the price of insurance) for individuals, groups, or classes of risks.

Insurance Trust—a trust composed partly or wholly of insurance policies. A common type is an ILIT, an irrevocable life insurance trust, designed to keep a life insurance policy out of the estate of the insured.

Insured—The person whose life is protected by the insurance policy and upon whose life the death benefit is predicated.

Insurer—The party of the insurance contract promising to pay the losses and benefits. It is a term used to refer to the company providing insurance to the public.

Integration—a coordination of the disability income insurance benefit with other disability income benefits such as Social Security through a specific formula to insure reasonable income replacement.

Interest Sensitive Whole Life—a policy type offering many of the guarantees found in traditional whole life, including a guaranteed death benefit and a minimum guaranteed interest crediting rate. When mortality and expense charges are guaranteed, the policy is often referred to as *interest-sensitive whole life,* because excess interest (credited interest minus guaranteed interest) credited to the cash value becomes the only non-guaranteed element in the contract.

Intestacy—the situation of dying without a will (intestate) in which the state assumes that the deceased had decided to have property disposed of under the laws of dissent and distribution. These are statutory ways of handling real property such as land and buildings (dissent laws) and personal property (distribution laws). The laws of intestacy differ by state.

Investment Income—income generated by a company's or person's portfolio of investments such as bonds or stocks.

Irrevocable Beneficiary—the beneficiary designation in a policy that cannot be changed without beneficiary permission or at the death of the beneficiary.

Joint Life Insurance—insurance on two or more persons, the benefits of which are payable on the first death.

Joint and Survivor Life Insurance—insurance on two or more persons, the benefits of which are payable on the second death.

Joint Tenancy—the undivided ownership of property by two or more people in such a manner that, upon the death of one, the survivor(s) take the entire property.

Juvenile Insurance—insurance on the life of a child applied for and issued to the person(s) having an insurable interest in the child.

Keogh (HR10) Account—an account to which a self-employed person can make annual tax-deductible contributions of the lesser of 25 percent of income or $30,000.

Key Person Insurance—insurance designed to protect a firm against the loss of business income resulting from the death or disability of an employee who is important to the company's operation.

Lapse Ratio—the ratio of the number of insurance policies lapsed without value or surrendered for cash during a year to those in force at the beginning of the year.

Lapsed Policy—a policy terminated by a company for nonpayment of premiums within the time required. Lapsing is sometimes limited to a termination occurring before the policy has a cash or other surrender value to pay the premium.

Lapse Rate—the probability that a policy in force at the start of a policy year will lapse by the end of the year.

Law of Large Numbers—the theory of probability that is the basis of insurance. The larger the number of risks or exposures, the more closely will the actual results obtained approach the probable results expected from an infinite number of exposures.

Leading Question—a type of question that steers the client toward a conclusion that the advisor, not the client, has already formulated. This type of question can be ineffective, dishonest, and manipulative.

Ledger Proposal—a printed illustration of a policy's premium rates, cash values, and any possible applicable dividends over a specified number of years.

Legal Reserve—the minimum reserve that a company must keep to meet future claims and obligations as they are calculated under the state insurance code.

Level Premium—a rating structure designed to keep the premium costs the same throughout the life of the policy.

Level Term Insurance—term insurance with a constant face value from the date of issue to the date of expiration.

License—certification by a state's insurance department that a company, agent, or broker has the right to do business with the public, by qualification and certification for a stated period of time.

Life Expectancy—the average number of years of life remaining for a group of persons of a given age, according to a particular mortality table.

Life Income Option—a life insurance settlement option under which the insurer uses the policy proceeds and interest to pay the beneficiary a series of payments for as long as the beneficiary shall live.

Life Insurance—the scientifically calculated pooling, growth, and distribution of money to satisfy two objectives: (1) paying benefits to survivors of someone who dies while covered, and (2) providing distribution of benefits by lump sum or with guaranteed lifetime payments.

Life Insurance Cost Indexes—measurements used to estimate the cost of a life insurance policy on a time-value-adjusted basis, assuming that the face amount of the policy would be paid at the end of a specific time period (net payment cost index) or that the policy will surrendered at the end of a specific time period (surrender cost index).

Life Insurance In Force—the sum of the face amounts plus dividend additions of life insurance policies outstanding at a given time. Additional amounts payable under accidental death or other special provisions are not included.

Life Settlement—a transaction of selling an existing life insurance policy by its owner to a third party. In exchange for a cash settlement, the policyowner transfers ownership and all other rights of the policy to that third party, to obtain a sum of money that exceeds the policy's cash value. The new owner keeps the policy in force by making subsequent premium payments, and collects the proceeds at the policy's maturity.

Limited Payment Life Insurance—ordinary life insurance having premiums that are scheduled for a specified number of years or until a specified age. Examples would be 10- or 20-pay life, single premium, or life payable to age 65.

Loan Interest—the rate of interest that the borrower must pay on the loan as specified in the policy. If the interest is not paid, it will be added to the policy loan.

Loan Value—the largest amount that can be borrowed by the policyowner on the security of the cash value of the policy without surrendering the contact.

Long-term Care—the continuum of broad-ranged maintenance and health services to the chronically ill, disabled, or retarded. Services may be provided on an inpatient (rehabilitation facility, nursing home, mental hospital), outpatient, or at-home basis.

Long-term Disability Income Insurance (LTD)—benefit plan that replaces earned income lost through the inability to work because of a disability caused by an accident or illness.

Loss—the occurrence of the event insured against.

Loss Ratio—in property and liability insurance, the percent to which losses bear to premiums for a given period.

Loss Reserve—the estimated liability on an insurer's balance sheet for unpaid insurance claims or losses that have occurred as of a given reporting date. On an individual claim, the loss reserve is the estimate of what will ultimately be paid out on that case.

Lump Sum—the method for payment of insurance proceeds of a policy wherein the whole amount due or still owing is payable to the beneficiary in one sum.

Managed Care Plans—a process to deliver cost-effective health care without sacrificing quality or access. Common characteristics include controlled access to providers, case management, preventive care, risk sharing, and high-quality care.

Manual Rates—the standard mortality rates for group life insurance that are based on the experience of an average group rather than being based on the experience of one particular group. Used typically for small groups and groups seeking coverage for the first time.

Marketing—the process of identifying needs that people have, clarifying those needs, and creating and supplying the products and services appropriate to satisfy those needs.

Master Policy—a policy that is issued to an employer or trustee, establishing a group insurance plan for designated members of an eligible group.

Material Misrepresentation—a misstatement by the applicant related to the insurer's acceptance of the risk. If the truth was known, the insurer would not have issued the policy or, at least, issued it on a different basis.

Maturity—the date when the endowment amount of a life policy becomes payable.

Medicaid—a government insurance program for persons of any age who have insufficient income and resources to pay for their own health care. It is state-administered and financed by both the state and the federal government through the Social Security Administration.

Medical Examination—the physical examination given by a qualified physician, to determine the insurability of the applicant.

Medical Examiner—a licensed and practicing MD appointed by an insurance company and authorized to make physical examinations of persons applying for insurance.

Medical Information Bureau (MIB)—a cooperative organization formed by life insurers to exchange information about the physical condition of prior applicants. It provides only physical and health information, not the underwriting decisions of other insurers.

Medical Underwriting—a practice used by insurers to determine the level of acceptability of applications, benefit levels, and premium rates based on the review of an applicant's medical history and/or current medical status.

Medicare—a federal government insurance plan attached to the Social Security Act in 1965 providing a health insurance program for the aged. It covers hospital benefits under Part A and medical benefits under Part B to persons aged 65 and older. It is designed to cover short-term, acute medical conditions rather than long-term, chronic conditions that require custodial care.

Misrepresentation—presenting an insurance policy as something else (a savings plan, cash accumulation fund, educational savings plan, or individual retirement plan) is illegal misrepresentation. Suggesting that a policy has certain features, benefits, values, or guarantees that are not specifically guaranteed in the written contract, or a failure to reveal limitations or exclusions of the coverage, is also misrepresentation.

Misstatement of Age—error in birth date given at time of policy issue.

Mode of Premium Payment—the frequency with which the premium for an insurance policy is paid. Modes include annual, semiannual, quarterly, monthly, and weekly.

Modified Endowment Contract—a life insurance contract that fails to meet the IRC's seven-pay test. Distributions receive less favorable tax treatment than other life insurance contracts. Gains are subject to a premature withdrawal penalty and gains are subject top tax on a LIFO basis.

Modified-Premium Whole Life Insurance—with this type of whole life insurance, the policyowner pays a lower than normal premium for a specified initial period of years. After the initial period, the premium increases to a stated amount that is somewhat higher than usual. The higher premium applies to the life of the policy.

Mortality—the actuarially expected rate of death of people by age and category. *Select* mortality reflects mortality of recently selected lives evaluated as good risks. *Ultimate* mortality reflects the mortality of those lives expected after the effects of underwriting selection has worn off over time.

Mortality, Interest, Expense—these factors represent the main variables that determine a life insurance policy premium, and ultimately the performance of the life insurance product over its lifetime. Actuarial assumptions about these factors are made in designing a product. As time passes, actual experience will determine if the product performs as projected.

Mortality Table—a statistical table showing the probable death rate at each age, usually expressed as so many per thousand people. Used to determine longevity and the probability of living or dying at each age, and consequently to determine the premium rate.

Mortgage Insurance—insurance purchased to protect the homeowner family should the breadwinner(s) die before the mortgage is retired. Customarily the benefit is used to pay the outstanding sum owed. When obtaining a mortgage, this insurance refers to insurance for the lender in the event the borrower dies with an outstanding mortgage.

Mortgage Redemption Insurance—a type of decreasing term insurance that covers the life of the mortgagee. Should this person die during the loan period, the policy proceeds will pay the approximate balance of the mortgage loan. Some policies are designed to target this through the loan's interest rate and equity increase.

Motivating Question—a question designed to make the prospect think about situations that need fixing. They uncover problems that the prospect must think about and act on.

Multiple Interview Selling—simply means that a sales process is begun and completed over more than one interview with the prospect. Complex situations, prospect expectations, not being prepared, or needing help can all lead to multiple interviews.

Multiple-Line Company—a company that writes a variety of basic or traditional lines of property and liability insurance such as auto, boat owners, homeowners, and commercial.

Multiple Table Extra Premium—the most common pricing method used for substandard risks. Standard risk is assumed to have 100-percent mortality. Risks assumed to have a mortality of above 100 percent pay higher premiums. Companies establish tables of extra percentages of risk in comparison to the standard.

Mutual Insurance Companies—insurance companies without capital stock, owned by the policyowners. A portion of surplus earnings may be returned to policyowners as dividends.

National Association of Insurance Commissioners (NAIC)—the national organization of state officials charged with regulating insurance. Although the group has no official power, it has a tremendous influence. Its mission is to provide national uniformity in insurance regulations.

NAIC Model Regulation—various insurance regulations promoted by the National Association of Insurance Commissioners intended for adoption by the states to create uniform regulation of insurance in all states. The Model Illustration Regulation, for example, establishes guidelines for companies and advisors regarding the content and presentation of sales illustrations.

Natural Markets—groups of people or businesses in which an advisor has easy access for reasons other than just direct personal knowledge or acquaintance.

Net Amount at Risk—the difference between the face amount of the insurance contract and the reserve.

Net Cash Value—an amount equal to the cash surrender value of a life insurance policy plus any paid-up additions, minus any existing indebtedness, including accrued interest.

Net Cost—the cost of life insurance after the deduction of dividends from the premium paid for a participating policy with a mutual company. Since there are no dividends on nonparticipating policies, the net cost is equal to the total premium paid.

Net Payment Index—A representation of the annual cost per $1,000 of insurance if a policy remains in force, considering the amount of premiums paid less dividends received and disregarding the cash value.

Net Surrender Cost—the ratio in a policy of premiums minus dividends minus cash surrender value at the end of a specific period.

New Business—new insurance policies for which applications are in the process of being issued by the home office.

New Money Rate—the rate of interest that a company can earn on new investments; the current rate.

Noncancelable Guaranteed Renewable Policy—an individual policy that the insured person has the right to continue in force until a specified age, such as 65, by the timely payment of premiums. During this period, the insurer has no right to unilaterally make any changes in any provision of the policy while it is in force, including the premium amount.

Noncontributory—a term used to describe an insurance plan in which the employer pays the employees' cost for protection.

Nonforfeiture Provisions—contractual policy provisions that allow the policyowner to receive the policy's cash value in the event that the policy is terminated for any reason other than the death of the insured. The options include lump-sum payment, extended term insurance, and reduced paid-up insurance.

Nonliquid Assets—assets that are not readily convertible into cash without a serious loss. An example would be real estate.

Nonmedical Limit—the maximum face value of a policy that a company will issue without the applicant providing further medical history by examination.

Nonparticipating Insurance—insurance that pays no dividends, such as the insurance contracts offered by stock insurance companies.

Nonverbal Behavior—nonlinguistic communication through the body and the voice which can indicate how a person feels about our proposals.

Not Taken (NT)—a policy that is not accepted by the policyowner and is returned to the company by the advisor or policyowner, or when the initial premium is not paid by a given date after policy issue.

OASHDI—the old age, survivors, disability, and health insurance program of the federal government. This program consists of Social Security and Medicare.

Objections—a fundamental concern of the prospect that the insurance is not needed, that the solution is not right, that it is too expensive, or that it is too much to be troubled with now. These concerns or questions must be resolved before the sale can proceed.

Occupational Hazards—physical dangers in the workplace of the insured, from which varying periods of absence from the occupation, due to the disability, can be expected.

Offer and Acceptance—The offer may be made by the applicant through the signing of an application, submitting to a physical examination, and prepayment of the first premium. Policy issuance, as applied for, then constitutes the acceptance by the company. The reverse also may be true, when the offer is made by the company by underwriting an application where no premium payment has been submitted. In this case, premium payment at the delivery of the policy constitutes acceptance by the applicant.

Open-ended Question—a question that forces the prospect to answer with an explanation, rather than a simple "yes" or "no." It solicits opinions, feelings, explanations, thoughts, ideas, and values.

Optional Renewable Policy—a health insurance contract that the insurer has the right to terminate at any policy anniversary or, in some instances, at any premium date.

Ordinary Life Insurance—the most common form of basic permanent life insurance in which coverage and premiums are paid to age 100. The policy is designed to build cash values equaling the face amount at age 100.

Orphan—a policyowner whose insurance agent is no longer available to provide client service on the policy.

Over Insurance—an amount of insurance that is excessive in relation to the loss insured against.

Paid-up Additions—units of single premium insurance purchased with dividends of participating policies; one of the customary dividend options.

Paid-up Insurance—Insurance on which all required premiums have been paid. The term is frequently used to mean the reduced paid-up insurance available as a nonforfeiture option, but can be applied to any policy meeting the requirement.

Paramedical Examination—The physical examination of an insurance applicant by a medically trained person other than a physician.

Partial Disability—The result of an illness or injury which prevents an insured from performing one or more of the functions of his or her regular job.

Participating Insurance—Insurance on which dividends may be payable to policyowners as determined by the company's board of directors.

Payor Benefit—An optional benefit as a rider offered by most companies, added to juvenile policies for an additional premium, providing for the waiving of premiums during total and permanent disability of the premium payor or in the event of the payor's death. The waived period extends to future premiums due between the date of benefit until the covered juvenile reaches a stated age, usually 20 or 25. At that time the juvenile will resume the premium payments.

Payroll Deductible Insurance—Employer-authorized deductions from salary earnings of an employee in amounts to cover the premium of individual life or disability income insurance policies. The employer forwards the premium to the company on a billing statement.

Pension Plan—An employer-sponsored system for the payment of annuities or pensions to qualified individuals during retirement, frequently using insurance.

Per Capita—literally meaning, "by head," the distribution of proceeds of an estate or life insurance to be divided equally among all survivors.

Period Certain—The specified time during which the insurer unconditionally guarantees that benefit payments will continue under a settlement option or annuity.

Permanent Life Insurance—Life insurance designed to be in force for the whole of a person's life. This refers to all insurance except term.

Persistency—the degree to which the life insurance business an advisor writes stays on the books through a specified period of time (usually measured at 13 months, 2 years, and other fixed time periods).

Personal History Interview Report—based on a personal interview with the proposed insured from the home office, this report contains the same types of information as an inspection report contains.

Per Stirpes—literally meaning "by branch," giving the share of the deceased child beneficiary of an estate or life insurance policy to his or her heirs equally.

Plan Document—the agreement between the sponsor of a retirement plan and the plan participants that contractually stipulates the definitions and provisions of the plan.

Policy—the printed legal document stating the terms of the insurance contract issued to the policyowner by the company.

Policy Acquisition Costs—costs directly attributable to the production of new business.

Policy Date—the effective date of the policy, which controls the premium due date and contract anniversaries. It may be different than the date of issue.

Policy Dividend—a refund of part of the premium on a participating life insurance policy reflecting the difference between the premium charged and actual experience.

Policy Fee—a fixed sum charged by the insurance company to the policyowner as part of the initial premium (or ongoing premiums) to help offset the underwriting and expenses. It is included and figured into the premium to the policyowner.

Policy Loan—a loan made by a life insurance company from its general funds to a policyowner on the security of the cash value of a policy.

Policy Reserves—the measure of the funds that a life insurance company holds specifically for fulfillment of its policy obligations. Reserves are required by law to be so calculated that, together with future premium payments and anticipated interest earnings, they will enable the company to pay all future claims.

Policyowner—one who owns an insurance policy. Also referred to as policyholder, it need not be the insured.

Policy Summary—Required to be delivered with the policy, this document defines the main features of the issued policy such as cash values (guaranteed and non-guaranteed), premium, guaranteed death benefit, and the policy's loan interest rate.

Pool—a group of reinsurers or insurers organizing to underwrite a particular risk by sharing premiums, losses, and expenses.

Portfolio Rate—the overall rate of return on the insurer's entire portfolio, excluding separate accounts. This rate represents the aggregate rate earned on investments made over many years, and tends to lag behind the changes in current or new money rates.

Preauthorized Check—one of a variety of names applied to a system whereby the policyowner authorizes the company to draw a check on his or her bank account to pay an insurance premium.

Preconditioning—the process of establishing the interest of the prospect to expect and be receptive to the advisor's request for an appointment.

Pre-existing Condition—a physical condition of the applicant existing prior to the issuance of an insurance contract that could determine the status of underwriting.

Preferred Risk—a prospect whose physical condition, occupation, mode of living, or other characteristics suggest above-average longevity,.

Preliminary Inquiry Form—a type of application form used when there is a high probability that a policy either will not be issued, or only issued with a high substandard rating. This is often called a trial or preliminary application.

Preliminary Term—insurance protection for a temporary period preceding the effective date of the permanent coverage.

Premium—the payment (consideration), or one of the periodic payments, a policyowner agrees to make for an insurance policy.

Premium Deposit—the cash deposit paid by an individual with application for insurance protection. It is usually equal to or greater than the first month's estimated premium and is applied to the actual premium due at billing.

Premium Due Date—the date specified for the payment of a premium.

Premium Loan—a policy loan made for the purpose of paying premiums.

Premium Rate—the price per unit of insurance.

Premium Receipt—the company's official receipt given to a policyowner when the premium is paid.

Premium Reserves—state insurance laws prescribe that there must be reserved from a company's admitted assets a sum equal to the amount due to its policyowners.

Present Value—the amount of money that must be invested on a certain day in order to accumulate at a specified rate of interest a specified amount at a later date.

Primary Beneficiary—the person(s) who have first rights to receive the policy benefits when the benefits of the insurance policy become payable.

Primary Insurance Amount (PIA)—the amount a worker will receive under Social Security if he or she retires at full retirement age or becomes disabled. It is the amount on which all other Social Security income benefits are based.

Principal Sum—the amount specified under an accident policy as the death benefit.

Probate—the process of proving the validity of a will in court and carrying out its provisions under the guidance of the court.

Proceeds—the face value of the policy and any increments payable at maturity, on death, or on surrender, less any indebtedness.

Profit-Sharing Plan—a type of defined-contribution plan where the employer agrees to contribute part of the company's profits for the benefit of its employees. Typically, the contributions will be held in a trust fund for distribution at death, disability, or retirement.

Professionalism—a professional is a person engaged in a field that requires (1) specialized knowledge not generally understood by the public, (2) a threshold entrance exam requirement, (3) a sense of altruism, and (4) a code of ethics.

Proposed Insured—the person on whose life the insurance is being applied.

Propriety—appropriateness, correct appearance, proper image, suitability, correctness, or "fit," meeting the expectations of what the prospect considers proper business customs, dress, and behavior; looking the part, appearance, manners, protocol (greetings, shaking hands, recognition of prospect's status), appropriate speech.

Prospect—the potential buyer identified by the advisor.

Prospecting—the continuous activity of exploring for new people to meet and talk to about the products the advisor sells.

Provision—a statement in the policy describing a feature, benefit, requirement, or condition of the contract.

Pure Endowment—a contract that pays a benefit only to those people who survive for a certain period of time. Because the non-survivors receive nothing, this type of insurance is generally considered illegal unless combined with some form of life insurance.

Qualified Retirement Plans—retirement plans that are qualified under law to avoid or postpone taxes until such time as the beneficiary retires and begins to take benefits, generally in a lower tax bracket.

Qualifying Prospects—As we collect facts and feelings about key financial issues and situations throughout the entire sales/planning process, we learn what will move the prospect from a possible (eligible) buyer to a probable buyer to an eager buyer, what the prospect is likely to buy, and when and why he or she will buy it.

Quarters of Coverage—the basis for benefit eligibility under OASDI. Credit for up to for quarters may be earned in any calendar year, based on earnings that are indexed annually.

Rapport—people want to do business with people they feel understand them, with whom they share something in common, whom are competent, and whom they can believe and trust. Rapport is a relationship marked by harmony and accord, aided by the advisor's friendly, interested concern.

Rate—the charge per unit, usually in increments of $1,000 for life insurance and $100 for disability income insurance, used to determine insurance premiums.

Rated Policy—sometimes called an extra-risk or substandard policy, it is an insurance policy issued at a higher-than-standard premium rate to cover the extra risk when, for example, an insured has impaired health or engages in a hazardous occupation.

Readjustment Income Period—an amount closely equivalent to the family's share of the producer's earnings at the time of his or her death. The length of the financial readjustment period depends largely on the magnitude of the changes the family will have to make in living standards.

Rebating—an insurance sales practice prohibited in most of the United States. In rebating, the advisor offers the prospect a special inducement to purchase a policy, usually as a share of the advisor's commission.

Reduced Paid-up Insurance—a form of insurance available as a nonforfeiture option, providing for continuation of the original insurance plan, but for a reduced face amount as determined by the cash value in the policy.

Reentry Term—a form of renewable term life insurance under which one rate schedule is used if the insured can prove continued insurability at favorable rates, and a higher schedule if the insured cannot or will not provide continued insurability.

Referred Lead—a person who may be interested in the products the advisor sells who has been suggested as a prospect by a present policyowner.

Reinstatement—a lapsed life or health insurance policy that has been restored to its original premium-paying status. Usually it requires evidence of good health and payment of past-due premiums and interest.

Reinsurance—the process of a company placing with another company excess insurance sold beyond the dollar limit they are willing to carry as a risk on a single life. Companies may also go to a reinsuring company to share a percentage of the risk on a rated application they have received.

Reinsurer—the insurance company that accepts the risk transferred from another company in a reinsurance transaction. Also known as an assuming insurer.

Renewable Term Insurance—term insurance providing the right to renew at the end of the term for another term (or terms) without evidence of insurability. The premium rates normally increase at each renewal as the age of the insured increases.

Renewal Commissions—those commissions paid to an advisor for a certain number of years after the first year. It is paid only on policies that stay in force and is usually much lower than the first-year commission.

Renewals—a policy renews each time an annual premium is paid or completed. A renewal commission is that commission paid to the agent after the first policy year. A renewal premium is any premium due after the first policy year.

Replacement—the substitution of one insurance contract for another.

Representations—any statement made before, during, or after a sales interview that materially represents the policy or plan of insurance offered. From the applicant's side, it is any statement made to the best of the knowledge and belief of that person, so it does not have to be true.

Reserve—the money set aside by a company to fulfill future obligations.

Retention—the net amount of risk retained by an insurance company for its own account or that of specified others and not reinsured.

Revocable Beneficiary—the named beneficiary whose rights in a policy are subject to the policyowner's right to revoke or change the designation, surrender, or make loans against the cash value.

Rider—an additional provision added to a policy, usually at issue, and for additional premium, to enhance or modify the benefits. These riders include, among others, waiver-of-premium, AD&D, spouse insurance, children's insurance, and guaranteed insurability.

Risk—the person insured in the case of life insurance. More generally it is considered the chance of loss.

Risk Tolerance—the degree of a client's willingness or reluctance to accept the risk that his or her investment may decline in value and that the premium may increase over time.

Risk Classification—the process by which a company decides how its premium rates for life insurance should differ according to the risk characteristics of individuals insured (age, occupation, sex, state of health) and then applies the resulting rules to the individual applications it receives.

Rule of 72—a mathematical rule based on the number 72 that allows the calculation of a variety of factors regarding the value of money over time. For instance, dividing 72 by an assumed rate of inflation will determine the number of years it takes to reduce the value of a fixed amount of money to half its present value. (72 divided by an assumed inflation rate of 8 percent will halve the value of today's dollar in 9 years.) It is also commonly used to estimate the time it takes for a principal sum to double.

Salary Continuation—the employee's salary is continued at retirement, at death, or at disability, and the employee is not taxed on the income until it is received, similar to deferred compensation. Also refers to a sick-leave plan, an uninsured arrangement to replace lost income for a limited period of time, often starting on the first day of disability.

Salary Deduction—a method of paying individual insurance premiums by the employees of one employer. An agreement between the employee and the employer stipulates the amount deducted per pay period to pay the insurance premiums. The employer in turn signs a master contract with the insurer stating that all such premium payments by these employees will be forwarded to the company.

Section 79—a group term life insurance plan that qualifies for federal income tax treatment under the Internal Revenue Code. The employer can deduct premiums paid for employee coverage, and there is no taxation to the employee for amounts of group term life up to $50,000.

Section 1035 Exchange—exchanging an existing policy for a new one in accordance with the IRC guidelines of Section 1035. No gain is attributed on the exchange. The adjusted basis of the old policy is carried over to the new one. Only the newly added premium will be measured for MEC status. A section 1035 exchange is allowed only when transferring cash values from an annuity to an annuity, life insurance to life insurance, or life insurance to an annuity contract.

Self-Administration—the procedure wherein an employer maintains all records regarding the employees covered under a group insurance plan.

Self-Insurance—setting aside of funds by an individual or organization to meet his or its losses, and accumulation of a fund to absorb fluctuations in the amount of losses being charged against the funds set aside or accumulated.

Selling/Planning Process—the eight-step procedure for the advisor to follow from selecting the prospect to completing the sale and servicing the client. It is very similar to the financial planning process.

Separate Account—an asset account established by a life insurance company separate from other funds, used primarily for pension plans and variable life products. This arrangement permits wider latitude in the choice of investments, particularly in equities.

Service Fee—compensation paid to an agent equal to a small percentage of the premiums payable after the renewal commissions have expired. Sometimes called a persistency fee.

Settlement Options—the several ways outlined in a policy, other than by a lump sum payment in cash, by which a policyowner or beneficiary may choose to have the contract's benefits paid.

Simplified Employee Pension (SEP)—a qualified retirement plan in which an employer contributes money to an IRA for each employee covered by the plan. The employee owns the contract.

Simple Plan—a plan available to businesses with less than 100 employees who may elect salary reduction or to receive non-elective contributions. This type of plan cannot exceed $6,000 per year. If the employer chooses to match the contribution, the match is generally up to 3 percent of the employees' compensation. If the non-elective contribution formula is chosen, the employer may simply contribute 2 percent of each eligible employee's compensation. All contributions must be fully vested. Contributions are not subject to income tax, and are subject to penalties for early withdrawal.

Simultaneous Death Act—state laws hat provide that if the insured and primary beneficiary both die under circumstances in which it is impossible to determine that one predeceased the other, the insured will be presumed to have survived the primary beneficiary.

Single Interview Selling—A particular need may be so prominent and in need of immediate attention that the total needs assessment will be postponed. The prospect may be concerned about a single need and wish to address it, so only one interview may be required to complete the sale. This would be also true if the client does not wish to divulge personal information for a total needs analysis.

Single Premium—the amount that would constitute the full future premium on a contract, at its inception.

Social Security—a federal government program, taxed to working citizens, to provide financial security for the general citizenship of the United States.

Social Style—a characteristic way a person behaves and reacts in different situations. Psychologist Dr. David Merrill described the characteristics of four different social styles: Driver, Expressive, Amiable, and Analytical.

Spendthrift Clause—a provision protecting the beneficiary of an insurance policy from attachments of the proceeds by others (creditors) excepting the federal government.

Split-dollar Insurance—life insurance funded in an agreement between two parties, usually an employer and employee, who agree to share premium costs, death proceeds, and perhaps cash value.

Spouse Rider—special term insurance coverage added to a policy for the spouse of the primary insured.

Standard Risk—a person who qualifies through a company's underwriting standards and practices for insurance protection without extra rating or any special restrictions.

State Insurance Department—a department of a state government whose duty is to regulate the business of insurance and give the public information on insurance.

Stock Life Insurance Company—an insurance company organized and owned by stockholders, as distinguished from the mutual insurance company form of ownership by policyowners.

Straight Life Insurance—whole life insurance on which premiums are payable for life.

Substandard Risk—the person who because of health history or physical impairments does not meet the underwriting qualifications for the issue of a company's standard life or health insurance policy. The policy may be issued at extra risk, requiring an additional premium for each unit of coverage.

Suicide Clause—a standard disclaimer of life insurance policies providing that the death benefit of a policy will not be paid if the insured dies because of suicide, governed by the rules of the state. Most states restrict this to, at most, 2 years from date of issue. If suicide occurs after the legal date the full death benefit is paid by the company. If suicide occurs before the time limit expires, the company's liability is limited to a return of premiums paid.

Suitability—is the appropriateness or the proper fit of the characteristics of a product to the needs and goals of a prospect. Fact-finding will help determine the client's risk tolerance. Some clients will accept far more risk in their insurance portfolio than others. Determining needs, goals, risk tolerance, and time horizon provides the advisor with information necessary to make a product recommendation.

Supplemental Security Income (SSI)—a Federally administered income assistance program authorized by Title XVI of the Social Security Act. SSI provides monthly cash payments in accordance with uniform nationwide eligibility requirements to needy aged, blind, and disabled individuals. Most people receiving SSI are automatically eligible for Medicaid benefits. To qualify for SSI payments, an individual must meet specified maximum income and resource standards and also must satisfy the program criteria for age, blindness, or disability.

Supplementary Contract—an agreement between a life insurance company and a policyowner or beneficiary by which the company retains the cash sum payable under an insurance policy and makes payments in accordance with the settlement option chosen.

Surplus—the amount by which an insurance company's assets exceed its liabilities and capital.

Surrender Charge—the difference between cash surrender value of a policy and the reserve held by the company. The charge will be higher in the early years of a policy to cover costs arising from underwriting.

Surrender Cost Index—a representation of the annual cost per $1,000 of insurance if the policy is surrendered for its cash value.

Suspense—money that has been received by a company that, for any of a variety of reasons, has not yet been applied to the proper account.

Target Market—an identifiable and accessible group of people or businesses who's members communicate with each other and who have common characteristics and common needs that can be answered by the advisor's products and services.

Tax Credits—credits applied after the tax due has been calculated and are used to directly reduce the actual amount of tax payable, generally available for investments and production assets such as plants and manufacturing equipment, research, and historical preservation.

Tax Deferral—the postponement of the tax that otherwise would have been placed on the investment or its interest earnings. Generally, the tax is payable at a future date when the money is constructively received by the owner.

Tax Exemptions—income tax deductibility of the interest, fees, and expenses involved in making an investment.

TEFRA Corridor—the required difference between a universal life insurance policy's face amount and that policy's cash value. Required by law, the difference is a specified percentage that depends on the insured's age. When the policy's cash value intrudes on the TEFRA corridor, the policy is considered an investment rather than life insurance and the taxation rules change accordingly.

Tenancy-in-Common—the holding of property by two or more people in such a manner that each has an undivided interest which, upon the death of one, is passed by will or intestate succession to another. It does not pass automatically to the surviving tenants-in-common.

Ten-Day Free Look—a policy provision notifying purchasers of new insurance that they have 10 days after delivery to inspect the policy and, if not satisfied, return it to the agent or company for a full refund of all premiums paid.

Term Life Insurance—life insurance providing a death benefit for a limited period of time on the life of the insured and expiring without value after the stated period.

Third-party Administrator (TPA)—administration of a group insurance plan by some person or firm other than the insurer or the policyowner.

Third-party Endorsement—in this method of marketing individual insurance to groups, a life insurance company makes an agreement with an organization such as a trade association, professional group, club, or university, to sell individual insurance contracts to employees or members. The organization endorses the company's products, but the purchase is voluntary.

Time/Tension Model—looks at the interaction of interpersonal relationship and the accomplishment of a task. The ease/uneasiness at a personal level is called relationship tension, and the ability/inability to work on business is task tension. You can help the rapport-building process by doing what you can to reduce relationship tension.

Total Disability—a health condition that prevents an individual from performing all duties of his or her occupation or any occupation. Definitions differ between companies and Social Security on what constitutes total disability.

Total-Needs Approach—the process of dealing with all life values and needs at the same time when working with a prospect or client in the sale of life insurance.

Trial Close—you get a feel for how a person is thinking by making "little" or trial closes. Getting the prospect's feedback provides valuable information about what the prospect wants from and likes about the plan and eases the final request to buy by asking for many small decisions, rather than one momentous one.

Transactional Selling—the immediate sale is the focus. Transactional selling focuses on the product and fits the prospect to the product. It is based on the salesperson talking and persuading, and his or her sales and closing skills. It creates sales pressure and an adversarial environment.

Trustee—the person to whom the legal title to property is conveyed for the benefit of another.

Trust—an arrangement by which property is held by a person or corporation (the trustee) for the benefit of others (the beneficiaries). The person who establishes the trust (the grantor) gives the trustee title to the trust assets (the corpus) subject to the terms of the agreement. Trusts can be established during life (inter vivos) or at death by will (testamentary). They can be changeable (revocable) or unchangeable (irrevocable).

Twisting—inducing a policyowner to drop an existing policy (especially one with another company) in order to take a similar policy from the advisor doing the twisting. The act is usually defined as not being in the policyowner's best interest. It may involve fraud and misrepresentation.

Unbundled Insurance Product—an insurance product where the mortality, investment, and expense factors used to calculate premium rates and cash values can be separately identified within the policy. This was first seen with the introduction of the universal life contract.

Underwriter—the employee of an insurance company who evaluates and rates the risks. The assignment is to authorize the sale of coverage that will produce an average risk of loss within an anticipated class of business.

Underwriting—the process by which insurance companies analyze risks to decide if they want to insure them, and at what rates.

Unearned Premium—the part of the premium payment applicable to the unexpired part of the policy period, usually due to the policyowner if the policy is canceled.

Unilateral Contract—a life insurance contract is unilateral because the promise of only one party to the contract is required to make it legal. The insurance company promises to fulfill the contract obligation. The policyowner's obligation is to pay premiums. See also: *Contract of Indemnity*.

Uninsurable Risk—an individual not acceptable to the company to qualify for insurance due to excessive risk.

Universal Life Insurance—a type of permanent life insurance under which the policyowner is allowed to vary the timing and amount of premiums as well as the death benefit. Premiums (less expenses) are credited to the policy account (cash value) from which mortality charges are deducted and to which interest is credited at a varying future rate.

Validation Period—the amount of time that it takes for a life insurance policy to become profitable or to begin adding to the company's surplus.

Variable Life Insurance—a type of permanent life insurance in which the death benefit and the policy's cash value may vary in relation to the investment experience of the selected fund in which the cash value is invested.

Variable Universal Life—a type of life insurance policy that combines the premium flexibility and design features of universal life insurance and policyowner-directed investment choices of variable life insurance.

Vesting—a participant's ownership rights to benefits from employer's contribution to a plan and not contingent upon continued specific employment with the employer.

Voluntary Payroll Deduction—a plan offered to employees under which they may purchase life, health or property and liability insurance with premiums paid through payroll deduction. The employer does not share in the premium cost. These plans often offer liberalized guaranteed issue, discounts, or liberal simplified underwriting, depending on the size of the group.

Waiver (Exclusion Endorsement)—an agreement, attached to the policy and accepted by the insured, to eliminate a specified pre-existing physical condition or specified hazard from coverage under the policy.

Waiver of Premium Provision—a statement of provision in a life or health insurance policy that the policy will be kept in force by the insurer without payment of further premiums if the insured becomes permanently and totally disabled as defined in the policy.

War Clause—a clause in an insurance contract relieving the insurer of liability, or reducing its liability, for loss caused by war.

Whole Life Insurance—another name for ordinary life insurance referring to premium payment for the whole period of a person's life.

Will—a document prepared by an individual in which instructions are made for the disposition of the property of the estate at death.

Workers' Compensation—insurance against liability imposed on certain employers to pay benefits and furnish care to injured employees and to pay benefits to dependents of employees killed in the course of or arising out of their employment.

Answers to Questions

Chapter 1

Answers to Review Questions

1-1. Common needs for life insurance include family/survivor income for readjustment and supplementing other income sources; cash to pay specific needs such as final expenses, establish an emergency fund, pay mortgage and other debts, or to make charitable gifts or specific gifts to heirs or others; an accumulation vehicle for supplementing education, retirement, or other purposes; and a tax-advantaged vehicle to accumulate money.

1-2. Solomon Huebner defined human life value as the production potential of the individual over his life expectancy, a measure of the actual future earnings or service of an individual. It can be measured and re-created by the capitalized value of an individual's net future earnings, after subtracting self-maintenance costs. From the standpoint of dependents, an individual's human life value is the measure of the value of benefits that the dependents can rightfully expect from their breadwinner or supporter. Human life value for insurance and financial planning purposes is the present value (today's value) of a life-long stream of net economic contributions a person will make to his or her family or dependents.

1-3. The benefits of life insurance include providing time and money to a family in the case of death to continue their lifestyle, preserve peace of mind, provide living benefits in cash value policies, allow for emergency money and an accumulation vehicle that provides financial flexibility and a financial foundation, guarantee policy values and benefits, and ensure tax advantaged benefits.

1-4. As the size of the sample increases, the actual loss experience will more closely approximate the true underlying probability. The insurer's statistical group must be large enough to produce reliable results and to produce results that are consistent with the underlying probability. Risk pooling means people exposed to a risk agree to share losses on an equitable basis, transferring the risk of loss to an insurance company.

Insurance is based on pooling the premiums of thousands of people and spreading the risk of losses across the entire pool.

1-5. Every life insurance product must take into account these three factors: mortality, interest, and expense. The assumptions made concerning these three factors will determine the premium and structure of the policy. Mortality predicts the number and timing of deaths in a group, interest assumes the investment earnings on reserves, and expense projects the cost of doing business over time, as a block of business matures.

1-6. The 2001 CSO (Commissioners Standard Ordinary) mortality tables are being introduced and will replace tables from 1980. Mortality has improved significantly over the past 25 to 30 years, so life insurance rates and premiums should be lower. The tables extend to age 120 rather than the current age 100. Mortality tables measure when and how many people will die over time.

1-7. Life insurance is a legally enforceable contract, so the language and provisions of the contract are extremely important. Insurance contracts are regulated by the states, so provisions are different from state to state, but similar due to NAIC regulations and similar state laws. Under the contract, the policyowner buys the right to a certain sum of money to be paid to a named beneficiary in the event of death, or to the owner if living at the end of a certain number of years. The policy contract provisions control the operation of the policy. They provide benefits and rights to the policyowner, and protection and obligations by the insurer. What happens under the insurance policy is ultimately dictated by those provisions within the policy.

1-8. *entire contract*—the entire contract consists of the policy, a copy of the application, and any reports of the insured's physical condition. The policy cannot be arbitrarily changed by the company after it is issued. Everything that controls the contract is included in the policy.

incontestability—This clause limits the period of time in which the insurer can use the defense of fraud, concealment, or material misrepresentation to end a contract. After a policy has been in effect for a period of time prescribed by the incontestable clause (typically 2 years), the insurance company cannot have the policy declared invalid.

automatic premium loan—The APL provides that if a premium has not been paid at the end of the grace period, the company will automatically take enough money out of the cash value (if there is value there) to pay the amount due.

reinstatement—Reinstatement allows a policyowner to put into force coverage under a policy that has lapsed. Lapsed policies may be reinstated (within a certain time frame, typically 3 years) if they have not been surrendered for cash and when proper evidence of insurability has been accepted by the company. Back and current premiums must be paid, with interest.

assignment—Policyowners may assign the ownership of their policies to another person or institution by following company provisions for temporary or permanent transfer of ownership. Normally the policyowner must notify the company in writing of his or her intention to make an assignment.

nonforfeiture options—If a policy is terminated for any reason other than the insured's death, the nonforfeiture provisions allow the policyowner to receive the policy's cash value in one of three ways:

- *Cash Surrender.* The cash value may be received as a lump-sum payment or as income under one of the settlement options offered by the company.
- *Reduced Paid-up Insurance.* Under this option, the cash value is used as a single premium on a policy of the same kind as the one being surrendered, except that the face amount is reduced. While no further premium payments are made, the policy cash values continue to grow.
- *Extended Term Insurance.* The cash value may also be used to buy extended term insurance of an amount equal to the face amount of the original policy for as long a period as the premium can be paid by the cash value. When the term period expires, there is no more protection. The extended term option is usually automatic upon lapse.

policy loan—gives the policyowner the right to borrow a percentage of the cash value that has accumulated in the policy. If a policy is surrendered with a loan outstanding, and if that loan, with other cash value, is greater than the cumulative premium payments made, then there will be a taxable gain. The loans do not have to be repaid, and if they are not, interest is charged by the company. Unpaid interest is automatically added to the principal loan and can further reduce the cash value. If the insured dies and has an outstanding loan, the balance and any accrued interest will be deducted from the policy proceeds at settlement and the balance will be paid to the beneficiary.

1-9. a. Premiums paid for individual life insurance policies are usually considered a personal expense and are not deductible for income tax purposes. Premiums are deductible when: paid in an alimony agreement; paid for a policy owned by a charity and the charity is the beneficiary, as a charitable contribution. In business, premiums are paid as a bonus to the employee, as a business expense. Also, if life insurance is part of a pension plan, the premiums are deductible as part of a contribution by the employer to a tax-qualified plan.

b. Generally, death proceeds from a life insurance policy are exempt from income taxation when paid in a lump sum. If the deceased had any incidents of ownership in the policy, it would be included in the estate for estate tax calculations.

c. It must be determined if the amount received from the policy over the life of the contract is in excess of the net premiums paid. Net premiums paid means the gross premium less any dividends received, less any outstanding loans. This is the cost basis, meaning the amount the policyowner paid with after-tax money. The total net premium is then subtracted from the amount of cash the policyowner receives upon surrender or maturity. Any excess or profit is fully reportable as ordinary taxable income in the year received.

d. This gives the policyowner the right to borrow a percentage of the cash value that has accumulated in the policy. If a policy is surrendered with a loan outstanding, and if that loan, with other cash value, is greater than the cumulative premium payments made, then there will be a taxable gain. Loans are otherwise not taxed when taken. Interest paid is personal and not deductible.

e. The cash dividend is taxable only when and if it exceeds the amount of premiums paid into the policy. Dividends are generally taxed on a first-in, first-out (FIFO) basis; that is, withdrawals are treated as a nontaxable return of capital to the extent of premiums paid. Withdrawals in excess of premiums paid are taxable.

Answers to Self-Test Questions

1-1. D
1-2. C
1-3. C
1-4. D
1-5. B
1-6. A
1-7. A
1-8. A
1-9. D
1-10. D

Chapter 2

Answers to Review Questions

2-1. The five steps in the buying cycle are:

- Recognize the problem or need. The buyer must recognize that there is a problem, an unfulfilled need or want.
- Desire a solution. A buyer must have a strong desire to solve the recognized problem now.

- Decide on the best available choice. A buyer must believe that the solution proposed is the most appropriate one for solving the problem now.
- Make the purchase. A buyer must be able and willing to exchange money in order to solve the problem.
- Take delivery. The purchase is completed when it is received in hand.

2-2. The eight steps of the selling/planning process are:
- identify the prospect
- approach the prospect
- meet the prospect
- gather information and establish goals
- analyze the information
- develop and present the plan
- implement the plan
- service the plan

2-3. The Six Steps in Financial Planning—General Model are:
- establish financial goals
- gather relevant data
- analyze the data
- develop a plan to achieve goals
- implement the program
- monitor the program

2-4. Elements of a Comprehensive Financial Plan are:
- personal data
- client goals and objectives
- identification of issues and problems
- assumptions
- balance sheet/net worth
- cash-flow management (budget)
- income tax
- risk management/insurance
- Investments
- financial independence, retirement planning, education, and other special needs
- estate planning
- recommendations
- implementation

2-5. The five parts are:

- selling yourself (rapport)
- selling your expertise and service (competence)
- finding the want or need (problem)
- selling the benefit (solution)
- selling the product (close)

People buy from, and share their lives with people they trust, respect, and come to know as people. Yet so often we skip that part of the sales presentation and get right down to business, without first selling ourselves. Say as little as possible and get the prospect to talk about themselves. This will help the relationship develop, and will give you significant information that may be of value later in the sales process. The sale of one's competence requires self-confidence, education, and enthusiasm. We must communicate success and expertise as well as earn the industry credentials. For any consumer to buy, he or she must recognize that a problem exists; the prospect's real unfulfilled wants must be identified. You must be open-minded and pose questions designed to determine the prospect's real dreams and wants. The solution, the benefit and the product are not the same thing. Prospects do not care about or understand the product. What they want to know is if the purchase of the product will solve their problems and satisfy their wants. We must distinguish between product features (what it is) and product benefits (what it does). Clients identify with benefits, so we must sell the benefits.

2-6. Traditional or transactional selling is salesperson oriented, emphasizing product, presentation skills, closing techniques, and sales skills. Persuasion and salesperson talk dominate. Discovery occurs through objections rather than listening and fact-finding to develop prospect needs. Client-focused selling is client oriented with emphasis on listening, prospect talking, fact and feeling finding and discovery of prospect needs. Helping, trust and relationship are emphasized.

2-7. Total-needs selling means collecting and analyzing detailed information about a client's life situation. It includes "feeling-finding" as well as fact-finding information. Facts include the objective personal details of a person's life, whereas feeling finding involves the subjective attitudes, values and emotions that lay behind the facts and give them meaning.

2-8. The financial advisor has responsibilities: (1) to his or her clients, (2) to himself or herself and the insurance profession, (3) to the insurance carrier, and (4) to the public. These include being professional, honest, following the law, regulations, and procedures, determining suitability, maintaining confidentiality, pursuing education and doing your best for all parties.

The following questions pertain to the case study of Dr. Robinson.

2-9. Over time at medical appointments, Rob struck up small talk about the stock market and what he did for a living.

2-10. He used an analogy to the Doctor's work, helping people with their financial well being rather than their physical well being. He did not push or apply sales pressure.

2-11. Rob placed emphasis on fact-finding and relating his work to the doctor's profession. He stated that he could not make a recommendation without fact finding, just as the doctor could not diagnose without a medical history. He focused on rapport building, fact-finding, a total needs approach, and client needs. He was not product oriented, but relationship oriented. He emphasized helping rather than selling, and solutions rather than closing.

Answers to Self-Test Questions

2-1. C
2-2. B
2-3. B
2-4. D
2-5. A
2-6. D
2-7. B
2-8. C
2-9. A
2-10. A

Chapter 3

Answers to Review Questions

3-1.
- Create a sense of rapport and credibility, and build trust
- Uncover insurance and other financial needs and determine priorities
- Establish your ability to help
- Obtain the prospect's permission to proceed and commitment to work with you

- Build an ongoing relationship. People want to do business with people they feel understand them, with whom they share something in common, whom are competent, and whom they can believe and trust. Discuss problems common to people in the prospect's situation, such as survivor income, saving for college and retirement, and so on, to see how the prospect feels about these issues. Explain what you do, how you do it, and the scope of your business. Set yourself apart from the competition. You must obtain agreement on what you and your prospect will do together. Image, rapport, and trust are the major elements of the relationship you are trying to build with your prospects.

3-2. Some of the documents you should ask about include the following: life insurance policies on all members of the family; disability income and health insurance policies, all coverage from an employer—life, health, retirement, bank account statements, CDs, credit union accounts, brokerage account statements, mutual fund statements, a copy of the latest will and living will or health care directive, mortgage(s) statements with some explanation of the terms and status for each, trusts and any other legal instruments for managing money, pension and profit-sharing plan statements, IRA accounts, 401(k) or 403(b) statements, loans, pledges, notes, or other liabilities indicating money owed to others.

3-3. You must be prepared for your interviews. You need to have resource papers and forms neatly gathered in your briefcase. Fact-finders are valuable for working with prospects in developing their total needs. Plan each interview, including which sales aids you will use. Practice and master your interviews ahead of time to build your self-confidence and polish your performance. Before you meet, review your material and go over all the information you have about the prospect. Review your objectives. Collect sales literature and prospectuses that may be relevant. Plan an agenda. Know what outcome you expect from this meeting. Preparation is the key to success.

3-4. There are four important areas that a person uses to determine if they will trust an advisor and allow rapport to develop:
- propriety—appropriateness, correct appearance, proper image, meeting the expectations of what the prospect considers proper business customs, dress, and behavior; looking the part
- commonality—shared experience, having things in common, harmony, agreement, comfort level, camaraderie, companionship, comradeship, friendship, a good "gut" feeling
- competence—skillful, knows what he/she is doing, inspires confidence, experienced, capable, expert

- intent—involves the perception of one's motives, the prospect's perception of an advisor's interest in helping and benefiting the client

3-5. Benefits of the total needs approach to you:

- *Multiple needs*—more sales opportunities—Identify all of their goals and the ways to achieve them. This approach to will motivate your clients to coordinate all of their protection for their families' interests.
- Professionalism and ethics—If you do not discuss their total situations and solve all their needs, you will fall short of the prospects' expectations, and professional standards that we not leave someone inadequately protected. Sell adequate amounts of the right kinds of protection.
- *Higher closing ratios*—A thorough understanding of the situation gives you the leverage to close the sale. There should be a clear understanding of and agreement on goals when the decision to buy is requested. Thoroughness leads your prospect to a feeling of appreciation and positive regard toward you, for you take the time to care, to educate, to explain, and to support your prospect in making the right choices.
- *Better markets*—The best prospects are those people who have more complex financial situations and incomes in the higher brackets. Services should be tailored to the needs of markets that want and can afford the products you offer.
- *Persistency from selling a comprehensive plan*—People who buy a plan of insurance buy the concepts of the plan and recognize that the policies are only vehicles to achieve the protection they want. They tend to keep their coverage intact, to make premium payments on time, and are less likely to accept any recommendations from someone who does not understand their total needs.
- *Prospecting Boost*—Prospecting is easier. Referrals are stronger. You will get a better response from the referrals when asking for appointments.
- Inviting repeat sales—Your clients will not want to work with anyone else. You become their trusted adviser, rather than just someone who sells them insurance.
- *Pride and satisfaction*—You know you have done everything you could to help your clients, and this brings you satisfaction. You are a professional, doing what a professional is expected to do.

3-6. The benefits of the total needs approach to your prospects:

- *Client understands their needs*—Prospects understand the needs they want to fulfill. Everything will have to dovetail into their overall plan. They will have a better grasp of their total life value after you help them work through the details of a well-conceived program.
- *Work from a plan*—The number of issues to consider makes insurance planning complex. Add to this the changing circumstances in the prospect's life, and the

need for a plan is evident. The sale of insurance becomes easier when the insurance becomes part of the solution.

- *Professionally monitored and serviced*—The policyowner recognizes the planner not only as a salesperson, but also as a trusted and respected professional adviser. Your knowledge of the dreams and realities of a family's life will help you in the services you may be called upon to provide someday in the future.
- *Customized solutions*—the greatest benefit is the satisfaction the client feels knowing that the plan was professionally prepared and implemented, was custom made to his or her needs and goals, and can be referred to as a basis of an ongoing planning process.

3-7. Final expenses, mortgage liquidation, education expenses, dependency period income, readjustment period income, retirement income, dependent income, and estate liquidation.

3-8. People find it increasingly necessary to consider their total financial picture when buying life insurance. Now it usually takes more than one interview to make a sale. This is due to a total needs selling approach and a movement toward comprehensive financial planning. A particular need may be so prominent and in need of immediate attention that the total needs assessment will be postponed. The prospect may be concerned about a single need and wish to address it. Situations for this may include: to fulfill an obligation, such as a condition for a loan or a divorce decree, where the client must have life insurance immediately. This does not mean that this is the prospect's only need; only that it is prominent and requires immediate attention. Where the prospect cannot afford to take care of all life insurance needs at once, but are prepared to focus on one or two of the most pressing dominant needs. Help your prospects identify their total life insurance needs, set priorities for solving them, and acquire solutions for the ones at the top of the list. in specific needs selling, although there may be other needs, the prospect is only interested in addressing one primary concern.

3-9. *Complex situations*—First, the sales situation may be complex. There is more to do than can be accomplished in a single sitting. It takes time to explain your concept of service and the relationship you wish to have as a professional with your clients. *Prospect expectations*—The prospect may consider his or her personal situation rather sophisticated. Many people want to be treated in a sophisticated and thorough manner. *Not prepared*—On occasion, you will find that either you or the prospect is not prepared for the initial interview. *You need help*—You may be new to the business, or uncover a situation where you are in need of help. In this type of case, you need to take information back to your office in order to do a case analysis and gather more information and advice.

3-10. As an expert in the products you sell, you should have confidence in your recommendations. You should have confidence in your clients. They need us as much as we need them. If we are providing a service, solving a problem, and establishing rapport, then we can develop confidence in what we do. Satisfied clients return to the advisor who helps them and services them. This means repeat business from clients.

3-11. Problems for prospects include the cost of waiting (higher premiums and lower cash values, negative insurability changes, increasing costs of insurance. Benefits include the ability to cover the costs of debts, final expenses, getting a plan started for future needs, tax-deferred growth, good current insurability and lower premiums than waiting.

3-12. The advisor focused on the cost of waiting. He asked the prospect to envision responsibilities 15 years into the future. Starting now will save a lot of time and avoid the risk of becoming uninsurable.

Answers to Self-Test Questions

3-1. A
3-2. A
3-3. B
3-4. C
3-5. C
3-6. D
3-7. C
3-8. B
3-9. D
3-10. A

Chapter 4

Answers to Review Questions

4-1. Objectives of the Information Gathering Interview include

- Gather relevant factual and objective information about the client's current situation, including important personal and employment information, assets and liabilities, financial information, and other related data.
- Gather subjective data, including important values, feelings, and attitudes toward financial issues. Most important here is determining client goals, objectives, and

needs, including prioritizing goals in terms of importance and completion target date(s). Risk tolerance, the client's attitude toward risk, and the expectations of the client for the results of the process are also important.

- Gain a dollar commitment, how much the client is willing and able to spend toward the accomplishment of the identified goals.

4-2. *Questioning and Listening*—Effective information gathering requires active listening and posing relevant questions. Demonstrate your genuine interest in the prospect's responses by giving feedback. Clarify your understanding of the prospect's experiences, behavior, and feelings by rephrasing, summarizing, and asking clarifying questions.

Motivating—Your success depends on your ability to establish rapport and to conduct interviews that help the buyer to identify, understand, and want to satisfy his or her needs. Questions can be designed to motivate the prospect into thinking about and acting on his or her needs.

Note-taking—When you record information, you want to get as much down on paper as possible without missing anything important.

Summarizing and Proposing—Briefly review and summarize the prospect's goals and priorities. These initial results will be developed in the analysis step into a discovery agreement. A discovery agreement is a written or verbal acknowledgment of the facts, feelings, values, and attitudes uncovered in the process. It states the prospect's present situation, what they want to accomplish financially, and the commitment to work together to achieve these objectives. Get a dollar commitment. You cannot make a sale unless the prospect agrees to spend money. Your ability to design a plan based on the prospect's needs and goals depends on knowing what the prospect is able and willing to commit to the solution. If appropriate, schedule a follow-up meeting.

4-3. For the advisor the sales process will be on a much firmer footing, because the prospect will become confident in the advisor thorough fact-finder process. Rapport improves as personal information is shared. The ultimate planning and solutions should be more customized and responsive to the prospect's situation, and thus more effective and more readily accepted. For the prospect, a thorough fact finder provides a professional analysis of his or her situation and solutions that should be effective and appropriate to his or her situation.

4-4. Prospects for life insurance are people who need protection from loss of life, can afford to pay the premiums for the protection, can be approached by you, and are insurable. But qualifying the prospect is not an event. It is not something that happens and then is done and the prospect is qualified forever. Instead, it is a process that starts at the first contact in the prospecting stage and continues through the delivery of the policy, and even beyond into the servicing stage as your prospect becomes a prospect for another product or service.

4-5. Communication always has a purpose: to understand the other person and to help them act in ways that are beneficial to them. Whatever your purpose, you should have a clear idea of why you are saying and doing the things you say and do—a desired objective or outcome. The first principle of effective communication is to have a goal. Relationship building is based on good and effective communication. It is the basis for increasing the trust and rapport necessary to gain the confidence of prospects. You will usually find that the best way to understand your prospect is to ask relevant questions. The need for empathy is critical. Demonstrating your understanding of the client's needs, goals, and values is the basis for establishing rapport and trust in the developing relationship. Qualities that contribute to building rapport include a friendly and interested concern; an unhurried, leisurely pace; an accepting and non-judgmental attitude; attentive, active listening; genuineness; and an equal and open relationship.

4-6. Nonverbal behavior is that aspect of communication other than words themselves. It has two main sources, the body and the voice. It is expressed through body position and movement, gestures, facial expressions, eye contact, voice pitch and voice tone. Most sociological research claims that non-verbal channels communicate about two-third of the total message, especially where emotions are concerned. You must recognize signals from your prospect and understand what they mean. All impressions of meaning and the significance of any body language must be checked out against other clues given by the client. Do not assume that you know what a given behavior means. Ask your prospect to explain. It is better to ask rather than make assumptions.

4-7. Active listening introduces a psychological involvement into listening or attending to others. It adds personal involvement in the message, putting the nonverbal behavior, the voice, the words, and the meaning of the message together. An active listener is an understanding listener, one who attempts to see the world from the other person's frame of reference. Active listening means involving yourself in the inner world of another person, while, at the same time, maintaining your own identity and being able to respond meaningfully to the messages of that other person. Attentive listening involves being alert, perceptive and creative in searching out what your prospects feel or think about their needs and desires. Ask good questions, then wait for an answer. Give feedback. Check for experiences, behaviors, and feelings. Use your own examples to clarify if necessary. Take a break and change your tack if you detect the prospect losing interest. Check nonverbal clues. Ask yourself what the prospect really means.

4-8. Open-ended questions allow the prospect to answer with something other than a simple yes or no. They elicit thinking and explanations from the prospect. Open-ended questions solicit opinions, thoughts, ideas, values, and feelings. Closed-ended questions limit the prospect to a specific, narrow response, often "yes" or "no," or short, factual answers. Combining an open-ended question occasionally with a closed-ended question can help you direct the interview and keep the prospect from lingering on one topic. By moving back and forth between closed-ended and open-ended questions, you can collect the facts and the feelings behind them. This keeps the information moving, it is more interesting for both parties, and you get a much fuller and meaningful understanding of the prospect's situation. One effective technique is to rephrase what the prospect said, and then ask if what you said is correct. Motivating questions are designed to make the prospect think about situations that need fixing. They uncover problems that the prospect must think about and act on.

4-9. A discovery agreement is a written or verbal acknowledgment of the facts, feelings, values, and attitudes uncovered in the sales/planning process to this point. It states the prospect's present situation, what they want to accomplish financially, and the commitment to work together to achieve these objectives. It confirms that you and the prospect understand his or her problems. This serves as a basis for proceeding forward to the next steps of the process. This process helps clarify the advisor/client relationship and the commitment necessary to complete the planning process. It helps the advisor and prospect come to a mutual understanding of the current situation and what the client wants to accomplish.

4-10. Insurance planning is the process of examining all of the client's needs, comparing needs with means, and selling, where appropriate, the types of policies and the amounts of insurance that best suit the client's purposes. Estate planning is the process of examining all the goals of the client regarding fulfilling their wishes upon their death. It encompasses the accumulation, conservation, and distribution of an estate and involves their financial desires in the context of their personal desires. Financial planning is the process of examining all the client's goals and objectives, doing a comprehensive analysis of all present aspects of the client's financial position (insurance, investments, savings, pending inheritances, and so on), assessing appropriate risk levels for investments, and planning redistribution and acquisition of assets to fulfill those needs and objectives. Retirement planning involves determining the desired amount of money one needs to accumulate to retire. Key issues in retirement are the amount of income needed, the age at which one can retire, the age at which one wants to retire, and the number of years until that retirement date.

4-11. The $100,000 life insurance policy of today may be only worth $60,000 10 years from now in terms of buying power because of inflation. To apply the Rule of 72 to inflation, divide 72 by an assumed rate of inflation to determine the number of years it takes to reduce a life insurance program to 50 percent of its current value. The Rule of 72 is a handy mathematical rule which helps to estimate approximately how many years it may take for the life insurance policy, due to inflation, to cut its buying power in half at a particular rate of inflation. For example, if a policyowner has an $80,000 policy and the rate of inflation is expected to average 8 percent, by dividing 72 by 8 (72 divided by 8 = 9), it can be determined that the $80,000 will be worth half, or $40,000, in 9 years. Conversely, the policyowner needs $160,000 of life insurance today to have the equivalent of $80,000 9 years from now.

Answers to Self-Test Questions

4-1. A
4-2. D
4-3. A
4-4. B
4-5. C
4-6. C
4-7. A
4-8. B
4-9. B
4-10. D

Chapter 5

Answers to Review Questions

5-1. After a data-gathering interview you will need to review and determine the prospect's situation in terms of their desires, concerns, objectives, needs, and priorities? Where is the prospect now in relation to established goals? How is the prospect's situation likely to change in the future? How far will existing life insurance and other benefit sources go toward meeting those needs? What additional life insurance or other recommendations are needed to make up the shortfall or to complete the plan? What possible product solution(s) may fit in this situation? How much can the prospect reasonably expect to pay for the protection? What objections can you anticipate? Who are the decision-makers in this sale?

5-2. Consider possible product solutions that may apply to this prospect's situation. A final decision of a product or products should not take place until the completion of your complete analysis. Make some initial "ballpark-type" generalizations to consider what may help the prospect. The best policy is the policy that most effectively meets your client's needs, and will be there when it is needed. Review the fact-gathering interview, the budget commitment and the financial and personal information about your prospect. Can the prospect reasonably afford the premium for the products you may propose? Is the product suitable for the prospect, based on the facts and feelings you have collected?

5-3. The cash needs analysis determines the amount of funding that would have to be set aside to pay for expenses the deceased would otherwise have paid. Cash needs at death include final expenses such as funeral, burial, or cremation; estate taxes; probate expenses; attorney fees; unpaid cost of a last illness; and operating expenses for the survivors' household. An emergency fund and a child-care and educational fund can also be provided. The income needs analysis determines the needs for income for survivors, and sources of income available to fund that need. If there is a shortfall of income, this method determines the amount of life insurance needed to cover the shortfall, using a capital conservation or capital distribution method. This, together with the cash needs analysis, will provide the funding for the lifestyle that the survivors will have in the future. Survivors' income needs include readjustment income, dependency period income, and income for the surviving spouse during the blackout period and for the remainder of life.

5-4. The capital needs analysis method

- identifies the needs a family would want to satisfy when death stops part or all of a family income
- estimates the funds necessary to cover the identified needs
- identifies existing sources of funds available to cover those needs
- subtracts those existing resources from the total needs
- creates a capital sum through life insurance to produce enough income the meet the identified needs of the family after a breadwinner's death

5-5. The capital distribution method uses both principal and interest to provide income for a certain period of time into the future, at which point the total capital is spent. This is also known as the liquidating approach, since all funds are distributed over time. Since the principal is used as income, this method requires a smaller amount of initial principal to provide the desired income than in the capital conservation method. The shortcoming of this method is that the entire capital sum may be consumed. This may be unacceptable if the income is expected to last for the lifetime of a designated beneficiary. This method would leave no room for contingencies, adjustment for inflation, or for any balance of principal to be passed on to other beneficiaries.

The capital conservation method preserves, rather than spends, capital. This method uses only interest generated from an investment to provide the desired income, thus, is also referred to as the non-liquidating or capital retention method. Capital is not invaded, so there is an investment amount that basically does not vary, if invested conservatively. The goal is to produce an after-tax income from the interest to meet the beneficiary's need. The principal remains intact to be used as a hedge against inflation or other contingencies, or to be passed on to the beneficiary's heirs.

5-6. Employee benefit plans may be contributory or noncontributory, have probationary periods, require full-time employment status, and generally not require evidence of insurability. Major types of plan benefits include group term life insurance, voluntary payroll deduction plans, accidental death and dismemberment, short-term and long-term disability, long-term care, medical expense and dental expense programs. Medical expense plans may come in the form of traditional major medical or Blue Cross/Blue Shield plans, or the managed care options of HMO, PPO, and POS organizations. Additional programs include employee stock ownership, salary continuation, deferred compensation, and cafeteria plans.

5-7. Employer-sponsored retirement plans typically make up a major part of an employee's retirement plan. Qualified retirement plans are employer-sponsored plans that meet federal tax regulations to qualify for tax-deductible contributions and tax-deferred growth. Under a defined-benefit plan, retirement benefits are determined by a formula. A contribution is calculated requiring annual deposits based on the benefits promised and the number of years in the accumulation period. Under defined-contribution plans, annual contributions are determined by a contribution formula applied to an employee's earnings. The future benefits paid to a participant depend on the size of the contributions made and the length of service under the plan. Defined-contribution plans make no guarantees about the size of the participant's monthly pension benefit, but will accumulate based on the contribution amount and earning on those deposits. In a profit sharing plan, the employer agrees to contribute part of the company's profits for the benefit of its employees. In a 401(k) plan, employees contribute to their own retirement accounts with before-tax dollars. The use of tax-deferred salary can lower an employee's current income tax, allowing employees to shelter part of their income and accumulate earnings tax-deferred until retirement. In some 401(k) plans, the employer also contributes to the employee's fund, thus significantly increasing the amount saved. 403(b) plans can only be sold to nonprofit 501(c)(3) organizations such as tax-exempt organizations and schools. SIMPLE and SEP plans are also available, primarily to small employers.

5-8. There are four major categories of benefits paid for through Social Security taxes: survivor, retirement, disability, and family benefits. In addition to a $255 lump-sum death benefit, eligible family members of a fully or currently insured worker receive income benefits. Surviving spouses receive income benefits if caring for children of the deceased worker under age 16 or disabled (before age 22). Each dependent, unmarried child under age 18, or age 19 if a student in elementary or secondary school, receives a monthly benefit. Disabled children of any age are eligible for benefits if disabled before age 22. The period between the last child's benefit and retirement eligibility for the surviving spouse is called the blackout period because no benefits are paid before age 60 to a widow or widower if there are no qualifying children. Benefits are reduced if taken prior to full retirement age. An ex-spouse could be eligible for widow(er)'s benefit if the marriage lasted at least 10 years. Also eligible is a parent age 62 or over that was a dependent of a deceased, fully insured worker. A worker who is fully insured under Social security is eligible to receive monthly retirement benefits as early as age 62. The amount of reduced benefit depends on how soon the worker retires before age 65 and ranges in months beginning with a 20-percent reduction at age 62. Full retirement benefits are payable when a participant attains full retirement age. A disabled worker under age 65, and dependent family members, may qualify for benefits if the worker is disability insured and is unable to engage in a substantially gainful activity, the disability must be expected to result in death or to last for at least 12 months. The waiting period for application is 5 months.

5-9. There are no benefits for the following personal and family needs from the income coverage offered through Social Security. Only a $255 maximum payment for final expenses to the insured. No payment for other family members who do not meet employment qualifications; No funds for emergency cash needs; No mortgage or rent protection for the family's home; No higher education funds for children or the surviving spouse; No income payments to the surviving spouse after children have reached the Social Security maximum age during the blackout period; No coverage for family members who may die or become disabled. Limited qualification restrictions for the insured.

5-10. The monthly benefit is determined by a worker's primary insurance amount (PIA). It is determined by the amount of contribution a worker makes through Social Security withholding taxes. In 2004, the average PIA for a retired worker is $922. A worker who has continually earned the maximum income subject to Social Security taxes can expect to have a PIA for retirement purposes of $1,825 if he or she retires at age 65 and 4 months in 2004. The maximum PIA in 2004 for purposes of disability and survivors benefits ranges from approximately $1,825 to $2,100. The higher PIA results for workers who are disabled or who die at younger ages. When a worker is fully insured and delays receipt of benefit payment after full retirement age because of continuation of work, the worker will receive special credit as a percentage added to benefits. It will vary depending on the worker's date of birth.

Dependent and survivor benefits as well as retirement and disability benefits for members of the insured worker's family are all figured as a percentage of the worker's PIA. The total amount is limited by the maximum family benefit for the worker's PIA eligibility.

Answers to Self-Test Questions

5-1. C
5-2. C
5-3. A
5-4. B
5-5. C
5-6. B
5-7. C
5-8. B
5-9. A
5-10. D

Chapter 6

Answers to Review Questions

6-1. Creating a solution to meet the prospect's needs depends heavily on the quality of the information gathered during the fact-finding process. The solution must be based on the prospect's circumstances and preferences. Thus, the importance of a thorough fact finder cannot be overemphasized. Plan design is a balancing act between the prioritized coverage needs of the prospect and his or her premium commitment. In preparing your recommendations, review the prospect's key issues discovered in the fact-finding.

Begin with the basic coverage design, creating an "ideal plan." Then adjust the plan to create an optimal solution that will best meet his or her priorities within the specific premium commitment. You should prepare a few alternatives in order to give the prospect choices based on the features and benefits of each option. Limit your choices to just a few so that you do not confuse the prospect. You can always customize further by using a few basic designs and illustrations as a starting point and introducing modifications (within cost parameters) by adding or subtracting certain features and benefits.

6-2. The key to an effective presentation is preparation. Take the time to prepare and put together a standardized sales presentation. You may organize it in a binder or portfolio if this is your style. Like in cooking, presentation is everything. The appearance and organization of your materials will go a long way toward the acceptance of your presentation. Do the following: Analyze your prospect. Create a summary of the fact-finding interview. Check your suggested plan alternatives. Collect any company-approved sales material you will use. Create policy illustrations for your recommendations. Put together any written proposals. Confirm the appointment time and location with the prospect.

6-3. There are two main components to every presentation. The first is to reestablish the prospect's need for life insurance; the second is to present possible solutions. Review the facts and planning assumptions. List the prospect's objectives. Outline the expected need for life insurance. Summarize the prospect's current plan. In presenting options, summarize your observations, make your recommendations, and outline the implementation plan. Stress the difference between product features, advantages, and benefits. Features are characteristics of the product itself—what it is. Features are descriptive, and are not given values. Advantages are what the product does, how it works. A benefit is what the prospect gets as a result of the feature and advantage. It is what the product does for the prospect and why he or she wants it. Benefits are value-laden and subjective. They are features that are wanted by that individual. When presenting a recommendation, you want to explain what it is, how it solves the problem, and what it does for the prospect. It is important to have the prospect's participation and involvement in the sales process. Insist on all decision-makers being present. Be alert for buying signals.

6-4. Despite recent product development, there are still only two basic types of individual life insurance on the market: permanent insurance and term insurance. They both provide protection that, once purchased and accepted, can only be canceled at the policyowner's option. Permanent insurance is intended to be for life; term is designed to provide protection for specific periods of time. Most permanent policies provide guaranteed cash value accumulation and nonforfeiture benefits that represent the policyowner's equity in the policy. With term, there is normally no cash value buildup. The insured is buying "pure" life insurance protection for a stated time. While premiums for permanent insurance are initially higher than they are for the same amount of term coverage, permanent premiums usually remain level, while term premiums generally increase as the insured ages. Term premiums can be higher in the later years than permanent premiums. The distinction between the two types of insurance can be summed up by analogy; owning a permanent policy is like buying a house; owning a term policy is like renting. By owning you build up equity in the home. With renting, you have no equity.

6-5. Term insurance policies provide a death benefit if death occurs during the period of time that the policy is in force. The policy period in term life insurance is expressed as a number of years (such as 1, 5 or 30) or until a certain age of the insured (such as 65 or 70). If the insured dies during the policy period, the specified amount (the face amount of the policy) will be paid to the designated recipient (beneficiary). If the insured survives until the end of the policy period, or term, the insurance company pays no benefit and the coverage ends. Term insurance is tied directly to the cost of mortality, which increases as the individual grows older. The premium is initially relatively low and increases periodically in most types of term insurance to reflect the increased mortality of the insured. The older a person is, and the longer the period of coverage, the higher the premium and mortality costs will be.

Level Term—The premium is averaged over the years to achieve a level rate. The premium remains level but builds up a reserve in the earlier, low mortality years to offset the higher mortality risk in the later years of the term.

Decreasing Term—The premium is level, but the face amount decreases over the policy period. While the premium is level, it is generally higher than for the same initial amount for level or annual renewable term insurance.

Reentry Term—This is a yearly renewable and convertible level death benefit term product. Periodically (every fourth, fifth, or tenth year, for example) the policy renews and the premium is subject to two schedules. The insured is allowed to reapply at company expense for a lower rate, subject to new evidence of insurability. Thus, the insured may be eligible for a new "select" rate at a substantially reduced premium. If the insured does not submit evidence of insurability, or does not meet the underwriting requirements for the lower rates, the existing policy is continued at the higher "ultimate" rates guaranteed in the contract.

6-6. A permanent life insurance policy is property in much the same way a stock certificate or bond is property. Rights of control or disposition are ownership rights, and ownership rights are what constitute property. The ownership rights provided by traditional permanent life insurance illustrate why a policy is valuable property. If a person has a long-term need for insurance, permanent insurance guarantees coverage for the rest of life at a predictable cost. If their estate is large enough to create an estate tax bill, heirs can use the death benefit to pay the IRS or other final expenses, providing estate liquidity. If a person wishes to leave a legacy to grandchildren or a charity, permanent insurance can provide a guarantee for accomplishing this. Providing a lifetime income to a surviving spouse can also be guaranteed.

In the early years of a permanent policy the premiums exceed the amount necessary to provide the face amount of protection. A cash reserve is accumulated to offset the increasing cost of protection in later years, and to pay other future obligations of the insurer. These cash values are available to the policyowner to borrow, or may be left to accumulate for future needs such as retirement. At any time the policyowner may surrender the policy for the cash value, or may borrow against it at an interest rate stated in the policy. If a policyowner should stop paying premiums, he or she has options. The policy may pay the unpaid premiums from its cash values by automatic premium loan provision. The policy may also be annuitized to produce an income. This is one of several settlement options, which is another way to continue the values in the policy, either during the life or at the death of the insured.

If the insured becomes disabled, the disability waiver-of-premium rider should pay the premium. For this reason, permanent life insurance is referred to as self-completing. The policyowner may convert the policy to a paid-up policy at a reduced face amount or continue the policy at the same original face amount as extended term coverage. The policyowner could also surrender the policy for its accumulated cash value. These options give the permanent insurance contract a degree of flexibility unavailable in any other financial vehicle a person might own. Policyowners may borrow accumulated cash values from the contract. The amount that may be borrowed at any time is stipulated by contract. Permanent insurance can also be used as collateral to back a loan.

6-7.

- *Ordinary life* provides level death benefit protection for a level premium. Premiums are paid to age 100, and the policy builds guaranteed cash values, which equal the face amount at age 100. At that time, if the insured is alive and has paid all the premiums, the policy will mature. The cash value will equal the face value of the original policy and will be paid to the policyowner. Ordinary life offers the most permanent protection for the least premium.
- *Limited pay life* policies are designed for people who need permanent protection but who want accelerated cash accumulation, or who prefer not to pay premiums to age 100. With limited pay plans, insurance protection extends to age 100, when the policy endows as it would with ordinary life. The differences are that the premium payments stop before age 100, resulting in higher premiums and cash values that build up at a faster rate. Generally, the shorter the premium payment period, the higher the premium and the faster the cash value accumulation. Single premium whole life is the ultimate limited pay plan. The entire premium for the policy is paid in a lump sum at issue

- *Modified life premiums* for the first several years are lower than they would be for the same amount of ordinary life (and higher than for comparable term insurance). After the initial period that can be almost any number of years, the premiums increase to a level higher than ordinary life would have been at the issue age but less than the premium would be at the attained age.
- *Graded-premium life* operates like modified life. Instead of having only two premium levels (an entry-level and ultimate level), however, graded-premium life usually has a series of increasing premium levels over 5, 10, or 20 years. At the end of the period of graded premiums, the policyowner pays the ultimate, level premium amount until age 100.
- *Adjustable life* insurance contains all of the same guarantees regarding cash values, mortality and expenses as traditional cash value insurance, but has the flexibility to allow the policyowner to adjust the plan of insurance, the premiums, and/or the face amount after it is in force. Adjustable life can be configured anywhere along the spectrum from short-duration term insurance through single premium whole life insurance. The policyowner can request a reconfiguration of the policy at specified intervals.

6-8.

- *Universal life* combines the features of renewable term insurance with a tax-deferred cash value account that earns competitive current interest rates. Policyowners can pay premiums on a flexible, nonscheduled basis. The current interest rate is applied to all premium deposits in the cash value account. The policy is designed as back-end loaded, meaning there are surrender charges during the first 10 to 15 years that are intended to recover company acquisition costs through charges to policies surrendered or lapsed during the earlier years. The policyowner can increase or decrease the amount of death benefit protection under the policy at any time within company and IRS rules. Two other features initiated with universal life policies are the policyowner's ability to withdrawal part of the cash and not be treated as a loan, and the choice of either a level death benefit design or an increasing death benefit design.
- *Current assumption whole life* is a variation of whole life that lies somewhere between adjustable life and universal life. It uses current mortality and interest earnings based on current yields rather than overall investment portfolio yields. In all other respects, it is identical to whole life, having many of the guarantees found in traditional whole life. There is a guaranteed death benefit and a minimum guaranteed interest rate to be credited on policy cash values. When mortality and expense charges are guaranteed, the policy is often referred to as interest-sensitive whole life, because excess interest (credited interest minus guaranteed interest) credited to the cash value becomes the only non-guaranteed element in the contract. Because many of these designs periodically reformulate the premium based on

recent experience, some of these policies are referred to as indeterminate premium whole life. There is a guaranteed maximum possible premium that could be charged, but actual mortality, interest, and expense result in lower premiums as a result of favorable experience in the policy.

- *Variable life* offers a combination of permanent life insurance protection and the growth potential of variable fund investments. The policy's cash value is invested in separate account funds of equities, money markets, and bonds. The policyowner decides in which separate account to invest the money (cash value) and may transfer funds from one fund to another. The policyowner chooses among the offered funds, but has no control over the assets purchased and sold within the individual funds. The policy guarantees a minimum death benefit, but the actual death benefit paid may be much higher if the investments perform well. The investment risk of the policy is shifted from the company to the policyowners. The cash values are not guaranteed and fluctuate daily with investment performance. Advisors who sell variable life insurance policies must be licensed as both life insurance agents and securities agents.
- *Variable universal life (VUL)* combines the investment features of variable life and the premium flexibility and adjustment features of universal life products. Most all of the features of those two products are combined into variable universal life. There are no interest rate or cash value guarantees in this policy.

6-9. Emphasis has been placed on proper formats of illustrations and a clear distinction of what is guaranteed in the contract and what is not. As a result of the NAIC Life Insurance Illustrations Model Regulations, insurers and state insurance departments require a full illustration, including all footnotes and explanation pages, of a product purchased by an individual to be signed by the prospect.

Policy illustrations are based on a variety of assumptions that may or may not occur in the future. The full explanation of the illustration is especially important when focusing on the projected cash values, dividends or interest accumulations in the future. Advisors must be able to explain to their clients how changes in interest rates, investment gains, mortality experience, cost of insurance, persistency, and expenses can affect the future performance of a life insurance policy and the policy illustration. For example, in looking at mortality assumptions, a company may use recent mortality experience, or assume mortality improvements in the future. Looking at interest, the policy illustration may assume that investment experience will improve, or use rates from an index not actually tied to company results. Some companies assume that lapse rates will improve, or take some other assumption that may be unrealistic, yet impact the illustration in most favorable ways.

6-10. The NAIC developed a Model Regulation to give consumers a way to compare the relative costs of different policies and to improve the quality of the cost information provided to consumers. The policy summary that you are required to deliver to your client must contain two cost indexes for the issued policy. In determining the cost of the life insurance, these indexes reflect the time value of money (interest), recognizing that money paid and received at different points in time has different values. The Model Regulation also endorses the use of a 5-percent interest rate, so that the cost of different policies can be better compared by using a specified interest assumption.

The net payment index represents the annual cost per $1,000 of insurance, adjusted for interest, if the policy remains in force over a given period of time. It considers the amount of premiums paid, less dividends received, if any, but disregards the cash value. This index is useful in comparing costs when death benefit protection is emphasized.

The surrender cost index represents the annual cost per $1,000 of insurance, adjusted for interest, if the policy is surrendered for its cash value. Unlike the net payment index, this index takes the cash value into consideration. It is most useful in comparing costs when cash accumulation is of primary interest. Policies whose net payment and surrender costs indexes are lower are generally better buys. Policies with higher index figures are probably less favorable buys, all other things being equal.

Answers to Self-Test Questions

6-1. B
6-2. D
6-3. C
6-4. A
6-5. D
6-6. C
6-7. A
6-8. B
6-9. A
6-10. A

Chapter 7

Answers to Review Questions

7-1. In preparing for the closing interview, you should review the information gathered previously and highlight key areas. Refresh your memory on the details discussed so that you are familiar with the client's information. Review your recommendations and the reasoning behind the solutions you have designed. Analyze the alternative plans you may have prepared, and be ready to discuss the benefits and drawbacks of each. Mentally walk through the presentation, anticipating objections, concerns, and points of resistance that the client may present. Be sure you have any presentation materials ready to go. Check your briefcase to be sure all application materials are in adequate supply.

Review with the client their needs, concerns, and objectives. Reconfirm the dollar commitment. You have presented or will present a solution and possibly alternative solutions. Present a summary that reviews all of the relevant features and the benefits.

You can now ask an open-ended question, such as "Where do we go from here?" "How would you like to proceed?" or "What's our next step?" You can also be more direct with a closed-ended question, such as "Would you like to start this plan today?" or "Is there any reason why you would not want to get this started?" Closing is seeking agreement that the solution proposed is a proper and acceptable plan to address the need or needs uncovered in the process.

Watch your client's interest level and buying signals. If the client is acting and speaking in ways that indicate they are ready to buy, stop talking and confirm the sale. Observe nonverbal cues. Stop occasionally during your presentation to elicit questions from your prospect, or to ask a few questions yourself. By getting prospects to say yes at several points during the interview, it will be easier for them to say yes again when it comes to signing the application and writing a check to bind the application. Watch for buying signals, signs that your prospects will make when it is time for you to take action.

7-2.
- *No Need*—is often expressed by people who truly believe they do not need the protection offered by life insurance. People who claim they have no need, but do, should be shown that they do have a need. By illustrating the risks associated with their present situations, you can shake prospects out of their complacency.
- *No Trust*—may refer to you, your agency, your product, or to life insurance in general. You are asking the prospect to make a major financial commitment based on your recommendations. A lack of trust on the prospect's part is a serious matter that can stop the sale if it is not addressed.
- *No Hurry*—The prospect may agree that the insurance is needed, but wants to wait to put the protection in force. It is often evidence of procrastination, associated with a fear of making the wrong decision.
- *No Money*—If people waited until they had plenty of money to spare, no one would buy life insurance. In dealing with this objection it is important to determine if the

person is objecting to buying the plan or really cannot afford the premium you have quoted.

7-3. The first step in answering an objection is to listen to the prospect. Listening to what the prospect has to say will help you understand the objection. Encourage the prospect to explain and tell you more about how he or she feels about the issue. In general, you should take a problem-solving approach to objections, focused on three things: building trust and rapport with the prospect, dealing with the needs involved, and instilling a sense of urgency.

The process for handling objections involves five steps: (1) Listen to the prospect. (2) Summarize or rephrase what the prospect tells you. (3) Wait for the prospect to respond. (4) Clarify and categorize the response. (5) Deal with it directly, honestly and completely; then resume your presentation.

Another technique for responding to client resistance is: (1) Acknowledge a concern. (2) Clarify a vague or negative response. (3) Resolve the concern by making appropriate recommendations. Another technique is Feel, Felt, Found. Respond to a prospect's concern by saying: "I understand exactly how you feel. Many of my prospects felt the same way, until they found that… (appropriate response, such as, this plan was a good solution for their situation)."

7-4.

- *Assumed or Implied Consent*—The decision to buy is assumed or implied; it is not directly asked or confronted. It presumes the prospect has decided to buy.
- *Alternative Choice*—Instead of asking the prospect to say yes or no to a proposal, present two or three options. Ask them which one they would prefer.
- *Fatal Alternatives or Forced-Choice*—offers two or more alternatives, none of which can be answered with a "yes" or "no," and all of which would mean the prospect has agreed to buy.
- *Silence*—Whenever you have asked a closing question, do not speak again. Wait in silence until your prospect reacts.
- *Direct Question*—Ask the person if they have made up their mind and wish to start the plan. Why? By asking such a question, you are shifting the pressure back to the prospect in order to regain control of the interview.
- *Ben Franklin Balance Sheet*—simply draw a "T" on a paper and on the left side write "pro" and on the right write "con." Under "pro" write all the positive reasons favoring the decision and on the right, under con, list those reasons against the decision. After listing all the reasons, evaluate the arguments for and against each.
- *Similar Situation*—Relate to your prospect a similar situation so that he or she can reflect on the possible consequences of not taking action now.
- *Medical Close*—If the person has had some medical history, that can be used to raise concern in the prospect about insurability. Another common use is to state

that medical underwriting is required and we can let the insurance company think it over as the prospect does, but with cash with the application, conditional coverage is in effect so there is nothing to lose and everything to gain.

7-5. A good case can be made for getting the prospect to give you the premium money at the time of application. The most compelling advantage to the applicant is putting the insurance in force. A conditional receipt is given in return for the applicant's first premium check. This is an acknowledgment that the insurance is in force from the date of the receipt (or medical examination, if later), assuming that the applicant is insurable at standard rates. By prepaying the insurance premium, the prospect is protected in case there are any changes in health before the policy is issued. Advantages to the advisor: you must realize that no sale is made until the customer pays for the product. Prepayment shows that the prospect is completely serious about wanting the life insurance. Policy delivery will be easier. The number of "not taken" policies is reduced.

7-6. After your initial selection through prospecting, your next role in the underwriting process is to provide the information to underwriters who then decide whether or not the risk is acceptable and what the appropriate premium will be. The information you gather and submit is contained in the application. This important document becomes a formal part of the contract between the company and the insured. The underwriters depend on you to make sure the information on the application is complete, detailed, and accurate. Explain the underwriting process to your prospect when taking the application so they will know what to expect. Explain the function of the Attending Physician's Statement (APS) (which may or may not be necessary) and the Medical Information Bureau (MIB) report. If you are able to write nonmedical applications, understand the responsibility you have in being certain that all questions on the application are answered and that all the responses are recorded in the presence of the applicant. If your questions reveal that the prospect has a serious medical problem, do not accept an initial premium payment. Your agency or underwriting guide can spell out where to draw this line. Your signature should appear as witness to the signing of the application, along with the date and location where it was signed.

7-7. The underlying principle of insurance is a sharing of a loss by those exposed to a common hazard through the creation of a common fund. If the plan is to be valid and equitable, each participant must pay into the fund a fair amount determined for people in the same risk classification. By spreading the risk of an individual's death among a larger group of insureds, the economic loss caused by death is shared by many instead of a few. An insurer's underwriting process must strike a balance. It must be flexible enough to allow people to become members of the large group of insureds at standard rates. However, it must remain selective enough to reject clearly unacceptable risks, while still accepting others who are substandard. If underwriting or selection is too severe, the company's advisors will lose their share of the market to the competition and may abandon that insurer. If selection is too liberal, mortality costs are likely to be excessive and the financial strength of that company may be threatened. For these reasons, deciding who will and who won't be insured, and at what rates, is a critical function.

To accomplish this, many underwriting requirements may be called for, depending on the age of the insured and the amount of insurance. Additional requirements may be called for as details of the prospective insured's life are revealed. The application as well as blood and urine specimens, medical tests, APSs, MIB reports, inspection reports and personal history interviews may be requested. The company must be able to counteract the tendencies of adverse selection. Adverse selection is the natural tendency for those who know they are highly vulnerable to a specific risk to be most inclined to acquire and retain insurance to cover that loss. This may result in a preponderance of poorer risks in the insured pool.

7-8. The underwriting department needs to evaluate and separate individual risks into one of three general risk classifications: standard, substandard, or preferred. A person who has statistically no greater a risk of dying than anyone else in that normal age group is considered a standard risk. A person who does have a statistically greater risk of death is usually considered to be a substandard risk. A person who is preferred has a statistically lower chance of death than people in the same normal age group. The criteria for determining these ratings vary greatly from one company to another, so it is sometimes difficult to compare and justify a rating from one company to another. Someone considered a substandard or unacceptable risk by one company may be considered standard by another because of differences in underwriting requirements and rules.

People who are considered substandard risks usually pay increased premiums. Substandard, or rated, policies are a small percentage of sales. Only 3 percent of issued policies are rated, while only another 2 percent are declined. The most common pricing method used for impaired or substandard risks is called the multiple table extra premium method. For each age and plan of insurance, a number of premium rates are established. The standard risk is assumed to have 100 percent mortality and pays the normal, standard premium. Risks that are assumed to have a mortality of above 100 percent pay higher premiums.

Another means of measuring the extra risk is by use of a flat extra premium. The regular premium is charged but an extra premium is also charged for the expected increased mortality. It is often used for occupational and avocational risks since the increased risk is accidental and not tied to the age of the applicant. It is most commonly used in situations where the amount at risk by the company is constant, as in level term insurance. Under a third type of substandard rating, the rated-up age plan, the applicant is assumed to be a specific number of years older than his or her actual age since the applicant's condition predicts a shorter life span. By adding to the age at issue of a policy, the company can equalize life expectancy for all risks. This is done to try to provide fairness in the insurance system, that those having higher risks must pay an additional premium.

Answers to Self-Test Questions

7-1. C
7-2. B
7-3. A
7-4. D
7-5. A
7-6. B
7-7. B
7-8. C
7-9. C
7-10. D

Chapter 8

Answers to Review Questions

8-1. The objectives of a polished policy delivery are as follows: reinforces the buying decision, builds trust, reopens the selling/planning process, obtains referred leads, and prevents lapses. Reemphasize the needs and reasons the prospect bought the policy. The client must understand why he or she bought the product, the solutions it provides, and the benefits he or she will derive from keeping it. Educate the policyowner about the policy. Send the client a thank you letter for his or her confidence in you, expressed through the purchase. In the letter, summarize the reasons for the purchase and the benefits provided by the plan. Promise a lot and deliver more. When you deliver service after the sale, the client's trust in you will grow.

Be sure that the client knows about all the products and services you offer. Even if you have already presented this information, review what you can do again. If you have a personal brochure or resume, be sure that the client has one. Periodically send compliance-approved articles, brochures, or reports based on what you know about the client's interests, business, or company. This will build rapport as well as generate or develop interest in further cross-selling opportunities. Help the client by sharing the specifics on the types of referrals that would be most helpful. Ask the client if he or she would be willing to be a reference for you. If appropriate, socialize with the client, building the relationship and sharing in a common interest. You must keep a customer satisfied in order to fight off competition.

8-2. The policy delivery should not be an afterthought or a casually dismissed step in the sales process. This interview should be taken as seriously as any other part of the selling/planning process. You must prepare and practice for the interview as you would with any other sales technique or it will not be as effective as it could be. Work to accomplish all the objectives mentioned here to maximize your effectiveness and efficiency.

Alert the client to future contact points at the delivery interview. If you use a client newsletter, show the client a sample or deliver an issue. Set the expectation of a mutually agreed upon review timetable, and inform the buyer of other typical times when you routinely contact your clients.

Check the policy when you receive it, before you call the applicant for delivery. Make sure it is exactly as applied for. Ask for an appointment time that will give you plenty of time to review the contract, ask for referrals, and set the stage for your continuing relationship. This meeting will reinforce the benefits of this purchase, so do not allow yourself to be rushed through it. You want to review all of the ideas you talked about in the past. Give your policy a professional appearance by delivering it in an attractive policy wallet. Review the policy contract, pointing out its key features.

8-3. Generally a Buyer's Guide is required to be delivered to the consumer with the policy. Some states require its delivery with the application. There are state variations in the forms themselves and state-specific requirements that must be followed. The Buyer's Guide is designed to give the consumer and prospective purchaser a clear explanation of products and how to shop for them. Most states require delivery of a Policy Summary with the policy. This form gives the main features of the currently issued policy and includes specific information on the policy values (guaranteed and non-guaranteed) of this particular contract.

The National Association of Insurance Commissioners (NAIC) drafted a Model Illustration Regulation, which establishes guidelines for companies and advisors regarding the content and presentations of sales illustrations. The regulation covers all life insurance products except face amounts under $10,000 and variable life. It requires that an illustration matching the issued policy be presented to the policyowner. The advisor and policyowner must sign this illustration; one copy is given to the policyowner, one is returned to the company, and one is retained in the advisor's client file.

Most companies and some states require the advisor and policyowner to sign policy delivery receipts. The delivery receipt contains information regarding guaranteed and non-guaranteed elements in the policy and information regarding proper policy delivery. A client file must be kept as long as a policy is in force. Once a policy is no longer in force because it lapsed, was surrendered, or a claim was paid, a file must be kept for 5 to 8 years, depending on jurisdiction. Where litigation or other disputes exist, files should be kept even longer if necessary. Documents to be maintained in files generally include: a signed NAIC illustration, any sales materials used in the sale, a fact-finder and suitability materials, replacement forms if appropriate, copies of policy delivery receipts, records of date and general content of all client contacts, and substantive correspondence concerning contractual changes or concerns of a client.

8-4. The delivery of the policy confirms for the client their decision to buy and completes the sales process in the eyes of the policyowner. This is why it is so important to meet with your new policyowner to deliver the contract in person. You establish a pattern of service for the future and you demonstrate and reinforce your personal approach and philosophy of selling and service. Explain the kinds of service the client can expect and reinforce the systems you have in place to accomplish that. Set an appointment for an annual review to express your commitment to these service goals and the goals and importance of this meeting. Then deliver on your promises.

Broaden the product portfolio you can offer to customers, developing strategic alliances with other producers who offer products and services you do not, including attorneys, accountants, bankers, and specialists in other lines of insurance, where you cannot or choose not to involve yourself. Broaden your areas of expertise. Pursue professional designations, add additional licenses, and generally improve your expertise and skills that make you more valuable to clients. Be sure to frequently tell your prospects and clients, through mail and personal contact, about your total product and service portfolio. Go back to every client, as least for regular review, and explain your total portfolio, particularly in areas you may not have previously addressed.

In planning reviews, the advisor and the client need to agree on the extent and the frequency of service and review activities, which may include, but are not limited to: identifying changes in conditions that would impact the current plan and recommendations made by the advisor, obtaining information from the client to determine changes in personal circumstances, reviewing work done by other professionals and providers of financial services, and reviewing the client's progress toward financial goals.

8-5. Generally, there are five types of beneficiary designations: the estate of the insured, a specifically named person or persons, a class or classes of persons, a business organization, or a trust. Care should be taken in making beneficiary choices that will accomplish what is intended. The advisor should check for the continued accuracy of the beneficiary designations at each annual review. Parents who wish their children to benefit from their life insurance should not name the youngsters as beneficiaries. A minor's capacity to receive and give a valid receipt for the proceeds of life insurance is limited by many laws and circumstances. It may be wise, for estate tax purposes, to have a trust own and be the beneficiary of the insurance, rather than having it paid directly to the spouse, children, or to the estate. If a policyowner names another person as beneficiary, gift taxes may result when the proceeds are paid to that person. Naming the insured's estate as beneficiary of life insurance is generally unwise, unless the proceeds are to be used by the executor to cover debts, taxes, funeral expenses, and other estate settlement costs. Such a designation will increase the probate assets of the estate by the amount of the insurance proceeds, thus exposing the proceeds to possible estate and inheritance taxes and to higher administration costs that can otherwise be avoided. A surviving spouse may be unable to use an appropriate payout option for long-term income if the proceeds are tied to estate settlement. The proceeds would also be available to the claims of creditors of the estate under these circumstances. These consequences can be avoided by designating a named beneficiary, such as the insured's spouse, to receive the entire proceeds. One way to avoid the problems inherent in naming multiple beneficiaries is to use a class beneficiary designation instead of listing specific individuals by name. How to pay proceeds to the heirs of deceased beneficiaries can be defined by using a per stirpes distribution or a per capita distribution. Life insurance proceeds can also be put in trust to be managed by a trustee for the benefit of another person. Insurable interest between the insured and the beneficiary must exist at the time of application.

8-6. When proceeds are to be paid under one of the settlement options other than the cash settlement, a new contract called a supplementary contract is issued. Insurance companies guarantee the safety of the funds and keep them invested at a contractual rate of return. Under the interest income settlement option the insurance company holds the proceeds and will make regular interest-income payments to the beneficiary based on a guaranteed rate of return. This selection preserves the capital for the future. The option can also be set up to enable the beneficiary to make cash withdrawals. It is the most flexible of all available settlement options.

The fixed-amount option pays out both policy proceeds and interest earned in installments over a specified period. The income received depends on the amount of proceeds and the period selected. The fixed-period payout offers no flexibility to the beneficiary and is not used unless a clearly defined purpose and time frame for need can be established.

Under the fixed-amount option, policy proceeds, plus interest, are used to pay out a specified amount of income at regular intervals for as long as the proceeds last: the larger the payment, the shorter the period of income. This option is similar to the fixed-period settlement choice except that excess interest above the return guaranteed by the company would extend the length of time for the payout.

The life income, no refund option pays a stated income as long as the beneficiary lives. At death the contract ends. This is a pure no-refund annuity. Whether the beneficiary lives many years or dies within the year, the annuity reverts to the company at death. For most, even though it may offer the highest return in income to the beneficiary during life, it would prove unsatisfactory without a guarantee of return built into the annuity.

The life-income with refund option guarantees payments for the life of the annuitant. If the annuitant should die before all the proceeds have been distributed, the balance of payments would be paid, either in a lump sum or installments, to the annuitant's beneficiary or even a third beneficiary, until all proceeds have been depleted. The annuitant is assured through this method that all proceeds will be paid out.

Under life income with period certain, the annuitant receives payments for his or her entire life. In addition, he or she is given a guarantee that if he or she should die within a certain period of time (such as 10, 15, 20, 25, or 30 years) the payment will be paid to a beneficiary for the balance of the time selected.

Under the joint and survivor life income option, income is provided for two people. Married couples use it most commonly for payment of retirement benefits. It can be set up to expire at the second death or to have the refund or period-certain guarantees built into the settlement.

8-7. Death proceeds of a life insurance contract generally become the property of the beneficiary without any income tax obligation. This income tax exclusion does not extend in full to all money paid to the beneficiary under a settlement option, since the payment would normally include both principal and interest. While the principal is not subject to income tax, the interest element of each settlement option payment is reportable for federal income tax purposes.

The interest option is the only one in which income is fully taxable to the recipient. This is because the money received is an extra benefit and is not the actual death proceeds. There is no tax advantage whatsoever. Both the guaranteed interest and any excess interest are fully reported, whether withdrawn or not, each tax year. Under the fixed period or fixed amount option, the monthly installments are taxed under a special rule. First, the total amount of guaranteed payments is computed. From this figure the amount of insurance proceeds is deducted. The difference is divided by the number of years for which benefits are guaranteed. The resulting amount must be reported as income for tax purposes each year.

If the option selected is a no-refund life-income option, to determine the taxable portion of any income received, multiply the monthly income times 12, times the beneficiary's life expectancy at the time the option is selected. This yields the total expected return. From this figure subtract the amount of proceeds from the life insurance that is placed under the option. The difference is divided by the life expectancy when the option is selected. The portion of each payment attributable to the life insurance proceeds is prorated over the beneficiary's life expectancy and is not subject to income tax. This portion of each payment is referred to as the excludable amount, since it represents a payment of the death proceeds over time. This excludable amount is not subject to income tax for the life of the beneficiary, even if the beneficiary lives beyond life expectancy and receives the total amount of insurance proceeds. A period certain life income option means that the proceeds of the policy will be paid out (or refunded) over a specified (certain) period of time, even if the initial beneficiary dies before the end of that period.

When using the period certain life income option, an additional calculation is required to determine the taxable portion of each payment. The value of the refund feature must be determined by referencing the Internal Revenue Service tables. The value of the refund is deducted from the proceeds to determine the value of the annuity feature. The annuity value is then deducted from the total expected return. (The total expected return is monthly income times 12 months, times life expectancy.) The difference between the total expected return and the value of the annuity is then divided by the life expectancy to determine the reportable income.

8-8. Typically used by senior clients, the life settlement is a way to release dormant cash values in a life insurance policy that is no longer needed or wanted. Seniors who need cash to pay for living expenses, long-term care expenses or other needs, may find this an attractive alternative. Through a life settlement a policyowner can obtain a higher value for their policies than to lapse, surrender, or borrow from them. A life settlement is a transaction of selling an existing life insurance policy by its owner to a third party. In exchange for a cash settlement, the policyowner transfers ownership and all other rights of the policy to that third party. The sale of the life insurance policy is completed through a broker or financial advisor to a settlement company or other provider, to obtain a sum of money that exceeds the policy's cash value. The provider keeps the policy in force by making subsequent premium payments, and collects the proceeds at the policy's maturity (the earlier of the maturity date or the death of the insured). All types of policies, as long as they are out of contesability, are life settlement candidates.

8-9. Since this is an emotional time for the beneficiary, you may find yourself offering services that you normally would not. You may offer to call the funeral director and help make the arrangements for the funeral. You may contact the deceased's other financial advisers or attorney. You may help in locating and procuring important papers, like certified copies of the death certificate or a copy of the most recent will. Contacts may need to be made with the local Veterans' and/or Social Security office and you may be the one who starts the process. The beneficiary may be entitled to Civil Service or employer benefits and may not even think about this aspect of the claims process. As the deceased's insurance advisor, you may need to contact several life insurance companies and help the beneficiaries file claims. You may find it helpful to have the following information on hand before contacting the companies involved:

- Policy number(s) and face amount(s)
- Social Security number of the deceased
- Full legal name and address of the deceased
- the deceased's occupation, last day worked, employer's name, address, and telephone number
- the deceased's date and place of birth
- the date, place, and cause of death
- the beneficiary's name, age, address, and Social Security number
- several certified copies of the death certificate

In any case, you need to be prepared to handle or find a resource for any matter that may cross your path in regard to the deceased. The advisor's job is not complete when death occurs, but in many cases is just beginning. Always remember that when you help your clients' beneficiaries select the most appropriate payout options for their circumstances, you will be doing the right thing and earning a reputation as a trustworthy professional who sticks with your clients and their families in good times and bad.

Answers to Self-Test Questions

8-1. A
8-2. B
8-3. C
8-4. D
8-5. C
8-6. C
8-7. D
8-8. A

8-9. B
8-10. D

Index

J

L

M

N

O

P

Q

R

S

T

U

V

W